Moishe Postone undertakes a fundamental reinterpretation of Karl Marx's mature critical theory. He calls into question many of the presuppositions of traditional Marxist analyses and offers new interpretations of Marx's central arguments. He does so by developing concepts aimed at grasping the essential character and historical development of modern society, and also at overcoming the familiar dichotomies of structure and action, meaning and material life.

These concepts lead him to an original analysis of the nature and problems of capitalism and provide the basis for a critique of "actually existing socialism." According to this new interpretation, Marx identifies the core of the capitalist system with an impersonal form of social domination generated by labor itself and not simply with market mechanisms and private property. Proletarian labor and the industrial production process are characterized as expressions of domination rather than as means of human emancipation. This reinterpretation entails a critical analysis of the historically dynamic character of modern social life. It relates the form of economic growth and the structure of social labor in modern society to the alienation and domination at the heart of capitalism. This reformulation, Postone argues, provides the foundation for a critical social theory that is more adequate to late twentieth-century capitalism.

Time, labor, and social domination

Time, labor, and social domination

A reinterpretation of Marx's critical theory

Moishe Postone
The University of Chicago

CAMBRIDGE
UNIVERSITY PRESS

Published by the Press Syndicate of the University of Cambridge
The Pitt Building, Trumpington Street, Cambridge CB2 IRP
40 West 20th Street, New York, NY 10011-4211, USA
10 Stamford Road, Oakleigh, Melbourne 3166, Australia

© Cambridge University Press 1996

First published 1993
Reprinted 1995
First paperback edition 1996

Printed in the United States of America

Library of Congress Cataloging-in-Publication Data is available.

A catalog record for this book is available from the British Library.

ISBN 0-521-39157-1 hardback
ISBN 0-521-56540-5 paperback

For my parents, Abraham and Evelyn Postone

Contents

**Part II Toward a reconstruction of the Marxian critique:
the commodity**

**Part III Toward a reconstruction of the Marxian critique:
capital**

Acknowledgments

This book had its origins some years ago, when, as a graduate student, I first came across Marx's *Grundrisse*. At the time, I was struck by its far-reaching implications, which suggested to me a fundamental reinterpretation of Marx's mature critical social theory, one that broke with some central assumptions of traditional Marxism. I also thought such a reinterpretation could provide the point of departure for a powerful and sophisticated analysis of modern society.

In my attempt to reappropriate Marx's theory, I have had the good fortune to receive considerable intellectual and moral support from many people. I was strongly encouraged to begin this project by two of my teachers at the University of Chicago, Gerhard Meyer and Leonard Krieger. I further developed my ideas during an extended stay in Frankfurt am Main, where I benefited greatly from the general theoretical atmosphere as well as from many intensive discussions with friends there. I owe special thanks to Barbara Brick, Dan Diner, and Wolfram Wolfer-Melior, who provided me with important personal and intellectual support and helped me refine my approach to many of the issues raised in this book. I would also like to thank Klaus Bergmann, Helmut Reinicke, and Peter Schmitt-Egner for many illuminating conversations. I completed an earlier version of this work as a dissertation for Fachbereich Gesellschaftswissenschaften at the J. W. Goethe Universität in Frankfurt, having received valuable guidance and encouragement from Iring Fetscher, and very useful and extensive critical comments from Heinz Steinert, Albrecht Wellmer, and Jeremy Gaines, as well as Gerhard Brandt and Jürgen Ritsert. Through the Canada Council, I received generous financial assistance from the Deutsche Akademischer Austauschdienst during my stay in Frankfurt.

The Center for Psychosocial Studies in Chicago subsequently provided me with a postdoctoral fellowship, as well as a lively and supportive intellectual environment, which enabled me to begin reworking my dissertation into this volume. I was afforded the rare opportunity of presenting my work in a series of seminars to a group of intellectually and academically diverse fellows; their reactions were very stimulating. I am grateful to Ed LiPuma, John Lucy, Beth Mertz, Lee Schlesinger, Barney Weissbourd, and Jim Wertsch, whose comments and criticisms helped me clarify my ideas further. I am especially thankful to Craig Calhoun and Ben Lee, who took the time to read carefully both the original manuscript and the revised version, and whose critical suggestions have been very helpful.

I completed this manuscript at the University of Chicago, and continue to benefit from the exciting, open, and intellectually rigorous climate created by my colleagues and students.

I owe a great deal to the following friends for their engagement with my work and, more generally, for their intellectual and moral support: Andrew Arato, Leora Auslander, Ike Balbus, Seyla Benhabib, Fernando Coronil, Norma Field, Harry Harootunian, Martin Jay, Bob Jessop, Tom McCarthy, György Márkus, Rafael Sanchez, George Steinmetz, Sharon Stephens, as well as John Boyer, Jean Cohen, Bert Cohler, Jean Comaroff, John Comaroff, Michael Geyer, Gail Kligman, Terry Shtob, and Betsy Traube. I also thank Fred Block, Cornelius Castoriadis, Geoff Eley, Don Levine, Bertell Ollman, and Terry Turner for their helpful comments.

Special thanks are due to my brother, Norman Postone, who accompanied and supported this project since its inception. I am particularly grateful to Patrick Murray, who read more versions of the manuscript than I care to remember, and whose comments have been both very helpful and generous. I have learned a great deal from our ongoing conversations.

Emily Loose, formerly of Cambridge University Press, responded very positively to this work and has been extremely helpful in preparing it for publication. Her many astute comments and recommendations contributed greatly to the finished manuscript. I thank Elvia Alvarez, Diane New, and Kitty Pucci for typing the various stages of the manuscript, as well as for their general helpfulness, and Ted Byfield for editing this volume. And I would also like to thank Anjali Fedson, Bronwyn McFarland, and Mike Reay for their help in proofreading and in preparing the index.

Finally, I wish to express my very deep gratitude to my wife, Margret Nickels. She has, for many years and in many ways, been intellectually and emotionally central to this project.

PART I

A critique of traditional Marxism

1. Rethinking Marx's critique of capitalism

Introduction

In this work I shall undertake a fundamental reinterpretation of Marx's mature critical theory in order to reconceptualize the nature of capitalist society. Marx's analysis of the social relations and forms of domination that characterize capitalist society can be most fruitfully reinterpreted by rethinking the central categories of his critique of political economy.[1] Toward that end, I shall seek to develop concepts that fulfill two criteria: First, they should grasp the essential character and historical development of modern society; and second, they should overcome the familiar theoretical dichotomies of structure and action, meaning and material life. On the basis of this approach, I shall try to reformulate the relation of Marxian theory to the current discourses of social and political theory in a way that has theoretical significance today, and provides a basic critique of traditional Marxist theories and of what was called "actually existing socialism." In doing so, I hope to lay the foundation for a different, more powerful critical analysis of the capitalist social formation, one adequate to the late twentieth century.

I shall attempt to develop such an understanding of capitalism by separating conceptually, on the basis of Marx's analysis, the fundamental core of capitalism from its nineteenth-century forms. Doing so, however, calls into question many basic presuppositions of traditional Marxist interpretations; for example, I do not analyze capitalism primarily in terms of private ownership of the means of production, or in terms of the market. Rather, as will become clear, I conceptualize capitalism in terms of a historically specific form of social interdependence with an impersonal and seemingly objective character. This form of interdependence is effected by historically unique forms of social relations that are constituted by determinate forms of social practice and, yet, become quasi-independent of the people engaged in these practices. The result is a new, increasingly abstract form of social domination—one that subjects people to

1. Patrick Murray and Derek Sayer recently wrote interpretations of Marx's theory that, in many respects, parallel my own as presented here; see Patrick Murray, *Marx's Theory of Scientific Knowledge* (Atlantic Highlands, N.J., 1988); and Derek Sayer, *Marx's Method* (Atlantic Highlands, N.J., 1979), and *The Violence of Abstraction* (Oxford, 1987).

3

impersonal structural imperatives and constraints that cannot be adequately grasped in terms of concrete domination (e.g., personal or group domination), and that generates an ongoing historical dynamic. In reconceptualizing the social relations and forms of domination that characterize capitalism, I shall attempt to provide the basis for a theory of practice capable of analyzing the systemic characteristics of modern society, such as its historically dynamic character, its processes of rationalization, its particular form of economic "growth," and its determinate mode of producing.

This reinterpretation treats Marx's theory of capitalism less as a theory of forms of exploitation and domination *within* modern society, and more as a critical social theory of the nature of modernity itself. Modernity is not an evolutionary stage toward which all societies evolve, but a specific form of social life that originated in western Europe and has developed into a complex global system.[2] Although modernity has taken different forms in different countries and areas, my concern is not to examine those differences but to explore theoretically the nature of modernity *per se*. Within the framework of a nonevolutionary approach, such an exploration must explain modernity's characteristic features with reference to historically specific social forms. I argue that Marx's analysis of the putative fundamental social forms that structure capitalism—the commodity and capital—provides an excellent point of departure for an attempt to ground *socially* the systemic characteristics of modernity and indicate that modern society can be fundamentally transformed. Moreover, such an approach is capable of systematically elucidating those features of modern society that, within the framework of theories of linear progress or evolutionary historical development, can seem anomalous: notable are the ongoing production of poverty in the midst of plenty, and the degree to which important aspects of modern life have been shaped by, and become subject to the imperatives of, abstract impersonal forces even as the possibility for collective control over the circumstances of social life has increased greatly.

My reading of Marx's critical theory focuses on his conception of the centrality of labor to social life, which is generally considered to lie at the core of his theory. I argue that the meaning of the category of labor in his mature works is different from what traditionally has been assumed: it is historically specific rather than transhistorical. In Marx's mature critique, the notion that labor constitutes the social world and is the source of all wealth does not refer to society in general, but to capitalist, or modern, society alone. Moreover, and this is crucial, Marx's analysis does not refer to labor as it is generally and transhistorically conceived—a goal-directed social activity that mediates between hu-

2. S. N. Eisenstadt has also formulated a nonevolutionary view of modernity. His primary concern is with the differences among various sorts of modern societies, whereas mine is with modernity itself as a form of social life. See, for example, S. N. Eisenstadt, "The Structuring of Social Protest in Modern Societies: The Limits and Direction of Convergence," in *Yearbook of the World Society Foundation*, vol. 2 (London, 1992).

mans and nature, creating specific products in order to satisfy determinate human needs—but to a peculiar role that labor plays in *capitalist* society alone. As I shall elaborate, the historically specific character of this labor is intrinsically related to the form of social interdependence characteristic of capitalist society. It constitutes a historically specific, quasi-objective form of social mediation that, within the framework of Marx's analysis, serves as the ultimate social ground of modernity's basic features.

It is this reconsideration of the significance of Marx's concept of labor that provides the basis of my reinterpretation of his analysis of capitalism. It places considerations of temporality and a critique of production at the center of Marx's analysis, and lays the foundation for an analysis of modern capitalist society as a directionally dynamic society structured by a historically unique form of social mediation that, though socially constituted, has an abstract, impersonal, quasi-objective character. This form of mediation is structured by a historically determinate form of social practice (labor in capitalism) and structures, in turn, people's actions, worldviews, and dispositions. Such an approach recasts the question of the relation between culture and material life into one of the relation between a historically specific form of social mediation and forms of social "objectivity" and "subjectivity." As a theory of social mediation, it is an effort to overcome the classical theoretical dichotomy of subject and object, while explaining that dichotomy historically.

In general, then, I am suggesting that the Marxian theory should be understood not as a universally applicable theory but as a critical theory specific to capitalist society. It analyzes the historical specificity of capitalism and the possibility of its overcoming by means of categories that grasp its specific forms of labor, wealth, and time.[3] Moreover, the Marxian theory, according to this approach, is self-reflexive and, hence, is itself historically specific: its analysis of the relation of theory and society is such that it can, in an epistemologically consistent manner, locate itself historically by means of the same categories with which it analyzes its social context.

This approach to Marx's mature critical theory has important implications which I shall attempt to unfold in the course of this work. I shall begin to do so by distinguishing between two fundamentally different modes of critical analysis: a critique of capitalism *from the standpoint of* labor, on the one hand, and a critique *of* labor in capitalism, on the other. The first, which is based upon a transhistorical understanding of labor, presupposes that a structural tension exists between the aspects of social life that characterize capitalism (for example, the

---

3. Anthony Giddens has drawn attention to the notion of the specificity of capitalist society that is implicit in Marx's treatment of noncapitalist societies in the *Grundrisse:* see Anthony Giddens, *A Contemporary Critique of Historical Materialism* (London and Basingstoke, 1981), pp. 76–89. I intend to ground that notion in Marx's categorial analysis, hence, in his conception of the specificity of labor in capitalism, in order to reinterpret his understanding of capitalism and rethink the very nature of his critical theory.

market and private property) and the social sphere constituted by labor. Labor, therefore, forms the basis of the critique of capitalism, the *standpoint* from which that critique is undertaken. According to the second mode of analysis, labor in capitalism is historically specific and constitutes the essential structures of that society. Thus labor is the *object* of the critique of capitalist society. From the standpoint of the second mode of analysis, it is clear that diverse interpretations of Marx hold several basic presuppositions of the first mode of analysis in common; consequently, I characterize these interpretations as "traditional." I shall investigate their presuppositions from the standpoint of my interpretation of Marx's theory as a critique *of* labor in capitalism in order to elucidate the limitations of the traditional analysis—and to do so in a way that will imply another, more adequate critical theory of capitalist society.

Interpreting Marx's analysis as a historically specific critique of labor in capitalism leads to an understanding of capitalist society which is very different from that of traditional Marxist interpretations. It suggests, for example, that the social relations and forms of domination that characterize capitalism, in Marx's analysis, cannot be understood sufficiently in terms of class relations, rooted in property relations and mediated by the market. Rather, his analysis of the commodity and capital—that is, the quasi-objective forms of social mediation constituted by labor in capitalism—should be understood as an analysis of this society's fundamental social relations. These impersonal and abstract social forms do not simply *veil* what traditionally has been deemed the "real" social relations of capitalism, that is, class relations; they *are* the real relations of capitalist society, structuring its dynamic trajectory and its form of production.

Far from considering labor to be the principle of social constitution and the source of wealth in *all* societies, Marx's theory proposes that what uniquely characterizes capitalism is precisely that its basic social relations are constituted by labor and, hence, ultimately are of a fundamentally different sort than those that characterize noncapitalist societies. Though his critical analysis of capitalism does include a critique of exploitation, social inequality, and class domination, it goes beyond this: it seeks to elucidate the very fabric of social relations in modern society, and the abstract form of social domination intrinsic to them, by means of a theory that grounds their social constitution in determinate, structured forms of practice.

This reinterpretation of Marx's mature critical theory shifts the primary focus of his critique away from considerations of property and the market. Unlike traditional Marxist approaches, it provides the basis for a critique of the nature of production, work, and "growth" in capitalist society by arguing that they are socially, rather than technically, constituted. Having thus shifted the focus of the critique of capitalism to the sphere of labor, the interpretation presented here leads to a critique of the industrial process of production—hence, to a reconceptualization of the basic determinations of socialism and a reevaluation of the political and social role traditionally accorded the proletariat in the possible historical overcoming of capitalism.

Inasmuch as this reinterpretation implies a critique of capitalism that is not bound to the conditions of nineteenth-century liberal capitalism, and entails a critique of industrial production as capitalist, it can provide the basis for a critical theory capable of illuminating the nature and dynamic of contemporary capitalist society. Such a critical theory could also serve as the point of departure for an analysis of "actually existing socialism" as an alternative (and failed) form of capital accumulation—rather than as a form of society that represented, however imperfectly, the historical negation of capitalism.

The crisis of traditional Marxism

This reconsideration has been developed against the background of the crisis of traditional Marxism and the emergence of what appears to be a new phase in the development of advanced industrial capitalism. In this work, the term "traditional Marxism" refers not to a specific historical tendency in Marxism but generally to all theoretical approaches that analyze capitalism from the standpoint of labor and characterize that society essentially in terms of class relations, structured by private ownership of the means of production and a market-regulated economy. Relations of domination are understood primarily in terms of class domination and exploitation. As is well known, Marx argued that in the course of capitalist development a structural tension, or contradiction, emerges between the social relations that characterize capitalism and the "forces of production." This contradiction has generally been interpreted in terms of an opposition between private property and the market, on the one hand, and the industrial mode of producing, on the other, whereby private property and the market are treated as the hallmarks of capitalism, and industrial production is posited as the basis of a future socialist society. Socialism is understood implicitly in terms of collective ownership of the means of production and economic planning in an industrialized context. That is, the historical negation of capitalism, is seen primarily as a society in which the domination and exploitation of one class by another are overcome.

This broad and preliminary characterization of traditional Marxism is useful inasmuch as it delineates a general interpretive framework shared by a wide range of theories that, on other levels, may differ considerably from one another. My intention in this work is to critically analyze the basic presuppositions of that general theoretical framework itself, rather than to trace the history of various theoretical directions and schools of thought within the Marxist tradition.

At the core of all forms of traditional Marxism is a transhistorical conception of labor. Marx's category of labor is understood in terms of a goal-directed social activity that mediates between humans and nature, creating specific products in order to satisfy determinate human needs. Labor, so understood, is considered to lie at the heart of all social life: it constitutes the social world and is the source of all social wealth. This approach attributes to social labor *transhistorically* what Marx analyzed as historically specific features of labor in capitalism. Such a transhistorical conception of labor is tied to a determinate understanding of the basic categories of Marx's critique of political economy and, hence, of his analysis of capitalism. Marx's theory of value, for example, has generally been interpreted as an attempt to show that social wealth is always and everywhere created by human labor, and that, in capitalism, labor underlies the nonconscious, "automatic," market-mediated mode of distribution.[4] His theory of surplus value, according to such views, seeks to demonstrate that, despite appearances, the surplus product in capitalism is created by labor alone and is appropriated by the capitalist class. Within this general framework, then, Marx's critical analysis of capitalism is primarily a critique of exploitation *from the standpoint of labor:* it demystifies capitalist society, first, by revealing labor to be the true source of social wealth, and second, by demonstrating that that society rests upon a system of exploitation.

Marx's critical theory, of course, also delineates a historical development that points to the emergent possibility of a free society. His analysis of the course of capitalist development, according to traditional interpretations, can be outlined as follows: The structure of free-market capitalism gave rise to industrial production, which vastly increased the amount of social wealth created. In capitalism, however, that wealth continues to be extracted by a process of exploitation and is distributed in a highly inequitable fashion. Nevertheless, a growing contradiction develops between industrial production and the existing relations of production. As a result of the ongoing process of capital accumulation, characterized by competition and crises, the mode of social distribution based on the market and private property becomes less and less adequate to developed industrial production. The historical dynamic of capitalism, however, not only renders the older social relations of production anachronistic but also gives rise to the possibility of a newer set of social relations. It generates the technical, social, and organizational preconditions for the abolition of private property and for centralized planning—for example, the centralization and concentration of the means of production, the separation of ownership and management, and the constitution and concentration of an industrial proletariat. These developments give rise to the historical possibility that exploitation and class domination could be abolished and that a new, just, and rationally regulated mode of distribution could be created. The focus of Marx's historical critique, according to this interpretation, is the mode of *distribution*.

---

4. See Paul Sweezy, *The Theory of Capitalist Development* (New York, 1969), pp. 52–53; Maurice Dobb, *Political Economy and Capitalism* (London, 1940), pp. 70–71; Ronald Meek, *Studies in the Labour Theory of Value* (2d ed., New York, 1956), p. 155.

This statement may seem paradoxical, because Marxism is generally considered to be a theory of *production*. Let us, therefore, briefly consider the role of production in the traditional interpretation. If the forces of production (which, according to Marx, come into contradiction with capitalist relations of production) are identified with the industrial mode of producing, then that mode is implicitly understood as a purely technical process, intrinsically independent of capitalism. Capitalism is treated as a set of extrinsic factors impinging on the process of production: private ownership and exogenous conditions of the valorization of capital within a market economy. Relatedly, social domination in capitalism is understood essentially as class domination, which remains external to the process of production. This analysis implies that industrial production, once historically constituted, is independent of capitalism and not intrinsically related to it. The Marxian contradiction between the forces and relations of production, when understood as a structural tension between industrial production, on the one hand, and private property and the market, on the other, is grasped as a contradiction between the mode of producing and the mode of distribution. Hence, the transition from capitalism to socialism is seen as a transformation of the mode of distribution (private property, the market), but not of production. On the contrary, the development of large-scale industrial production is treated as the historical mediation linking the capitalist mode of distribution to the possibility of another social organization of distribution. Once developed, though, the industrial mode of production based upon proletarian labor is considered historically final.

This interpretation of the trajectory of capitalist development clearly expresses an affirmative attitude toward industrial production as a mode of producing which generates the conditions for the abolition of capitalism and constitutes the foundation of socialism. Socialism is seen as a new mode of politically administering and economically regulating the *same* industrial mode of producing to which capitalism gave rise; it is thought to be a social form of distribution that is not only more just, but also more *adequate* to industrial production. This adequacy is thus considered to be a central historical precondition for a just society. Such a social critique is essentially a historical critique of the mode of distribution. As a *theory* of production, traditional Marxism does not entail a *critique* of production. Quite the opposite: the mode of producing provides the standpoint of the critique and the criterion against which the historical adequacy of the mode of distribution is judged.

Another way of conceptualizing socialism, implied by such a critique of capitalism, is a society in which labor, unhindered by capitalist relations, structures social life openly, and the wealth it creates is distributed more justly. Within the traditional framework, the historical "realization" of labor—its full historical development and its emergence as the basis of social life and wealth—is the fundamental condition of general social emancipation.

This vision of socialism as the historical realization of labor is also evident

in the notion that the proletariat—the laboring class intrinsically related to industrial production—will come into its own as the universal class in socialism.
That is, the structural contradiction of capitalism is seen, on another level, as a
class opposition between the capitalists, who own and control production, and
the proletarians, who with their labor create the wealth of society (and of the
capitalists), yet must sell their labor power to survive. This class opposition,
because it is grounded in the structural contradiction of capitalism, has a historical dimension: Whereas the capitalist class is the dominant class of the present order, the working class is rooted in industrial production and, hence, in the
historical foundations of a new, socialist order. The opposition between these
two classes is seen at once as an opposition between exploited and exploiters
and as one between universal and particularistic interests. The general social
wealth produced by the workers does not benefit all members of society under
capitalism, but is appropriated by the capitalists for their particularistic ends.
The critique of capitalism from the standpoint of labor is a critique in which
the dominant social relations (private property) are criticized as particularistic
from a universalistic position: what is universal and truly social is constituted
by labor, but is hindered by particularistic capitalist relations from becoming
fully realized. The vision of emancipation implied by this understanding of capitalism is, as we shall see, a totalizing one.

Within this basic framework, which I have termed "traditional Marxism,"
there have been extremely important theoretical and political differences: for
example, deterministic theories as opposed to attempts to treat social subjectivity and class struggle as integral aspects of the history of capitalism; council
communists versus party communists; "scientific" theories versus those seeking in various ways to synthesize Marxism and psychoanalysis, or to develop
a critical theory of culture or of everyday life. Nevertheless, to the extent they
all have rested on the basic assumptions regarding labor and the essential characteristics of capitalism and of socialism outlined above, they remain bound
within the framework of traditional Marxism. And however incisive the diverse
social, political, historical, cultural, and economic analyses this theoretical
framework has generated, its limitations have become increasingly evident in
light of various twentieth-century developments. For example, the theory has
been able to analyze the historical trajectory of liberal capitalism leading to
a stage characterized by the partial or total supersession of the market by the
interventionist state as the primary agent of distribution. But because the traditional critique's focus is the mode of distribution, the rise of state-
interventionist capitalism has posed serious problems for this theoretical
approach. If the categories of the critique of political economy apply only to
a self-regulating market-mediated economy and the private appropriation of
the surplus, the growth of the interventionist state implies that these categories
have become less suited to a contemporary social critique. They no longer
grasp social reality adequately. Consequently, traditional Marxist theory has

become less and less capable of providing a historical critique of postliberal capitalism and is left with two options. It can bracket the qualitative transformations of capitalism in the twentieth century and concentrate on those aspects of the market form that continue to exist—and thereby implicitly concede that it has become a partial critique—or it can limit the applicability of the Marxian categories to nineteenth-century capitalism and try to develop a new critique, one presumably more adequate to contemporary conditions. In the course of this work, I shall discuss the theoretical difficulties involved in some attempts of the latter sort.

Traditional Marxism's weaknesses in dealing with postliberal society are particularly apparent in to analyze systematically "actually existing socialism." Not all forms of traditional Marxism affirmed "actually existing socialist" societies, such as the Soviet Union. Nevertheless, this theoretical approach does not allow for an adequate critical analysis of that form of society. The Marxian categories, as traditionally interpreted, are of little use in formulating a social critique of a society that is regulated and dominated by the state. Thus the Soviet Union was often considered socialist because private property and the market had been abolished; continued unfreedom was attributed to repressive bureaucratic institutions. This position suggests, however, that there is no relation between the nature of the socioeconomic sphere and the character of the political sphere. It indicates that the categories of Marx's social critique (such as value), when understood in terms of the market and private property, cannot grasp the grounds for continued or increased unfreedom in "actually existing socialism," and cannot, therefore, provide the basis for a historical critique of such societies. Within such a framework, the relationship of socialism to freedom has become contingent; this, however, implies that a historical critique of capitalism undertaken from the standpoint of socialism can no longer be considered a critique of the grounds of unfreedom and alienation from the standpoint of general human emancipation.[5] These fundamental problems indicate the limits of the traditional interpretation. They show that an analysis of capitalism that focuses exclusively on the market and private property can no longer serve as an adequate basis for an emancipatory critical theory.

As this fundamental weakness has become more evident, traditional Marxism increasingly has been called into question. Moreover, the theoretical basis of its social critique of capitalism—the claim that human labor is the social source of all wealth—has been criticized in light of the growing importance of scientific knowledge and advanced technology in the process of production. Not only does traditional Marxism fail to provide the basis for an adequate historical analysis of "actually existing socialism" (or of its collapse), but its critical analysis of

---

5. A similar point could be made regarding the relationship of socialism, when determined in terms of economic planning and public ownership of the means of production, and the overcoming of gender-based domination.

capitalism and its emancipatory ideals have become increasingly remote from the themes and sources of current social dissatisfaction in advanced industrialized countries. This is particularly true of its exclusive and positive focus on class, and its affirmation of industrial proletarian labor and the specific forms of production and technological "progress" that mark capitalism. At a time of growing criticism of such "progress" and "growth," heightened awareness of ecological problems, widespread discontent with existing forms of labor, increased concern with political freedom, and the growing importance of non–class-based social identities (gender or ethnicity, for example), traditional Marxism seems increasingly anachronistic. In both the East and the West, it has been revealed as historically inadequate by the developments of the twentieth century.

The crisis of traditional Marxism, however, in no way obviates the need for a social critique that is adequate to contemporary capitalism.[6] On the contrary, it draws attention to the need for such a critique. Our historical situation can be understood in terms of a transformation of modern, capitalist society that is as far-reaching—socially, politically, economically, and culturally—as the earlier transformation of liberal to state-interventionist capitalism. We seem to be entering yet another historical phase of developed capitalism.[7] The contours of this new phase are not yet clear, but the past two decades have witnessed the relative decline in importance of the institutions and centers of power that had been at the heart of state-interventionist capitalism—a form characterized by centralized production, large industrial labor unions, ongoing government intervention in the economy, and a vastly expanded welfare state. Two apparently opposed historical tendencies have contributed to this weakening of the central institutions of the state-interventionist phase of capitalism: on the one hand, a partial decentralization of production and politics, and with it the emergence of a plurality of social groupings, organizations, movements, parties, subcultures; and on the other, a process of the globalization and concentration of capital that has taken place on a new, very abstract level, far removed from immediate experience and apparently, for now, beyond the effective control of the state.

These tendencies should not, however, be understood in terms of a linear historical process. They include developments that highlight the anachronistic and inadequate character of the traditional theory—for example, the rise of

---

6. See Stanley Aronowitz, *The Crisis in Historical Materialism* (New York, 1981).

7. For attempts to delineate and theorize this newer phase of capitalism, see David Harvey, *The Condition of Postmodernity* (Oxford and Cambridge, Mass., 1989); Scott Lash and John Urry, *The End of Organized Capitalism* (Madison, Wisc., 1987); Claus Offe, *Disorganized Capitalism,* ed. John Keane (Cambridge, Mass., 1985); Michael J. Piore and Charles F. Sabel, *The Second Industrial Divide* (New York, 1984); Ernest Mandel, *Late Capitalism,* trans. Joris De Bres (London, 1975); Joachim Hirsch and Roland Roth, *Das neue Gesicht des Kapitalismus* (Hamburg, 1986).

new social movements such as mass ecology movements, women's movements, minority emancipation movements, as well as growing disaffection with (and polarization regarding) existing forms of labor and traditional value systems and institutions. Yet our historical situation since the early 1970s has also been characterized by the reemergence of "classical" manifestations of industrial capitalism, such as worldwide economic dislocations and intensifying inter-capitalist rivalry on a global scale. Taken together, these developments suggest that a critical analysis adequate to contemporary capitalist society must be able to grasp its significant new dimensions *and* its underlying continuity as capitalism.

Such an analysis, in other words, must avoid the theoretical one-sidedness of more orthodox versions of traditional Marxism. These are frequently able to indicate that crises and intercapitalist rivalry are continuing characteristics of capitalism (despite the emergence of the interventionist state); but they do not address qualitative historical changes in the identity and nature of the social groupings expressing discontent and opposition, or in the character of their needs, dissatisfactions, aspirations, and forms of consciousness. Yet an adequate analysis must also avoid the equally one-sided tendency to address only the latter changes, either by ignoring the "economic sphere" or by simply assuming that, with the rise of the interventionist state, economic considerations have become less important. Finally, no adequate critique can be formulated by simply bringing together analyses that have continued to focus on economic issues with those that have addressed qualitative social and cultural changes—so long as the basic theoretical presuppositions of such a critique remain those of the traditional Marxist theory. The increasingly anachronistic character of traditional Marxism and its grave weaknesses as an emancipatory critical theory are intrinsic to it; ultimately, they are rooted in its failure to grasp capitalism adequately.

That failure has become clearer in light of the current transformation of modern capitalist society. Just as the Great Depression revealed the limits of market-mediated economic "self-regulation" and demonstrated the deficiencies of conceptions that equated capitalism with liberal capitalism, the crisis-ridden period which ended the postwar era of prosperity and economic expansion highlighted the limits of the interventionist state's ability to regulate the economy; this has cast into doubt linear conceptions of the development of capitalism from a liberal phase to a state-centered one. The expansion of the welfare state after World War II was made possible by a long-term upswing of the capitalist world economy, which has since proved to have been a phase of capitalist development; it was *not* an effect of the political spheres having successfully and permanently gained control of the economic sphere. Indeed, the development of capitalism in the past two decades has reversed the previous period's overt trends by weakening and imposing limits on state interventionism. This became manifest in the crisis of the welfare state in the West—which heralded the demise of Keynesianism and manifestly reaffirmed the contradictory dynamic of capitalism—as well as in the crisis and collapse of most communist states and parties in the East.[8]

It is noteworthy that, compared to the situation after the collapse of liberal capitalism in the late 1920s, the worldwide crises and dislocations associated with this newest transformation of capitalism have precipitated little critical analysis undertaken from a position that points to the possible overcoming of capitalism. This can be interpreted as an expression of theoretical uncertainty. The crisis of state-interventionist capitalism indicates that capitalism continues to develop with a quasi-autonomous dynamic. This development therefore demands a critical reconsideration of those theories which had interpreted the displacement of the market by the state as signifying the effective end of economic crises. However, the underlying nature of capitalism, of the dynamic process that, once again, manifestly has asserted itself, is not clear. It no longer is convincing to claim that "socialism" represents the answer to the problems of capitalism, when what is meant is simply the introduction of central planning and state (or even public) ownership.

The frequently invoked "crisis of Marxism" does not, then, express only disillusioned rejection of "actually existing socialism," disappointment in the proletariat, and uncertainty regarding any other possible social agents of fundamental social transformation. More fundamentally, it is an expression of a deep uncertainty regarding the essential nature of capitalism and what overcoming it could mean. A variety of theoretical positions from the past decades—the dogmatism of many New Left groups in the late 1960s and early 1970s, the purely political critiques that reemerged subsequently, and many contemporary "postmodern" positions—can be seen as expressions of such uncertainty about the nature of capitalist society and even of a turning away from the very attempt to grasp it. This uncertainty can be understood, in part, as an expression of a basic failure of the traditional Marxist approach. Its weaknesses not only have been revealed by its difficulties with "actually existing socialism" and with the needs and dissatisfactions expressed by new social movements; more fundamentally, it has become clear that that theoretical paradigm does not provide a satisfactory conception of the nature of capitalism itself, one that grounds an adequate analysis of the changing conditions of capitalism, and grasps its fundamental structures in a way that points to the possibility of their historical transformation. The transformation implied by traditional Marxism is no longer plausible as a "solution" to the ills of modern society.

8. The historical relation between the two implicitly indicates that "actually existing socialism" as well as the welfare systems in the West should be conceived not as fundamentally different social formations but as importantly different variations of the general state-interventionist form of twentieth-century world capitalism. Far from demonstrating the victory of capitalism over socialism, the recent collapse of "actually existing socialism" could be understood as signifying the collapse of the most rigid, vulnerable, and oppressive form of state-interventionist capitalism.

If modern society is to be analyzed as capitalist and, hence, as transformable on a fundamental level, then, the fundamental core of capitalism must be reconceptualized. On that basis, a different critical theory of the nature and trajectory of modern society could be formulated—one that attempts to grasp socially and historically the grounds of unfreedom and alienation in modern society. Such an analysis would also contribute to democratic political theory. The history of traditional Marxism has shown only too clearly that the question of political freedom must be central to any critical position. Nevertheless it is still the case that an adequate democratic theory requires a historical analysis of the social conditions of freedom, and cannot be undertaken from an abstractly normative position, or from one that hypostatizes the realm of politics.

Reconstructing a critical theory of modern society

My reconceptualization of the nature of Marx's critical theory is a response to the historical transformation of capitalism and to the weaknesses of traditional Marxism outlined above.[9] My reading of Marx's *Grundrisse,* a preliminary version of his fully developed critique of political economy, has led me to reevaluate the critical theory he developed in his mature writings, particularly in *Capital.* That theory, in my judgment, is different from and more powerful than traditional Marxism; it also has more contemporary significance. The reinterpretation of Marx's conception of the basic structuring relations of capitalist society presented in this work could, in my view, serve as the starting point for a critical theory of capitalism that could overcome many of the shortcomings of the traditional interpretation, and address in a more satisfactory way many recent problems and developments.

This reinterpretation both has been influenced by, and is intended as a critique of, the approaches developed by Georg Lukács (especially in *History and Class Consciousness*) and members of the Frankfurt School of critical theory. Those approaches, based on sophisticated understandings of Marx's critique, responded theoretically to the historical transformation of capitalism from a liberal, market-centered form to an organized, bureaucratic, state-centered form, by reconceptualizing capitalism. Within this interpretive tradition, Marx's theory is not considered to be one of material production and class structure alone, much less one of economics. Instead, it is understood as a theory of the historical

---

9. Iring Fetscher also has criticized some central tenets of the notions of socialism implied by more traditional critiques of capitalism. He has called for a renewed democratic critique of capitalism, as well as of "actually existing socialism," that would be critical of runaway growth and contemporary techniques of production; concerned with the social and political conditions for genuine individual and cultural heterogeneity; and sensitive to the issue of an ecologically sound relationship of humans to nature. See Iring Fetscher, "The Changing Goals of Socialism in the Twentieth Century," *Social Research* 47 (Spring 1980). For an earlier version of this position, see Fetscher, *Karl Marx und der Marxismus* (Munich, 1967).

constitution of determinate, reified forms of social objectivity and subjectivity; his critique of political economy is taken to be an attempt to analyze critically the cultural forms and social structures of capitalist civilization.[10] Additionally, Marx's theory is thought to grasp the relationship of theory to society self-reflexively, by seeking to analyze its context—capitalist society—in a way that locates itself historically and accounts for the possibility of its own standpoint. (This attempt to ground socially the possibility of a theoretical critique is seen as a necessary aspect of any attempt to ground the possibility of oppositional and transformative social action.)

I sympathize with their general project of developing a broad and coherent social, political, and cultural critique adequate to contemporary capitalist society by means of a self-reflexive social theory with emancipatory intent. Nevertheless, as I shall elaborate, some of their basic theoretical assumptions prevented Lukács as well as members of the Frankfurt School, in different ways, from fully realizing their theoretical aims. On the one hand, they recognized the inadequacies of a critical theory of modernity that defined capitalism solely in nineteenth-century terms, that is, in terms of the market and private property; on the other, though, they remained bound to some presuppositions of that very sort of theory, in particular, to its transhistorical conception of labor. Their programmatic aim of developing a conception of capitalism adequate to the twentieth century could not be realized on the basis of such an understanding of labor. I intend to appropriate the critical thrust of this interpretive tradition by reinterpreting Marx's analysis of the nature and significance of labor in capitalism.

Although the Marxian analysis of capitalism does entail a critique of exploitation and the bourgeois mode of distribution (the market, private property), it is not undertaken from the standpoint of labor, according to my reinterpretation; rather, it is based upon a critique of labor in capitalism. Marx's critical theory tries to show that labor in capitalism plays a historically unique role in mediating social relations, and to elucidate the consequences of that form of mediation. His focus on labor in capitalism does not imply that the material process of production is necessarily more important than other spheres of social life. Rather, his analysis of labor's specificity in capitalism indicates that production in capitalism is not a purely technical process; it is inextricably related to, and molded by, the basic social relations of that society. The latter, then, cannot be understood with reference to the market and private property alone. This inter-

---

10. For elaborations of this position, see, for example, Georg Lukács, *History and Class Consciousness*, trans. Rodney Livingstone (London, 1971); Max Horkheimer, "Traditional and Critical Theory," in Max Horkheimer, *Critical Theory*, trans. Matthew J. O'Connell et al. (New York, 1972) [this translation is not adequate]; Herbert Marcuse, "Philosophy and Critical Theory," in Stephen Bronner and Douglas Kellner, eds., *Critical Theory and Society* (New York and London, 1989); Theodor Adorno, *Negative Dialectics*, trans. E. B. Ashton (New York, 1973); Alfred Schmidt, "Zum Erkenntnisbegriff der Kritik der politischen Ökonomie," in Walter Euchner and Alfred Schmidt, eds., *Kritik der politischen Ökonomie heute: 100 Jahre Kapital* (Frankfurt, 1968).

pretation of Marx's theory provides the basis for a critique of the form of production and the form of wealth (that is, value) that characterize capitalism, rather than simply calling into question their private appropriation. It characterizes capitalism in terms of an abstract form of domination associated with the peculiar nature of labor in that society and locates in that form of domination the ultimate social ground for runaway "growth," and for the increasingly fragmented character of work and even of individual existence in that society. It also suggests that the working class is *integral to* capitalism rather than the embodiment of its negation. As we shall see, such an approach reinterprets Marx's conception of alienation in light of his mature critique of labor in capitalism—and places this reinterpreted conception of alienation at the center of his critique of that society.

Clearly, such a critique of capitalist society differs entirely from the sort of "productivist" critique, characteristic of many traditional Marxist interpretations, which affirms proletarian labor, industrial production, and unfettered industrial "growth." Indeed, from the standpoint of the reconsideration presented here, the productivist position does not represent a fundamental critique: not only does it fail to point beyond capitalism to a possible future society, but it affirms some central aspects of capitalism itself. In this regard, the reconstruction of Marx's mature critical theory undertaken in this work provides the standpoint for a critique of the productivist paradigm in the Marxist tradition. I shall indicate that what the Marxist tradition has generally treated affirmatively is precisely the object of critique in Marx's later works. I intend not merely to indicate this difference in order to point out that Marx's theory was *not* productivist— and therefore to call into question a theoretical tradition that purports to rely on Marx's texts—but also to show how Marx's theory itself provides a powerful critique of the productivist paradigm which does not merely reject that paradigm as false, but seeks to render it understandable in social and historical terms. It does so by theoretically grounding the possibility of such thought in the structuring social forms of capitalist society. In this way, Marx's categorial[11] analysis of capitalism lays the basis for a critique of the paradigm of production as a position that does indeed express a moment of the historical reality of capitalist society—but does so in a transhistorical and, hence, uncritical and affirmative way.

I shall present a similar interpretation of Marx's theory of history. His notion of an immanent logic of historical development is also not transhistorical and affirmative in his mature works, but is critical and refers specifically to capitalist society. Marx locates the ground of a particular form of historical logic in the specific social forms of capitalist society. His position neither affirms the exis-

---

11. In order to avoid misunderstandings that could be encouraged by the term "categorical," I use "categorial" to refer to Marx's attempt to grasp the forms of modern social life by means of the categories of his mature critique.

tence of a transhistorical logic of history nor denies the existence of any sort of historical logic. Instead, it treats such a logic as a characteristic of capitalist society which can be, and has been, projected onto all of human history.

Marx's theory, in seeking to render forms of thought socially and historically plausible in this manner, reflexively attempts to render plausible its own categories. Theory, then, is treated as part of the social reality in which it exists. The approach I propose is an attempt to formulate a critique of the paradigm of production on the basis of the social categories of the Marxian critique of production, and thereby to tie the critique of theory to a possible social critique. This approach provides the basis for a critical theory of modern society that entails neither an abstractly universalistic, rationalist affirmation of modernity nor an antirationalist and antimodern critique. Rather, it seeks to surpass both of these positions by treating their opposition as historically determinate and rooted in the nature of capitalist social relations.

The reinterpretation of Marx's critical theory presented here is based upon a reconsideration of the fundamental categories of his critique of political economy—such as value, abstract labor, the commodity, and capital. These categories, according to Marx, "express the forms of being [*Daseinsformen*], the determinations of existence [*Existenzbestimmungen*] ... of this specific society."[12] They are, as it were, categories of a critical ethnography of capitalist society undertaken from within—categories that purportedly express the basic forms of social objectivity and subjectivity that structure the social, economic, historical, and cultural dimensions of life in that society, and are themselves constituted by determinate forms of social practice.

Very frequently, however, the categories of Marx's critique have been taken to be purely economic categories. Marx's "labor theory of value," for example, has been understood as an attempt to explain, "first, relative prices and the rate of profit in equilibrium; secondly, the condition of possibility of exchange value and profit; and lastly, the rational allocation of goods in a planned economy."[13] Such a narrow approach to the categories, if it deals with the social, historical, and cultural-epistemological dimensions of Marx's critical theory at all, understands them only with reference to passages explicitly dealing with those dimensions, taken out of their context in his categorial analysis. The breadth and systematic nature of Marx's critical theory, however, can only be fully grasped through an analysis of its categories, understood as determinations of social being in capitalism. Only when Marx's explicit statements are understood with reference to the unfolding of his categories can the inner logic of his critique be reconstructed adequately. I shall, therefore, devote considerable attention to reconsidering the determinations and implications of the basic categories of Marx's critical theory.

12. Karl Marx, *Grundrisse: Foundations of the Critique of Political Economy,* trans. Martin Nicolaus (London, 1973), p. 106 (translation amended).
13. Jon Elster, *Making Sense of Marx* (Cambridge, 1985), p. 127.

In reinterpreting the Marxian critique, I shall try to reconstruct its systematic nature and recover its internal logic. I shall not examine the possibility of divergent or contradictory tendencies in Marx's mature works, nor trace the development of his thought. Methodologically, my intention is to interpret the fundamental categories of Marx's critique of political economy in as logically coherent and systematically powerful a way as possible, in order to work out the theory of the core of capitalism—that which defines capitalism as such throughout its various stages—implied by those categories. My critique of traditional Marxism is one part of this reconceptualization of the Marxian theory at its most coherent level.

This approach could also serve as the point of departure for an effort to locate Marx's own works historically. Such a reflexive attempt could examine possible internal tensions and "traditional" elements in those works from the standpoint of the theory, implied by his fundamental categories, of the underlying nature and trajectory of capitalism. Some of those internal tensions could then be understood in terms of a tension between, on the one hand, the logic of Marx's categorial analysis of capitalism as a whole, and on the other, his more immediate critique of liberal capitalism—that is, in terms of a tension between two different levels of historical locatedness. In this work, however, I shall write as though Marx's self-understanding were that implied by the logic of his theory of the core of the capitalist social formation. Since I hope here to contribute to the reconstitution of a systematic critical social theory of capitalism, the question of whether Marx's actual self-understanding was indeed adequate to that logic is, for present purposes, of secondary importance.

This work is conceived of as the initial stage of my reinterpretation of the Marxian critique. It is intended primarily as a work of fundamental theoretical clarification, rather than as a fully elaborated exposition of that critique, much less as a developed theory of contemporary capitalism. I shall not, therefore, directly address the newest phase of developed capitalist society in this work. Instead, I shall try to interpret Marx's conception of the fundamental structuring relations of modern society, as expressed by his categories of the commodity and capital, so as not to limit them to any of the major phases of developed capitalism—and perhaps thereby permit them to illuminate the underlying nature of the social formation as a whole. This could provide the basis for an analysis of twentieth-century modern society in terms of a growing separation of capitalism from its earlier bourgeois form.

I shall begin with a general outline of my reinterpretation, based upon an analysis of several sections of Marx's *Grundrisse*. On that basis, in Chapter Two I shall proceed to examine more closely the fundamental assumptions of traditional Marxism. In order further to clarify my approach and to indicate its relevance to a contemporary critical theory, I shall in Chapter Three examine attempts by members of the Frankfurt School circle—in particular, Friedrich Pollock and Max Horkheimer—to develop a critical social theory adequate to important changes in twentieth-century capitalist society. I shall examine, with reference to my interpretations of traditional Marxism and of Marx, the theoretical dilemmas and weaknesses involved in their attempts; these, I argue, indicate the limits of a theory attempting to come to grips with postliberal capitalism while retaining certain fundamental presuppositions of traditional Marxism.

My analysis of those limits is intended as a critical response to the theoretical dilemmas of Critical Theory. Jürgen Habermas's work, of course, can be understood as another such response; but he too retains what I regard as a traditional understanding of labor. My critique of that understanding, then, seeks also to point to the possibility of a reconstituted critical social theory that differs from Habermas's. Such a theory would seek to dispense with evolutionary conceptions of history and with the notion that human social life is based upon an ontological principle that "comes into its own" in the course of historical development (for example, labor in traditional Marxism, or communicative action in Habermas's recent work).[14]

In the second half of this work, I shall begin with my reconstruction of the Marxian critique, which will clarify, if retrospectively, the basis for my critique of traditional Marxism. In *Capital* Marx attempts to elucidate capitalist society by locating its fundamental social forms and, on that basis, carefully developing a set of interrelated categories with which to explain its underlying workings. Beginning with categories that he presumes grasp the core structures of the social formation—such as commodity, value, and abstract labor—Marx then unfolds them systematically to encompass ever more concrete and complex levels of social reality. My intention here is to clarify the fundamental categories with which Marx begins his analysis, that is, the most abstract and basic level of that analysis. Many interpreters, in my opinion, have proceeded too quickly to the analytic level of immediate concrete social reality and, consequently, have overlooked some crucial aspects of the fundamental structuring categories themselves.

I examine the category of abstract labor in Chapter Four, and that of abstract time in Chapter Five. On that basis, I critically examine Habermas's critique of Marx in Chapter Six, and then, in Chapters Seven, Eight, and Nine, reconstruct the initial determinations of Marx's concept of capital and his notions of contradiction and historical dynamic. In these chapters I attempt to clarify the most basic categories of the Marxian theory so as to ground my critique of traditional Marxism, and to justify my contention that the logic of the categorial unfolding in *Capital* points in a direction consonant with the *Grundrisse*'s presentation of capitalism's contradiction and the nature of socialism. In establishing the foundation for the further development of my reconstruction, I also shall sometimes

---

14. See Jürgen Habermas, *The Theory of Communicative Action,* vol. 1: *Reason and the Rationalization of Society,* trans. Thomas McCarthy (Boston, 1984), and vol. 2: *Lifeworld and System: A Critique of Functionalist Reason,* trans. T. McCarthy (Boston, 1987).

extrapolate from my arguments to indicate their implications for an analysis of contemporary society. Such extrapolations are abstract and initial determinations of aspects of modern capitalism, based on my reconstruction of the most fundamental level of Marx's critical theory; they do not represent an attempt to analyze directly, without any mediations, a more concrete level of social reality on the basis of the most abstract categories.

On the basis of what I have developed here, I intend to pursue my project of reconstruction in a future work. In my view, this work demonstrates the plausibility of my reinterpretation of Marx's critique of political economy and of the critique of traditional Marxism associated with it. It indicates the theoretical power of the Marxian theory and its possible relevance to the reconstruction of a critical theory of modern society. Nevertheless, the approach must be more fully developed before the question of the viability of its categories of a critical theory of contemporary society can be addressed adequately.

The *Grundrisse*:
rethinking Marx's conception of capitalism and its overcoming

My reinterpretation of Marx's mature critical theory proceeds from a consideration of the *Grundrisse der Kritik der politischen Ökonomie,* a manuscript written by Marx in 1857–58.[15] The *Grundrisse* is well suited to serve as the point of departure for such a reinterpretation: It is easier to decipher than *Capital,* which is subject to misunderstanding inasmuch as it is structured in a tightly logical manner as an immanent critique—that is, one undertaken from a standpoint that is immanent to, rather than outside, its object of investigation. Because the *Grundrisse* is not structured as rigorously, the general strategic intent of Marx's categorial analysis is more accessible, particularly in those sections where he presents his conception of the primary contradiction of capitalist society. His analysis there of the essential core of capitalism and of the nature of its historical overcoming has contemporary significance; it casts doubt on interpretations of his theory that center on considerations of the market and class domination and exploitation.[16]

I shall try to show how these sections of the *Grundrisse* indicate that the categories of Marx's theory are historically specific, that his critique of capitalism is directed at both its mode of producing and its mode of distribution, and that his notion of the basic contradiction of capitalism cannot be conceived of

---

15. Some of the arguments presented in this section were first developed in Moishe Postone, "Necessity, Labor and Time," *Social Research* 45 (Winter 1978).

16. The possible contemporary significance of the *Grundrisse* has also been recognized by Herbert Marcuse in *One-Dimensional Man* (Boston, 1964) and, more recently, by André Gorz in *Paths to Paradise: On the Liberation from Work,* trans. Malcolm Imrie (Boston, 1985). For a rich and extensive analysis of the *Grundrisse* and its relation to *Capital,* see Roman Rosdolsky, *The Making of Marx's "Capital,"* trans. Pete Burgess (London, 1977).

simply as one between the market and private property, on the one hand, and industrial production, on the other. In other words, my discussion of Marx's treatment of the contradiction of capitalism in the *Grundrisse* points to the need for a far-reaching reconsideration of the nature of his mature critical theory: In particular, it will suggest that his analysis of labor in capitalism is historically specific, and his mature critical theory is a critique of labor in capitalism, not a critique of capitalism from the standpoint of labor. Having established this, I shall be able to address the problem of why, in Marx's critique, the fundamental categories of social life in capitalism are categories of labor. This is by no means self-evident, and it cannot be justified merely by pointing to the obvious importance of labor to human social life in general.[17]

In the *Grundrisse,* Marx's analysis of the contradiction between the "relations of production" and the "forces of production" in capitalism differs from that of traditional Marxist theories, which focus on the mode of distribution and understand the contradiction as one between the spheres of distribution and production. He explicitly criticizes those theoretical approaches that conceptualize historical transformation in terms of the mode of distribution without considering the possibility that the mode of producing could be transformed. Marx takes as an example of such approaches John Stuart Mill's statement that "the laws and conditions of the production of wealth partake of the character of physical truths. . . . It is not so with the distribution of wealth. That is a matter of human institutions solely."[18] This separation, according to Marx, is illegitimate: "The 'laws and conditions' of the production of wealth and the laws of the 'distribution of wealth' are the same laws under different forms, and both change, undergo the same historic process; are as such only moments of a historic process."[19]

Marx's notion of the mode of distribution, however, does not refer only to the way in which goods and labor are socially distributed (for example, by means of the market); he goes on to describe "the workers' propertylessness, and the . . . appropriation of alien labour by capital,"[20] that is, capitalist property relations, as "modes of distribution [that] are the relations of production themselves, but *sub specie distributionis.*"[21] These passages indicate that Marx's notion of the mode of distribution encompasses capitalist property relations. They also imply that his notion of the "relations of production" cannot be understood in terms of the mode of distribution alone, but must also be considered *sub specie productionis*—in other words, that the relations of production should not be understood as they traditionally have been. If Marx considers property relations to be

17. One could make a similar argument with regard to theories that place language at the center of their analyses of social life.
18. John Stuart Mill, *Principles of Political Economy* (2d ed., London, 1849), vol. 1, pp. 239–40 (quoted in Marx, *Grundrisse,* p. 832).
19. *Grundrisse,* p. 832.
20. Ibid.
21. Ibid.

relations of distribution,[22] it follows that his concept of the relations of production cannot be fully grasped in terms of capitalist class relations, rooted in the private ownership of the means of production and expressed in the unequal social distribution of power and wealth. Rather, that concept must also be understood with reference to the mode of producing in capitalism.[23]

If the process of production and the fundamental social relations of capitalism are interrelated, however, then the mode of producing cannot be equated with the forces of production, which eventually come into contradiction with the capitalist relations of production. Instead, the mode of producing itself should be seen as intrinsically related to capitalism. These passages suggest, in other words, that the Marxian contradiction should not be conceived as one between industrial production, on the one hand, and the market and capitalist private property, on the other; his understanding of the forces and relations of production must, therefore, be rethought fundamentally. Marx's notion of the overcoming of capitalism apparently involves a transformation not merely of the existing mode of distribution but also of the mode of production. It is precisely in this regard that he approvingly points to the significance of Charles Fourier's thought: "Labour cannot become play, as Fourier would like, although it remains his great contribution to have expressed the suspension not of distribution, but of the mode of production itself, in a higher form, as the ultimate object."[24]

Assuming that the "ultimate object" is the "suspension" or overcoming of the mode of production itself, this mode must embody capitalist relations. And, indeed, Marx's critique of those relations points later to the possibility of a historical transformation of production:

It requires no great penetration to grasp that, where e.g. free labour or wage labour arising out of the dissolution of bondage is the point of departure, there machines can only *arise* in antithesis to living labour, as property alien to it, and as power hostile to it; i.e., that they must confront it as capital. But it is just as easy to perceive that machines will not cease to be agencies of social production when they become e.g. property of the associated workers. In the first case, however, their distribution, i.e., that they *do not belong* to the worker, is just as much a condition of the mode of production founded on wage labour. In the second case the changed distribution would start from a *changed* foundation of production, a new foundation first created by the process of history.[25]

22. For purposes of simplicity, I shall refer to the "relations of production *sub specie distributionis*" as the "relations of distribution."
23. As I shall discuss further, the distinction between the relations of production proper and the relations of distribution is important in understanding the relationship between the categories of Volume 1 of *Capital* such as value, surplus value, valorization process, and accumulation, and those of Volume 3 such as price, profit, and revenue. The former categories purportedly express the underlying social relations of capitalism, its fundamental "relations of production"; the latter categories, according to Marx, are categories of distribution.
24. *Grundrisse*, p. 712.
25. Ibid., pp. 832–33.

In order to understand more clearly the nature of Marx's analysis, and to grasp what he means by a transformation of the mode of production, we must examine his conception of the "foundation" of (capitalist) production. That is, we must analyze his notion of "the mode of production founded on wage labor" and consider what a "changed foundation of production" could mean.

The fundamental core of capitalism

My investigation of Marx's analysis of capitalism begins with a crucially important section of the *Grundrisse* entitled "Contradiction between the *foundation* of bourgeois production (*value as measure*) and its development."[26] Marx begins this section as follows: "The exchange of living labour for objectified labour—i.e., the positing of social labour in the form of the contradiction of capital and wage labour—is the ultimate development of the *value relation* and of production resting on value."[27] The title and initial sentence of this section of the *Grundrisse* indicate that, for Marx, the category of value expresses the basic relations of production of capitalism—those social relations that specifically characterize capitalism as a mode of social life—as well as that production in capitalism is based on value. In other words, value, in Marx's analysis, constitutes the "foundation of bourgeois production."

A peculiarity of the category of value is that it purportedly expresses both a determinate form of social relations and a particular form of wealth. Any examination of value, then, must elucidate both of these aspects. We have seen that value, as a category of wealth, generally has been conceived of as a category of the market; yet when Marx refers to "exchange" in the course of considering the "value relation" in the passages quoted, he does so with regard to the capitalist process of production itself. The exchange to which he refers is not that of circulation, but of production—"the exchange of living labour for objectified labour." This implies that value should not be understood merely as a category of the mode of distribution of commodities, that is, as an attempt to ground the automatism of the self-regulating market; rather, it should be understood as a category of capitalist production itself. It seems, then, that the Marxian notion of the contradiction between the forces and relations of production must be reinterpreted as referring to differentiable moments of the production process. "Production resting on value" and "the mode of production founded on wage labour" seem closely related. This requires further examination.

When Marx discusses production resting on value, he describes it as a mode of production whose "presupposition is—*and remains*—the mass of direct labour time, the quantity of labour employed, as the determinant factor in the

26. Ibid., p. 704 (first emphasis added).
27. Ibid.

production of wealth.''[28] What characterizes value as a form of wealth, according to Marx, is that it is constituted by the expenditure of direct human labor in the process of production, it remains bound to such expenditure as the determining factor in the production of wealth, and it possesses a temporal dimension. Value is a social form that expresses, and is based on, the expenditure of direct labor time. This form, for Marx, is at the very heart of capitalist society. As a category of the fundamental social relations that constitute capitalism, value expresses that which is, and remains, the basic foundation of capitalist production. Yet a growing tension arises between this foundation of the capitalist mode of production and the results of its own historical development:

But to the degree that large industry develops, the creation of real wealth comes to depend less on labour time and on the amount of labour employed than on the power of the agencies set in motion during labour time, whose "powerful effectiveness" is itself . . . out of all proportion to the direct labour time spent on their production, but depends rather on the general state of science and on the progress of technology. . . . Real wealth manifests itself, rather . . . in the monstrous disproportion between the labour time applied, and its product, as well as in the qualitative imbalance between labour, reduced to a pure abstraction, and the power of the production process it superintends.[29]

The contrast between value and "real wealth"—that is, the contrast between a form of wealth that depends on "labour time and on the amount of labour employed" and one that does not—is crucial to these passages and to understanding Marx's theory of value and his notion of the basic contradiction of capitalist society. It clearly indicates that value does not refer to wealth in general, but is a historically specific and transitory category that purportedly grasps the foundation of capitalist society. Moreover, it is not merely a category of the market, one that grasps a historically particular mode of the social distribution of wealth. Such a market-centered interpretation—which relates to Mill's position that the mode of distribution is changeable historically but the mode of production is not—implies the existence of a transhistorical form of wealth that is distributed differently in different societies. According to Marx, however, value is a historically specific form of social wealth and is intrinsically related to a historically specific mode of production. That forms of wealth can be historically specific implies, obviously, that social wealth is not the same in all societies. Marx's discussion of these aspects of value suggests, as we shall see, that the form of labor and the very fabric of social relations differ in various social formations.

In the course of this work, I shall investigate the historical character of value and try to clarify the relationship Marx posits between value and labor time. To jump ahead for a moment, many arguments regarding Marx's analysis of the uniqueness of labor as the source of value do not acknowledge his distinction

28. Ibid., p. 704 (emphasis added).
29. Ibid., pp. 704–5.

between "real wealth" (or "material wealth") and value. Marx's "labor theory of value," however, is not a theory of the unique properties of labor in general, but is an analysis of the historical specificity of value as a form of wealth, and of the labor that supposedly constitutes it. Consequently, it is irrelevant to Marx's endeavor to argue for or against his theory of value as if it were intended to be a labor theory of (transhistorical) wealth—that is, as if Marx had written a political economy rather than a *critique* of political economy.[30] This is not to say, of course, that the interpretation of Marx's category of value as a historically specific category proves his analysis of modern society to be correct; but it *does* require that Marx's analysis be considered in its own historically determinate terms and not as if it were a transhistorical theory of political economy of the sort he severely criticized.

Value, within the framework of Marx's analysis, is a critical category that reveals the historical specificity of the forms of wealth and production characteristic of capitalism. The paragraph quoted above shows that, according to Marx, the form of production based on value develops in a way that points to the possible historical negation of value itself. In an analysis that seems quite relevant to contemporary conditions, Marx argues that, in the course of the development of capitalist industrial production, value becomes less and less adequate as a measure of the "real wealth" produced. He contrasts value, a form of wealth bound to human labor time expenditure, to the gigantic wealth-producing potential of modern science and technology. Value becomes anachronistic in terms of the potential of the system of production to which it gives rise; the realization of that potential would entail the abolition of value.

This historical possibility does not, however, mean merely that ever greater masses of goods could be turned out on the basis of the existing industrial mode of production, and that they could be distributed more equitably. The logic of the growing contradiction between "real wealth" and value, which points to the possibility of the former superseding the latter as the determining form of social wealth, also implies the possibility of a different process of production, one based upon a newer, emancipatory structure of social labor:

Labour no longer appears so much to be included within the production process; rather, the human being comes to relate more as watchman and regulator to the production process itself.... He steps to the side of the production process instead of being its chief actor. In this transformation, it is neither the direct human labour he himself performs, nor the time during which he works, but rather the appropriation of his own general productive power, his understanding of nature and his mastery over it by virtue of his

---

30. Jon Elster provides an example of such an argument. He argues against Marx's theory of value and surplus value by denying "that the workers have a mysterious capacity to create *ex nihilo*"; he maintains, instead, that "man's ability to tap the environment makes possible a surplus over and above any given consumption level" (*Making Sense of Marx*, p. 141). In addressing the issue of the creation of wealth in a transhistorical manner, Elster's argument implicitly takes value to be a transhistorical category, and thereby conflates value and wealth.

presence as a social body—it is, in a word, the development of the *social individual* which appears as the great foundation-stone of production and of wealth. The *theft of alien labour time, on which the present wealth is based,* appears a miserable foundation in face of this new one, created by large-scale industry itself.[31]

The section of the *Grundrisse* we have been considering makes abundantly clear that, for Marx, overcoming capitalism involves the abolition of value as the social form of wealth, which, in turn, entails overcoming the determinate mode of producing developed under capitalism. He explicitly asserts that the abolition of value would signify that labor time no longer would serve as the measure of wealth, and that the production of wealth no longer would be effected primarily by direct human labor in the process of production: "As soon as labour in the direct form has ceased to be the great well-spring of wealth, labour time ceases and must cease to be its measure, and hence exchange value [must cease to be the measure] of use value."[32]

With his theory of value, in other words, Marx analyzes the basic social relations of capitalism, its form of wealth, and its material form of production, as interrelated. Because production resting on value, the mode of production founded on wage labor, and industrial production based on proletarian labor are intrinsically related, according to Marx's analysis, his conception of the increasingly anachronistic character of value is also one of the increasingly anachronistic character of the industrial process of production developed under capitalism. Overcoming capitalism, according to Marx, entails a fundamental transformation of the material form of production, of the way people work.

Clearly, this position differs fundamentally from traditional Marxism. The latter, as noted, focuses its critique on the transformation of the mode of distribution alone and treats the industrial mode of production as a technical development that becomes incompatible with capitalism. Here, however, it is obvious that Marx did *not* see the contradiction of capitalism as one between industrial production and value, that is, between industrial production and capitalist social relations. Rather, he saw the former as molded by the latter: industrial production is the "mode of production based on value." It is in *this* sense that, in his later writings, Marx refers explicitly to the industrial mode of production as a "specifically capitalist form of production . . . (at the technological level too),"[33] and in doing so implies that it is to be transformed with the overcoming of capitalism.

Obviously, the meaning of Marx's basic categories cannot be summed up in a few sentences. The second half of this book will be concerned with elaborating his analysis of value and its role in shaping the process of production. At this

---

31. *Grundrisse,* p. 705 (second emphasis added).
32. Ibid.
33. Marx, *Results of the Immediate Process of Production,* trans. Rodney Livingstone, in Marx, *Capital,* vol. 1, trans. Ben Fowkes (London, 1976), p. 1024 (see also pp. 1034–35).

point, I should simply note that Marx's critical theory, as expressed in these passages in the *Grundrisse,* is not a form of technological determinism, but treats technology and the process of production as socially constituted, in the sense that they are shaped by value. They should not, therefore, be simply identified with his notion of the "forces of production" that come into contradiction with capitalist social relations. They do nevertheless embody a contradiction: Marx's analysis distinguishes between the *actuality* of the form of production constituted by value, and its *potential*—a potential that grounds the possibility of a new form of production.

It is clear from the passages cited that when, in the *Grundrisse,* Marx describes the overcoming of capitalism's contradiction and states that the "mass of workers must themselves appropriate their own surplus labour,"[34] he is referring not only to the expropriation of private property and the use of the surplus product in a more rational, humane, and efficient way. The appropriation of which he speaks goes far beyond this, for it also involves the reflexive application of the forces of production developed under capitalism to the process of production itself. That is, he envisages that the potential embedded in advanced capitalist production could become the means by which the industrial process of production itself could be transformed; the system of social production in which wealth is created through the appropriation of direct labor time and workers labor as cogs of a productive apparatus could be abolished. These two aspects of the industrial capitalist mode of production are related, according to Marx. Hence, overcoming capitalism, as presented in the *Grundrisse,* implicitly involves overcoming both the formal and material aspects of the mode of production founded on wage labor. It entails the abolition of a system of distribution based upon the exchange of labor power as a commodity for a wage with which means of consumption are acquired; it also entails the abolition of a system of production based upon proletarian labor, that is, upon the one-sided and fragmented labor characteristic of capitalist industrial production. Overcoming capitalism, in other words, also involves overcoming the concrete labor done by the proletariat.

This interpretation, by providing the basis for a historical critique of the concrete form of production in capitalism, sheds light on Marx's well-known assertion that the capitalist social formation marks the conclusion of the prehistory of human society.[35] The notion of overcoming proletarian labor implies that "prehistory" should be understood as referring to those social formations in which ongoing surplus production exists and is based primarily on direct human labor. This characteristic is shared by societies in which the surplus is created by slave, serf, or wage labor. Yet the formation based upon wage labor, ac-

34. *Grundrisse,* p. 708.
35. Marx, *A Contribution to the Critique of Political Economy,* trans. S. W. Ryazanskaya (Moscow, 1970), pp. 21–22.

cording to Marx, is uniquely characterized by a dynamic from which arises the historical possibility that surplus production based on human labor as an internal element of the process of production can be overcome. A new social formation can be created in which the "*surplus labour of the mass* has ceased to be the condition for the development of general wealth, just as the *non-labour of the few,* for the development of the general powers of the human head."[36]

For Marx, then, the end of prehistory signifies the overcoming of the separation and opposition between manual and intellectual labor. Within the framework of his historical critique, however, that opposition cannot be overcome merely by fusing existing manual and intellectual labor together (as was promulgated, for example, in the Peoples' Republic of China in the 1960s). His treatment of production in the *Grundrisse* implies that not only the separation of these modes of labor, but also the determining characteristics of each, are rooted in the existing form of production. Their separation could be overcome only by transforming existing modes of both manual and intellectual labor, that is, by the historical constitution of a new structure and social organization of labor. Such a new structure becomes possible, according to Marx's analysis, when surplus production no longer is necessarily based primarily on direct human labor.

Capitalism, labor, and domination

Marx's social theory—as opposed to a traditional Marxist position—thus entails a critical analysis of the form of production developed under capitalism, and of the possibility of its radical transformation. It clearly does not involve the productivist glorification of that form. That Marx treats value as a historically determinate category of a specific mode of production, and not as one of distribution alone, suggests—and this is crucial—that the labor which constitutes value should not be identified with labor as it may exist transhistorically. Rather, it is a historically specific form that would be abolished, not realized, with the overcoming of capitalism. Marx's conception of the historical specificity of labor in capitalism requires a fundamental reinterpretation of his understanding of the social relations that characterize that society. Those relations are, according to Marx, constituted by labor itself and, consequently, have a peculiar, quasi-objective character; they cannot be grasped fully in terms of class relations.

The differences between the "categorial" and the "class-centered" interpretations of the fundamental social relations of capitalism are considerable. The former is a critique of labor in capitalism, the latter a critique of capitalism from the standpoint of labor; these imply very different conceptions of the determining mode of domination in capitalism and, hence, of the nature of its overcoming. The consequences of these differences will become clearer as I analyze more closely Marx's discussion of how the specific character of labor in capi-

36. *Grundrisse*, p. 705.

talism constitutes its basic social relations, and how it underlies both the specificity of value as a form of wealth and the nature of the industrial mode of
producing. The specific character of labor also—to jump ahead for a moment—
constitutes the basis for a historically specific, abstract, and impersonal form of
social domination.

In Marx's analysis, social domination in capitalism does not, on its most
fundamental level, consist in the domination of people by other people, but in
the domination of people by abstract social structures that people themselves
constitute. Marx sought to grasp this form of abstract, structural domination—
which encompasses, and extends beyond, class domination—with his categories
of the commodity and capital. This abstract domination not only determines the
goal of production in capitalism, according to Marx, but its material form as
well. Within the framework of Marx's analysis, the form of social domination
that characterizes capitalism is not ultimately a function of private property, of
the ownership by the capitalists of the surplus product and the means of production; rather, it is grounded in the value form of wealth itself, a form of social
wealth that confronts living labor (the workers) as a structurally alien and dominant power.[37] I shall try to show how, for Marx, this opposition between social
wealth and people is based on the unique character of labor in capitalist society.

According to Marx, the process by which labor in capitalism constitutes abstract social structures that dominate people is what induces a rapid historical development in the productive power and knowledge of humanity. Yet it does so by
fragmenting social labor—that is, at the expense of narrowing and emptying the
particular individual.[38] Marx argues that value-based production creates enormous
possibilities of wealth, but only by "positing . . . an individual's entire time as
labour time, [which results in] his degradation therefore to mere worker."[39]
Under capitalism the power and knowledge of humanity is increased greatly,
but in an alienated form that oppresses people and tends to destroy nature.[40]

A central hallmark of capitalism, then, is that people do not really control their
own productive activity or what they produce but ultimately are dominated by the
results of that activity. This form of domination is expressed as an opposition between individuals and society, which is constituted as an abstract structure.
Marx's analysis of this form of domination is an attempt to ground and explain
what, in his early writings, he referred to as alienation. Without entering into an
extensive discussion of the relationship of Marx's early writings to his later critical theory, I shall attempt to show that he did not later abandon all central
themes of those early works but that some—for example, alienation—remain central to his theory. Indeed, it is only in the later works that Marx rigorously grounds
the position he presents in the *Economic and Philosophic Manuscripts of 1844*—

37. Ibid., p. 831.
38. *Capital,* vol. 1, pp. 458, 469, 481–82, 486, 547.
39. *Grundrisse,* p. 708.
40. *Capital,* vol. 1, pp. 376, 638.

namely, that private property is not the social cause but the consequence of alienated labor and that, therefore, overcoming capitalism should not be conceived in terms of the abolition of private property alone, but must entail the overcoming of such labor.[41] He grounds this position in his later works with his analysis of the specific character of labor in capitalism. Nevertheless, that analysis also entails a modification of his earlier notion of alienation. The theory of alienation implied by Marx's mature critical theory does not refer to the estrangement of what had previously existed as a property of the workers (and should, therefore, be reclaimed by them); rather, it refers to a process of the historical constitution of social powers and knowledge that cannot be understood with reference to the immediate powers and skills of the proletariat. With his category of capital, Marx analyzed how these social powers and knowledge are constituted in objectified forms that become quasi-independent of, and exert a form of abstract social domination over, the individuals who constitute them.

This process of self-generated structural domination cannot be fully grasped in terms of class exploitation and domination, nor can it be understood in static, nondirectional, "synchronic" terms. The fundamental form of social domination characterizing modern society, that which Marx analyzed in terms of value and capital, is one that generates a historical dynamic beyond the control of the individuals constituting it. A central thrust of Marx's analysis of the specificity of labor in capitalist society is to explain this historical dynamic; not simply a theory of exploitation, or of the workings of the economy, narrowly understood, Marx's critical theory of capital is a theory of the nature of the history of modern society. It treats that history as being socially constituted and, yet, as possessing a quasi-autonomous developmental logic.

This preliminary discussion implies an understanding of the overcoming of alienation very different from that posited by traditional Marxism. It suggests that Marx regarded the industrial mode of production developed under capitalism and the intrinsic historical dynamic of that society as characteristic of the capitalist social formation. The historical negation of that social formation would, then, entail the abolition of both the historically dynamic system of abstract domination and the industrial capitalist mode of production. In the same vein, the developed theory of alienation implies that Marx saw the negation of the structural core of capitalism as allowing for the appropriation by people of the powers and knowledge that had been historically constituted in alienated form. Such appropriation would entail the material transcendence of the earlier split between the narrowed and impoverished individual and the alienated general

41. Marx, *Economic and Philosophic Manuscripts of 1844,* in Karl Marx and Frederick Engels, *Collected Works,* vol. 3: *Marx and Engels: 1843–44* (New York, 1975), p. 279ff. A more complete discussion of the relation of Marx's early manuscripts to his later works would show that many other themes of the former (for example, the relations between people and nature, women and men, work and play) remain implicitly central to the latter, yet are transformed by his analysis of the historically specific character of labor in capitalism.

productive knowledge of society by an incorporation of the latter into the former. This would allow the "mere worker"[42] to become the "social individual"[43]— one who incorporates the human knowledge and potential first developed historically in alienated form.

The notion of the social individual expresses Marx's idea that overcoming capitalism entails overcoming the opposition between individual and society. According to his analysis, both the bourgeois individual and society as an abstract whole confronting the individuals were constituted as capitalism superseded earlier forms of social life. For Marx, though, overcoming this opposition entails neither the subsumption of the individual under society nor their unmediated unity. The Marxian critique of the relation of individual and society in capitalism is not, as has been commonly assumed, limited to a critique of the isolated and fragmented bourgeois individual. Just as Marx did not criticize capitalism from the standpoint of industrial production, he did not positively evaluate the collectivity, in which all persons are parts, as the standpoint from which to criticize the atomized individual. In addition to relating the historical constitution of the monadic individual to the sphere of commodity circulation, Marx also analyzes the meta-apparatus in which persons are mere cogs as *characteristic* of the sphere of capital-determined production.[44] Such a collectivity does not at all represent the overcoming of capitalism. The opposition of the atomized individual to the collectivity (as a sort of "supersubject"), then, does not represent the opposition between the mode of social life in capitalism and that in a postcapitalist society; rather, it is the opposition of two one-sided determinations of the relationship of individual to society which, together, constitute yet another antinomy of the capitalist social formation.

For Marx, the social individual represents the overcoming of this opposition. This notion does not simply refer to a person who labors communally and altruistically with other people; rather, it expresses the possibility of every person existing as a full and richly developed being. A necessary condition for the realization of this possibility is that the labor of each person is full and positively self-constituting in ways that correspond to the general richness, varigatedness, power, and knowledge of society as a whole; individual labor would no longer be the fragmented basis for the richness of society. Overcoming alienation, then, entails not the reappropriation of an essence that had previously existed but the appropriation of what had been constituted in alienated form.

Thus far, this discussion implies that Marx saw proletarian labor itself as a materialized expression of alienated labor. Such a position suggests that it would be ideological at best to claim that the emancipation of labor is realized when private property is abolished and people have a collective, socially re-

42. *Grundrisse*, p. 708.
43. Ibid., p. 705.
44. *Capital*, vol. 1, pp. 477, 547, 614.

sponsible attitude toward their labor—if the concrete labor of each remains the same as under capitalism. On the contrary, the emancipation of labor presupposes a new structure of social labor; within the framework of Marx's analysis, labor can be constitutive of the social individual only when the productive forces' potential is used in a way that completely revolutionizes the organization of the labor process itself. People must be able to step outside of the direct labor process in which they had previously labored as parts, and control it from above. The control of the "process of nature, transformed into an industrial process"[45] must be available not only to society as a whole, but to all of its members. A necessary material condition for the full development of all individuals is that "labour in which a human being does what a thing could do has ceased."[46]

Marx's notion of the appropriation by "the mass of workers . . . of their own surplus labour,"[47] then, entails a process of self-abolition as a process of material self-transformation. Far from entailing the *realization* of the proletariat, overcoming capitalism involves the material *abolition* of proletarian labor. The emancipation of labor requires the emancipation from (alienated) labor.

In the course of our investigations, we shall see that capitalism, in Marx's analysis, is a social formation in which social production is for the sake of production, whereas the individual labors in order to consume. My discussion thus far implies that Marx envisaged its negation as a social formation in which social production is for consumption, whereas the labor of the individual is sufficiently satisfying to be pursued for its own sake.[48]

---

45. *Grundrisse*, p. 705.
46. Ibid., p. 325.
47. Ibid., p. 708.
48. As I shall discuss in Chapter Nine, below, it is important to distinguish two forms of necessity and freedom in Marx's analysis of social labor. That he thought social labor in a future society could be structured so as to be satisfying and enjoyable does not mean, as we have seen, that he thought such labor could become play. Marx's notion of nonalienated labor is that it is free of relations of direct and of abstract social domination; it can thereby become an activity for self-realization, hence more playlike. Yet this freedom from domination does not imply freedom from *all* constraints, since any human society requires labor in some form in order to survive. That labor can never be a sphere of absolute freedom, however, does not mean that nonalienated labor is unfree in the same way and to the same extent as labor constrained by forms of social domination. In other words, Marx, in denying that absolute freedom could exist in the realm of labor, was not reverting to Adam Smith's undifferentiated opposition of labor to freedom and happiness. (See *Grundrisse*, pp. 611–12.)

   It is clear, of course, that all one-sided and fragmented work could not be abolished immediately with the overcoming of capitalism. Moreover, it is conceivable that some such work could never be abolished fully (although the time it would require could be reduced drastically, and such tasks could be rotated among the population). Nevertheless, in order to highlight what I consider to be the main thrust of Marx's analysis of labor in capitalism and his related notion of labor in a future society, I shall not consider such problems in this work. (For a brief discussion of such problems, see Gorz, *Paths to Paradise*, p. 47ff.)

The contradiction of capitalism

Socialist society, according to Marx, does not emerge as the result of a linear, evolutionary historical development. The radical transformation of the process of production outlined above is *not* an automatic consequence of the rapid increase in scientific and technical knowledge or its application. It is, rather, a possibility that arises from a growing intrinsic social contradiction.

What is the nature of that contradiction? It is clear that for Marx, in the course of capitalist development the possibility emerges for a new emancipatory structure of social labor, but that its general realization is impossible under capitalism.

Capital itself is the moving contradiction, [in] that it presses to reduce labour time to a minimum, while it posits labour time, on the other side, as sole measure and source of wealth. Hence it diminishes labour time in the necessary form so as to increase it in the superfluous form; hence posits the superfluous in growing measure as a condition—question of life or death—for the necessary.[49]

I shall consider the question of "necessary" and "superfluous" labor time in more detail below. Here it suffices to note that, according to Marx, although capitalism tends to develop powerful forces of production whose potential increasingly renders obsolete an organization of production based upon direct labor time expenditure, it cannot allow the full realization of these forces. The only form of wealth that constitutes capital is one based upon direct labor time expenditure. Hence, value, despite its growing inadequacy as a measure of the material wealth produced, is not simply superseded by a new form of wealth. Instead, according to Marx, it remains the necessary structural precondition of capitalist society (although, as he argues in Volume 3 of *Capital,* this is not manifestly the case). So, although capitalism is characterized by an intrinsic developmental dynamic, that dynamic remains bound to capitalism; it is not self-overcoming. What becomes "superfluous" on one level remains "necessary" on another: in other words, capitalism *does* give rise to the possibility of its own negation, but it *does not* automatically evolve into something else. That the expenditure of direct human labor time remains central and indispensable for capitalism, despite being rendered anachronistic by the development of capitalism, gives rise to an internal tension. As I shall elaborate, Marx analyzes the nature of industrial production and its developmental trajectory with reference to this tension.

This important dimension of the fundamental contradiction of capitalism, as understood by Marx, indicates that it should not be identified immediately with concrete social relations of antagonism or conflict, such as those of class struggle. A fundamental contradiction is intrinsic to the structuring elements of capitalist society; it imparts a contradictory dynamic to the whole and gives rise to

49. *Grundrisse,* p. 706.

the immanent possibility of a new social order. The passages quoted indicate, further, that Marx's notion of the structural contradiction between the forces and relations of production should not be interpreted in the traditional way, where in "relations of production" are understood only in terms of the mode of distribution, and the "forces of production" are identified with the industrial mode of production, seen as a purely technical process. Within such an interpretation, the results of liberating those "forces" from their relational "fetters" would presumably be an acceleration of the dynamic of production, based on the same concrete form of the process of production and of the structure of labor. Yet the passages of the *Grundrisse* discussed above suggest that Marx treats the industrial mode of production and the historical dynamic of capitalism as characteristic features of capitalist society, and not as historical developments pointing beyond, but inhibited by, capitalist relations. His understanding of the contradiction of capitalism seems not to refer most essentially to a contradiction between private appropriation and socialized production,[50] but to a contradiction *within* the sphere of production itself, whereby that sphere includes the immediate process of production *and* the structure of social relations constituted by labor in capitalism. With regard to the structure of social labor, then, the Marxian contradiction should be understood as a growing contradiction between the sort of labor people perform under capitalism and the sort of labor they could perform if value were abolished and the productive potential developed under capitalism were reflexively used to liberate people from the sway of the alienated structures constituted by their own labor.

In the course of this work, I shall show how Marx grounds this contradiction in the fundamental structuring social form of capitalism (that is, the commodity), and shall elaborate as well how, for Marx, "freeing" the forces of production from the "fetters" of the relations of production requires the abolition of both value and the specific character of labor in capitalism. This would entail the negation of the intrinsic historical logic, as well as of the industrial mode of production characteristic of the capitalist social formation.

This preliminary exposition of Marx's notion of alienation and of the contradiction of capitalism indicates that his analysis seeks to grasp the course of capitalist development as a double-sided development of enrichment and impoverishment. It implies that this development cannot be understood adequately in a one-dimensional fashion, either as the progress of knowledge and happiness, or as the "progress" of domination and destruction. According to his analysis, although the historical *possibility* that the mode of social labor could be enrich-

---

50. The argument that the primary contradiction of capitalism is, for Marx, structural and does not refer simply to social antagonism has been made by Anthony Giddens as well. However, he locates that contradiction between private appropriation and socialized production, that is, between bourgeois relations of distribution and industrial production: see Anthony Giddens, *Central Problems in Social Theory* (Berkeley and Los Angeles, 1979), pp. 135–41. My reading of the *Grundrisse* supports a very different interpretation.

ing for everyone emerges, social labor has *actually* become impoverishing for the many. The rapid increase in scientific and technical knowledge under capitalism does not, therefore, signify linear progress toward emancipation. According to Marx's analysis of the commodity and capital, such increased knowledge—itself socially constituted—has led to the fragmentation and emptying of individual labor and to the increasing control of humanity by the results of its objectifying activity; yet it has also increased the possibility that labor could be individually enriching and that humanity could exert greater control over its fate. This double-sided development is rooted in the alienated structures of capitalist society and can be overcome. Marx's dialectical analysis, then, should not in any way be identified with the positivist faith in linear scientific progress and in social progress, or in the correlation of the two.[51]

Marx's analysis thus implies a notion of overcoming capitalism that entails neither uncritically affirming industrial production as the condition of human progress nor romantically rejecting technological progress per se. By indicating that the potential of the system of production developed under capitalism could be used to transform that system itself, Marx's analysis overcomes the opposition of these stances and shows that each takes one moment of a more complex historical development to be the whole. That is, Marx's approach grasps the opposition of the faith in linear progress and its romantic rejection as expressing a historical antinomy which, in *both* of its terms, is characteristic of the capitalist epoch.[52] More generally, his critical theory argues for neither simply retaining nor for abolishing what was constituted historically in capitalism. Rather, his theory points to the possibility that what was constituted in alienated form be appropriated and, thereby, fundamentally transformed.

Social movements, subjectivity, and historical analysis

This interpretation of Marx's analysis of capitalism and of the nature of its fundamental contradiction recasts the problem of the relation of social class, social movements, and the possibility of overcoming capitalism. By contravening analyses in which the industrial mode of production is seen as fundamentally in tension with capitalism, this approach rejects the idea that the proletariat represents a social counterprinciple to capitalism. According to Marx, manifestations of class struggle between the representatives of capital and the workers over working-time issues or the relationship of wages and profits, for example, are structurally intrinsic to capitalism, hence an important constitutive

---

51. In chapters Four and Five, I shall deal more extensively with this position as it has been propounded by Jürgen Habermas in *Knowledge and Human Interests,* trans. Jeremy Shapiro (Boston, 1971), and Albrecht Wellmer in *Critical Theory of Society,* trans. John Cumming (New York, 1974).
52. *Capital,* vol. 1, pp. 568–69, 798ff.

element of the dynamic of that system.[53] Nevertheless, his analysis of value necessarily implies that the basis of capital is and remains proletarian labor. That labor, then, is not the basis of the potential negation of the capitalist social formation. The contradiction of capitalism presented in the *Grundrisse* is not between proletarian labor and capitalism, but between proletarian labor—that is, the existent structure of labor—and the possibility of another mode of production. The critique presented in this work of socialism conceived as a more efficient, humane, and just way of administering the industrial mode of production that arose under capitalism is thus a critique as well of the notion of the proletariat as the revolutionary Subject, in the sense of a social agent that both constitutes history and realizes itself in socialism.

This implies that there is no linear continuum between the demands and conceptions of the working class historically constituting and asserting itself, and the needs, demands, and conceptions that point beyond capitalism. The latter—which might include a need for self-fulfilling activity, for example—would not be limited to the sphere of consumption and to issues of distributive justice, but would call into question the nature of work and the structure of objective constraints that characterize capitalism. This suggests that a critical theory of capitalism and of its possible overcoming must entail a theory of the social constitution of such needs and forms of consciousness—one able to address qualitative historical transformations in subjectivity and to understand social movements in those terms. Such an approach could shed new light on Marx's notion of the self-abolition of the proletariat, and could be useful in analyzing the new social movements of the past two decades.

The categories of Marx's critical theory, when interpreted as categories of structured forms of practice that are determinations of both social "objectivity" and "subjectivity" (rather than as categories of social "objectivity" alone, much less as economic categories), can provide the basis for such a historical theory of subjectivity. In such a reading, the analysis of the dynamic character of capitalism is also, potentially, an analysis of the historical transformations of subjectivity. If, moreover, the social forms that structure capitalist society can be shown to be contradictory, it becomes possible to treat critical and oppositional consciousness as being socially constituted.

This interpretation of the Marxian contradiction as being both "objective" and "subjective" should not, however, be taken as implying that oppositional consciousness will necessarily emerge, much less that emancipation will automatically be achieved. My concern here is not with the theoretical level of *probability,* for example, the probability that such consciousness will emerge; rather, I am considering the level of *possibility,* that is to say, the more fundamental formulation of an approach to the problem of the social constitution of subjectivity, including the possibility of critical or oppositional consciousness.

53. Ibid., p. 344.

The notion of contradiction allows for a theory that grounds the possibility of such consciousness socially. If capitalist society is not thought of as a unitary whole and its social forms are not considered "one-dimensional," one can analyze critical and oppositional forms of consciousness as socially constituted possibilities.

Such a theory of the social constitution of subjectivity (including subjectivity critical of its own context) stands opposed to the implicitly functionalist notion that only consciousness which affirms or perpetuates the existent order is socially formed. It opposed as well the notion, covertly related to the first, that the possibility of critical, oppositional, or revolutionary consciousness must be rooted ontologically or transcendentally—or, at the very least, in elements of social life that purportedly are noncapitalist. The approach I shall outline does not deny the existence or importance of residual, noncapitalist tendencies, which may introduce some heterogeneity into the dominant order and promote critical distance to it; but it *does* provide the basis for a critique of those theoretical attempts that focus exclusively on such tendencies *because* they consider capitalism to be a unitary whole. Whereas such approaches to the problem of resistance and opposition conceive of capitalist society only as reified and deforming, and treat critical thought and practices as historically indeterminate, the analysis of capitalism as a contradictory society seeks to indicate that the possibilities for critical distance and heterogeneity are generated socially from within the framework of capitalism itself. It lays the groundwork for a historical theory of subjectivity (including oppositional forms of subjectivity) that, in my judgment, is much more powerful than theoretical efforts that presuppose a simple antagonism between the existing social order and critical forms of subjectivity and practices. Such an approach allows one to investigate the relation of various critical conceptions and practices to their historical context—in terms of the constitution of such conceptions and practices, as well as in terms of their possible historical effects—and thereby allows one to consider the role such oppositional subjectivity and practices might play in relation to the possible determinate negation of capitalism. In short, such an approach allows one to analyze the possibility that the existing order might be transformed.

Seeing capitalism as contradictory in these terms allows for a social critique that is self-reflexively consistent and understands itself with reference to its context. This approach allows one to analyze the intrinsic relation, however mediated, between critical theory and the emergence of capital-negating needs and oppositional forms of consciousness on a popular level. Such a reflexive social theory of subjectivity contrasts sharply with those critiques that cannot ground the possibility of fundamentally oppositional consciousness in the existing order, or do so only objectivistically, implicitly positing a privileged position for critical thinkers whose knowledge inexplicably has escaped social deformation. Such approaches fall back into the antinomies of Enlightenment materialism, already criticized by Marx in his "Theses on Feuerbach," whereby a population is divided into the many, who are socially determined, and the critical few who, for some reason, are not.[54] They implicitly represent an epistemologically inconsistent mode of social critique that cannot account for its own existence and must present itself in the form of tragic stance or avant-garde pedagogy.

Some present-day implications

At this point I would like briefly to indicate some further implications of the interpretation of Marx's critical theory, based on the *Grundrisse,* that I have begun to outline. Focusing on the historically specific form of labor in capitalism lays the groundwork for a concept of capital and an understanding of the dynamic of the capitalist social formation that do not depend essentially on the market-mediated mode of distribution—in other words, it allows for an analysis of capitalism that is not bound to its nineteenth-century forms. Such an approach could provide the basis for analyzing as capitalist the nature and dynamic of modern society in a period when state institutions and other large bureaucratic organizations have become significant, sometimes primary, agents of social regulation and distribution. It could also serve as the point of departure for understanding current global social and economic transformations as transformations of capitalism.

Focusing on the critique of production, moreover, allows one to recover Marx's notion of socialism as a *post*capitalist form of social life. I have argued that the historical relationship of socialism to capitalism, for Marx, is not simply a question of the historical preconditions for the abolition of private ownership of the means of production, and the replacement of the market by planning. This relationship should also be conceived in terms of the growing possibility that the historically specific role of labor in capitalism could be superseded by another form of social mediation. This possibility, according to Marx, is grounded in an increasing tension generated by capitalist development between value and "real wealth." This tension points to the possible systemic abolition of value and, hence, of abstract domination, of the abstract necessity of a particular form of "growth," and of direct human labor as an internal element of production. The material foundation of a classless society, according to Marx's exposition in the *Grundrisse,* is a form of production in which the surplus product no longer is created primarily by direct human labor. According to this approach, the crucial question of socialism is not whether a capitalist class exists but whether a proletariat still exists.

Critical theories of capitalism that deal only with overcoming the bourgeois

---

54. Marx, "Theses on Feuerbach," in Karl Marx and Frederick Engels, *Collected Works,* vol. 5: *Marx and Engels: 1845–47* (New York, 1976), pp. 5–8.

mode of distribution cannot fully grasp this dimension of capitalism and, worse, can veil the fact that overcoming class society entails overcoming the foundation of the mode of production. Thus, one variant of traditional Marxism became an ideology of legitimation for those social forms—the "actually existing social-ist" countries—in which the liberal bourgeois mode of distribution was abol-ished but the capital-determined mode of production was not, and the abolition of the former served ideologically to veil the existence of the latter.[55]

Marx's notion of a postcapitalist society, then, must be distinguished from state-directed modes of capital accumulation. The interpretation outlined above, with its emphasis on the specific form of labor as constituting capital, is con-sonant with a historical analysis of the rise of the "actually existing socialist" countries in terms of the interrelation between the development of industrial capitalism in the metropolitan centers of the world economy and the increasing role of the state in "peripheral" countries. It could be argued that, for a phase of global capitalist development, the state served to effect the creation of total capital nationally. In such a situation, the suspension of the free circulation of commodities, money, and capital did not imply socialism. Rather, it was one of the few, if not the only, means by which a "capital revolution" was able to succeed in the periphery of a world market context, where the original historical connection of bourgeois revolution and the consolidation of total national capital no longer existed. The result, however, was not, and could not have been, post-capitalist society. Capital-determined society is not simply a function of the market and private property; it cannot be reduced sociologically to the domi-nation of the bourgeoisie.

Clearly, considering statist organizations of modern society in terms of the development of the capitalist social formation, rather than as the negation of

---

55. I shall not, in this work, pursue the implications of my reconsideration of Marx's conception of the basic parameters of capitalism for the question of the stages or forms of postcapitalist society (for example, "socialism" and "communism"). I should, however, note that the terms of the question change when the forms of social domination and exploitation central to, and characteristic of, capitalism are no longer located in the private ownership of the means of production, but rather in the alienated structures of social relations expressed by the categories of the commodity and capital, as well as when the process of alienation is understood as a form of social and historical constitution, rather than as the estrangement of a pre-given human essence. For a different approach to the question, see Stanley Moore, *Marx on the Choice between Socialism and Communism* (Cambridge, Mass., and London, 1980). Moore identifies exploitation with capitalist private ownership, and on that basis he argues for the superiority of a society with exchange but no private ownership of the means of production (his determination of "socialism") to one with neither ("communism"): see pp. viii–ix, 34–35, 82. Moore's intent is to argue against the view that socialism, so determined, is merely an incomplete form of postcapitalist society, a prelude to "communism." In so doing, he seeks to undermine an ideological justification of political, social, and cultural repression in "actually existing social-ist" societies (p. x). In that sense, there is a parallel in strategic intent between Moore's ap-proach and the very different interpretation of Marx presented here, according to which such societies should not be considered postcapitalist at all.

capitalism, also recasts the problem of postcapitalist democracy. This analysis grounds a mode of abstract compulsions and constraints, historically specific to capitalism, in the social forms of value and capital. That the social relations expressed by these categories are not fully identical with the market and private property implies that those compulsions could continue to exist in the absence of bourgeois relations of distribution. If this is so, the question of postcapitalist democracy can not be posed adequately in terms of an opposition between statist and nonstatist conceptions of politics alone. Rather, one must consider a further critical dimension: the nature of the constraints imposed upon political decisions by the forms of value and capital. That is to say, the approach I shall begin to develop in this work suggests that postcapitalist democracy entails more than democratic political forms in the absence of private ownership of the means of production. It would require as well the abolition of the abstract social compulsions rooted in the social forms grasped by the Marxian categories.

Such a reconstruction of the Marxian theory renders it more fruitful today as a way of critically analyzing modern society. It is intended both as a critique of traditional Marxism and as an attempt to lay the groundwork for a critical social theory able to respond to the pessimistic analyses of such great social thinkers as Georg Simmel, Émile Durkheim, and Max Weber, each of whom identified and analyzed elements of the negative aspects of the development of modern society. (For example, Simmel's examination of the growing gap between the richness of "objective culture" and the relative narrowness of individual, "subjective culture"; Durkheim's investigation of the increase in anomie with the supersession of mechanical by organic solidarity; and Weber's analysis of the rationalization of all spheres of social life.) Writing during the transition from a more liberal form of capitalism to a more organized form, each maintained in his own way that a critical theory of capitalism—understood as a critique of private property and the market—can not adequately grasp essential features of modern society; and each recognized that centrally important aspects of modern industrial social life are left untouched when only the mode of distribution and the relations of class power are transformed. For these thinkers, the supersession of capitalism by socialism, as envisioned by traditional Marxism, involved a nonessential transformation of the social formation, if not a heightening of its negative aspects.

The reinterpretation of Marx's critical theory I present here is an attempt to meet the challenge posed by their various critiques of modern society by developing a broader and deeper theory of capitalism, one capable of encompassing those critiques. Such an approach, instead of considering various processes—such as the growth of a gap between "objective" and "subjective" culture, or the increasing instrumental rationalization of modern life—as necessary and irreversible results of a fatelike development, would allow one to ground such processes socially in historically determinate forms of social practice, and to grasp their developmental trajectory as nonlinear, and transformable.

This reinterpretation of Marx also entails, as noted, a sociohistorical theory of subjectivity, on the basis of which one could develop a powerful approach to the Weberian problematic of modernity and rationalization. While according importance to the forms of thought that were crucial to the development of capitalism, and to the ongoing processes of differentiation and rationalization, such an approach could also address that thought and those processes themselves in terms of the forms of social life expressed by the Marxian categories. Finally, we shall also see that Marx's theory of the constitution of the social structures and historical dynamic of modern society by historically determinate forms of practice can be read as a sophisticated theory of the sort proposed recently by Pierre Bourdieu—that is, as a theory of the mutually constituting relationship between social structure and everyday forms of practice and thought.[56] Such a theory would be able to overcome the currently widespread antinomy of functionalism and methodological individualism, neither of which is capable of relating intrinsically the objective and subjective dimensions of social life.

Most important, though, a theory of the socially constituted character of the structures and the historical processes of capitalism is also a theory of their possible overcoming. This overcoming can be conceived in terms of the dialectical reversal outlined above, as the subjective appropriation of objective culture and its transformation, made possible by the overcoming of the structure of abstract social compulsion which is rooted ultimately in alienated labor. The difference between capitalism, defined thus, and its possible historical negation can, then, justifiably be treated as that between one social formation and another.

56. Pierre Bourdieu, *Outline of a Theory of Practice,* trans. Richard Nice (Cambridge, 1977), pp. 1–30, 87–95.

2. Presuppositions of traditional Marxism

Value and labor

The approach I have begun to outline represents a fundamentally different sort of critical theory than the traditional Marxist critique of capitalism. It calls into question the traditional understanding of the nature of capitalism and its basic contradiction between the "forces" and the "relations" of production, as well as the traditional conception of socialism and the historical role of the working class. This approach does not merely supplement the traditional view of capitalism—that is, the primary emphasis on the market and private property—with a critique of the form of production.[1] Rather, it reconceptualizes the nature of capitalist society itself on the basis of an interpretation of Marx's theory as a historically specific critical theory of modern, capitalist society—one that rests upon a critique of labor, of the form of mediation and of the mode of producing in that society. Such an approach, suggested by the reading of the *Grundrisse* outlined above, entails a critique of the basic assumptions of traditional Marxist interpretations, and implies the need for a fundamental reinterpretation of the central categories of Marx's mature critical theory.

In order to elucidate the various dimensions of such a categorial reinterpretation, I shall begin by analyzing more closely the presuppositions of the traditional Marxist critique. (As noted above, this work is not a survey of Marxist thought but, in part, an explication of the assumptions underlying all forms of traditional Marxism, however those forms may differ in other respects.) This investigation will make clear that the approach presented in this work and that of traditional Marxism are fundamentally different forms of social critique—the latter a critique of capitalism from the standpoint of labor, and the former a critique of the historically determinate character of labor in capitalism as con-

---

1. The tensions between these two critical approaches inform Ernest Mandel's *Late Capitalism* (trans. Joris De Bres, [London and New York, 1978]), a major study of the historical trajectory of modern capitalism. Although his investigation of the contemporary phase of capitalism, the period marked by the "third technological revolution," is based upon Marx's analysis of the contradiction of capitalism in the *Grundrisse,* he does not consistently draw out the implications of that analysis. Instead, his treatment of the various epochs of capitalist development focuses on issues of competition and "uneven development" in a manner that implicitly remains bound to a traditional Marxist understanding of capitalism and of the Soviet Union as socialist.

stituting that society. (In the course of this examination, I will necessarily refer to Marxian categories, such as value, whose full meaning can only be developed in the second half of this work.)

The social relations that characterize capitalism, which Marx terms the capitalist "relations of production," purportedly are grasped by the basic categories of his mature critique of political economy. Marx begins his critical analysis of modern, capitalist society with the category of the commodity. Within the framework of his analysis, this category refers not only to a product but also to the most fundamental structuring social form of capitalist society, a form constituted by a historically determinate mode of social practice. Marx then goes on to unfold a series of categories, such as money and capital, with which he attempts to explain the nature and developmental dynamic of capitalism. He analyzes the category of the commodity itself in terms of an opposition between what he terms "value" and "use value."[2] I shall examine these categories more extensively below but here it suffices to recall that, in the *Grundrisse,* Marx treats value as a category expressing both the determinate form of social relations and the particular form of wealth that characterize capitalism. It is the initial and logically most abstract determination of capitalist social relations in Marx's analysis.[3] We have also seen that Marx's category of value and, hence, his conception of capitalist relations of production, cannot be understood adequately in terms of the mode of distribution alone, but must be grasped in relation to the mode of production as well.

This being said, we can proceed to examine the categorial presuppositions of traditional Marxism by analyzing several well-known interpretations of Marx's category of value, the "law of value" and the character of value-constituting labor. In *The Theory of Capitalist Development,* Paul Sweezy emphasizes that value should not be understood as an economic category in the narrower sense, but as "an outward form of the social relation between the commodity owners."[4] The basic nature of this social relation, according to Sweezy, is that "individual producers, each working in isolation, are in fact working for each other."[5] In other words, although social interdependence does exist, it is not expressed overtly in the organization of society but functions indirectly. Value is the outward form of that nonovert interdependence. It expresses an indirect mode of the social distribution of labor and its products. Sweezy, then, interprets the category of value solely in terms of the market. Consequently, he describes the Marxian law of value as follows: "What Marx called the 'law of value' summarizes those forces at work in a commodity-producing society which regulate a) the exchange ratios among commodities, b) the quantity of each produced, and c) the allocation of the labor force to

2. Marx, *Capital,* vol. 1, trans. Ben Fowkes (London, 1976), p. 125ff.
3. Ibid., p. 174n3.
4. Sweezy, *The Theory of Capitalist Development* (New York, 1969), p. 27.
5. Ibid.

the various branches of production."[6] According to this interpretation, the law of value is "essentially a theory of general equilibrium."[7] One of its primary functions "is to make clear that in a commodity-producing society, in spite of the absence of centralized and coordinated decision-making, there is order and not simply chaos."[8] The law of value according to Sweezy, then, is an attempt to explain the workings of the self-regulating market, which implies that value is a category of distribution alone, an expression of the non-conscious, "automatic," market-mediated mode of distribution in capitalism. It is not surprising, therefore, that Sweezy abstractly opposes value, as the principle of capitalism, to planning, as the principle of socialism.[9] The mode by which distribution is effected is the essential critical focus of such an interpretation.

It is undeniable that overcoming capitalism, for Marx, does involve overcoming an "automatic" mode of distribution. Nevertheless, the category of value cannot be adequately understood in terms of the mode of distribution alone; Marx analyzes not only how distribution is effected, but what is distributed as well. As we have seen, he treats value as a historically specific form of wealth, opposing it to "real wealth" in the *Grundrisse*. However, when value is regarded essentially as a category of market-mediated distribution, it is treated as a historically specific *mode of the distribution of wealth,* but not as a specific *form of wealth* itself. We shall see that the emergence of value as a form of wealth may have been related historically to the rise of a particular mode of distribution, according to Marx, but it does not remain bound to that mode. Once fully established socially, it can be distributed in various ways. Indeed, I shall argue that, contrary to the assumptions of Sweezy, Ernest Mandel,[10] and others, there is not even a necessary logical opposition between value and planning. The existence of the latter need not signify the absence of the former; value can be distributed by means of planning as well.

Because the traditional interpretation of value as a category of the distribution of wealth overlooks Marx's opposition of value to what he variously calls "material wealth" or "real wealth," it cannot analyze the historical specificity of the form of labor that constitutes value. If value is a historically specific form of wealth, the labor that creates it also must be historically determinate. (An analysis of that specificity would allow for an analysis of how the value-form structures the sphere of production as well as that of distribution.) If, however, value were simply a category of the distribution of wealth, the labor that creates that wealth would not differ intrinsically from labor in noncapitalist formations.

6. Ibid., pp. 52–53.
7. Ibid., p. 53.
8. Ibid.
9. Ibid., pp. 53–54.
10. Ernest Mandel, *The Formation of the Economic Thought of Karl Marx* (New York and London, 1971), p. 98.

The difference between them would be extrinsic—merely a matter of how they are coordinated socially.

It should come as no surprise, therefore, that traditional attempts to specify the character of labor in capitalism do so in terms of this extrinsic difference. Vitali Vygodski, for example, who, like Sweezy, interprets value as a category of market distribution, describes the specificity of labor in capitalism as follows: "although social like all labour, under the conditions of private ownership of the means of production . . . it does not have a directly social character."[11] Before analyzing what Vygodski means by "social," it should be noted that his characterization implies that labor in capitalism is intrinsically similar to labor in all societies; it differs only inasmuch as its social character is not expressed directly. Ernest Mandel presents a similar interpretation. Although he differs from Vygodski over the centrality of private property to capitalism,[12] he too characterized the specificity of labor in capitalism in terms of its indirectly social character: "When individual labor is directly recognized as social labor—and this is one of the fundamental features of socialist society—it is obviously absurd to take the roundabout route through the market in order to 'rediscover' the social quality of this labor."[13] The purpose of Marx's theory of value, according to Mandel, is to express the indirect manner by which the social quality of labor is established in capitalism.[14]

Such interpretations, which characterize labor in capitalism as being indirectly social, are very common.[15] Note, however, that what they present as the specific social "character" or "quality" of labor in capitalism is actually the mode of its distribution. Such a determination remains extrinsic to labor itself. Marx's characterization of labor in capitalism as simultaneously private and social can help to clarify the distinction between an extrinsic and an intrinsic determination of the specificity of that labor.[16]

The various passages cited above suggest that when value is interpreted as a market category, the description of labor in capitalism as both private and social is taken to mean that labor is social because people "actually" are working for each other as members of a larger social organism—but that in a society structured by the market and private property it *appears* to be private, because people work directly for themselves and only indirectly for others. Inasmuch as labor is mediated by capitalist relations of production, its social character cannot ap-

---

11. Vitali Solomonovich Vygodski, *The Story of a Great Discovery* (Berlin, 1973), p. 54.
12. Mandel, *Formation of the Economic Thought,* p. 98.
13. Ibid., p. 97.
14. Ibid.
15. See, for example, Helmut Reichelt, *Zur logischen Struktur des Kapitalbegriffs bei Karl Marx* (Frankfurt, 1970), pp. 146–47; Anwar Shaikh, "The Poverty of Algebra," in Ian Steedman, Paul Sweezy, et al., *The Value Controversy* (London, 1981), p. 271.
16. Marx, *A Contribution to the Critique of Political Economy*, trans. S. W. Ryazanskaya (Moscow, 1970), p. 34.

pear as such. "Social" in such a scheme, however, is simply that which is not "private," that which purportedly pertains to the collectivity rather than to the individual. The specific nature of the social relations involved is not interrogated, nor is the opposition of social and private entailed by such a generic conception of "the social."

Such interpretations imply that overcoming capitalism would involve the supersession of a mediated form of social relations by a direct unmediated form. Labor could then realize its social character directly. This sort of critical analysis is a critique of the individuated, indirectly social character of labor in capitalism from the standpoint of its "true," directly social, and totalizing character. It is, more generally, a critique of mediated social relations from the standpoint of unmediated ("direct") social relations.

Contrary to such interpretations, however, Marx's characterization of labor in capitalism as both private and social is not a critique of its private dimension from the standpoint of its social dimension. It refers not to the difference between the true, transhistorical "essence" of labor and its form of appearance in capitalism but, rather, to two moments of labor in capitalism itself: "The labour which expresses itself in exchange-value is presupposed as the labour of the isolated individual. It becomes social by assuming the form of its immediate opposite, the form of abstract generality."[17] Marx's characterization here is part of his analysis of what he called the "twofold" or "double" character of commodity-determined labor; it is the "labour of the isolated individual" and it "assumes the form of abstract generality." (As we shall see, Marx defines the latter form as directly or immediately social.) Note that Marx's description of the dual character of labor in capitalism implies an approach very different from that based upon the undifferentiated notion of "the social" outlined above. His concern is to grasp the specificity of a particular form of social life. Far from treating the opposition of the social and the private as one between what is potentially noncapitalist and what is specific to capitalist society, he treats the opposition itself, and both of its terms, as peculiarly characteristic of labor in capitalism and of capitalist society itself. In other words, the opposition of private and directly social labor is of one-sided terms that complement and depend on each other. This suggests that it is precisely labor in capitalism that has a directly social dimension, and that "directly social labor" exists only within a social framework marked by the existence of "private labor" as well. Contrary to the interpretation outlined above, Marx explicitly asserts that the immediately social character of labor in capitalist society is at the core of that society. He considers this directly social character of labor to be central to the historical processes that characterize capitalism, processes in which socially general powers and wealth are developed, but at the cost of the individuals:

17. Ibid. (translation amended).

In fact, in that epoch of history that directly precedes the conscious reconstruction of human society, it is only through the most tremendous waste of individual development that the development of humanity in general is secured and pursued. Since the whole of the economizing we are discussing here arises from the social character of labor, *it is precisely this immediately social character of labour that produces this waste of the worker's life and health.*[18]

We have begun to uncover a remarkable opposition. According to interpretations of value as a market category, labor is directly social in all societies *except* in capitalism; yet, according to Marx, it is *only* in capitalism that labor also has a directly social dimension. That which would be realized in overcoming capitalism, according to the traditional approach, is precisely that which should be abolished, according to Marx.

A central concern of this work will be to elaborate this basic difference by analyzing Marx's conception of the directly social dimension of labor in capitalism. I shall anticipate that analysis by summarizing it here: Within the framework of Marx's mature critical theory, labor in capitalism is directly social because it acts as a socially mediating activity. This social quality, which is historically unique, distinguishes labor in capitalism from labor in other societies and determines the character of social relations in the capitalist formation. Far from signifying the absence of social mediation (that is, the existence of unmediated social relations), the directly social character of labor constitutes a determinate form of social mediation specific to capitalism.

Marx's critique of capitalist society, as noted, should not be understood as a critique of the atomized mode of individual social existence in that society from the standpoint of the collectivity in which people are component parts. Instead, it analyzes capitalist society in terms of an opposition between the isolated individuals and the social collectivity. The critique is of *both* terms; it maintains that they are structurally related and that they form an opposition specific to capitalism. Marx's critical analysis of this opposition is undertaken from the standpoint of the historical possibility of its overcoming, a standpoint represented by Marx's notion of the social individual. By the same token, we now see that the Marxian critique of labor in capitalism is not one of the private character of labor from the standpoint of directly social labor; rather, it is a critique of private labor and immediately social labor as complementary, as one-sided terms of an elemental opposition that characterizes capitalist society.

This interpretation of Marx suggests that it is inadequate to conceive of social relations—that is, forms of social interdependence—as being either direct or indirect. Marx's critique is of the nature of social mediation in capitalism, not of the mere circumstance that social relations are mediated. Social interdependence is always mediated (nonmediated interdependence is a contradiction in

18. Marx, *Capital,* vol. 3, trans. David Fernbach (Harmondsworth, England, 1981), p. 182 (translation amended, emphasis added).

terms). What characterizes a society is the specific character of that mediation, of its social relations. Marx's analysis is a critique of labor-mediated social relations from the standpoint of the historically emergent possibility of other social and political mediations. As such, it is a critical theory of forms of social mediation, not a critique of mediation from the standpoint of immediacy. Construing it thus avoids the possible pitfalls of the latter position: A vision of a possible postcapitalist society in terms of overcoming mediation per se can lead to a vision of socialism that is essentially apolitical, whether of a statist or of a utopian communitarian variety.[19] Moreover, the Marxian critique, seen as one of a specific form of mediation rather than of mediation per se, is consonant with a concern with the possible forms of social and political mediation in a postcapitalist society; indeed, by grounding such a concern socially and historically, this theory renders it able to assess the historical viability and social consequences of possible postcapitalist forms.

I have outlined, then, a theory whose essential object of critical investigation is the historically specific form of labor, and one for which the form of labor remains an unexamined point of departure for a critical examination of forms of distribution. These differences are related to the divergence between the vision of socialism presented in the *Grundrisse*—wherein the forms of wealth and labor specific to capitalism would be abolished with the overcoming of that formation—and that implied by an interpretation of value as a category of the market, according to which the *same* forms of wealth and of labor that are distributed mediately in capitalism would be coordinated directly in socialism. The extent of this divergence requires that I further investigate the assumptions of critical theories of the mode of distribution alone. I shall do so by comparing Marx's critique with that of classical political economy.

Ricardo and Marx

In *Political Economy and Capitalism,* Maurice Dobb provides a definition of the law of value similar to that given by Sweezy: "The law of value was a principle of exchange relations between commodities, including labour power. It was simultaneously a determinant of the mode in which labour was allocated between different industries in the general social division of labour and of the distribution of the products among classes."[20] By interpreting value as a market category, Dobb characterizes capitalism essentially as a system of nonconscious social regulation. The law of value, according to Dobb, indicates that "a system of com-

---

19. For a more extensive discussion of this point, see Jean Cohen, *Class and Civil Society: The Limits of Marxian Critical Theory* (Amherst, Mass., 1982). Although Cohen identifies the traditional view of overcoming mediation with Marx's critique, her strategic intent in criticizing the notion that mediation itself could be transcended parallels that of my interpretation in this regard.

20. Dobb, *Political Economy and Capitalism* (London, 1940), pp. 70–71.

modity production and exchange can operate of itself without collective regulation or single design.''[21] He describes the workings of this ''automatic'' mode of distribution with reference to the theories of classical political economy:[22] the law of value shows that ''this disposition of the social labour-force was not arbitrary but followed a determinate law of cost by virtue of Adam Smith's 'unseen hand' of competitive forces.''[23] Dobb's formulation makes explicit what is implicit in such interpretations of Marx's law of value—that this law is basically similar to the ''invisible hand'' of Adam Smith. The question, however, is whether the two indeed can be equated. Put more generally: What is the difference between classical political economy and Marx's critique of political economy?

The classical economists, according to Dobb, ''had, in demonstrating the laws of *laissez-faire,* provided a critique of previous orders of society; but they had not provided a historical critique of capitalism itself.''[24] The latter task was Marx's contribution.[25] As it stands, there is little to object to in Dobb's statement. Nevertheless it is necessary to specify what Dobb means by social critique in general and the critique of capitalism in particular.

According to Dobb, the critical thrust of political economy was to indicate that regulation of society by the state, though considered essential under mercantilism, was unnecessary.[26] Furthermore, by showing that the relationships controlling the behavior of exchange values are relationships among people as producers, political economy became primarily a theory of production.[27] It implied that a consuming class, which bore no active relation to the production of commodities, played no positive economic role in society.[28] Thus the Ricardians, for example, could use the theory to attack the landed interests since, in their view, the only active factors in production are labor and capital—but not land rent.[29] Dobb's notion of social critique, in other words, is a critique of nonproductive social groupings from the standpoint of productiveness.

Marx's historical critique of capitalism, according to Dobb, involved taking the classical theory of value and, by refining it, turning it against the bourgeoisie. Marx, he argues, went beyond the Ricardians by showing that profit could not be explained with reference to any inherent property of capital, and that only labor was productive.[30] At the crux of Marx's argument is the concept of surplus value. He proceeded from an analysis of the class structure of capitalist society—in which the members of one major class have no property and are thus compelled to

21. Ibid., p. 37.
22. Ibid., p. 9.
23. Ibid., p. 63.
24. Ibid., p. 55.
25. Ibid.
26. Ibid., p. 49.
27. Ibid., pp. 38–39.
28. Ibid., p. 50.
29. Ibid.
30. Ibid., p. 58.

sell their labor power in order to survive—and then showed that the value of labor power as a commodity (the amount necessary for its reproduction) is less than the value that labor in action produces.[31] The difference between the two constitutes the "surplus" value that is appropriated by the capitalists.

In locating the difference between Marx's analysis and classical political economy in the theory of surplus value, Dobb assumes that they share substantially identical theories of value and of the law of value. Thus, he claims that Marx "took-over" the theory of value from classical political economy[32] and developed it further by showing profit to be a function of labor alone.[33] Consequently, "the essential difference between Marx and classical Political Economy lay . . . in the theory of surplus-value."[34] According to this very common interpretation, Marx's theory of value is essentially a refined and more consistent version of Ricardo's labor theory of value.[35] His law of value, therefore, also has a similar function—to explain the workings of the laissez-faire mode of distribution in terms of labor. However, Dobb himself points out that although the category of value and the law of value developed by classical political economy provide a critique of earlier orders of society, they do not, in and of themselves, provide the basis for a historical critique of capitalism.[36] The implication of such a position, then, is that Marx's critique of capitalism is not yet expressed by the categories with which he began his critique of political economy—categories such as the commodity, abstract labor, and value, that are developed on the initial logical level of his analysis.[37] Rather, this level of his analysis is implicitly taken to be a prolegomenon to a critique; it presumably only prepares the ground for the "real critique," which begins with the introduction of the category of surplus value.[38]

The question of whether the initial categories of the Marxian analysis express

31. Ibid., pp. 58–62.
32. Ibid., p. 67.
33. Ibid., pp. 56, 58.
34. Ibid., p. 75.
35. See, for example, Mandel, *The Formation of the Economic Thought,* pp. 82–88; Paul Walton and Andrew Gamble, *From Alienation to Surplus Value* (London, 1972), p. 179; George Lichtheim, *Marxism: A Historical and Critical Study* (New York and Washington, 1965), p. 172ff.
36. Dobb, *Political Economy and Capitalism,* p. 55.
37. Such a position is closely bound to the spurious interpretation of the first chapters of *Capital* as an analysis of a precapitalist stage of "simple commodity production." I shall discuss this more extensively below.
38. Martin Nicolaus provides a more recent example of this approach: in the introduction to his translation of the *Grundrisse,* Nicolaus states that "with the conception of 'labour power', Marx resolves the inherent contradiction of the classical theory of value. He preserves what is sound in it, namely the determination of value by working time. . . . By . . . bursting through the limitations contained in it, Marx turned the old theory into its opposite; from a legitimation of bourgeois rule into the theory . . . explaining how the capitalist class grows wealthy from the workers' labour" (Martin Nicolaus, Introduction, in Karl Marx, *Grundrisse: Foundations of the Critique of Political Economy,* trans. Martin Nicolaus [London, 1973], p. 46).

a critique of capitalism is related to the question of whether they ground theoretically the historical dynamic characteristic of that society.[39] According to Oskar Lange, for example, the "real superiority" of Marxian economics is "in the field of explaining and anticipating a process of economic evolution."[40] Yet, proceeding from an interpretation of the law of value similar to that of Dobb and Sweezy, Lange argues that "the economic meaning of the labour theory of value . . . is nothing but a static theory of economic equilibrium."[41] As such, it is really applicable only to a precapitalist exchange economy of small independent producers and is incapable of explaining capitalist development.[42] The real basis of Marx's analysis of the dynamic of capitalism, according to Lange, is an "institutional datum": the division of the population into a class that owns the means of production and one that owns only its labor power.[43] It is for this reason that capitalist profit can exist only in a progressive economy.[44] Technical progress results from the needs of capitalists to prevent wages from rising so as to swallow profits.[45] In other words, proceeding from the common interpretation of Marx's theory of value as being essentially similar to that of classical political economy, Lange argues that a gap exists between the static "specific economic concepts" used by Marx and his "definite specification of the institutional framework in which the economic process goes on in capitalist society."[46] Only the latter can explain the historical dynamic of the social formation. The law of value, according to Lange, is a theory of equilibrium; as such, it has nothing to do with the developmental dynamics of capitalism.

We have thus seen that if the Marxian theory of value is basically the same as that of classical political economy, it does not and cannot directly provide the basis for a historical critique of capitalism or for an explanation of its dynamic character. (By implication, then, my reinterpretation must show that the basic Marxian categories developed on the initial logical level of his analysis are indeed critical of capitalism and do imply an immanent historical dynamic.)

According to the interpretations outlined above, Marx's labor theory of value demystifies (or "defetishizes") capitalist society by revealing labor to be the true source of social wealth. That wealth is distributed "automatically" by the market and is appropriated by the capitalist class in a nonovert manner. The essential thrust of Marx's critique is, accordingly, to reveal beneath the appear-

---

39. See Henryk Grossmann, *Marx, die klassische Nationalökonomie und das Problem der Dynamik* (Frankfurt, 1969).
40. Oskar Lange, "Marxian Economics and Modern Economic Theory," in David Horowitz, ed., *Marx and Modern Economics* (London, 1968), p. 76. (This article first appeared in the June 1935 issue of *The Review of Economic Studies*.)
41. Ibid.
42. Ibid., pp. 78–79.
43. Ibid., p. 81.
44. Ibid., p. 82.
45. Ibid., p. 84.
46. Ibid., p. 74.

ance of the exchange of equivalents the existence of class exploitation. The market and private ownership of the means of production are considered to be the essential capitalist relations of production, which are expressed by the categories of value and surplus value. Social domination is treated as a function of class domination which, in turn, is rooted in "private property in land and capital."[47] Within this general framework, the categories of value and surplus value express how labor and its products are distributed in a market-based class society. They are not, however, interpreted as categories of *particular* forms of wealth and labor.

What is the basis of such a critique of the bourgeois mode of distribution and appropriation? It is, in Dobb's terms, a "theory of production."[48] As we have seen, Dobb considers such a theory to be one that, by identifying those classes which truly contribute productively to economic society, provides a basis for calling into question the role of nonproductive classes. Classical political economy, at least in the Ricardian form, showed that the class of large landowners was not productive; Marx, in developing the theory of surplus value, did the same with the bourgeoisie.

It should be noted—and this is crucial—that such a position implies that the character of Marx's critique of capitalism is basically identical to that of the bourgeois critique of previous orders of society. The critique in both cases is of social relations from the standpoint of labor. But if labor is the standpoint of the critique, it is not and cannot be its object. What Dobb calls a "theory of production" entails a critique not of production but of the mode of distribution, and does so based upon an analysis of the "true" productive source of wealth—labor.

At this point, one can ask whether the Marxian critique is indeed fundamentally similar in structure to that of classical political economy. As we have seen, this understanding presupposes that Marx's theory of value is the same as that of political economy; hence, his critique of capitalism is not yet expressed by the initial logical level of his analysis. Marx's critique, seen thus, begins later in the exposition of his theory in *Capital,* namely, with his distinction between the categories of labor and labor power and, relatedly, his argument that labor is the sole source of surplus value. In other words, his critique is taken to be one primarily concerned with demonstrating that exploitation is structurally intrinsic to capitalism. The presupposition that Marx's category of value is basically the same as Ricardo's implies further that their conceptions of the labor that constitutes value must also be basically identical. The idea that labor is both the source of all wealth and the standpoint of a social critique is, as noted, typical of bourgeois social critique. It dates at least as far back as John Locke's writings and found its most consistent expression in Ricardo's political econ-

47. Dobb, *Political Economy and Capitalism,* p. 78.
48. Ibid., p. 39.

omy. The traditional reading of Marx—which interprets his categories as those of distribution (the market and private property) and identifies the forces of production in capitalism with the (industrial) process of production—depends ultimately on the identification of Ricardo's notion of labor as the source of value with that of Marx.

This identification, however, is specious. The *essential* difference between Marx's critique of political economy and classical political economy is precisely the treatment of labor.

It is true that, in examining Ricardo's analysis, Marx praises him as follows:

> The basis, the starting point for the physiology of the bourgeois system . . . is the determination of *value by labour-time.* Ricardo starts with this and forces science . . . to examine how matters stand with the contradiction between the apparent and actual movements of the system. This then is Ricardo's great historical significance for science.[49]

This homage, however, in no way implies that Marx adopts Ricardo's labor theory of value. Neither should the differences between the two be understood in terms of their different methods of analytic presentation alone. It is true that, as far as Marx is concerned, Ricardo's exposition moved too quickly and directly from the determination of the magnitude of value by labor time to a consideration of whether other economic relations and categories contradict or modify that determination.[50] Marx himself proceeds differently: at the end of the first chapter of *A Contribution to the Critique of Political Economy,* he lists the most common objections to the labor theory of value and states that those objections will be met by his theories of wage labor, capital, competition, and rent.[51] These theories are then unfolded categorially in the course of the three volumes of *Capital.* It would, nevertheless, be misleading to maintain, as Mandel does, that they represent "Marx's own contribution to the development of economic theory"[52]—as if Marx had merely ironed out Ricardo's theory and had not developed a fundamental critique of it.

The main difference between Ricardo and Marx is far more fundamental. Marx does not merely render "the determination of exchange-value by labor-

---

49. Marx, *Theories of Surplus Value,* part 2, trans. Renate Simpson (Moscow, 1968), p. 166.
50. Ibid., p. 164.
51. The objections he lists are as follows: First, given labor time as the intrinsic measure of value, how are wages to be determined on this basis? Second, how does production on the basis of exchange value solely determined by labor time lead to the result that the exchange value of labor is less than the exchange value of its product? Third, how on the basis of exchange value does a market price differing from this exchange value come into being? (In other words, values and prices necessarily are not identical.) Fourth, how does it come about that commodities which contain no labor possess exchange value? (See *A Contribution to the Critique,* pp. 61–63.) Many critics of Marx's theory of value seem to be unaware that he even acknowledges these problems, not to mention the nature of his proposed solutions.
52. Mandel, *The Formation of the Economic Thought,* pp. 82–83.

time'' more consistent.[53] Rather than take over and refine Ricardo's labor theory of value, Marx criticizes Ricardo for having posited an undifferentiated notion of ''labor'' as the source of value without having further examined the specificity of commodity-producing labor:

Ricardo starts out from the determination of the relative values (or exchangeable values) of commodities by *''the quantity of labour.''* ... But *Ricardo does not examine* the form—the peculiar characteristic of labour that creates exchange value or manifests itself in exchange values—the nature of this labour.[54]

Ricardo did not recognize the historical determinateness of the form of labor associated with the commodity form of social relations but, rather, transhistoricized it: ''the bourgeois form of labour is regarded by Ricardo as the eternal natural form of social labour.''[55] And it is precisely such a transhistorical conception of value-constituting labor that hinders an adequate analysis of the capitalist social formation:

The value-form of the product of labour is the most abstract, but also the most general form of the bourgeois mode of production. This mode is thereby characterized as a particular sort of social production and, therefore, as historically specific. If one then makes the mistake of treating it as the eternal natural form of social production, one necessarily overlooks the specificity of the value-form, and consequently of the commodity form together with its further developments, the money form, the capital form, etc.[56]

An adequate analysis of capitalism is possible, according to Marx, only if it proceeds from an analysis of the historically specific character of labor in capitalism. The initial and basic determination of that specificity is what Marx calls the ''double character'' of commodity-determined labor.

What is best about my book is 1. (*all* understanding of the facts depends upon this) the *double-character of labour,* depending on whether it expresses itself in use-value or exchange-value—as is already emphasized in the *first* chapter; 2. the treatment of surplus-value *independent of its particular forms* as profit, interest, rent, etc.[57]

I shall undertake an extensive discussion of Marx's notion of the ''double character'' of labor in capitalism in the second part of this book. At this point I shall only note that, according to Marx's own account, his critique of capitalism does not commence with the introduction of the category of surplus

53. *A Contribution to the Critique,* p. 61.
54. *Theories of Surplus Value,* part 2, p. 164.
55. *A Contribution to the Critique,* p. 60.
56. *Capital,* vol. 1, p. 174n34 (translation amended).
57. Marx to Engels, August 24, 1867, in *Marx-Engels Werke* (hereafter *MEW*), vol. 31 (Berlin, 1956–1968), p. 326.

value; it begins in the very first chapter of *Capital* with his analysis of the specificity of commodity-determined labor. This marks the fundamental distinction between Marx's critique and classical political economy, one upon which "*all* understanding of the facts depends." Smith and Ricardo, according to Marx, analyzed the commodity in terms of an undifferentiated notion of "labour,"[58] as "*Arbeit sans phrase.*"[59] If its historical specificity is not recognized, labor in capitalism is considered in a transhistorical, ultimately noncritical fashion as " 'the' labour,"[60] that is, as "the productive activity of human beings in general, by which they mediate the material metabolism with nature, divested . . . of every social form and determinate character."[61] According to Marx, though, social labor per se—"the productive activity of human beings in general"—is a mere phantom, an abstraction that, taken by itself, does not exist at all.[62]

Contrary to common interpretation, then, Marx does not take over Ricardo's labor theory of value, render it more consistent, and use it to prove that profit is created by labor alone. He writes a *critique* of political economy, an immanent critique of the classical labor theory of value itself. Marx takes the categories of classical political economy and uncovers their unexamined, historically specific social basis. He thereby transforms them from transhistorical categories of the constitution of wealth into critical categories of the specificity of the forms of wealth and social relations in capitalism. By analyzing value as a historically determinate form of wealth and uncovering the "twofold" nature of the labor that constitutes it, Marx argues that value-creating labor cannot be grasped adequately as labor as it is commonly understood, that is, as an intentional activity that changes the form of matter in a determinate fashion.[63] Rather, labor in capitalism possesses an additional social dimension. The problem, according to Marx, is that although commodity-determined labor is socially and historically specific, it appears in transhistorical form as an activity mediating humans and nature, as "labor." Classical political economy, then, based itself on the transhistorical form of appearance of a historically determinate social form.

The difference between an analysis based on the notion of "labor," as in classical political economy, and one based on the concept of the double character of concrete and abstract labor in capitalism is crucial; it is, in Marx's phrase,

58. Marx, *Results of the Immediate Process of Production*, trans. Rodney Livingstone, in *Capital*, vol. 1, trans. Ben Fowkes (London, 1976), p. 992.
59. Marx to Engels, January 8, 1868, *MEW*, vol. 32, p. 11.
60. *Capital*, vol. 3, p. 954 (translation amended).
61. Ibid. (translation amended).
62. Ibid.
63. "The economists, without exception, have missed the simple point that, if the commodity is a duality of use-value and exchange-value, the labour represented in the commodity must also possess a double-character, whereas the mere analysis of labour *sans phrase*, as in Smith, Ricardo, etc. is bound to come up everywhere against the inexplicable. This is in fact the whole secret of the critical conception" (Marx to Engels, January 8, 1868, *MEW*, vol. 32, p. 11).

"the whole secret of the critical conception."[64] It delineates the difference between a social critique that proceeds from the standpoint of "labor," a standpoint that itself remains unexamined, and one in which *the form of labor itself* is the object of critical investigation. The former remains confined within the bounds of the capitalist social formation, whereas the latter points beyond it.

If classical political economy provides the basis for a critique of society from the standpoint of "labor," the critique of political economy entails a critique of that standpoint. Hence, Marx does not accept Ricardo's formulation of the aim of political-economic investigation, namely, to "determine the laws which regulate this distribution" of social wealth among the various classes of society,[65] for such an investigation takes the form of labor and of wealth for granted. Instead, in his critique, Marx redetermines the object of investigation. The center of his concern becomes the forms of wealth, labor, and production in capitalism, rather than the form of distribution alone.

Marx's fundamental redetermination of the object of critical investigation also implies an important analytic reconceptualization of the structure of the capitalist social order.

Classical political economy expressed the growing historical differentiation between the state and civil society, and concerned itself with the latter sphere. It has been argued that Marx's analysis was a continuation of this undertaking, and that he identified civil society as the social sphere governed by the structuring forms of capitalism.[66] As I shall later elaborate, however, the differences between Marx's approach and that of classical political economy suggest that he tries to move beyond conceiving of capitalist society in terms of the opposition between the state and civil society. Marx's critique of political economy (written after the rise of large-scale industrial production) implicitly argues that what is central to capitalist society is its directionally dynamic character, a dimension of modern social life that cannot be grounded adequately in either of those differentiated spheres of modern society. Rather, he attempts to grasp this dynamic by delineating *another* social dimension of capitalist society. This is the fundamental significance of his analysis of production. Marx does investigate the sphere of civil society but in terms of bourgeois relations of *distribution*. His analysis of the specificity of labor in capitalism and of the capitalist relations of *production* has another theoretical goal; it is an attempt to ground and explain the *historical dynamic* of capitalist society. Hence, Marx's analysis of the sphere of production should neither be understood in terms of "labor" nor taken to privilege the "point of production" over other spheres of social life. (Indeed, he indicates that production in capitalism is not a purely technical process which is regulated by social relations but a process

---

64. Ibid.
65. David Ricardo, *Principles of Political Economy and Taxation,* ed. P. Sraffa and M. Dobb (Cambridge, 1951), p. 5.
66. See, for example, Cohen, *Class and Civil Society.*

that incorporates such relations; it determines and is determined by them.) As an attempt to elucidate the historically dynamic social dimension of capitalist society. Marx's analysis of production implicitly argues that this dimension cannot be grasped in terms of the state or civil society. On the contrary, the historical dynamic of developed capitalism increasingly embeds and transforms both of those spheres. At issue, therefore, is not the relative importance of "the economy" and "the state," but the nature of social mediation in capitalism, and the relation of that mediation to the directional dynamic characteristic of that society.

"Labor," wealth, and social constitution

Interpreting value as primarily a category of the market-mediated mode of distribution—as traditional Marxism does—implies that Marx's category of value and his understanding of value-creating labor are identical to those of classical political economy. We have seen, however, that Marx distinguishes his analysis from that of political economy precisely with regard to the question of value-constituting labor, and criticizes political economy for conceptualizing labor in capitalism as transhistorical "labor." This distinction is fundamental, for it underlies the differences between two basically different forms of social critique. The significance of these differences will become clearer as I elaborate the role that "labor" plays in the traditional critique and outline some theoretical implications of that role.

I have argued that if "labor" is the standpoint of a critical theory, the focus of the critique necessarily becomes the mode of the distribution and appropriation of labor and its products.[67] On the one hand, the social relations that characterize capitalism are seen as extrinsic to labor itself (for example, property relations); on the other hand, what is represented as the specificity of labor in capitalism is actually the specificity of the way in which it is distributed.[68]

---

67. An extreme example of this is afforded by Dobb: "More essentially even than with Ricardo, his [Marx's] concern was with the movements of the main class revenues of society, as key to the 'laws of motion of capitalist society', which his analysis was primarily designed to reveal" (Dobb, *Political Economy and Capitalism*, p. 23). In Marx's analysis, however, the problem of revenue—the distribution among the various classes of society of the surplus value created by only one of those classes—is investigated in Volume 3 of *Capital*, that is, after the value form of production and its immanent dynamic had been investigated. The latter represents the logical level on which the "laws of motion" are developed; the former is part of an attempt to indicate how those "laws" prevail behind the backs of the social actors—that is, although they are unaware of value and its workings.

68. The one-sided critique of the mode of distribution has rarely been recognized as such. This can be seen, for example, in an article by Rudolf Hilferding—"Zur Problemstellung der theoretischen Ökonomie bei Karl Marx," *Die Neue Zeit* 23, no. 1 (1904–1905), pp. 101–112—in which he tries to elucidate the differences between Marx and Ricardo. In the process, he criticizes those socialists who, like Ricardo, concern themselves primarily with the problem of distribution (p. 103). Yet, despite appearances, Hilferding's criticism is not made from the standpoint of a critique of

Marx's theory, however, entails a very different conception of the basic social relations of capitalism. Moreover, as we shall see, what he analyzes as specific to labor in capitalism is what traditional Marxism attributes to "labor" understood transhistorically, as an activity that mediates the interactions of humans with nature. Consequently, the traditional critique invests labor per se with enormous significance for human society and for history—and does so in a way that, from the standpoint of the interpretation developed in this work, is essentially metaphysical and obscures the specific social role that labor plays in capitalism.

In the first place, the traditional interpretation takes "labor" to be the transhistorical source of social wealth. This presupposition underlies interpretations like that of Joan Robinson, who maintains that, according to Marx, the labor theory of value will come into its own under socialism.[69] It also, however, is characteristic of positions such as that of Dobb, who does not ascribe transhistorical validity to the category of value but does interpret it solely in terms of the market. Such a position, which considers the category of value to be a historically determinate form of *the distribution of* wealth rather than a historically specific *form of* wealth, is transhistorical, in another way, for it implicitly posits a transhistorical correlation between human labor and social wealth; it

production. He does emphasize that, unlike Marx, Ricardo did not inquire into the form of wealth in capitalism (p. 104), posited the relations of production as given, natural, and immutable (p. 109), and was concerned only with distribution (p. 103). Only at first glance, however, does his position appear the same as that argued here. Closer examination reveals that Hilferding's interpretation is also basically one of a critique of the mode of distribution: his investigation of the form of wealth is not related to an examination of production, which he considers only in terms of the relationship of people and nature (pp. 104–105); rather, he interprets the form of wealth only in terms of the form the product socially assumes *after* it has been produced, as a function of the self-regulating market (p. 105ff.). Hence, Hilferding does not really have a notion of value as a social form of wealth that differs from material wealth; instead, he regards value as a different *form of appearance* of (the same form of) wealth (p. 104). In a similar vein, he interprets the law of value in terms of the workings of the market, and understands the relations of production only as the market-mediated, nonconsciously regulated social relations of private producers (pp. 105–110). Finally, Hilferding later specifies and narrows his charge that Ricardo was interested only in distribution, by saying he is referring to Ricardo's focus on the distribution of products in the existing order rather than on the distribution of people into opposed classes in the various spheres of production (p. 110). In other words, Hilferding's criticism of socialists who emphasize the problem of distribution is directed against those concerned with the just distribution of goods within the existing mode of production. He does so from a standpoint that calls the structure of bourgeois distribution into question but not the structure of capitalist production. He criticizes a quantitative critique of distribution in the name of a qualitative critique of the relations of distribution, but misunderstands the latter to be a critique of the relations of production.

69. Joan Robinson, *An Essay on Marxian Economics* (2d ed., London, Melbourne, and Toronto, 1967), p. 23. This sort of misinterpretation of the historical character of value in Marx's analysis renders impossible an understanding of the significance of that category within the critique of political economy.

implies that although the "value form"—the market-mediated form of distribution, in this interpretation—would be overcome in socialism, direct human labor in the process of production necessarily would continue to be the source of social wealth. Unlike Marx's approach in the *Grundrisse,* this sort of analysis does not question historically the "necessary" connection between direct human labor and social wealth; nor does it address categorially the problem of the wealth-creating potential of science and technology. Hence, the Marxian critique of capitalist production lies outside of its purview. This position has led to considerable confusion over why labor alone should be seen as constituting value, and how science and technology should be taken into account theoretically.

In this view, "labor" is considered to be not only the transhistorical source of wealth but also that which primarily structures social life. The relationship between the two is evident, for example, in Rudolf Hilferding's reply to Eugen Böhm-Bawerk's critique of Marx. Hilferding writes, "Marx proceeds from a consideration of labor in its significance as that element which constitutes human society and . . . determines, in the final analysis, the development of society. In so doing, he grasps, with his principle of value, that factor whose quality and quantity . . . causally controls social life."[70]

"Labor" here has become the ontological ground of society—that which constitutes, determines, and causally controls social life. If, as traditional interpretations maintain, labor is the only source of wealth and the essential constituting element of social life in all societies, the difference among various societies could only be a function of the different ways in which this regulating element prevails—whether in a veiled and "indirect" form or (preferably) in an open and "direct" form. As Hilferding puts it:

The purview of economic analysis is restricted to that particular epoch of social development . . . where the good becomes a commodity, that is, where labor and the power of disposition over it have not been consciously raised to the regulating principle of social metabolism and social predominance, but where this principle prevails unconsciously and automatically as a material attribute of things.[71]

This passage makes explicit a central implication of positions that characterize labor in capitalism in terms of its indirect social character and consider value to be a category of distribution. "Labor" is taken to be the transhistorical regulating principle of "social metabolism" and the distribution of social power. The difference between socialism and capitalism, then, aside from whether private ownership of the means of production exists, is understood essentially as

70. Rudolf Hilferding, "Böhm-Bawerk's Criticism of Marx," in Paul M. Sweezy, ed., *"Karl Marx and the Close of His System" by Eugen Böhm-Bawerk, and "Böhm-Bawerk's Criticism of Marx" by Rudolf Hilferding* (New York, 1949), p. 133 (translation amended).
71. Ibid., p. 133 (translation amended).

a matter of whether labor is recognized as that which constitutes and regulates society—and is consciously dealt with as such—or whether social regulation occurs nonconsciously. In socialism, then, the ontological principle of society appears openly, whereas in capitalism it is hidden.

Such a critique from the standpoint of "labor" has implications for the question of the relation of form and content. To say that the category of value expresses the nonconscious, automatic fashion in which "labor" prevails in capitalism, is to say that a transhistorical, ontological content takes on various historical forms in various societies. An example of this interpretation is afforded by Helmut Reichelt, who writes:

Where, however, the *content* of value and of the magnitude of value is consciously raised to the principle of the economy, the Marxian theory will have lost its object of investigation, which can only be presented and grasped as a *historical* object when that content is conceived as the content of other forms and therefore can be described separate from its historical form of appearance.[72]

Like Hilferding, Reichelt argues that the content of value in capitalism will be "consciously raised to the principle of the economy" in socialism. The "form" (value) is thus completely separable from the "content" ("labor"). It follows that the form is a determination not of labor but of the mode of its social distribution; there is no intrinsic relation, according to this interpretation, between form and content—nor could there be, given the presumably transhistorical character of the latter.

This interpretation of the relation between form and content is, at the same time, one of the relation of appearance and essence. Value, in Marx's analysis, both expresses and veils a social essence—in other words, as a form of appearance, it is "mystifying." Within the framework of interpretations based upon the notion of "labor," the function of critique is to demystify (or defetishize) theoretically, that is, to reveal that, despite appearances, labor is actually the transhistorical source of social wealth and the regulatory principle of society. Socialism, then, is the practical "demystification" of capitalism. As Paul Mattick remarks, such a position maintains that, "it is only the *mystification* of the social organization of production as a 'law of value' which comes to an end with the end of capitalism. Its *demystified* results reappear in a consciously regulated economy."[73] In other words, when "labor" is taken to be the transhistorical essence of social life, mystification necessarily is understood as follows: the historically transitory form that mystifies and is to be abolished (value) is independent of the transhistorical essence it veils ("labor"). Demystification, then, is understood as a process whereby the essence openly and directly appears.

72. Helmut Reichelt, *Zur logischen Struktur,* p. 145.
73. Paul Mattick, *Marx and Keynes: The Limits of the Mixed Economy* (Boston, 1969), p. 32.

As I shall attempt to show, however, the features I have outlined of a social critique from the standpoint of "labor" differ fundamentally from those of Marx's mature critique of political economy. We shall see that labor is indeed socially constituting and determining, according to Marx, but *only* in capitalism. This is so because of its historically specific character and not simply because it is an activity that mediates the material interactions of humans and nature. What theorists such as Hilferding attribute to "labor" is, in Marx's approach, a transhistorical hypostatization of the specificity of labor in capitalism. Indeed, inasmuch as Marx's analysis of labor's specificity indicates that what appears to be a transhistorical, ontological ground of social life is actually historically determinate, that analysis entails a critique of the sort of social ontology that characterizes traditional Marxism.

Marx's analysis of the specificity of labor in capitalism also entails an approach to the relation of social form and content in capitalism diametrically opposed to the approach associated with a critique from the standpoint of "labor." We have seen that the notion of "labor" implies a conception of mystification according to which no intrinsic relationship exists between the social "content" and its mystified form. In Marx's analysis, however, forms of mystification (of what he termed the "fetish") most definitely *are* related intrinsically to their "content"—they are treated as *necessary* forms of appearance of an "essence" they both express and veil.[74] Commodity-determined social relations, for example, necessarily are expressed in fetishized form, according to Marx: social relations appear "*as what they are*, i.e.,...as objective [*sachliche*] relations between persons and social relations between objects."[75] In other words, the quasi-objective, impersonal social forms expressed by categories such as the commodity and value do not simply disguise the "real" social relations of capitalism (that is, class relations); rather, the abstract structures expressed by those categories *are* those "real" social relations.

The relationship between form and content in Marx's critique, then, is necessary, not contingent. The historical specificity of the form of appearance implies the historical specificity of what it expresses, for that which is historically determinate cannot be the necessary form of appearance of a transhistorical "content." At the core of this approach is Marx's analysis of the specificity of labor in capitalism: the social "content" (or "essence") in Marx's analysis is not "labor" but a historically specific form of labor.

Marx charges political economy with having been unable to address the question of the intrinsic, necessary relationship of social form and content in capitalism: "But it has never once even asked the question why this content has assumed that particular form, that is to say, why labour is expressed in value,

74. See Marx's discussion of the relative and equivalent value forms in *Capital*, vol. 1, pp. 138–63.
75. Ibid., p. 166 (translation amended).

and why the measurement of labour by its duration is expressed in the magnitude of the value of the product.''[76] His analysis of the specificity of the historically determinate content, of labor in capitalism, provides the point of departure for his answer to that question. As we shall discuss below, the character of labor in capitalism, according to Marx, is such that it must exist in the form of value (which, in turn, appears in still other forms). Labor in capitalism necessarily appears in a form that both expresses and veils it. Interpretations based upon an undifferentiated, transhistoricized notion of "labor," however, imply a contingent relationship between that "content" and the value form; consequently, they are no more able to deal with the question of the relationship of social content and form, of labor and value, than was classical political economy.

The necessary relationship between social form and content in Marx's critique indicates that it is contrary to his analysis to conceive of overcoming capitalism—its real demystification—in a manner that does not involve a transformation of the "content" that necessarily appears in mystified form. It implies that overcoming value and the abstract social relations associated with it are inseparable from overcoming value-creating labor. The "essence" grasped by Marx's analysis is not that of human society but that of capitalism; it is to be abolished, not realized, in overcoming that society. As we have seen, however, when labor in capitalism is hypostatized as "labor," overcoming capitalism is considered in terms of the liberation of the "content" of value from its mystified form, which thereby allows that "content" to be "consciously raised to the principle of economy." This is merely a somewhat sophisticated expression of the abstract opposition of planning, as the principle of socialism, to the market, as the principle of capitalism, which I criticized above. It addresses neither what is to be planned nor the degree to which planning is truly conscious and free of the imperatives of structural domination. The one-sided critique of the mode of distribution and the transhistorical social ontology of labor are related.

By formulating a critique of labor in capitalism on the basis of his analysis of its historical specificity, Marx transformed the nature of the social critique based upon the labor theory of value from a "positive" to a "negative" critique. The critique of capitalism which retains the starting point of classical political economy—a transhistorical, undifferentiated notion of "labor"—and uses it to prove the structural existence of exploitation is, in terms of its form, a "positive" critique. Such a critique of existing social conditions (exploitation) and structures (the market and private property) is undertaken on the basis of what also already exists ("labor" in the form of industrial production). It purports to reveal that, despite appearances, labor "actually" is social and not private, and that profit "actually" is a function of labor alone. This is bound to an understanding of social mystification according to which there is no intrinsic relation between what really underlies capitalist society ("labor") and the social forms

---

76. Ibid., p. 174 (translation amended).

of appearance that veil it. A positive critique—which criticizes what exists on the basis of what also exists—points ultimately to another variation of the existent capitalist social formation. We shall see how the Marxian critique of labor in capitalism provides the basis for a "negative" critique—one that criticizes what is on the basis of what could be—which points to the possibility of another social formation. In this sense (and only in this non–sociologically reductive sense), the difference between the two forms of social critique is that between a "bourgeois" critique of society, and a critique of bourgeois society. From the viewpoint of the critique of the specificity of labor in capitalism, the critique from the standpoint of "labor" implies a vision of socialism which entails the realization of the essence of capitalist society.

The critique of society from the standpoint of labor

These two forms of social critique also differ in their normative and historical dimensions. As we have seen, the argument that Marx adopted the classical labor theory of value, refined it, and thereby proved surplus value (and, hence, profit) to be a function of labor alone, is based upon a historically undifferentiated notion of "labor." His critique is taken to be one of the mode and the relations of distribution—a nonconscious, "anarchic" mode of distribution, and the nonmanifest, private appropriation of the surplus by the capitalist class. Social domination is conceived essentially in terms of class domination. Overcoming value is thus understood in terms of the abolition of a mediated, nonconscious, form of distribution, thereby allowing for a mode of social life that is consciously and rationally regulated. Overcoming surplus value is conceived in terms of the abolition of private property and, hence, of the expropriation by a nonproductive class of the general social surplus, which is created by labor alone: the productive working class could then reappropriate the results of its own collective labor.[77] In socialism, then, labor would emerge openly as the regulatory principle of social life, which would provide the basis for the realization of a rational and just society, based on general principles.

We have seen that the character of such a critique is essentially identical to that of the early bourgeois critique of the landed aristocracy and of earlier forms of society. It is a normative critique of nonproductive social groupings from the standpoint of those groupings that are "truly" productive; it makes "productiveness" the criterion of social worth. Moreover, because it presupposes that society is constituted as a whole by labor, it identifies labor (hence, the working classes) with the general interests of society and regards the interests of the capitalist class as particular and opposed to those general interests. As a result, the theoretical attack on a social order characterized as a class society, in which nonproductive groupings play an important or dominant role, has the character

77. See, for example, Dobb, *Political Economy and Capitalism,* pp. 76–78.

of a critique of the particular in the name of the general.[78] Finally, because labor, in this view, constitutes the relationship between humanity and nature, it serves as the standpoint from which the social relations among people can be judged: Relations that are in harmony with labor and reflect its fundamental significance are considered socially "natural." The social critique from the standpoint of "labor" is, therefore, a critique from a quasi-natural point of view, that of a social ontology. It is a critique of what is artificial in the name of the "true" nature of society. The category of "labor" in traditional Marxism, then, provides a normative standpoint for a social critique in the name of justice, reason, universality, and nature.

The standpoint of "labor" also implies a historical critique. This critique does not merely condemn existing relations but seeks to show that they become increasingly anachronistic and that the realization of the good society becomes a real possibility with the development of capitalism. When "labor" is the standpoint of the critique the historical level of the development of production is taken to determine the relative adequacy of those existing relations, which are interpreted in terms of the existing mode of distribution. Industrial production is not the object of the historical critique, but is posited as the "progressive" social dimension that, increasingly "fettered" by private property and the market, will serve as the basis of socialist society.[79] The contradiction of capitalism is seen as one between "labor" and the mode of distribution purportedly grasped by the categories of value and surplus value. Within this framework, the course of capitalist development leads to the growing anachronism of the market and private property—they become less and less adequate to conditions of industrial production—and gives rise to the possibility of their abolition. Socialism, then, entails the establishment of a mode of distribution—public planning in the absence of private property—that is adequate to industrial production.

When socialism is seen as a transformation of the mode of distribution which renders it *adequate* to the industrial mode of production, this historical adequacy implicitly is considered to be the condition of general human freedom. The latter is thus grounded in the industrial mode of production, once freed from the fetters of "value" (that is, the market) and private property. Emancipation, in this view, is grounded in "labor"—it is realized in a social formation in which "labor" has realized its directly social character and has emerged openly as the essential

---

78. This point indicates the internal relation of classical political economy and the social critique of Saint-Simon. Moments of both complement aspects of Hegel's thought. Whereas the mature Marxian analysis of capitalism entails an immanent critique that points beyond the well-known triad of British political economy, French social theory, and German philosophy, and treats them as forms of thought that remain within the bounds of capitalist civilization, the traditional Marxist position discussed here is, in some respects, their "critical" synthesis.

79. See, for example, Karl Kautsky, *Karl Marx's oekonomische Lehren* (Stuttgart, 1906), pp. 262–63.

element of society. This understanding, of course, is tied inseparably to that of socialist revolution as the "coming to itself" of the proletariat: as the productive element of society, the working class realizes itself as the universal class in socialism.

The normative and historical critique based on "labor" is thus positive in character; its standpoint is an already existing structure of labor and the class that performs it. Emancipation is realized when a structure of labor already in existence no longer is held back by capitalist relations and used to satisfy particularistic interests but is subject to conscious control in the interests of all. Hence, the capitalist class is to be abolished in socialism, but not the working class; the private appropriation of the surplus and the market mode of distribution are to be negated historically, but not the structure of production.[80]

From the viewpoint of a critique of the specific character of labor in capitalism, however, the critique of one dimension of the existing social formation from the standpoint of another of its existing dimensions—that is, the critique of the mode of distribution from the standpoint of industrial production—has serious weaknesses and consequences. Rather than pointing beyond the capitalist social formation, the traditional positive critique, made from the standpoint of "labor," hypostatizes and projects onto all histories and societies the forms of wealth and labor that are historically specific to capitalism. Such a projection hinders consideration of the specificity of a society in which labor plays a unique constituting role and renders unclear the nature of the possible overcoming of that society. The difference between the two modes of social critique is that between a critical analysis of capitalism as a form of class exploitation and domination *within modern society,* and a critical analysis of *the form of modern society itself.*

These different understandings of capitalism imply different approaches to the normative dimension of the critique. For example, my assertion that a critique based upon "labor" entails a transhistorical projection of what is specific to capitalism implies, on another level, a historical rethinking of the conceptions of reason, universality, and justice, which serve as the normative standpoint of that critique. Within the framework of the positive critique of capitalism, those conceptions (which were expressed historically as the ideals of the bourgeois revolutions) represent a noncapitalist moment of modern society; they have not been realized in capitalist society because of the particularistic interests of the capitalist class, but presumably would be realized in socialism. Socialism, then, is thought to entail the general social realization of the ideals of modern society and, in that sense, represents the full realization of modern society itself. In the second part of this work I shall argue that the ideals of reason, universality, and

---

80. See Dobb, *Political Economy and Capitalism,* pp. 75–79. I shall return below to the notion of the forces of production as the standpoint of the critique, but in the context of an attempt to outline a negative critique whose standpoint is not production as it is but as it could be.

justice, as understood by both the traditional Marxist social critique and earlier bourgeois social critiques, do not represent a noncapitalist moment of modern society; rather, they should be understood in terms of the sort of social constitution effected by labor in capitalism. Indeed, the very opposition, which characterizes the traditional critique—between abstract universality and concrete particularity—is not one between ideals that point beyond capitalism and the reality of that society; rather, as an opposition, it is a feature of that society and is rooted in its labor-mediated mode of social constitution itself.

To argue that such normative conceptions can be related to the form of social constitution characteristic of capitalist society, and that they do not truly point beyond the bounds of the capitalist social formation, does not mean that they are shams that disguise ideologically the interests of the capitalist class, or that the gap between such ideals and the reality of capitalist existence has no emancipatory significance. It does mean, however, that that gap and the form of emancipation implicitly associated with it remain within the bounds of capitalism. At issue is the level at which the critique engages capitalism—whether capitalism is understood as a form of society or merely as a form of class domination, and whether social values and conceptions are treated in terms of a theory of social constitution rather than in functionalist (or idealist) terms. Both the notion that these normative conceptions represent a noncapitalist moment of modern society and the idea that they are mere shams share a common understanding of capitalism as a mode of class exploitation and domination within modern society.

Unlike the traditional critique, the social critique of the specific character of labor in capitalism is a theory of the determinate structuring and structured forms of social practice that constitute modern society itself. It is an attempt to understand the specificity of modern society by grounding both the ideals and the reality of modern society in those social forms, and to avoid the unhistorical position that the ideals of bourgeois society will be realized in socialism, as well as its antinomic opposite—the notion that the ideals of bourgeois society are shams. This theory of social constitution is the basis of the negative critique that I shall outline. I shall try to locate the possibility of theoretical and practical critique not in the gap between the ideals and the reality of modern capitalist society, but in the contradictory nature of the form of social mediation that constitutes that society.

The normative aspect of the traditional critique is intrinsically related to its historical dimension. The notion that the ideals of modern society represent a noncapitalist moment of that society parallels the idea that there is a structural contradiction between the proletarian-based industrial mode of producing, as a noncapitalist moment of modern society, and the market and private property. This adopts "labor," as the standpoint of its critique, and lacks a conception of the historical specificity of wealth and of labor in capitalism. It therefore implies that the same form of wealth, which under capitalism is expropriated by a class of private owners, would be appropriated collectively and regulated consciously in socialism. By the same token, it suggests that the mode of producing in socialism will be essentially the same as in capitalism; the proletariat and its labor will "come into their own" in socialism.

The idea that the mode of producing is intrinsically independent of capitalism implies a one-dimensional, linear understanding of technical progress—"labor's progress"—which, in turn, frequently is equated with social progress. This understanding differs considerably from Marx's position that the capital-determined industrial mode of producing greatly increased humanity's productive power, but in an alienated form; hence this increased power also dominates the laboring individuals and is destructive of nature.[81]

The difference between the two forms of critique is also evident in the ways they conceive of the fundamental form of social domination characteristic of capitalism. The social critique from the standpoint of "labor" understands that form of domination essentially in terms of class domination, rooted in private ownership of the means of production; the social critique of labor in capitalism, however, characterizes the most fundamental form of domination in that society as an abstract, impersonal, structural form of domination underlying the historical dynamic of capitalism. This approach grounds that abstract form of domination in the historically specific social forms of value and value-producing labor.

The latter reading of Marx's critical theory of capitalism provides the basis for a far-reaching critique of abstract domination—of the domination of people by their labor—and, relatedly, for a theory of the social constitution of a form of social life characterized by an intrinsic directional dynamic. In the hands of traditional Marxism, however, the critique is flattened out and reduced to a critique of the market and private property that projects forward into socialism the form of labor and the mode of production characteristic of capitalism. "Labor's" development, according to traditional theory, has reached its historical endpoint with industrial production; once the industrial mode of production is freed from the shackles of the market and private property, "labor" will come to itself as the quasi-natural constitutive principle of society.

As noted, traditional Marxism and early bourgeois critiques share a notion of historical progress that, paradoxically, is a movement toward the "naturally" human, toward the possibility that the ontologically human (for example, Reason, "labor") will come into its own and prevail over existing artificiality. In this regard, then, the social critique based on "labor" is open to the criticism Marx leveled at aspects of Enlightenment thought in general and of classical political economy in particular: "The economists have a singular way of proceeding. For them, there are only two kinds of institutions, artificial and natural. The institutions of feudalism are artificial institutions, those of the bourgeoisie

---

81. *Capital*, vol. 1, p. 638.

are natural institutions.... Thus there has been history, but there is no longer any."[82] What is seen as a natural institution, of course, is not the same for "the economists" and traditional Marxist theory. The form of thought, however, is the same: both naturalize what is socially constituted and historically specific, and see history as a movement toward the realization of what they regard as the "naturally human."

As we have seen, interpretations of the determining relations of capitalism in terms of the self-regulating market and private ownership of the means of production are based upon an understanding of the Marxian category of value that remains bound within the framework of classical political economy. Consequently, that form of critical social theory itself—the social critique from the standpoint of "labor"—remains bound within that framework. It does differ in some respects from political economy, of course: for example, it does not accept the bourgeois mode of distribution as final, and calls it into question historically. Nevertheless, the sphere of distribution remains the focus of its critical concern. Whereas the form of labor (hence, of production) is the object of Marx's critique, an unexamined "labor" is, for traditional Marxism, the transhistorical source of wealth and the basis of social constitution. The result is not a *critique of political economy* but a *critical political economy,* that is, a critique solely of the mode of distribution. It is a critique which, in terms of its treatment of labor, merits the name "Ricardian Marxism."[83]) Traditional Marxism replaces Marx's critique of the mode of production and distribution with a critique of the mode of distribution alone, and his theory of the self-abolition of the proletariat with a theory of the self-realization of the proletariat. The difference between the two forms of critique is profound: what in Marx's analysis is the central object of the critique of capitalism becomes the social basis of freedom for traditional Marxism.

This "reversal" cannot be explained adequately with reference to exegetical method—for example, the claim that Marx's writings were not properly interpreted in the Marxist tradition. It requires a social and historical explanation, which should proceed on two levels. First, it should seek to theoretically ground the possibility of the traditional critique of capitalism. For example, it could, following Marx's procedure, attempt to ground the possibility of that theory in the ways in which the social relations of capitalism are manifest. I shall take a step in this direction below, by showing how the historically specific character of labor in capitalism is such, according to Marx, that it appears to be transhistorical "labor." A further step—which I shall only touch upon in this work— would show how the relations of distribution could become the exclusive focus of a social critique. It would do so by unfolding the implications of the relation

82. Ibid., p. 175n35.
83. For an extensive critique of what he calls "Left-Ricardianism," see Hans Georg Backhaus, "Materialien zur Rekonstruktion der Marxschen Werttheorie," *Gesellschaft: Beiträge zur Marxschen Theorie* (Frankfurt), no. 1 (1974), no. 3 (1975), and no. 11 (1978).

between volumes 1 and 3 of *Capital.* Marx's analysis in the former of the
categories of value and capital addresses the underlying social relations of capitalism, its fundamental relations of production; his analysis in the latter of the
categories of prices of production and profit addresses the relations of distribution. The relations of production and of distribution are related but are not
identical. Marx indicates that the relations of distribution are categories of immediate everyday experience, manifest forms of the relations of production that
both express and veil those relations in a way that can lead the former to be
taken for the latter. When the Marxian concept of the relations of production is
interpreted only in terms of the mode of distribution, as in traditional Marxism,
the manifest forms are taken to be the whole. This sort of systematic misrecog-
nition, which is rooted in the determinate forms of appearance of capitalist social
relations, is what Marx attempts to grasp with his notion of the "fetish."

Second, having established the possibility of such a "critical political economy" in the forms of appearance of the social relations themselves (instead of
attributing it to muddled thinking), one could then try to elucidate the historical
conditions for the emergence of such a form of thought.[84] An important element
of such an attempt most likely would involve an analysis of the formulation and
appropriation of social theory in the late nineteenth and early twentieth centuries
by working-class movements in their struggle to constitute themselves, achieve
recognition, and effect social and political changes. It is clear that the position
outlined above seeks to assert the dignity of labor and contribute to the realization of a society in which labor's essential importance is recognized in material and moral terms. It posits direct human labor in the process of production
as the transhistorical source of wealth, and therefore conceives of overcoming
value not in terms of overcoming direct human labor in production, but in terms
of direct human labor's nonmystified social assertion. The result is a critique of
the unequal distribution of wealth and power, and the lack of social recognition
given to the unique significance of direct human labor as an element of production—rather than a critique of that labor and an analysis of the historical
possibility that it be abolished. This, however, is understandable: in the process
of formation and consolidation of the working classes and their organizations,
the question of their self-abolition and the labor they perform could hardly have

84. Although this proposed procedure would entail using Marx's analysis to examine Marxism, it
has only the most external similarities with Karl Korsch's notion of the application of "Marx's
principle of dialectical materialism . . . to the whole history of Marxism" (*Marxism and Philosophy,* trans. Fred Halliday [New York and London, 1970], p. 56). Korsch does not make
use of the epistemological dimension of *Capital,* in which forms of thought are related to the
forms of the social relations of capitalism. Neither is he concerned primarily with the problem
of the substantive character of the social critique—the critique of production and distribution,
as opposed to that of distribution alone. Korsch's procedure remains more extrinsic: he seeks
to establish a correlation between revolutionary periods and a more holistic and radical social
critique, and between nonrevolutionary periods and a fragmented, more academic and passive
social critique (ibid., pp. 56–67).

been a central issue. The notion of the self-realization of the proletariat, based upon an affirmation of "labor" as the source of social wealth, was adequate to the immediacy of that historical context, as was the related critique of the free market and private ownership. This notion, however, was projected into the future as a determination of socialism; it implies the developed existence of capital, however, rather than its abolition.

For Marx, the abolition of capital is the necessary precondition for the dignity of labor, for only then could another structure of social labor, another relation of work and recreation, and other forms of individual labor become socially general. The traditional position accords dignity to labor that is fragmented and alienated. It may very well be the case that such dignity, which is at the heart of classical working-class movements, has been important for workers' self-esteem and a powerful factor in the democratization and humanization of industrialized capitalist societies. The irony of such a position, though, is that it implicitly posits the perpetuation of such labor and the form of growth intrinsically related to it as necessary to human existence. Whereas Marx saw the historical overcoming of the "mere worker" as a precondition for the realization of the full human being,[85] the implication of the traditional position is that the full human being is to be realized as the "mere worker."

The interpretation that I present in this work must also be understood historically. The critique of capitalism based upon an analysis of the specificity of the forms of labor and wealth in that society should be seen in the context of the historical developments outlined in Chapter One above, which have revealed the inadequacies of traditional interpretations. As I have tried to make clear, my critique of traditional Marxism is not merely retrospective: it seeks to validate itself by developing an approach that would avoid the shortcomings and pitfalls of traditional Marxism *and* ground the traditional interpretation of the categories in its own categorial interpretation. It would thereby begin to ground its own possibility socially.

Labor and totality: Hegel and Marx

I must now, once again, jump ahead in order to round out this brief examination of traditional Marxism's fundamental assumptions. There has been a great deal of critical discussion recently about the proletariat as the Subject of history and the concept of totality in Marxism—that is, the politically problematic consequences of positing that concept affirmatively, as the standpoint of a social critique.[86] The meaning and importance of both conceptions in Marx's analysis are bound intrinsically to the question of the relationship of his mature critique

---

85. *Grundrisse,* p. 708.
86. For a very good discussion of this problematic in Western Marxism, see Martin Jay, *Marxism and Totality* (Berkeley and Los Angeles, 1984).

to Hegel's philosophy. An extensive discussion of this problematic would far exceed the boundaries of this work, but a cursory outline of that relationship, reinterpreted in light of the preceding discussion, is necessary. I shall describe briefly Marx's notion of the Subject and his concept of totality as they are implied by his analysis of the specificity of labor in capitalism, and contrast these concepts to those implied by the traditional critique based on "labor."

Hegel attempts to overcome the classical theoretical dichotomy of subject and object with his theory that all of reality, natural as well as social, subjective as well as objective, is constituted by practice—more specifically, by the objectifying practice of the *Geist,* the world-historical Subject. The *Geist* constitutes objective reality by means of a process of externalization or self-objectification, and, in the process, reflexively constitutes itself. Because both objectivity and subjectivity are constituted by the *Geist* as it unfolds dialectically, they are of the same substance, rather than necessarily disparate: both are moments of a general whole that is substantially homogeneous—a totality.

For Hegel, then, the *Geist* is simultaneously subjective and objective—it is the identical subject-object, the "substance" that is at the same time "Subject": "The living *substance* is, further, that Being which is in truth *Subject* or, what is the same thing, which is in truth actual only insofar as it is the movement of positing itself, or the mediation of the process of becoming different from itself with itself."[87]

The process by which this self-moving substance/Subject, the *Geist,* constitutes objectivity and subjectivity as it unfolds dialectically is a historical process, which is grounded in the internal contradictions of the totality. That historical process of self-objectification, according to Hegel, is one of self-alienation, and leads ultimately to the reappropriation by the *Geist* of that which had been alienated in the course of its unfolding. That is, historical development has an endpoint: the realization by the *Geist* of itself as a totalizing and totalized Subject.

In his brilliant essay, "Reification and the Consciousness of the Proletariat," Georg Lukács attempts to appropriate Hegel's theory in a "materialist" fashion, restricting its validity to social reality. He does so in order to place the category of practice at the center of a dialectical social theory. Lukács's appropriation of Hegel is central to his general theoretical attempt to formulate a critique of capitalism that would be adequate to twentieth-century capitalism. In this context, Lukács adopts Max Weber's characterization of modern society in terms of a historical process of rationalization, and attempts to embed that analysis within the framework of Marx's analysis of capitalism. He does so by grounding the process of rationalization in Marx's analysis of the commodity form as the basic structuring principle of capitalist society. In this way, Lukács

---

87. G. W. F. Hegel, Preface to the *Phenomenology,* in Walter Kaufmann, ed., *Hegel: Texts and Commentary* (Garden City, N.Y., 1966), p. 28 (translation amended, emphasis added).

seeks to show that the process of rationalization is socially constituted, that is develops in a nonlinear fashion, and that what Weber described as the "iron cage" of modern life is not a necessary concomitant of any form of "post-traditional" society but a function of capitalism—and, hence, could be transformed. Thus, Lukács responds to Weber's argument that property relations are not the most fundamental structuring feature of modern society by incorporating it into the framework of a broader conception of capitalism.

Some aspects of Lukács's arguments are very rich and promising. By characterizing capitalist society in terms of the rationalization of all spheres of life, and grounding those processes in the commodity form of social relations, he implicitly points to a conception of capitalism that is deeper and broader than that of a system of exploitation based on private property. Moreover, by means of his materialist appropriation of Hegel, Lukács makes explicit the idea that Marx's categories represent a powerful attempt to overcome the classical subject-object dualism. They refer to structured forms of practice that are simultaneously forms of objectivity and subjectivity. This approach permits an analysis of the ways in which historically specific social structures both constitute and are constituted by practice. It also, as I shall elaborate later in this work, points toward a theory of forms of thought and their transformation in capitalism which avoids the materialist reductionism entailed by the base-superstructure model as well as the idealism of many culturalist models. On the basis of this approach, Lukács critically analyzes the thought and institutions of bourgeois society, as well as the deterministic Marxism of the Second International.

Yet, for all its brilliance, Lukács's attempt to reconceptualize capitalism is deeply inconsistent. Although his approach points beyond traditional Marxism, it remains bound to some of its basic theoretical presuppositions. His materialist appropriation of Hegel is such that he analyzes society as a totality, constituted by labor, traditionally understood. This totality, according to Lukács, is veiled by the fragmented and particularistic character of bourgeois social relations, and will be realized openly in socialism. The totality, then, provides the standpoint of his critical analysis of capitalist society. Relatedly, Lukács identifies the proletariat in "materialized" Hegelian terms as the identical subject-object of the historical process, as the historical Subject, constituting the social world and itself through its labor. By overthrowing the capitalist order, this historical Subject would realize itself.[88]

The idea that the proletariat embodies a possible postcapitalist form of social life only makes sense, however, if capitalism is defined essentially in terms of private ownership of the means of production, and if "labor" is considered to be the standpoint of the critique. In other words, although Lukács's analysis

---

88. Georg Lukács, "Reification and the Consciousness of the Proletariat," in *History and Class Consciousness,* trans. Rodney Livingstone (London, 1971), pp. 102–21, 135, 145, 151–53, 162, 175, 197–200. For a very good discussion of the essay, see Andrew Arato and Paul Breines, *The Young Lukács and the Origins of Western Marxism* (New York, 1979), pp. 111–60.

implies that capitalism cannot be defined in traditional terms if its critique is to be adequate as a critical theory of modernity, he undermines his implicit insight by continuing to regard the standpoint of the critique in precisely those traditional terms.

A more complete discussion of Lukács's approach would show in greater detail how the nature of his materialist appropriation of Hegel undercuts his attempt to analyze historical processes of rationalization in terms of the commodity form. Rather than undertake such a discussion directly, however, I wish only to indicate an important difference between Lukács's approach and that of Marx. Lukács's reading, in particular his identification of the proletariat with the identical subject-object, has very frequently been identified with Marx's position.[89] Nevertheless, his understanding of the identical subject-object is as distant from Marx's theoretical approach as is Ricardo's labor theory of value. Marx's critique of political economy is based upon a very different set of presuppositions that those underlying Lukács's reading. In *Capital,* Marx does indeed attempt to explain socially and historically that which Hegel seeks to grasp with his concept of *Geist.* His approach, however, differs fundamentally from Lukács's, that is, from one that views totality affirmatively, as the standpoint of critique, and identifies Hegel's identical subject-object with the proletariat. The differences between Marx's historical critique of Hegel and Lukács's materialist appropriation of him relate directly to the differences between the two forms of social critique we investigated. It has far-reaching ramifications regarding the concepts of totality and the proletariat, and more generally for an understanding of the basic character of capitalism and of its historical negation.

The nature of Marx's critique of Hegel is very different in his mature theory than it had been in his early works.[90] He no longer proceeds in the Feuerbachian manner of inverting subject and object as he had in the *Critique of Hegel's Philosophy of Right* (1843); nor does he treat labor transhistorically as in the *Economic and Philosophic Manuscripts of 1844* where he argues that Hegel metaphysicized labor as the labor of the Concept. In *Capital* (1867), Marx does not simply invert Hegel's concepts in a "materialist" fashion. Rather, in an effort to grasp the peculiar nature of social relations in capitalism, Marx analyzes

---

89. See, for example, Paul Piccone, General Introduction, in Andrew Arato and Eike Gebhardt, eds., *The Essential Frankfurt School Reader* (New York, 1978), p. xvii.

90. As will become evident in the course of this work, my interpretation rejects those readings, such as Althusser's, that posit a break between Marx's early works as "philosophical" and his later works as "scientific." It also, however, rejects the humanist reaction to structuralist neo-objectivism, which fails to recognize the major changes in the development of Marx's critical analysis. In the early works, Marx's categories are still transhistorical; although his early concerns remain central to his later works—his analysis of alienation, for example—they become historicized and thereby transformed. The centrality of the historical specificity of the social forms in Marx's mature works, coupled with his critique of theories that transhistoricize this specificity, indicate that the categories of the early works cannot be identified directly with, or used directly to elucidate, those of the critique of political economy.

the social validity for capitalist society of precisely those idealist Hegelian concepts which he earlier had condemned as mystified inversions. So, whereas in *The Holy Family* (1845) Marx criticizes the philosophical concept of "substance" and, in particular, Hegel's understanding of the "substance" as "Subject,"[91] at the beginning of *Capital* he himself makes use of the category of "substance." He refers to value as having a "substance," which he identifies as abstract human labor.[92] Marx, then, no longer considers "substance" to be simply a theoretical hypostatization, but now conceives of it as an attribute of labor-mediated social relations, as expressing a determinate sort of social reality. He investigates the nature of that social reality in *Capital* by unfolding logically the commodity and money forms from his categories of use value, value, and its "substance." On that basis, Marx begins to analyze the complex structure of social relations expressed by his category of capital. He initially determines capital in terms of value—he describes it in categorial terms as self-valorizing value. At this point in his exposition, Marx describes his concept of capital in terms that clearly relate it to Hegel's concept of *Geist*:

It [value] is constantly changing from one form into the other without becoming lost in this movement; it thus transforms itself into an *automatic subject*. . . . In truth, however, value is here the *subject* of a process in which, while constantly assuming the form in turn of money and of commodities, it changes its own magnitude, . . . and thus valorizes itself. . . . For the movement in the course of which it adds surplus-value is its own movement, its valorization is therefore self-valorization. . . . [V]alue suddenly presents itself as a *self-moving substance* which passes through a process of its own, and for which the commodity and money are both mere forms.[93]

Marx, then, explicitly characterizes capital as the self-moving substance which is Subject. In so doing, Marx suggests that a historical Subject in the Hegelian sense does indeed exist in capitalism, yet he does not identify it with any social grouping, such as the proletariat, or with humanity. Rather, Marx analyzes it in terms of the structure of social relations constituted by forms of objectifying practice and grasped by the category of capital (and, hence, value). His analysis suggests that the social relations that characterize capitalism are of a very peculiar sort—they possess the attributes that Hegel accorded the *Geist*. It is in this sense, then, that a historical Subject as conceived by Hegel exists in capitalism.

It should be clear from the preliminary determinations of Marx's concept of capital that it cannot be understood adequately in physical, material terms, that is, in terms of the stock of buildings, materials, machines, and money owned by the capitalists; rather, it refers to a form of social relations. Yet, even un-

91. Marx, *The Holy Family*, in Lloyd D. Easton and Kurt H. Guddat, eds., *Writings of the Young Marx on Philosophy and Society* (Garden City, N.Y., 1967), pp. 369–73.
92. *Capital*, vol. 1, p. 128.
93. Ibid., pp. 255–56 (translation amended, emphasis added).

derstood in social terms, the passage cited above indicates that the Marxian category of capital cannot be apprehended fully in terms of private property, of the exploitation and domination of the proletariat by the bourgeoisie. Marx, by suggesting that what Hegel sought to conceptualize with his concept of *Geist* should be understood in terms of the social relations expressed by the category of capital, implies that the social relations that characterize capitalism have a peculiar, dialectical, and historical character, which cannot be conceptualized adequately in terms of class alone. He also suggests that these relations constitute the social basis for Hegel's conception itself. Both moments indicate a shift in the nature of Marx's critical theory—hence, in the nature of his materialist critique of Hegel as well—with important implications for his treatment of the epistemological problem of the relation of subject and object, the question of the historical Subject, and the notion of totality.

Marx's interpretation of the historical Subject with reference to the category of capital indicates a shift from a theory of social relations understood essentially in terms of class relations to a theory of forms of social mediation expressed by categories such as value and capital. This difference is related to that between the two forms of social critique I have discussed in this chapter, that is, to the difference between understanding capitalism as a system of class exploitation and domination within modern society, on the one hand, and as constituting the very fabric of modern society, on the other. The "Subject," for Marx, is a conceptual determination of that fabric. As we have seen, the difference between Hegel's idealist concept of the Subject and what Marx presents as the materialist "rational core" of that concept is not that the former is abstract and suprahuman, whereas the latter is concrete and human. Indeed, to the degree that Hegel's notion of the Subject does have historical and social validity, according to Marx, that Subject is *not* a concrete human social agent, collective or individual. Rather, the historical Subject analyzed by Marx consists of objectified relations, the subjective-objective categorial forms characteristic of capitalism, whose "substance" is abstract labor, that is, the specific character of labor as a socially mediating activity in capitalism. Marx's Subject, like Hegel's, then, is abstract and cannot be identified with any social actors. Moreover, both unfold in time in a way that is independent of individual will.

In *Capital,* Marx tries to analyze capitalism in terms of a dialectic of development that is indeed independent of individual will and, therefore, presents itself as a logic. He investigates the unfolding of that dialectical logic as a real expression of alienated social relations which are constituted by practice and, yet, exist quasi-independently. He does not treat that logic as an illusion or simply as a consequence of insufficient knowledge on the part of people. As he points out, knowledge alone does not change the character of such relations.[94] We shall see that such a logic of development, within the framework of his

94. Ibid., p. 167.

analysis, is ultimately a function of the social forms of capitalism and is not characteristic of human history as such.[95]

As the Subject, capital is a remarkable "subject." Whereas Hegel's Subject is transhistorical and knowing, in Marx's analysis it is historically determinate and blind. Capital, as a structure constituted by determinate forms of practice, may in turn be constitutive of forms of social practice and subjectivity; yet, as the Subject, it has no ego. It is self-reflexive and, as a social form, may induce self-consciousness, but unlike Hegel's *Geist* it does not possess self-consciousness. Subjectivity and the sociohistorical Subject must, in other words, be distinguished in Marx's analysis.

The identification of the identical subject-object with determinate structures of social relations has important implications for a theory of subjectivity. It indicates that Marx has moved away from the subject-object paradigm and epistemology to a social theory of consciousness. That is, inasmuch as he does not simply identify the concept of the identical subject-object (Hegel's attempt to overcome the subject-object dichotomy of classical epistemology) with a social agent, Marx changes the terms of the epistemological problem. He shifts the focus of the problem of knowledge from the knowing individual (or supra-individual) subject and its relation to an external (or externalized) world to the forms of social relations, seen as determinations of social subjectivity as well as objectivity. The problem of knowledge now becomes a question of the relation between forms of social mediations and forms of thought. Indeed, as I shall touch upon below, the Marxian analysis of the capitalist social formation implies the possibility of analyzing socially and historically the classical epistemological question itself, predicated as it is on the notion of an autonomous subject in sharp contradiction to an objective universe.[96] This sort of critique of the classical subject-object dichotomy is characteristic of the approach Marx

95. Louis Althusser's position in this regard can be considered the one-sided opposite to that of Lukács. Whereas Lukács subjectivistically identified Hegel's *Geist* with the proletariat, Althusser claimed that Marx owed to Hegel the idea that history is a process without a subject. In other words, Althusser transhistorically hypostatized as History, in an objectivistic way, that which Marx analyzed in *Capital* as a historically specific, constituted structure of social relations. Neither Lukács's nor Althusser's position is able to grasp the category of capital adequately. See Louis Althusser, "Lenin before Hegel," in *Lenin and Philosophy*, trans. Ben Brewster (New York and London, 1971), pp. 120–25.

96. Although Marx's turn away from the subject-object paradigm is crucial, it has been overlooked. Thus Habermas has justified his turn to a theory of communicative action as an attempt to lay the groundwork for a critical theory with emancipatory intent that is not tied to the subjectivistic and cognitive-instrumental implications of the classical subject-object paradigm—a paradigm that, in his opinion, crippled Marxism (see Jürgen Habermas, *The Theory of Communicative Action*, vol. 1: *Reason and the Rationalization of Society*, trans. Thomas McCarthy [Boston, 1984], p. xl). As I shall argue below, however, Marx did indeed provide a critique of the subject-object paradigm—by turning to a theory of historically specific forms of social mediation which, in my view, provides a more satisfactory point of departure for a critical social theory than Habermas's turn to a transhistorical evolutionary theory.

implicitly develops in his mature critical theory. It differs from other sorts of critiques—for example, those rooted in the phenomenological tradition—that refute the classical notion of the disembodied and decontextualized subject by arguing that "in reality" people are always embedded in determinate contexts. Rather than simply dismissing positions such as the classical subject-object dualism as results of mistaken thinking (which leaves unanswered the source of the "superior" insight of the refuting position), the Marxian approach seeks to explain them historically, by rendering them plausible with reference to the nature of their context—that is, by analyzing them as forms of thought related to the structured and structuring social forms that are constitutive of capitalist society.

Marx's critique of Hegel, then, is quite different from Lukács's materialist appropriation of Hegel, for it does not identify a concrete, conscious, social Subject (for example, the proletariat) that unfolds itself historically, achieving full self-consciousness through a process of self-reflexive objectification. Doing so would implicitly posit "labor" as the constituting substance of a Subject, which is prevented by capitalist relations from realizing itself. As I implied in my discussion of "Ricardian Marxism," the historical Subject in that case would be a collective version of the bourgeois subject, constituting itself and the world through "labor." The concepts of "labor" and the bourgeois subject (whether interpreted as the individual, or as a class) are intrinsically related: they express a historically specific social reality in ontological form.

Marx's critique of Hegel breaks with the presuppositions of such a position (which, nevertheless, became dominant within the socialist tradition). Rather than viewing capitalist relations as extrinsic to the Subject, as that which hinder its full realization, Marx analyzes those very relations as constituting the Subject. This fundamental difference is related to the one outlined earlier: the quasi-objective structures grasped by the categories of Marx's critique of political economy do not *veil* either the "real" social relations of capitalism (class relations) or the "real" historical Subject (the proletariat). Rather, those structures *are* the fundamental relations of capitalist society that, because of their peculiar properties, *constitute* what Hegel grasps as a historical Subject. This theoretical turn means that the Marxian theory neither posits nor is bound to the notion of a historical meta-Subject, such as the proletariat, which will realize itself in a future society. Indeed, the move from a theory of the collective (bourgeois) Subject to a theory of alienated social relations implies a critique of such a notion. It is one aspect of a major shift in critical perspective from a social critique on the basis of "labor" to a social critique of the peculiar nature of labor in capitalism, whereby the former's standpoint becomes the latter's object of critique.

This shift becomes clearer still in considering the concept of totality. This should not simply be thought of indeterminately, as referring to the "whole" in general. For Hegel, the *Geist* constitutes a general, substantially homogeneous totality which not only is the Being of the beginning of the historical process but, unfolded, is the result of its own development. The full unfolding and coming to itself of the *Geist* is the endpoint of its development. We have seen that traditional assumptions regarding labor and social relations in capitalism lead the Hegelian concept of totality to be adopted and translated into "materialist" terms as follows: Social totality is constituted by "labor," but is veiled, apparently fragmented, and prevented from realizing itself by capitalist relations. It represents the *standpoint* of the critique of the capitalist present, and will be realized in socialism.

Marx's categorial determination of capital as the historical Subject, however, indicates that the totality has become the *object* of his critique. As shall be discussed below, social totality, in Marx's analysis, is an essential feature of the capitalist formation and an expression of alienation. The capitalist social formation, according to Marx, is unique inasmuch as it is constituted by a qualitatively homogeneous social "substance"; hence, it exists as a social totality. Other social formations are not so totalized: their fundamental social relations are not qualitatively homogeneous. They cannot be grasped by the concept of "substance," cannot be unfolded from a single structuring principle, and do not display an immanent, necessary historical logic.

Marx's assertion that capital, and not the proletariat or the species, is the total Subject clearly implies that the historical negation of capitalism would not involve the *realization*, but the *abolition*, of the totality. It follows that the contradiction driving the unfolding of his totality also must be conceived very differently—it presumably drives the totality not toward its full realization but toward the possibility of its historical abolition. That is, the contradiction expresses the temporal finiteness of the totality by pointing beyond it. (I shall discuss the differences between this understanding of contradiction and that of traditional Marxism below.) Marx's conception of the historical negation of capitalism in terms of the abolition, rather than the realization, of the totality is related to his notion that socialism represents the beginning, rather than the end, of human history, and to the idea that the negation of capitalism entails overcoming a determinate form of social mediation rather than overcoming social mediation per se. Considered on another level, it indicates that Marx's mature understanding of history cannot be grasped adequately as an essentially eschatological conception in secular form.

Finally, the notion that capital constitutes the historical Subject also suggests that the realm of politics in a postcapitalist society should not be seen in terms of a totality that is hindered in capitalism from emerging fully. Indeed, it implies the contrary—that an institutionally totalizing form of politics should be interpreted as an expression of the political coordination of capital as the totality, subject to its constraints and imperatives, rather than as the overcoming of capital. The abolition of the totality would, then, allow for the possible constitution of very different, non-totalizing, forms of the political coordination and regulation of society.

At first glance, the determination of capital as the historical Subject may seem to deny the history-making practices of humans. It is, however, consistent with an analysis that seeks to explain the directional dynamic of capitalist society with reference to alienated social relations, that is, social relations that are constituted by structured forms of practice yet acquire a quasi-independent existence and subject people to determinate quasi-objective constraints. This interpretation also possesses an emancipatory moment not available to interpretations that explicitly or implicitly identify the historical Subject with the laboring class. "Materialist" interpretations of Hegel that posit the class or the species as the historical Subject seem to enhance human dignity by emphasizing the role of practice in the creation of history; but they are only apparently emancipatory, because the call for the full realization of the Subject can only mean the full realization of an alienated social form. On the other hand, many currently popular positions that criticize the affirmation of totality in the name of emancipation do so by denying the existence of the totality.[97] To the extent that such approaches deal with totality as a mere artifact of determinate theoretical positions and ignore the reality of alienated social structures, they can neither grasp the historical tendencies of capitalist society nor formulate an adequate critique of the existent order. From the perspective I am arguing for, those positions that assert the existence of a totality only to affirm it, on the one hand, and those that recognize that the realization of a social totality would be inimical to emancipation and therefore deny its very existence, on the other, are antinomically related. Both sorts of positions are one-sided, for both posit, in opposed ways, a transhistorical identity between what is and what should be.

The Marxian critique of totality is a historically specific critique that does not conflate what is and what should be. It does not approach the issue of totality in ontological terms; that is, it neither affirms ontologically the transhistorical existence of totality nor denies that totality exists (which, given the existence of capital, could only be mystifying). Rather, it analyzes totality in terms of the structuring forms of capitalist society. In Hegel, totality unfolds as the realization of the Subject; in traditional Marxism, this becomes the realization of the proletariat as the concrete Subject. In Marx's critique, totality is grounded as historically specific, and unfolds in a manner that points to the possibility of its abolition. Marx's historical explanation of the Subject as capital, and not as a class, attempts to ground Hegel's dialectic socially and thereby to provide its critique.[98]

97. Martin Jay provides a useful overview of such positions, which especially in France, have become increasingly popular in the past decade. See Jay, *Marxism and Totality,* pp. 510–37.
98. For a similar argument, see Iring Fetscher, "Vier Thesen zur Geschichtsauffassung bei Hegel und Marx," in Hans Georg Gadamer, ed., *Stuttgarter Hegel-Tage 1970* (Bonn, 1974), pp. 481–88.

The structure of the dialectical unfolding of Marx's argument in *Capital* should be read as a metacommentary on Hegel. Marx did not "apply" Hegel to classical political economy but contextualized Hegel's concepts in terms of the social forms of capitalist society. That is, Marx's mature critique of Hegel is immanent to the unfolding of the categories in *Capital*—which, by paralleling the way Hegel unfolds these concepts, implicitly suggests the determinate sociohistorical context of which they are expressions. In terms of Marx's analysis, Hegel's concepts of dialectic, contradiction, and the identical subject-object express fundamental aspects of capitalist reality but do not adequately grasp them.[99] Hegel's categories do not elucidate capital, as the Subject of an alienated mode of production, nor do they analyze the historically specific dynamic of the forms, driven forward by their particular immanent contradictions. Instead, Hegel posits the *Geist* as the Subject and the dialectic as the universal law of motion. In other words, Marx implicitly argues that Hegel did grasp the abstract, contradictory social forms of capitalism *but not in their historical specificity*. Instead, he hypostatized and expressed them in an idealist way. Hegel's idealism, nevertheless, does expreses those forms, even if inadequately: it presents them by means of categories that are the identity of subject and object, and appear to have their own life. This critical analysis is very different from the sort of materialism that would simply invert these idealist categories anthropologically; the latter approach does not permit an adequate analysis of those alienated social structures characteristic of capitalism which do dominate people and are indeed independent of their wills.

Marx's mature critique, therefore, no longer entails a "materialist," anthropological inversion of Hegel's idealistic dialectic but, in a sense, is its materialist "justification." Marx implicitly attempts to show that the "rational core" of Hegel's dialectic is precisely its idealist character:[100] it is an expression of a mode of social domination constituted by structures of social relations which, because they are alienated, acquire a quasi-independent existence vis-à-vis individuals, and which, because of their peculiar dualistic nature, are dialectical in character. The historical Subject, according to Marx, is the alienated structure of social mediation that constitutes the capitalist formation.

Capital, then, is a critique of Hegel as well as of Ricardo—two thinkers who, in Marx's opinion, represented the furthest development of thought that remains bound within the existent social formation. Marx did not simply "radicalize" Ricardo and "materialize" Hegel. His critique—proceeding from the historically specific "double character" of labor in capitalism—is essentially historical. He argues that, with their respective conception of "labor" and the *Geist,*

---

99. This point has also been made by Alfred Schmidt and Iring Fetscher. See their comments in W. Euchner and A. Schmidt, eds., *Kritik der politischen Ökonomie heute: 100 Jahre Kapital* (Frankfurt, 1968), pp. 26–57. See also Hiroshi Uchida, *Marx's Grundrisse and Hegel's Logic,* ed. Terrell Carver (London and Boston, 1988).

100. See M. Postone and H. Reinicke, "On Nicolaus," *Telos* 22 (Winter 1974–75), p. 139.

Ricardo and Hegel posited as transhistorical, and therefore could not fully grasp, the historically specific character of the objects of their investigations. The form of exposition of Marx's mature analysis, then, is no more an "application" of Hegel's dialectic to the problematic of capital than his critical investigation of the commodity indicates that he "took over" Ricardo's theory of value. On the contrary, his argument is an immanently critical exposition that seeks to ground and render plausible the theories of Hegel and Ricardo with reference to the peculiar character of the social forms of their context.

Marx's own analysis, paradoxically, seeks to move beyond the limits of the present totality by limiting itself historically. As I shall argue below, his immanent critique of capitalism is such that the indication of the historical specificity of the object of thought reflexively implies the historical specificity of his theory, that is, the thought itself that grasps the object.

In summary, what I have termed "traditional Marxism" can be considered a "materialist," critical Ricardo-Hegel synthesis. An affirmation in social theory of the Hegelian concept of totality and of the dialectic (as undertaken by Lukács, for example) may indeed provide an effective critique of one aspect of capitalist society as well as of the evolutionist, fatalistic, and deterministic tendencies of the Marxism of the Second International. Nevertheless, it by no means should be seen as delineating a critique of capitalism from the standpoint of its historical negation. The identification of the proletariat (or the species) with the historical Subject rests ultimately on the same historically undifferentiated notion of "labor" as does "Ricardian Marxism." "Labor" is posited as the transhistorical source of social wealth and, as the substance of the Subject, is presumed to be that which constitutes society. The social relations of capitalism are understood as hindering the Subject from realizing itself. The standpoint of the critique becomes the totality, as it is constituted by "labor," and Marx's dialectic is transformed from the historically specific, self-driven movement of the alienated social forms of capitalist society into the expression of the history-making practice of humanity. Any theory that posits the proletariat or the species as Subject implies that the activity constituting the Subject is to be fulfilled rather than overcome. Hence, the activity itself cannot be seen as alienated. In the critique based on "labor," alienation must be rooted outside of labor itself, in its control by a concrete Other, the capitalist class. Socialism then involves the realization of itself by the Subject and the reappropriation of the same wealth that, in capitalism, had been privately expropriated. It entails the coming to itself of "labor."

Within such a general interpretation, the character of the Marxian critique is essentially one of "unmasking." It purportedly proves that, despite appearances, "labor" is the source of wealth and the proletariat represents the historical Subject, that is, self-constituting humanity. Such a position is closely related to the notion that socialism entails the realization of the universalistic ideals of the bourgeois revolutions, ideals that were betrayed by the particularistic interests of the bourgeoisie.

I shall endeavor below to show how the Marxian critique does include such unmasking, but as a moment of a more fundamental theory of the social and historical constitution of the ideals *and* reality of capitalist society. Marx analyzes the constitution by labor of social relations and of a historical dialectic as characteristic of the deep structure of capitalism—and not as the ontological grounds of human society that shall be realized fully in socialism. Any critique, then, that transhistorically argues that labor uniquely generates wealth and constitutes society, that opposes positively the ideals of bourgeois society to its reality, and that formulates a critique of the mode of distribution from the standpoint of "labor," necessarily remains within the bounds of the totality. The contradiction such a critique posits between the market and private property, on the one hand, and industrial, proletarian-based production, on the other, points to the abolition of the bourgeois class—but it does not point beyond the social totality. Rather, it points to the historical overcoming of earlier bourgeois relations of distribution by a form that may be more adequate on a national level to developed capitalist relations of production. That is, it delineates the supersession of an earlier, apparently more abstract form of the totality by an apparently more concrete form. If the totality itself is understood as capital, such a critique is revealed as one that, behind its own back, points to the full realization of capital as a quasi-concrete totality rather than to its abolition.

3. The limits of traditional Marxism and the pessimistic turn of Critical Theory

In the previous chapters I examined some fundamental assumptions underlying traditional Marxism's interpretation of the basic contradiction of capitalism as one between the market and private ownership, on the one hand, and industrial production, on the other. The limits and dilemmas of such an interpretation increasingly have become manifest in the course of the historical development of postliberal capitalism. In this chapter, I shall investigate those limits more closely by critically examining some basic aspects of one of the richest and most powerful theoretical responses to that historical development—the approach that has come to be known as that of the "Frankfurt School," or "Critical Theory."[1]

Those who formulated the general framework of Critical Theory—Theodor W. Adorno, Max Horkheimer, Leo Lowenthal, Herbert Marcuse, Friedrich Pollock, and others who had been associated with the Institut für Sozialforschung in Frankfurt or its journal, the *Zeitschrift für Sozialforschung*—sought to develop a fundamental social critique that would be adequate to the transformed conditions of postliberal capitalism. Influenced in part by Georg Lukács's *History and Class Consciousness* (though without adopting his identification of the proletariat as the identical subject-object of history), they proceeded from a sophisticated understanding of Marx's theory as a critical and self-reflexive analysis of the intrinsic interrelation of the social, economic, political, and cultural dimensions of life in capitalism. In the course of confronting and conceptualizing the significant transformations of capitalism in the twentieth century, they developed and placed at the center of their concern a critique of instrumental reason and the domination of nature, a critique of culture and ideology, and a critique of political domination. These attempts considerably broadened and deepened the scope of social critique and called into question the adequacy of traditional Marxism as a critique of postliberal modern society. Yet, in seeking to formulate a more adequate critique, Critical Theory ran into serious theoretical difficulties and dilemmas. These became manifest in a theoretical turn taken in the late 1930s, wherein postliberal capitalism came to be conceived as

1. Some of the arguments presented in this chapter were first developed in Barbara Brick and Moishe Postone, "Critical Pessimism and the Limits of Traditional Marxism," *Theory and Society* 11 (1982).

a completely administered, integrated, one-dimensional society, one that no longer gives rise to any immanent possibility of social emancipation.

I shall elucidate the problems entailed by that pessimistic turn and argue they indicate that although Critical Theory was based upon an awareness of the limitations of the traditional Marxist critique of capitalism, it was unable to move beyond the most fundamental assumptions of that critique. An analysis of that theoretical turn, therefore, will serve both to clarify the limits of traditional Marxism and to imply the conditions for a more adequate critical theory of modern society.

In my examination of Critical Theory's pessimistic vision of postliberal capitalism, I shall try to clarify its theoretical basis in terms of the distinction, discussed earlier, between a social critique from the standpoint of "labor" and a critique of the historically specific nature of labor in capitalism. This approach, then, will not consider the pessimism of Critical Theory only with immediate reference to its larger historical context. That context—the failure of revolution in the West, the development of Stalinism, the victory of National Socialism and, later, the character of postwar capitalism—certainly makes a pessimistic reaction understandable. Nevertheless, the specific character of the pessimistic analysis of Critical Theory cannot be fully understood in terms of historical events alone, not even World War II and the Holocaust. While these events did have a major effect on the theory, an understanding of that analysis also requires an understanding of the fundamental theoretical assumptions on the basis of which those major developments were interpreted.[2] I shall show how Critical Theory's pessimistic theoretical response to those historical events and eruptions was rooted deeply in a number of traditional presuppositions regarding the nature and course of capitalist development. Those who formulated Critical Theory recognized the significance of the changed morphology of postliberal capitalism very early on and analyzed some of its dimensions incisively. They interpreted this change, however, in terms of the constitution of a new form of social totality, one without an intrinsic structural contradiction, hence, without an intrinsic historical dynamic from which the possibility of a new social formation could arise.[3] Consequently, the pessimism to which I refer was not contingent;

2. For an interpretation that emphasizes more strongly the direct effects of historical changes on the development of Critical Theory, see Helmut Dubiel, *Theory and Politics: Studies in the Development of Critical Theory*, trans. Benjamin Gregg (Cambridge, Mass., and London, 1985). For more general treatments of Critical Theory, see Martin Jay's pioneering work, *The Dialectical Imagination* (Boston and Toronto, 1973), as well as Andrew Arato and Eike Gebhardt, eds., *The Essential Frankfurt School Reader* (New York, 1978); Seyla Benhabib, *Critique, Norm, and Utopia: On the Foundations of Critical Social Theory* (New York, 1986); David Held, *Introduction to Critical Theory* (London, Melbourne, Sydney, Auckland, Johannesburg, 1980); Douglas Kellner, *Critical Theory, Marxism and Modernity* (Baltimore, 1989); and Rolf Wiggershaus, *Die Frankfurter Schule* (Munich and Vienna, 1986).
3. In focusing on the problem of contradiction, I shall deal with the question of the form and dynamic of capitalism as a totality rather than more directly with that of class struggle and the

it did not merely express doubt about the likelihood of significant political and social change. Rather, it was an integral moment of Critical Theory's analysis of the far-reaching changes in twentieth-century capitalist society. That is, it was a *necessary* pessimism; it concerned the immanent historical *possibility* that capitalism could be superseded—and not only the *probability* that this could occur.[4] This pessimistic analysis rendered problematic the basis of Critical Theory itself.

I shall investigate the basic assumptions of this necessary pessimism by examining several articles written by Friedrich Pollock and Max Horkheimer in the 1930s and 1940s which were of central significance in the development of Critical Theory. In particular, I shall investigate the relationship between Pollock's analysis of the changed relation of state to civil society in postliberal capitalism and the changes in Horkheimer's understanding of a critical theory of society between 1937 and 1941. Focusing on the issue of social contradiction, I shall show how Pollock's work in the 1930s provided the implicit political-economic presuppositions of the pessimistic turn in Horkheimer's theory and the changes in his conception of social critique. More generally, on the basis of an examination of Pollock's investigations, I shall discuss the intrinsic relation of the political-economic dimension of Critical Theory to its social, political, and epistemological dimensions.[5] As we shall see, Pollock's interpretation of postliberal capitalism did cast doubt on the adequacy of traditional Marxism as a critical theory, and indicated its limits as a theory of emancipation; but his approach did not entail a sufficiently far-reaching reconsideration of the basic presuppositions of that theory and, hence, remained bound to some of those presuppositions. I shall then argue that, when Horkheimer adopted an analysis

---

problem of the proletariat as revolutionary Subject. The historical dialectic of capitalism in Marx's analysis encompasses, but cannot be reduced to, class struggle. A position that maintains that the social totality no longer possesses an intrinsic contradiction thus goes beyond the claim that the working class has become integrated.

4. Marcuse represents a partial exception in this regard. He continued to try to locate an immanent possibility of emancipation even when he viewed postliberal capitalism as a one-dimensional totality. Thus, for example, in *Eros and Civilization* (New York, 1962), he sought to locate that possibility by transposing the locus of contradiction to the level of psychic formation (see pp. 85–95, 137–43).

5. On the basis of a similar analysis of the importance of Pollock's political-economic presuppositions to the development of Horkheimer's critical social theory, Jeremy Gaines has undertaken an illuminating investigation of the relationship between those presuppositions, as mediated by that theory, and the aesthetic theories of Adorno, Lowenthal, and Marcuse. See "Critical Aesthetic Theory" (Ph.D. dissertation, University of Warwick, 1985).

For the relationship of Pollock's political-economic analyses and other dimensions of Critical Theory, see also Andrew Arato, Introduction, in A. Arato and E. Gebhardt, eds., *The Essential Frankfurt School Reader*, p. 3; Helmut Dubiel, Einleitung, *Friedrich Pollock: Stadien des Kapitalismus* (Munich, 1975), pp. 7, 17, 18; Giacomo Marramao, "Political Economy and Critical Theory," *Telos* 24 (Summer 1975), pp. 74–80; Martin Jay, *The Dialectical Imagination*, pp. 152–58.

of postliberal capitalism essentially similar to Pollock's, the character of his critical theory was transformed in a way that undermined the possibility of its epistemological self-reflection and resulted in its fundamental pessimism. In Horkheimer's pessimistic analysis we can find the limits, theoretically and historically, of approaches based upon traditional Marxist presuppositions.

By examining the limits of the traditional Marxist understanding of capitalism and the extent to which Critical Theory remained bound to it, I intend to call into question the necessary pessimism of the latter theory.[6] My analysis of the theoretical dilemmas of Critical Theory points in the direction of a reconstituted critical social theory that would appropriate important aspects of the approaches of Lukács and the Frankfurt School within the framework of a fundamentally different form of social critique. It differs from Jürgen Habermas's recent attempt to resuscitate theoretically the possibility of a critical social theory with emancipatory intent, which has also been formulated against the background of the theoretical dilemmas of Critical Theory,[7] inasmuch as it rests on a different understanding of traditional Marxism and the limitations of Critical Theory. Indeed, on the basis of that analysis and the first stages of my reconstruction of Marx's theory, I shall argue that Habermas himself has adopted several of Critical Theory's traditional assumptions, and that this has weakened his effort to reconstitute a critical theory of modern society.

Critique and contradiction

Before examining that fundamental pessimism, I must briefly elaborate on the notion of contradiction and its centrality to an immanent social critique. If a theory, such as Marx's, that is critical of society and assumes that people are socially constituted is to remain consistent, it cannot proceed from a standpoint that, implicitly or explicitly, purports to lie outside of its own social universe; rather, it must view itself as embedded within its context. Such a theory is an immanent social critique. It cannot take a normative position extrinsic to that which it investigates (which is the context of the critique itself)—indeed, it must regard the very notion of a decontextualized, Archimedean standpoint as spurious. The concepts used by such a social theory, then, must be related to its context. When that context itself is the object of investigation, the nature of those concepts is intrinsically bound to the nature of their object. This means that an immanent critique does not judge critically what "is" from a conceptual position outside of its object—for example, a transcendent "ought." Instead, it

---

6. My critique of the fundamental pessimism of Critical Theory is intended as an investigation of the limits of the traditional interpretation in analyzing capital. It should not be taken as implying that a more adequate social theory necessarily would entail an optimistic evaluation of the *likelihood* that a postcapitalist society will be realized.

7. Jürgen Habermas, *The Theory of Communicative Action* vol. 1: *Reason and the Rationalization of Society,* trans. Thomas McCarthy (Boston, 1984), pp. 339–99.

must be able to locate that "ought" as a dimension of its own context, as a possibility immanent to the existent society. Such a critique must also be immanent in the sense that it must be able to reflexively grasp itself and ground the possibility of its own existence in the nature of its social context. That is, if it is to be internally consistent, it must be able to ground its own standpoint in the social categories with which it grasps its object, and not simply posit or assume that standpoint. The existent, in other words, must be grasped in its own terms in a way that encompasses the possibility of its critique: the critique must be able to show that the nature of its social context is such that this context generates the possibility of a critical stance toward itself. It follows, then, that an immanent social critique must show that its object, the social whole of which it is a part, is not a unitary whole. Furthermore, if such a critique is to ground historical development socially, and avoid hypostatizing history by positing a transhistorical evolutionary development, it must show the fundamental relational structures of the society to be such that they give rise to an ongoing directional dynamic.

The notion that the structures, the underlying social relations, of modern society are contradictory provides the theoretical basis for such an immanent historical critique. It allows the immanent critique to elucidate a historical dynamic that is intrinsic to the social formation, a dialectical dynamic that points beyond itself—to that realizable "ought" that is immanent to the "is" and serves as the standpoint of its critique. Social contradiction, according to such an approach, then, is the precondition of both an intrinsic historical dynamic and the existence of the social critique itself. The possibility of the latter is intrinsically related to the socially generated possibility of other forms of critical distance and opposition—on the popular level as well. That is, the notion of social contradiction also allows for a theory of the historical constitution of popular oppositional forms that point beyond the existent order. The significance of the notion of social contradiction thus goes beyond its narrower economic interpretation as the basis of economic crises in capitalism. As I argued above, it should not be understood simply as the social antagonism between laboring and expropriating classes; rather, social contradiction refers to the very fabric of a society, to a self-generating "nonidentity" intrinsic to its structures of social relations—which do not, therefore, constitute a stable unitary whole.

The classical critical social theory based on the notion that an intrinsic social contradiction characterizes its social universe is, of course, Marx's. I shall discuss below how Marx attempts to analyze capitalist society as intrinsically contradictory and directionally dynamic, and to root those basic characteristics in the historically specific character of labor in capitalism. In so doing, Marx both grounds the possibility of his critique in a self-reflexive, epistemologically consistent manner, and breaks with all notions of the intrinsic developmental logic of human history as a whole.

Marx's immanent critique of capitalism, as noted, does not consist simply in opposing the reality of that society to its ideals. Such an understanding of immanent critique assumes that the essential purpose of the critique is to unmask bourgeois ideologies, such as that of equal exchange, and reveal the sordid reality they disguise—exploitation, for example. This, obviously, is related to the critique of capitalism from the standpoint of "labor" outlined above.[8] The critique based upon the analysis of the specificity of labor in capitalism, however, has a different character; it does not seek merely to peer behind the level of appearances of bourgeois society in order to critically oppose that surface (as "capitalist") to the underlying social totality constituted by "labor." Rather, the immanent critique Marx unfolds in *Capital* analyzes that underlying totality itself—not merely the surface level of appearances—as characteristic of capitalism. The theory seeks to grasp both surface and underlying reality in a way that points to the possible historical overcoming of the whole—which means, on another level, that it attempts to explain both the reality and the ideals of capitalist society, indicating the historically determinate character of both. Historically specifying the object of the theory in this way implies historically specifying the theory itself.

Immanent social critique also has a practical moment: it can understand itself as contributing to social and political transformation. Immanent critique rejects positions that affirm the given order, the "is," as well as utopian critiques of that order. Because the standpoint of the critique is not extraneous to its object but, rather, is a possibility immanent to it, the character of the critique is neither theoretically nor practically exhortative. The real consequences of social and political actions are always codetermined by the context within which they take place, regardless of the justifications and goals of such actions. Inasmuch as immanent critique, in analying its context, reveals its immanent possibilities, it contributes to their realization. Revealing the potential in the actual helps action to be socially transformative in a conscious way.

The adequacy of an immanent social critique depends on the adequacy of its categories. If the fundamental categories of the critique (value, for example) are to be considered critical categories adequate to capitalist society, they must express the specificity of that society. Furthermore, as categories of a historical critique, the categories must be shown to grasp the grounds of an intrinsic dynamic of that society, leading to the possibility of its historical negation—to the

---

8. The idea that an immanent critique reveals the gap between the ideals and the reality of modern capitalist society is presented, for example, by Theodor Adorno in "On the Logic of the Social Sciences," *The Positivist Dispute in German Sociology*, trans. Glyn Adey and David Frisby (London, 1976), p. 115. In general, Critical Theory and its sympathetic commentators strongly emphasize the immanent character of Marx's social critique; however, they understand the nature of that immanent critique as being one that judges the reality of capitalist society on the basis of its liberal bourgeois ideals. See, for example, Steven Seidman, Introduction, in Seidman, ed., *Jürgen Habermas on Society and Politics* (Boston, 1989), pp. 4–5. The latter understanding reveals the extent to which Critical Theory remains bound to some basic presuppositions of the traditional critique from the standpoint of "labor."

"ought" that emerges as a historical possibility immanent to the "is." Relatedly, if one supposes the society to be contradictory, the categories one uses to express its basic forms of social relations must express this contradiction. As we saw in the previous chapter, this contradiction must be such that it points beyond the existent of the totality. Only if the categories themselves express such a contradiction can the critique avoid being positive, in other words, one that criticizes what is on the basis of what also is and, hence, does not really point beyond the existent totality. The adequate, negative critique is not undertaken on the basis of what is but of what could be, as a potential immanent to the existent society. Finally, categories of an immanent social critique with emancipatory intent must adequately grasp the determinate grounds of unfreedom in capitalism, so that the historical abolition of what they express would imply the possibility of social and historical freedom.

These conditions of an adequate immanent critique are not fulfilled by the social critique from the standpoint of "labor." Pollock's and Horkheimer's attempts to analyze the changed character of postliberal capitalism reveal that the traditional critique's categories are not adequate expressions of the core of capitalism or of the grounds of unfreedom in that society, and that the contradiction they express does not point beyond the present totality to an emancipated society. Having shown these categories to be inadequate, though, Pollock and Horkheimer did not then call into question their traditional presuppositions. As a result, they were unable to reconstitute a more adequate social critique. It was the combination of these two elements of their approach that resulted in the pessimism of Critical Theory.

Friedrich Pollock and "the primacy of the political"

I shall begin my discussion of the pessimistic turn of Critical Theory by examining the political-economic presuppositions of Friedrich Pollock's analysis of the transformation of capitalism associated with the rise of the interventionist state. Pollock first develops this analysis in the early 1930s with Gerhard Meyer and Kurt Mandelbaum, and he extends it further in the course of the following decade. Faced with the Great Depression and the resultant increasingly active role of the state in the socioeconomic sphere, as well as the Soviet experience with planning, Pollock concludes that the political sphere has superseded the economic sphere as the locus of both economic regulation and the articulation of social problems. He characterizes this shift as the primacy of the political over the economic.[9] This notion, which has since become widespread,[10] implies

9. Friedrich Pollock, "Is National Socialism a New Order?" *Studies in Philosophy and Social Science* 9 (1941), p. 453.
10. Jürgen Habermas, for example, presents a version of this position in "Technology and Science as 'Ideology,' " in *Towards a Rational Society,* trans. Jeremy J. Shapiro (Boston, 1970), and further develops it in *Legitimation Crisis,* trans. Thomas McCarthy (Boston, 1975).

that the Marxian critique of political economy was valid for the period of laissez-faire capitalism but has since become anachronistic in the repoliticized society of postliberal capitalism. Such a position may appear to be a self-evident consequence of the transformation of capitalism in the twentieth century. As I shall show, though, it is based upon a set of questionable assumptions which give rise to serious problems in the analysis of postliberal capitalism. My critique does not question Pollock's basic insight—that the development of the interventionist state entailed far-reaching economic, social, and political consequences—but it does reveal the problematic implications of Pollock's theoretical framework for analyzing those changes, that is, his understanding of the economic sphere and of the basic contradiction between the forces and relations of production.

Pollock develops his conception of the social order emerging from the Great Depression in two, increasingly pessimistic, phases. His point of departure in analyzing both the fundamental causes of the Great Depression and its possible historical results is the traditional interpretation of the contradictions of capitalism. In two essays written in 1932–1933—"Die gegenwärtige Lage des Kapitalismus und die Aussichten einer planwirtschaftlichen Neuordnung"[11] and "Bemerkungen zur Wirtschaftskrise"[12]—Pollock characterizes the course of capitalist development in the traditional terms of an increasing contradiction between the forces of production (interpreted as the industrial mode of production) and private appropriation mediated socially by the "self-regulatory" market.[13] This growing contradiction underlies economic crises that, by violently diminishing the forces of production (for example, by the use of machinery at less than full capacity, the destruction of raw materials, and the unemployment of thousands of workers), are the means by which capitalism tries "automatically" to resolve the contradiction.[14] In this sense, the world depression represents nothing new. Yet the intensity of the depression and the crassness of the gap between the social wealth produced, which potentially could serve the satisfaction of general human needs, and the impoverishment of large segments of the population mark the end of the era of free market or liberal capitalism.[15] They indicate that "the present economic form is incapable of using the forces which it itself developed for the benefit of all members of society."[16] Because this development is not historically contingent but results from the dynamic of liberal capitalism itself, any attempt to reconstitute a social organization based on liberal economic mechanisms would historically be doomed to failure: "Ac-

---

11. Pollock, "Die gegenwärtige Lage des Kapitalismus und die Aussichten einer planwirtschaftlichen Neuordnung," *Zeitschrift für Sozialforschung* 1 (1932).
12. Pollock, "Bemerkungen zur Wirtschaftskrise," *Zeitschrift für Sozialforschung* 2 (1933).
13. "Die gegenwärtige Lage," p. 21.
14. Ibid., p. 15.
15. Ibid., p. 10.
16. "Bemerkungen," p. 337.

cording to all indications, it would be a wasted effort to attempt to reestablish the technical, economic and social-psychological conditions for a free market economy."[17]

Although liberal capitalism cannot be reconstituted, according to Pollock, it has given rise to the possibility of a new social order that could resolve the difficulties of the older one: the dialectic of the forces and relations of production underlying the development of free-market capitalism has given rise to the possibility of a centrally planned economy.[18] Yet—and this is the decisive turning point—such an economy need not be socialist. Pollock maintains that laissez-faire and capitalism are not necessarily identical and that the economic situation can be stabilized within the framework of capitalism itself, through massive and ongoing intervention of the state in the economy.[19] Instead of identifying socialism with planning, Pollock distinguishes two main types of planned economic systems: "a capitalist planned economy on the basis of private ownership of the means of production and hence within the social framework of class society, and a socialist planned economy characterized by social ownership of the means of production within the social framework of a classless society."[20]

Pollock rejects any theory of the automatic breakdown of capitalism and emphasizes that socialism does not necessarily follow capitalism. Its historical realization depends not only on economic and technical factors but on the power of resistance of those who carry the burden of the existing order. And, for Pollock, massive resistance on the part of the proletariat is unlikely in the near future as a result of the diminished weight of the working class in the economic process, changes in weapons-technology, and the newly developed means for the psychic and cultural domination of the masses.[21]

Pollock considers a capitalist planned economy, rather than socialism, to be the most likely result of the Great Depression: "What is coming to an end is not capitalism, but its liberal phase."[22] At this stage of Pollock's thought, the difference between capitalism and socialism in an age of planning has been reduced to that between private and social ownership of the means of production. In both cases, the free-market economy would be replaced by state regulation.

Even the distinction based on forms of property, however, has become problematic. In describing the reaction of capitalism to the crisis, Pollock refers to the violent diminishing of the forces of production and a "loosening of the fetters"—a modification of the "relations of production"—through state intervention.[23] He claims, on the one hand, that it might be possible for both to occur

17. Ibid., p. 332.
18. "Die gegenwärtige Lage," pp. 19–20.
19. Ibid., p. 16.
20. Ibid., p. 18.
21. "Bemerkungen," p. 350.
22. Ibid.
23. Ibid., p. 338.

without the basis of the capitalist system—private property and its valorization—being touched.[24] On the other hand, he notes that continuous state intervention involves a more or less drastic limitation of the individual owner's
power of disposal over his capital, and associates that with the tendency, already
present before World War I, for ownership and effective management to become
separated.[25] The determination of capitalism in terms of private property has,
then, become somewhat ambiguous. Pollock effectively dispenses with it in his
essays of 1941, in which the theory of the primacy of the political is fully
developed.

In these essays—"State Capitalism" and "Is National Socialism a New Order?"[26]—Pollock analyzes the newly emergent social order as state capitalism.
His method here is to construct ideal types: whereas in 1932 he opposes a
socialist to a capitalist planned economy, in 1941 he opposes totalitarian and
democratic state capitalism as the two primary ideal types of the new order.[27]
(In 1941 Pollock describes the Soviet Union as a state capitalist society.)[28] In
the totalitarian form, the state is in the hands of a new ruling stratum, an amal-
gamation of leading bureaucrats in business, state, and party;[29] in the democratic
form it is controlled by the people. Pollock's ideal-typical analysis concentrates
on the totalitarian state capitalist form. When stripped of those aspects specific
to totalitarianism, his examination of the fundamental change in the relation of
state to civil society can be seen as constituting the political-economic dimension
of a general critical theory of postliberal capitalism, which Horkheimer, Marcuse, and Adorno develop more fully.

The central characteristic of the state capitalist order, according to Pollock, is
the supersession of the economic sphere by the political realm. Balancing production and distribution has become a function of the state rather than of the
market.[30] Although a market, a price system, and wages may remain in existence, they no longer serve to regulate the economic process.[31] Furthermore,
even if the legal institution of private property is retained, its economic functions
have been effectively abolished, inasmuch as the right of disposal over individual capital has been transferred in large measure from the individual capitalist
to the state.[32] The capitalist has been transformed into a mere rentier.[33] The state
formulates a general plan and compels its fulfillment. As a result, private prop-

24. Ibid., p. 349.
25. Ibid., pp. 345–46.
26. Pollock, "State Capitalism," *Studies in Philosophy and Social Science* 9 (1941); "Is National
   Socialism."
27. "State Capitalism," p. 200.
28. Ibid., p. 211n1.
29. Ibid., p. 201.
30. Ibid.
31. Ibid., pp. 204–205; "Is National Socialism," p. 444.
32. "Is National Socialism," p. 442.
33. "State Capitalism," pp. 208–9.

erty, the law of the market, or other economic "laws"—such as the equalization of the rate of profit or its tendency to fall—do not retain their previously essential functions.[34] No autonomous, self-moving economic sphere exists in state capitalism. Problems of administration, therefore, have replaced those of the process of exchange.[35]

This transition, according to Pollock, has broad social implications. He maintains that all social relations under liberal capitalism are determined by the market; people and classes confront one another in the public sphere as quasi-autonomous agents. In spite of the inefficiencies and injustices of the system, the market relation implies that the rules governing the public sphere are mutually binding. Law is the doubled rationality, applying to rulers as well as to ruled. Such an impersonal legal realm contributes to the separation of the public and private spheres and, by implication, to the formation of the bourgeois individual. Social position is a function of the market and income. Employees are impelled to work by their fear of hunger and the wish for a better life.[36]

Under state capitalism, the state becomes the determinant of all spheres of social life;[37] the hierarchy of bureaucratic political structures occupies the center of social existence. Market relations are replaced by those of a command hierarchy in which a one-sided technical rationality reigns in the place of law. The majority of the population becomes, in effect, paid employees of the political apparatus; they lack political rights, powers of self-organization, and the right to strike. The impetus to work is effected by political terror, on the one hand, and psychic manipulation, on the other. Individuals and groups, no longer autonomous, are subordinated to the whole; because of their productivity, people are treated as means rather than as ends in themselves. This is veiled, however, for they are compensated for their loss of independence by the socially sanctioned transgression of some earlier social norms, especially sexual ones. By breaking down the wall separating the intimate sphere from society and the state, such compensation allows for further social manipulation.[38]

Both the market and private property—that is, the basic capitalist social relations (traditionally understood)—have been effectively abolished in state capitalism, according to Pollock. The social, political, and cultural consequences, however, have not necessarily been emancipatory. Expressing this view in Marxian categories, Pollock claims that production in state capitalism no longer entails the production of commodities, but has become oriented toward use. The

34. Ibid.
35. Ibid., p. 217.
36. Ibid., p. 207; "Is National Socialism," pp. 443, 447.
37. "State Capitalism," p. 206.
38. "Is National Socialism," pp. 448–49. In many respects, Pollock's brief comments on this matter foreshadow what Marcuse later develops more fully with his concept of repressive desublimation.

latter determination, however, does not guarantee that production serves "the needs of free humans in an harmonious society."[39]

Given Pollock's analysis of the nonemancipatory character of state capitalism and his claim that a return to liberal capitalism is impossible, the problem now is whether state capitalism could be superseded by socialism.[40] That possibility can no longer be considered immanent to the present society—that is, as emerging from the unfolding of an intrinsic contradiction underlying a self-moving economy—because, according to Pollock, the economy has become totally manageable. He claims that the command economy, as opposed to free-market capitalism, has at its disposal the means to check the economic causes of depressions.[41] Pollock repeatedly emphasizes that there are no economic laws or functions that could hinder or set a limit to the functionings of state capitalism.[42]

If this is the case, is there no possibility that state capitalism can be overcome? In his tentative answer, Pollock sketches the beginnings of a theory of political crises—crises in political legitimation. State capitalism, according to Pollock, arose historically as the solution to the economic ills of liberal capitalism. Hence, the primary tasks of the new social order will be to maintain full employment and to enable the forces of production to develop unhindered, while maintaining the basis of the old social structure.[43] The replacement of the market by the state means that mass unemployment immediately would entail a political crisis, one that would call the system into question. State capitalism necessarily requires full employment to legitimate itself.

The totalitarian variant of state capitalism is confronted with additional problems. That order represents the worst form of an antagonistic society "in which the power interests of the ruling class prevents the people from fully using the productive forces for their own welfare and from having control of the organization and activities of society."[44] Because of the intensity of this antagonism, totalitarian state capitalism cannot allow the general standard of living to rise appreciably, because such a rise would free people to reflect on their situation critically, which could lead to the emergence of a revolutionary spirit, with its demands for freedom and justice.[45]

---

39. "Is National Socialism," p. 446.
40. Ibid., pp. 452–55.
41. Ibid., p. 454.
42. "State Capitalism," p. 217.
43. Ibid., p. 203.
44. Ibid., p. 223.
45. Ibid., p. 220. Pollock seems to consider mass consciousness in an era of the primacy of the political only in terms of external manipulation and a vague notion of the possible revolutionary effects of a rise in the standard of living. It appears that, in dealing with state-determined society, he has no concept of social consciousness as an immanent aspect of that form (although that is perhaps not the case in his consideration of market-determined society). It could be argued that Pollock has no adequately worked out notion of the relation between social subjectivity and objectivity. He, therefore, only specifies the most external "material conditions" that would

Totalitarian state capitalism is, therefore, faced with the problem of maintaining full employment, promoting further technical progress, yet *not* allowing the standard of living to rise appreciably. According to Pollock, only a permanent war economy could achieve these tasks simultaneously. The greatest threat to the totalitarian form is peace. In a peace economy, the system could not maintain itself, despite mass psychological manipulation and terror.[46] It could not tolerate a high standard of living and could not survive mass unemployment. A high standard of living could be maintained by democratic state capitalism, but Pollock describes that form as unstable and transitory: either class differences would assert themselves, in which case democratic state capitalism would develop in the direction of the totalitarian form, or democratic control of the state would result in the abolition of the last remnants of class society, thereby leading to socialism.[47] The latter possibility, however, seems unlikely within the framework of Pollock's approach—that is, his thesis of the manageability of the economy and his awareness that a policy of military "preparedness," which allows for a permanent war economy without war, is a hallmark of the state capitalist era.[48] Pollock's analysis of state capitalism cannot ground his hope that democratic state capitalism can be established and developed further in the direction of socialism. His position is fundamentally pessimistic: the overcoming of the new order cannot be derived immanently from the system itself but, rather, has become dependent on an unlikely "extrinsic" circumstance—world peace.

Assumptions and dilemmas of Pollock's thesis

Several aspects of Pollock's analysis are problematic. His examination of liberal capitalism indicates its dynamic development and historicity. It shows how the immanent contradiction between its forces and relations of production gave rise to the possibility of an economically planned society as its historical negation. Pollock's analysis of state capitalism, however, lacks this historical dimension; rather, it is static and merely describes various ideal types. Pollock's initial formulation of a political crisis theory did, to be sure, seek to uncover moments of instability and conflict, yet they are not related to any sort of immanent historical dynamic from which the contours and the possibility of another social formation could emerge. We must thus consider why, for Pollock, the stage of capitalism characterized by the "primacy of the economic" is contradictory and dynamic while that characterized by the "primacy of the political" is not.

This problem can be elucidated by considering Pollock's understanding of the economic. In postulating the primacy of politics over economics, he con-

allow for critical thought, but cannot indicate why that thought might be critical in a particular direction.
46. Ibid.
47. Ibid., pp. 219, 225.
48. Ibid., p. 220.

ceptualizes the latter in terms of the quasi-automatic market-mediated coordination of needs and resources, whereby price mechanisms direct production and distribution.[49] Under liberal capitalism, profits and wages direct the flow of capital and the distribution of labor power within the economic process.[50] The market is central to Pollock's understanding of the economic. His assertion that economic "laws" lose their essential function when the state supersedes the market indicates that, in his view, such laws are rooted only in the market mode of social regulation. The centrality of the market to Pollock's notion of the economic is also indicated on a categorial level, by his interpretation of the commodity: a good is a commodity only when circulated by the market, otherwise it is a use value. This approach, of course, implies an interpretation of the Marxian category of value—purportedly the fundamental category of the relations of production in capitalism—solely in terms of the market. In other words, Pollock understands the economic sphere and, implicitly, the Marxian categories only in terms of the mode of distribution.

Pollock interprets the contradiction between the forces and relations of production accordingly, as one between industrial production and the bourgeois mode of distribution (the market, private property). Thus, he maintains that the growing concentration and centralization of production renders private ownership increasingly dysfunctional and anachronistic,[51] whereas the periodic crises indicate that the "automatic" mode of regulation is not harmonious and that the anarchic operations of economic laws have become increasingly destructive.[52] This contradiction, then, gives rise to a dynamic that both requires and makes possible the supersession of the bourgeois mode of distribution by a form characterized by planning and the effective absence of private property.

It follows from this interpretation that when the state supplants the market as the agency of distribution, the economic sphere is essentially suspended. Hence, according to Pollock, economics as a social science loses the object of its investigation: "Whereas the economist formerly racked his brain to solve the puzzle of the exchange process, he meets, under state capitalism, with mere problems of administration."[53] With state planning, in other words, a conscious mode of social regulation and distribution has replaced the nonconscious economic mode. Underlying Pollock's notion of the primacy of the political is an understanding of the economic which presupposes the primacy of the mode of distribution.

It should now be clear why state capitalism, according to such an interpretation, possesses no immanent dynamic. An immanent dynamic implies a logic of development, above and beyond conscious control, which is based on a con-

49. Ibid., p. 203.
50. "Is National Socialism," p. 445ff.
51. "Bemerkungen," p. 345ff.
52. "Die gegenwärtige Lage," p. 15.
53. "State Capitalism," p. 217.

tradiction intrinsic to the system. In Pollock's analysis, the market is the source of all nonconscious social structures of necessity and regulation; as a result, it constitutes the basis of the "laws of motion" of the capitalist social formation. Pollock maintains, moreover, that planning alone implies full conscious control and, hence, is not limited by any economic laws. It follows, then, that the supersession of the market by state planning must signify the end of any blind logic of development: historical development is now consciously regulated. Furthermore, an understanding of the contradiction between the forces and relations of production as one between distribution and production—expressed by the growing inadequacy of the market and private property to conditions of developed industrial production—implies that a mode based upon planning and the effective abolition of private property *is* adequate to those conditions. Within the framework of a theory which proceeds from the traditional, distribution-oriented interpretation of the relations of production, an intrinsic social contradiction no longer exists between these new "relations of production" and the industrial mode of production. Hence, the Marxian notion of the contradictory character of capitalism is relegated implicitly to the period of liberal capitalism. Pollock's notion of the primacy of the political thus refers to an antagonistic society possessing no immanent dynamic that points toward the possibility of socialism as its negation; the pessimism of his theory is rooted in its analysis of postliberal capitalism as an unfree but noncontradictory society.

Pollock's analysis indicates the problems with a critique of the social formation that assumes the primacy of the mode of distribution. According to Pollock's ideal-typical analysis, with the development of state capitalism, value has been superseded and private property effectively has been abolished. Yet the abolition of these social relations does not necessarily lay the foundations of the "good society"; on the contrary, it can and does lead to forms of greater oppression and tyranny, forms that no longer can be criticized adequately by means of the category of value. Furthermore, according to his interpretation, overcoming the market means that the system of commodity production has been replaced by one of use value production. Yet Pollock shows that to be an insufficient determination of emancipation; it does not necessarily mean that the "needs of free humans in a harmonious society" are being met. Value and the commodity, however, can be considered critical categories adequate to the capitalist social formation only when they ground an immanent dynamic of that social form leading to the possibility of its historical negation. They must sufficiently grasp the core of that contradictory society so that their abolition implies the social basis of freedom. Pollock's analysis indicates that the Marxian categories, understood in terms of the mode of distribution, do not grasp adequately the grounds of unfreedom in capitalism. He does not, however, reconsider the source of these limitations of the categories, namely, the one-sided emphasis on the mode of distribution; instead, he retains that emphasis while implicitly limiting the validity of Marx's categories to liberal capitalism.

Pollock's traditional assumption of the primacy of distribution, however, gives rise to serious theoretical difficulties in his treatment of state capitalism. As we have seen, capitalism—as state capitalism—can exist, according to Pollock, in the absence of the market and private property. These, however, are its two essential characteristics, as defined by traditional Marxist theory. What, in the absence of those "relations of production," characterizes the new phase as capitalist? Pollock lists the following grounds for his characterization: "State capitalism is the successor of private capitalism,... the state assumes important functions of the private capitalist,... profit interests still play a significant role, and ... it is not socialism."[54] It appears, at first glance, that the key to Pollock's specification of postliberal class society as capitalist is his statement that profit interests continue to play an important role. Although, according to Pollock, such interests do become subordinate to a general plan, "no state capitalist government can or will dispense with the profit motive":[55] its abolition would destroy "the character of the entire system."[56] It seems that the specific character of the "entire system" could be clarified by a consideration of profit.

Such a clarification, however, is not offered by Pollock. Instead of undertaking an analysis of profit, which would help to determine the capitalist character of the new social form, Pollock treats that category in an indeterminate fashion:

Another aspect of the changed situation under state capitalism is that the profit motive is superseded by the power motive. Obviously the profit motive is a specific form of the power motive.... The difference, however, is ... that the latter is essentially bound up with the power position of the ruling group while the former pertains to the individual only.[57]

Leaving aside considerations of the weaknesses of positions that implicitly derive relations of power from a motive for power, it is clear that this approach merely underlines the political character of state capitalism without further elucidating its capitalist dimension. That the economic sphere, according to Pollock, no longer plays an essential role is reflected in his basically empty treatment of profit. Economic categories (profit) have become subspecies of political categories (power).

The ultimate ground for Pollock's characterization of postliberal society as state capitalist is that it remains antagonistic, that is, a class society.[58] The term "capitalism," however, requires a more specific determination than that of social antagonism, for all developed historical forms of society have been antagonistic in the sense that the social surplus is expropriated from its immediate

54. Ibid., p. 201.
55. Ibid., p. 205.
56. Ibid.
57. Ibid., p. 207.
58. Ibid., p. 219.

producers and not used for the benefit of all. Moreover, the term "class" also requires a more specific determination; it does not refer simply to social groups that exist in such antagonistic relations. Rather, as I shall show, the Marxian notions of class and class struggle acquire their full significance only as categories of an inherently contradictory and dynamic system. Social antagonism and social contradiction, in other words, are not identical.

The concept of state capitalism necessarily implies that what is being politically regulated is capitalism; it demands, therefore, a concept of capital. Such considerations, however, are not to be found in Pollock's treatment. His strategic intention in using the term "state capitalism" seems clear—to emphasize that the abolition of the market and private property does not suffice for the transformation of capitalism into socialism. Yet Pollock cannot ground adequately his characterization of postliberal antagonistic society as capitalist.

Pollock's position, moreover, cannot explain the source of continuing class antagonism in postliberal capitalism. His understanding of the economic sphere renders opaque the material conditions underlying the differences between state capitalism and socialism. In the traditional Marxist analysis, the system based upon the market and private property necessarily implies a specific class system; overcoming these relations of production is understood as the economic presupposition of a classless society. A fundamentally different social organization is bound to a fundamentally different economic organization. Whereas Pollock proceeds from the same assumptions regarding the structure of liberal capitalism, the intrinsic connectedness of the economic organization and the social structure is severed in his treatment of postliberal societies. Although he characterizes state capitalism as a class system, he considers its basic economic organization (in the broader sense) to be the same as that of socialism: central planning and the effective abolition of private property under conditions of developed industrial production. This, however, implies that the difference between a class system and a classless society is not related to fundamental differences in their economic organization; rather, it is simply a function of the mode and goal of its administration. The basic structure of society has thus presumably become independent of its economic form. Pollock's approach implies that there is no longer any relation between social structure and economic organization.

This paradoxical result is latent in Pollock's theoretical point of departure. If the Marxian categories and the notion of the relations of production are understood in terms of the mode of distribution, the conclusion is inescapable that the dialectic of economic development has run its course when the market and private property are overcome. The politically mediated economic organization that emerges thus represents the historical endpoint of the mode of distribution. The further existence of class society in such a situation, therefore, cannot be grounded in this mode of distribution—which, presumably, would underlie a classless society as well. Nor, for that matter, can class antagonism be rooted in the sphere of production. As we have seen, in the traditional interpretation of the Marxian categories, the transformation of the relations of production entails not a transformation of the industrial mode of production but an "adjustment" adequate to that mode of production which, supposedly, had already acquired its historically final form. Within this framework, then, the continued existence of class society cannot be grounded in either production or distribution.

Economic organization, in other words, has become a historical invariable in Pollock's analysis, one that underlies various possible political forms and no longer is related to social structure. Given the absence of any relation between social structures and economic organization in his analysis of postliberal society, Pollock has to posit a political sphere that not only maintains and reinforces class differences but is their source. Class relations are reduced to power relations, the source of which remain obscure. Given his point of departure, however, it seems that Pollock has little choice in so reductively analyzing the repoliticization of social life in postliberal society.

Finally, the limits of Pollock's underlying assumptions in adequately grasping the changed morphology of postliberal capitalism become clear in his treatment of the capitalist relations of production. The notion itself refers to that which characterizes capitalism as capitalism, that is, to the essence of the social formation. The logic of Pollock's interpretation should have induced a fundamental reconsideration: if the market and private property are, indeed, to be considered the capitalist relations of production, the ideal-typical postliberal form should not be considered capitalist. On the other hand, characterizing the new form as capitalist, despite the (presumed) abolition of those relational structures, implicitly demands a different determination of the relations of production essential to capitalism. Such an approach, in other words, should call into question the identification of the market and private property with the essential relations of production of capitalist society—even for the liberal phase of capitalism.

Pollock, however, does not undertake such a reconsideration. Instead, he modifies the traditional determination of the relations of production by limiting its validity to the liberal phase of capitalism, and postulates its supersession by a political mode of distribution. The result is a new set of theoretical problems and weaknesses which points to the need for a more radical reexamination of the traditional theory. If one maintains, as Pollock does, that the capitalist social formation possesses successively different sets of "relations of production," one necessarily posits a core of that formation that is not fully grasped by any of those sets of relations. This separation of the essence of the formation from all determinate relations of production indicates, however, that the latter have been inadequately determined. Moreover, what in Pollock's analysis remains the essence—"class" antagonism—is too historically indeterminate to be of use in specifying the capitalist social formation. Both weaknesses indicate the inadequacy and limits of Pollock's point of departure, that is, locating the relations of production only in the sphere of distribution.

Pollock's analysis of the significant transformations of social life and the structure of domination associated with the development of postliberal capitalism contains many important insights. His analysis, however, must be placed on a firmer theoretical basis. Such a basis, I shall argue, would also call into question the necessary character of Pollock's pessimism.

It should, however, be clear that I regard as inadequate a critique of Pollock that proceeds from the presuppositions of traditional Marxism. Such an approach could reintroduce a dynamic to the analysis by pointing out that market competition and private property have by no means disappeared or lost their functions under state-interventionist capitalism. (This, of course, would not apply to the "real existing socialist" variants of state capitalism. One weakness of traditional Marxism is that it cannot provide the basis for an adequate critique of such societies.) Indeed, on a less immediately empirical level, one could ask whether it would at all be possible for bourgeois capitalism to reach a stage in which all elements of market capitalism are overcome. Nevertheless, reintroducing a dynamic to the analysis of state-interventionist capitalism on the basis of the continued significance of the market and private property does not get to the roots of Pollock's pessimism; it simply avoids the fundamental problems raised when that development is thought through to its endpoint—the abolition of these "relations of production." The question must then be faced whether that abolition is indeed a sufficient condition for socialism. As I have sought to show, Pollock's approach, despite its frozen character and questionable theoretical foundations, does indicate that an interpretation of the relations of production and, hence, value, in terms of the sphere of distribution does not grasp sufficiently the core of unfreedom in capitalism. To criticize him from the standpoint of that interpretation would, therefore, be a step back from the level of the problem as it has emerged in the consideration of Pollock's analysis.[59]

In spite of the difficulties associated with Pollock's ideal-typical approach, it has the unintended heuristic value of allowing a perception of the problematic character of the assumptions of traditional Marxism. Within the framework of a one-sided critique of the mode of distribution from the standpoint of "labor," the Marxian categories cannot critically grasp the social totality. This, however, only becomes historically evident when the market loses its central role as the agency of distribution. Pollock's analysis shows that any attempt based on the

59. See, for example, Giacomo Marramao, "Political Economy and Critical Theory." I agree with Marramao's general thesis relating Pollock's work to that of Horkheimer, Marcuse, and Adorno, as well as with his general conclusion that Pollock is not able to locate the "dialectical elements" within the new stage of capitalism. However, although Marramao approvingly presents aspects of Henryk Grossmann's analysis as an interpretation of Marx very different from that dominant in the Marxist tradition (p. 59ff.), he does not follow through its implications. Instead, by identifying Pollock's interpretation of the conflict between the forces and relations of production with that of Marx, he implicitly accepts it (p. 67). This does not allow him to support his charge—that Pollock mistakes as essence the illusory level of appearance (p. 74)—from a standpoint that would move beyond the limits of traditional Marxism.

traditional interpretation to characterize the resultant politically regulated social order as capitalist must remain indeterminate. It also renders clear that the abolition of the market and private property alone and, hence, the "coming into its own" of industrial production is an insufficient condition for human emancipation. Pollock's treatment of postliberal capitalism thus inadvertently indicates that the market and private property are not adequate determinations of the most basic social categories of capitalism, hence, that the traditional Marxist categories are inadequate as critical categories of the capitalist social totality. The abolition of that which they express does not constitute the condition of general freedom.

Pollock's analysis highlights precisely those limitations of the traditional Marxist interpretation, and shows as well that the Marxian notion of contradiction as a hallmark of the capitalist social formation is not identical with the notion of social antagonism. Whereas an antagonistic social form can be static, the notion of contradiction necessarily implies an intrinsic dynamic. By considering state capitalism to be an antagonistic form that does not possess such a dynamic, Pollock's approach draws attention to the problem of social contradiction as one that must be located structurally in a way that extends beyond considerations of class and ownership. Finally, Pollock's refusal to consider the new form in its most abstract contours merely as one that is not yet fully socialist enables him to uncover its new, more negative modes of political, social, and cultural domination.

Pollock and the other members of the Frankfurt School do break with traditional Marxism in one decisive respect. One of Pollock's basic insights is that a system of central planning in the effective absence of private property is not, in and of itself, emancipatory, although such a form of distribution is adequate to industrial production. This implicitly calls into question the idea that "labor"—for example, in the form of the industrial mode of production or, on another level, the social totality constituted by labor—is the basis of general human freedom. Yet Pollock's analysis remains too bound to some fundamental propositions of traditional Marxism to constitute its adequate critique. Because he adopts its one-sided emphasis on the mode of distribution, Pollock's break with the traditional theory does not really overcome its basic assumptions regarding the nature of labor in capitalism. Instead, he retains the notion of "labor," but implicitly reverses his evaluation of its role. According to Pollock, the historical dialectic has run its course: "Labor" has come into itself. The totality has been realized, but the result is anything but emancipatory. His analysis suggests that that result must, therefore, be rooted in the character of "labor." Whereas "labor" had been regarded as the locus of freedom, it now implicitly comes to be seen as a source of unfreedom. This reversal is expressed more explicitly in Horkheimer's works, as I shall demonstrate. Both the optimistic and the pessimistic positions I have been examining share an understanding of labor in capitalism as "labor," an understanding that falls behind the level of Marx's mature critique of Ricardo and of Hegel. Pollock retains this notion and continues to envision the contradiction of capitalism as one between production and distribution. He therefore concludes that there is no immanent contradiction in state capitalism. His analysis results in a conception of an antagonistic and repressive social totality that has become essentially noncontradictory and no longer possesses an immanent dynamic. It is a conception that casts doubt on the emancipatory role attributed to "labor" and to the realization of the totality, but ultimately, it does not move beyond the horizons of the traditional Marxist critique of capitalism.

Max Horkheimer's pessimistic turn

The qualitative transformation of capitalist society—hence, of the object of social critique—implied by Pollock's analysis of postliberal capitalism as a noncontradictory totality entails a transformation of the nature of the critique itself. I shall investigate this transformation and its problematic aspects by considering the implications of Pollock's analysis for Max Horkheimer's conception of Critical Theory. This transformation of Critical Theory has been described in terms of the supersession of the critique of political economy by the critique of politics, the critique of ideology, and the critique of instrumental reason.[60] It frequently has been understood as a shift from a critical analysis of modern society whose focus is restricted to one sphere of social life, to a broader and deeper approach. Yet my discussion suggests that this evaluation must be modified. We have seen that the starting point of Critical Theory, as articulated by Pollock, was a traditional understanding of Marx's basic categories, coupled with the recognition that these traditional categories had been rendered inadequate by the development of twentieth-century capitalism. Nevertheless, because this recognition did not lead to a fundamental reconceptualization of the Marxian categories themselves, Critical Theory's broadening of the social critique of capitalism involved a number of serious theoretical difficulties. It also weakened the ability of the theory to grasp aspects of capitalist society that were central concerns of Marx's critique of political economy.

It is a mistake, in other words, to see the difference between the critique of political economy and the critique of instrumental reason (and so on) as simply a matter of the relative importance attributed to particular spheres of social life. Labor is central to Marx's analysis not because he assumes material production as such to be the most important aspect of social life or the essence of human society, but because he considers the peculiarly abstract and directionally dynamic character of capitalist society to be its central hallmark, and maintains that those basic features could be grasped and elucidated in terms of the historically specific nature of labor in that society. Through his analysis of that his-

---

60. See A. Arato, Introduction, in *The Essential Frankfurt School Reader,* pp. 12, 19.

torically specific nature, Marx seeks to clarify and to ground socially an abstract form of social relations and of domination as characteristic of capitalism. His critique does so in a way that shows capitalism to be a totality that is intrinsically contradictory and, thus, immanently dynamic. In this regard, a critique of political institutions or instrumental reason could be seen as superseding (rather than extending or supplementing) Marx's critique of political economy, only if it were also capable of accounting for the historical dynamism of the social formation—by indicating, for example, a contradiction intrinsic to the nature of its object of investigation. This is an exceedingly unlikely proposition, in my opinion. Furthermore, the shift in the focus of Critical Theory outlined above was related precisely to the assumption that because the postliberal social totality had become noncontradictory, it was without any intrinsic historical dynamic. That analysis not only resulted in a fundamentally pessimistic position, but it also undermined the possibility that Critical Theory could be consistently self-reflexive as an immanent critique. Moreover, it has proven retrospectively to have been questionable historically.

I shall elaborate these contentions and investigate the transformation of the nature of critique associated with an analysis of state capitalism as a noncontradictory society by examining two essays written by Horkheimer in 1937 and 1940. In his classical essay, "Traditional and Critical Theory,"[61] Horkheimer still grounds critical theory in the contradictory character of capitalist society. He proceeds from the assumption that the relation of subject and object should be understood in terms of the social constitution of both:

In fact, social practice always contains available and applied knowledge. The perceived fact is therefore co-determined by human ideas and concepts even prior to its conscious assimilation by the knowing individual.... At the higher stages of civilization, conscious human practice unconsciously determines not only the subjective side of perception but, to an increasing degree, the object as well.[62]

Such an approach implies that thought is historically determinate, and it demands, therefore, that both traditional as well as critical theory be grounded sociohistorically. Traditional theory, according to Horkheimer, is an expression of the fact that although subject and object are always intrinsically related within a historically constituted totality, this intrinsic relation is not manifest in capitalism. Because the form of social synthesis in that society is mediate and abstract, what is constituted by cooperative human activity is alienated and thus appears as quasi-natural facticity.[63] This alienated form of appearance finds theoretical expression, for example, in the Cartesian assumption of the essential

61. Max Horkheimer, "Traditional and Critical Theory," in Horkheimer, *Critical Theory,* trans. Matthew J. O'Connell et al. (New York, 1972), pp. 188–243.
62. Ibid., pp. 200–1 (translation amended).
63. Ibid., pp. 199, 204, 207.

immutability of the relation of subject, object, and theory.[64] Such a hypostatized dualism of thought and being does not, Horkheimer asserts, allow traditional theory to conceptualize the unity of theory and practice.[65] The form of social synthesis characteristic of capitalism, moreover, is such that the various areas of productive activity do not appear related, constituting a whole but are fragmented and exist in a mediate, apparently contingent relation to one another. The result is an illusion of the independence of each sphere of productive activity, similar to that of the freedom of the individual as economic subject in bourgeois society.[66] Consequently, in traditional theory, scientific and theoretical developments are seen as immanent functions of thought or of independent disciplines, and are not understood with reference to real social processes.[67]

Horkheimer asserts that the problem of the adequacy of thought and being must be dealt with in terms of a theory of their constitution by social activity.[68] Kant began to develop such an approach, according to Horkheimer, but in an idealist fashion: Kant claimed that sensuous appearances have already been formed by the transcendental Subject, that is, rational activity, when they are perceived and consciously evaluated.[69] Horkheimer argues that the concepts Kant developed have a double character: they express unity and goal-directedness, on the one hand, and an opaque and nonconscious dimension, on the other. This duality is expressive of capitalist society, according to Horkheimer, but not self-consciously so; it corresponds to the "contradictory form of human activity in the modern era":[70] "The cooperation of people in society is the mode of existence of their reason. . . . At the same time, however, this process, along with its results, is alienated from them and appears, with all its waste of labor power and human life, to be . . . an unalterable natural force, a fate beyond human control."[71]

Horkheimer grounds this contradiction in that between the forces and relations of production. Within the theoretical framework he presents, collective human production constitutes a social whole that potentially is rationally organized. Yet the market-mediated form of social interconnection and class domination based on private property impart a fragmented and irrational form to that social whole.[72] Thus, capitalist society is characterized by blind, mechanical, developmental necessity, and by the utilization of the developed human powers of controlling nature for particular and conflicting interests rather than for the gen-

64. Ibid., p. 211.
65. Ibid., p. 231. Horkheimer is not referring to the unity of theory and practice simply in terms of political activity but, more fundamentally, on the level of social constitution.
66. Ibid., p. 197.
67. Ibid., pp. 194–95.
68. Ibid., p. 202.
69. Ibid.
70. Ibid., p. 204 (translation amended).
71. Ibid. (translation amended).
72. Ibid., pp. 207, 217.

eral interest.[73] According to Horkheimer's account of the trajectory of capitalism, the economic system based upon the commodity form was characterized in its early stages by the notion of the congruence of individual and social happiness; as that system emerged and became consolidated, it entailed the unfolding of human powers, the emancipation of the individual, and an increasing control over nature. Its dynamic, however, has since given rise to a society that no longer furthers human development but increasingly checks it, and drives humanity in the direction of a new barbarism.[74] Within this framework, production is socially totalizing, but is alienated, fragmented, and increasingly arrested in its development by the market and private property. Capitalist social relations hinder the totality from realizing itself.

This contradiction, Horkheimer asserts, is the condition under which critical theory becomes possible. Critical theory does not accept the fragmented aspects of reality as necessary givens but seeks to grasp society as a whole. This necessarily entails a perception of its internal contradictions, of that which fragments the totality and hinders its realization as a rational whole. Grasping the whole thus implies an interest in superseding its present form with a rational human condition rather than merely modifying it.[75] Critical theory, then, accepts neither the given social order nor the utopian critique of that order.[76] Horkheimer describes critical theory as an immanent analysis of capitalism which, on the basis of the intrinsic contradictions of that society, uncovers the growing discrepancy between what is and what could be.[77]

Reason, social production, totality, and human emancipation are intertwined and provide the standpoint of a historical critique in Horkheimer's essay. For him, the idea of a rational social organization adequate to all of its members—a community of free persons—is a possibility immanent to human labor.[78] If, in the past, the misery of large segments of the producing population was in part conditioned by the low level of technical development—hence, was in a sense "rational"—this is no longer the case. Negative social conditions such as hunger, unemployment, crises, and militarization are now based only "on relations, no longer adequate to the present, under which production occurs."[79] Those relations now hinder "the application of all intellectual and physical means for the mastery of nature."[80] General social misery, caused by anachronistic, particularist relations, has become irrational in terms of the potential of the forces of production. Inasmuch as this potential gives rise to the possibility

---

73. Ibid., pp. 213, 229.
74. Ibid., pp. 212–13, 227.
75. Ibid., pp. 207, 217.
76. Ibid., p. 216.
77. Ibid., pp. 207, 219.
78. Ibid., pp. 213, 217.
79. Ibid., p. 213 (translation amended).
80. Ibid.

that rationally planned social regulation and development might supplant the blind, market-mediated form of regulation characteristic of capitalism, it reveals that this form is irrational as well.[81] Finally, on another level, the historical possibility of a rational social organization based on labor also shows the dichotomous relation of subject and object in the present society to be irrational: "The mysterious correspondence of thought and being, understanding and sensuousness, human needs and their satisfaction in the present, chaotic economy—a correspondence which appears to be accidental in the bourgeois epoch—shall, in the future epoch, become the relation of rational intention and realization."[82]

The immanent dialectical critique outlined by Horkheimer is an epistemologically sophisticated version of traditional Marxism. The forces of production are identified with the social process of production, which is hindered from realizing its potential by the market and private property. Those relations, according to this approach, fragment and veil the wholeness and connectedness of the social universe constituted by labor. Labor is simply identified by Horkheimer with control over nature. He questions the mode of its organization and application but not its form. Thus, whereas for Marx (as we shall see), the constitution of the structure of social life in capitalism is a function of labor mediating the relations among people as well as the relations between people and nature, for Horkheimer it is a function of the latter mediation alone, of "labor." The standpoint of his critique of the existing order in the name of reason and justice is provided by "labor;" Horkheimer grounds the possibility of emancipation and the realization of reason in "labor" coming to itself and openly emerging as that which constitutes the social totality.[83] Hence, the object of critique is the structure of relations that hinders that open emergence. Such a position is closer to the sort of Ricardo-Hegel synthesis outlined above than it is to Marx's critique.

This positive view of "labor" and of the totality later gives way, in Horkheimer's thought, to a more negative evaluation of the effects of the domination of nature, once he comes to consider the relations of production as having become adequate to the forces of production. Throughout, however, he conceptualizes the process of production only in terms of the relation of humanity to nature.

---

81. Ibid., pp. 208, 219.
82. Ibid., p. 217 (translation amended).
83. In *Dämmerung* (occasional notes written between 1926 and 1931 and published in 1934 under the pseudonym of Heinrich Regius), Horkheimer criticizes the maxim that "one who does not work should also not eat" as an ascetic ideology that supports the status quo in capitalism. Nevertheless, he claims that it *would be* valid for a future rational society. His critique calls into question the justification of the capitalist order on the basis of the maxim—not, however, the notion that labor is the fundamental constituting principle of social life. See Horkheimer, *Dawn and Decline,* trans. Michael Shaw (New York, 1978), pp. 83–84.

The later pessimistic turn in Horkheimer's thought should not be related too directly and exclusively to the failure of proletarian revolution and the defeat of working-class organizations by fascism, for Horkheimer writes "Traditional and Critical Theory" long after National Socialism's seizure of power. He nevertheless continues to interpret the social formation as essentially contradictory, which is to say, he continues to develop an immanent critique. Although his evaluation of the political situation is certainly pessimistic, this pessimism has not yet acquired a necessary character. Horkheimer asserts that due to the setbacks, ideological narrowness, and corruption of the working class, critical theory is momentarily carried by a small group of persons.[84] Yet the fact that he continues to ground the possibility of a critical theory in the contradictions of the present order implies that the integration or defeat of the working class does not, in and of itself, signify that the social formation no longer is contradictory. In other words, the notion of contradiction for Horkheimer refers to a deeper structural level of society than that of immediate class antagonism. Thus, he claims that critical theory, as an element of social change, exists as part of a dynamic unity with the dominated class but is not immediately identical with that class.[85] Were critical theory merely to formulate passively the current feelings and visions of that class, it would be no different structurally than the disciplinary sciences.[86] Critical theory deals with the present in terms of its immanent potential; it cannot, therefore, be based on the given alone.[87] Horkheimer's pessimism at this point clearly has to do with the *probability* that a socialist transformation would occur in the foreseeable future; but the *possibility* of such a transformation remains, in his analysis, immanent to the contradictory capitalist present.

He does argue that the changed character of capitalism demands changes in the *elements* of critical theory—and proceeds to outline the new possibilities for conscious social domination available to the small circle of the very powerful as a result of the vastly increased concentration and centralization of capital. He then argues that this change is related to a historical tendency for the sphere of culture to lose its previous position of relative autonomy and become more directly embedded in the framework of social domination.[88] Horkheimer lays the ground here for a critical focus on political domination, ideological manipulation, and the culture industry. Yet he insists that the *basis* of the theory remains unchanged inasmuch as the basic economic structure of society has not changed.[89]

At this point, Horkheimer does not propose that the society has changed so

---

84. Horkheimer, "Traditional and Critical Theory," pp. 214–15, 241.
85. Ibid., p. 215.
86. Ibid., p. 214.
87. Ibid., pp. 219–20.
88. Ibid., pp. 234–37.
89. Ibid., pp. 234–35.

fundamentally that the economic sphere has been replaced by the political. On the contrary, he argues that private property and profit still play decisive roles and that people's lives are now even more immediately determined by the economic dimension of social life, whose unchained dynamic gives rise to new developments and misfortunes at an ever increasing tempo.[90] This proposed shift in critical theory's object of investigation, the increased emphasis on conscious domination and manipulation, is tied to the notion that the market—hence, the indirect and veiled form of domination associated with it—no longer plays the role it had in liberal capitalism. This shift is not yet bound, however, to the view that the immanent contradiction of the forces and relations of production has been overcome. Horkheimer's critique remains immanent. Its character, however, changes following the outbreak of World War II. This change is related to the change in theoretical evaluation expressed by Pollock's notion of the primacy of the political.

In his essay, "The Authoritarian State," written in 1940,[91] Horkheimer describes the new social form as "state capitalism, . . . the authoritarian state of the present."[92] The position developed here is basically similar to Pollock's, although Horkheimer more explicitly characterizes the Soviet Union as the most consistent form of state capitalism, and considers fascism to be a mixed form inasmuch as the surplus value won and distributed under state control is transmitted to industrial magnates and large landowners under the old title of profit.[93] All forms of state capitalism are repressive, exploitative, and antagonistic.[94] And although he predicts that state capitalism would not be subject to economic crises because the market had been overcome, he nevertheless claims that the form was ultimately transitory rather than stable.[95]

In discussing the possible transitory character of state capitalism, Horkheimer expresses a new, deeply ambiguous attitude toward the emancipatory potential of the forces of production. The essay does contain passages in which Horkheimer still describes the forces of production (traditionally interpreted) as potentially emancipatory; he argues that they are held back consciously as a condition of domination.[96] The increased rationalization and simplification of production, distribution, and administration have rendered the existing form of political domination anachronistic and, ultimately, irrational. To the extent that the state has become potentially anachronistic, it must become more authoritarian, that is, it must rely to a greater degree on force and the permanent threat

90. Ibid., p. 237.
91. Horkheimer, "The Authoritarian State," in Arato and Gebhardt, eds., *The Essential Frankfurt School Reader,* pp. 95–117.
92. Ibid., p. 96.
93. Ibid., pp. 101–2.
94. Ibid., p. 102.
95. Ibid., pp. 97, 109–10.
96. Ibid., pp. 102–3.

of war in order to maintain itself.[97] Horkheimer does foresee a possible collapse of the system, which he grounds in the restriction of productivity by the bureaucracies. He claims that the utilization of production in the interests of domination rather than to satisfy human needs would result in a crisis. The crisis would not, however, be economic (as was the case in market capitalism), but would be an international political crisis tied to the constant threat of war.[98]

Horkheimer does, then, allude to the fetters imposed on the forces of production. Yet the gap he describes between what is and what could be the case, were it not for those fetters, only highlights the antagonistic and repressive nature of the system: it no longer has the form of an intrinsic contradiction. Horkheimer does not treat the international political crisis he outlines as an emergent moment of the possible determinate negation of the system; rather, he represents it as a dangerous result that *demands* such a negation. Horkheimer speaks of collapse but does not specify its preconditions. Instead, he seeks to elucidate those democratic, emancipatory possibilities that are not realized, or are crushed in state capitalism, in the hope that people would oppose the system out of their misery and the threat to their existence.

The dominant tendency of the article, moreover, is to maintain that there is, indeed, no contradiction or even necessary disjuncture between the developed forces of production (traditionally understood) and authoritarian political domination. On the contrary, Horkheimer now skeptically writes that, although the development of productivity *may* have increased the possibility of emancipation, it certainly *has* led to greater repression.[99] The forces of production, freed from the constraints of the market and private property, have not proved to be the source of freedom and a rational social order: "With each bit of realized planning, a bit of repression was originally supposed to become superfluous. Instead, even more repression has emerged through the administration of the plans."[100]

The adequacy of a new mode of distribution to the developed forces of production had proved to be negative in its consequences. Horkheimer's statement that "state capitalism at times appears almost as a parody of classless society"[101] implies that repressive state capitalism and emancipatory socialism possess the same "material" basis, thus indicating the dilemma of traditional Marxist theory upon reaching its limits. Faced with this dilemma, however, Horkheimer (like Pollock) does not reconsider the basic determinations of that theory. Instead, he continues to equate the forces of production with the industrial mode of production.[102] As a result, he is compelled to reevaluate production and to rethink the relationship of history and emancipation. Horkheimer now radically calls

97. Ibid., pp. 109–11.
98. Ibid.
99. Ibid., pp. 106–7, 109, 112.
100. Ibid., p. 112 (translation amended).
101. Ibid., p. 114 (translation amended).
102. Ibid.

into question any social uprising based upon the development of the forces of production: "The bourgeois upheavals did indeed depend on the ripeness of the situation. Their successes, from the Reformation to the legal revolution of fascism, were tied to the technical and economic achievements that mark the progress of capitalism."[103]

Here he evaluates the development of production negatively, as the basis for the development of domination within capitalist civilization. Horkheimer now begins to turn to a pessimistic theory of history. Because the laws of historical development, driven on by the contradiction between the forces and relations of production, have led only to state capitalism, a revolutionary theory based upon that historical development—a theory that demands that "the first attempts at planning should be reinforced, and distribution made more rational"—could only hasten the transition to the state capitalist form.[104] Consequently, Horkheimer reconceptualizes the relation of emancipation and history by according social revolution two moments:

Revolution brings about what would also happen without spontaneity: the societalization of the means of production, the planned management of production and the unlimited control of nature. And it also brings about what would never happen without active resistance and constantly renewed efforts to achieve freedom: the end of exploitation.[105]

That Horkheimer accords these two moments to revolution, however, indicates that he has fallen back to a position characterized by an antinomy of necessity and freedom. His view of history has become completely determinist: he now presents it as a fully automatic development in which labor comes to itself— but not as the source of emancipation. Freedom is grounded in a purely voluntarist fashion, as an act of will against history.[106] Horkheimer now assumes, as is clear from these passages, that the material conditions of life in which freedom for all could be fully achieved are identical to those in which freedom for all is negated; that those conditions are, therefore, essentially irrelevant to the question of freedom; and that they automatically emerge. One need not disagree with his proposition that freedom is never achieved automatically to question these assumptions. Bound by a traditional Marxist vision of the material conditions of capitalism and socialism, Horkheimer does not question the presupposition that a publicly planned mode of industrial production in the absence of private property is a sufficient material condition for socialism. Nor does he consider whether industrial production itself might not best be considered in social terms, as having been molded by the social form of capital. Were the latter the case, achieving another form of production would be no more auto-

---

103. Ibid., p. 106 (translation amended).
104. Ibid., p. 107.
105. Ibid. (translation amended).
106. Ibid., pp. 107–8, 117.

matic than achieving freedom. Having undertaken no such reconsideration, though, Horkheimer no longer considers freedom as a determinate historical possibility but one which is historically and therefore socially indeterminate:

Critical Theory . . . confronts history with that possibility which is always visible within it. . . . The improvement of the means of production may have improved not only the chances of oppression but also of its elimination. But the consequence that follows from historical materialism today as it did then from Rousseau or the Bible, that is, the insight that "now or in a hundred years" the horror will come to an end, was always timely.[107]

This position emphasizes that a greater degree of freedom has always been possible, but its historically indeterminate character does not permit one to consider the relation among various sociohistorical contexts, different conceptions of freedom, and the kind (rather than degree) of emancipation that can be achieved within a particular context. This position does not question, to use one of Horkheimer's examples, whether the sort of freedom that might have been obtained had Thomas Münzer and not Martin Luther been successful, is comparable to that conceivable today.[108] Horkheimer's notion of history has become indeterminate; it is unclear whether he is referring to the history of capitalism in the passage quoted above, or to history as such. This lack of specificity is related to the historically indeterminate notion of labor as the mastery of nature that underlies Horkheimer's earlier positive attitude toward the development of production, as well as its later negative complement.

In conceiving of state capitalism as a form in which the contradictions of capitalism have been overcome, Horkheimer comes to realize the inadequacy of traditional Marxism as a historical theory of emancipation. Yet he remains too bound to its presuppositions to undertake a reconsideration of the Marxian critique of capitalism, which would allow for a more adequate historical theory. This dichotomous theoretical position is expressed by the antinomic opposition of emancipation and history, and by Horkheimer's departure from his earlier, dialectically self-reflexive epistemology. If emancipation is no longer grounded in a determinate historical contradiction, a critical theory with emancipatory intent must also step outside of history.

We have seen that Horkheimer's theory of knowledge had been based upon the assumption that social constitution is a function of "labor," which in capitalism is fragmented and hindered from fully unfolding by the relations of production. He now begins to consider the contradictions of capitalism to have been no more than the motor of a repressive development, which he expresses categorially with his statement that "the self-movement of the concept of the commodity leads to the concept of state capitalism just as for Hegel the certainty

107. Ibid., p. 106 (translation amended).
108. Ibid.

of sense data leads to absolute knowledge.''[109] Horkheimer has thus come to the conclusion that a Hegelian dialectic, in which the contradictions of the categories lead to the self-unfolded realization of the Subject as totality (rather than to the abolition of totality), could only result in the affirmation of the existing order. Yet he does not formulate his position in a way that would go beyond the limits of that order, for example, in terms of Marx's critique of Hegel and of Ricardo. Instead, Horkheimer reverses his earlier position: "labor" and the totality, which earlier had been the standpoint of the critique, now become the grounds of oppression and unfreedom.

The result is a series of ruptures. Not only does Horkheimer locate emancipation outside of history but, to save its possibility, he now feels compelled to introduce a disjuncture between concept and object: "The identity of the ideal and reality is universal exploitation. . . . The difference between concept and reality—not the concept itself—is the foundation for the possibility of revolutionary practice.''[110] This step is made necessary by the conjunction of Horkheimer's continued passion for general human emancipation with his analysis of state capitalism as an order in which the intrinsic contradiction of capitalism has been overcome. (Although, as we have seen, this analysis is not completely unequivocal in 1940.) As outlined above, an immanent social critique presupposes that its object—the social universe that is its context—and the categories that grasp that object are not one-dimensional. The belief that the contradiction of capitalism has been overcome implies, however, that the social object *has* become one-dimensional. Within such a framework, the "ought" no longer is an immanent aspect of a contradictory "is," hence, the result of an analysis that grasps what is would necessarily be affirmative. Now that Horkheimer no longer considers the whole to be intrinsically contradictory, he posits the difference between concept and actuality in order to make room for another possible actuality. This position converges in some respects with Adorno's notion of the totality as necessarily affirmative (rather than contradictory and pointing beyond itself even when fully unfolded). In taking this step, Horkheimer weakens the epistemological consistency of his own argument.

As is indicated by his statements on the self-movement of the concept of the commodity and the identity of the ideal and reality, Horkheimer does not suddenly adopt a position that concepts are one thing, reality another. His statements imply, rather, that concepts are indeed adequate to their objects, but in an affirmative rather than critical way. Given the fundamental presuppositions of such a position, the concept that presumably no longer fully corresponds to its object cannot be considered an exhaustive determination of the concept, if the theory is to remain self-reflexive. Horkheimer's position—that the critique is to be grounded outside the concept—necessarily posits indeterminacy as the basis of

109. Ibid., p. 108.
110. Ibid., pp. 108–9.

the critique. Such a position essentially argues that because the totality does not subsume all of life, the possibility of emancipation, however dim, is not extinguished. Yet it cannot point to the possibility of a determinate possible negation of the existing social order; nor can it account for itself as a determinate possibility and, hence, as an adequate critical theory of its social universe.

Horkheimer's critical theory could have maintained its self-reflexive character only if it would have embedded the affirmative relation it posited between the concept and its object within another, more encompassing set of concepts that would have continued to allow theoretically for the immanent possibility of critique and historical transformation. Horkheimer, however, did not proceed with such a reconsideration, which, on another level, would have entailed a critique of the traditional Marxist categories on the basis of a more essential, "abstract," and complex set of categories. Instead, Horkheimer, by positing the nonidentity of the concept and actuality in the interest of preserving the possibility of freedom within a presumed one-dimensional social universe, undercut the possible self-reflexive explanation of his own critique. The disjunction of concept and actuality he asserted rendered his own position similar to that of traditional theory, which he criticized in 1937 when he pointed out that theory is not understood as a part of the social universe in which it exists, but is accorded a spurious independent position. Horkheimer's understanding of the disjunction of concept and reality hovers mysteriously above its object. It cannot explain itself.

The epistemological dilemma entailed in this pessimistic turn retrospectively highlights a weakness in Horkheimer's earlier epistemology, which had seemed consistent. In "Traditional and Critical Theory," the possibility of an all-encompassing social critique, as well as of the overcoming of the capitalist formation, was grounded in the contradictory character of that society. Yet that contradiction was interpreted as one between social "labor" and those relations that fragment its totalistic realization and inhibit its full development. In such an interpretation, the Marxian categories such as value and capital express those inhibiting social relations and are ultimately extrinsic to the concept of "labor" itself. This indicates, however, that, within such an interpretation, the categories of commodity and capital do not really grasp the social totality while expressing its contradictory character. Instead, they specify only one dimension of capitalist society, the relations of distribution, which eventually comes to oppose its other dimension, social "labor." In other words, when the Marxian categories are understood only in terms of the market and private property, they are essentially one-dimensional from the outset: they do not grasp the contradiction but only one of its terms. This implies that even in Horkheimer's earlier essay the critique is external to, rather than grounded in, the categories. It is a critique from the standpoint of "labor" of the social forms expressed by the categories.

In a sophisticated version of the traditional Marxist critique—one that treats the Marxian categories as determinate forms of social being and of social consciousness—the implicit understanding of those categories as one-sided is reflected by the term "reification" as used by Lukács. Although it lies beyond the bounds of this work to elaborate on this, I should note that the term represents a convergence of the traditional Marxist interpretation and Weber's notion of rationalization—two strands that have one-dimensionality in common. The ambiguous legacy of Weber in strains of Western Marxism, as mediated by Lukács, involves the "horizontal" broadening of the scope of the Marxian categories to include dimensions of social life ignored in more narrowly orthodox interpretations and, at the same time, their "vertical" flattening. In *Capital,* the categories are expressions of a contradictory social totality; they are two-dimensional. The notion of reification in Western Marxism, however, implies one-dimensionality; hence, the possible determinate negation of the existent order cannot be rooted in the categories that purportedly grasp it.

In spite of its apparently dialectical character, then, Horkheimer's earlier critical theory did not succeed in grounding itself as critique in the concept. That would have required recovering the contradictory character of the Marxian categories, an undertaking that would have required reconceptualizing those categories so as to incorporate the historically determinate form of labor as one of their dimensions. Such an effort, which would formulate more adequate categories of the commodity and capital, differs fundamentally from any view that treats "labor" in a transhistorical fashion as a quasi-natural social process, as simply a matter of the technical domination of nature by means of the cooperative effort of humans. Without such a reconsideration, the self-reflexive analysis of capitalism can be critical only if it grounds itself in the contradiction between the categorial forms and "labor," rather than in the categorial forms of commodity and capital themselves. The former constitutes a positive critique; the latter is the categorial condition of a negative critique.

Horkheimer's traditional Marxist point of departure meant from the very beginning, then, that the adequacy of concept to actuality was implicitly affirmative—but of only one dimension of the totality. Critique was grounded outside of the categories, in the concept of "labor." When "labor" no longer seemed to be the principle of emancipation, given the repressive results of the abolition of the market and private property, the previous weakness of the theory emerged manifestly as a dilemma.

The dilemma, however, illuminates the inadequacy of the point of departure. In discussing Pollock, I argued that the weaknesses of his attempt to characterize postliberal society as state capitalism reveals that the determination of the essential capitalist relations of production in terms of the market and private property had always been inadequate. By the same token, the weaknesses of Horkheimer's self-reflexive social theory indicate the inadequacy of a critical theory based upon a notion of "labor." The weaknesses of each indicate that the Ricardian and Hegelian forms of Marxism I criticized in the previous chapter are conceptually related. The identification of the relations of production with those of distribution is based upon the Ricardian labor theory of value. Over-coming those bourgeois relations of distribution alone does not, however, signify overcoming capital, but the emergence of a more concrete mode of its total existence, mediated by gigantic bureaucratic organizations rather than by liberal forms. Similarly, a materialist dialectical theory based upon the notion of "la-bor" ultimately affirms the unfolded totality. Whereas Marx attempts to uncover the social relations that are mediated by labor in capitalism and, in turn, shape labor's concrete form, the concept of "labor" at the heart of Ricardian-Hegelian Marxism implies that the mediating activity is grasped affirmatively, as that which stands opposed to the social relations of capitalism. The result is a critique adequate only to liberal capitalism, and only from the standpoint of a historical negation that does not overcome capital—state capitalism.

Horkheimer became aware of the inadequacy of that theory without, however, reconsidering its assumptions. The result was a reversal of an earlier traditional Marxist position. In 1937, Horkheimer still positively regards "labor" as that which, in its contradiction to the social relations of capitalism, constitutes the ground for the possibility of critical thought, as well as of emancipation; in 1940 he had come to see—if equivocally—the development of production as the progress of domination. In *Dialectic of Enlightenment* (1944), and in *Eclipse of Reason* ("Zur Kritik der instrumentellen Vernunft," 1946), Horkheimer's eval-uation of the relationship between production and emancipation becomes more unequivocally negative: "Advance in technical facilities for enlightenment is accompanied by a process of dehumanization."[111] He claims that the nature of social domination has changed and increasingly has become a function of tech-nocratic or instrumental reason, which he grounds in "labor."[112] Production has become the source of unfreedom. Horkheimer does assert that the contemporary decline of the individual, and the dominance of instrumental reason, should be attributed not to technics or production as such but to the forms of social rela-tions in which they occur.[113] His notion of such forms, however, remains empty. He treats technological development in a historically and socially indeterminate way, as the domination of nature. Following Pollock, Horkheimer regards post-liberal capitalism as an antagonistic society in which usefulness for the power structure, rather than for the needs of all, is the measure of economic impor-tance.[114] He treats social form in postliberal capitalism reductively, in terms of power relations and the particularistic political practices of the leaders of the economy.[115] Such a notion of social form can be related to technology only extrinsically, in terms of the use to which it is applied; it cannot, however, be related intrinsically to the form of production. Yet a social, as opposed to a

111. Horkheimer, *Eclipse of Reason* (New York, 1974), p. vi.
112. Ibid., p. 21.
113. Ibid., p. 153.
114. Ibid., p. 154.
115. Ibid., p. 156.

technical, explanation of the instrumentalization of the world can be made only on the basis of such an intrinsic relation. Hence, despite Horkheimer's disclaimer that the dominance of instrumental reason and the destruction of individuality should be explained in social terms and should not be attributed to production as such, I would argue that he does indeed associate instrumental reason and "labor."[116]

The possibilities of emancipation in the postliberal universe described by Horkheimer have become very meager. Elaborating an idea developed by Marcuse in 1941,[117] Horkheimer suggests that perhaps just those economic and cultural processes that destroy individuality can lay the groundwork for a new, less ideological and more humane, age. He quickly adds, however, that the signs of such a possibility are very weak indeed.[118] Deprived of the possibility of an immanent historical critique, the task of critical philosophy becomes reduced to uncovering those anti-instrumentalist values sedimented in language, that is, to drawing attention to the gap between the reality and the ideals of the civilization in the hope of inducing greater popular self-awareness.[119] The critical theory no longer can delineate the social foundations of an order in which a more humane existence would be possible. The attempt to attribute a determination to language that, if realized, would have emancipatory consequences[120] is rather weak and cannot veil the fact that the theory has become exhortative.

This exhortative character, though, is not an unfortunate but "necessary" consequence of the transformation of twentieth-century industrial capitalism— it is a function of the assumptions with which that transformation was interpreted. Pollock and Horkheimer were aware of the negative social, political, and cultural consequences of the emergence of the new form of the totality as bureaucratic and state capitalist. The new phase of the social formation provided the "practical refutation," as it were, of traditional Marxism as a theory of emancipation. Because Pollock and Horkheimer retained some basic assumptions of the traditional theory, however, they were unable to incorporate that "refutation" into a more fundamental and adequate critique of capitalism. Consequently, their resulting position was characterized by a number of theoretical

---

116. Ibid., pp. 21, 50, 102.
117. In "Some Social Implications of Modern Technology," *Studies in Philosophy and Social Science* 9 (1941), Marcuse describes the negative, dehumanizing effects of modern technology. He maintains that this technology is social rather than technical and continues to discuss its possible emancipatory effects (pp. 414, 436–39). Marcuse also, however, does not determine this purportedly social character more closely; he does not ground the possible emancipatory moment of modern technology in an intrinsic contradiction but in the possible positive effects of precisely such negative developments as standardization, dequalification, and so on. The notion that a situation of total alienation can give rise to its opposite is one that Marcuse then pursued further in *Eros and Civilization*.
118. *Eclipse of Reason*, pp. 160–61.
119. Ibid., pp. 177–82, 186–87.
120. Ibid., pp. 179–80.

weaknesses. The critique of reason developed by Horkheimer and Adorno in the mid-1940s, for example, reflexively confronted Critical Theory with a dilemma. Gerhard Brandt, among others, has noted that in *Dialectic of Enlightenment,* "the reified character of bourgeois thought is no longer grounded in the production of commodities, as had been the case in the materialist critique of ideology from Marx to Lukács. Rather, it is now grounded in the interaction of humanity with nature, in its history as a species."[121] The consequences of such a position weaken the very project of a critical theory; they undermine the possibility that such a theory could ground socially the conditions of its own existence and, relatedly, the conditions of a possible historical transformation.

The analysis presented in this work provides a plausible interpretation of the presuppositions underlying this dilemma. As we have seen, in 1937 Horkheimer proceeded from the assumption that "labor" transhistorically constitutes society, and that the commodity is a category of the mode of distribution. On that basis, he grounded the difference between reified bourgeois thought and emancipatory reason in the opposition between the capitalist mode of distribution and "labor." According to Pollock's state capitalism thesis, which Horkheimer subsequently adopted, this opposition no longer existed. Labor had come to itself—yet both oppression and the domination of reified reason had grown stronger. Because the source of this development, as I have shown, could now only be located in "labor" itself, it follows that the origins of reified reason, being grounded in "labor," must be located prior to the spread and dominance of the commodity form. It must be located in the very process of human interaction with nature. Lacking a conception of the specific character of labor in capitalism, Critical Theory ascribed its consequences to labor per se. The frequently described shift of Critical Theory from the analysis of political economy to a critique of instrumental reason does not, then, signify that the theorists of the Frankfurt School simply abandoned the former in favor of the latter.[122] Rather, that shift followed from, and was based upon, a particular analysis of political economy, more specifically, a traditional understanding of Marx's critique of political economy.

Pollock's and Horkheimer's analysis of the social totality as both noncontradictory—that is, one-dimensional—and antagonistic and repressive implies that history has come to a standstill. I have sought to argue that it indicates, instead, the limits of any critical theory resting on the notion of "labor." The critical pessimism, so strongly expressed in *Dialectic of Enlightenment* and *Eclipse of Reason,* cannot be understood only with reference to its historical

121. Gerhard Brandt, "Max Horkheimer und das Projekt einer materialistischen Gesellschafts-theorie," in A. Schmidt and N. Altwicker, eds., *Max Horkheimer heute: Werke und Wirkung* (Frankfurt a. M., 1986), p. 282. Brandt goes on to argue that Horkheimer's notes from 1950 until 1969 indicate that he later began to emphasize the critical potential of a focus on the historical specificity of the objects of social investigation.
122. See S. Seidman, Introduction, in Seidman, ed., *Jürgen Habermas on Society and Politics,* p. 5.

context. It also must be seen as expressing an awareness of the limits of traditional Marxism in the absence of a fundamental reconstitution of the dialectical critique of what, despite significant transformations, remains a dialectical social totality.

This view has been reinforced by the current historical transformation of capitalism, which has dramatically made manifest the limits of the welfare state in the West (and of the totalistic party-state in the East), and can be seen, in turn, as a "practical refutation" of the thesis of the primacy of the political. It retrospectively shows that Critical Theory's quasi-Weberian analysis of the earlier major transformation of capitalism was too linear, and strongly suggests that the totality has indeed remained dialectical.

I shall try, in the succeeding sections of this work, to outline a theoretical basis for the notion of a postliberal dialectical totality which will ground my critique of traditional Marxism. In the course of my exposition, I shall distinguish my effort to move theoretically beyond the necessary pessimism of Critical Theory from Habermas's approach to this problem. The theoretical turn analyzed in this chapter—Horkheimer's pessimism, his critique of instrumental reason, and the suggested beginnings of a "linguistic turn"—was an important dimension of the theoretical context within which Jürgen Habermas began, in the 1960s, to call into question the socially synthetic and constitutive role attributed to labor. His strategic intent can be seen as an attempt to overcome the pessimism of Critical Theory by questioning the centrality of labor—once it had presumably been shown to be an inadequate basis for freedom. His intent, in other words, has been to reestablish theoretically the possibility of emancipation. I shall deal with some aspects of Habermas's early critique of Marx below. At this point I should note that Habermas, in attempting to overcome Critical Theory's pessimism, retains the traditional understanding of labor shared by Pollock and Horkheimer, and then attempts to limit the scope of its social significance. He proceeds from precisely that notion of "labor" for which Marx criticized Ricardo. Marx's analysis of the double character of labor in capitalism, however, can serve as the foundation for a critique of late capitalism which, in my view, is more adequate than one that proceeds from the traditional interpretation of labor in capitalism—whether that "labor" is evaluated positively as emancipatory or, more negatively, as instrumental activity.

PART II

Toward a reconstruction of the Marxian critique: the commodity

4. Abstract labor

Requirements of a categorial reinterpretation

The exposition thus far has laid the groundwork for a reconstruction of Marx's critical theory. As we have seen, the passages of the *Grundrisse* presented in Chapter One suggest a critique of capitalism whose assumptions are very different from those of the traditional critique. These passages do not represent utopian visions that later were excluded from Marx's more "sober" analysis in *Capital* but are a key to understanding that analysis; they provide the point of departure for a reinterpretation of the basic categories of Marx's mature critique that can overcome the limits of the traditional Marxist paradigm. My examination of the presuppositions of this paradigm has highlighted certain requirements such a reinterpretation must meet.

I have examined approaches that, proceeding from a transhistorical notion of "labor" as the standpoint of the critique, conceptualize the social relations characterizing capitalism in terms of the mode of distribution alone, and locate the system's fundamental contradiction between the modes of distribution and production. Central to this examination was the argument that the Marxian category of value should not be understood merely as expressing the market-mediated form of the distribution of wealth. A categorial reinterpretation, therefore, must focus on Marx's distinction between value and material wealth; it must show that value is not essentially a market category in his analysis, and that the "law of value" is not simply one of general economic equilibrium. Marx's statement that in capitalism "direct labor time [is the] decisive factor in the production of wealth,"[1] suggests that his category of value should be examined as a form of wealth whose specificity is related to its temporal determination. An adequate reinterpretation of value must demonstrate the significance of the temporal determination of value for Marx's critique and for the question of the historical dynamic of capitalism.

Related to the problem of value is that of labor. As I have shown, so long as one assumes that the category of value—hence, the capitalist relations of production—are adequately understood in terms of the market and private property,

---

1. Marx, *Grundrisse: Foundations of the Critique of Political Economy,* trans. Martin Nicolaus (London, 1973), p. 704.

the meaning of labor seems to be clear. These relations, so conceived, supposedly are the means by which labor and its products are socially organized and distributed; they are, in other words, extrinsic to labor itself. Consequently, labor in capitalism can be taken to be labor as it is commonly understood: a purposive social activity involving the transformation of material in a determinate fashion which is an indispensable condition for the reproduction of human society. Labor is thus understood in a transhistorical fashion; what varies historically is the mode of its social distribution and administration. Accordingly, labor and, thus, the process of production are "forces of production," embedded in varying sets of "relations of production" that purportedly remain extrinsic to labor and production.

A different approach would reformulate value as a historically specific form of wealth, different from material wealth. This implies that value-constituting labor cannot be understood in terms that are valid transhistorically for labor in all social formations; rather, such labor must be seen as possessing a socially determinate character specific to the capitalist social formation. I shall analyze that specific quality by elucidating Marx's conception of the "double character" of labor in capitalism, referred to above, which will allow me to distinguish such labor from the traditional conception of "labor." On that basis I shall be able adequately to determine value as a historically specific form of wealth and of social relations, and to show that the process of production incorporates both the "forces" and "relations" of production, and does not merely embody the forces of production alone. I shall do so by demonstrating that, according to Marx's analysis, the mode of producing in capitalism is not simply a technical process, but is molded by the objectified forms of social relations (value, capital). From this it will become clear that the Marxian critique is a critique of labor in capitalism, rather than merely a critique of labor's exploitation and mode of social distribution, and that the fundamental contradiction of the capitalist totality should be seen as intrinsic to the realm of production itself, and not simply a contradiction between the spheres of production and distribution. In short, I intend to redetermine the Marxian categories in such a way that they do indeed grasp the core of the social totality as contradictory—and do not refer just to one of its dimensions, which then is opposed to, or is subsumed by, that of "labor." By reinterpreting the Marxian contradiction in this way, the approach based on a critique of the notion of "labor" could avoid the dilemmas of Critical Theory, and could show that postliberal capitalism is not "one-dimensional." The adequacy of concept to its object could thus remain critical; it would not have to be affirmative. Hence, social critique would not have to be grounded in the disjuncture between the concept and its object, as Horkheimer came to think, but could be grounded in the concept itself, in the categorial forms. This, in turn, could reestablish the self-reflexive epistemological consistency of the critique.

The categories of the adequate critique, as I have argued, must grasp not only the contradictory character of the totality but also the basis of the sort of unfreedom that characterizes it. The historical abolition of the social forms expressed categorially must be shown to be a determinate possibility that implies the social basis of freedom. Capitalism's characteristic form of social domination, according to Marx, relates to the form of social labor. In the *Grundrisse,* he outlines three basic historical social forms. The first, in its many variations, is based on "relations of personal dependence."[2] It has been superseded historically by the "second great form" of society—capitalism, the social formation based on the commodity form,[3] which is characterized by *personal independence* in the framework of a system of *objective [sachlicher] dependence.*[4] What constitutes that "objective" dependence is social; it is "nothing more than social relations which have become independent and now enter into opposition to the seemingly independent individuals; i.e., the reciprocal relations of production separated from and autonomous of individuals."[5]

A characteristic of capitalism is that its essential social relations are social in a peculiar manner. They exist not as overt interpersonal relations but as a quasi-independent set of structures that are opposed to individuals, a sphere of impersonal "objective" necessity and "objective dependence." Consequently, the form of social domination characteristic of capitalism is not overtly social and personal: "These *objective* dependency relations also appear,. . . in such a way that individuals are now ruled by *abstractions,* whereas earlier they depended on one another."[6] Capitalism is a system of abstract, impersonal domination. Relative to earlier social forms, people appear to be independent; but they actually are subject to a system of social domination that seems not social but "objective."

The form of domination peculiar to capitalism is also described by Marx as the domination of people by production: "Individuals are subsumed under social production, which exists, like a fate, outside of them; but social production is not subsumed under the individuals and is not managed by them as their common power and wealth."[7] This passage is of central importance. To say that individuals are subsumed under production is to say that they are dominated by social labor. This suggests that social domination in capitalism cannot be apprehended sufficiently as the domination and control of the many and their labor by the few. In capitalism social labor is not only the *object* of domination and exploitation but is itself the essential *ground* of domination. The nonpersonal,

2. Ibid., p. 158.
3. Ibid.
4. Ibid. Marx characterizes the third great social form, capitalism's possible supersession, in terms of "free individuality based on the universal development of individuals and on their subordination of their communal, social productivity as their social wealth" (ibid.).
5. Ibid., p. 164.
6. Ibid.
7. Ibid. (translation amended).

abstract, "objective" form of domination characteristic of capitalism apparently is related intrinsically to the domination of the individuals *by* their social labor.

Abstract domination, the form of domination that characterizes capitalism, cannot simply be equated with the workings of the market; it does not refer simply to the market-mediated way in which class domination is effected in capitalism. Such a market-centered interpretation assumes that the invariable ground of social domination is class domination, and that what varies is only the form in which it prevails (directly or via the market). This interpretation is closely related to those positions which assume "labor" to be the source of wealth and to constitute society transhistorically, and which examine critically only the mode in which "labor's" distribution is effected.

According to the interpretation presented here, the notion of abstract domination breaks with such conceptions. It refers to the domination of people by abstract, quasi-independent structures of social relations, mediated by commodity-determined labor, which Marx tries to grasp with his categories of value and capital. In his mature works, these forms of social relations represent the fully elaborated sociohistorical concretization of alienation as self-generated domination. In analyzing Marx's category of capital, I shall try to show that these social forms underlie a dynamic logic of historical development that is constraining and compelling for the individuals. Such relational forms cannot be grasped adequately in terms of the market; nor, because they are quasi-independent forms that exist above and in opposition to individuals and classes, can they be understood fully in terms of overt social relations (for example, class relations). As we shall see, although capitalism is, of course, a class society, class domination is not the ultimate ground of social domination in that society, according to Marx, but itself becomes a function of a superordinate, "abstract" form of domination.[8]

In discussing the trajectory of Critical Theory, I have already touched upon the question of abstract domination. Pollock, in postulating the primacy of the political, maintained, in effect, that the system of abstract domination grasped by Marx's categories had been superseded by a new form of direct domination. Such a position assumes that every form of objective dependence and every

8. In *Legitimation Crisis* (trans. Thomas McCarthy [Boston, 1975]), Habermas deals with abstract domination but not as a form of domination, different from direct social domination, that entails the domination of people by abstract, quasi-independent social forms within which the relations among individuals and classes are structured. Instead, he treats it as a different *form of appearance* of direct social domination, as class domination that is veiled by the nonpolitical form of exchange (p. 52). The existence of this form of domination, according to Habermas, provided the basis for Marx's attempt to grasp the crisis-prone development of the social system by means of an economic analysis of the laws of motion of capital. With the repoliticization of the social system in postliberal capitalism, domination once again becomes overt; the validity of Marx's attempt, therefore, is limited implicitly to liberal capitalism (ibid.). Habermas's notion of abstract domination, then, is that of traditional Marxism—class domination mediated by the self-regulating market.

nonconscious structure of abstract social necessity analyzed by Marx is rooted in the market. To question this is to question the assumption that, with the supersession of the market by the state, conscious control has not merely re-placed nonconscious structures in particular spheres, but that it has overcome all such structures of abstract compulsion and, hence, the historical dialectic.

How abstract domination is understood, in other words, is closely tied to how the category of value is interpreted. I shall try to show that value, as a form of wealth, is at the core of structures of abstract domination whose significance extends beyond the market and the sphere of circulation (into that of production, for example). Such an analysis implies that when value remains the form of wealth planning itself is subject to the exigencies of abstract domination. That is, public planning does not, in and of itself, suffice to overcome the system of abstract domination—the impersonal, nonconscious, nonvolitional, mediate form of necessity characteristic of capitalism. Public planning, then, should not be abstractly opposed to the market, as the principle of socialism to that of capitalism.

This suggests that we should reconceptualize the fundamental social precon-ditions for the fullest possible realization of general human freedom. Such a realization would involve overcoming forms of overtly social, personal domi-nation as well as structures of abstract domination. Analyzing the structures of abstract domination as the ultimate grounds of unfreedom in capitalism, and redetermining the Marxian categories as critical categories that grasp those struc-tures, would be first steps in reestablishing the relationship between socialism and freedom, a relationship that has become problematic in traditional Marxism.

In this part of this work, I shall begin to reconstruct the Marxian theory on the initial and most abstract logical level of his critical presentation in *Capital,* that of his analysis of the commodity form. As opposed to the traditional inter-pretations examined in Chapter Two, I shall try to show that the categories with which Marx begins his analysis are indeed critical and do imply a historical dynamic.

The historically determinate character of the Marxian critique

Marx begins *Capital* with an analysis of the commodity as a good, a use value, that, at the same time, is a value.[9] He then relates these two dimensions of the commodity to the double character of the labor it incorporates. As a particular use value, the commodity is the product of a particular concrete labor; as a value, it is the objectification of abstract human labor.[10] Before proceeding with an investigation of these categories—especially that of the double character of commodity-producing labor, which Marx regards as "the crucial point . . . upon

9. Marx, *Capital,* vol. 1, trans. Ben Fowkes (London, 1976), pp. 125–29.
10. Ibid., pp. 128–37.

which an understanding of political economy is based"[11]—it is important to emphasize their historical specificity.

Marx's analysis of the commodity is not an examination of a product that happens to be exchanged regardless of the society in which that takes place; it is not an investigation of the commodity torn from its social context or as it contingently may exist in many societies. Instead, Marx's analysis is of the *"form of the commodity* as the generally necessary social form of the product,"[12] and as the *"general elementary form of wealth."*[13] According to Marx, though, the commodity is the general form of the product *only* in capitalism.[14]

Hence, Marx's analysis of the commodity is of the general form of the product and the most elementary form of wealth in capitalist society.[15] If, in capitalism, "the dominant and determining characteristic of its product is that it is a commodity,"[16] this necessarily implies that "the worker himself exists only as a seller of commodities, and thus as a free wage-labourer, that labour exists in general as wage-labour."[17] In other words, a commodity as examined by Marx in *Capital* presupposes wage labor and, hence, capital. Thus, "commodity production in its universal, absolute form [is] capitalist commodity production."[18]

Roman Rosdolsky has pointed out that in Marx's critique of political economy the existence of capitalism is assumed from the very beginning of the unfolding of the categories; each category presupposes those which follow.[19] I shall discuss the significance of this mode of presentation below, but should note here that if Marx's analysis of the commodity presupposes the category of capital, his determinations of the former category do not pertain to the commodity per se, but only to the commodity as a general social form, that is, as it exists in capitalism. Thus, the mere existence of exchange, for example, does not signify that the commodity exists as a structuring social category and that social labor has a double character. Only in capitalism does social labor have a twofold character[20] and value exist as a specific social form of human activity.[21]

Marx's mode of presentation in the first chapters of *Capital* has frequently been seen as historical, for it begins with the category of the commodity and proceeds to consider money and, then, capital. This progression, however, should not be interpreted as an analysis of an immanently logical historical

11. Ibid., p. 132 (translation amended).
12. Marx, *Results of the Immediate Process of Production*, trans. Rodney Livingstone, in *Capital*, vol. 1, p. 949 (translation amended).
13. Ibid., p. 951 (translation amended).
14. Ibid.
15. Ibid., p. 949.
16. Marx, *Capital*, vol. 3, trans. David Fernbach (Harmondsworth, England, 1981), p. 1019.
17. Ibid. (translation amended).
18. Marx, *Capital*, vol. 2, trans. David Fernbach (London, 1978), p. 217.
19. Roman Rosdolsky, *The Making of Marx's Capital*, trans. Pete Burgess (London, 1977), p. 46.
20. *Capital*, vol. 1, p. 166.
21. Marx, *Theories of Surplus Value*, part 1, trans. Emile Burns (Moscow, 1963), p. 46.

development leading from the first appearance of commodities to a fully developed capitalist system. Marx explicitly states that his categories express the social forms not as they first appear historically but as they exist, fully developed, in capitalism:

As in the theory the concept of value precedes that of capital, but requires for its pure development a mode of production founded on capital, so the same thing takes place in practice.[22]

It would therefore be . . . wrong to let the economic categories follow one another in the same sequence as that in which they were historically decisive. Their sequence is determined, rather, by their relation to one another in modern bourgeois society, which is precisely the opposite of that . . . which corresponds to historical development.[23]

To the extent that a logical historical development leading toward capitalism is presented—as in the analysis of the value form in the first chapter of *Capital*[24] —this logic must be understood as being *retrospectively apparent* rather than *immanently necessary*. The latter form of historical logic does exist, according to Marx, but, as we shall see, it is an attribute of the capitalist social formation alone.

The categorially grasped social forms of Marx's critique of political economy are thus historically *determinate* and cannot simply be applied to other societies. They are also historically *determining*. At the outset of his categorial analysis, Marx states explicitly that it must be understood as an investigation of the specificity of capitalism: "The value-form of the product of labour is the most abstract, but also the most general form of the bourgeois mode of production. This mode is thereby characterized as a particular sort of social production and, hence, as historically specific."[25]

The analysis of the commodity with which Marx begins his critique, in other words, is an analysis of a historically specific social form. He goes on to treat the commodity as a structured and structuring form of practice that is the initial and most general determination of the social relations of the capitalist social formation. If the commodity, as a general and totalizing form, is the "elementary form" of the capitalist formation,[26] an investigation of it should reveal the essential determinations of Marx's analysis of capitalism and, in particular, the specific characteristics of the labor that underlies, and is determined by, the commodity form.

---

22. *Grundrisse*, p. 251.
23. Ibid., p. 107.
24. *Capital*, vol. 1, pp. 138–63. The asymmetry of the value form (relative and equivalent forms), which is so important in Marx's development of the fetish of commodities, presupposes money and indicates that Marx's analysis of commodity exchange has nothing to do with direct barter.
25. Ibid., p. 174n34 (translation amended).
26. Ibid., p. 125.

Historical specificity: value and price

Marx, as we have seen, analyzes the commodity as a generalized social form at the core of capitalist society. It is not legitimate in terms of his self-understanding, then, to assume that the law of value and, hence, the generalization of the commodity form, pertain to a precapitalist situation. Yet Ronald Meek, for example, proceeds from the assumption that Marx's initial formulation of the theory of value entails postulating a model of a precapitalist society in which "although commodity production and free competition were assumed to reign more or less supreme, the labourers still owned the whole produce of their labour."[27] Unlike Oskar Lange, whose position was outlined in Chapter Two, Meek does not simply relegate the validity of the law of value to such a society. Nor does he maintain, as Rudolf Schlesinger does, that such a point of departure is the source of a fundamental error inasmuch as Marx seeks to develop laws valid for capitalism on the basis of those that apply to a simpler and historically earlier society.[28] Instead, Meek assumes that the precapitalist society that Marx presumably postulates was not intended to be an accurate representation of historical reality in anything more than the broadest sense. That model—which Meek sees as essentially similar to Adam Smith's "early and rude" society inhabited by deer and beaver hunters—is, rather, "clearly part of a quite complex analytical device."[29] By analyzing the way in which capitalism impinges on such a society, "Marx believed one would be well on the way to reveal the real essence of the capitalist mode of production."[30] In Volume 1 of *Capital,* according to Meek, Marx proceeds from the postulated precapitalist model,[31] a system of "simple commodity production";[32] in Volume 3 he "deals with commodity and value relations which have become 'capitalistically modified' in the fullest sense.

---

27. Ronald Meek, *Studies in the Labour Theory of Value* (2d ed., New York and London, 1956), p. 303.
28. For this argument, see Rudolf Schlesinger, *Marx: His Time and Ours* (London, 1950), pp. 96–97. George Lichtheim suggests a similar argument: "It is arguable that, in applying a labour-cost theory of value derived from primitive social conditions to an economic model belonging to a higher stage, the classics were guilty of confusing different levels of abstraction" (*Marxism* [2d ed., New York and Washington, 1963], pp. 174–75). In this section, Lichtheim does not distinguish between "the classics" and Marx. His own presentation brings together different, opposing, interpretations of the relationship between Volumes 1 and 3 of *Capital* without synthesizing them or overcoming their differences. In this passage, he implies that the law of value in Volume 1 is based on a precapitalist model, yet several pages later he follows Maurice Dobb's lead and describes that level of analysis as a "sensible qualification of a theoretical first approximation" (p. 15).
29. Meek, *Studies in the Labour Theory,* p. 303.
30. Ibid.
31. Ibid., p. 305.
32. Ibid., p. xv.

His 'historical' starting point here is a fairly well developed capitalist system."[33]

Marx's analysis of value, however, is much more historically specific than Meek's interpretation acknowledges. Marx seeks to grasp the core of capitalism with the categories of commodity and value. The very notion of a precapitalist stage of simple commodity circulation is spurious, within the framework of Marx's critique of political economy; as Hans Georg Backhaus has pointed out, this notion stems not from Marx but from Engels.[34] Marx explicitly and emphatically rejects the notion that the law of value was valid for, or derived from, a precapitalist society of commodity owners. Although Meek identifies the law of value used by Adam Smith with that used by Marx, Marx criticizes Smith precisely for relegating the validity of the law of value to precapitalist society:

Although Adam Smith determines the value of the commodity by the labour-time it embodies, he then transfers the real validity of this determination of value to pre-adamite times. In other words, what he regards as evident when considering the simple commodity becomes unclear to him as soon as he examines the higher and more complex forms of capital, wage-labour, rent, etc. This is expressed by him in the following way: the value of commodities was measured by labour-time in the paradise lost of the bourgeoisie, where people did not confront one another as capitalists, wage-labourers, land-owners, tenant farmers, usurers, and so on, but as simple producers and exchangers of commodities.[35]

According to Marx, however, a society composed of independent commodity producers has never existed:

Original production is based on anciently arisen communal entities in which private exchange appears only as a completely superficial and secondary exception. With the historical dissolution of such communal entities, however, relations of domination and subjugation emerge at once. Such relations of violence stand in sharp contradiction to mild commodity circulation and its corresponding relations.[36]

Marx neither postulates such a society as a hypothetical construct from which to derive the law of value nor seeks to analyze capitalism by investigating how it "impinges" upon a social model in which the law of value is presumed to operate in pure form. Rather, as Marx's critique of Robert Torrens and Adam Smith clearly indicates, he regards the law of value to be valid only for capitalism:

33. Ibid., p. 308.
34. Hans Georg Backhaus, "Materialien zur Rekonstruktion der Marxschen Werttheorie," *Gesellschaft: Beiträge zur Marxschen Theorie* (Frankfurt), no. 1 (1974), p. 53.
35. Marx, *A Contribution to the Critique of Political Economy,* trans. S. W. Ryazanskaya (Moscow, 1970), p. 59 (translation amended).
36. Marx, "Fragment des Urtextes von *Zur Kritik der politischen Ökonomie,*" in Marx, *Grundrisse der Kritik der politischen Ökonomie* (Berlin, 1953), p. 904.

Torrens . . . reverts to Adam Smith . . . according to whom the value of commodities was determined by the labor-time embodied in them 'in that early period' when people confronted one another only as owners and exchangers of commodities, but not when capital and property in land have been evolved. This would mean . . . that the law which is valid for commodities *qua* commodities, no longer is valid for them once they are regarded as capital, or as products of capital. . . . *On the other hand, the product wholly assumes the form of the commodity . . . only with the development and on the basis of capital production.* Thus the law of the commodity is supposed to be valid for a type of production which produces no commodities (or produces them only to a limited extent), and not to be valid for a type of production which is based on the existence of the product as a commodity.[37]

The commodity form and, hence, the law of value, are fully developed only in capitalism and are fundamental determinations of that social formation, according to Marx. When they are considered valid for other societies the result is that, *"the truth of the law of appropriation of bourgeois society must be transposed to a time when this society itself did not yet exist."*[38]

For Marx, then, the theory of value grasps the "truth of the law of appropriation" of the capitalist social formation and does not apply to other societies. It is thus clear that the initial categories of *Capital* are intended as historically specific; they grasp the underlying social forms of capitalism. A complete discussion of the historical specificity of these basic categories should, of course, consider why they do not appear to be valid for the "higher and more complex forms of capital, wage-labor, rent, etc."[39] I shall outline Marx's attempt to address this problem by analyzing the relation of his investigation of value in Volume 1 of *Capital* to his investigation of price and, hence, of these "higher and more complex forms" in Volume 3. Although this problem cannot be fully analyzed in this work, a preliminary discussion of the issues involved is in order here.

The debate on the relation of Volume 3 to Volume 1 was initiated by Eugen von Böhm-Bawerk in 1896.[40] Böhm-Bawerk notes that, when analyzing capitalism in value-based terms in Volume 1, Marx assumed that the "organic composition of capital" (the ratio of living labor, expressed as "variable capital," to objectified labor, expressed as "constant capital") is equal in the various branches of production. This, however, is not the case—as Marx himself later recognized. This caused him, in Volume 3, to concede a divergence of prices

37. Marx, *Theories of Surplus Value*, part 3, trans. Jack Cohen and S. W. Ryazanskaya (Moscow, 1971), p. 74 (translation amended, emphasis added).
38. "Fragment des Urtextes," p. 904.
39. *A Contribution to the Critique*, p. 59.
40. Eugen von Böhm-Bawerk, "Karl Marx and the Close of His System," in Paul M. Sweezy, ed., *"Karl Marx and the Close of His System," by Eugen Böhm-Bawerk, and "Böhm-Bawerk's Criticism of Marx" by Rudolf Hilferding* (New York, 1949). The article originally appeared as *Zum Abschluss des Marxschen Systems*, in Otto von Boenigk, ed., *Staatswissenschaftliche Arbeiten* (Berlin, 1896).

from values which, according to Böhm-Bawerk, directly contradicts the original labor theory of value and indicates its inadequacy. Since Böhm-Bawerk's critique, there has been considerable discussion of the "transformation problem" (of values into prices) in *Capital*,[41] much of which, in my opinion, has suffered from the assumption that Marx intended to write a critical political economy.

As regards Böhm-Bawerk's argument, two initial points should be made. First, contrary to Böhm-Bawerk's assumption, Marx did not first complete Volume 1 of *Capital* and only later, while writing Volume 3, come to realize that prices diverge from values, thus undermining his point of departure. Marx wrote the manuscripts for Volume 3 in 1863–1867, that is, *before* Volume 1 was published.[42]

Second, as noted in Chapter Two, far from being surprised or embarrassed by the divergence of prices from values, as early as 1859 Marx wrote in *A Contribution to the Critique of Political Economy* that, at a later stage of his analysis, he would deal with objections to his labor theory of value which are based on the divergence of the market prices of commodities from their exchange values.[43] Indeed, Marx not only recognized this divergence, but insisted on its centrality to an understanding of capitalism and its mystifications. As he wrote to Engels: "As far as Herr Dühring's modest objections to the determination of value are concerned, he will be very surprised to see, in Volume II, how little the determination of value is 'immediately' valid in bourgeois society."[44]

A difficulty with much of the discussion on the transformation problem is that it is generally assumed that Marx intended to operationalize the law of value in order to explain the workings of the market. It seems clear, however, that Marx's intention was different.[45] His treatment of the relation of value to price is not, as Dobb would have it, one of "successive approximations" to the reality of capitalism;[46] rather, it is part of a very complex argumentative strategy to render plausible his analysis of the commodity and capital as constituting the fundamental core of capitalist society, while accounting for the fact that the category of value does not seem to be empirically valid for capitalism (which is why Adam Smith relegated its validity to precapitalist society). In *Capital* Marx tries to solve this problem by showing that those phenomena (such as prices, profits, and rents) that contradict the validity of what he had postulated

41. See Sweezy's summary of that discussion in *The Theory of Capitalist Development* (New York, 1969), pp. 109–33.
42. See Engels's introduction to Volume 3 of *Capital*, p. 93; see also ibid., p. 278n27.
43. *A Contribution to the Critique*, p. 62.
44. Marx to Engels, January 8, 1868, in *Marx-Engels Werke* (hereafter *MEW*), vol. 32 (Berlin, 1956–1968), p. 12.
45. Joseph Schumpeter recognizes that to criticize Marx on the basis of the deviation of prices from values is to confuse Marx with Ricardo: see *History of Economic Analysis* (New York, 1954), pp. 596–97.
46. Dobb, *Political Economy and Capitalism* (London, 1940), p. 69.

as the fundamental determinations of the social formation (value and capital)
are actually expressions of these determinations—to show, in other words, that
the former both express and veil the latter. In this sense, the relation between
what the categories of value and price grasp is presented by Marx as a relation
between an essence and its form of appearance. One peculiarity of capitalist
society, which makes its analysis so difficult, is that this society has an essence,
objectified as value, which is veiled by its form of appearance:

The vulgar economist does not have the slightest idea that the real, daily relations of
exchange and the magnitudes of value *cannot be immediately identical*. . . . The vulgar
one then believes he has made a great discovery when he opposes the position which
uncovers the *inner nexus of connections* by insisting that, on the manifest level, things
appear differently. In fact he insists on holding onto the appearances and taking them to
be ultimate.[47]

The level of social reality expressed by prices represents, in Marx's analysis,
a form of appearance of value which veils the underlying essence. The category
of value is neither a rough, first approximation of capitalist reality nor a category
valid for precapitalist societies; rather, it expresses the "inner nexus of connections" (*inneren Zusammenhang*) of the capitalist social formation.

The movement of Marx's presentation from the first to the third volume of
Capital should, therefore, be understood not as a movement approaching the
"reality" of capitalism but as one approaching its manifold forms of surface
appearances. Marx does not preface the third volume with a statement that he
will now examine a fully developed capitalist system, nor does he assert that
he will now introduce a new set of approximations in order to grasp more
adequately capitalist reality. He states, rather, that "the various forms of capital,
as evolved in this book, thus approach step by step *the form which they assume
on the surface of society,* in the action of different capitals upon one another,
in competition, and in the ordinary consciousness of the agents of production
themselves."[48] Whereas Marx's analysis of value in Volume 1 is the analysis
of capitalism's essence, his analysis of price in Volume 3 is of how that essence
appears on the "surface of society."

The divergence of prices from values should, then, be understood as integral
to, rather than as a logical contradiction within, Marx's analysis: his intention
is not to formulate a price theory but to show how value induces a level of
appearance that disguises it. In Volume 3 of *Capital,* Marx derives empirical
categories such as cost price and profit from the categories of value and surplus
value, and shows how the former appear to contradict the latter. Thus, in Volume
1, for example, he maintains that surplus value is created by labour alone; in
Volume 3, however, he shows how the specificity of value as a form of wealth,

47. Marx to L. Kugelmann, July 11, 1868, in *MEW,* vol. 32, p. 553 (second emphasis added).
48. *Capital,* vol. 3, p. 25 (emphasis added).

and the specificity of the labor that constitutes it, are veiled. Marx begins by noting that the profit accruing to an individual capital unit is not, in fact, identical to the surplus value generated by the labor it commands. He attempts to explain this by arguing that surplus value is a category of the social whole which is distributed among individual capitals according to their relative shares of total social capital. This means that on the level of immediate experience, however, the profit of an individual capital unit indeed is a function not of labor alone ("variable capital") but of total capital forwarded;[49] hence, on an immediately empirical level, the unique features of value as a form of wealth and social mediation constituted by labor alone are hidden.

Marx's argument has many dimensions. I have mentioned the first already, namely, that the categories he develops in Volume 1 of *Capital,* such as the commodity, value, capital, and surplus value, are categories of the deep structure of capitalist society. On the basis of these categories, he seeks to elucidate the fundamental nature of that society and its "laws of motion," that is, the process of the constant transformation in capitalism of production and of all aspects of social life. Marx argues that this level of social reality cannot be elucidated by means of economic "surface" categories such as price and profit. He also unfolds his categories of the deep structure of capitalism in a way that indicates how the phenomena that contradict these structural categories are actually forms of their appearance. In this way, Marx tries to validate his analysis of the deep structure and, at the same time, to show how the "laws of motion" of the social formation are veiled on the level of immediate empirical reality.

The relation between what is grasped by the analytic level of value and that of price can be understood, moreover, as constituting a theory (never fully completed)[50] of the mutual constitution of deep social structures and everyday action and thought. This process is mediated by the forms of appearance of these deep structures, which constitute the context of such action and thought: Everyday action and thought are grounded in the manifest forms of the deep structures and, in turn, reconstitute those deep structures. Such a theory attempts to explain how the "laws of motion" of capitalism are constituted by individuals and prevail, even though those individuals are unaware of their existence.[51]

In elaborating this, Marx also seeks to indicate that theories of political econ-

---

49. Ibid., pp. 157–59.
50. Engels edited for publication the manuscripts that became volumes 2 and 3 of *Capital.*
51. In this sense, the Marxian theory is similar to the sort of theory of practice outlined by Pierre Bourdieu (*Outline of a Theory of Practice,* trans. Richard Nice [Cambridge, 1977]), which deals with "the dialectical relationship between the objective structures and the cognitive and motivating structures which they produce and which tend to reproduce them" (p. 83), and attempts "to account for a practice objectively governed by rules unknown to the agents [in a way that] does not mask the question of the mechanisms producing this conformity in the absence of the intention to conform" (p. 29). The attempt to mediate that relationship by means of a sociohistorical theory of knowledge and an analysis of the forms of appearance of the "objective structures" is consonant with, but not identical to, Bourdieu's approach.

omy as well as everyday "ordinary consciousness" remain bound to the level of appearances, that the objects of investigation of political economy are the mystified forms of appearance of value and capital. It is in Volume 3, in other words, that Marx completes his critique of Smith and Ricardo, his critique of political economy in the narrower sense. Ricardo, for example, begins his political economy as follows:

The produce of the earth—all that is derived from its surface by the united application of labor, machinery and capital—is divided among three classes of the community; namely, the proprietor of the land, the owner of the stock or capital necessary for its cultivation, and the laborers by whose industry it is cultivated. . . . [I]n different stages of society, the proportion of the whole produce of the earth which will be allotted to each of these classes under the names of rent, profit, wages, will be . . . different. . . . [T]o determine the laws which regulate this distribution, is the principal problem in Political Economy.[52]

Ricardo's point of departure, with its one-sided emphasis on distribution and its implicit identification of wealth with value, presupposes the transhistorical nature of wealth and labor. In Volume 3 of *Capital,* Marx seeks to explain that presupposition by showing how the socially and historically specific structuring forms of social relations in capitalism appear on the surface in a naturalized and transhistorical form. Thus, as noted, Marx argues that the historically unique social role of labor in capitalism is hidden by virtue of the fact that the profit gained by individual capital units does not depend only upon labor, but is a function of total capital forwarded (the various "factors of production," in other words). That value is created by labor alone is, according to Marx, further veiled by the wage form: wages seem to be compensation for the value of labor rather than for the value of labor power. This, in turn, renders opaque the category of surplus value as the difference between the amount of value created by labor and the value of labor power. Consequently, profit does not appear to be ultimately generated by labor. Marx then goes on to show how capital, in the form of interest, appears to be self-generating and independent of labor. Finally, he shows how rent, a form of revenue in which surplus value is distributed to landowners, appears to be related intrinsically to the land. In other words, the empirical categories upon which theories of political economy are based—profits, wages, interest, rents and so on—are forms of appearance of value and commodity-producing labor that belie the historical and social specificity of what they represent. Toward the end of Volume 3, after a long and complicated analysis that begins in Volume 1 with an examination of the reified "essence" of capitalism and moves to increasingly mystified levels of appearance, Marx sums up that analysis by examining what he terms the "trinity formula":

52. Ricardo, *Principles of Political Economy and Taxation,* ed. P. Sraffa and M. Dobb (Cambridge, England, 1951), p. 5.

Capital–profit (or better still capital–interest), land–ground-rent, labor–wages, this economic trinity as the connection between the components of value and wealth in general and its sources, completes the mystification of the capitalist mode of production, the reification of social relations, and the immediate coalescence of the material relations of production with their historical and social specificity.[53]

Marx's critique, then, ends with the derivation of Ricardo's point of departure. Consistent with his immanent approach, Marx's technique of criticizing theories such as Ricardo's no longer has the form of a refutation; rather, he embeds those theories within his own, by rendering them plausible in terms of his own analytic categories. Put another way, he grounds in his own categories the fundamental assumptions that Smith and Ricardo make regarding labor, society, and nature, in a manner that explains the transhistorical character of these assumptions. And he shows, further, that those theories' more specific arguments are based upon "data" that are the misleading manifestations of a deeper, historically specific structure. By proceeding from the "essence" to the "surface" of capitalist society, Marx tries to show how his own categorial analysis can account for both the problem and Ricardo's formulation of it, thereby indicating the latter's inadequacy as an attempt to grasp the essence of the social totality. By elucidating as forms of appearance that which served as the basis of Ricardo's theory, Marx seeks to provide the adequate critique of Ricardo's political economy.

According to Marx, then, the tendency of some political economists, such as Smith and Torrens, to transpose the validity of the law of value to models of precapitalist society is not merely a result of bad thinking. It is, rather, grounded in a peculiarity of the capitalist social formation: its essence appears *not* to be valid for the "higher and more complex forms of capital, wage-labor, and rent." The failure to penetrate theoretically the level of appearance and to determine its relation to the historically specific social essence of the capitalist formation can lead to a transhistorical application of value to other societies, on the one hand, and to an analysis of capitalism only in terms of its "illusory appearance," on the other.

One consequence of Marx's turn to a reflexive and historically specific approach, then, is that the critique of theories that posit transhistorically what is historically determinate becomes central to his investigations. Once he claims to have discovered the historically specific core of the capitalist system, Marx has to explain why this historical determinateness is not evident. As we shall see, central to this epistemological dimension of his critique is the argument that social structures specific to capitalism appear in "fetishized" form—that is, they appear to be "objective" and transhistorical. To the degree that Marx shows that the historically specific structures he analyzes present themselves in transhistorical manifest forms, and that these manifest forms serve as the object of various theories—especially those of Hegel and Ricardo—he is able to ac-

---

53. *Capital*, vol. 3, pp. 968–69.

count for and criticize such theories in social and historical terms, as forms of thought that express, but do not fully apprehend, the determinate social forms at the heart of their context (capitalist society). The historically specific character of Marx's immanent social critique implies that what is "false" is the temporarily valid form of thought that, lacking self-reflection, fails to perceive its own historically specific ground, and therefore considers itself to be "true," that is, transhistorically valid.

The unfolding of Marx's argument in the three volumes of *Capital* should be understood, on one level, as presenting what he describes as the only fully adequate method of a critical materialist theory: "It is, in reality, much easier to discover by analysis the earthly kernel of the misty creations of religion than to do the opposite, i.e. to develop from the actual, given relations of life the forms in which these have been apotheosized. The latter method is the only materialist, and therefore the only scientific one."[54] An important aspect of Marx's method of presentation is that he develops from value and capital—that is, from the categories of "the actual, given relations of life"—the surface forms of appearance (cost price, profit, wages, interest, rent, and so on) that have been "apotheosized" by political economists and social actors. He thereby tries to render his deep structural categories plausible while explaining the surface forms.

By logically deriving the very phenomena that seem to contradict the categories with which he analyzes capitalism's essence from the unfolding of these same categories, and by demonstrating that other theories (and the consciousness of most social actors directly involved) are bound to the mystified forms of appearance of that essence, Marx provides a remarkable display of the rigor and power of his critical analysis.

Historical specificity and immanent critique

The historical specificity of the categories, then, is central to Marx's mature theory and marks a very important distinction between it and his early works.[55] This shift to historical determinateness has far-reaching implications for the nature of Marx's critical theory—implications that are inherent in the point of departure of his mature critique. In the introduction to his translation of the

---

54. *Capital*, vol. 1, p. 494n4.
55. I shall not discuss extensively the differences between Marx's early writings and his later writings in this work. My treatment of his mature critique of political economy will, however, suggest that many of the explicit themes and concepts of the early writings (such as the critique of alienation, the concern with the possibility of forms of human activity not defined narrowly in terms of work, play, or leisure, and the theme of the relations between men and women) remain central, if implicit, in Marx's later works. Nevertheless, as I shall discuss with reference to the notion of alienation, some of these concepts were fully worked out—and were modified— only when Marx clearly developed a historically specific social critique based upon an analysis of the specificity of labor in capitalism.

Grundrisse, Martin Nicolaus draws attention to this shift by arguing that Marx's introduction to the manuscript proved to be a false start, for the categories used are simply direct translations of Hegelian categories into materialist terms. For example, where Hegel begins his *Logic* with pure, indeterminate *Being,* which immediately calls forth its opposite, *Nothing,* Marx begins his introduction with *material production* (in general), which calls forth its opposite, *consumption.* In the course of the introduction, Marx indicates his dissatisfaction with this starting point and, after writing the manuscript, he begins anew, in the section entitled "Value" (which he added at the end). He does so with a different point of departure, one that he retains in *A Contribution to the Critique of Political Economy* and *Capital*—the commodity.[56] In the course of writing the *Grundrisse,* Marx discovers the element with which he then structures his mode of presentation, the point of departure from which he unfolds the categories of the capitalist formation in *Capital.* From a transhistorical starting point, Marx moves to a historically determinate one. The category "commodity," in Marx's analysis, does not simply refer to an object, but to a historically specific, "objective" form of social relations—a structuring and structured form of social practice that constitutes a radically new form of social interdependence. This form is characterized by a historically specific duality purportedly at the core of the social system: use value and value, concrete labor and abstract labor. Proceeding from the category of the commodity as this dualistic form, this nonidentical unity, Marx seeks to unfold from it the overarching structure of capitalist society as a totality, the intrinsic logic of its historical development, as well as the elements of immediate social experience that veil the underlying structure of that society. That is, within the framework of Marx's critique of political economy, the commodity is the essential category at the heart of capital; he unfolds it in order to illuminate the nature of capital and its intrinsic dynamic.

With this turn to historical specificity, Marx now historicizes his earlier, transhistorical conceptions of social contradiction and the existence of an intrinsic historical logic. He now treats them as specific to capitalism, and roots them in the "unstable" duality of material and social moments with which he characterizes its basic social forms, such as the commodity and capital. In my analysis of *Capital,* I shall show how this duality, according to Marx, becomes externalized and gives rise to a peculiar historical dialectic. By describing his object of investigation in terms of a historically specific contradiction, and grounding the dialectic in the double character of the peculiar social forms underlying the capitalist social formation (labor, the commodity, the process of production, and so on), Marx now implicitly rejects the idea of an immanent logic of human history and any form of transhistorical dialectic, whether inclusive of nature or restricted to history. In Marx's mature works, the historical dialectic does not result from the interplay of subject, labor, and nature, from the reflexive work-

56. Martin Nicolaus, Introduction, in *Grundrisse,* pp. 35–37.

ings of the material objectifications of the Subject's "labor" upon itself; rather, it is rooted in the contradictory character of capitalist social forms.

A transhistorical dialectic must be grounded ontologically, either in Being as such (Engels) or in social Being (Lukács). In light of Marx's historically specific analysis, however, the idea that reality or social relations in general are essentially contradictory and dialectical is now revealed to be one that cannot be explained or grounded; it can only be assumed metaphysically.[57] In other words, by analyzing the historical dialectic in terms of the peculiarities of the fundamental social structures of capitalism, Marx removes it from the realm of the philosophy of history and places it within the framework of a historically specific social theory.

The move from a transhistorical to a historically specific point of departure implies that not only the categories but also the very form of the theory are historically specific. Given Marx's assumption that thought is socially embedded, his turn to an analysis of the historical specificity of the categories of capitalist society—his own social context—involves a turn to a notion of the historical specificity of his own theory. The historical relativization of the object of investigation is also reflexive for the theory itself.

This implies the necessity for a new, self-reflexive sort of social critique. Its standpoint cannot be located transhistorically or transcendentally. In such a conceptual framework, no theory—including Marx's—has absolute, transhistorical validity. The impossibility of an extrinsic or privileged theoretical standpoint is also not to be contravened implicitly by the form of the theory itself. For that reason, Marx now feels compelled to construct his critical presentation of capitalist society in a rigorously immanent fashion, analyzing that society in its own terms, as it were. The standpoint of the critique is immanent to its social object; it is grounded in the contradictory character of capitalist society, which points to the possibility of its historical negation.

Marx's mode of argumentation in *Capital* should, then, be understood as an attempt to develop a form of critical analysis that is consonant with the historical specificity both of its object of investigation—that is, its own context—and, reflexively, of its concepts. As we shall see, Marx attempts to reconstruct the social totality of capitalist civilization by beginning with a single structuring principle—the commodity—and dialectically unfolding from it the categories of money and capital. This mode of presentation, viewed in terms of his new self-understanding, itself expresses the peculiarities of the social forms being investigated. Such a method itself expresses, for example, that a peculiar characteristic of capitalism is that it exists as a homogeneous totality that can be unfolded from a single structuring principle; the dialectical character of the presentation purportedly expresses that the social forms are uniquely constituted in

57. See M. Postone and H. Reinicke, "On Nicolaus," *Telos* 22 (Winter 1974–75) pp. 135–36.

a way that grounds a dialectic. *Capital,* in other words, is an attempt to construct an argument that does not have a logical form independent of the object being investigated, when that object is the context of the argument itself. Marx describes this method of presentation as follows:

Of course the mode of presentation must differ in form from that of inquiry. The latter has to appropriate the material in detail, to analyze its different forms of development and to track down their inner connection. Only after this work has been done can the real movement be appropriately presented. If this is done successfully, if the life of the subject matter is now reflected in the ideas, then it may appear as if we have before us an *a priori* construction.[58]

What appears as an "*a priori* construction" is a mode of argument intended to be adequate to its own historical specificity. The nature of the Marxian argument, then, is not supposed to be that of a logical deduction: it does not begin with indubitable first principles from which everything else may be derived, for the very form of such a procedure implies a transhistorical standpoint. Rather, Marx's argument has a very peculiar, reflexive form: The point of departure, the commodity—which is posited as the fundamental structuring core of the social formation—is validated retroactively by the argument as it unfolds, by its ability to explain the developmental tendencies of capitalism, and by its ability to account for the phenomena that apparently contradict the validity of the initial categories. That is, the category of the commodity presupposes that of capital and is validated by the power and rigor of the analysis of capitalism for which it serves as the point of departure. Marx briefly described this procedure as follows:

If there were no chapter on "value" in my book, the analysis of the real relations that I provide contains the proof and the evidence of the real value relation. The blather about the necessity to prove the concept of value rests upon complete ignorance of the issues involved as well as of the methods of science.... Science entails developing how the law of value prevails. If one wished to "explain" from the very beginning all the phenomena that apparently contradict the law, one would have to present the science *prior* to the science.[59]

In this light, Marx's actual argument regarding value as well as the nature and the historicity of capitalist society should be understood in terms of the full unfolding of the categories of *Capital.* It follows that his explicit arguments deriving the existence of value in the first chapter of that work are not in-

---

58. Marx, "Postface to the Second Edition," *Capital,* vol. 1, p. 102.
59. Marx to L. Kugelmann, July 11, 1868, in *MEW,* vol. 32, pp. 552–53.

tended—and should not be seen—as "proof" of the concept of value.[60] Rather, *those arguments are presented by Marx as forms of thought characteristic of the society whose underlying social forms are being critically analyzed.* As I shall show in the following section, those arguments—for example, the initial determinations of "abstract labor"—are transhistorical; that is, they already are presented in mystified form. The same holds true for the *form* of the arguments: it represents a mode of thinking, typified by Descartes, that proceeds in a decontextualized, logically deductive manner, discovering a "true essence" behind the changing world of appearances.[61] I am suggesting, in other words, that Marx's arguments deducing value should be read as part of an ongoing metacommentary on forms of thought characteristic of capitalist society (for example, of the tradition of modern philosophy, as well as of political economy). That "commentary" is immanent to the unfolding of the categories in his presentation, and thereby implicitly relates those forms of thought to the social forms of the society that is their context. Inasmuch as Marx's mode of presentation is intended to be immanent to its object, the categories are presented "in their own terms"—in this case, as decontextualized. The analysis, then, purports to takes no standpoint outside of its context. The critique only fully emerges in the course of the presentation itself which, in unfolding the basic structuring social forms of its object of investigation, shows the historicity of that object.

The drawback of such a presentation is that Marx's reflexive, immanent approach is easily subject to misinterpretation. If *Capital* is read as anything other than an immanent critique, the result is a reading that interprets Marx as affirming that which he attempts to criticize (for example, the historically determinate function of labor as socially constitutive).

This dialectical mode of presentation, then, is intended to be the mode of presentation adequate to, and expressive of, its object. As an immanent critique, the Marxian analysis claims to be dialectical because it shows its object to be so. This presumed adequacy of the concept to its object implies a rejection of both a transhistorical dialectic of history and any notion of the dialectic as a universally valid method applicable to various particular problems. Indeed, as we have seen, *Capital* is an attempt to provide a critique of such conceptions

60. Marx "deduces" value in the first chapter of *Capital* by arguing that various commodities must have a nonmaterial element in common. The manner of his deduction is decontextualized and essentializing: value is deduced as the expression of a *substance* common to all commodities (with "substance" meant in the traditional philosophical sense): see *Capital,* vol. 1, pp. 126–28.

61. John Patrick Murray has pointed out the similarity between the structure of Marx's argument deriving value and Descartes's derivation, in the *Second Meditation,* of abstract, primary-quality matter as the substance underlying the changing appearance of a piece of wax. Murray also regards this similarity as the expression of an implicit argument by Marx: see "Enlightenment Roots of Habermas' Critique of Marx," *The Modern Schoolman,* 57, no. 1 (November 1979), p. 13ff.

of decontextualized, nonreflexive methods—whether dialectical (Hegel) or not (classical political economy).

Marx's turn to historical specificity also changes the character of the critical consciousness expressed by the dialectical critique. The point of departure of a dialectical critique presupposes its result. As mentioned, for Hegel, the Being of the beginning of the dialectical process is the Absolute, which, unfolded, is the result of its own development. Consequently, the critical consciousness that is obtained when the theory becomes aware of its own standpoint necessarily must be absolute knowledge.[62] The commodity, as the point of departure of the Marxian critique, also presupposes the full unfolding of the whole; yet its historically determinate character implies the finitude of the unfolding totality. The indication of the historicity of the object, the essential social forms of capitalism, implies the historicity of the critical consciousness that grasps it; the historical overcoming of capitalism would also entail the negation of its dialectical critique. The turn to the historical specificity of the basic structuring social forms of capitalism thus signifies the self-reflexive historical specificity of Marx's critical theory—and thereby both frees the immanent critique from the last vestiges of the claim to absolute knowledge and allows for its critical self-reflection.

By specifying the contradictory character of his own social universe, Marx is able to develop an epistemologically consistent critique and finally to move beyond the dilemma of earlier forms of materialism he outlined in the third thesis on Feuerbach:[63] A theory that is critical of society and assumes humans and, therefore, their modes of consciousness to be socially formed must be able to account for the very possibility of its own existence. The Marxian critique grounds this possibility in the contradictory character of its categories, which purport to express the essential relational structures of its social universe and, simultaneously, to grasp forms of social being and of consciousness. The critique is thus immanent in another sense: showing the nonunitary character of its own context allows the critique to account for itself as a possibility immanent to that which it analyzes.

One of the most powerful aspects of Marx's critique of political economy is the way it locates itself as a historically determinate aspect of that which it examines rather than as a transhistorically valid positive science that constitutes a historically unique (hence, spurious) exception standing above the interaction of social forms and forms of consciousness it analyzes. This critique does not

---

62. In *Knowledge and Human Interests* (trans. Jeremy Shapiro [Boston, 1971]), Habermas criticizes Hegel's identification of critical consciousness and absolute knowledge as one that undermines critical self-reflection. Habermas attributes this identification to Hegel's presupposition of the absolute identity of subject and object, including nature. He does not, however, proceed to consider the negative implications for epistemological self-reflection of any transhistorical dialectic, even when nature is excluded. See p. 19ff.

63. Marx, "Theses on Feuerbach," in Karl Marx and Frederick Engels, *Collected Works,* vol. 5: *Marx and Engels: 1845–47* (New York, 1976), p. 4.

adopt a standpoint outside of its object and is, therefore, self-reflexive and epistemologically consistent.

Abstract labor

My contention that Marx's analysis of the historically specific character of labor in capitalism lies at the heart of his critical theory is central to the interpretation presented in this work. I have shown that the Marxian critique proceeds from an examination of the commodity as a dualistic social form, and that he grounds the dualism of the fundamental structuring social form of capitalist society in the double character of commodity-producing labor. At this point, that double character, especially the dimension Marx terms "abstract labor," must be analyzed.

The distinction Marx makes between concrete, useful labor, which produces use values, and abstract human labor, which constitutes value, does not refer to two different sorts of labor, but to two aspects of the same labor in commodity-determined society: "It follows from the above that the commodity does not contain two different sorts of labour; the *same* labour, however, is determined as different and as opposed to itself, depending on whether it is related to the *use-value* of the commodity as its product, or to the *commodity-value* as its mere objectified expression."[64] Marx's immanent mode of presentation in discussing this dual character of commodity-producing labor, however, makes it difficult to understand the importance he explicitly attributes to this distinction for his critical analysis of capitalism. Moreover, the definitions he provides of abstract human labor in *Capital,* Chapter One, are very problematic. They seem to indicate that it is a biological residue, that it is to be interpreted as the expenditure of human physiological energy. For example:

On the one hand, all labour is an expenditure of human labour-power in the physiological sense, and it is in this quality of being equal, or abstract, human labour that it forms the value of commodities. On the other hand, all labour is an expenditure of human labour-power in a particular form and with a definite aim, and it is in this quality of being concrete useful labour that it produces use-values.[65]

If we leave aside the determinate quality of productive activity, and therefore the useful character of the labour, what remains is its quality of being an expenditure of human labour-power. Tailoring and weaving, although they are qualitatively different productive activities, are both a productive expenditure of human brains, muscles, nerves, hands etc., and in this sense both human labour. They are merely two different forms of the expenditure of human labour-power.[66]

64. Marx, *Das Kapital,* vol. 1 (1st ed., 1867), in Iring Fetscher, ed., *Marx-Engels Studienausgabe,* vol. 2 (Frankfurt, 1966), p. 224.
65. *Capital,* vol. 1, p. 137.
66. Ibid., pp. 134–35.

Yet, at the same time, Marx clearly states that we are dealing with a *social* category. He refers to abstract human labor, which constitutes the value dimension of commodities, as their *"social substance,* which is common to them all."[67] Consequently, although commodities as use values are material, as values they are purely social objects:

Not an atom of matter enters into the object-ness of commodities as values; in this it is the direct opposite of the coarsely sensuous object-ness of commodities as physical objects.... However, let us remember that commodities possess value object-ness only in so far as they are all expressions of the same social unity, human labour; their object-ness as values is therefore purely social.[68]

Furthermore, Marx explicitly emphasizes that this social category is to be understood as historically determinate—as the following passage, cited before, indicates: "The value-form of the product of labour is the most abstract, but also the most general form of the bourgeois mode of production. This mode is thereby characterized as a particular sort of social production and, hence, as historically specific."[69]

If, however, the category of abstract human labor is a social determination, it cannot be a physiological category. Furthermore, as my interpretation of the *Grundrisse* in Chapter One indicated and this passage confirms, it is central to Marx's analysis that value be understood as a historically specific form of social wealth. That being the case, its "social substance" could not be a transhistorical, natural residue, common to human labor in all social formations. As Isaak I. Rubin argues:

One of two things is possible: if abstract labor is an expenditure of human energy in physiological form, then value also has a reified-material character. Or value is a social phenomenon, and then abstract labor must also be understood as a social phenomenon connected with a determined social form of production. It is not possible to reconcile a physiological concept of abstract labor with the historical character of the value which it creates.[70]

The problem, then, is to move beyond the physiological definition of abstract human labor provided by Marx and analyze its underlying social and historical meaning. An adequate analysis, moreover, must not only show *that* abstract human labor has a social character; it must also investigate the historically specific social relations that underlie value in order to explain *why* those relations appear and, therefore, are presented by Marx, as being physiological—as transhistorical, natural, and thus historically empty. Such an approach, in other words, would

67. Ibid., p. 128 (emphasis added).
68. Ibid., pp. 138–39 (translation amended).
69. Ibid., p. 174n34 (translation amended).
70. Isaak Illich Rubin, *Essays on Marx's Theory of Value,* trans. Milos Samardzija and Fredy Perlman (Detroit, 1972), p. 135.

examine the category of abstract human labor as the initial and primary determination underlying the "commodity fetish" in Marx's analysis—that social
relations in capitalism appear in the form of the relations among objects and,
hence, seem to be transhistorical. Such an analysis would show that, for Marx,
even categories of the "essence" of the capitalist social formation such as
"value" and "abstract human labor" are reified—and not only their categorial
forms of appearance such as exchange value and, on a more manifest level, price
and profit. This is extremely crucial, for it would demonstrate that the categories
of Marx's analysis of the essential forms underlying the various categorial forms
of appearance are intended not as ontological, transhistorically valid categories,
but purportedly grasp social forms that themselves are historically specific. Because of their peculiar character, however, these social forms appear to be ontological. The task confronting us, then, is to uncover a historically specific form
of social reality "behind" abstract human labor as a category of essence. We
must then explain why this specific reality exists in this particular form, which
appears to be ontologically grounded and, hence, historically nonspecific.

The centrality of the category of abstract labor to an understanding of Marx's
critique also has been argued by Lucio Colletti in his essay, "Bernstein and the
Marxism of the Second International."[71] Colletti claims that contemporary conditions have revealed the inadequacies of the interpretation of the labor theory
of value first developed by the Marxist theorists of the Second International.
That interpretation, according to Colletti, is still prevalent; it reduces Marx's
theory of value to that of Ricardo and leads to a narrow understanding of the
economic sphere.[72] Like Rubin, Colletti maintains that what has rarely been
understood is that Marx's theory of value is identical to his theory of the fetish.
What must be explained is why the product of labor assumes the form of the
commodity and why, therefore, human labor appears as a value of things.[73] The
concept of abstract labor is central to such an explanation, yet, according to
Colletti, most Marxists—including Karl Kautsky, Rosa Luxemburg, Rudolf Hilferding, and Paul Sweezy—have never really elucidated this category. Abstract
labor has been treated implicitly as a mental generalization of various sorts of
concrete labor rather than as an expression of something real.[74] If such were the
case, however, value would also be a purely mental construction, and Böhm-
Bawerk would have been right in arguing that value is use value in general and
not, as Marx had argued, a qualitatively distinct category.[75]

71. Lucio Colletti, "Bernstein and the Marxism of the Second International," in *From Rousseau
    to Lenin*, trans. John Merrington and Judith White (London, 1972), pp. 45–110.
72. Ibid., p. 77.
73. Ibid., pp. 77–78.
74. Ibid., pp. 78–80. Sweezy, for example, defines the category as follows: "Abstract labor, in
    short, is, as Marx's own usage clearly attests, equivalent to 'labor in general'; it is what is
    common to all productive human activity" (*The Theory of Capitalist Development*, p. 30).
75. Colletti, "Bernstein and the Marxism of the Second International," p. 81.

To show that abstract labor does indeed express something real, Colletti examines the source and significance of the abstraction of labor. In so doing, he concentrates on the process of exchange: he argues that, in order to exchange their products, people must equalize them, which, in turn, entails an abstraction from the physical-natural differences among the various products and, therefore, from the differences among the various labors. This process, which constitutes abstract labor, is one of alienation: such labor becomes a force in itself, separated from the individuals. Value, according to Colletti, is not only independent of people, but also dominates them.[76]

Colletti's argument parallels some aspects of that developed in this work. Like Georg Lukács, Isaak Rubin, Bertell Ollman, and Derek Sayer, he considers value and abstract labor to be historically specific categories and regards Marx's analysis as concerned with the forms of social relations and of domination that characterize capitalism. Nevertheless, he does not really ground his description of alienated labor and does not pursue the implications of his own interpretation. Colletti does not proceed from an examination of abstract labor to a more fundamental critique of the traditional Marxist interpretation, and thereby develop a critique of the form of production and of the centrality of labor in capitalism. This would have required rethinking the traditional Marxist conception of labor and seeing that Marx's analysis of labor in capitalism is one of a historically specific form of social mediation. Only by developing a critique centered on the historically unique role of labor in capitalism could Colletti—and other theorists who have argued for the historical specificity of value and abstract labor—have effected a basic theoretical break with traditional Marxism. Instead, Colletti remains well within the limits of a social critique from the standpoint of "labor": the function of social critique, he says, is to "defetishize" the world of commodities and thereby to aid wage labor to recognize that the essence of value and capital is an objectification of itself.[77] It is telling that, although Colletti begins this section of his essay with a critique of Sweezy's notion of abstract labor, he nevertheless concludes the section by approvingly citing Sweezy's absolute and historically abstract opposition of value as the principle of capitalism to planning as the principle of socialism.[78] That is, Colletti's reconsideration of the problem of abstract labor does not significantly alter the conclusions at which he arrives: the problem of abstract labor is effectively reduced to one of interpretative detail. Despite his assertion that most Marxist interpretations of the labor theory of value have been Ricardian, and his insistence on the centrality of abstract labor as alienated labor in Marx's analysis, Colletti ends up reproducing, in a more sophisticated fashion, the position he had criticized. His critique remains one of the mode of distribution.

76. Ibid., pp. 82–87.
77. Ibid., pp. 89–91.
78. Ibid., p. 92.

The theoretical problem facing us, then, is to reconsider the category of abstract labor so as to provide the basis for a critique of the mode of production—a critique, in other words, that *does* differ fundamentally from the Marxism of the Second International, whether in historically specific or transhistorical form.

Abstract labor and social mediation

We can begin to understand Marx's interrelated categories of the commodity, value, and abstract labor by approaching them as categories of a determinate form of social interdependence. (By not beginning with certain common questions—for example, whether market exchange is regulated by relative quantities of objectified labor, by considerations of utility, or by other factors—this approach avoids treating Marx's categories too narrowly as political-economic categories that presuppose what he is actually attempting to explain.)[79] A society in which the commodity is the general form of the product, and hence value is the general form of wealth, is characterized by a unique form of social interdependence—people do not consume what they produce but produce and exchange commodities in order to acquire other commodities:

In order to become a commodity, the product must cease to be produced as the immediate means of subsistence of the producer himself. Had we gone further, and inquired under what circumstances all, or even the majority of products take the form of commodities, we would have found that this only happens on the basis of one particular mode of production, the capitalist one.[80]

We are dealing with a new sort of interdependence, one that emerged historically in a slow, spontaneous, and contingent way. Once the social formation based upon this new form of interdependence became fully developed, however (which occurred when labor power itself became a commodity),[81] it acquired a necessary and systematic character; it has increasingly undermined, incorporated, and superseded other social forms, while becoming global in scale. My

---

79. Marx's theory should, on one level, be seen as an attempt to analyze the underlying structural bases of a society characterized by the universal exchangeability of products—that is, one in which all goods, and the relations of people to goods, have become "secular" in the sense that, unlike in many "traditional" societies, all goods are considered "objects," and people can theoretically choose among all goods. Such a theory differs fundamentally from theories of market exchange—whether labor theories of value or utility theories of equivalence—that presuppose as a background condition precisely what Marx's analysis of the commodity seeks to explain. Moreover, as we shall see, Marx's analysis of the commodity is intended to provide the basis for an elucidation of the nature of capital—which is to say, his theory attempts to explain the historical dynamic of capitalist society. As I shall elaborate, that dynamic is rooted in the dialectic of abstract and concrete labor, according to Marx, and cannot be grasped by theories that focus on market exchange alone.

80. *Capital,* vol. 1, p. 273.

81. Ibid., p. 274.

concern is to analyze the nature of this interdependence and its constituting principle. In examining this peculiar form of interdependence and the specific role played by labor in its constitution, I shall elucidate Marx's most abstract determinations of capitalist society. On the basis of Marx's initial determinations of the form of wealth, the form of labor, and the form of social relations that characterize capitalism, I shall then be able to clarify his notion of abstract social domination by analyzing how these forms confront the individuals in a quasi-objective fashion, and how they give rise to a particular mode of production and an intrinsic historical dynamic.[82]

In commodity-determined society, the objectifications of one's labor are means by which goods produced by others are acquired; one labors in order to acquire other products. One's product, then, serves someone else as a good, a use value; it serves the producer as a means of acquiring the labor products of others. It is in this sense that a product is a commodity: it is simultaneously a use value for the other, and a means of exchange for the producer. This signifies that one's labor has a dual function: On the one hand, it is a specific sort of labor that produces particular goods for others, yet, on the other hand, labor, independent of its specific content, serves the producer as the means by which the products of others are acquired. Labor, in other words, becomes a peculiar means of acquiring goods in commodity-determined society; the specificity of the producers' labor is *abstracted* from the products they acquire with their labor. There is no intrinsic relation between the specific nature of the labor expended and the specific nature of the product acquired by means of that labor.

This is quite different from social formations in which commodity production and exchange do not predominate, where the social distribution of labor and its products is effected by a wide variety of customs, traditional ties, overt relations of power, or, conceivably, conscious decisions.[83] Labor is distributed by mani-

---

82. Diane Elson also has argued that the object of Marx's theory of value is labor and that, with his category of abstract labor, Marx attempts to analyze the foundations of a social formation in which the process of production has mastery over people, rather than vice versa. On the basis of this approach she does not, however, call into question the traditional understanding of the basic relations of capitalism. See "The Value Theory of Labour," in Elson, ed., *Value: The Representation of Labour in Capitalism* (London, 1979), pp. 115–80.

83. Karl Polanyi also emphasizes the historical uniqueness of modern capitalist society: in other societies, the economy is embedded in social relations, but in modern capitalism, social relations are embedded in the economic system. See *The Great Transformation* (New York and Toronto, 1944), p. 57. However, Polanyi focuses almost exclusively on the market and claims that fully developed capitalism is defined by the fact that it is based on a fiction: human labor, land, and money are treated as if they were commodities, which they are not (p. 72). He thereby implies that the existence of labor products as commodities is, somehow, socially "natural." This very common understanding differs from that of Marx, for whom nothing is a commodity "by nature," and for whom the category of the commodity refers to a historically specific form of social relations rather than to things, people, land, or money. Indeed, this form of social relations refers first and foremost to a historically determinate form of social labor. Polanyi's approach, with its implicit social ontology and exclusive focus on the market, deflects attention away

fest social relations in noncapitalist societies. In a society characterized by the universality of the commodity form, however, an individual does not acquire goods produced by others through the medium of overt social relations. Instead, labor itself—either directly or as expressed in its products—replaces those relations by serving as an "objective" means by which the products of others are acquired. *Labor itself constitutes a social mediation in lieu of overt social relations.* That is, a new form of interdependence comes into being: No one consumes what one produces, but one's own labor or labor products, nevertheless, function as the necessary means of obtaining the products of others. In serving as such a means, labor and its products in effect preempt that function on the part of manifest social relations. Hence, rather than being mediated by overtly or "recognizably" social relations, commodity-determined labor is mediated by a set of structures that—as we shall see—it itself constitutes. Labor and its products mediate themselves in capitalism; they are self-mediating socially. This form of social mediation is unique: within the framework of Marx's approach, it sufficiently differentiates capitalist society from all other existent forms of social life, so that, relative to the former, the latter can be seen as having common features—they can be regarded as "noncapitalist," however else they may differ from one another.

In producing use values, labor in capitalism can be regarded as an intentional activity that transforms material in a determinate fashion—what Marx terms "concrete labor." The *function* of labor as a socially mediating activity is what he terms "abstract labor." Various sorts of what we would consider labor exist in all societies (even if not in the general "secularized" form implied by the category of concrete labor), but abstract labor is specific to capitalism and therefore warrants closer examination. It should already be clear that the category of abstract labor refers neither to a particular sort of labor, nor to concrete labor in general; rather, it expresses a particular, unique social function of labor in capitalism in addition to its "normal" social function as a productive activity.

Labor, of course, has a social character in all social formations, but as noted in Chapter Two, this social character cannot be grasped adequately only in terms of whether it is "direct" or "indirect." In noncapitalist societies, laboring activities are social by virtue of the matrix of overt social relations in which they are embedded. That matrix is the constituting principle of such societies; various labors gain their social character through these social relations.[84] From the standpoint of capitalist society, relations in precapitalist formations can be described as personal, overtly social, and qualitatively particular (differentiated according to social grouping, social standing, and so on). Laboring activities, accordingly, are determined as overtly social and qualitatively particular; various labors are imbued with meaning by the social relations that are their context.

from consideration of the "objective" form of social relations and intrinsic historical dynamic characteristic of capitalism.

84. *Capital,* vol. 1, pp. 170–71.

In capitalism, labor itself constitutes a social mediation in lieu of such a matrix of relations. This means that labor is *not* accorded a social character by overt social relations; rather, because labor mediates itself, it both constitutes a social structure that replaces systems of overt social relations and accords its social character to itself. This reflexive moment determines the specific nature of labor's self-mediated social character as well as of the social relations structured by this social mediation. As I shall show, this self-grounding moment of labor in capitalism imparts an "objective" character to labor, its products, and the social relations it constitutes. The character of social relations and the social character of labor in capitalism come to be determined by a social function of labor which replaces that of overt social relations. In other words, labor grounds its own social character in capitalism by virtue of its historically specific function as a socially mediating activity. In that sense, *labor in capitalism becomes its own social ground.*

In constituting a self-grounding social mediation, labor constitutes a determinate sort of social whole—a totality. The category of totality and the form of universality associated with it can be elucidated by considering the sort of generality related to the commodity form. Each producer produces commodities that are particular use values and, at the same time, function as social mediations. A commodity's function as a social mediation is independent of its particular material form and is true of all commodities. A pair of shoes is, in this sense, identical to a sack of potatoes. Thus, each commodity is both particular, as a use value, and general, as a social mediation. As the latter, the commodity is a value. Because labor and its products are not mediated and accorded their social character and meaning by direct social relations, they acquire two dimensions: they are qualitatively particular, yet they also possess an underlying general dimension. This duality corresponds to the circumstance that labor (or its product) is bought for its qualitative specificity but is sold as a general means. Consequently, commodity-producing labor is both particular—as concrete labor, a determinate activity that creates specific use values—and socially general, as abstract labor, a means of acquiring the goods of others.

This initial determination of the double-character of labor in capitalism should not be understood out of context as implying simply that all the various forms of concrete labor are forms of labor in general. Such a statement is analytically useless inasmuch as it could be made of laboring activities in all societies, even those in which commodity production is only of marginal significance. After all, all forms of labor have in common that they are labor. But such an indeterminate interpretation does not and cannot contribute to an understanding of capitalism precisely because abstract labor and value, according to Marx, are specific to that social formation. What makes labor general in capitalism is not simply the truism that it is the common denominator of all various specific sorts of labor; rather, *it is the social function of labor which makes it general.* As a socially mediating activity, labor is abstracted from the specificity of its product, hence, from the specificity of its own concrete form. In Marx's analysis, the category of abstract labor expresses this real social process of abstraction; it is not simply based on a conceptual process of abstraction. As a practice that constitutes a social mediation, labor is labor in general. We are dealing, moreover, with a society in which the commodity form is generalized and therefore socially determining; the labor of *all* producers serves as a means by which the products of others can be obtained. Consequently, "labor in general" serves in a socially general way as a mediating activity. Yet labor, as abstract labor, is not only socially general in the sense that it constitutes a mediation among all producers; the *character* of the mediation is socially general as well.

This requires further elucidation. The labor of all commodity producers, taken together, is a collection of various concrete labors; each is the particular part of a whole. Likewise, their products appear as an "immense collection of commodities"[85] in the form of use values. At the same time, all of their labors constitute social mediations; but because each individual labor functions in the *same* socially mediating way that all the others do, their abstract labors taken together do *not* constitute an immense collection of various abstract labors but a *general* social mediation—in other words, socially total abstract labor. Their products thus constitute a *socially total mediation—value*. The mediation is general not only because it connects all producers, but also because its character is general—abstracted from all material specificity as well as any overtly social particularity. The mediation has, therefore, the same general quality on the individual level as on the level of society as a whole. Viewed from the perspective of society as a whole, the concrete labor of the individual is particular and is *part* of a qualitatively heterogeneous *whole;* as abstract labor, however, it is an individuated *moment* of a qualitatively homogeneous, general social mediation constituting *a social totality*.[86] This duality of the concrete and the abstract characterizes the capitalist social formation.

Having established the distinction between concrete labor and abstract labor, I can now modify what I said above about labor in general, and note that the constitution of the duality of the concrete and the abstract by the commodity form of social relations entails the constitution of two different sorts of generality. I have outlined the nature of the abstract general dimension, which is rooted in labor's function as a socially mediating activity: all forms of labor

---

85. Ibid., p. 125.
86. It should be noted that, this interpretation—as opposed to Sartre's, for example—does not presuppose the concepts of "moment" and "totality" ontologically; it does not claim that, in general, the whole should be grasped as being present in its parts: see Jean-Paul Sartre, *Critique of Dialectical Reason* (London, 1976), p. 45. Unlike Althusser, however, this interpretation does not ontologically reject these concepts: see Louis Althusser, *For Marx* (New York, 1970), pp. 202–204. Rather, it treats the relation of moment and totality as historically constituted, a function of the peculiar properties of the social forms analyzed by Marx with his categories of value, abstract labor, commodity, and capital.

and labor products are rendered equivalent. This social function of labor, however, also establishes another form of commonality among the particular sorts of labor and labor products—it entails their de facto classification as labor and as labor products. Because any particular sort of labor can function as abstract labor and any labor product can serve as a commodity, activities and products that, in other societies, might not be classified as similar *are* classified in capitalism as similar, as varieties of (concrete) labor or as particular use values. In other words, the abstract generality historically constituted by abstract labor also establishes "concrete labor" and "use value" as general categories; but this generality is that of a heterogeneous whole, made up of particulars, rather than that of a homogeneous totality. This distinction between these two forms of generality, of the totality and the whole, must be kept in mind in considering the dialectic of historically constituted forms of generality and particularity in capitalist society.

Society is not simply a collection of individuals; it is made up of social relations. Central to Marx's analysis is the argument that the relations that characterize capitalist society are very different from the forms of overt social relations—such as kinship relations or relations of personal or direct domination—that characterize noncapitalist societies. The latter sorts of relations are not only manifestly social, they are qualitatively particular; no single, abstract, homogeneous sort of relation underlies every aspect of social life.

According to Marx, though, the case is different with capitalism. Overt and direct social relations do continue to exist, but capitalist society is ultimately structured by a new, underlying level of social interrelatedness which cannot be grasped adequately in terms of the overtly social relations among people or groups—including classes.[87] The Marxian theory does, of course, include an analysis of class exploitation and domination, but it goes beyond investigating the unequal distribution of wealth and power within capitalism to grasp the very nature of its social fabric, its peculiar form of wealth, and its intrinsic form of domination.

What renders the fabric of that underlying social structure so peculiar, for Marx, is that it is constituted by labor, by the historically specific quality of labor in capitalism. Hence, the social relations specific to, and characteristic of, capitalism exist only in the medium of labor. Since labor is an activity that necessarily objectifies itself in products, commodity-determined labor's function as a socially mediating activity is inextricably intertwined with the act of objectification: commodity-producing labor, in the process of objectifying itself as concrete labor in particular use values, also objectifies itself as abstract labor in social relations.

87. While class analysis remains basic to the Marxian critical project, the analysis of value, surplus value, and capital as social forms cannot be fully grasped in terms of class categories. A Marxist analysis that remains limited to considerations of class entails a serious sociological reduction of the Marxian critique.

According to Marx, then, one hallmark of modern, or capitalist society is that, because the social relations that essentially characterize this society are constituted by labor, they exist only in objectified form. They have a peculiar objective and formal character, are not overtly social, and are characterized by the totalizing antinomic duality of the concrete and the abstract, the particular and the homogeneously general. The social relations constituted by commodity-determined labor do not bind people to one another in an overtly social fashion; rather, labor constitutes a sphere of objectified social relations which has an apparently nonsocial and objective character and, as we shall see, is separate from, and opposed to, the social aggregate of individuals and their immediate relations.[88] Because the social sphere that characterizes the capitalist formation is objectified, it cannot be grasped adequately in terms of concrete social relations.

Corresponding to the two forms of labor objectified in the commodity are two forms of social wealth: value and material wealth. Material wealth is a function of the products produced, of their quantity and quality. As a form of wealth, it expresses the objectification of various sorts of labor, the active relation of humanity to nature. Taken by itself, however, it neither constitutes relations among people nor determines its own distribution. The existence of material wealth as the dominant form of social wealth implies, therefore, the existence of overt forms of social relations that mediate it.

Value, on the other hand, is the objectification of abstract labor. It is, in Marx's analysis, a self-distributing form of wealth: the distribution of commodities is effected by what seems to be inherent to them—value. Value is, then, a category of mediation: it is at once a historically determinate, self-distributing form of wealth and an objectified, self-mediating form of social relations. Its measure, as we shall see, is very different from that of material wealth. Moreover, as noted, value is a category of the social totality: the value of a commodity is an individuated moment of the objectified general social mediation. Because it exists in objectified form, this social mediation has an objective character, is not overtly social, is abstracted from all particularity, and is independent of directly personal relations. A social bond results from the function of labor as a social mediation, which, because of these qualities, does not depend on immediate social interactions but can function at a spatial and temporal distance. As the objectified form of abstract labor, value is an essential category of capitalist relations of production.

The commodity, which Marx analyzed as both use value and value, is thus the material objectification of the double character of labor in capitalism—as concrete labor and as a socially mediating activity. It is the fundamental structuring principle of capitalism, the objectified form of both the relations of people with nature as well as with each other. The commodity is both a product and a

---

88. *Grundrisse*, pp. 157–62.

social mediation. It is not a use value that *has* value but, as the materialized objectification of concrete and abstract labor, it is a use value that *is* a value and, therefore, has exchange value. This simultaneity of substantial and abstract dimensions in the form of labor and its products is the basis of the various antinomic oppositions of capitalism and, as I shall show, underlies its dialectical and, ultimately, contradictory character. In its double-sidedness as concrete and abstract, qualitatively particular and qualitatively general-homogeneous, the commodity is the most elementary expression of capitalism's fundamental character. As an object, the commodity *has* a material form; as a social mediation, it *is* a social form.

Having considered the very first determinations of Marx's critical categories, it should be noted here that his analysis in Volume 1 of *Capital* of the commodity, value, capital, and surplus value does not sharply distinguish "micro" and "macro" levels of investigation, but analyzes structured forms of practice on the level of society as a whole. This level of social analysis, of the fundamental forms of social mediation that characterize capitalism, also allows for a sociohistorical theory of forms of subjectivity. This theory is nonfunctionalist and does not attempt to ground thought merely with reference to social position and social interests. Rather, it analyzes thought or, more broadly, subjectivity, in terms of historically specific forms of social mediation, that is, in terms of determinately structured forms of everyday practice that constitute the social world.[89] Even a form of thought such as philosophy, which seems very far removed from immediate social life, can, within this framework, be analyzed as socially and culturally constituted, in the sense that this mode of thought itself can be understood with reference to historically determinate social forms.

89. In this work, I shall begin to outline aspects of the subjective dimension of Marx's theory of the constitution of modern social life by determinate structured forms of social practice, but I shall not address issues of the possible role of language in the social constitution of subjectivity—whether in the form of the (Sapir-Whorf) linguistic relativity hypothesis, for example, or discourse theory. For attempts to relate culturally specific forms of thought to linguistic forms, see Edward Sapir, *Language* (New York, 1921), and Benjamin L. Whorf, *Language, Thought and Reality* (Cambridge, Mass., 1956). The notion that language does not simply transport preexisting ideas but codetermines subjectivity can be brought together with social and historical analyses only on the basis of theories of language and society which allow for such mediation in the way they conceive of their objects. My intention here is first to explicate a social-theoretical approach that focuses on the form of social mediation rather than on social groups, material interests, and so on. Such an approach could serve as one starting point for considering the relation of society and culture in the modern world in a way that moves beyond the classical opposition of materialism and idealism—an opposition that has been recapitulated between economistic or sociologistic theories of society and idealist theories of discourse and language. A resultant social theory could be more intrinsically capable than more conventionally "materialist" approaches of addressing issues raised by linguistically oriented theories. It also implicitly demands of theories of the relation of language and subjectivity that they acknowledge and be intrinsically capable of addressing issues of historical specificity and large-scale ongoing social transformations.

As I have suggested, Marx's unfolding of the categories of his critique can also be read as an immanent metacommentary on the social constitution of philosophical thought in general, and Hegel's philosophy in particular. For Hegel, the Absolute, the totality of the subjective-objective categories, grounds itself. As the self-moving "substance" that is "Subject," it is the true *causa sui* as well as the endpoint of its own development. In *Capital,* Marx presents the underlying forms of commodity-determined society as constituting the social context for notions such as the difference between essence and appearance, the philosophical concept of substance, the dichotomy of subject and object, the notion of totality, and, on the logical level of the category of capital, the unfolding dialectic of the identical subject-object.[90] His analysis of the double character of labor in capitalism, as a productive activity and as a social mediation, allows him to conceive of this labor as a nonmetaphysical, historically specific "*causa sui.*" Because such labor mediates itself, it grounds itself (socially) and therefore has the attributes of "substance" in the philosophical sense. We have seen that Marx explicitly refers to the category of abstract human labor with the philosophical term "substance," and that it expresses the constitution of a social totality by labor. The social form is a totality because it is not a collection of various particularities but, rather, is constituted by a general and homogeneous "substance" that is its own ground. Since the totality is self-grounding, self-mediating, and objectified, it exists quasi-independently. As I shall show, on the logical level of the category of capital this totality becomes concrete and self-moving. Capitalism, as analyzed by Marx, is a form of social life with metaphysical attributes—those of the absolute Subject.

90. The rise of philosophy in Greece has been related by Alfred Sohn-Rethel, among others, to the development of coinage and the extension of the commodity form in the sixth and fifth centuries B.C.: see Alfred Sohn-Rethel, *Geistige und körperliche Arbeit* (Frankfurt, 1972); George Thomson, *The First Philosophers* (London, 1955); and R.W. Müller, *Geld und Geist* (Frankfurt, 1977). A revised version of Sohn-Rethel's book appeared in English as *Intellectual and Manual Labour: A Critique of Epistemology,* trans. Martin Sohn-Rethel (Atlantic Highlands, N.J., 1978.) Sohn-Rethel, however, does not distinguish between a situation such as that in fifth-century Attica, where commodity production was widespread but by no means the dominant form of production, and capitalism, a situation in which the commodity form is totalizing. He is, therefore, unable to ground socially the distinction, emphasized by Georg Lukács, between Greek philosophy and modern rationalism. The former, according to Lukács, "was no stranger to certain aspects of reification [but did not experience them] as universal forms of existence; it had one foot in the world of reification while the other remained in a 'natural' society." The latter was characterized by "its increasingly insistent claim that it has discovered the principle which connects up all phenomena which in nature and society are found to confront mankind" (*History and Class Consciousness,* trans. Rodney Livingstone [London, 1971], pp. 111, 113). Nevertheless, because of his assumptions regarding "labor" and, therefore, his affirmation of totality, Lukács himself is not sufficiently historical with regard to the capitalist epoch: he is unable to analyze Hegel's notion of the dialectical unfolding of the *Weltgeist* as an expression of the capitalist epoch; and he interprets it instead as an idealist version of a form of thought that *transcends* capitalism.

This does not mean that Marx treats social categories in a philosophical manner; rather, he treats philosophical categories with reference to the peculiar attributes of the social forms he analyzes. According to his approach, the attributes of the social categories are expressed in hypostatized form as philosophical categories. His analysis of the double character of labor in capitalism, for example, implicitly treats self-groundedness as an attribute of a historically specific social form rather than as the attribute of an Absolute. This suggests a historical interpretation of the tradition of philosophical thought that demands self-grounded first principles as its point of departure. The Marxian categories, like those of Hegel, grasp the constitution of subject and object with reference to the unfolding of an identical subject-object. In Marx's approach, however, the latter is determined in terms of the categorial forms of the social relations in capitalism, which are rooted in the duality of commodity-determined labor. What Hegel sought to grasp with his concept of the totality is, according to Marx, not absolute and eternal, but historically determinate. A *causa sui* does indeed exist, but it is social; and it is not the true endpoint of its own development. That is, there is no final end point: overcoming capitalism would entail the abolition—not the realization—of the "substance," of labor's role in constituting a social mediation, and, hence, the abolition of the totality.

To sum up: In Marx's mature works, the notion that labor is at the core of social life does not simply refer to the fact that material production is always a precondition of social life. Nor does it imply that production is the historically specific determining sphere of capitalist civilization—if production is understood only as the production of goods. In general, the sphere of production in capitalism should not be understood only in terms of the material interactions of humans with nature. While it is obviously true that the "metabolic" interactions with nature effected by labor is a precondition of existence in any society, what determines a society is also the nature of its social relations. Capitalism, according to Marx, is characterized by the fact that its fundamental social relations are constituted by labor. Labor in capitalism objectifies itself not only in material products—which is the case in all social formations—but in objectified social relations as well. By virtue of its double character, it constitutes as a totality an objective, quasi-natural societal sphere that cannot be reduced to the sum of direct social relations and, as we shall see, stands opposed to the aggregate of individuals and groups as an abstract Other. In other words, the double character of commodity-determined labor is such that the sphere of labor in capitalism mediates relations that, in other formations, exist as a sphere of overt social interaction. It thereby constitutes a quasi-objective social sphere. Its double character signifies that labor in capitalism has a socially synthetic character, which labor in other formations does not possess.[91] Labor as such does *not* constitute society per se; labor in capitalism, however, *does* constitute that society.

91. As I shall further elaborate, the analysis of the double character of commodity-producing labor

Abstract labor and alienation

We have seen that, according to Marx, the objective and general quality of capitalism's essential social relations are such that they constitute a totality. It can be unfolded from a single structuring form, the commodity. This argument is an important dimension of Marx's presentation in *Capital,* which attempts to reconstruct theoretically the central features of capitalist society from that basic form. Proceeding from the category of the commodity and the initial determination of labor as a social mediation, Marx then develops further determinations of the capitalist totality by unfolding the categories of money and capital. In the process, he shows that the labor-mediated form of social relations characteristic of capitalism does not simply constitute a social matrix within which individuals are located and related to one another; rather, the mediation, initially analyzed as a means (of acquiring others' products), acquires a life of its own, independent, as it were, of the individuals that it mediates. It develops into a sort of objective system over and against the individuals, and it increasingly determines the goals and means of human activity.[92]

It is important to note that Marx's analysis does not ontologically presuppose the existence of this social "system" in a conceptually reified manner. Rather, as I have shown, it grounds the systemlike quality of the fundamental structures of modern life in determinate forms of social practice. The social relations that fundamentally define capitalism are "objective" in character and constitute a "system," because they are constituted by labor as a historically specific socially mediating activity, that is, by an abstract, homogeneous, and objectifying form of practice. Social action is conditioned, in turn, by the forms of appearance of these fundamental structures, by the way in which these social relations are manifest to and shape immediate experience. Marx's critical theory, in other words, entails a complex analysis of the reciprocal constitution of system and action in capitalist society which does not posit the transhistorical existence of that very opposition—between system and action—but grounds it and each of its terms in the determinate forms of modern social life.

The system constituted by abstract labor embodies a new form of social domination. It exerts a form of social compulsion whose impersonal, abstract, and

shows that *both* positions in the debate initiated by Habermas's *Knowledge and Human Interests* (trans. Jeremy Shapiro [Boston, 1971])—that is, on whether labor is a social category sufficiently synthetic to fulfill all that Marx demanded of it, or whether the sphere of labor must be supplemented conceptually by a sphere of interaction—deal with labor as "labor" in an undifferentiated transhistorical fashion, rather than with the specific and historically unique synthetic structure of labor in capitalism, as analyzed in the critique of political economy.

92. In this work, I shall not address the question of the relationship between the constitution of capitalist society as a social totality with an intrinsic historical dynamic and the growing differentiation of various spheres of social life that characterizes that society. For one approach to this problem, see Georg Lukács, "The Changing Function of Historical Materialism," in *History and Class Consciousness,* esp. p. 229ff.

objective character is historically new. The initial determination of such abstract social compulsion is that individuals are compelled to produce and exchange commodities in order to survive. This compulsion exerted is not a function of direct social domination, as is the case, for example, with slave or serf labor; it is, rather, a function of "abstract" and "objective" social structures, and represents a form of *abstract, impersonal domination.* Ultimately, this form of domination is not grounded in any person, class or institution; its ultimate locus is the pervasive structuring social forms of capitalist society that are constituted by determinate forms of social practice.[93] Society, as the quasi-independent, abstract, universal Other that stands opposed to the individuals and exerts an impersonal compulsion on them, is constituted as an alienated structure by the double character of labor in capitalism. The category of value, as the basic category of capitalist relations of production, is also the initial determination of alienated social structures. Capitalist social relations and alienated structures are identical.[94]

It is well known that, in his early writings, Marx maintains that labor objectifying itself in products need not be alienating, and criticizes Hegel for not having distinguished between alienation and objectification.[95] Yet how one conceptualizes the relation of alienation and objectification depends on how one understands labor. If one proceeds from a transhistorical notion of "labor," the difference between objectification and alienation necessarily must be grounded in factors *extrinsic* to the objectifying activity—for example, in property relations, that is, in whether the immediate producers are able to dispose of their own labor and its products, or whether the capitalist class appropriates them. Such a notion of alienated labor does not adequately grasp the sort of socially constituted abstract necessity I have begun to analyze. In Marx's later writings, however, alienation is rooted in the double character of commodity-determined labor, and as such, is *intrinsic* to the character of that labor itself. Its function as a socially mediating activity is externalized as an independent, abstract social sphere that exerts a form of impersonal compulsion on the people who constitute it. Labor in capitalism gives rise to a social structure that dominates it. This form of self-generated reflexive domination is alienation.

Such an analysis of alienation implies another understanding of the difference between objectification and alienation. This difference, in Marx's mature works,

93. This analysis of the form of domination entailed by the social forms of commodity and capital in Marx's theory provides a different approach to the sort of impersonal, intrinsic, and pervasive form of power Michel Foucault sees as characteristic of modern Western societies. See *Discipline and Punish: The Birth of the Prison,* trans. Alan Sheridan (New York, 1977).

94. In his sophisticated and extensive study of the notion of alienation as a central structuring principle of Marx's critique, Bertell Ollman also has interpreted the category of value as one that grasps capitalist social relations as relations of alienation. See *Alienation* (2d ed., Cambridge, 1976), pp. 157, 176.

95. Marx, *Economic and Philosophic Manuscripts of 1844,* in Karl Marx and Frederick Engels, *Collected Works,* vol. 3: *Marx and Engels: 1843–44* (New York, 1975), pp. 329–35, 338–46.

is not a function of what occurs to concrete labor and its products; rather, his analysis shows that *objectification is indeed alienation—if what labor objectifies are social relations.* This identity, however, is historically determinate: it is a function of the specific nature of labor in capitalism. Hence, the possibility exists that it could be overcome.

Thus, once again, it is clear that Marx's mature critique succeeds in grasping the "rational core" of Hegel's position—in this case that objectification *is* alienation—by analyzing the specificity of labor in capitalism. I noted earlier that a "materialist transformation" of Hegel's thought on the basis of an historically undifferentiated notion of "labor" can apprehend socially Hegel's conception of the historical Subject only in terms of a social grouping, but not in terms of a suprahuman structure of social relations. We now see that it also fails to grasp the intrinsic (albeit historically determinate) relation between alienation and objectification. In both cases, Marx's analysis of the double character of labor in capitalism permits a more adequate social appropriation of Hegel's thought.[96]

Alienated labor, then, constitutes a social structure of abstract domination, but such labor should not necessarily be equated with toil, oppression, or exploitation. The labor of a serf, a portion of which "belongs to" the feudal lord, is, in and of itself, not alienated: the domination and exploitation of that labor is not intrinsic to the labor itself. It is precisely for this reason that expropriation in such a situation *was and had to be* based upon direct compulsion. Nonalienated labor in societies in which a surplus exists and is expropriated by nonlaboring classes necessarily is bound to direct social domination. By contrast, exploitation and domination are integral moments of commodity-determined labor.[97] Even the labor of an independent commodity producer is alienated, if not to the same degree as that of an industrial worker, because social compulsion is effected abstractly, as a result of the social relations objectified by labor when it functions as a socially mediating activity.

96. Marx's discussion of alienated labor in the *Economic and Philosophic Manuscripts of 1844* indicates that he has not yet fully worked out the basis for his own analysis. On the one hand, he explicitly states that alienated labor is at the core of capitalism, and is not based on private property, but that, on the contrary, private property is the product of alienated labor (pp. 279–280). On the other hand, he has not yet clearly worked out a conception of the specificity of labor in capitalism and, hence, cannot really ground that argument: his argument regarding alienation is only fully worked out later, on the basis of his conception of the twofold character of labor in capitalism. This conception, in turn, modifies his notion of alienation itself.

97. Giddens notes that in precapitalist, "class-divided" societies, the dominated classes do not need the dominant class in order to carry on the process of production, but that in capitalism the worker does need an employer to gain a livelihood: see *A Contemporary Critique of Historical Materialism* (London and Basingstoke, 1981), p. 130. This describes a very important dimension of the specificity of the domination of labor in capitalism. My intention in this work, however, is to delineate another dimension of this specificity, that of the domination of labor *by* labor. This form can be overlooked when one focuses only on the ownership of the means of production.

The abstract domination and the exploitation of labor characteristic of capitalism are grounded, ultimately, not in the appropriation of the surplus by the nonlaboring classes, but in the form of labor in capitalism.

The structure of abstract domination constituted by labor acting as a socially mediating activity does not appear to be socially constituted; rather, it appears in naturalized form. Its social and historical specificity is veiled by several factors. The form of social necessity exerted—of which I have only discussed the first determination—exists in the absence of any direct, personal, social domination. Because the compulsion exerted is impersonal and "objective," it seems not to be social at all but "natural," and, as I shall explain later, conditions social conceptions of natural reality. This structure is such that one's own needs, rather than the threat of force or other social sanctions, appear to be the source of such necessity.

This naturalization of abstract domination is reinforced by the overlapping of two very different sorts of necessity associated with social labor. Labor in some form is a necessary precondition—a transhistorical or *"natural"* social necessity—of human social existence as such. This necessity can veil the specificity of commodity-producing labor—that, although one does not consume what one produces, one's labor is nevertheless the necessary social means of obtaining products to consume. The latter necessity is a *historically determinate social necessity*. (The distinction between these two sorts of necessity is important for understanding Marx's conception of freedom in postcapitalist society, as will become clear.) Because the specific social mediating role played by commodity-producing labor is veiled, and such labor appears as labor per se, these two sorts of necessity are conflated in the form of an apparently valid transhistorical necessity: one must labor to survive. Hence, a form of social necessity specific to capitalism appears as the "natural order of things." This apparently transhistorical necessity—that the individual's labor is the necessary means to their (or their family's) consumption—serves as the basis for a fundamental legitimating ideology of the capitalist social formation as a whole, throughout its various phases. As an affirmation of capitalism's most basic structure, such an ideology of legitimation is more fundamental than those that are more closely tied to specific phases of capitalism—for example, those related to the market-mediated exchange of equivalents.

Marx's analysis of the specificity of labor in capitalism has further implications for his conception of alienation. The meaning of alienation varies considerably depending upon whether one considers it in the context of a theory based on the notion of "labor" or in the context of an analysis of the duality of labor in capitalism. In the former case, alienation becomes a concept of a philosophical anthropology; it refers to the externalization of a preexisting human essence. On another level, it refers to a situation in which capitalists possess the power of disposal over the workers' labor and its products. Within the framework of such a critique, alienation is an unequivocally negative process—although it is grounded in circumstances that can be overcome.

In the interpretation presented here, alienation is the process of the objectification of abstract labor. It does not entail the externalization of a preexisting human essence; rather, it entails the coming into being of human powers in alienated form. In other words, alienation refers to a process of the historical constitution of human powers which is effected by labor objectifying itself as a socially mediating activity. Through this process, an abstract, objective social sphere emerges, which acquires a life of its own and exists as a structure of abstract domination over and against the individuals. Marx, in elucidating and grounding central aspects of capitalist society in terms of this process, evaluates its results as two-sided, rather than as unequivocally negative. So, for example, in *Capital* he analyzes the constitution by alienated labor of a universal social form that is both a structure in which human capacities are created historically *and* a structure of abstract domination. This alienated form induces a rapid accumulation of the social wealth and productive power of humanity, and it entails as well the increasing fragmentation of labor, the formal regimentation of time, and the destruction of nature. The structures of abstract domination constituted by determinate forms of social practice give rise to a social process that lies beyond human control; yet they also give rise, in Marx's analysis, to the historical possibility that people could control what they had constituted socially in alienated form.

This two-sidedness of the process of alienation as a process of social constitution can also be seen in Marx's treatment of universality and equality. As noted, it has commonly been assumed that Marx's critique of capitalist society contrasts the values articulated in the bourgeois revolutions of the seventeenth and eighteenth centuries with the particularistic and inequitable underlying reality of capitalist society, or that he criticizes the universalistic forms of bourgeois civil society as serving to mask the particularistic interests of the bourgeoisie.[98] The Marxian theory, however, does not simply—and affirmatively—oppose the universal to the particular, nor does it dismiss the former as a mere sham; rather, as a theory of social constitution, it examines critically and grounds socially the character of modern universality and equality. According to Marx's analysis, the universal is not a transcendent idea but is historically constituted with the development and consolidation of the commodity-determined form of social relations. What emerges historically is not, however, the universal per se but a specific universal form, one that is related to the social forms of which it is a part. Thus in *Capital,* for example, Marx describes the spread and generalization of capitalist relations as a process that abstracts from the concrete specificities of various labors and, at the same time, reduces them

98. See, for example, Jean Cohen, *Class and Civil Society: The Limits of Marxian Critical Theory* (Amherst, Mass., 1982), pp. 145–46.

to their common denominator as human labor.[99] This universalizing process, according to Marx, constitutes the sociohistorical precondition for the emergence of a popular notion of human equality upon which, in turn, modern theories of political economy are based.[100] In other words, the modern idea of equality is rooted in a social form of equality that has arisen historically concomitantly with the development of the commodity form—that is, with the process of alienation.

This historically constituted form of equality has a double-sided character. On the one hand, it is universal: It establishes commonality among people, but it does so in a form abstracted from the qualitative specificity of particular individuals or groups. An opposition of the universal to the particular arises which is grounded in a historical process of alienation. The universality and equality constituted thus have had positive political and social consequences; but because they entail a negation of specificity, they also have had negative results. There are many examples of the ambiguous consequences of this opposition. For example, the history of the Jews in Europe following the French Revolution can, on one level, be seen as that of a group caught between an abstract form of universalism, which allows for the emancipation of people only qua abstract individuals, and its concrete, antiuniversalistic antithesis, whereby people and groups are identified particularistically and judged—for example, in a hierarchical, exclusionary, or Manichaean manner.

This opposition between the abstract universality of the Enlightenment and particularistic specificity should not be understood in a decontextualized fashion; it is a historically constituted opposition, rooted in the determinate social forms of capitalism. To regard abstract universality, in its opposition to concrete specificity, as an ideal that can only be realized in a postcapitalist society, is to remain bound within the framework of an opposition characteristic of that society.

The form of domination related to this abstract form of the universal is not merely a class relation concealed by a universalistic facade. Rather, the domination Marx analyzes is that of a specific, historically constituted form of universalism itself, which he tries to grasp with his categories of value and capital. The social framework he analyzes thus is also characterized by the historically constituted opposition of the abstract social sphere and individuals. In commodity-determined society, the modern individual is historically constituted—a person independent of personal relations of domination, obligation, and dependence who no longer is embedded overtly in a quasi-natural fixed social position and so, in a sense, is self-determining. Yet this "free" individual is confronted by a social universe of abstract objective constraints that function in a lawlike fashion. In Marx's terms, from a precapitalist context marked by relations of

99. *Capital*, vol. 1, pp. 159–60.
100. Ibid., p. 152.

personal dependence a new one emerged characterized by individual personal freedom within a social framework of "objective dependence."[101] The modern opposition between the free, self-determining individual and an extrinsic sphere of objective necessity is, according to Marx's analysis, a "real" opposition that is historically constituted with the rise and spread of the commodity-determined form of social relations, and is related to the more general constituted opposition between a world of subjects and a world of objects. This opposition, however, is not solely one between individuals and their alienated social context: it also can be seen as one within the individuals themselves or, better, as one between different determinations of individuals in modern society. These individuals are not only self-determining "subjects," acting on the basis of will; they are also subjected to a system of objective compulsions and constraints that operates independent of their will—and in this sense, are also "objects." Like the commodity, the individual constituted in capitalist society has a dual character.[102]

The Marxian critique, then, does not simply "expose" the values and institutions of modern civil society as a facade that masks class relations, but grounds them with reference to the categorially grasped social forms. The critique calls for neither the implementation nor the abolition of the ideals of bourgeois society;[103] and it points neither to the realization of the abstract homogeneous universality of the existent formation nor to the abolition of universality. Instead, it elucidates as socially grounded the opposition of abstract universalism and particularistic specificity in terms of determinate forms of social relations—and as we shall see, it is their development that points to the possibility of another form of universalism, one not based upon an abstraction from all concrete specificity. With the overcoming of capitalism, the unity of society already constituted in alienated form could then be effected differently, by forms of political practice, in a way that need not negate qualitative specificity.

(It would be possible, in light of this approach, to interpret some strains within recent social movements—notably, among women and various minorities—as efforts to move beyond the antinomy, associated with the social form of the commodity, of an abstract, homogeneous universalism and a form of particularism that excludes universality. An adequate analysis of such movements should, of course, be historical: it should be able to relate them to developments of the underlying social forms in a way that accounts for the historical emergence of such attempts to surpass this antinomy that characterizes capitalism.)

There is a conceptual parallel between Marx's implicit critique of historically constituted abstract universality and his analysis of industrial production as in-

---

101. *Grundrisse,* p. 158.
102. The Marxian framework, then, implies an approach to the problem of the subject/object nature of the individual in modern society different from that developed by Michel Foucault in his extensive discussion of modern "Man" as an empiricotranscendental doublet. See *The Order of Things* (New York, 1973), pp. 318ff.
103. *Grundrisse,* pp. 248–49.

trinsically capitalist. As I noted in discussing the *Grundrisse,* overcoming capitalism, for Marx, would entail neither a new mode of distribution based on the same industrial mode of production nor the abolition of the productive potential developed in the course of the past centuries. Rather, the form as well as the goal of production in socialism would be different. In its analysis both of universality and of the process of production, then, the Marxian critique avoids hypostatizing the existent form and positing it as the sine qua non of a future free society, while also avoiding the notion that what was constituted in capitalism will be completely abolished in socialism. The two-sided quality of the process of alienation signifies, in other words, that its overcoming entails the appropriation by people—rather than the simple abolition—of what had been socially constituted in alienated form. The Marxian critique differs from both abstract rationalist and romantic critiques of capitalism in this regard.

The process of alienation in Marx's later works, then, is integral to a process by which structured forms of practice historically constitute the basic social forms, forms of thought, and cultural values of capitalist society. The notion that values are historically constituted should not, of course, be taken as an argument that because they are not eternal, they are a sham or merely conventional and without validity. A self-reflexive theory of the ways in which forms of social life are constituted must move beyond such an opposition of abstract absolutist and abstract relativist approaches, both of which suggest that humans can somehow act and think outside of their social universes.

According to Marx's theory of capitalist society, that the social relations constituted in alienated form by labor undermine and transform earlier social forms, indicates that those earlier forms are also constituted. Nevertheless, one should differentiate between the sorts of social constitution involved. People in capitalism constitute their social relations and their history by means of labor. Although they also are controlled by what they have constituted, they "make" these relations and this history in a different and more emphatic sense than people "make" precapitalist relations (which Marx characterizes as spontaneously arisen and quasi-natural [*naturwüchsig*]). If one were to relate Marx's critical theory and Vico's dictum that people can know history, which they have made, better than they can know nature, which they have not,[104] one should do so in a manner that distinguishes between "making" capitalist society and precapitalist societies. The alienated, labor-mediated mode of social constitution not only weakens traditional social forms, but does so in a way that introduces a new sort of social context characterized by a form of distance between individuals and society that allows for—and perhaps induces—social reflection on, and analysis of, society as a whole.[105] Because of the intrinsic dynamic logic of

104. See, for example, Martin Jay, *Marxism and Totality* (Berkeley and Los Angeles, 1984), pp. 32–37.
105. In this sense, one could argue that the rise and spread of the commodity form is related to the transformation and partial supersession of what Bourdieu calls "the field of doxa," which

capitalism, moreover, such reflection need not remain retrospective once the capital form is fully developed. By substituting an alienated, dynamic structure of "made" relations for traditional "quasi-natural" social forms, capitalism allows for the objective and subjective possibility that a still newer form of "made" relations be established, one no longer "automatically" constituted by labor.

Abstract labor and the fetish

I can now turn to address the problem of why Marx presents abstract labor as physiological labor in his immanent analysis. We have seen that labor, in its historically determinate function as a socially mediating activity, is the "substance of value," the determining essence of the social formation. It is by no means self-evident to speak of the essence of a social formation. The category of essence presupposes the category of form of appearance. It is not meaningful to speak of an essence where no difference exists between what is and the way it appears. What characterizes an essence, then, is that it does not and cannot directly appear, but must find expression in a distinct form of appearance. This implies a *necessary* relation between essence and appearance; the essence must be of such a quality that it necessarily appears in the manifest form that it does. Marx's analysis of the relation of value to price, for example, is one of how the former is expressed and veiled by the latter. My concern here is with a prior logical level—that of labor and value.

We have seen that labor constitutes social relations in capitalism. Labor, however, is an objectifying social activity that mediates between humans and nature. It necessarily is as such an objectifying activity, then, that labor effects its function in capitalism as a socially mediating activity. Labor's specific social role in capitalism, therefore, must *necessarily* be expressed in forms of appearance that are the objectifications of labor as a productive activity. The historically specific social dimension of labor, however, is both expressed and veiled by labor's apparently transhistorical "material" dimension. Such manifest forms are necessary forms of appearance of labor's unique function in capitalism. In other societies, laboring activities are embedded within an overt social matrix and, hence, are neither "essences" nor "forms of appearance." It is labor's unique role in capitalism that constitutes labor both as an essence and as a form of appearance. In other words, because the social relations characterizing capitalism are mediated by labor, it is a peculiarity of that social formation that it has an essence.

"Essence" is an ontological determination. The essence I am considering

he characterizes as "a quasi-perfect correspondence between the objective order and the subjective principles of organization (as in ancient societies) [whereby] the natural and social world appears as self-evident" (*Outline of a Theory of Practice*, p. 164).

here, however, is historical—a historically specific social function of labor. Yet this historical specificity is not apparent. We have seen that the social relations mediated by labor are self-grounding, have an essence, and appear not to be social at all but objective and transhistorical. They appear, in other words, to be ontological. Marx's immanent analysis is *not* a critique from the standpoint of a social ontology; rather, it provides a critique of such a position by indicating that what seems to be ontological is actually historically specific to capitalism.

Earlier in this work I examined critically those positions that interpret the specificity of labor in capitalism to be its indirect character and formulate a social critique from the standpoint of "labor." It is clear now that such positions take the ontological appearance of the basic social forms of capitalism at "face value," for labor is a social essence only in capitalism. That social order cannot be historically overcome without abolishing the essence itself, that is, the historically specific function and form of labor. A noncapitalist society is not constituted by labor alone.

Positions that do not grasp the particular function of labor in capitalism, attribute to labor as such a socially synthetic character: They treat it as the transhistorical essence of social life. Why labor as "labor" should constitute social relations cannot, however, be explained. Moreover, the relationship we have just examined, between appearance and essence, cannot be elucidated by such critiques from the standpoint of "labor." As we have seen, such interpretations postulate a separation between forms of appearance which are historically variable (value as a market category) and a historically invariable essence ("labor"). According to such positions, while all societies are constituted by "labor," a noncapitalist society would presumably be directly and overtly so constituted. In Chapter Two, I argued that social relations can *never* be direct, unmediated. At this point, I can supplement that criticism by noting that social relations constituted by labor can never be overtly social, but necessarily must exist in objectified form. By hypostatizing the essence of capitalism as the essence of human society, traditional positions cannot explain the intrinsic relation of the essence to its forms of appearance and, therefore, cannot consider that a hallmark of capitalism may be that it has an essence.

The misinterpretation just outlined is certainly understandable, for it is a possibility immanent to the form under consideration. We have just seen that value is an objectification not of labor per se but of a historically specific function of labor. Labor does not play such a role in other social formations, or does so only marginally. It follows, then, that the function of labor in constituting a social mediation is not an intrinsic attribute of labor itself; it is not rooted in any characteristic of human labor as such. The problem, however, is that when the analysis proceeds from an examination of commodities in order to uncover what constitutes their value, it can come upon labor—but not its mediating function. This specific function does not, and cannot, appear as an attribute of labor; nor can it be uncovered by examining labor as a productive activity, because what we term labor is a productive activity in all social formations. Labor's unique social function in capitalism cannot appear directly as an attribute of labor, for labor, in and of itself, is not a socially mediating activity; only an overt social relation can appear as such. The historically specific function of labor can only appear objectified, as value in its various forms (commodity, money, capital).[106] It is, therefore, impossible to uncover a manifest form of labor as a socially mediating activity by looking *behind* the form—value—in which it is *necessarily* objectified, a form that itself can only appear materialized as the commodity, money, and so on. Labor, of course, does appear—but the form of its appearance is not as a social mediation, but simply as "labor" itself.

One cannot discover the function of labor as constituting a medium of social relations by examining labor itself; one must investigate its objectifications. This is why Marx began his presentation not with labor but with the commodity, the most basic objectification of capitalist social relations.[107] However, even in the investigation of the commodity as a social mediation, appearances can deceive. As we have seen, a commodity is a good and an objectified social mediation. As a use value, or good, the commodity is particular, the objectification of a particular concrete labor; as a value, the commodity is general, the objectification of abstract labor. Commodities, however, *cannot* simultaneously fulfill both determinations: They cannot function as particular goods and a general mediation at once.

This implies that the general character of each commodity as a social mediation must have a form of expression that is separate from the particular character of each commodity. This is the starting point for Marx's analysis of the value form, leading to his analysis of money.[108] The existence of each commodity as a general mediation acquires an independent materialized form as an equivalent among commodities. The value dimension of all commodities becomes externalized in the form of one commodity—money—which acts as a universal equivalent among all other commodities: it appears as the universal mediation. Thus, the duality of the commodity as a use value and as a value becomes externalized and appears in the form of the commodity, on the one hand, and money, on the other. As a result of this externalization, however, the commodity does not appear to be a social mediation itself. Instead, it appears as a pure "thingly" object, a good, which is socially mediated by money. By the same token, money does not appear as a materialized externalization of the abstract, general dimension of the commodity (and of labor)—that is, as an expression of a determinate form of social mediation—but as a universal

106. According to Marx's analysis of price and profit, even the value level of objectified appearances is overlaid with a more superficial level of appearances.
107. Marx, "Marginal Notes on Adolf Wagner's *Lehrbuch der politischen Ökonomie*," in Karl Marx and Frederick Engels, *Collected Works*, vol. 24: *Marx and Engels: 1874–83* (New York, 1975), pp. 544–45.
108. *Capital*, vol. 1, pp. 137–63.

mediation in and of itself, one that is external to social relations. The object-mediated character of social relations in capitalism, then, is expressed and veiled by its manifest form as an externalized mediation (money) among objects; the existence of that mediation can then be taken to be a result of convention.[109]

The appearance of the commodity simply as a good or a product conditions, in turn, conceptions of value and value-creating labor. That is, the commodity seems not to *be* a value, a social mediation, but rather a use value that *has* exchange value. It is no longer apparent that value is a particular form of wealth, an objectified social mediation, which is materialized in the commodity. Just as the commodity appears to be a good that is mediated by money, value then appears to be (transhistorical) wealth that, in capitalism, is distributed by the market. This displaces the analytic problem from one of the nature of social mediation in capitalism to one of the determinations of exchange ratios. One can then argue whether the ratios of exchange are ultimately determined by factors extrinsic to the commodities, or whether they are intrinsically determined, for example, by the relative amount of labor that went into their production. In either case, however, the specificity of the social form—that value is an objectified social mediation—will have become blurred.

If value is taken to be wealth mediated by the market, and it is assumed that that wealth is constituted by labor, then value-constituting labor seems simply to be wealth-creating labor in a situation where its products are exchanged. In other words, if, as a result of their manifest forms, the determinate nature of the basic social forms of capitalism is not grasped, then even if value is seen as a property of the commodity, it is not of the commodity as a social mediation but as a product. Consequently, value seems to be created by labor as productive activity—labor as it produces goods and material wealth—rather than by labor as a socially mediating activity. Since labor apparently creates value regardless of its concrete specificity, it then appears to do so simply by virtue of its capacity as productive activity in general. Value, then, seems to be constituted by the expenditure of labor per se. To the extent that value is considered to be historically specific, it is as a form of distribution of that which is constituted by the expenditure of "labor."

The peculiar social function of labor, which renders its indeterminate expenditure constitutive of value, cannot, then, be uncovered directly. As I have argued, this function cannot be revealed by seeking it behind the form in which it necessarily is objectified; what one discovers, instead, is that value appears to be constituted by the mere expenditure of labor, without reference to the function of labor that renders it value-constituting. The difference between material wealth and value, which is rooted in the difference between labor mediated by social relations in noncapitalist societies, and labor mediated by labor itself

109. Ibid., pp. 188–243.

in capitalism, becomes indistinct. In other words, when the commodity appears to be a good with exchange value and, therefore, value appears to be market-mediated wealth, value-creating labor appears not to be a socially mediating activity but wealth-creating labor in general. Hence, labor seems to create value merely by virtue of its expenditure. Abstract labor thus appears in Marx's immanent analysis as that which "underlies" all forms of human labor in all societies: the expenditure of muscle, nerve, and so on.

I have shown how the social "essence" of capitalism is a historically specific function of labor as a medium of social relations. Yet, within the framework of Marx's mode of presentation—which is already immanent to the categorial forms and proceeds from the commodity to examine the source of its value—the category of abstract labor appears to be an expression of labor per se, of concrete labor in general. The historically specific "essence" of capitalism appears in the immanent analysis as a physiological, ontological essence, a form that is common to all societies: "labor." The category of abstract labor presented by Marx is thus an initial determination of what he explicates with his notion of the fetish: because the underlying relations of capitalism are mediated by labor, hence are objectified, they appear not to be historically specific and social but transhistorically valid and ontologically grounded forms. The appearance of labor's mediational character in capitalism as physiological labor is the fundamental core of the fetish of capitalism.

The fetishized appearance of labor's mediating role as labor in general, taken at face value, is the starting point for the various social critiques from the standpoint of "labor" I have termed "traditional Marxism." The possibility that the object of Marx's critique can be transformed into what traditional Marxism affirms with its "paradigm of production" is rooted in the circumstance that the core of capitalism, according to Marx, has a necessary form of appearance that can be hypostatized as the essence of social life. In this way, the Marxian theory points to a critique of the paradigm of production which is able to grasp its historical "rational core" in the social forms specific to capitalism.

This analysis of the category of abstract human labor is a specific elaboration of the immanent nature of Marx's critique. His physiological definition of this category is part of an analysis of capitalism *in its own terms,* that is, as the forms present themselves. The critique takes no standpoint outside of its object, but rests, instead, on the full unfolding of the categories and their contradictions. In terms of the self-understanding of the Marxian critique, the categories that grasp the forms of social relations are at once categories of social objectivity and subjectivity, and are themselves expressions of this social reality. They are not descriptive, that is, external to their object, hence, they do not exist in a contingent relation to it. It is precisely because of this immanent character that the Marxian critique can be so easily misunderstood, and that quotes and concepts torn out of context can so easily be used to construct a positive "science."[110] The traditional interpretation of Marx and a fetishized understanding of capitalism are parallel and interrelated.

The *Materie* in Marx's "materialist" critique, then, is social—the forms of social relations. Mediated by labor, the characterizing social dimension in capitalism can appear *only* in objectified form. By uncovering the historical and social content of the reified forms, the Marxian analysis becomes as well a critique of those varieties of materialism which hypostatize these forms of labor and its objects. His analysis provides a critique of both idealism and materialism by grounding each in historically specific, reified and alienated social relations.

Social relations, labor, and nature

The forms of social relations that characterize capitalism are not manifestly social and, thus, appear not to be social at all, but "natural" in a way that involves a very specific notion of nature. The forms of appearance of capitalist social relations not only condition understandings of the social world but, as the approach presented here suggests, of the natural world as well. In order to extend the discussion of the Marxian sociohistorical theory of subjectivity introduced above and to suggest an approach to the problem of the relation of conceptions of nature to their social contexts—which I shall only be able to touch upon here—I shall now examine further the quasi-objective character of capitalist relations by considering briefly the question of the meaning accorded labor and its objects.

For heuristic purposes, I shall proceed from the highly simplified comparison of traditional and capitalist social relations with which I began. As noted, in traditional societies, laboring activities and their products are mediated by, and embedded in, overt social relations, whereas in capitalism labor and its products mediate themselves. In a society where labor and its products are embedded in a matrix of social relations, they are informed, and accorded their social character, by those relations—yet the social character accorded various labors seems to be intrinsic to them. In such a situation, productive activity does not exist as a pure means, nor do tools and products appear as mere objects. Instead, informed by social relations, they are imbued with meanings and significances— whether manifestly social or quasi-sacred—that seem to be intrinsic to them.[111]

110. Cornelius Castoriadis, for example, overlooks the immanent nature of Marx's critique when he assumes that it is metaphysical and involves an ontologization of labor: see "From Marx to Aristotle," *Social Research* 45, no. 4, (Winter 1978), esp. pp. 669–84. Castoriadis implicitly reads Marx's negative critique as a positive science and then criticizes it on this basis; he does not consider the relation between Marx's categorial analysis and his notion of the commodity fetish, and imputes an implausible degree of inconsistency to Marx. He implies that, in one and the same chapter of *Capital,* Marx holds the very quasi-natural, nonhistorical position he analyzes critically in his discussion of the fetish.

111. See György Márkus's excellent discussion of the relation of direct, explicit norms, social structures, and objects and tools in precapitalist societies in "Die Welt menschlicher Objekte:

This entails a remarkable inversion. An activity, implement, or object that is *determined* nonconsciously by social relations appears, because of its resultant symbolic character, to possess a socially *determining* character. Within a rigidly traditional social framework, for example, the object or activity seems to embody and determine social position and gender definition.[112] Laboring activities in traditional societies do not simply appear as labor, but each form of labor is socially imbued and appears as a particular determination of social existence. Such forms of labor are very different from labor in capitalism: they cannot be understood adequately as instrumental action. Moreover, the social character of such labor should not be confused with what I have described as the specific social character of labor in capitalism. Labor in noncapitalist societies does not constitute society, for it does not possess the peculiar synthetic character that marks commodity-determined labor. Although social, it does not constitute social relations but is constituted by them. The social character of labor in traditional societies is, of course, seen as "natural." However, this notion of the natural—thus of nature as well—is very different from that in a society where the commodity form prevails. Nature in traditional societies is endowed with a character that is as "essentially" variegated, personalized, and nonrational as the social relations characterizing the society.[113]

As we have seen, labor in capitalism is not mediated by social relations but, rather, itself constitutes a social mediation. *If, in traditional societies, social relations impart meaning and significance to labor, in capitalism labor imparts an "objective" character to itself and to social relations.* This objective character is historically constituted when labor, which is accorded various specific meanings by overt social relations in other societies, mediates itself and thereby negates those meanings. In this sense, objectivity can be seen as the nonovertly social "meaning" that arises historically when objectifying social activity reflexively determines itself socially. Within the framework of this approach, then, social relations in traditional societies determine labors, implements, and objects that, inversely, appear to possess a socially determining character. In capitalism, labor and its products create a sphere of objective social relations: they are in fact socially determining but do not appear as such. Rather, they appear to be purely "material."

This latter inversion merits further examination. I have shown that the specific mediating role of labor in capitalism necessarily appears in objectified form and not directly as an attribute of labor. Instead, because labor in capitalism accords

Zum Problem der Konstitution im Marxismus," in Axel Honneth and Urs Jaeggi, eds., *Arbeit, Handlung, Normativität* (Frankfurt, 1980), esp. pp. 24–38.

112. Márkus, for example, mentions societies in which objects belonging to one group are not even touched by members of other groups—for example, the men's weapons are not to be touched by women and children (ibid., p. 31).

113. Lukács has suggested such an approach to conceptions of nature: see "Reification and the Consciousness of Proletariat," in *History and Class Consciousness*, p. 128.

its social character to itself, it appears simply as labor in general, stripped of the aura of social meaning accorded various labors in more traditional societies. Paradoxically, precisely because the social dimension of labor in capitalism is reflexively constituted, and is not an attribute accorded it by overt social relations, such labor does not appear to be the mediating activity it actually is in this social formation. It appears, rather, only as one of its dimensions, as concrete labor, a technical activity that can be applied and regulated socially in an instrumental fashion.

This process of the "objectification" of labor in capitalist society is also a process of the paradoxical "secularization" of the commodity as a social object. Although the commodity as an object does not acquire its social character as a result of social relations but, rather, is intrinsically a social object (in the sense of being a materialized social mediation), it appears to be a mere thing. As noted, although the commodity is simultaneously a use value and a value, the latter social dimension becomes externalized in the form of a universal equivalent, money. As a result of this "doubling" of the commodity into commodity and money, the latter appears as the objectification of the abstract dimension, whereas the former appears to be merely a thing. In other words, the fact that the commodity is itself a materialized social mediation implies the absence of overt social relations that imbue objects with a "suprathingly" (social or sacred) significance. As a mediation, the commodity is itself a "suprathingly" thing. The externalization of its mediational dimension results, therefore, in the appearance of the commodity as a *purely* material object.[114]

This "secularization" of labor and its products is a moment of the historical process of the dissolution and transformation of traditional social bonds by a social mediation with a dual—concrete-material and abstract-social—character. The precipitation of the former dimension proceeds apace with the construction of the latter. Hence, as we have seen, it is only apparently the case that with the overcoming of the determinations and limits associated with overt social relations and forms of domination, humans now freely dispose of their labor. Because labor in capitalism is not really free of nonconscious social determination, but itself has become the medium of such determination, people are

114. I shall not, on this abstract level of the analysis, address the question of the meaning accorded to use values in capitalism, other than to suggest that any examination of this question should take into account the very different relationships between objects (and labor) and social relations in capitalist and noncapitalist societies. It seems that objects are accorded significance in capitalism in a different sense than in traditional societies. Their meaning is not so much seen as intrinsic to them, an "essential" attribute; rather, they are "thingly" things that *have* meaning—they are like signs in the sense that no necessary relationship exists between the signifier and the signified. One could attempt to relate the differences between the "intrinsic" and the "contingent," "suprathingly" attributes of objects, as well as the historical development of the social importance of judgments of taste to the development of the commodity as the totalizing social form of capitalist society. This theme, however, cannot be treated in this work.

confronted with a new compulsion, one grounded in precisely that which overcame the compelling bonds of traditional social forms: the alienated, abstract social relations that are mediated by labor. These relations constitute a framework of "objective," apparently nonsocial constraints within which self-determining individuals pursue their interests—whereby "individuals" and "interests" seem to be ontologically given rather than socially constituted. That is, a new social context is constituted that appears neither to be social nor contextual. Put simply, *the form of social contextualization characteristic of capitalism is one of apparent decontextualization.*

(Overcoming nonconscious social compulsion in an emancipated society, then, would entail "freeing" secularized labor from its role as a social mediation. People could then dispose of labor and its products in a manner free from both traditional social limits and alienated objective social compulsions. On the other hand, labor, although secular, could once again be imbued with significance—not as a result of nonconscious tradition but because of its recognized social importance as well as the substantial satisfaction and meaning it could afford individuals.)

According to Marx's analysis of capitalism, then, the dual character of commodity-determined labor constitutes a social universe characterized by concrete and abstract dimensions. The former appears as the variegated surface of immediate sensuous experience, and the latter exists as general, homogeneous, and abstracted from all particularity—but both dimensions are accorded an objective character by the self-mediating quality of labor in capitalism. The concrete dimension is constituted as objective in the sense of being objectlike, "material" or "thingly." The abstract dimension also has an objective quality, in the sense of being a qualitatively homogeneous general sphere of abstract necessity that functions in a lawful manner, independent of will. The structure of social relations that characterize capitalism has the form of a quasi-natural opposition between "thingly" nature and abstract, universal, "objective" natural laws, an opposition from which the social and historical have vanished. The relation of these two worlds of objectivity can then be construed as that of essence and appearance, or as that of an opposition (as has been expressed historically, for example, in the opposition between romantic and positive-rational modes of thought).[115]

115. See M. Postone, "Anti-Semitism and National Socialism," in A. Rabinbach and J. Zipes, eds., *Germans and Jews Since the Holocaust* (New York and London, 1986), pp. 302–14, where I analyze modern anti-Semitism with reference to this quasi-natural opposition in capitalist society between a concrete "natural" sphere of social life and an abstract universal one. The opposition of its abstract and the concrete dimensions allows capitalism to be perceived and understood in terms of its abstract dimension alone; its concrete dimension can thereby be apprehended as noncapitalist. Modern anti-Semitism can be understood as a fetishized, one-sided form of anticapitalism that grasps capitalism in terms of its abstract dimension alone, and biologistically identifies that dimension with the Jews, and the concrete dimension of capitalism with the "Aryans."

There are many similarities between the characteristics of these social forms, as analyzed thus far, and those of nature as conceptualized by seventeenth-century natural science, for example. They suggest that when the commodity, as a structured form of social practice, becomes widespread, it conditions the way in which the world—natural as well as social—is conceived.

The world of commodities is one in which objects and actions are no longer imbued with sacred significance. It is a secular world of "thingly" objects bound together by, and revolving around, the glittering abstractum of money. It is, to use Weber's phrase, a disenchanted world. One could reasonably hypothesize that the practices that constitute and are constituted by such a social world could also generate a conception of nature as deanimated, secularized, and "thingly," one whose further characteristics, moreover, can be related to the particular character of the commodity as a concrete object and an abstract mediation. Dealing with commodities on an everyday level establishes a social commonality among goods as "thingly" and involves as well a continuous act of abstraction. Each commodity has not only its specific concrete qualities, measured in concrete material quantities, but all commodities share in common value, a nonmanifest abstract quality with (as we shall see) a temporally determined magnitude. The magnitude of their value is a function of abstract measure rather than of concrete material quantity. As a social form, the commodity is completely independent of its material content. This form is not, in other words, the form of qualitatively specific objects but is abstract and can be grasped mathematically. It possesses "formal" characteristics. Commodities are both particular, sensual objects (and are valued as such by the buyer) and values, moments of an abstractly homogeneous substance that is mathematically divisible and measurable (for example, in terms of time and money).

Similarly, in classical modern natural science, behind the concrete world of manifold qualitative appearances is a world consisting of a common substance in motion, which possesses "formal" qualities and can be grasped mathematically. Both levels are "secularized." That of the underlying essence of reality is an "objective" realm in the sense that it is independent of subjectivity and operates according to laws that can be grasped by reason. Just as the value of the commodity is abstracted from its qualities as a use value, true nature, according to Descartes, for example, consists in its "primary qualities," matter in motion, which can only be grasped by abstracting from the level of appearances of qualitative particularity ("secondary qualities"). The latter level is a function of the sense organs, the "eye of the beholder." Objectivity and subjectivity, mind and matter, form and content, are constituted as substantially different and opposed. Their possible correspondence now becomes an issue—they now must be mediated.[116]

---

116. As mentioned above, it is noteworthy in this regard that the form of Marx's initial "derivation" of value in its opposition to use value closely parallels Descartes's derivation of primary qualities in opposition to secondary qualities.

One could describe and analyze further the points of similarity between the commodity as a form of social relations and modern European conceptions of nature (such as its impersonal, lawlike mode of functioning). On this basis, one could then hypothesize that not only the paradigms of classical physics but also the emergence of a specific form and concept of Reason in the seventeenth and eighteenth centuries are related to the alienated structures of the commodity form. One could even try to relate changes in forms of thought in the nineteenth century to the dynamic character of the fully developed capital form. I do not, however, intend to pursue such an investigation at this point. This brief outline is intended merely to suggest that conceptions of nature and paradigms of natural science can be socially and historically grounded. Although, in discussing the problem of abstract time, I shall continue to examine certain epistemological implications of the categories, I cannot investigate more extensively in this work the relation of conceptions of nature to their social contexts. It should, however, be clear that what I have outlined here has very little in common with attempts to examine social influences on science in which the social is understood in an immediate sense—group or class interests, "priorities," and so on. Although such considerations are very important in examining the application of science, they cannot account for conceptions of nature or scientific paradigms themselves.

The nonfunctionalist sociohistorical theory of knowledge suggested by the Marxian critique maintains that the ways in which people perceive and conceive of the world in capitalist society is shaped by the forms of their social relations, understood as structured forms of everyday social practice. It has little in common with the "reflection" theory of knowledge. The emphasis on the *form* of social relations as an epistemological category also distinguishes the approach suggested here from attempts at a materialist explanation of the natural sciences such as those of Franz Borkenau and Henryk Grossmann. According to Borkenau, the rise of modern science, of "mathematical-mechanistic thought," was closely related to the emergence of the system of manufacture—the destruction of the artisanal system and the concentration of labor under one roof.[117] Borkenau does not attempt to explain the relationship he postulates between the natural sciences and manufacture in terms of utility; rather, he notes that science played a negligible role in the process of production during the period of manufacture, that is, until the emergence of large-scale industrial production. The relationship between production and science Borkenau postulates was indirect: he claims that the labor process developed in manufacture at the beginning of the seventeenth century served as a model of reality for natural philosophers. That labor process was characterized by an extreme detail-division of labor into relatively unskilled activities, giving rise to an underlying substratum of ho-

---

117. For the following summary, see Franz Borkenau, "Zur Soziologie des mechanistischen Welt-
    bildes," *Zeitschrift für Sozialforschung* 1 (1932), pp. 311–35.

mogeneous labor in general. This, in turn, allowed for the development of a conception of social labor and, hence, for the quantitative comparison of labor time units. Mechanistic thought, according to Borkenau, arose from the experience of a mechanistic organization of production.

Leaving aside Borkenau's attempt to derive the category of abstract labor directly from the organization of concrete labor, it is by no means clear why people should have begun to conceive of the world in terms similar to the organization of production in manufacture. In describing the social conflicts of the seventeenth century, Borkenau does point out that the new worldview was of advantage to those groupings associated with, and struggling for, the new emerging social, economic, and political order. Its ideological *function,* however, can hardly explain the *ground* of such a form of thought. A consideration of the structure of concrete labor, supplemented by one of social conflict, does not suffice as the basis of a sociohistorical epistemology.

Henryk Grossmann criticizes Borkenau's interpretation, but his criticisms are restricted to the empirical level.[118] Grossmann argues that the organization of production which Borkenau attributes to the period of manufacture actually came into being only with industrial production; in general, manufacture did not entail the breakdown and homogenization of labor, but brought together skilled artisans in one factory without appreciably changing their mode of labor. In addition, he claims that the emergence of mechanistic thought should not be sought in the seventeenth century, but earlier, with Leonardo da Vinci. Grossmann then suggests another explanation for the origins of such thought: it emerged from the practical activity of skilled handicraftsmen in inventing and producing new mechanical devices.

What Grossmann's hypothesis has in common with that of Borkenau is that it attempts to derive a form of thought directly from a consideration of labor as productive activity. Yet, as Alfred Sohn-Rethel points out in *Geistige und körperliche Arbeit,* Grossmann's approach is inadequate because, in his essay, the devices that supposedly give rise to mechanistic thought are already understood and explained in terms of the logic of such thought.[119] The origins of particular forms of thought must be sought on a deeper level, according to Sohn-Rethel. Like the interpretation outlined in this work, his approach is to analyze underlying structures of thought—for example, those which Kant posited ahistorically as transcendental *a priori* categories—in terms of their constitution by forms of social synthesis. However, Sohn-Rethel's understanding of social constitution differs from that presented in this work: he does not analyze the specificity of labor in capitalism as being socially constituting but, rather, posits two forms of social synthesis—one effected by means of exchange, and one by means of

118. See Henryk Grossmann, "Die gesellschaftlichen Grundlagen der mechanistischen Philosophie und die Manufaktur," *Zeitschrift für Sozialforschung,* 4 (1935), pp. 161–229.
119. Sohn-Rethel, *Geistige und körperliche Arbeit,* p. 85n20.

labor. He argues that the sort of abstraction and form of social synthesis entailed in the value form is not a labor abstraction but an exchange abstraction.[120] According to Sohn-Rethel, there is a labor abstraction in capitalism but it occurs in the process of production rather than in the exchange process.[121] Sohn-Rethel, however, does not relate the notion of labor abstraction to the creation of alienated social structures. Instead, he evaluates positively the mode of social synthesis purportedly effected by labor in industrial production as noncapitalist and opposes it to the mode of societalization effected by exchange, which he assesses negatively.[122] The latter mode of social synthesis alone, according to Sohn-Rethel, constitutes the essence of capitalism. This version of a traditional interpretation of the contradiction of capitalism leads Sohn-Rethel to claim that a society is potentially classless when it acquires the form of its synthesis directly through the process of production and not through exchange-mediated appropriation.[123] It also weakens his sophisticated attempt at an epistemological reading of Marx's categories.

Within the framework of this work, the synthesis of societalization is never a function of "labor" but of the form of social relations in which production takes place. Labor effects that function only in capitalism, as a result of the historically specific quality we have uncovered in examining the commodity form. Sohn-Rethel, however, interprets the commodity form as being extrinsic to commodity-determined labor, and then attributes to production as such a role in societalization which it does not possess. This prevents him from grasping adequately the character of these alienated social structures created by labor-mediated societalization and the specificity of the process of production in capitalism.

In Chapter Five I shall examine the social compulsion exerted by abstract time as a further basic determination of the alienated social structures grasped by the category of capital. It is precisely these structures, however, that Sohn-Rethel evaluates positively as noncapitalist: "The functional necessity of a unitary organization of time, which characterizes the modern continuous labor process, contains the elements of a new synthesis of societalization."[124] Such an evaluation is consistent with an approach that understands abstraction as a market phenomenon completely extrinsic to labor in capitalism, and, hence, implicitly regards labor in capitalism as "labor." The form of alienated social synthesis that is indeed effected by labor in capitalism is, thereby, assessed positively as a noncapitalist form of societalization, effected by labor per se.

This position also hinders Sohn-Rethel from dealing with nineteenth- and twentieth-century forms of thought in which the form of capital-determined pro-

120. Ibid., pp. 77–78.
121. Ibid.
122. Ibid., pp. 123, 186.
123. Ibid., p. 123.
124. Ibid., p. 186.

duction itself takes on a fetishized form. His emphasis on exchange, which excludes any examination of the implications of the commodity form for labor, restricts his social epistemology to a consideration of forms of static, abstract mechanical thought. This necessarily excludes many forms of modern thought from the purview of his critical social epistemology. The failure to consider the mediating role of labor in capitalism indicates that Sohn-Rethel's understanding of the form of synthesis differs from that of the form of social relations I have developed here. Although my interpretation parallels, in some respects, Sohn-Rethel's attempt to relate the historical emergence of abstract thought, philosophy, and natural science to abstract social forms, it is based upon a different understanding of the character and constitution of those forms.

Nevertheless, a theory of social forms is of central importance to a critical theory. A theory based on an analysis of the commodity form of social relations can, in my judgment, account at a high level of logical abstraction for the conditions under which scientific thought shifted, with the rise of capitalist civilization, from a concern with quality (use value) and questions addressing the substantive ''what'' and ''why'' to a concern with quantity (value) and questions dealing with the more instrumental ''how.''

Labor and instrumental action

I have argued that the forms of capitalist social relations have ''cultural'' significance: they condition understandings of nature as well as of the social world. A basic characteristic of modern natural science is its instrumental character—its preoccupation with questions of how nature functions to the exclusion of questions of meaning, its ''value-free'' character with regard to substantive goals. Although I shall not continue to pursue directly the question of the social grounding of such a natural science at this point, this question can be illuminated indirectly by examining the problem of whether labor should be considered instrumental activity, and by considering the relation between such activity and the form of social constitution that characterizes capitalism.

In *Eclipse of Reason,* Max Horkheimer relates labor to instrumental reason, which he characterizes as that reduced form of reason which has become dominant with industrialization. Instrumental reason, according to Horkheimer, is concerned only with the question of the correct or most efficient means to a given end. It is related to Weber's notion of formal, as opposed to substantive, rationality. Goals themselves are not seen as ascertainable by means of reason.[125] The idea that reason itself is meaningfully valid only in relation to instruments, or is itself an instrument, is closely tied to the positivist deification of the natural sciences as the only model of knowledge.[126] Such an idea results in complete

125. Horkheimer, *Eclipse of Reason* (New York, 1974), pp. 3–6.
126. Ibid., pp. 59ff., 105.

relativism with regard to substantive goals and systems of morals, politics, and economics.[127] Horkheimer relates this instrumentalization of reason to the development of increasingly complex methods of production:

The complete transformation of the world into a world of means rather than of ends is itself the consequence of the historical development of the methods of production. As material production and social organization grow more complicated and reified, recognition of means as such becomes increasingly difficult, since they assume the appearance of autonomous entities.[128]

Horkheimer does state that this process of increasing instrumentalization is not a function of production per se, but of its social context.[129] As I have argued, however, Horkheimer, despite some equivocations, identifies labor in and of itself with instrumental action. While I agree that there is a connection between instrumental action and instrumental reason, I take issue with his identification of the former with labor as such. Horkheimer's explanation for the increasing instrumental character of the world in terms of the growing complexity of production is less than convincing. Labor may always be a pragmatic technical means for achieving particular goals, in addition to whatever meaning it may be accorded, but this can hardly explain the growing instrumental character of the world—the growing domination of "value-free" means over substantive values and goals, the transformation of the world into one of means. Only at first glance does labor appear to be the example par excellence of instrumental action. Both György Márkus and Cornelius Castoriadis, for example, have argued convincingly that social labor is never simply instrumental action.[130] In terms of the argument I have developed here, that proposition can be modified: Social labor as such is *not* instrumental action; labor in capitalism, however, *is* instrumental action.

The transformation of the world into one of means rather than ends, a process that extends even to people,[131] is related to the particular character of commodity-determined labor as a means. Although social labor is always a means to an end, this alone does not render it instrumental. As noted, in precapitalist societies, for example, labor is accorded significance by overt social relations and is shaped by tradition. Because commodity-producing labor is not mediated by such relations it is, in a sense, de-signified, "secularized." This development may be a necessary condition for the growing instrumentalization of the world, but it is not a sufficient condition for labor's instrumental character—that it

127. Ibid., p. 31.
128. Ibid., p. 102.
129. Ibid., pp. 153–54.
130. Cornelius Castoriadis, *Crossroads in the Labyrinth,* trans. Kate Soper and Martin H. Ryle (Cambridge, Mass., 1984), pp. 244–49; György Márkus, "Die Welt menschlicher Objekte," p. 24ff.
131. Horkheimer, *Eclipse of Reason,* p. 151.

exists as a pure means. That character is a function of the sort of means labor in capitalism is.

As we have seen, commodity-determined labor is, as concrete labor, a means for producing a particular product; moreover and more essentially, as abstract labor, it is self-mediating—it is a *social means* of acquiring the products of others. Hence, for the producers, labor is abstracted from its concrete product: it serves them as a pure means, an instrument to acquire products that have no intrinsic relation to the substantive character of the productive activity by means of which they are acquired.[132]

The goal of production in capitalism is neither the material goods produced nor the reflexive effects of laboring activity on the producer, but value, or, more precisely, surplus value. Value, however, is a purely quantitative goal; there is no qualitative difference between the value of wheat and that of weapons. Value is purely quantitative because as a form of wealth it is an objectified means: it is the objectification of abstract labor—of labor as an objective means of acquiring goods it has not produced. Thus production for (surplus) value is production where the goal itself is a means.[133] Hence, production in capitalism necessarily is quantitatively oriented, toward ever-increasing amounts of surplus value. This is the basis of Marx's analysis of production in capitalism as production for the sake of production.[134] The instrumentalization of the world, within such a framework, is a function of the determination of production and social relations by this historically specific form of social mediation—it is not a function of the increasing complexity of material production as such. Production for the sake of production signifies that production is no longer a means to a substantive end but a means to an end that is itself a means, a moment in a never-ending chain of expansion. *Production in capitalism becomes a means to a means.*

The emergence of a goal of social production which is actually a means underlies the increasing domination of means over ends, noted by Horkheimer. It is not rooted in the character of concrete labor as a determinate material means of creating a specific product; rather, it is rooted in the character of labor in

132. This analysis of abstract labor provides an abstract and initial logical determination for the development in the twentieth century, noted by André Gorz and Daniel Bell, among others, of workers' self-conceptions as being worker/consumers rather than worker/producers. See André Gorz, *Critique of Economic Reason,* trans. Gillian Handyside and Chris Turner (London and New York, 1989), p. 44ff.; and Daniel Bell, "The Cultural Contradictions of Capitalism," in *The Cultural Contradictions of Capitalism* (New York, 1978), pp. 65–72.

133. The rise of social and political, as well as theoretical, formalism could be investigated with reference to this process of the separation of form and content, whereby the former dominates the latter. On another level, Giddens has suggested that, because the process of commodification both destroys traditional values and modes of life and entails this separation of form and content, it induces widespread feelings of meaninglessness. See *A Contemporary Critique of Historical Materialism,* pp. 152–53.

134. *Capital,* vol. 1, p. 742; *Results of the Immediate Process of Production,* pp. 1037–38.

capitalism as a social means that is quasi-objective and supersedes overtly social relations. Horkheimer, in effect, attributes a consequence of the specific character of labor in capitalism to labor in general.

Although the process of instrumentalization is logically implied by the twofold character of labor in capitalism, this process is greatly intensified by the transformation of humans into means. As I shall elaborate, the first stage of this transformation is the commodification of labor itself as labor power (what Marx calls the "formal subsumption of labor under capital"), which does not necessarily transform the material form of production. The second stage is when the process of producing surplus value molds the labor process in its image (the "real subsumption of labor under capital").[135] With real subsumption, the goal of capitalist production—which is actually a means—molds the material means of its realization. The relation of the material form of production and its goal (value) are no longer contingent. Rather, abstract labor begins to quantify and shape concrete labor in its image; the abstract domination of value begins to be materialized in the labor process itself. A hallmark of real subsumption, according to Marx, is that, despite appearances, the actual raw materials of the process of production are not the physical materials that are transformed into material products, but the *workers* whose objectified labor time constitutes the lifeblood of the totality.[136] With real subsumption this determination of the valorization process is materialized: the person has, quite literally, become a means.

The goal of production in capitalism exerts a form of necessity on the producers. The goals of labor—whether defined in terms of the products or the effects of labor on the producers—are neither given by social tradition nor decided upon consciously. Rather, *the goal has escaped human control:* people cannot decide on value (or surplus value) as a goal, for this goal confronts them as an external necessity. They can decide only which products are most likely to maximize the (surplus) value obtained; the choice of material products as goals is a function of neither their substantive qualities, nor the needs to be fulfilled. Yet the "battle of the gods"—to borrow Weber's term—that does actually reign among the substantive goals only *appears* to be pure relativism; the relativism that prevents one from judging on substantive grounds the merits of one goal of production relative to another stems from the fact that, in capital-determined society, *all* products embody the same underlying goal of production—value. This actual goal, however, is itself not substantive; hence the appearance of pure relativism. The goal of production in capitalism is an absolute given that, paradoxically, is only a means—but one that has no end other than itself.

As the duality of concrete labor and labor-mediated interaction, labor in capitalism has a socially constituting character. This confronts us with the follow-

135. *Results of the Immediate Process of Production,* p. 1034ff.
136. *Capital,* vol. 1, pp. 296–97, 303, 425, 548–49.

ing, only apparently paradoxical, conclusion: it is precisely because of its socially mediating character that labor in capitalism is instrumental action. Because the mediating quality of labor in capitalism cannot appear directly, instrumentality then appears as an objective attribute of labor as such.

The instrumental character of labor as self-mediating is, at the same time, the instrumental character of labor-mediated social relations. Labor in capitalism constitutes the social mediation that characterizes this society; as such it is a "practical" activity. We are now confronted with a further paradox: labor in capitalism is instrumental action precisely because of its historically determinate "practical" character. Conversely, the "practical" sphere, that of social interaction, is fused with that of labor and has an instrumental character. In capitalism, then, the instrumental character of both labor and social relations is rooted in labor's specific social role in that formation. Instrumentality is rooted in the (labor-mediated) form of social constitution in capitalism.

This analysis, however, need not imply the necessary pessimism of Critical Theory discussed in Chapter Three. Because the instrumental character we have investigated is a function of the double character of labor in capitalism—and not of labor per se—it can be analyzed as an attribute of an internally contradictory form. The growing instrumental character of the world need not be understood as a linear, endless process bound to the development of production. The social form can be seen as one that not only accords itself an instrumental character but, from the same duality, gives rise to the possibility of its fundamental critique and to the conditions of the possibility of its own abolition. The concept of the double character of labor, in other words, provides the starting point for a reconsideration of the meaning of the fundamental contradiction of capitalist society.

Abstract and substantive totality

I have analyzed value as a category expressing the self-domination of labor, that is, the domination of the producers by the historically specific mediating dimension of their own labor. Except in the brief discussion of the subsumption of labor under capital in the previous section, my analysis up to this point has treated the alienated social totality constituted by labor in capitalism as formal rather than as substantive—it is the externalized social bond among individuals which results from the simultaneous determination of labor as a productive activity and as a socially mediating activity. If the investigation were to stop here, it might seem as though what I have analyzed as the alienated social bond in capitalism does not—given its formal character—differ fundamentally from the market. The analysis of alienation presented thus far could be appropriated and reinterpreted by a theory that would focus on money as the medium of exchange rather than on labor as a mediating activity.

However, in continuing this investigation, and examining Marx's category of surplus value, hence, of capital as well, we shall see that the alienated social bond in capitalism does not remain formal and static, in his analysis. It has, rather, a directionally dynamic character. That capitalism is characterized by an immanent historical dynamic is due, in the Marxian analysis, to the form of abstract domination intrinsic to the value form of wealth and of social mediation. As noted, an essential characteristic of that dynamic is an ever-accelerating process of production for the sake of production. What characterizes capitalism is that, on a deep systemic level, production is not for the sake of consumption. Rather, it is driven, ultimately, by a system of abstract compulsions constituted by the double character of labor in capitalism, which posit production as its own goal. In other words, the "culture" that ultimately mediates production in capitalism is radically different than in other societies inasmuch as it itself is constituted by labor.[137] What distinguishes the critical theory based on the notion of labor as a socially mediating activity from approaches that focus on the market or on money is the former's analysis of capital—its ability to grasp the directional dynamic and trajectory of production of modern society.

As I investigate Marx's category of capital, it will become clear that the social totality acquires its dynamic character by incorporating a substantive social dimension of labor. Up to this point, I have considered a specific, abstract, social dimension of labor in capitalism as a socially mediating activity. This dimension should not be confused with the social character of labor as a productive activity. The latter, according to Marx, includes the social organization of the process of production, the average skill of the working population, the level of the development, and the application of science, among other factors.[138] This dimen-

---

137. In this sense, the criticism that Marx neglects to incorporate in his theory an analysis of the historical and cultural specificity of use values in capitalism—or, more generally, an analysis of culture in mediating production—focuses on a different logical level of social life in capitalism than that which Marx seeks to elucidate in his mature critique. This criticism, moreover, overlooks the fact that Marx regards the essential characteristic and driving force of the capitalist social formation as being a historically unique form of social mediation that results in production for the sake of production rather than for consumption. This analysis, as we shall see, does address the category of use value, although it is not identified with consumption alone. Nevertheless, it does argue that theories of consumption-driven production cannot account for the necessary dynamism of capitalist production. (The interpretation I present in this work casts doubt on recent tendencies in social theory to identify consumption as the locus of culture and subjectivity—which implies that production is to be considered essentially technical and "objective"; and more fundamentally, it casts doubt on any notion of "culture" as a transhistorical universal category, which everywhere and at all times is constituted in the same manner.) Such criticisms do, however, indicate that other considerations of use value—with regard to consumption, for example—are important in investigating capitalist society on a more concrete level. It is crucial, though, to distinguish among levels of analysis and work out their mediations. For the above criticisms of Marx, see Marshall Sahlins, *Culture and Practical Reason* (Chicago, 1976), pp. 135, 148ff.; and William Leiss, *The Limits to Satisfaction* (Toronto and Buffalo, 1976), pp. xvi–xx.
138. *Capital*, vol. 1, p. 130.

sion—the social character of concrete labor as productive activity—has remained outside of my considerations until now; I have treated the function of labor as a socially mediating activity independently of the specific concrete labor performed. However these two social dimensions of labor in capitalism do not simply exist alongside one another. In order to analyze how they determine each other, I shall first examine the quantitative and temporal dimension of value; this will allow me to show—in elucidating the dialectic of labor and time— that, with the capital form, the social dimension of concrete labor is incorporated into the alienated social dimension constituted by abstract labor. The totality, which I have treated only as abstract thus far, acquires a substantive character by virtue of its appropriation of the social character of productive activity. I shall undertake this analysis in the third part of this work in order to provide the basis for an understanding of Marx's category of capital. In the course of this investigation, I shall show that the social totality expressed by the category of capital also possesses a "double character"—abstract and substantive— rooted in the two dimensions of the commodity form. The difference is that, with capital, *both* social dimensions of labor are alienated and, together, confront individuals as a compelling force. This duality is the reason that the totality is not static but possesses an intrinsically contradictory character that underlies an immanent, historically directional dynamic.

This analysis of the alienated social forms as at once formal and substantive yet contradictory differs from approaches, such as that of Sohn-Rethel, that seek to locate capitalism's contradiction between its abstract formal dimension and a substantive dimension—the proletarian-based industrial process of production— and presume the latter not to be capital-determined. At the same time, my approach implies that any fundamentally pessimistic notion of the totality as a "one-dimensional" structure of domination (one without intrinsic contradiction) is not fully adequate to the Marxian analysis. Rooted in the double character of commodity-determined labor, the alienated social totality is not, as Adorno for example would have it, the identity that incorporates the socially nonidentical in itself so as to make the whole a noncontradictory unity, leading to the universalization of domination.[139] To establish that the totality is intrinsically contradictory is to show that it remains an essentially contradictory identity of identity and nonidentity, and has not become a unitary identity that has totally assimilated the nonidentical.

139. Theodor W. Adorno, *Negative Dialectics,* trans. E. B. Ashton (New York, 1973).

5. Abstract time

The magnitude of value

In examining Marx's analysis of the essential structuring social forms of capitalist society, I have focused thus far on his category of abstract labor and on some basic implications of his argument that the social relations characteristic of capitalism are constituted by labor. What also characterizes these social forms, according to Marx, is their temporal dimension and quantifiability. Marx introduces these aspects of the commodity form early in his discussion, when he considers the problem of the magnitude of value.[1] In discussing his treatment of that problem, I shall show its central significance in Marx's analysis of the nature of capitalist society. On this basis, I will consider more closely the differences between value and material wealth, and begin examining the issue of capitalism and temporality—which will lay the groundwork for my consideration, in the last part of this book, of Marx's conception of the trajectory of capitalist development. In the process, I shall also develop further aspects of the sociohistorical theory of knowledge and subjectivity outlined above. This will set the stage for a critical examination of Jürgen Habermas's critique of Marx, which will conclude my discussion of the trajectory of Critical Theory as an attempt to formulate a social critique adequate to the twentieth century. At that point I will be in a position to begin reconstructing Marx's category of capital.

The problem of the magnitude of value appears, at first glance, to be far simpler and more direct than that of the categories of value and abstract human labor. It has been treated by Franz Petry, Isaak Illich Rubin, and Paul Sweezy, for example, as the "quantitative theory of value" in contradistinction to the "qualitative theory of value."[2] They draw this distinction to emphasize that Marx's intention in developing his theory of value was not merely economic, in the narrower sense, but to elucidate the structure of social relations in capi-

---

1. Marx, *Capital,* vol. 1, trans. Ben Fowkes (London, 1976), pp. 129ff.
2. Franz Petry, *Der soziale Gehalt der Marxschen Werttheorie* (Jena, 1916), pp. 3–5, 16; Isaak Illich Rubin, *Essays on Marx's Theory of Value,* trans. Milos Samardzija and Fredy Perlman (Detroit, 1972), pp. 67, 119, 173; Paul Sweezy, *The Theory of Capitalist Development* (New York, 1969), p. 25.

talism. Leaving aside critical considerations of their specific analyses of these social relations, though, such theories do not go far enough. They undertake a qualitative analysis of the social content of value but treat the magnitude of value only in quantitative terms. The analysis of value as a historically specific social form should, however, change the terms with which the magnitude of value is considered.[3] Marx not only writes—as has frequently been cited—that political economy "has never once even asks the question why labour is expressed in value," but he also asks why "the measurement of labour by its duration is expressed in the magnitude of the value of the product."[4] The second question implies that it is not enough to undertake a qualitative examination of the form of value alone, and thereby to exclude the problem of the magnitude of value—for the latter problem also entails a qualitative social analysis.

The above-mentioned interpretations of Marx do not, to be sure, treat the problem of the magnitude of value in a narrow quantitative sense—that is, in terms of the problem of relative exchange values alone—as does political economy. They do, however, treat it only as the quantification of the qualitative dimension of value, rather than as a further qualitative determination of the social formation. Sweezy, for example, writes, "Beyond the mere determination of exchange ratios . . . the quantitative value problem . . . is nothing more or less than the investigation of the laws which govern the allocation of the labor force to different spheres of production in a society of commodity producers."[5] If, for Sweezy, the task of qualitative value theory is to analyze these laws in terms of the nature of social relations and modes of consciousness, that of quantitative value theory is to consider their nature in purely quantitative terms.[6] In a similar fashion, Rubin states:

The basic error of the majority of Marx's critics consists of: 1) their complete failure to grasp the qualitative sociological side of Marx's theory of value and 2) their confining the quantitative side to the examination of exchange ratios. . . . [T]hey ignore the quantitative interrelations among the quantities of social labor distributed among the different branches of production and different enterprises. [The] magnitude of value [is] a regulator of the quantitative distribution of social labor.[7]

3. Generally, the point of departure for positions that emphasize a qualitative analysis of the category of value has been Marx's criticism of classical political economy for neglecting such an analysis: "It is one of the chief failings of classical political economy that it has never succeeded, through an analysis of the commodity, and in particular, of its value, in discovering the form of value. . . . Even its best representatives, Adam Smith and Ricardo, treat the form of value as something of indifference, something external to the nature of the commodity itself. The explanation for this is not simply that their attention is entirely absorbed by the analysis of the magnitude of value" (*Capital,* vol. 1, p. 174n34 [translation amended]). This, however, does not mean that political economy's analysis of the magnitude of value can be retained and simply supplemented by a qualitative analysis of the value form.
4. *Capital,* vol. 1, p. 174.
5. Sweezy, *The Theory of Capitalist Development,* pp. 33–34.
6. Ibid., p. 41.
7. Rubin, *Essays on Marx's Theory of Value,* pp. 73–74.

Petry, on the other hand, sees the "quantitative value problem" in terms of the distribution of the total value produced by the proletariat among the various classes of society in the form of revenue.[8]

These interpretations of the quantitative value problem emphasize exclusively the nonconscious regulation of the social distribution of commodities and labor (or of revenue). Such approaches, which interpret the categories of value and the magnitude of value solely in terms of the lack of conscious social regulation of distribution in capitalism, implicitly conceive of the historical negation of capitalism only in terms of public planning in the absence of private property. They do not provide an adequate basis for a categorial critique of the capital-determined form of production. The Marxian analysis of the magnitude of value is, however, an integral element of precisely such a critique: it entails a qualitative determination of the relation of labor, time, and social necessity in the capitalist social formation. By investigating the temporal dimension of Marx's categories, I shall be able to demonstrate my earlier assertion that the law of value, far from being a theory of equilibrium market mechanisms, implies both a historical dynamic and a particular material form of production.

The measure of value, according to Marx, is of a very different sort than that of material wealth. The latter form of wealth, created by the action of various sorts of concrete labor on raw materials, can be measured in terms of the objectifications of those labors, that is, by the quantities and qualities of the particular goods produced. This mode of measurement is a function of the qualitative specificity of the product, the activity that produces it, the needs it may satisfy, as well as custom—in other words, the mode of measurement of material wealth is particular and not general. For it to be the dominant measure of wealth, it therefore must be mediated by various sorts of social relations. Material wealth does not mediate itself socially; where it is the dominant social form of wealth, it is "evaluated" and distributed by overt social relations—traditional social ties, relations of power, conscious decisions, considerations of needs, and so forth. The dominance of material wealth as the social form of wealth is related to an overtly social mode of mediation.

Value, as we have seen, is a peculiar form of wealth inasmuch as it is not mediated by overt social relations but, rather, *is itself a mediation:* it is the self-mediating dimension of commodities. This is expressed by its measure, which is not a direct function of the amount of goods produced. Such a material measure, as noted, would imply a manifestly social mode of mediation. Although value, like material wealth, is an objectification of labor, it is an objectification of abstract labor. As that which constitutes a general, "objective" social mediation, abstract labor is neither expressed in terms of the objectifications of

---

8. Petry, *Der soziale Gehalt,* pp. 29, 50. Marx deals with the distribution of total value among the various classes in the form of revenue, however, on the logical level of price and profit, not that of value.

particular concrete labors nor measured by their quantity. Its objectification is value—a form separable from that of objectified concrete labor, that is, particular products. Similarly, the magnitude of value, the quantitative measure of the objectification of abstract labor, differs from the various physical quantities of the various commodities produced and exchanged (50 yards of cloth, 450 tons of steel, 900 barrels of oil, and so on). Yet that measure can be translated into such physical quantities. The consequent qualitative and quantitative commensurability of the commodities is an expression of the objective social mediation: it constitutes and is constituted by this mediation. Value, then, is measured not in terms of the particular objectifications of various labors, but in terms of what they all have in common, regardless of their specificity—the expenditure of labor. The measure of the expenditure of human labor that is not a function of the quantity and nature of its products is, in Marx's analysis, time: "How, then, is the magnitude of this value to be measured? By means of the quantity of the 'value-forming substance', the labour, which it contains. This quantity is measured by its duration, and the labour-time is itself measured on the particular scale of hours, days, etc."[9]

Thus, when labor itself acts as the general quasi-objective means of mediating products, this constitutes a general quasi-objective measure of wealth which is independent of the particularity of the products and, hence, of overt social ties and contexts. This measure, according to Marx, is the socially necessary expenditure of human labor time. This time, as we shall see, is a determinate, "abstract" form of time. Because of the mediating character of labor in capitalism, its measure has a socially mediating character as well. The form of wealth (value) *and* its measure (abstract time) are constituted by labor in capitalism as "objective" social mediations.

The category of abstract human labor refers to a social process that entails an abstraction from the specific qualities of the various concrete labors involved, as well as a reduction to their common denominator as human labor.[10] Similarly, the category of the magnitude of value refers to an abstraction from the physical quantities of the products exchanged as well as a reduction to a nonmanifest common denominator—the labor time involved in their production. In Chapter Four, I touched upon some social-epistemological implications of Marx's analysis of the commodity form understood as an analysis of structured forms of everyday practice that involve an ongoing process of abstraction from the concrete specificity of objects, activities, and persons, and their reduction to a general "essential" common denominator. I indicated that the emergence of the modern opposition between abstract universalism and concrete particularism could be understood in terms of that analysis. This social process of abstraction to which the commodity form refers also entails a determinate process of

9. *Capital*, vol. 1, p. 129 (translation amended).
10. Ibid., pp. 159–60.

quantification. I shall address this dimension of the commodity form of social relations in the course of investigating time itself as measure.

It is important to note at this point that Marx's assertion, in Chapter One of *Capital,* that socially necessary labor time expenditure is the measure of value, is not his full demonstration of that position. As I pointed out in Chapter Four, Marx's argument in *Capital* is immanent to his mode of presentation, to the full unfolding of the categories, wherein what is unfolded is intended to justify retroactively that which preceded it, and from which it logically was developed. We shall see that Marx seeks to support retroactively his assertion that the magnitude of value is determined in terms of socially necessary labor time by analyzing, on the basis of his initial determinations of value and its measure, the process of production in capitalism and its trajectory of development. His argument thereby seeks to justify the temporal determination of the magnitude of value as a categorial determination of both production and the dynamic of the whole, and not—as it might seem at first—simply as one of the regulation of exchange.

Abstract time and social necessity

Because abstract human labor constitutes a general social mediation, in Marx's analysis, the labor time that serves as the measure of value is not individual and contingent, but *social* and *necessary:*

The total labour-power of society, which is manifested in the values of the world of commodities, counts here as one homogeneous mass of human labour-power.... Each of these individual labour-powers is the same as the others, to the extent that it has the character of socially average labour-power ... i.e., only needs, in order to produce a commodity, the labour-time which is necessary on an average, or in other words is socially necessary.[11]

Marx defines socially necessary labor time as follows: "Socially-necessary labour-time is the labour-time required to produce any use-value under the prevailing socially normal conditions of production and with the prevalent socially average degree of skill and intensity of labour."[12] The value of a single commodity is a function not of the labor time expended on that individual object but of the amount of labor time that is socially necessary for its production: "What exclusively determines the magnitude of the value of any article is therefore the amount of labour socially necessary, or the labour-time socially necessary for its production."[13]

The determination of a commodity's magnitude of value in terms of socially

11. Ibid., p. 129 (translation amended).
12. Ibid. (translation amended).
13. Ibid.

necessary, or average, labor time indicates that the reference point is society as a whole. I shall not, at this point, address the problem of how this average is constituted—that it is the result of a "social process that goes on behind the backs of the producers," and that "these proportions therefore appear to the producers to have been handed down by tradition"[14]—other than to note that this "social process" involves a socially general mediation of individual action. It entails the constitution by individual action of a general external norm that acts reflexively on each individual.

The sort of necessity expressed by the term "socially necessary labor time" is a function of this reflexive, general mediation. Only at first glance does it seem to be simply a descriptive statement of the average amount of time required to produce a particular commodity. Closer consideration, however, reveals that the category is a further determination of the form of social domination constituted by commodity-determined labor—what I have termed "historically determinate" social necessity, over and against transhistorical, "natural" social necessity.

The time expended in producing a particular commodity is mediated in a socially general manner and transformed into an average that determines the magnitude of the value of the product. The category of socially necessary labor time, then, expresses a general temporal norm resulting from the action of the producers, to which they must conform. Not only is one compelled to produce and exchange commodities in order to survive, but—if one is to obtain the "full value" of one's labor time—that time must equal the temporal norm expressed by socially necessary labor time. As a category of the totality, socially necessary labor time expresses a quasi-objective social necessity with which the producers are confronted. It is the temporal dimension of the abstract domination that characterizes the structures of alienated social relations in capitalism. The social totality constituted by labor as an objective general mediation has a temporal character, wherein *time becomes necessity.*

I noted above that the level of logical abstraction of Marx's categories in Volume 1 of *Capital* is very high; it deals with the "essence" of capitalism as a whole. One strategic intention of his categorial analysis in that volume is to ground historically, in terms of the forms of social relations in capitalism, the modern opposition between the free, self-determining individual and society as an extrinsic sphere of objective necessity. This opposition is intrinsic to the value form of wealth and of social relations. Although value is constituted by the production of particular commodities, the magnitude of value of a particular commodity is, reflexively, a function of a constituted general social norm. The value of a commodity, in other words, is an individuated moment of a general social mediation; its magnitude is a function not of the labor time actually required to produce that particular commodity but of the general social mediation expressed

14. Ibid., p. 135.

by the category of socially necessary labor time. Unlike the measure of material wealth, which is a function of the quantity and quality of particular goods, then, the measure of value expresses a determinate *relation*—namely, a relation between the particular and the abstract-general that has the form of a relation between moment and totality. Both terms of this relation are constituted by labor functioning as a productive activity and as a socially mediating activity. This double character of labor underlies the quasi-objective, abstract temporal measure of social wealth in capitalism; and it also gives rise to an opposition between the range of particular products or labors and an abstract general dimension that constitutes and is constituted by those particular labors.

On another level, the commodity as a dominant social form necessarily implies a tension and opposition between individual and society which points to a tendency toward the subsumption of the former by the latter. When labor mediates and constitutes social relations, it becomes the central element of a totality that dominates individuals—who, nevertheless, are free from relations of personal domination: "Labour, which is thus measured by time, does not seem, indeed, to be the labour of different subjects, but on the contrary the different working individuals seem to be mere organs of the labour."[15]

Capitalist society is constituted as a totality that not only stands opposed to the individuals but also tends to subsume them: they become "mere organs" of the whole. This initial determination of the subsumption of individuals by the totality in Marx's analysis of the commodity form foreshadows his later critical investigation of the process of production in capitalism as the concrete materialization of this subsumption. Far from criticizing the atomized character of individual existence in capitalism from the standpoint of the totality, as traditional interpretations imply, Marx analyzes the subsumption of individuals under abstract objective structures as a feature of the social form grasped by the category of capital. He sees this subsumption as the antinomic complement of individual atomization and argues that both moments, as well as their opposition, are characteristic of the capitalist formation. Such an analysis reveals the dangerous one-sidedness of any notion of socialism that, equating capitalism with the bourgeois mode of distribution, posits socialist society as the totality openly constituted by labor, under which individuals are subsumed.

This discussion of the temporal determination of value has been preliminary; I shall develop it more fully when I consider Marx's category of capital. Nevertheless, I can at this point consider more adequately the significance of the difference between value and material wealth in Marx's analysis. I shall then return to examining capitalism and temporality by investigating the sort of time expressed by the category of socially necessary labor time, and the more general implications of this category for a theory of social constitution.

15. Marx, *A Contribution to the Critique of the Political Economy,* trans. S. W. Ryazanskaya (Moscow, 1970), p. 30 (translation amended).

Value and material wealth

In distinguishing value from material wealth, I have analyzed the former as a form of wealth that is also an objectified social relation—which is to say, it mediates itself socially. On the other hand, the existence of material wealth as the dominant form of wealth implies the existence of overt social relations that mediate it. As we have seen, these two forms of social wealth have different measures: the magnitude of value is a function of the expenditure of abstract labor time, whereas material wealth is measured in terms of the quantity and quality of products created. This difference has significant implications for the relationship between value and the productivity of labor, and, ultimately, for the nature of the fundamental contradiction of capitalism.

The magnitude of the value of an individual commodity is, as noted, a function of the socially necessary labor time required for its production. An increase in average productivity increases the average number of commodities produced per unit of time. It thereby decreases the amount of socially necessary labor time required for the production of a single commodity and, hence, the value of each commodity. In general, "the magnitude of value of a commodity, therefore, varies directly with the quantity, and inversely with the productivity, of the labour which is realized within the commodity."[16]

Increased productivity leads to a decrease in the value of each commodity produced because less socially necessary labor time is expended. This indicates that the total value yielded in a particular period of time (for example, an hour) remains constant. The inversely proportional relationship between average productivity and the magnitude of value of a single commodity is a function of the fact that the magnitude of total value produced depends only on the amount of abstract human labor time expended. Changes in average productivity do not change the total value created in equal periods of time. Thus, if average productivity doubles, twice as many commodities are produced in a given time period, each with half the previous value, because the total value in that time period remains the same. The only determinant of total value is the amount of abstract labor time expended, measured in constant temporal units. It is, therefore, independent of changes in productivity: "The same labour, therefore, performed for the same length of time, always yields the same amount of value, independently of any changes in productivity. But it provides different quantities of use-values during equal periods of time; more, if productivity rises; fewer, if it falls."[17]

We shall see that the question of the relationship between productivity and abstract time is more complicated than indicated by this initial determination. It has, nevertheless, become clear that the Marxian category of value is not merely

16. *Capital,* vol. 1, p. 131 (translation amended).
17. Ibid., p. 137.

material wealth that, in capitalism, is mediated by the market. Qualitatively and quantitatively, value and material wealth are two very different forms of wealth, which can even be opposed: "In itself, an increase in the quantity of use-values constitutes an increase in material wealth. Two coats will clothe two men, one coat will only clothe one man, etc. Nevertheless, an increase in the amount of material wealth may correspond to a simultaneous fall in the magnitude of its value."[18]

This examination of the category of value has shown that the dominant form of social wealth in capitalism is nonmaterial, although it must be expressed in the commodity as its materialized "carrier."[19] It is an immediate function not of the use value dimension—of the material mass or quality of goods—but of the expenditure of labor time. Thus, Marx has shown that the statement with which *Capital* begins—"[t]he wealth of societies in which the capitalist mode of production prevails, appears as an 'immense collection of commodities' "[20]— is only apparently valid. In capitalism, abstract temporal measure rather than concrete material quantity is the measure of social wealth. This difference is the first determination of the possibility in capitalism that, not only for the poor, but for society as a whole, poverty (in terms of value) can exist in the midst of plenty (in terms of material wealth). Material wealth in capitalism is, ultimately, only apparent wealth.

The difference between material wealth and value is central to the Marxian critique of capitalism. It is rooted, according to Marx, in the double character of labor in that social formation.[21] Material wealth is created by concrete labor, but labor is not the sole source of material wealth;[22] rather, this form of wealth results from the transformation of matter by people with the aid of natural forces.[23] Material wealth, then, arises from the interactions of humans and nature, as mediated by useful labor.[24] As we have seen, its measure is a function of the quantity and quality of what is objectified by concrete labor, rather than of the temporal expenditure of direct human labor. Consequently, the creation of material wealth is not bound necessarily to such labor time expenditure. Increased productivity results in increased material wealth, whether or not the amount of labor time expended is increased.

It is important to note that the concrete or useful dimension of labor in capitalism has a social character different from that of the historically specific dimension of labor as socially constituting activity, that is, of abstract labor. Marx

18. Ibid., pp. 136–37.
19. Ibid., p. 126.
20. Ibid., p. 125.
21. Ibid., p. 137.
22. Ibid., pp. 134, 136–37.
23. Ibid.
24. Marx, "Critique of the Gotha Program," in Karl Marx and Frederick Engels, *Collected Works,* vol. 24: *Marx and Engels: 1874–1883* (New York, 1975), p. 81.

analyzes productivity, the "force of production of labor" [*Produktivkraft der Arbeit*] as the productivity of useful, concrete labor.[25] It is determined by the social organization of production, the level of the development and application of science, and the acquired skills of the working population, among other factors.[26] In other words, the concrete dimension of labor, as conceived by Marx, has a social character that is informed by, and encompasses aspects of, social organization and social knowledge—what I have termed the "social character of labor as productive activity"—and is not restricted to the expenditure of direct labor. Productivity, in Marx's analysis, is an expression of that social character, of the acquired productive abilities of humanity. It is a function of the concrete dimension of labor, and not of labor as it constitutes a historically specific social mediation.

The determinations of value, the dominant form of wealth in capitalism, are very different from those of material wealth. Value is peculiar in that, though a form of wealth, it does not express directly the relation of humans to nature but the relations among people as mediated by labor. Hence, according to Marx, nature does not enter directly into value's constitution at all.[27] As a social mediation, value is constituted by (abstract) labor alone: it is an objectification of the historically specific social dimension of labor in capitalism as a socially mediating activity, as the "substance" of alienated relations. Its magnitude is, then, not a direct expression of the quantity of products created or of the power of natural forces harnessed; it is, rather, a function only of abstract labor time. In other words, although increased productivity does result in more material wealth, it does not result in more value per unit of time. As a form of wealth that is also a form of social relations, value does not express directly the acquired productive abilities of humanity. (Later, in discussing Marx's conception of the category of capital, I shall examine how these productive abilities, which are determinations of the use value dimension of labor, become attributes of capital.) If value is constituted by labor alone, and the only measure of value is direct labor time, it follows that the *production of value, unlike that of material wealth, necessarily is bound to the expenditure of direct human labor.*

This distinction between value and material wealth is, as we shall see, crucial to Marx's analysis of capitalism. However, before proceeding, I should note that Marx also argues that, on the level of immediate experience, this distinction is not evident. We have seen that one of Marx's intentions in the manuscript, posthumously published and edited as Volume 3 of *Capital* is to show, on the basis of his theory of value itself, that this theory does not seem to be valid— in particular, that labor alone appears not to constitute value. One aim of Marx's discussion in Volume 3 of ground rent, for example, is to show how nature

25. *Capital*, vol. 1, p. 137.
26. Ibid., p. 130.
27. Ibid., p. 138.

can seem to be a factor in the creation of value; as a result, the distinction between the specific character of labor in capitalism and labor in general becomes unclear, as does the difference between value and material wealth.[28]

(A full exposition of Marx's analysis of the nature and development of capitalism's contradictory character should, therefore, elucidate how a categorial distinction—such as that between value and material wealth—is indeed operative socially, although the actors may be unaware of it. One would need to show how people, acting on the basis of forms of appearance that disguise the underlying essential structures of capitalism, reconstitute these underlying structures. Such an exposition would also show how these structures, as mediated by their forms of appearance, not only constitute practices that are socially constituting, but do so in a way that imparts a determinate dynamic and particular constraints to the society as a whole. However, because I seek only to clarify the nature of Marx's critical analysis of capitalist society in terms of his basic categories, I cannot address these questions fully in this work.)

The differences between value and material wealth, as expressions of the two dimensions of labor, bears on the problem of the relation between value and technology and the question of the basic contradiction of capitalism. Marx's treatment of machines should be seen in the context of his analysis of value as a historically specific form of wealth, different from material wealth. Although machines do yield increased material wealth, according to Marx, they do not create new value. Rather, they only transmit the amount of value (direct labor time) that went into their production, or they indirectly decrease the value of labor power (by decreasing the value of workers' means of consumption), and thereby increase the amount of value appropriable as surplus by the capitalists.[29] That machines create no new value is neither a paradox nor an indication of a reductionist insistence on Marx's part to posit the primacy of direct human labor as the essential social constituent of wealth, regardless of technological developments. Rather, it is based upon the difference between material wealth and value, a difference that lays the basis for what Marx analyzes as a growing contradiction between the two social dimensions expressed by the commodity form. Indeed, as we shall see, the potential of machine production plays an important role in Marx's understanding of that contradiction.

In Chapter One, I examined passages in the *Grundrisse* which indicate that capitalism's basic contradiction is not between industrial production and bourgeois relations of distribution, according to Marx, but lies within the sphere of production itself. On that basis, I argued that his analysis is a critique of labor and of production in capitalism, not a critique from the standpoint of ''labor.'' The distinction Marx makes at the beginning of *Capital* between value and

28. Marx, *Capital,* vol. 3, trans. David Fernbach (Harmondsworth, England, 1981), pp. 751–970.
29. Marx, *Grundrisse: Foundations of the Critique of Political Economy,* trans. Martin Nicolaus (London, 1973), p. 701.

material wealth is completely consonant with, and reinforces, this interpretation. Indeed, one can infer the basic contradiction presented in the *Grundrisse* from his distinction between these two forms of wealth, as well as from the complex relationship entailed between value, productivity, and material wealth.

On the one hand—as I shall elucidate more thoroughly later—Marx's analysis indicates that the system of production grounded in value gives rise to ever-increasing levels of productivity based on changes in the organization of labor, technological developments, and the increased application of science to production. With advanced technological production, material wealth becomes a function of a high level of productivity, which depends on the wealth-creating potential of science and technology. The expenditure of direct human labor time no longer stands in any meaningful relationship to the production of such wealth. Nevertheless, according to Marx, the greater mass of material wealth produced does not, in and of itself, mean that a greater amount of the determining form of social wealth in capitalism—that is, value—has been created. Indeed, the difference between the two is crucial to Marx's argument regarding the fundamental contradiction of capitalism. Increased productivity does not, as noted, yield greater amounts of value per unit of time. For this reason, all means of increasing productivity, such as applied science and technology, do *not* increase the amount of value yielded per unit of time, but they *do* increase greatly the amount of material wealth produced.[30] What underlies the central contradiction of capitalism, according to Marx, is that value remains the determining form of wealth and of social relations in capitalism, regardless of developments in productivity; however, value also becomes increasingly anachronistic in terms of the material wealth–producing potential of the productive forces to which it gives rise.

A central moment of this contradiction is the role that direct human labor plays in the process of production. On the one hand, by inducing an enormous increase in productivity, the social forms of value and capital give rise to the possibility of a new social formation in which direct human labor would no longer be the primary social source of wealth. On the other hand, these social forms are such that direct human labor remains necessary to the mode of production and becomes increasingly fragmented and atomized. (I shall discuss the structural grounds for that persisting necessity, together with its implications for an analysis of the material form of the process of production, in Part III of this work.) According to this interpretation, Marx does not posit a necessary connection between direct human labor and social wealth, regardless of technological developments. Rather, his immanent critique claims that it is capitalism itself that does so.

The contradiction of capitalism Marx outlines in the *Grundrisse* can thus be

---

30. For purpose of simplicity and clarity, I am not considering questions of surplus value or the intensification of labor at this point.

understood in terms of a growing contradiction between value and material wealth—one, however, that does not appear to be such, inasmuch as the difference between these two forms of wealth is blurred on the "surface" of society, the level of immediate experience. Ultimately, one can grasp Marx's analysis of this contradiction—as should now be clear—only if one understands value as a historically specific form of wealth, measured by the expenditure of human labor time. The distinction Marx draws between value and material wealth supports my contention that his category of value is not intended to show that social wealth is always and everywhere a function of direct human labor; nor that, in capitalism, this transhistorical "truth" is veiled by various forms of mystification; nor that, in socialism, this "truth" of human existence will emerge openly. Marx *does* seek to show that, beneath the surface of appearances, the dominant social form of wealth in capitalism is indeed constituted by (abstract) labor alone—but this "essential" form itself, and not simply the surface forms that veil it, is the object of his critique. By drawing attention to the distinction between value and material wealth, I have begun to show that the critical function of Marx's "labor theory of value" is not simply to "prove" that the social surplus in capitalism is created by means of the exploitation of the working class. Rather, it provides a historical critique of the socially synthetic role played by labor in capitalism so as to point to the possibility of its abolition.

By now it should be clear that much of the discussion on how applicable Marx's categories are to the analysis of contemporary developments has been limited by the failure to distinguish between value and material wealth. This is particularly true regarding the question of the relationship between technology and value. Because the category of value has frequently been equated with that of social wealth in general, prevailing tendencies have tended to argue either that labor always is the sole social source of wealth, thereby subsuming material wealth under value, or that value is not a function of labor alone, but can be created directly by the application of science and technological knowledge, thereby subsuming value under material wealth. Paul Walton and Andrew Gamble, for example, have defended Marx's approach by emphasizing labor's unique value-creating ability. However, rather than taking into account the particularity of this form of wealth, they argue as if labor, by virtue of its special qualities, were transhistorically a unique source of social wealth.[31] Why machines do not produce value—understood simply as wealth—cannot, however, be explained convincingly. Conversely, in an attempt to account for the obvious wealth-creating possibilities of science and technology today, Joan Robinson criticizes Marx for maintaining that only human labor produces surplus value.[32] Robinson, however, also interprets the Marxian categories of value and capital in terms of

31. P. Walton and A. Gamble, *From Alienation to Surplus Value* (London, 1972), pp. 203–204.
32. Joan Robinson, *An Essay on Marxian Economics* (2d ed., London, Melbourne, Toronto, 1967), p. 18.

wealth in general, rather than as specific forms of wealth and of social relations. Hence she does not distinguish between what produces material wealth and what produces value. Instead, she reifies capital as wealth per se: "It is more cogent to say that capital, and the application of science to industry, are immensely productive, and that the institutions of private property, developing into monopoly, are deleterious precisely because they prevent us from having as much capital, and the kind of capital, that we need."[33] By equating value and capital with material wealth, Robinson's approach necessarily identifies the social relations of capitalism in a traditional manner, with private property.

Interpretations that posit the Marxian category of value as a transhistorically valid category of wealth or, conversely, interpret its increasingly anachronistic character as an indication of the theoretical inadequacy of the category, conflate value and material wealth. Such approaches empty Marx's category of value of its historical specificity and cannot grasp his conception of the contradictory character of the basic social forms underlying capitalist society. They tend to view the mode of production as an essentially technical process impinged upon by social forces and institutions; and they tend to see the historical development of production as a linear technological development that may be restrained by extrinsic social factors such as private property, rather than as an intrinsically technical-social process whose development is contradictory. Such interpretations, in short, fundamentally misunderstand the nature of Marx's critical analysis.

Marx's analysis of the differences between value and material wealth is central to his conception of the contradictory character of capitalist society. He argues that value indeed is not adequate to the wealth-producing potential of science and technology and, yet, that it remains the basic determination of wealth and social relations in capitalism. This contradiction is ultimately rooted in the duality of labor in capitalism. It structures a growing internal tension that gives form to a broad range of historical developments and social phenomena in capitalist society. In Part III of this work, I shall address the questions of the intrinsic dynamic of capitalist society, and of the concrete configuration of capitalism's process of production in terms of this internal tension. I shall argue that the mode of production in capitalism should be understood not in terms of technical "forces of production" separate from social "relations of production" but in terms of the contradiction between value and material wealth, that is, as a materialized expression of both dimensions of labor in capitalism and, hence, of both the forces and the relations of production.[34] (I shall also suggest that

---

33. Ibid., p. 19.
34. In his attempt to conceptualize recent changes in capitalist society, Claus Offe treats the two dimensions of labor in capitalism as two different sorts of labor, which he distinguishes on the basis of whether their products are created for the market. (See Claus Offe, "Tauschverhältnis und politische Steuerung: Zur Aktualität des Legitimationsproblems," in *Strukturprobleme des kapitalistischen Staates* [Frankfurt, 1972], pp. 29–31.) He defines abstract labor as "produc-

that contradiction provides a point of departure for analyzing, on a very abstract level, the problem of the historical transformation of needs and consciousness as expressed, for example, by different social movements.)

I shall interpret the dynamic of capitalism in terms of a dialectic of labor and time which is rooted in the duality of the structuring social forms of this society. In order to do so, however, I must first examine the abstract form of time associated with socially necessary labor time and consider the social-epistemological implications of my discussion of the temporal dimension of Marx's categories.

Abstract time

In discussing the magnitude of value, I have examined the "social" as well as the "necessary" aspects of socially necessary labor time. But which sort of time are we dealing with? As is well known, notions of time vary culturally and historically—the most commonly expressed distinction being that between cyclical and linear conceptions of time. For example, G. J. Whitrow points out that time understood as a kind of linear progression measured by the clock and calendar generally superseded cyclical conceptions of time in Europe only within the past several centuries.[35] I shall consider various forms of time (as well as various conceptions of time) and distinguish them in another way—namely,

tive," that is, surplus value–producing labor, and concrete labor as "nonproductive" labor. Offe argues that the growth of state and service sectors in late capitalism involves an increase of "concrete labor" that neither produces commodities nor is a commodity. This results in a dualism of capitalist and noncapitalist elements (p. 32). According to Offe, although such forms of "concrete labor" may ultimately be functional for the creation of value, they are not bound to the commodity form and, thus, lead to an erosion of social legitimation based on the exchange of equivalents.

Offe's approach differs from Marx's in several important respects. The Marxian categories of abstract and concrete labor do not refer to two different kinds of labor; moreover, the category of productive labor and that of labor power as a commodity are not identical. Whereas the Marxian dialectic of the two dimensions of labor in capitalism points to the historical possibility of a society based on very different forms of labor, what Offe calls noncapitalist labor does not represent such a qualitatively different form. It seems that Offe's intention is to account for popular dissatisfaction with existing forms of labor by arguing that greater identification with, and importance of, job content characterizes the service sector (p. 47). While this may be true of some very specific parts of that sector, this thesis is questionable as a general explanation in light of the fact that the greatest increases in the service sector apparently have been in the areas of janitorial, cleaning, kitchen, and domestic work (see Harry Braverman, *Labor and Monopoly Capitalism* [New York and London, 1974], p. 372). The main thrust of Offe's argument is that the essential determinant of capitalism and the basis of its social legitimation is the market, which is increasingly undermined with the growth of the state and service sectors. His basic assumption is that the Marxian critique of capitalism can be adequately grasped as a critique of its form of legitimation—and that the basis of that legitimation can be identified with the market.

35. G. J. Whitrow, *The Nature of Time* (Harmondsworth, England, 1975), p. 11.

whether time is a dependent or an independent variable—in order to investigate the relation of the category of socially necessary labor time to the nature of time in modern capitalist society and to the historically dynamic character of that society.

I shall term "concrete" the various sorts of time that are functions of events: They are referred to, and understood through, natural cycles and the periodicities of human life as well as particular tasks or processes, for example, the time required to cook rice or to say one *paternoster*.[36] Before the rise and development of modern, capitalist society in Western Europe, dominant conceptions of time were of various forms of concrete time: time was not an autonomous category, independent of events, hence, it could be determined qualitatively, as good or bad, sacred or profane.[37] Concrete time is a broader category than is cyclical time, for there are linear conceptions of time which are essentially concrete, such as the Jewish notion of history, defined by the Exodus, the Exile, and the coming of the Messiah, or the Christian conception in terms of the Fall, the Crucifixion, and the Second Coming. Concrete time is characterized less by its direction than the fact that it is a dependent variable. In the traditional Jewish and Christian notions of history, for example, the events mentioned do not occur within time, but structure and determine it.

The modes of reckoning associated with concrete time do not depend on a continuous succession of constant temporal units but either are based on events—for example, repetitive natural events such as days, lunar cycles, or seasons—or on temporal units that vary. The latter mode of time reckoning—which probably was first developed in ancient Egypt, spread widely throughout the ancient world, the Far East, the Islamic world, and was dominant in Europe until the fourteenth century—used units of variable length to divide day and night into a fixed number of segments.[38] That is, daily periods of daylight and darkness were each divided equally into twelve "hours" that varied in length with the seasons.[39] Only on the equinoxes was a daylight "hour" equal to a

---

36. E. P. Thompson, "Time, Work-Discipline and Industrial Capitalism," *Past and Present* 38 (1967), p. 58. Thompson's article, which is rich in ethnographic and historical materials, is an excellent account of the changes in time apprehension, time measure, and the relation of labor and time concomitant with the development of industrial capitalism.

37. Aaron J. Gurevich, "Time as a Problem of Cultural History," in L. Gardet et al., *Cultures and Time* (Paris, 1976), p. 241.

38. Whitrow, *The Nature of Time*, p. 23; Gustav Bilfinger, *Die mittelalterlichen Horen und die modernen Stunden* (Stuttgart, 1892), p. 1.

39. The Babylonians and the Chinese apparently had a system of subdividing the day into constant temporal units: see Joseph Needham, Wang Ling, and Derek de Solla Price, *Heavenly Clockwork: The Great Astronomical Clocks of Medieval China* (2d ed., Cambridge, England, 1986), p. 199ff.; Gustav Bilfinger, *Die babylonische Doppelstunde: Eine chronologische Untersuchung* (Stuttgart, 1888), pp. 5, 27–30. Nevertheless, as I shall briefly explain later, these constant time units cannot be equated with modern constant hours and do not imply a conception of time as an independent variable.

nocturnal "hour." These variable time units are frequently referred to as "variable" or "temporal" hours.[40] Such a form of time reckoning seems to be related to modes of social life strongly dominated by agrarian, "natural" rhythms of life and work that depend on the cycles of the seasons and of day and night. A relationship exists between the measure of time and the sort of time involved. The fact that the time unit is not constant, but itself varies, indicates that this form of time is a dependent variable, a function of events, occurrences, or actions.

"Abstract time," on the other hand, by which I mean uniform, continuous, homogeneous, "empty" time, is independent of events. The conception of abstract time, which became increasingly dominant in Western Europe between the fourteenth and seventeenth centuries, was expressed most emphatically in Newton's formulation of "absolute, true and mathematical time [which] flows equably without relation to anything external."[41] Abstract time is an independent variable; it constitutes an independent framework within which motion, events, and action occur. Such time is divisible into equal, constant, nonqualitative units.

The conception of time as an independent variable with phenomena as its function was developed only in modern Western Europe, according to Joseph Needham.[42] Such an understanding, which is related to the idea of motion as a change of place functionally dependent on time, did not exist in ancient Greece, the Islamic world, early medieval Europe, India, or China (although constant time units did exist in the latter). The division of time into commensurable, interchangeable segments would have been alien to the world of antiquity and the early Middle Ages.[43] Abstract time, then, is historically unique—but under what conditions did it emerge?

The origins of abstract time should be sought in the prehistory of capitalism, in the late Middle Ages. It can be related to a determinate, structured form of social practice that entailed a transformation of time's social significance in some spheres of European society in the fourteenth century and, by the end of the seventeenth century, was well on its way to becoming socially hegemonic. More specifically, the historical origins of the conception of abstract time should be seen in terms of the constitution of the social reality of such time with the spread of the commodity-determined form of social relations.

40. Whitrow, *The Nature of Time*, p. 23; Bilfinger, *Die mittelalterlichen Horen*, p. 1.
41. Isaac Newton, *Principia*, as quoted in L. R. Heath, *The Concept of Time* (Chicago, 1936), p. 88. Newton did, to be sure, distinguish between absolute time and relative time. He referred to relative time as "some sensible and external . . . measure of duration by the means of motion . . . which is commonly used instead of true time, such as the hour, a day, a month, a year" (ibid.). The fact that he did not distinguish among those units, however, implies that Newton considered relative time to be a mode of sensuous approximation to absolute time, rather than another form of time.
42. Joseph Needham, *Science in Traditional China* (Cambridge, Mass., and Hong Kong, 1981), p. 108.
43. Gurevich, "Time as a Problem of Cultural History," p. 241.

As noted, in medieval Europe until the fourteenth century, as in antiquity, time was not conceptualized as continuous. The year was divided qualitatively according to the seasons and the zodiac—whereby each time period was considered to exert its own particular influence[44]—and the day was divided into the variable hours of antiquity, which served as the basis for the *horae canonicae,* the canonical hours of the Church.[45] To the extent that time was kept in medieval Europe, then, it was the Church's time that was kept.[46] This mode of time reckoning was transformed dramatically in the course of the fourteenth century: according to Gustav Bilfinger, modern, or constant, hours began to appear in European literature in the first half of that century and, by the beginning of the fifteenth century, generally had displaced the variable hours of classical antiquity and the canonical hours.[47] This historical transition from a mode of time reckoning based on variable hours to one based on constant hours implicitly marks the emergence of abstract time, of time as an independent variable.

The transition in time reckoning to a system of commensurable, interchangeable, and invariable hours is very closely related to the development of the mechanical clock in Western Europe in the very late thirteenth century or the early fourteenth century.[48] The clock, in Lewis Mumford's words, "dissociated time from human events."[49] Nevertheless, the emergence of abstract time cannot be accounted for solely with reference to a technical development such as the invention of the mechanical clock. Rather, the appearance of the mechanical clock itself must be understood with reference to a sociocultural process that it, in turn, strongly reinforced.

Many historical examples indicate that the development of a mode of time reckoning based upon such interchangeable and invariable time units must be understood socially and cannot be understood in terms of the effects of technology alone. Until the development of the mechanical clock (and its refinement in the seventeenth century by Christiaan Huygens's invention of the pendulum clock), the most sophisticated widely known form of timekeeper was the clepsydra, or water clock. Various kinds of water clocks were used in Hellenistic

44. Whitrow, *The Nature of Time,* p. 19.
45. David S. Landes, *Revolution in Time* (Cambridge, Mass., and London, 1983), p. 403n15; Bilfinger, *Die mittelalterlichen Horen,* pp. 10–13. According to Bilfinger, the origins of the canonical hours are to be sought in the Romans' division of the day into four watches, which were based on the "temporal" hours and to which an additional two time points were added in the early Middle Ages.
46. Landes, *Revolution in Time,* p. 75; Jacques Le Goff, "Merchant's Time and Church's Time in the Middle Ages," in *Time, Work, and Culture in the Middle Ages,* trans. Arthur Goldhammer (Chicago and London, 1980), pp. 29, 30, 36.
47. Bilfinger, *Die mittelalterlichen Horen,* p. 157.
48. Landes, *Revolution in Time,* pp. 8, 75; Bilfinger, *Die mittelalterlichen Horen,* p. 157; Le Goff, "Labor Time in the 'Crisis' of the Fourteenth Century," in *Time, Work, and Culture in the Middle Ages,* p. 43.
49. Lewis Mumford, *Technics and Civilization* (New York, 1934), p. 15.

and in Roman society and were widespread in both Europe and Asia.[50] What is significant for our purposes is the fact that, although water clocks operated on the basis of a roughly uniform process—the flow of water—they were used to indicate variable hours.[51] This generally was effected by constructing those parts of the clock that indicated the time in such a way that, although the rate of the water's flow remained constant, the indicator varied with the seasons. Less frequently, a complicated mechanism was devised that allowed the flow of water itself to be varied seasonally. On this basis, complex water clocks that marked the (variable) hours with ringing bells were constructed. (Such a clock apparently was sent as a gift by Caliph Haroun al-Rashid to Charlemagne in 807.)[52] In either case, it would have been technically simpler to mark constant uniform hours with water clocks. That variable hours were marked was, therefore, clearly not because of technical constraints. Rather, the grounds seems to have been social and cultural: variable hours apparently were significant, whereas equal hours were not.

The example of China clearly indicates that the problem of the emergence of abstract time and the mechanical clock is a social and cultural one, and not merely a matter of technical ability or of the existence of any sort of constant time units. In many respects, the level of technological development in China was higher than that of medieval Europe prior to the fourteenth century. Indeed, some Chinese innovations such as paper and gunpowder were seized upon by the West, with important consequences.[53] Yet the Chinese did not develop the mechanical clock or any other timekeeping device that both marked equal hours *and* was used primarily for that purpose in organizing social life. This seems particularly puzzling inasmuch as the older system of variable hours, which had been in use after about 1270 B.C. in China, had been superseded by a system of constant hours: one system of time reckoning used in China after the second century B.C. was the Babylonian system of dividing the full day into twelve equal, constant "double hours."[54] Moreover, the Chinese developed the technical ability to measure such constant hours. Between A.D. 1088 and 1094, Su Sung, a diplomat and administrator, coordinated and planned the construction of a gigantic water-driven astronomical "clocktower" for the Chinese emperor.[55] This "clock" was perhaps the most sophisticated of various clockwork drive mechanisms developed in China between the second and the fifteenth

---

50. Landes, *Revolution in Time*, p. 9.
51. Bilfinger, *Die mittelalterlichen Horen*, p. 146; Landes, *Revolution in Time*, pp. 8, 9.
52. Bilfinger, *Die mittelalterlichen Horen*, pp. 146, 158–59; Landes, *Revolution in Time*, fig. 2 (following p. 236).
53. Needham, *Science in Traditional China*, p. 122.
54. See Needham et al., *Heavenly Clockwork*, pp. 199–203; Bilfinger, *Die babylonische Doppelstunde*, pp. 45–52. (I am indebted to Rick Biernacki for drawing my attention to the problem of the constant hours used in China.)
55. Landes, *Revolution in Time*, pp. 17–18; Needham et al., *Heavenly Clockwork*, pp. 1–59.

centuries.[56] It was primarily a mechanism for displaying and studying the movements of the heavenly bodies, but it also showed constant hours and "quarters" (*k'o*).[57] Nevertheless, neither this device nor its marking of equal hours seems to have had much social effect. No such devices—not even smaller and modified versions—were produced on a large scale and used to regulate daily life. Neither a lack of technological sophistication nor ignorance of constant hours, then, can account for the fact that the mechanical clock was not invented in China. What seems more important is that the constant "double hours" were apparently not significant in terms of the organization of social life.

According to David Landes, there was little social need in China for time expressed in constant units, such as hours or minutes. Life in the countryside and in the cities was regulated by the diurnal round of natural events and chores, and the notion of productivity, in the sense of output per unit time, was unknown.[58] Moreover, to the extent that urban timekeeping was regulated from above, it seems to have been with reference to the five "night watches," which were variable time periods.[59]

If this was the case, what was the significance of the constant "double hours" used in China? Although a full discussion of this problem lies beyond the bounds of this work, it is significant that those time units were not numbered serially, but bore names.[60] This not only meant that there were no unambiguous ways to announce each hour (for example, by drum or gong), but suggests that those time units, although equal, were not abstract—that is, commensurable and interchangeable. This impression is reinforced by the fact that the twelve "double hours" were linked in a one-to-one correspondence with the astronomical succession of signs of the zodiac, which are certainly not interchangeable units.[61] There was a conscious paralleling of the daily and yearly course of the sun, with the "months" and the "hours" bearing the same names.[62] Together, this system of signs designated a harmonious, symmetrical cosmic system.

It seems, however, that this "cosmic system" did not serve to organize what we would regard as the "practical" realm of everyday life. We have already seen that the Chinese waterwheel towers were intended not primarily as clocks but as astronomical devices. Hence, as Landes notes, their accuracy was checked "not by comparing the time with the heavens, but a copy of the heavens with the heavens."[63] This apparent separation between that aspect of the cosmic system inscribed in the Chinese clockwork mechanisms and the "practical"

56. Needham et al., *Heavenly Clockwork*, pp. 60–169.
57. Landes, *Revolution in Time*, pp. 18, 29–30.
58. Ibid., p. 25.
59. Ibid., p. 26, p. 396n24; Needham et. al., *Heavenly Clockwork*, pp. 199, 203–5.
60. Landes, *Revolution in Time*, p. 27.
61. Needham et al., *Heavenly Clockwork*, p. 200.
62. Bilfinger, *Die babylonische Doppelstunde*, pp. 38–43.
63. Landes, *Revolution in Time*, p. 30.

realm is also suggested by the fact that, although the Chinese measured the solar year, they used a lunar calendar to coordinate social life.[64] They also did not use the twelve "houses" of their "Babylonian" zodiac to locate the position of heavenly bodies, but used a twenty-eight-part "moon-zodiac" to that end.[65] Finally, as already noted, the constant "double hours" used in China apparently did not serve to organize everyday social life; that Su Sung's technical device made no difference in this regard suggests, therefore, that the constant "Babylonian" time units used in China were not the same sorts of constant time units as those associated with the mechanical clock. They were not really units of abstract time, of time as an independent variable with phenomena as its function; rather, they might best be understood as units of "heavenly" concrete time.

The origin of abstract time, then, seems to be related to the organization of social time. Abstract time, apparently, cannot be understood solely in terms of invariable time units any more than its origins can be attributed to technical devices. Just as the Chinese waterwheel towers effected no change in the temporal organization of social life, the introduction of mechanical clocks into China in the late sixteenth century by the Jesuit missionary Matteo Ricci was without effect in this regard. Large numbers of European clocks were imported into China for members of the Imperial Court and other high-ranking persons, and inferior copies even were produced there. However, they apparently were regarded and used essentially as toys; they seem not to have acquired practical social significance.[66] Neither life nor work in China had been organized on the basis of constant time units or became so organized because of the introduction of the mechanical clock.[67] The mechanical clock, then, does not, in and of itself, necessarily give rise to abstract time.

This conclusion is further reinforced by the example of Japan. There, the older, variable hours were retained after the mechanical clock was adopted from the Europeans in the sixteenth century. The Japanese even modified the mechanical clock by constructing movable numerals on the dials of their clocks, which were adjusted to indicate the traditional variable hours.[68] When constant hours were adopted in Japan in the latter third of the nineteenth century, it was not as a result of the introduction of the mechanical clock, but as part of the program of economic, social, and scientific adjustment to the capitalist world which marked the Meiji Restoration.[69]

One final example from Europe should suffice to demonstrate that the historical emergence of constant hours of abstract time should be understood in terms

64. Bilfinger, *Die babylonische Doppelstunde,* pp. 33, 38.
65. Ibid., p. 46.
66. Landes, *Revolution in Time,* pp. 37–52; Carlo M. Cipolla, *Clocks and Culture, 1300–1700* (London, 1967), p. 89.
67. Landes, *Revolution in Time,* p. 44.
68. Ibid., p. 77.
69. Ibid., p. 409n13; Wilhelm Brandes, *Alte japanische Uhren* (Munich, 1984), pp. 4–5.

of their social significance. The *Libros del Saber de Astronomia,* a book pre-pared for King Alfonso X of Castile in 1276, describes a clock that was to be driven by a weight attached to a wheel internally divided into compartments partially filled with mercury, which would act as an inertial brake.[70] Although the mechanism was such that this clock could have shown invariable hours, the dial was to be constructed to indicate variable hours.[71] And although the bells that were to be attached to this clock would, because of the nature of the mech-anism, have struck regular hours, the book's author did not see these as mean-ingful time units.[72]

The dual problem of the origins of time understood as an independent variable and of the development of the mechanical clock should, then, be examined in terms of the circumstances under which constant invariable hours became mean-ingful forms of the organization of social life.

Two institutionalized contexts of social life in medieval Europe were char-acterized by a heightened concern with time and its measurement: monasteries and the urban centers. In the monastic orders in the West, prayer services had been temporally ordered and bound to the variable hours by the Benedictine rule in the sixth century.[73] This ordering of the monastic day became established more firmly, and the importance of time discipline became emphasized more strongly in the eleventh, twelfth, and thirteenth centuries. This was particularly true of the Cistercian order, founded at the beginning of the twelfth century, which undertook relatively large-scale agricultural, manufacturing, and mining projects, and which emphasized time discipline in the organization of work as much as in the organization of prayer, eating, and sleeping.[74] Time periods were marked off for the monks by bells, which were rung by hand. There seems to have been a relation between this increased emphasis on time and an increased demand for, and improvements in, water clocks in the twelfth and thirteenth centuries. The water clocks presumably were needed in order to ascertain more accurately when the (variable) hours should be struck. In addition, crude forms of "timers," outfitted with bells, which may have been mechanically driven, were used to awaken the monks who rang the bells for the night service.[75]

In spite of the monastic emphasis on time discipline and the improvements of timekeeping mechanisms associated with it, however, the transition from a system of variable hours to one of constant hours, and the development of the mechanical clock, apparently did not originate in the monasteries, but in the urban centers of the late Middle Ages.[76] Why was this the case? By the begin-

70. Landes, *Revolution in Time,* p. 10.
71. Bilfinger, *Die mittlelalterlichen Horen,* p. 159.
72. Ibid., p. 160.
73. Landes, *Revolution in Time,* p. 61.
74. Ibid., pp. 62, 69.
75. Ibid., pp. 63, 67–69.
76. Ibid., pp. 71–76; Bilfinger, *Die mittelalterlichen Horen,* pp. 160–65; Le Goff, "Labor Time in the 'Crisis,' " pp. 44–52.

ning of the fourteenth century, the urban communes of Western Europe, which had grown and benefited greatly from the economic expansion of the previous centuries, began using a variety of striking bells to regulate their activities. City life was increasingly marked by the pealings of a broad array of bells that signaled the opening and closing of various markets, indicated the beginning and end of the workday, heralded various assemblies, marked the curfew and the time after which alcohol no longer could be served, and warned of fire or danger, and so on.[77] Like the monasteries, the towns, then, had developed a need for greater time regulation.

However, the fact that a system of *constant* hours arose in the towns but not in the monasteries indicates a significant difference. That difference, according to Bilfinger, was rooted in the very different interests involved with regard to maintaining the older system of time reckoning. At issue was the relation of the definition and social control of time to social domination. Bilfinger argues that the Church may have been interested in measuring time, but was not at all interested in changing the old system of variable hours (the *horae canonicae*), which had become closely tied to its dominant position in European society.[78] The towns, on the other hand, had no such interest in maintaining that system and, therefore, were able to exploit fully the invention of the mechanical clock in introducing a new system of hours.[79] The development of constant hours, then, was rooted in the transition from a churchly division of time to a secular one, according to Bilfinger, and was related to the flowering of the urban bourgeoisie.[80] This argument, in my opinion, is underspecified. Bilfinger focuses on the factors that hindered the Church's adoption of a system of constant hours, and notes the lack of such constraints among the urban bourgeoisie. This implies that the system of constant hours resulted from a technical innovation in the absence of social constraints. As I have indicated, however, the technical means for measuring constant hours existed long before the fourteenth century. Moreover, the mere absence of reasons not to adopt constant hours does not seem sufficient to explain why they were adopted.

David Landes has suggested that the system of constant hours was rooted in the temporal organization of the "man-made" day of town dwellers, which differed from that of the "natural" day of peasants.[81] However, the differences between an urban and a rural environment, and between the sorts of work done in each, are an insufficient explanation: after all, large cities existed in many parts of the world long before the rise of a system of constant hours in Western European cities. Landes himself notes of China, that the pattern of life and work in the cities and the countryside were regulated by the same diurnal round of

77. Bilfinger, *Die mittelalterlichen Horen,* pp. 163–65.
78. Ibid., pp. 158–60.
79. Ibid., p. 163.
80. Ibid., p. 158.
81. Landes, *Revolution in Time,* p. 72.

natural events.[82] Moreover, the urban workday in medieval European towns until the fourteenth century—which was marked off approximately by the *horae canonicae*—was also defined in terms of variable "natural" time, from sunrise until sunset.[83]

The transition from variable to constant time units in the European urban centers in the fourteenth century cannot, then, be understood adequately in terms of the nature of town life *per se*. Rather, a more specific reason, one that can ground this transition socially, is needed. The different relationship to time implied by the two systems is not only a matter of whether or not time discipline plays an important role in structuring the daily course of life and work; such discipline, as we have seen, was very much a feature of monastic life. Rather, the difference between a system of variable hours and one of constant hours also is expressed in two different sorts of time discipline. Although the form of life developed in the medieval monasteries was regulated strictly by time, this regulation was effected in terms of a series of time points, which marked when various activities were to be done. This form of time discipline does not demand, imply, or depend upon constant time units; it is quite distinct from a form of time discipline in which time units serve as the *measure* of activity. As I shall show, the transition to constant time units should be further specified in terms of a new form of social relations, a new social form that cannot be grasped fully in terms of sociological categories such as "peasant life" and "urban life," and that is bound to abstract time.

Jacques Le Goff, in his investigation of this transition—which he describes as the transition from Church's time to merchants' time,[84] or from medieval time to modern time[85]—focuses on the proliferation of various sorts of bells in medieval European towns, especially the work bells, which appeared and spread quickly in the cloth-producing towns of the fourteenth century.[86] On the basis of Le Goff's discussion, I shall briefly suggest how the work bells might have played an important role in the emergence of a system of constant time units and, relatedly, of the mechanical clock. The work bells themselves were an expression of a new social form that had begun to emerge, particularly within the medieval cloth-making industry. This industry did not produce primarily for the local market, like most medieval "industries," but, along with the metal industry, was the first that engaged in large-scale production for export.[87] The craftsmen of most other industries sold what they produced, but in the textile industry there was a strict separation between the cloth merchants, who distrib-

82. Ibid., p. 25.
83. Le Goff, "Labor Time in the 'Crisis,' " p. 44.
84. Le Goff, "Merchant's Time," pp. 29–42.
85. Le Goff, "Labor Time in the 'Crisis,' " pp. 43–52.
86. Ibid., pp. 47–48. David Landes also focuses on the significance of the work bells: See *Revolution in Time*, pp. 72–76.
87. Henri Pirenne, *Belgian Democracy*, trans. J. V. Saunders (Manchester, 1915), p. 92.

uted the wool to the workers, collected the finished cloth from them and sold it, and the workers, many of whom were "pure" wage earners, possessing only their labor power. The work generally was done in small workrooms that belonged to master weavers, fullers, dyers, and shearmen, who owned or rented the equipment, such as the looms, received the raw material as well as the wages from the cloth merchants, and supervised the hired workers.[88] The organizing principle of the medieval cloth industry, in other words, was an early form of the capital–wage labor relationship. It was a form of relatively large-scale, privately controlled production for exchange (that is, for profit) based upon wage labor, and it both presupposed and contributed to the growing monetarization of some sectors of medieval society. Implicit in this form of production is the importance of productivity. The merchants' goal, profit, depended in part on the difference between the worth of the cloth produced and the wages they paid— that is, on the productivity of the labor they had hired. Thus, productivity— which, according to Landes, had been an unknown category in China (as opposed to "busyness")[89]—was constituted, at least implicitly, as an important social category in the textile industry of medieval Western Europe.

The productivity of labor depended, of course, on the degree to which it could be disciplined and coordinated in a regularized fashion. This, according to Le Goff, became an increasingly contentious issue between textile workers and employers as a result of the economic crisis of the late thirteenth century, which strongly affected the cloth-making industry.[90] Because workers were paid by the day, conflict became focused on the length and definition of the work day.[91] It seems that it was the workers who, at the beginning of the fourteenth century, demanded initially that the work day be lengthened in order to increase their wages, which had declined in real value as a result of the crisis. Very quickly, however, the merchants seized upon the issue of the length of the work day and tried to turn it to their advantage by regulating it more closely.[92] It was in this period, according to Le Goff, that work bells, which publicly marked the beginning and end of the work day, as well as the intervals for meals, spread throughout the textile-producing towns of Europe.[93] One of their primary functions was to coordinate the working time of large numbers of workers. The cloth-producing towns of Flanders of the time were like large factories. Their streets were filled in the morning with thousands of workers on their way to the workshops, where they began and ended their work to the stroke of the municipal work bell.[94]

88. Ibid., pp. 92, 96, 97.
89. Landes, *Revolution in Time,* p. 25.
90. Le Goff, "Labor Time in the 'Crisis,' " pp. 45–46.
91. Landes, *Revolution in Time,* pp. 73–74.
92. Le Goff, "Labor Time in the 'Crisis,' " p. 45.
93. Ibid.
94. Eleanora Carus-Wilson, "The Woolen Industry," in M. Postan and E. E. Rich, eds., *The Cambridge Economic History of Europe* (Cambridge, 1952), vol. 2, p. 386.

Equally important, the work bells marked a time period—the work day—that previously had been determined "naturally," by sunrise and sunset. The workers' demands for a longer work day (that is, longer than the daylight period), already implied a loosening of the tie to "natural" time and the emergence of a different measure of duration. To be sure, this did not mean that a system of standard, equal hours was introduced immediatcly; there was a transition period during which it is not clear whether the hours of the working day continued to be the older variable hours, which changed with the seasons, or were standardized initially at a summer length and a winter length.[95] Nevertheless, it could be argued that the move toward equal time units was potentially present once a regularized and standardized work day no longer bound directly to the diurnal cycle was constituted historically. The work day had come to be defined in terms of a temporality that was not a dependent variable of the seasonal variations in the length of daylight and darkness. This is the significance of the fact that the focal issue of workers' struggles in the 14th century was the duration of the work day.[96] The length of the work day is not an issue when it is determined "naturally," by sunrise and sunset; that it became an issue and was determined by the outcome of struggle rather than by tradition implies a transformation in the social character of temporality. The struggle over the length of the work day not only is, as Anthony Giddens notes, "the most direct expression of class conflict in the capitalist economy,"[97] but it also expresses and contributes to the social constitution of time as an abstract measure of activity.

Temporality as a measure of activity is different from a temporality measured by events. It implicitly is a uniform sort of time. The system of work bells, as we have seen, developed within the context of large-scale production for exchange, based upon wage labor. It expressed the historical emergence of a de facto social relationship between the level of wages and labor output as measured temporally—which, in turn, implied the notion of productivity, of labor output per unit time. In other words, with the rise of early capitalist forms of social relations in the cloth-producing urban communes of Western Europe, a form of time emerged that was a measure of, and eventually a compelling norm for, activity. Such a time is divisible into constant units; and within a social framework constituted by the emerging commodity form, such units also are socially meaningful.

I am suggesting, then, that the emergence of such a new form of time was related to the development of the commodity form of social relations. It was rooted not only in the sphere of commodity production but in that of commodity circulation as well. With the organization of commercial networks in the Med-

---

95. Sylvia Thrupp, "Medieval Industry 1000–1500," in Carlo M. Cipolla, ed., *The Fontana Economic History of Europe* (Glasgow, 1972), vol. 1, p. 255.

96. Le Goff, "Labor Time in the 'Crisis,' " p. 47.

97. Anthony Giddens, *A Contemporary Critique of Historical Materialism* (London and Basingstoke, 1981), p. 120.

iterranean and the region dominated by the Hanseatic League, increased emphasis was placed on time as a measure. This occurred because of the crucial question of the duration of labor in production, and because factors such as the duration of a commercial voyage or the fluctuation of prices in the course of a commercial transaction became increasingly important objects of measurement.[98]

It was within this social context that mechanical clocks were developed in Western Europe. The introduction of striking clocks placed on towers and owned by the municipalities (not the Church) occurred shortly after the system of work bells had been introduced, and spread very rapidly throughout the major urbanized areas of Europe in the second quarter of the fourteenth century.[99] Mechanical clocks certainly did contribute to the spread of a system of constant hours; by the end of the fourteenth century the sixty-minute hour was firmly established in the major urbanized areas of Western Europe, replacing the day as the fundamental unit of labor time.[100] This account has suggested, however, that the origins of such a temporal system and the eventual emergence of a conception of abstract mathematical time cannot be attributed to the invention and spread of the mechanical clock. Rather, this technical invention itself, as well as the conception of abstract time, must be understood in terms of the "practical" constitution of such time, that is, with reference to an emergent form of social relations that gave rise to constant time units and, hence, abstract time, as socially "real" and meaningful.[101] As A. C. Crombie notes, "By the time Henri de Vick's mechanical clock, divided into 24 equal hours, had been set up on the Palais Royale in Paris in 1370, the time of practical life was on the way to becoming abstract mathematical time of units on a scale that belongs to the world of science."[102]

Although abstract time arose socially in the late Middle Ages, it did not become generalized until much later. Not only did rural life continue to be governed by the rhythms of the seasons, but even in the towns, abstract time impinged directly upon only the lives of merchants and the relatively small number of wage earners. Moreover, abstract time remained local time for centuries; that large areas share the same time is a very recent development.[103] Even

---

98. Le Goff, "Merchant's Time," p. 35; Kazimierz Piesowicz, "Lebensrhythmus und Zeitrechnung in der vorindustriellen und in der industriellen Gesellschaft," *Geschichte in Wissenschaft und Unterricht* 31, no. 8 (1980), p. 477.

99. Le Goff, "Labor Time in the 'Crisis,' " p. 49.

100. Ibid.

101. David Landes, for example, seems to have grounded the change in the units of time in the mechanical clock itself: see *Revolution in Time,* pp. 75–78.

102. A. C. Crombie, "Quantification in Medieval Physics," in Sylvia Thrupp, ed., *Change in Medieval Society* (New York, 1964), p. 201. E. P. Thompson also notes that the timing of work preceded the diffusion of the clock: see "Time, Work-Discipline, and Industrial Capitalism," p. 61.

103. Le Goff, "Labor Time in the 'Crisis,' " p. 49.

the zero hour, the beginning of the day, varied widely after the spread of the mechanical clock, until it finally was standardized at midnight, that is, at an "abstract" time point independent of the perceptible transitions of sunrise and sunset. It was the standardization of this abstract zero hour which completed the creation of what Bilfinger calls the "bourgeois day."[104]

The "progress" of abstract time as a dominant form of time is closely tied to the "progress" of capitalism as a form of life. It became increasingly prevalent as the commodity form slowly became the dominant structuring form of social life in the course of the following centuries. It was only in the seventeenth century that Huygens's invention of the pendulum clock made the mechanical clock into a reliable measuring instrument, and that the notion of abstract mathematical time was formulated explicitly. Nevertheless, the changes in the early fourteenth century that I have outlined did have important ramifications then. The equality and divisibility of constant time units abstracted from the sensuous reality of light, darkness, and the seasons became a feature of everyday urban life (even if it did not affect all town dwellers equally), as did the related equality and divisibility of value, expressed in the money form, which is abstracted from the sensuous reality of various products. These moments in the growing abstraction and quantification of everyday objects—indeed, of various aspects of everyday life itself—probably played an important role in changing social consciousness. This is suggested, for example, by the new significance accorded time, the increased importance of arithmetic in fourteenth-century Europe,[105] and

---

104. G. Bilfinger, *Der bürgerliche Tag* (Stuttgart, 1888), pp. 226–31, cited in Kazimierz Piesowicz, "Lebensrhythmus und Zeitrechnung in der vorindustriellen und in der industriellen Gesellschaft," p. 479.

105. Landes makes this point but concentrates only on the equality of time, which he grounds in the mechanical clock itself (see *Revolution in Time*, pp. 77–78). He thereby overlooks the other dimensions of the emerging commodity form. I have suggested some other implications of Marx's categorial analysis for a sociohistorical theory of knowledge. Consideration of the relationship between forms of social relations and forms of subjectivity need not be limited to forms of thought; it can be extended to other dimensions of subjectivity and to historical changes in modes of subjectivity. The effects of the processes of abstraction and abstract quantification as everyday processes, and of the related forms of rationality that became prevalent with the growing domination of the commodity form, could also, for example, be examined with reference to the form of schooling and the changed determinations of childhood which emerged in the early modern period (see Philippe Ariès, *Centuries of Childhood* [New York, 1962]). Additional dimensions of historical changes in subjectivity that could be examined with reference to a categorial analysis of capitalist civilization include the psychic and social-habitual changes in the same period, such as the lowering of the threshold of shame, described by Norbert Elias in *The Civilizing Process* (New York, 1982), or those encompassed by Marcuse's thesis that the performance principle is the specific historical form of the reality principle in capitalist society (*Eros and Civilization* [New York, 1962]). In general, it seems to me that a theory of social forms could be useful in approaching the social and historical constitution of subjectivity on the level of psychic structures and tacit ways of being in the world, as well as of forms of thought.

the beginnings of the modern science of mechanics, with the development of the impetus theory by the Paris School.[106]

The abstract form of time associated with the new structure of social relations also expressed a new form of domination. The new time proclaimed by the clocktowers—which frequently were erected opposite the church belltowers—was the time associated with a new social order, dominated by the bourgeoisie, who not only controlled the cities politically and socially but also had begun to wrest cultural hegemony away from the Church.[107] Unlike the concrete time of the Church, a form of temporality controlled overtly by a social institution, abstract time, like other aspects of domination in capitalist society, is "objective." It would, however, be mistaken to regard this "objectivity" as no more than a veil that disguises the concrete particularistic interests of the bourgeoisie. As with the other categorial social forms investigated in this work, abstract time is a form that emerged historically with the development of the domination of the bourgeoisie and has served the interests of that class; but it has also helped to constitute those interests historically (indeed, the very category of "interests"), and it expresses a form of domination beyond that of the dominating class. The temporal social forms, as I shall show, have a life of their own, and are compelling for all members of capitalist society—even if in a way that benefits the bourgeois class materially. Although constituted socially, time in capitalism exerts an abstract form of compulsion. As Aaron Gurevich puts it:

> The town had become master of its own time . . .in the sense that time had been wrestled from the control of the Church. But it is also true that it was precisely in the town that man ceased to be master of time, for time, being now free to pass by independently of man and events, established its tyranny, to which men are constrained to submit.[108]

The tyranny of time in capitalist society is a central dimension of the Marxian categorial analysis. In my consideration of the category of socially necessary labor time thus far, I have shown that it does not simply describe the time expended in the production of a particular commodity; rather, it is a category that, by virtue of a process of general social mediation, determines the amount of time that producers *must* expend if they are to receive the full value of their labor time. In other words, as a result of general social mediation, labor time expenditure is transformed into a temporal norm that not only is abstracted from, but also stands above and determines, individual action. Just as labor is transformed from an action of individuals to the alienated general principle of the totality under which the individuals are subsumed, time expenditure is trans-

106. Le Goff, "Labor Time in the 'Crisis,' " p. 50.
107. Le Goff, ibid., p. 46; Bilfinger, *Die mittelalterlichen Horen,* pp. 142, 160–63; Gurevich, "Time as a Problem of Cultural History," p. 241.
108. Gurevich, "Time as a Problem of Cultural History," p. 242. See also Guy Debord, *Society of the Spectacle* (Detroit, 1983).

formed from a result *of* activity into a normative measure *for* activity. Although, as we shall see, the magnitude of socially necessary labor time is a dependent variable of society as a whole, it is an independent variable with regard to individual activity. This process, whereby a concrete, dependent variable of human activity becomes an abstract, independent variable governing this activity, is real and not illusory. It is intrinsic to the process of alienated social constitution effected by labor.

I have suggested that this form of temporal alienation involves a transformation of the nature of time itself. Not only is socially necessary labor time constituted as an "objective" temporal norm, which exerts an external compulsion on the producers, but time itself has been constituted as absolute and abstract. The amount of time that determines a single commodity's magnitude of value is a dependent variable. The time itself, however, has become independent of activity—whether individual, social, or natural. It has become an independent variable, measured in constant, continuous, commensurable, and interchangeable conventional units (hours, minutes, seconds), which serves as an absolute measure of motion and of labor qua expenditure. Events and action in general, labor and production in particular, now take place within and are determined by time—a time that has become abstract, absolute, and homogeneous.[109]

The temporal domination constituted by the forms of the commodity and capital is not restricted to the process of production but extends into all areas of life. Giddens writes:

The commodification of time . . . holds the key to the deepest transformations of day-to-day social life that are brought about by the emergence of capitalism. These relate both to the central phenomenon of the organization of production processes, and to the "workplace", and also the intimate textures of how daily social life is experienced.[110]

I shall not, in the present work, address the effects of this temporal domination on the texture of experience in everyday life.[111] Instead, I shall discuss some of

---

109. Lukács also analyzes abstract time as a product of capitalist society. He considers such time to be essentially spatial in character: "Thus time sheds its qualitative, variable, flowing nature; it freezes into an exactly delimited, quantifiable continuum filled with quantifiable 'things' . . . in short, it becomes space" (*History and Class Consciousness,* trans. Rodney Livingstone [London, 1971], p. 90). The problem with Lukács's analysis is that he opposes the static quality of abstract time to historical process, as if the latter, in and of itself, represents a noncapitalist social reality. However, as I shall discuss in Part III, capitalism is characterized not only by unchanging abstract time but also by a historical dynamic beyond human control. Historical process as such cannot be opposed to capitalism. Lukács's position indicates the degree to which his understanding of the category of capital is inadequate and is related to his identification of Hegel's identical subject-object with the proletariat.

110. Giddens, *A Contemporary Critique,* p. 131.

111. David Gross, following Lukács in some respects, considers the effects of abstract time on everyday life in terms of the "spatialization of thought and experience," by which he means

the social-epistemological implications of our investigation of temporality thus far; then, in Part III, I shall return to the question of the social constitution of time in capitalist society by investigating the temporal dualism of the underlying social forms of capitalism and, on that basis, outlining the conception of history implied by Marx's categorial theory.

The opposition between abstract and concrete time overlaps, but is not fully identical, with the opposition between time in capitalist society and time in precapitalist societies. The rise of capitalism does, to be sure, entail the supersession of earlier forms of concrete time by abstract time. E. P. Thompson, for example, describes the domination of a task-oriented notation of time in preindustrial societies, and its supersession by the timing of labor with the development of industrial capitalism.[112] In the former case, time is measured by labor, whereas in the latter it measures labor. I have chosen to speak of concrete and abstract time in order to emphasize that two different sorts of time are involved rather than merely two different modes of measuring time. Moreover, as I shall elaborate in Chapter Eight, abstract time is not the only form of time that is constituted in capitalist society; a peculiar form of concrete time is constituted as well. We shall see that the dialectic of capitalist development is, on one level, a dialectic of the two sorts of time constituted in capitalist society and, therefore, cannot be understood adequately in terms of the supersession by abstract time of all forms of concrete time.

Forms of social mediation and forms of consciousness

Marx's determination of the magnitude of value, in my interpretation, implies that time as an independent variable, the homogeneous, absolute mathematical time that has come to organize much of social life in our society, has been constituted socially. This attempt to relate abstract mathematical time as well as its concept to the commodity-determined form of social relations is an instance of the sociohistorical theory of knowledge and subjectivity presented in this

"the tendency to condense time relations . . . into space relations" ("Space, Time, and Modern Culture," *Telos* 50 [Winter 1981–82], p. 59). Gross regards the social consequences of this "spatialization" as extremely negative, entailing the loss of historical memory and the progressive destruction of the possibilities of social critique in contemporary society (pp. 65–71). Gross's critical description is illuminating, but he does not ground the historical constitution of "spatialization" in the forms of social relations characteristic of capitalism. Instead, because he understands these relations only as class relations, he attempts to ground spatialization in the development of urbanization and technology per se (p. 65), and in the interests of controlling elites (p. 72). However, as I have sought to show, consideration of the former alone, without reference to forms of social relations, does not suffice; it cannot, for example, account adequately for the origins of abstract time. Moreover, recourse to considerations of the interests of the ruling strata cannot explain the genesis, nature, and social efficacy of forms that may very well constitute and serve those interests.

112. Thompson, "Time, Work-Discipline, and Industrial Capitalism," pp. 58–61.

work, which analyzes both social objectivity and social subjectivity as socially constituted by historically specific structured forms of practice. Such a theory transforms the classical epistemological problem of the subject-object relation, and entails a reconceptualization and critique of the terms of that problem itself.

The notion of the constitution by the subject of the object of knowledge is central to Kant's "Copernican turn" from examining the object to considering the subjective conditions of knowledge, which he undertakes after elucidating the antinomies generated by the subject-object problematic, as classically conceived. Kant conceives of constitution in terms of the constituting role of the subject. Arguing that reality in itself, the noumenon, is not available to human knowledge, Kant maintains that our knowledge of things is a function of transcendental *a priori* categories with which perception is organized. That is, to the degree that our knowledge and perception are organized by such subjective categories, we co-constitute the phenomena we perceive. This process of constitution, however, is not a function of action and does not refer to the object; rather, it is a function of the subjective structures of knowing. Time and space, according to Kant, are such transcendental *a priori* categories.

Hegel, criticizing Kant, claims that his epistemology results in a dilemma: it requires knowledge of the cognitive faculties as a precondition of knowledge.[113] Using a different theory of the constitution by the subject of the object of knowledge, Hegel seeks to overcome the subject-object dichotomy by demonstrating their intrinsic connection. I have discussed how he treats all of reality, including nature, as constituted by practice—as an externalization, a product and expression, of the world-historical Subject: the *Geist,* in its unfolding, constitutes objective reality as a determinate objectification of self, which, in turn, reflexively effects determinate developments in consciousness of self. The *Geist,* in other words, constitutes itself in the process of constituting objective reality: it is the identical subject-object. Adequate categories, according to Hegel, do not express the subjective forms of finite cognition and the appearances of things, as Kant would have it; they grasp, instead, the identity of subject and object as the structures of absolute knowing. The Absolute is the totality of the subjective-objective categories; it expresses itself and prevails in individual consciousness. Hegel's notion of the identical subject-object is central to his attempt to solve the epistemological problem of the possible relation of subject and object, consciousness and reality, with a theory of the constitution of objectivity and subjectivity which would avoid the dilemma of having to know the cognitive faculty before knowing.

Marx also seeks to establish the intrinsic connectedness of objectivity and subjectivity by means of a theory of their constitution through practice. The universe so constituted, however, is social. Unlike Hegel, Marx rejects the idea

---

113. See Jürgen Habermas, *Knowledge and Human Interests,* trans. Jeremy Shapiro (Boston, 1971), p. 7.

of absolute knowledge and denies that nature as such is constituted. Marx's theory of constitution through practice is social, but not in the sense that it is a theory of the constitution of a world of social objectivity by a human historical Subject. Rather, it is a theory of the ways in which humans constitute structures of social mediation which, in turn, constitute forms of social practice. Thus, as we have seen, although Marx does posit the existence in capitalism of what Hegel identified as a historical Subject—that is, an identical subject-object—he identifies it as the form of alienated social relations expressed by the category of capital rather than as a human subject, whether individual or collective. He thereby shifts the problem of knowledge from the possible correlation between "objective reality" and the perception and thought of the individual or supra-individual subject, to a consideration of the constitution of social forms. His approach analyzes social objectivity and subjectivity not as two ontologically different spheres that must be related but as intrinsically related dimensions of the forms of social life that are grasped by his categories. By transforming the ways in which constitution and constituting practice are understood, this shift of focus transforms the problem of knowledge into one of social theory.

I have shown, for example, that Marx's determination of the magnitude of value implies a sociohistorical theory of the emergence of absolute mathematical time as a social reality and as a conception. In other words, this approach implicitly treats as socially constituted the level of structured preknowledge that Kant interprets as a transcendental *a priori* condition of knowledge.[114] Marx's theory of social constitution tries to overcome what Hegel identifies as the circular dilemma of Kant's transcendental epistemology— that one must know (the cognitive faculties) as a precondition of knowing— without, however, taking recourse to Hegel's notion of absolute knowledge. Marx's theory implicitly analyzes as social the condition of self-knowledge (that is, in order to know explicitly, one already must have known). It grasps this preknowledge as a preconscious structure of consciousness which is socially formed, and neither posits it as a universal, transcendental *a priori* nor bases it on an assumed absolute knowledge. This sociohistorical theory of knowledge is not restricted to examining the social and historical determinations of the subjective conditions of perception and knowledge. Although Marx's critical theory rejects the possibility of absolute knowledge, it does not imply a sort of socially and historically relativized Kantian epistemology, for it seeks to grasp the constitution of forms of social objectivity along with their related forms of subjectivity.

The Marxian critique, then, does not imply a theory of knowledge in the proper sense but, rather, one of the constitution of historically specific social forms that are forms of social objectivity and subjectivity simultaneously. Within

---

114. Jacques Le Goff makes a similar argument regarding the social constitution of three-dimensional space as well: see "Merchant's Time," p. 36.

the framework of such a theory, categories of apprehending the world and norms of action can be seen as connected inasmuch as both ultimately are rooted in the structure of social relations. This interpretation suggests that epistemology becomes, in Marx's theory, radical as social epistemology.[115]

The unfolding of the categorially grasped social forms in Marx's *Capital* is the full elaboration of the theory of social practice he had only posited earlier, in the "Theses on Feuerbach":

The chief defect of all previous materialism . . . is that the object, actuality, sensuousness is conceived only in the form of the *object, or of contemplation* [*Anschauung*], but not as *sensuous human activity, practice* [*Praxis*], not subjectively.

The question whether objective [*gegenständliche*] truth can be attributed to human thinking is not a question of theory but is a practical question.

All social life is essentially *practical*.[116]

115. This interpretation of the epistemological implications of Marx's theory differs from Habermas's, which I shall outline in Chapter Six. On a more general level, my interpretation of the Marxian categories—as expressions of the intrinsic connectedness of historical forms of social being and consciousness—implicitly separates objective validity from any notion of the absolute and historically relativizes it. Yet because this position relativizes both the objective as well as subjective dimensions, it rejects the notion of an opposition between historical relativity and objective validity. The criterion of the latter is social, rather than absolute, validity. Thus Marx can say that "forms of this kind constitute the categories of bourgeois economics. They are forms of thought which are socially valid, and hence objective, for the relations of production of this historically determinate mode of social production, i.e., commodity production" (*Capital*, vol. 1, p. 169 [translation amended]).

The question of the standards by which that which exists can be criticized cannot be fully dealt with here. It should be clear, however, that in Marx's approach the source and standards of critique also must be a function of existing forms of social reality. It could be argued that an understanding of historical relativity as implying that "anything goes" is itself bound to the assumption that objective validity requires an absolute grounding. In this sense, the opposition of the two can be conceived as similar to that between abstract rationalism and skepticism. In both cases, the turn to social theory illuminates the intrinsic relation of the terms of the opposition, indicates that they do not define the universe of possibilities, and transforms the terms of the problem. For a powerful critique of the assumptions that underlie such abstract oppositions different from, but consonant with, the critique suggested in this work, see Ludwig Wittgenstein, *Philosophical Investigations*, trans. G. E. M. Anscombe (New York, 1958).

The problem for social theory of the standards of critique is, of course, difficult. Yet the Marxian approach does offer the possibility of consistent epistemological self-reflection on the part of the theory, which thereby avoids the pitfalls of those forms of critical social thought which presume to view society with a set of standards outside of their social universe—and which therefore cannot explain themselves. Indeed, the Marxian approach implies that the attempt to ground critique in an extrasocial, immutable realm (as, for example, in the classical tradition of Natural Law theory) can itself be analyzed in terms of social forms that present themselves as nonsocial and transhistorical.

116. "Theses on Feuerbach," in Karl Marx and Frederick Engels, *Collected Works*, vol. 5: *Marx and Engels: 1845–1847* (New York, 1976), pp. 3–5 (translation amended).

The mature Marxian critique analyzes the relation of objectivity and subjectivity in terms of structures of social mediation, determinate modes of constituting and constituted social practice. The "praxis" to which Marx refers, as should be clear, is not only revolutionary practice but practice as socially constituting activity. Labor constitutes the forms of social life grasped by the categories of Marx's critique. However, this socially constituting practice cannot be understood adequately in terms of labor per se, that is, concrete labor in general. It is not concrete labor alone that creates the world Marx analyzes, but the mediating quality of labor, which constitutes alienated social relations characterized by an antinomy of an abstract, general, objective dimension and a concrete, particular dimension, even as it objectifies itself in products. This duality gives rise to a sort of unified field of social being in capitalism. An identical subject-object (capital) exists as a totalizing historical Subject and can be unfolded from a single category, according to Marx, because two dimensions of social life—the relations among people and the relations between people and nature—are conflated in capitalism inasmuch as both are mediated by labor. This conflation shapes both the form of production and the form of social relations in capitalism, and it relates them intrinsically. That the categories of Marx's critique of political economy express both dimensions of social life in a single unified form (which is, nevertheless, intrinsically contradictory) stems from this real conflation.

Marx's mature theory of social practice in capitalism, then, is a theory of labor's constitution of social forms that mediate people's relations with each other and with nature, and are, at once, forms of being and consciousness. It is a theory of the social and historical constitution of determinate, structured forms of social practice as well as of social knowledge, norms, and needs that shape action. Although the social forms Marx analyzes are constituted by social practice, they cannot be grasped on the level of immediate interaction alone. Marx's theory of practice is a theory of the constitution and possible transformation of forms of social mediation.

This interpretation of Marx's theory transforms the traditional problem of the relation between labor and thought by formulating it in terms of the relation between labor-mediated forms of social relations and forms of thought, rather than between concrete labor and thought. I have argued that, just as social constitution is not a function of concrete labor alone, in Marx's analysis the constitution of consciousness by social practice should not be understood solely in terms of the labor-mediated interactions of individual subjects or social groupings with their natural environment. This applies even to conceptions of natural reality: they are not won pragmatically, merely from struggles with and transformations of nature, but, as I have tried to indicate, also are rooted in the character of the determinate social forms that structure these interactions with nature. In other words, labor as productive activity does not, in and of itself, accord meaning; rather, as I have argued, even labor acquires its meaning from the social relations in which it is embedded. When these social relations are constituted by labor itself, labor exists in "secular" form and can be analyzed as instrumental action.

The notion that labor is socially constitutive is not, then, based on a reduction by Marx of social praxis to labor qua material production, whereby the interaction of humanity with nature becomes the paradigm of interaction.[117] This would, indeed, have been the case if Marx had understood praxis in terms of "labor." However, Marx's conception in his mature works of labor as socially constituting practice is linked to his analysis of labor's mediation of dimensions of social life that, in other societies, are not so mediated. This analysis, according to Marx, is the sine qua non of an adequate critical understanding of the specificity of the forms of social relations, production, and consciousness in the capitalist social formation. The above-mentioned conflation of two dimensions of social life in capitalism allows Marx to analyze social constitution in terms of one form of practice (labor) and to investigate the intrinsic relation of social objectivity and subjectivity in terms of a single set of categories of structured practice. It is conceivable that in another society, where production and social relations are not constituted as a totalizing sphere of social objectivity by a single structuring principle, the notion of a single form of constituting practice would have to be modified and the relationship between forms of consciousness and forms of social being would have to be grasped differently.

Jürgen Habermas and Alfred Schmidt have also argued that Marx's analysis entails a theory of the constitution of social objectivity and social subjectivity. Although they evaluate Marx's theory of practical constitution very differently, both consider this process of constitution only in terms of "labor," that is, in terms of the transformation of external physical nature and, reflexively, of humans themselves, as a result of concrete labor.[118]

The traditional notion, mistakenly attributed to Marx, that labor is socially constituting solely by virtue of its function as productive activity can itself be

---

117. Albrecht Wellmer formulates this critique in his essay, "Communication and Emancipation: Reflections on the Linguistic Turn in Critical Theory," in John O'Neill, ed., *On Critical Theory* (New York, 1976), pp. 232–33.

118. See Habermas, *Knowledge and Human Interests*, pp. 25–63; Alfred Schmidt, *Der Begriff der Natur in der Lehre von Marx* (Frankfurt, 1971), pp. 107–28. Schmidt's position is very similar to that of Horkheimer in "Traditional and Critical Theory" (in *Critical Theory*, trans. Matthew J. O'Connell et al. [New York, 1972]). He emphasizes the role of concrete labor in constituting both the subjective human capacity for knowledge as well as the experiental world. Schmidt does, to be sure, cite approvingly statements by Arnold Hauser, Ernst Bloch, and Marx to the effect that the concept of nature is also a function of the structure of society (p. 126). This position, however, is not systematically integrated into the body of his argument. In discussing the natural sciences, Schmidt focuses on experimentation and applied natural science, to the exclusion of a consideration of paradigms of natural reality (pp. 118–19). The latter, I have argued, cannot be derived from concrete social labor alone but must be elucidated in terms of the forms of social relations which serve as the context of their emergence.

explained by the Marxian critique in terms of the specificity of the social forms in capitalism. As we have seen, although commodity-determined labor is marked by a peculiar, historically specific dimension, it can seem to both the theorist and the social actor to be "labor." This is also true of the epistemological dimension of labor as social practice. I have maintained, for example, that two moments of humans' relation to nature must be distinguished: the transformation of nature, materials and the environment, as a result of social labor, and people's conceptions of the character of natural reality. The second, I have argued, cannot be explained as a direct consequence of the first alone, that is, of the labor-mediated interactions of humans with nature, but also must be considered with reference to the forms of social relations within which such interactions take place. In capitalism, however, both moments of people's relation to nature are a function of labor: the transformation of nature by concrete social labor can, therefore, seem to condition the notions people have of reality, as though the source of meaning is the labor-mediated interaction with nature alone. Consequently, the undifferentiated notion of "labor" can be taken to be the principle of constitution, and knowledge of natural reality can be presumed to develop as a direct function of the degree to which humans dominate nature. The fact that this position, which was held by Horkheimer in 1937, has been attributed to Marx stems in part from the affirmation by traditional socialist working class parties of "labor," and in part from Marx's immanent mode of presentation.

What I have presented as the traditional Marxist theory of social constitution by "labor" can be understood, on one level, as an attempt to resolve the opposition of objectivity and subjectivity. That is, it remains ultimately within the framework of the terms of the problem as formulated by classical modern philosophy. Marx's approach, as I have presented it, however, is not an attempt to resolve this opposition. Rather, it transforms the terms of the problem by analyzing socially the relation of objectivity and subjectivity so as to ground the presuppositions of the classical problematic itself—the opposition of an external lawlike sphere of objectivity and the individual, self-determining subject—in the social forms of modern capitalist society.[119]

Further differences between these two approaches to the problem of social constitution are expressed in their divergent understandings of the process of alienation and its relation to subjectivity. The understanding commonly associated with the notion of social constitution by "labor" can be seen in Hilferding's reply to Böhm-Bawerk, which I cited earlier. Hilferding posits "labor" as the regulatory principle of human society which is veiled in capitalism and which,

---

119. In this sense, the Marxian approach differs from other critiques of the subject-object dichotomy which maintain that the idea of a knowing, decontextualized, and decorporealized subject makes no sense, and that people are always embedded in a preconscious background. While it is also critical of the subject-object dichotomy, the Marxian approach does not simply refute positions that posit a decontextualized subject but seeks to account for such positions by analyzing apparent decontextualization as a characteristic of the determinate context of capitalist society.

in socialism, will emerge openly as the causal principle of human life. Inasmuch as "labor" remains the constant substratum of society, the form in which it appears in capitalism is separable from its content, from "labor" itself.

This conception of social constitution effected by "labor" implies the existence of a concrete historical Subject, and is related to an understanding of alienation as the estrangement of what already exists as a property of this Subject. That is, alienation is treated as a process entailing the simple reversal of subject and object. This is also the case regarding perception and consciousness. In describing the mystification of the commodity form, Hilferding writes, "The social characters of persons appear as the objective [*gegenständliche*] attributes of things, just as the subjective forms of human perception (time and space) appear as objective [*objektive*] attributes of things."[120]

The analogy Hilferding draws between "the social characters of persons" and the Kantian transcendental *a priori* categories ("the subjective forms of human perception") indicates that in both cases he presupposes a preexisting, rather than a socially constituted, structure of subjectivity. Capitalism's specificity seems, then, to lie in the fact that what already exists as a property of the subjective dimension appears to be a property of the objective dimension. Hilferding thus understands the Marxian theory of alienation as "the exchange of the subjective with the objective and vice-versa."[121] This position implicitly understands Marx's notion of the fetish of commodities as referring to a sort of illusion, whereby attributes of the subjects appear to be attributes of that which they create. This relates directly to Hilferding's notion that the commodity form is simply a mystified form of "labor." When labor in capitalism is analyzed in transhistorical terms as "labor," its specificity is understood only extrinsically, in terms of the mode of distribution, and alienation is apprehended as a reversal that mystifies what already exists. Overcoming alienation, within such a framework, is seen as a process of demystification and reappropriation, as the reemergence of that which is socially ontological from behind the veil of its mystified form of appearance. Overcoming alienation, in other words, entails the historical Subject's realization of itself.

In the interpretation I present here, the categories of Marx's critique do not express the "exchange" of the subjective with the objective but, rather, the constitution of each of these dimensions. As I argued in the case of abstract time, determinate subjective forms, together with the objectivity they grasp, are constituted with determinate alienated forms of social relations; they are not preexistent, universal forms that, because they are alienated, appear to be the objective attributes of things. This further reinforces my contention that, with

120. Hilferding, "Böhm-Bawerk's Criticism of Marx," in Paul M. Sweezy, ed., *"Karl Marx and the Close of His System"* by Eugen Böhm-Bawerk and *"Böhm-Bawerk's Criticism of Marx"* by Rudolf Hilferding (New York, 1949), p. 195 (translation amended).

121. Colletti, "Bernstein and the Marxism of the Second International," in *From Rousseau to Lenin,* trans. John Merrington and Judith White (London, 1972), p. 78.

his analysis of the twofold character of labor in capitalism, Marx developed the theory of alienation as one of a historically specific mode of social constitution, whereby determinate social forms—characterized by the opposition of an abstract universal, objective, lawlike dimension and a "thingly," particular dimension—are constituted by structured forms of practice and, in turn, shape practice and thought in their image. These social forms are contradictory. It is this quality that renders the totality dynamic and gives rise to the possibility of its critique and possible transformation.

Integral to this theory of the socially and historically determinate constitution of social objectivity and subjectivity by a process of alienation is a critical analysis of the specificity of the various dimensions of social life in capitalism. This theory does not simply condemn the estrangement from the Subject—or subjects—of what already had existed as their property. Rather, it analyzes the historical constitution of human powers in alienated form. Overcoming alienation, in this view, involves the *abolition of the self-grounding, self-moving Subject* (capital) and of the form of labor that constitutes and is constituted by structures of alienation; this would allow humanity to appropriate what had been constituted in alienated form. Overcoming the historical Subject would allow people, for the first time, to become the subjects of their own social practices.

Marx's notion of the fetish is centrally related to his theory of alienation as social constitution. This notion does not refer merely to socially constructed illusions, but attempts to socially account for various forms of subjectivity. It is integral to Marx's theory of social constitution, which relates forms of thought, worldviews, and beliefs to the forms of social relations and the ways in which they appear to immediate experience. In *Capital,* Marx tries to grasp the constitution of historically specific deep social structures by forms of social practice that, in turn, are guided by beliefs and motivations grounded in the forms of appearance engendered by these structures. The whole, however, is not statically circular and doxic, but dynamic and contradictory. An adequate elaboration of Marx's theory of the constitution of forms of subjectivity and objectivity in capitalism would analyze the interaction of structure and practice in terms of the nature of the contradictory dynamic of the totality; on this basis, one could develop a theory of the historical transformation of subjectivity that would elucidate the social constitution and historical development of needs and perceptions—both those that tend to perpetuate the system and those that call it into question.

Such a theory of the constitution of consciousness and social being has little in common with interpretations in which "labor" or the economy form the "base" of society and thought is a "superstructural" element. It is a nonfunctionalist social theory of subjectivity which, ultimately, is based on an analysis of the forms of social relations, rather than on considerations of social position and social interest, including class position and class interest. The former analysis provides the general, historically changing framework of forms of consciousness within which the latter considerations can be examined. Such an approach assumes that if social meaning and social structure are to be related, the categories that grasp them must be related intrinsically—in other words, that the pervasive theoretical dichotomy of the material and cultural dimensions of social life cannot be overcome extrinsically, on the basis of concepts that already contain within them that opposition.[122] This position distinguishes the social and historical theory of subjectivity presented here from those attempts to relate thought and "social conditions" which can explain the social function and social consequences of a particular form of thought, but cannot ground socially the specificity of this thought and relate it intrinsically to its context. The Marxian theory attempts to do so. In general, it treats meaning neither in a reductive materialist manner, as an epiphenomenal reflex of a physical material base nor—of course—in an idealist manner, as a self-grounded and completely autonomous sphere. Rather, it seeks to grasp social life with categories that allow it to treat the structure of meaning as an intrinsic moment of the constituted and constituting structure of social relations.[123]

122. This approach is very different than that expressed by Max Weber in his well-known metaphor that ideas create world-images that determine, like switchmen, the tracks along which action is pushed by the dynamic of interest (see "The Social Psychology of the World Religions," in H. H. Gerth and C. W. Mills, eds., *From Max Weber* [New York, 1958], p. 280). This metaphor relates the social, or material, dimension and the cultural dimension only extrinsically and contingently. To the extent that the position it expresses does recognize a subjective aspect of material life, it does so in a way similar to many economistic theories—it identifies this dimension with considerations of interest alone. As a result, what should be analyzed as a specific, socially, and historically constituted form of subjectivity ("interest") is presupposed as given, while other forms of subjectivity are treated in an idealist manner. This inability to grasp the intrinsic relation of forms of subjectivity and forms of social relations is related to an approach which does not grasp material life in terms of the determinate forms by which social life is mediated.

123. Émile Durkheim, in *The Elementary Forms of the Religious Life* (trans. Joseph Ward Swain [New York, 1965]), also proposes a theory of knowledge which attempts to ground the categories of thought socially. On the basis of his approach, Durkheim is able to indicate the power of a social theory of knowledge in addressing and changing the terms of epistemological problems, as they had been formulated classically. However (leaving aside its functionalist aspects), Durkheim's theory focuses on the social organization of society rather than on the forms of social mediation—hence, he lacks a conception of categories of social life which could simultaneously be categories of subjectivity and objectivity. Durkheim's approach is ambivalent as regards the issue of the relation of social context and thought. It both is critical of natural scientific understandings of social life, which disregard the issue of social meaning, and is itself transhistorical and objectivistic. Although Durkheim does suggest that science itself is embedded socially, he does not treat as a determinate system of meaning the tendency of science to view all of reality in object-terms. Rather, he takes it to be an expression of the evolutionary development of society.

It is possible to grasp Durkheim's own dualistic interpretations of social life in terms of the Marxian approach presented here. His oppositions of society and the individual, soul and body, the abstract, general and the concrete particular—whereby only the first, abstract term of each opposition is understood as social—can be grasped as hypostatizations and projections of the commodity form. See *The Elementary Forms of the Religious Life*, pp. 21–33, 169–73, 258–60, 306–308, 467–94.

6. Habermas's critique of Marx

On the basis of what I have developed thus far regarding Marx's analysis of labor in capitalist society, the difference between value and material wealth, and the sort of sociohistorical theory of consciousness and subjectivity implied by his categorial analysis, I shall now conclude my discussion of the trajectory of Critical Theory by considering some aspects of Jürgen Habermas's critique of Marx. This critique is integral to Habermas's effort to reconstruct a critical social theory adequate to the changed nature of postliberal capitalism that would also move beyond the pessimism of Critical Theory discussed in Chapter Three.[1] As I have mentioned, though, Habermas's critique of Marx, which was closely tied in his earlier works to the distinction he had begun to develop between labor and interaction,[2] is predicated upon some basic assumptions that informed the works of Pollock and Horkheimer. Habermas tries to surpass the limits of their work by calling into question the central constitutive role they, in traditional Marxist fashion, accorded "labor"; he does not, however, criticize the notion of "labor" itself. Although Habermas has modified his approach to social theory since his early critique of Marx, his traditional understanding of labor has continued to inform his work. This, I argue, has weakened his attempt to formulate a critical social theory adequate to modern society. What follows is not a full discussion of the development of Habermas's theory; rather, it is an attempt to extend my earlier argument regarding the limitations of any social critique that seeks to respond to the changed nature of contemporary capitalism while remaining tied to the traditional conception of "labor"—even if, like Habermas's, it successfully avoids the fundamental pessimism of Critical Theory.

---

1. See J. Habermas, *Knowledge and Human Interests*, trans. Jeremy Shapiro (Boston, 1971), pp. 60–63; *Communication and the Evolution of Society,* trans. Thomas McCarthy (Boston, 1979); *The Theory of Communicative Action,* vol. 1: *Reason and the Rationalization of Society,* trans. Thomas McCarthy (Boston, 1984), and vol. 2: *Lifeworld and System: A Critique of Functionalist Reason,* trans. Thomas McCarthy (Boston, 1987).
2. See Habermas, "Labor and Interaction: Remarks on Hegel's Jena *Phenomenology of Mind,*" in *Theory and Practice,* trans. John Viertel (Boston, 1973); and "Technology and Science as 'Ideology,'" in *Towards a Rational Society,* trans. Jeremy J. Shapiro (Boston, 1970).

Habermas's early critique of Marx

One of Habermas's central concerns in his early works was to examine the possibility of critical consciousness within the framework of a theory capable of grasping critically the technocratic nature of postliberal capitalism and the bureaucratic and repressive nature of "actually existing socialism". In *Knowledge and Human Interests,* he approaches this problematic in terms of the question of a radical critique of knowledge. He maintains that such a critique is necessary in order to undermine the positivist identification of knowledge with science—itself an expression of, and contributing factor to, the increasingly technocratic organization of society—and to show instead that science should be understood as only one possible mode of knowledge.[3] Habermas claims that such a radical critique of knowledge is possible only as social theory, and notes that that idea is already implicitly present in Marx's theory of society.[4] Nevertheless, according to Habermas, Marx does not adequately ground such a critique, inasmuch as his methodological self-understanding obscures the difference between rigorous empirical science and critique. For that reason Marx was unable to develop a theory that could contest the victory of positivism.[5]

Habermas develops his arguments regarding Marx's theory against the background of his reading of Hegel's critique of Kant. In this critique, according to Habermas, Hegel opened the possibility of a radical critique of knowledge, one characterized by self-reflection.[6] Hegel criticized Kant's epistemology for being caught in the circle of having to know the cognitive faculty before knowing, and he uncovered several of the implicit, unreflected presuppositions of this epistemology.[7] These presuppositions include a normative concept of science, a fixed, knowing subject, and the distinction between theoretical and practical reason. Hegel argued that epistemology is not—and cannot be—free of presuppositions, as Kant claims, but actually bases itself on a critical consciousness that results from a process of self-formation. The critique of knowledge, therefore, must become aware of its own self-formative process and know that it itself is incorporated in the experience of reflection as one of its elements. This process of reflection develops as a process of determinate negation in which theoretical and practical reason are one: the categories of understanding the world and norms of behavior are connected.[8] By subjecting the presuppositions of epistemology to self-criticism, Hegel radicalized it. Nevertheless, according to Habermas, he did not proceed further in this direction. Instead of unambiguously radicalizing the critique of knowledge, Hegel negated it abstractly; he

---

3. Habermas, *Knowledge and Human Interests,* pp. 3–5.
4. Ibid., p. vii.
5. Ibid., pp. 24, 61.
6. Ibid., pp. 5, 19.
7. Ibid., p. 7.
8. Ibid., pp. 13–19.

attempted, on the basis of the presuppositions of the philosophy of identity (of the world and the knowing subject) and its associated notion of absolute knowledge, to overcome the critique of knowledge as such, rather than to transform it.[9]

Marx, according to Habermas, did not share the basic assumptions of the philosophy of identity, for he assumed the externality of nature.[10] He was, therefore, in a position to develop a radical critique of knowledge—but he failed to do so. The grounds for this failure, Habermas argues, are rooted in the philosophical foundations of Marx's materialism, in particular, the role accorded labor.[11] Habermas maintains that labor, in Marx's social theory, is an epistemological category as well as one of human material existence: not only is it a necessary precondition of the reproduction of social life, but, inasmuch as it constitutes the nature around us as an objective nature for us, it also creates the "transcendental conditions of the possible objectivity of the objects of experience."[12] Thus, labor both regulates material exchange with nature and constitutes a world: its function is synthesis.

The Marxian notion of synthesis through labor, according to Habermas, entails a materialist transformation of Fichte's philosophy of the ego, according to which the ego is constructed in the very act of self-consciousness: the original ego posits the ego by positing a nonego in opposition to itself.[13] In Marx's theory, the laboring subject confronts a nonego, its environment, which obtains its identity through labor. The subject thus gains its own identity by interacting with a nature that has been the object of its labor and the labor of preceding generations. In this sense, the human species posits itself as a social subject in the process of production.[14] With this notion of the self-development of humanity through labor, Marx undercut both philosophical anthropology and transcendental philosophy.[15]

Nevertheless, Habermas argues, such a materialist conception of synthesis does not provide an adequate basis for a radicalized critique of knowledge.[16] If synthesis takes place by means of labor, the substratum in which its results are expressed is not a connection of symbols but the system of social labor.[17] Labor, according to Habermas, is instrumental action. Hence, the concept of synthesis through social labor can lead to an instrumentalist theory of knowledge: The condition of possibility of the objectivity of natural scientific knowledge is

9. Ibid., pp. 9, 20, 23, 24.
10. Ibid., pp. 24, 33, 34.
11. Ibid., p. 42.
12. Ibid., p. 28.
13. Ibid., p. 38.
14. Ibid., p. 39.
15. Ibid., pp. 28–29.
16. Ibid., p. 42.
17. Ibid., p. 31.

rooted in labor. However, phenomenological experience, hence self-reflection, exist in another dimension, that of symbolic interaction.[18] Habermas claims that Marx did, to be sure, incorporate this social dimension—which is that of the relations of production—in his material investigations; on the categorial level, however, within his philosophical frame of reference, the self-generative act of the human species is reduced to labor.[19] Marx, according to Habermas, conceived of the process of reflection according to the model of production and, hence, reduced this process to the level of instrumental action. He thereby eliminated reflection as a motive force of history—for, within such a materialist theory, the subject, in confronting the nonego, not only confronts a product of the ego but also some portion of the contingency of nature.[20] Consequently, the act of appropriation, as conceived by Marx, is not identical with the reflective reintegration of some previously externalized part of the subject itself. As a result of the notion of synthesis through social labor, then, the possibility of a radical critique of knowledge was undermined and the logical status of the natural sciences was not distinguished from that of critique.[21]

Habermas maintains that such a materialist conception of synthesis leads to a notion of social theory as technically exploitable knowledge and, therefore, serves to support social engineering and technocratic control.[22] Quoting a long passage from the *Grundrisse*[23] that deals with the emancipation of humanity from alienated labor on the basis of the transformation of the labor process into a scientific process, Habermas claims that the position it expresses presupposes both that the history of the species has been constructed solely by synthesis through social labor, and that the development of natural science and technology is transposed automatically into the self-consciousness of the social subject. The result is the reciprocal subsumption of the human sciences and natural science, which the young Marx envisioned.[24] Habermas's argument, in other words, is that Marx's theory of social synthesis through labor does not provide an adequate basis for a critical theory of a world characterized by technocratic domination, social engineering, and bureaucratization—indeed that, the nature of his theory is such that it can be and has been used to further such developments.

The way out of this impasse, according to Habermas, is a reconstruction of the history of the species that would conceive of its self-constitution from a double perspective, that of labor and of interaction.[25] The problem with Marx's

---

18. Ibid., pp. 35–36, 42.
19. Ibid., pp. 42, 53.
20. Ibid., p. 44.
21. Ibid.
22. Ibid., p. 47.
23. Marx, *Grundrisse: Foundations of the Critique of Political Economy,* trans. Martin Nicolaus (London, 1973), pp. 704–5; quoted in the present volume in Chapter One, "Rethinking Marx's Critique of Capitalism," p. 25.
24. Habermas, *Knowledge and Human Interests,* pp. 48–50.
25. Ibid., pp. 53, 60, 62.

attempt to grasp both with the dialectic of the forces and relations of production (that is, in terms of the sphere of labor alone) is that the institutional framework resisting a new stage of reflection is not immediately the result of a labor process, but rather represents a relation of social forces, of class domination.[26] For Habermas, Marx's theory of social synthesis through labor collapses the sphere of interaction into that of labor, thereby undermining the possibility of critical consciousness and, hence, of emancipation. Habermas therefore proposes a historical reconstruction based upon a theory of two forms of social synthesis: synthesis through labor (that is, through instrumental action), whereby reality is interpreted from the technical viewpoint, and synthesis through struggle (as the institutionalized form of interaction), whereby it is interpreted from a practical viewpoint.[27] He maintains that synthesis through labor alone historically leads to the organization of society as an automaton, whereas synthesis through interaction can lead to an emancipated society, which he describes in terms of an organization of society on the basis of decisions made in discussions free from domination.[28] The sphere of interaction, then, provides the basis for critique and for the possibility of emancipation.

Habermas's proposed reconstruction of the history of the species should be seen as an attempt to move beyond the fundamental pessimism of Critical Theory and to resuscitate the possibility of an emancipatory critique of contemporary society in a twofold way—by criticizing the notion of synthesis through labor and supplementing it with one of synthesis through interaction. In light of my exposition thus far, however, it should be clear that his critique of Marx's conception of synthesis through labor is based upon an understanding of labor as concrete labor per se, that is, as "labor." It does not deal with the Marxian analysis of the double character of labor. Given this traditional presupposition, it is not surprising that the passages Habermas cites to present Marx's position are taken from either his early works (in which, it can be argued, Marx himself had a transhistorical concept of "labor") or, for example, from a section in Volume 1 of *Capital* in which Marx describes the material elements of the labor process in transhistorical terms.[29] As I shall show in Part III, however, the latter passages should be understood in light of Marx's strategy of presentation. Proceeding from the indeterminate, transhistorical description of the labor process that Habermas cites, Marx subsequently spends the better part of Volume 1 indicating that all of its terms become reversed in capitalism. He thereby demonstrates that production in capitalist society *cannot* be understood simply in transhistorical terms, that is, in terms of the interaction of humans and nature, because the form and goal of the labor process are shaped by abstract labor,

26. Ibid., pp. 52, 55.
27. Ibid., pp. 55–56.
28. Ibid.
29. Ibid., pp. 25–29.

that is, by the process of creating surplus value.[30] Marx's analysis of labor and of production in capitalism, in other words, cannot be interpreted adequately if it is understood in precisely those transhistorical terms that he demonstrated to be invalid for capitalist society.

I have argued that, in his mature works, Marx does indeed present a theory of social synthesis by labor, but as the basis for an analysis of the *specificity* of the social forms of capitalist society. The labor that Marx analyzes not only regulates the material exchange with nature, as is the case in all social formations, but also constitutes those social relations that characterize capitalism. It is because of its peculiar twofold character that labor in capitalism—*not* "labor"—underlies a dialectic of the forces and relations of production.[31] The world constituted by such labor is not only the material environment, formed by concrete social labor, but the social world as well. Hence, to return to the Fichtean model described above, the nonego posited by abstract labor is indeed a product of the ego: it is a structure of alienated social relations. Contrary to the distinction Habermas draws between the categorial level in Marx's work and the level of his material investigations, the former level in Marx's mature critique is not that of "labor" but of the commodity, abstract labor, value, and so on—that is, forms of social relations mediated by labor. As such, it does incorporate the interactional dimension that Habermas maintains is included only in Marx's "material investigations."

Marx, as I have argued, does not reduce social practice to labor and posit productive activity as the paradigm of interaction. Rather, he analyzes how what might be two dimensions of social life in other societies are conflated in capitalism, inasmuch as both are mediated by labor. On this basis, he specifies the forms of social relations and of consciousness in capitalist society, and analyzes the inner logic of development of that society. Habermas, as I shall outline briefly, proceeds on the basis of the transhistorical notion of "labor" and overlooks Marx's conception of the specificity of the forms of wealth, production, and social relations in capitalism; he also misunderstands Marx's sociohistorical theory of knowledge. The issue is not simply whether Habermas is "fair" to Marx; it is a question of the adequacy of a critical social theory to its object. If the process of social constitution by labor does indeed specify capitalism, then to project this mode of constitution transhistorically (as traditional Marxism has), or to replace it with an equally transhistorical scheme of the existence of two separate but interdependent spheres (labor and interaction, instrumental and communicative action) is to obscure the specificity of commodity-determined labor and, hence, of what characterizes capitalism. More generally, the meth-

---

30. Marx, *Capital,* vol. 1, trans. Ben Fowkes (London, 1976), pp. 283–639.
31. In a long footnote (*Knowledge and Human Interests,* p. 327n14), Habermas criticizes Marx's attempt to analyze "productive activity" and "relations of production" as different aspects of the same process. He considers this process, however, only in terms of "labor" and not in terms of the specific, socially constitutive character of labor in capitalism.

odological and epistemological implications of Marx's categorial analysis of capitalism raise serious questions about any attempt to develop a social theory on the basis of a set of categories presumed to be applicable generally to the history of the human species.

I can begin to elucidate the differences between the two approaches by examining Habermas's treatment of the category of value. In discussing some implications of technological change in an early essay, Habermas, relying to some extent on Joan Robinson, equates value and material wealth.[32] It is worth looking at his arguments more closely, for they refer to the sections of Marx's *Grundrisse* that I discussed Chapter One. Recall that, in the *Grundrisse* (as well as in *Capital*), Marx does not deal with value as a category of wealth in general, or in terms of a quasi-automatic self-regulating market, but as the essence of a mode of production whose "presupposition is—*and remains*—the mass of direct labour time, the quantity of labour employed, as the determinant factor in the production of wealth."[33] With the development of industrial capitalism and the rapid growth of productivity, material wealth increasingly becomes a function of the general state of science and its application to production, rather than of the amount of labor time and, hence, direct human labor employed.[34] The difference between material wealth and value becomes an increasingly acute opposition, according to Marx, because value remains the essential determination of wealth in capitalism even though material wealth becomes ever less dependent on the expenditure of direct human labor. Hence, direct human labor is retained as the basis of production and becomes even more fragmented, although it has become "superfluous" in terms of the potential of the forces of production that have come into being.[35] The enormous increase in productivity under capitalism, then, does not result in a corresponding reduction of labor time and a positive transformation of the nature of work. The basic contradiction in capitalism, seen thus, is grounded in the fact that the form of social relations and wealth, as well as the concrete form of the mode of production, remain determined by value even as they become anachronistic from the viewpoint of the material wealth-creating potential of the system. In other words, the social order mediated by the commodity form gives rise, on the one hand, to the historical possibility of its own determinate negation—a different form of social mediation, another form of wealth, and a newer mode of production no longer based on fragmented direct human labor as an integral part of the process of production. On the other hand, this possibility is not automatically realized; the social order remains based on value.

In his essay, however, Habermas mistakenly interprets these passages in the

32. Habermas, "Between Philosophy and Science: Marxism as Critique," in *Theory and Practice*, pp. 222–35.
33. *Grundrisse*, p. 704 (emphasis added).
34. Ibid., pp. 704–705.
35. Ibid., p. 706.

Grundrisse as an assertion by Marx that the "scientific development of the technical forces of production are to be considered as a possible source of value."[36] He bases his argument on the following statement of Marx's: "But to the degree that large industry develops, the creation of real wealth comes to depend less on labour time and on the amount of labour employed than on the power of the agencies set in motion during labour time."[37] In this passage Marx clearly opposes the *real wealth*–producing potential of the forces of production developed under capitalism to the *value* form of wealth, which remains a function of direct labor time. Yet Habermas misses this point by assuming that Marx was positing a changed determination of *value*—one no longer based on direct human labor. Consequently, he argues that Marx later dropped this "revisionist" idea, and that it did not enter into the final version of the labor theory of value.[38] In an attempt to "save" the theory of value and render it adequate to conditions of modern technology, Habermas suggests that the value expression for constant capital (machinery and so on) should be modified to take into account the "advance in technical knowledge" that goes into its creation.[39]

Habermas, in other words, does not grasp Marx's distinction between value and material wealth, and, thus, between the abstract and concrete dimensions of commodity-producing labor. He assumes that Marx's labor theory of value was similar to that of classical political economy—an attempt to explain social wealth in general. Habermas maintains, therefore, that the labor theory was valid only for the stage of development of the technical forces of production when the creation of real wealth did, indeed, depend essentially on labor time and the amount of labor employed. With the rise of highly developed technology, value is based increasingly on science and technology rather than on direct human labor.[40] Unlike those positions that posit labor as the transhistorical source of wealth, Habermas recognizes the *wealth*-creating potentials of science and technology, and their growing relevance to contemporary social life. He claims, however, that they constitute a new basis of *value*, and thereby conflates what Marx had distinguished.

This conflation prevents Habermas from understanding the Marxian conception of the contradiction of capitalism as one that arises within capitalist production as a result of the growing discrepancy between value and wealth.[41] As

36. Habermas, "Between Philosophy and Science," p. 226.
37. *Grundrisse*, p. 704.
38. Habermas, "Between Philosophy and Science," p. 227.
39. Ibid., p. 226.
40. Ibid., p. 229.
41. Wolfgang Müller begins a very similar critique of Habermas's interpretation of the *Grundrisse* passages in question and of his interpretation of the category of value: see "Habermas und die 'Anwendbarkeit' der 'Arbeitswerttheorie,'" *Sozialistische Politik* 1 (April 1969), pp. 39–54. Yet, following his exposition of the difference between value and material wealth and the emergence of their contradiction, Müller breaks with the logic of his own analysis. He does

I shall elaborate, the Marxian dialectic of production is socially determinate and contradictory, rooted in the twofold character of the fundamental social forms of capitalism. Habermas, however, interprets the *Grundrisse* passages cited immediately above as expressing an evolutionary transformation of the basis of value.[42] The labor theory of value, according to Habermas, was once valid for a stage of technical development; it is now no longer valid and should be superseded by a "science and technology theory of value." Habermas's notion that the basis of "value" changes as technology does necessarily implies a linear notion of the course of capitalist production, possessing no intrinsic contradictions and limits. In the critique of political economy, Marx seeks to ground and explain the dialectical course of capitalist development in terms of the nature of its underlying social forms; Habermas, however, takes recourse to a basically evolutionary conception, to a notion of a linear, transhistorical development of production (and of interaction), which he does not ground socially.

Habermas's approach represents an attempt to conceptualize critically significant changes that have occurred in modern capitalist society. In terms of Marx's analysis, however, a theory based upon the identification of value with wealth in general (and the linear, evolutionary conception of development this implies), does not adequately grasp the specific nature of contemporary capitalist production and the course of its development. The general problem involved—a problem to which I shall return in the next chapters—is the formulation of a theory able to do justice to modern society's major transformations in the twentieth century and to its continuing identity as capitalism. Neither a "labor theory of wealth" nor a "science and technology theory of value" can, in my view, provide the basis for a theory that is able to analyze both moments adequately.

Habermas's evolutionary conception of development is an expression of a fundamental reversal of Marx's analysis. For Marx, value is a historically specific social category that expresses the essential social relations of capitalism, in terms of which its forms of production and subjectivity, and its dynamic

---

not reconsider the Marxian critique in light of this contradiction; rather, in the course of his discussion of the German Democratic Republic, Müller presents the traditional Marxist position. He characterizes capitalism as a system in which "the *societalization* of labor . . . remains subsumed under the forms of *private* appropriation" (p. 50). Müller's critique of Habermas, in other words, does not lead him to place labor at the center of the critique of capitalism; instead, he places private property (and the market) there. This position, however, implies a notion of "labor" in terms of which any critique of Habermas—as of Pollock—is ultimately inadequate, as it ignores the specificity of commodity-producing labor. For other critiques of Habermas's understanding of Marx, see Rick Roderick, *Habermas and the Foundations of Critical Theory* (New York, 1986); Ron Eyerman and David Shipway, "Habermas on Work and Culture," *Theory and Society* 10, no. 4, (July 1981); Anthony Giddens, "Labour and Interaction," in John B. Thompson and David Held, eds., *Habermas: Critical Debates* (Cambridge, Mass., 1982); John Keane, "Habermas on Work and Interaction," *New German Critique* 6 (Fall 1975); and Richard Winfield, "The Dilemmas of Labor," *Telos* 24 (Summer 1975).

42. Habermas, "Between Philosophy and Science," pp. 229–30.

historical development, can be understood. Habermas understands the category of value as a quasi-natural, transhistorical, technical category of wealth, and maintains that the rate of surplus value in the Marxian analysis is a magnitude that is "naturally" grounded, a fact of "natural history"[43]—its basis merely expresses the technical level of production. Although, in other works, Habermas does not always treat value as a transhistorical category of wealth but, at times, as a historically specific category of the market,[44] he does not grasp value as a specific form of wealth and of social relations, and consider it with reference to the specificity of labor in capitalism. Instead, he treats value either as wealth in general or as a specific form of the distribution of wealth. This position is, of course, related intrinsically to an understanding of the category of labor in Marx's analysis of capitalism as concrete labor in general, as a technical activity that mediates the relationship of humans with nature. Habermas's misinterpretation of Marx's analysis of value and of commodity-determined labor reinforces, and is logically consistent with, his failure to develop a conception of the social form of production and technology and, hence, to develop a critique of the process of production in capitalism. Instead, Habermas regards the form and development of production and technology in technical and evolutionary terms, and rejects as romantic all attempts to specify them socially.[45]

Habermas's treatment of the *Grundrisse* passages discussed in Chapter One illustrates his identification of labor, understood as productive activity, with the labor-mediated social relations that Marx analyzed. As I have shown, Habermas misinterprets as an evolutionary development the contradiction outlined by Marx between production based on value and the form that production would be able to take were it not for value. In addition, Habermas interprets these passages as implying that the transformation of science into machinery leads automatically to the liberation of a self-conscious general Subject.[46] He imputes to Marx, in

43. Ibid., pp. 227, 229–231. Unfortunately, the translation on pp. 229–30 is very misleading. The word "only" has been omitted in the following sentence: "With the introduction of a corresponding corrective factor the rate of surplus value would not *only* cease to be a prior given as a 'natural magnitude.' "

44. See for example, "Technology and Science as 'Ideology,' " pp. 100–2.

45. See for example, *Knowledge and Human Interests*, p. 61; "Technology and Science as 'Ideology,' " pp. 83–90. In the latter, Habermas rejects Marcuse's position that the rationality of science and technology incorporates a historical and hence transitory, *a priori*. Instead, he claims that they follow invariant rules of logic and feedback-controlled action. The arguments Habermas provides, however, are far from convincing. He argues—questionably—that Marcuse's conception of another science and technology is tied to a notion of communication with a resurrected nature. More important, Habermas implies that any critique of the existing forms of science and technology must necessarily entail such a romantic notion, which is by no means the case. The Marxian analysis of the social determinations of capitalism's process of production, and the sociohistorical theory of knowledge implied by this analysis, certainly are not romantic. Habermas himself simply ignores the question of the social and cultural determinations of production as well as of conceptions of nature.

46. Habermas, *Knowledge and Human Interests*, pp. 50–51.

other words, a notion of emancipation as a quasi-automatic technical consequence of the linear development of material production. In his early essay,
"Labor and Interaction," Habermas had already called such a technocratic
vision of social emancipation into question: "Liberation from hunger and misery does not necessarily converge with liberation from servitude and degradation, for there is no automatic developmental relation between labor and
interaction."[47]

Overcoming material want alone is not a sufficient condition for freedom from
domination, according to Habermas—hence, the development of production
alone does not lead automatically to emancipation, even when it is used to free
people from material deprivation. On the contrary, as we have seen, the logical
endpoint of the development of labor, for Habermas, is society as an automaton,
managed technocratically. Because of this interpretation of the nature and consequences of social synthesis through labor, Habermas regards Marx's distinction in the *Grundrisse* between the self-conscious control of social life by the
collective producers, on the one hand, and the automatic regulation of the process of production that has become independent of the producers, on the other,
as the expression of another position on Marx's part, one not consonant with
the analytic centrality he accords labor.[48]

Contrary to Habermas's interpretation, however, the distinction between the
self-conscious and the automatic regulation of social life is completely consistent
with Marx's analysis of the form of social constitution effected by commodity-
determined labor, as well as with his description of the growing contradiction
between production that remains based on value and the potential of its own
results. I have shown that Marx's critique is very much directed against the
automatic regulation of production and of society. Such regulation, however, is
not rooted in production per se, according to Marx; it is not a function of labor
as such. Rather, it is a function of specific social forms, the value form of wealth,
and commodity-determined labor. In Part III, I shall show how Marx also analyzes the directionality of capitalist society and its mode of producing in terms
of this abstract and automatic form of regulation—he shows that the developmental course of production in that society is not technical and linear but social
and dialectical. Science and technology are embedded in a value-determined
mode of production that they both reinforce and contradict, according to Marx:
they are not automatically transposed into the self-consciousness of the social
subject.

Social constitution by labor in Marx's analysis, then, is not transhistorical but,
rather, a historically specific mode that underlies the automatic regulation of
social life in capitalism. This form of social constitution is the object, not the
standpoint, of his critique. It, therefore, follows that emancipation would require

---

47. Habermas, "Labor and Interaction," p. 169.
48. Habermas, *Knowledge and Human Interests,* pp. 50–51.

not the *realization* but the *overcoming* of the consequences of this mode of social constitution. Overcoming the contradiction outlined in the *Grundrisse* does not, then, imply emancipation from hunger and toil alone: overcoming the capitalist relations of production, as expressed by the categories of value and capital, also entails overcoming the automatic regulation of society. Although this may not be a sufficient condition for establishing the self-conscious control of social life, overcoming abstract domination certainly is a necessary presupposition for the realization of such social self-determination. Marx's analysis of the historically specific process of social constitution by labor thus involves a critique of precisely what Habermas maintains Marx's theory affirms.

Habermas's critique of Marx is a critique of the traditional Marxist notion of social constitution by labor from the standpoint of a position that shares some traditional assumptions.[49] His concern is to develop a notion of emancipation in terms of liberating the many from material deprivation, as well as establishing the self-conscious control by people of social and political life—in sharp contradistinction to any technocratic conception. Yet, because Habermas fails to distinguish a historically specific social form—commodity-determined labor—from labor understood transhistorically as productive activity, he is less able than Marx, in my judgment, to ground the "automatism" of modern life and, hence, the conditions of its possible overcoming.

Labor in capitalism may be a form of instrumental action, as Habermas claims, but not by virtue of the fact that it is productive activity. It may very well be the case that, whatever their other significance, various labors and their tools in all societies can also be seen as technical means to achieving particular ends. This, however, does not constitute the basis for instrumental reason: there is no necessary correlation between the level of technical sophistication in various societies and the existence and strength of what can be called "instrumental reason." The character of labor is not transhistorically given but a function of the social relations in which it is embedded. We have seen that, within the framework of Marx's analysis, it is labor's self-mediating quality in capitalism that accords an instrumental character to labor and imparts an objective nature to the social relations characterizing this society. Such an approach, unlike those of Horkheimer and Habermas, casts the technical and means-oriented character of instrumental reason and action in social and historical terms, rather than as a result of the development of production, understood technically.

The problematic determinations of the technical and the social in Habermas's earlier works are related to his transhistorical treatment of labor, and highlight

49. For an explicit example of these assumptions, see, for example, "Technology and Science as 'Ideology,' " p. 96, where Habermas describes capitalism as having given rise to a mode of production "that could be freed from the institutional framework of capitalism and connected to mechanisms other than that of the valorization of capital in private form" (translation amended). In other words, he considers the process of production in capitalism to be a technical process, and deems the relations of production to be exogenous to it, that is, private property.

what has always been a paradox of traditional Marxism. On the one hand, Habermas deals with labor as "labor" and does not grasp Marx's analysis of the historical specificity of labor in capitalism. His approach to labor and production entails treating as socially indeterminate and technical what for Marx is, but does not appear to be, socially determined and determining in capitalism. On the other hand, Habermas does retain the notion of labor as socially synthetic (even if he limits its scope by supplementing it with a notion of interaction). As a result, he is led to attribute to labor per se, to a purportedly technical activity, properties that labor in capitalism possesses because of its historically specific social function, according to Marx, which are not everywhere and always properties of laboring activity. Habermas, in other words, hypostatizes transhistorically the alienated character of labor in capitalism as an attribute of labor per se. Consequently, his understanding of the relations of production in capitalism is crucially underspecified, for it lacks precisely their central, characterizing moment—their alienated and objective character—which he attributes to "labor" by seeing it as instrumental action.

To attribute instrumentality to labor in and of itself is to naturalize that which is socially constituted and to project transhistorically what is historically determinate. In Marxian language, it is to succumb to the appearance of the fetish by attributing a quality of the abstract value dimension of the social forms of capitalism to their concrete, use value dimension, thereby rendering opaque their social and historical specificity. At issue is not only whether labor always and everywhere is instrumental action but, rather, whether instrumental reason and action themselves, regardless of how constituted, should be considered transhistorically rather than as expressions of a particular form of social life.[50]

Unlike more orthodox versions of Marxism, both Habermas's approach and the Marxian theory share a critical attitude toward the consequences of social synthesis by labor. Because Marx's conception of social synthesis by labor is historically specific, however, it points to consequences that are very different from those attributed to it by Habermas; and it allows for an analysis of, for example, the growth of instrumental reason and action, or of the quasi-automatic regulation of capitalist society, more satisfactory than that proposed by Habermas in his early critique. It seeks to elucidate such developments with reference to the specificity of capitalism's social forms rather than in terms of socially indeterminate categories that purportedly describe the interactions among humans and between humans and nature in all societies and at all times.

---

50. That Habermas more recently has referred to social labor as a combination of communicative and instrumental action does not obviate this critique of the transhistorical nature of his notion of instrumental reason and action, whether considered to be rooted in "labor" or not. See Habermas, "A Reply to my Critics," in Thompson and Held, eds., *Habermas: Critical Debates,* pp. 267–68. Moreover, one must distinguish between seeing instrumental reason and action as historically specific forms, and seeing them as transhistorical but socially dominant only in modern capitalist society.

A transhistorical approach also tends not to distinguish between labor as socially constitutive and as individually self-constituting. Thus, orthodox forms of traditional Marxism evaluate both positively: socialism is conceived as a society in which social constitution by labor will function openly and coincide with individual self-constitution by labor. Yet Habermas's negative evaluation of the effects of social constitution by labor, because of its similarly transhistorical character, implicitly accords no creative, positively self-reflexive possibilities to individual labor. When social synthesis by labor is seen as historically specific, however, these two moments can be separated. We have seen that for Marx, overcoming capitalism would entail the abolition of value and allow for a radical transformation of the nature of social labor. This suggests that individual labor could be much more positively self-constituting when labor no longer functioned as a socially constituting activity. Unlike both the orthodox position and Habermas's, moreover, this interpretation does not evaluate as either unequivocally positive or negative the consequences of the mode of social constitution effected by labor; rather, as I noted in my discussion of alienation, these consequences are seen as two-sided.

Habermas's misinterpretation of the historical specificity of the form of labor in Marx's critique of political economy also has far-reaching consequences for a consideration of the epistemological dimension of that theory. Habermas accuses Marx of not having sufficiently distinguished natural science and social theory. He provides as one proof Marx's claim to have uncovered the economic laws of motion of capitalism as a natural law that operates independently of human will.[51] Such a claim on Marx's part, however, does not indicate that he understood human society as such to follow quasi-natural laws. It reflects, rather, his analysis of the *capitalist* formation as governed by such laws because its fundamental social relations are alienated: they are objectified, have a "life of their own," and exert a sort of quasi-natural compulsion on the individuals. Habermas, however, does not interpret Marx's statement as referring to an abstract domination historically specific to capitalism—for example, to the process of capital accumulation that constantly revolutionizes all aspects of social life on a worldwide scale, a process that indeed is independent of individual will. He takes Marx's statement, rather, as expressing a transhistorical position according to which the science of society in general and natural science are essentially similar.

Marx's position, however, implies a relationship between natural science and society very different from what Habermas imputes to it. Far from considering natural science to be the only model of knowledge, including knowledge of society, it implies a historical theory of all forms of knowledge, including natural science. Marx's categorial analysis of the social relations of capitalism as mediated by labor implies not that society is like nature,[52] but that there is a sim-

51. Habermas, *Knowledge and Human Interests*, pp. 45–46.
52. Ibid., p. 47.

ilarity between these forms of social relations and modern forms of thought, including the natural sciences.[53] Marx's theory of the fetish does not merely unmask the legitimation of power in bourgeois society, as Habermas would have it;[54] rather, it is a social theory of subjectivity that relates forms of consciousness to the manifest forms of social relations in a society where labor mediates itself and thereby constitutes people's relations among each other as well as with nature. The reason Marx's critique of political economy does not separate sharply the system of meaning, a "connection of symbols," from the system of social labor is because of his analysis of the historically specific constitutive role of labor in capitalism—not because of any ontological presuppositions regarding labor. Marx grounds both systems in the structure of labor-mediated social relations.

Habermas apparently does not at this point have a comparable social theory of knowledge. (As noted, he does not have a conception of the social constitution of the process of production.) Although Habermas argues in his early works that the category of labor alone is insufficient to grasp social synthesis, he does seem to accept the notion that knowledge of nature arises directly out of the labor-mediated interaction of humans with nature. He thus implicitly treats natural science as a form of knowledge that is pragmatically won and, hence, not socioculturally formed. I have argued that conceptions of reality cannot be derived from concrete labor alone, because labor itself does not impart meaning but, rather, is accorded meaning by the structure of its social universe. In terms of what I have suggested thus far, it could be argued that a theory that grounds conceptions of nature in concrete labor—such as the one Habermas apparently accepts in his earlier works—is itself a form of thought that expresses a social situation in which labor functions as a social mediation.[55]

I have argued that Habermas, in his earlier works, emphasizes the epistemological dimension of critical social theory in order to criticize the increasingly technocratic nature of domination in the modern world, as well as technocratic tendencies within the Marxist tradition, and to provide a theoretical standpoint of critique that would allow a contemporary critical theory to move beyond the sort of fundamental pessimism that characterized Critical Theory after 1940.

---

53. For an explicit indication that Marx does interpret natural-scientific thought in terms of forms of social relations and not simply as a function of the interaction of concrete social labor with nature, see *Capital,* vol. 1, p. 512n27, where he speaks of Descartes as seeing "with the eyes of the period of manufacture."

54. Habermas, *Knowledge and Human Interests,* p. 60.

55. The fundamental issue is one of the social constitution of culturally specific forms of thought, and not simply of whether conceptions of nature, for example, are won pragmatically out of the interaction with nature. In this sense, my criticism of an approach that does not consider the social and cultural determinateness of forms of thought would also apply to the sort of position Habermas apparently has subscribed to more recently—that is, understanding the development of natural science in terms of discourses about the pragmatic interaction with nature, for example, but not analyzing these discourses as socially and culturally determinate.

However, the nature of Habermas's critique of the notion of synthesis by labor does not, in my opinion, provide a satisfactory alternative to what he criticizes. The notion of a radical epistemology promulgated in *Knowledge and Human Interests* does not entail a sociohistorical theory of knowledge and subjectivity, a theory of determinate forms of consciousness. The nature of critical consciousness, therefore, remains underspecified socially.

Moreover, Habermas's interpretation of labor and interaction contains a fundamental ambiguity. As I have shown, Habermas grounds the growth of instrumental reason and action not socially, in a structure of labor-mediated social relations, but in labor as such. He claims that instrumentality has extended beyond its "proper" realm (for example, the sphere of production) and is invading other spheres of social life; yet it remains unclear why the extension of instrumentality into the sphere of interaction, which presumably results from the growing importance and complexity of production in the modern world, is not inexorable and irreversible. In other words, Habermas does not clarify how it is that social self-determination can take place at all in a situation of advanced technological development, given that a result of this development would likely be the growing tendency for society to be organized as an automaton. Put simply, there is an ambiguity in Habermas's earlier works as to whether practical reason *is* or *should be* dominant in the sphere of interaction. If the former, then it is unclear how practical reason could have succumbed in the face of "labor's progress." However, if the instrumentalization of the world is bound necessarily to the development of production as such, it is not evident why the appeal to practical reason could be more than an exhortation.

Habermas's early attempt to reconstitute the possibility of a critical social theory can be seen in light of Horkheimer's pessimistic turn, examined in Chapter Three. There, I showed that, in 1937, Horkheimer still regarded synthesis through labor to be emancipatory. The totality it constitutes allows for a rational and just organization of social life; this totality, however, is fragmented and hindered from realizing itself by (capitalist) social relations. Following his adoption of the thesis of the primacy of the political,[56] Horkheimer became deeply skeptical regarding "labor" as a source of emancipation—without, however, reconsidering his transhistorical understanding of that category. Habermas has retained Horkheimer's traditional understanding of "labor," and also has adopted his later negative evaluation of it as instrumental action, as the source of technocratic domination. In order to avoid Horkheimer's fundamental pessimism, Habermas's strategy has been to limit theoretically the scope of "labor's" significance by supplementing it with a conception of interaction. By arguing that the latter social sphere serves as the standpoint of the critique, Habermas theoretically grounds the possibility of emancipation in a sphere of social rela-

---

56. Habermas also adopted this thesis and, hence, its one-sided emphasis on the mode of distribution as socially determining: see "Technology and Science as 'Ideology,'" pp. 100–2.

tions outside of that of labor. He characterizes that sphere as a social dimension "which does not coincide with that of instrumental action," one within which "phenomenological experience moves."[57] In a sense, Habermas reverses the relationship among labor, social relations, and emancipation posited by Hork-heimer in 1937.

Because Habermas interprets Marx's conception of social synthesis through labor in terms of instrumental action, his early critique of Marx is strongly reminiscent of Horkheimer's polemic in *Eclipse of Reason* against the (certainly nondialectical and noncritical) forms of scientism and faith in automatic progress he saw as dominant in the United States. Horkheimer criticized pragmatism for making experimental physics the prototype of all scientific knowledge.[58] He also polemicized against positivism for regarding natural science as the automatic guarantor of social progress, and criticized the technocratic assumption that the-oretical social criticism is superfluous because technological development will automatically solve all human problems.[59] These charges are basically similar to Habermas's early critique of Marx.[60] While this critique may be justified with regard to more orthodox variants of Marxism, it can only be applied to Marx if the meaning and implication of value, the central category of the critique of political economy, is overlooked or reductively interpreted as a market category. Moreover, although Habermas attributes to Marx the same notions of natural science, production, and labor criticized by Horkheimer in pragmatism and pos-itivism, Habermas himself adopts precisely these notions in his treatment of the sphere of labor, and then attempts to limit the extent of their social validity by positing a countervailing sphere of interaction. The result is a historically in-determinate interpretation of the sphere of labor as one of instrumental action, an underspecified theory of forms of social relations and forms of consciousness, and a return to a transhistorical theory of social and historical development.

The Theory of Communicative Action and Marx

Habermas's *Theory of Communicative Action* (1981) represents the culmina-tion to date of his efforts to lay the foundation for a new critical theory of modern society. It entails a reconstruction of the history of the human species in the context of an attempt to transform the fundamental presuppositions of modern social theory. Compared to his earlier works, Habermas's critical ap-proach in this work is no longer based so strongly on the ideal of critical self-reflection and does not focus primarily on the critique of scientism; it does not place as much emphasis on labor as instrumental action; it has a more funda-

57. Habermas, *Knowledge and Human Interests,* p. 42.
58. Horkheimer, *Eclipse of Reason* (New York, 1974), p. 50.
59. Ibid., pp. 59, 74ff., 151.
60. For a similar critique, see Albrecht Wellmer, "The Latent Positivism of Marx's Philosophy of History," in *Critical Theory of Society,* trans. John Cumming (New York, 1971).

mentally worked out theory of interaction (as a theory of communicative action and reason); and it combines a historically specific analysis with a transhistorical approach in a more differentiated manner.[61] Nevertheless, the basic themes, concerns, and orientations of *The Theory of Communicative Action* remain continuous with those of Habermas's early works. As in these early works, Habermas's reading of Marx is constitutive of his approach; the traditional nature of this reading has weakened his theory in ways that suggest that a fundamental rethinking of the Marxian critique is important for contemporary critical theory.[62]

I have noted that Habermas's attempt to reconstitute a fundamental social critique with emancipatory intent should be seen in the context of Critical Theory's trajectory. Indeed, he himself describes his project of reconstituting a critical theory adequate to contemporary postliberal society in this work as a "second attempt to appropriate Weber in the spirit of Western Marxism."[63] He has sought to incorporate Max Weber's analysis of modernity as a process of societal rationalization, while avoiding the theoretical limitations of the earlier critical appropriation of Weber's analysis undertaken by Georg Lukács and theorists associated with the Frankfurt School, such as Max Horkheimer and Theodor Adorno. Habermas argues that a new theoretical approach able to move beyond those limitations cannot be developed simply by modifying the older approach; rather, it requires a fundamental reorientation of social theory. He attempts to effect such a reorientation with his theory of communicative action; on this basis, he attempts to transform social theory's categorial framework from one resting upon the subject-object paradigm—and, hence, a notion of action as essentially purposive-rational—to one resting upon a paradigm of intersubjectivity.

Habermas states at the outset of this work that his general intentions in developing the theory of communicative action are threefold.[64] First, he wishes to reestablish theoretically the possibility of a social critique. The standpoint of critical theory, according to Habermas, must be universalistic and based on reason—which, for him, means that it must be nonrelativistic. Nevertheless, he seeks to ground the possibility of such a standpoint socially, rather than transcendentally. To this end, Habermas formulates a social theory of rationality. He distinguishes various forms of reason by developing a concept of communicative rationality which is different from, even opposed to, cognitive-

61. For a discussion of the development of Habermas's project in the 1960s and 1970s, see Thomas McCarthy's excellent account, *The Critical Theory of Jürgen Habermas* (Cambridge, Mass., 1978).

62. A version of the following analysis of *The Theory of Communicative Action* appeared in M. Postone, "History and Critical Social Theory," *Contemporary Sociology* 19, no. 2 (March 1990), pp. 170–76.

63. Habermas, *The Theory of Communicative Action*, vol. 2, p. 302.

64. Ibid., vol. 1, p. xl.

instrumental rationality. He roots both forms of reason in determinate modes of social action and, on this basis, formulates a theory of historical development in terms of two distinguishable processes of rationalization (rather than in terms of the development of purposive rationalization alone). Habermas seeks to ground the possibility of a critical social theory in the development of communicative reason. In doing so, he attempts simultaneously to defend (communicative) reason against postmodernist and poststructuralist positions—which he regards as irrationalist—and provide a critique of the growing domination of cognitive-instrumental forms of rationality in postliberal capitalism.

Habermas's second major concern is to grasp modern society by means of a two-level theory, based on differentiating forms of action and of reason. This theory is an effort to integrate approaches that view social life in terms of a "lifeworld"—an idea deriving from the phenomenological and hermeneutic traditions—with approaches that view society as a "system." He argues that modern society should be understood in terms of both dimensions, as differentiated modes of social integration, and relates each of these dimensions to a determinate form of rationality ("communicative" and "cognitive-instrumental"). He attempts to do justice to the notion of people as social actors, as well as to the idea that modern society is characterized by emergent forms of social integration (for example, the capitalist economy, the modern state) that function quasi-independently of actors' intentions and, frequently, of their awareness and understanding.

Habermas's third concern is to construct on this basis a theory of postliberal modern society which affirmatively apprehends the historical development of modernity as a process of rationalization and differentiation, and yet also views critically the negative, "pathological," aspects of existing forms of modern society. He interprets such "pathologies" in terms of a selective process of rationalization under capitalism which leads to the growing domination and penetration of the communicatively structured lifeworld by quasi-autonomous, formally organized systems of action.

These three interrelated thematic concerns, which refer to three different levels of historical specificity, define the contours of a theory based on the conception of communicative action. With it, Habermas criticizes the main theoretical tendencies in contemporary social scientific inquiry as well as the tradition of Western Marxism. He tries to redeem the intentions of that latter tradition by questioning some of its fundamental theoretical propositions. He begins anew, as it were, by appropriating major currents of twentieth-century philosophy and social theory—speech-act theory and analytic philosophy, classical social theory, hermeneutics, phenomenology, developmental psychology, systems theory—in order to transform the basic paradigm of social theory and formulate a critical theory adequate to the contemporary world. Nevertheless, he does so with an understanding of Marx that leads him, in the process of appropriation, to adopt presuppositions that ultimately are in tension with the critical thrust of his theory. This, in turn, raises the question whether a socially grounded critical theory of modernity which overcomes the limitations of earlier Critical Theory requires the sort of social ontology and evolutionary approach that Habermas proposes.

In order to elaborate this contention, I must outline briefly Habermas's complex argumentative strategy in *The Theory of Communicative Action*. The conceptual point of departure for his critical theory of modernity is an immanent critique of Weber's theory of rationalization and its reception by Lukács, Horkheimer, and Adorno. As Habermas notes, Weber analyzed modernization as a process of societal rationalization that involved the institutionalization of purposive-rational action in Europe between the sixteenth and eighteenth centuries.[65] This development, for Weber, presupposed a process of cultural rationalization involving the differentiation of individual value spheres—of scientific, artistic, legal, and moral representations—that began to follow their own independent and autonomous logics.[66] The paradoxical result of these processes of rationalization, in Weber's account, is that modern life increasingly becomes an "iron cage," characterized by a loss of meaning—of any theoretical and ethical unification of the world—as well as a loss of freedom due to the institutionalization of cognitive-instrumental rationality in the economy and the state.[67]

Habermas adopts Weber's analysis of modernity in terms of processes of rationalization but maintains that the "iron cage" is not a necessary feature of all forms of modern society. Rather, what Weber attributed to rationalization as such should be grasped in terms of a selective pattern of rationalization in capitalism which leads to the dominance of purposive rationality.[68] Habermas claims that Weber's own theory provides the basis for such an approach, for it implicitly presupposed, as its standpoint, a more complex notion of reason from which it criticized the increasing dominance of purposive rationality; however, it never explicitly clarified that standpoint.[69]

Habermas makes explicit this implicit critical standpoint by reconstructing the theory of cultural rationalization suggested by Weber's treatment of the world religions.[70] His two-stage reconstruction postulates a universal-historical process of the rationalization of worldviews, which sets the stage for the historically specific transposition of cultural rationalization into social rationalization in the West.[71] Habermas adopts and modifies this evolutionary theory of worldview development. First, he distinguishes the universal *inner logic* of the historical

65. Ibid., p. 216.
66. Ibid., pp. 166, 175.
67. Ibid., p. 241.
68. Ibid., pp. 181–83.
69. Ibid., pp. 220–22.
70. Ibid., pp. 166, 195.
71. Ibid., pp. 174–77.

development of worldview structures from the *empirical dynamic* of worldview development, which depends on external factors.[72] (This distinction is fundamental to Habermas's reconceptualization of critical social theory.) Second, Habermas claims that Weber's focus in analyzing modernization as rationalization was too narrow: he did not adequately consider the implications of the differentiation of value spheres, each characterized by a single universal validity claim (truth, normative rightness, beauty) and form of rationality (cognitive-instrumental, moral-practical, and aesthetic).[73]

This critical appropriation of Weber's approach points toward a broader conception of rationality, rooted in the purportedly inner logic of rationalization and differentiation. It allows Habermas to distinguish what was empirically actualized in capitalist society from the possibilities contained in the modern structures of consciousness that resulted from the process of disenchantment.[74] Habermas is thus able to present the rise to preeminence of cognitive-instrumental rationality, at the expense of moral-practical and aesthetic-practical rationality, as an expression of the partial character of rationalization in capitalism, rather than of rationalization per se.[75]

It is important to note that, within the framework of Habermas's reconstruction, the possibilities resulting from the process of disenchantment are present at the *beginning* of capitalism. This implies that capitalism represents a *deformation* of what had become possible as a result of a universal inner logic of historical development. The standpoint of the critique, in other words, is *outside* of capitalism, in what Habermas earlier had termed the "sphere of interaction," now interpreted as a universal social potential. Similarly, capitalism is implicitly understood in terms of cognitive-instrumental reason alone (what Habermas had considered the sphere of labor in his earlier works)—that is, as one-dimensional.

Habermas begins to explicate the preconditions of his reconstruction by uncovering two basic reasons for Weber's failure to realize the explanatory potential of his own theory. He argues that Weber's theory of action is too narrow: Weber based it on a model of purposive action and cognitive-instrumental rationality. The understanding of the rationalization of worldviews suggested by Weber's approach could be fully developed, however, only on the basis of another theory of action—one of communicative action. Habermas asserts, moreover, that a theory of modern society cannot be based on a theory of action alone. What characterizes modern society is that important dimensions of social life (for example, the economy and the state) are integrated in a quasi-objective way; they cannot be grasped by action theory, but must be understood systemically. Hence, a critical theory of the present requires a theory of com-

72. Ibid., pp. 179–97.
73. Ibid.
74. Ibid., p. 198.
75. Ibid., p. 223.

municative action as well as a theory of society able to combine an action-theoretic with a systems-theoretic approach.[76]

Lukács and the members of the Frankfurt School did attempt to incorporate Weber's analysis of rationalization in a theory of systematic integration. Nevertheless, according to Habermas, their efforts were unsuccessful. Central to those attempts was Lukács's concept of reification, with which he sought, on the basis of Marx's analysis of the commodity, to separate Weber's analysis of societal rationalization from its action-theoretical framework, and to relate it to anonymous processes of capital realization.[77] Using this concept, Lukács argued that economic rationalization is not an example of a more general process, but that, on the contrary, commodity production and exchange underlie the basic phenomenon of societal rationalization.[78] The latter, therefore, should not be seen as a linear and irreversible process.

Habermas does not confront directly Lukács's Marxian analysis of rationalization; rather, he criticizes his Hegelian "solution" to the problem, which entailed a dogmatic deification of the proletariat as the identical subject-object of history.[79] Horkheimer and Adorno also rejected this Hegelian logic in their respective attempts to develop further a critical theory based on the concept of reification.[80] As Habermas notes, however, their critique of instrumental reason in the 1940s raised problems regarding the normative foundations of critical theory. They assumed that the rationalization of the world had become total, and rejected Lukács's appeal to objective reason; consequently, they no longer grounded reification in a historically specific and transformable form (the commodity), but rooted it transhistorically in the labor-mediated confrontation of humanity with nature. Habermas points out that, with this turn, Critical Theory no longer could articulate the standards of its critique.[81]

The problem with all of these efforts, Habermas claims, is that they remained bound to the subject-object paradigm (which he calls the "paradigm of the philosophy of consciousness"). Their theoretical difficulties reveal the limits of any social theory based on this paradigm and indicate the need for a fundamental theoretical change to a paradigm of intersubjective communication.[82]

In some respects, Habermas's critique of Western Marxism parallels the interpretation I present here. What he terms the "philosophy of consciousness" is related to the concept of "labor" I have analyzed; both approaches are critical of theories based on the subject-object paradigm and place considerations of social relations at the center of analysis. Nevertheless, Habermas's critique leads

76. Ibid., p. 270.
77. Ibid., p. 354.
78. Ibid., p. 359.
79. Ibid., p. 364.
80. Ibid., p. 369.
81. Ibid., pp. 377–83.
82. Ibid., p. 390.

to an analysis of communication as such, whereas mine leads to a consideration of the determinate form of social mediation that constitutes modern society. I shall consider some implications of this difference somewhat later.

Habermas tries to provide the basis for the theoretical change to a paradigm of intersubjectivity by developing the concepts of communicative reason and communicative action. He argues that the modern understanding of the world—which, unlike mythic forms of thoughts, is reflexively aware of itself and entails differentiated objective, social, and subjective worlds—is both socially grounded and yet has universal significance.[83] Making tacit use of Jean Piaget's theory of the ontogenesis of structures of consciousness, Habermas maintains that the modern worldview results from a universal-historical process of the rationalization of worldviews that takes place by means of historical learning processes.[84] This process of rationalization does not only entail the growth of cognitive-instrumental rationality but is primarily associated with the development of communicative rationality. Habermas grasps the latter in procedural terms (not in terms of content), as relating a decentered understanding of the world to the possibility of communication based on uncoerced agreement.[85]

Using speech-act theory, Habermas then argues that reaching understanding is the most essential aspect of language, although not every linguistically mediated interaction is oriented to that end. Moreover, he maintains that speech-acts can coordinate interactions *rationally*—that is, independently of external forces, such as sanctions and traditional norms—when the validity claims they raise are criticizable. Finally, Habermas also argues that, in coming to an understanding, actors necessarily claim validity for their speech acts.[86]

In other words, Habermas roots communicative rationality in the very nature of language-mediated communication and, thereby, implicitly claims that it has universal significance. It represents the more complex form of reason which would allow for a critique of the one-dimensional form of rationalization Habermas sees as characteristic of capitalist society. Indeed, the potential for critique is built into the very structure of communicative action; this does not allow questions of meaning to be separated from those of validity.[87]

Having grounded the possibility of communicative rationality abstractly, Habermas then attempts to provide a genetic account of its development by apprehending the universal-historical rationalization process in terms of the rationalization of the lifeworld.[88] In order to do so with concepts outside of the

---

83. Ibid., pp. 48, 64, 70.
84. Ibid., pp. 67–69.
85. Ibid., pp. 70–74.
86. Ibid., pp. 287–88; 297–308.
87. Ibid., pp. 104–6; 295–305.
88. Ibid., pp. 70, 336.

subject-object paradigm, Habermas appropriates and modifies George Herbert Mead's communication-theoretic approach[89] and interweaves it with an analysis of Emile Durkheim's notion of the sacred roots of morality and his account of the change in the form of societal integration from mechanical to organic solidarity. Habermas thus develops a theory of the inner logic of sociocultural development as a process of the "linguistification of the sacred."[90] He characterizes this process as one in which the rationality potential of communicative action is released; such action then supersedes the older sacred normative core as that which effects cultural reproduction, social integration, and socialization. This process of the supersession of a mode based on normatively ascribed agreement to one based on communicatively achieved agreement results in a rationalized lifeworld—that is, in the rationalization of worldviews, the generalization of moral and legal norms, the growth of individuation, and the growing reflexivity of symbolic reproduction.[91]

Habermas, in other words, conceptualizes the development of the modern worldview in terms of a process by which linguistically mediated communication increasingly "realizes itself" (like Hegel's *Geist*) and comes into its own as that which structures the lifeworld. This logic of social evolution is the standard against which the actuality of modern development can be judged.[92] The standpoint of Habermas's critique, then, is universal; although social, essentially it is not formed culturally, socially or historically, but is grounded in the ontological character of communicative action as it unfolds in time. Language, then, occupies a place in Habermas's theory that is directly analogous to that occupied by "labor" in affirmative forms of traditional Marxism.

Although this approach does entail a change of paradigm within the theory of action, it grasps only one dimension of modern society, according to Habermas: it can explain the symbolic reproduction of the lifeworld, but not the reproduction of society as a whole. Actions, as Habermas notes, are coordinated not only by processes of reaching understanding but also through functional interconnections that are not intended and frequently not perceived.[93] He therefore proposes a theory of social evolution according to which society become differentiated both as a system and as a lifeworld.[94] Habermas distinguishes the rationalization of the lifeworld from systemic evolution, which is measured by increases in a society's steering capacity, and he claims that increases in systemic complexity ultimately depend on the structural differentiation of the lifeworld. He grounds the latter in an evolutionary development of moral con-

89. Ibid., vol. 2, pp. 10–13, 61–74.
90. Ibid., pp. 46, 110.
91. Ibid., pp. 46, 77, 107, 146.
92. Ibid., p. 110.
93. Ibid., pp. 113, 150.
94. Ibid., p. 153ff.

sciousness that is the necessary condition for releasing the rationality potential in communicative action.[95]

This development, according to Habermas, eventually undermines the normative steering of social interactions. Consequently, interaction becomes coordinated in two very different ways: either by means of explicit communication, or by means of what Talcott Parsons characterized as the steering media of money and power—quasi-objective social mediations that encode purposive-rational attitudes and detach interchange processes from the normative contexts of the lifeworld. The result, then, is an uncoupling of system integration (effected by the steering media of money and power) from social integration (effected by communicative action). This uncoupling of system and lifeworld, which involves the differentiation of state and economy, characterizes the modern world.[96]

After presenting this two-sided approach, Habermas notes that most approaches in social theory have been one-sided, in that they seek to grasp modern society with concepts that apply to only one of its two dimensions. He implicitly presents his own approach as the third major attempt, after those of Marx and Parsons, to do justice to both aspects of modern social life. Although Marx's theory of value, according to Habermas, was an attempt to connect the systemic dimension of anonymous interdependencies with the lifeworld context of actors, it ultimately reduced the former to the latter inasmuch as it viewed the systemic dimension of capitalism as no more than the fetishized form of class relations. Hence, Marx could neither see the positive aspects of systemic differentiation nor deal adequately with bureaucratization.[97] For this reason Habermas turns to Parsons's attempt to bring together system-theoretic and action-theoretic paradigms. He tries to embed this attempt within the framework of a more critical approach that at once entails a reconceptualization of action theory and, unlike Parsons's approach, addresses the "pathological" aspects of capitalist modernization.[98]

On the basis of this two-sided approach, Habermas then outlines a critical theory of postliberal capitalism. He begins by reformulating Weber's diagnosis of modernity and his thesis of the paradox of rationalization, rejecting conservative positions that attribute the pathologies of modernity either to secularization or to the structural differentiation of society.[99] Instead, Habermas distinguishes two forms of modernization: a "normal" form, which he characterizes as a "mediatization" of the lifeworld by system imperatives, wherein a progressively rationalized lifeworld is uncoupled from, and made to depend on, increasingly complex, formally organized domains of action (like the econ-

95. Ibid., p. 173ff.
96. Ibid., pp. 154, 180ff.
97. Ibid., pp. 202, 336ff.
98. Ibid., p. 199ff.
99. Ibid., p. 330.

omy and the state), and a "pathological" form, which he calls the "colonization" of the lifeworld. What characterizes the latter is that cognitive-instrumental rationality, by means of monetarization and bureaucratization, extends beyond the economy and the state into other spheres and achieves dominance at the expense of moral-practical and aesthetic-practical rationality. This results in disturbances in the symbolic reproduction of the lifeworld.[100] Habermas reformulates Weber's notion of the loss of meaning and loss of freedom in terms of his thesis that the lifeworld is colonized by the system world. This thesis serves as the basis for his analysis of postliberal capitalism.[101]

Habermas claims that this reinterpretation of the developmental logic suggested by Weber provides the justification for describing the phenomena he describes as pathologies. Further, the concept of communicative rationality also theoretically provides a social grounding for resistance against the colonization of the lifeworld (which characterizes many contemporary social movements).[102] Nevertheless, he asserts, one must also understand the developmental dynamics of the modern world—that is, explain why such pathologies appear. In order to do so, Habermas adopts Marx's notion of an accumulation process that is an end in itself, uncoupled from orientations toward use values.[103] Having incorporated the dynamic of capital accumulation into his model of the interchange relations between system and lifeworld, Habermas then addresses issues in late capitalism that have eluded more orthodox Marxist attempts, such as state interventionism, mass democracy, the welfare state, and the fragmented consciousness of everyday life.[104] Coming full circle, as it were, he concludes with an agenda for a critical theory of society, which takes up some of the themes developed in the 1930s as the research program of the (Frankfurt) Institute for Social Research.

Despite the breadth and sophistication of Habermas's exposition, certain aspects of the theoretical framework he proposes in *The Theory of Communicative Action* are problematic. It attempts to apprehend a twofold social reality by bringing together two approaches that essentially are one-sided. Habermas criticizes Parsons for projecting an uncritical picture of developed capitalist societies,[105] and attributes this to a theoretical construction that blurs the distinction between system and lifeworld; yet he does not seem to acknowledge that the very attempt to theorize "economy" and "state" in systems-theoretic terms ("steering media") limits the scope of his social critique. The categories of "money" and "power" do not grasp the determinate structure of the economy and polity, but simply express the fact that they exist in quasi-objective form

100. Ibid., p. 303ff.
101. Ibid., p. 318ff.
102. Ibid., p. 333.
103. Ibid., p. 328.
104. Ibid., p. 343ff.
105. Ibid., p. 299.

The commodity

and are not mere projections of the lifeworld. These categories cannot, for example, elucidate the nature of production, or of the developmental dynamic of the capitalist social formation; nor do they allow for a critique of existing forms of administration. Hence, although Habermas does presuppose capital accumulation and state development, and criticizes the existing organization of the economy and public administration, the systems-theoretic framework he adopts does not allow him to ground these presuppositions and critical attitudes.

Habermas clearly seeks to indicate that, contrary to all romantic critiques of capitalism, any complex society requires some form of "economy" and "state." However, by adopting the notion of steering media, he presents the existing forms of these spheres of modern social life as necessary. His critique of state and economy is restricted to situations in which their organizing principles overstep their bounds. However, the notion of a quasi-ontological boundary between those aspects of life which safely can be "mediatized" and those that only can be "colonized" is very problematic. The idea that only those domains of action that fulfill economic and political functions can be converted over to steering media[106]—in other words, that the system can successfully colonize spheres of material reproduction, but not of symbolic reproduction—implies that one can conceive of material reproduction as not being symbolically mediated. This separation of material life and meaning, which continues the quasi-ontological distinction between labor and interaction Habermas drew in his earlier works, reveals that Habermas still implicitly adheres to the concept of "labor." Like Horkheimer, he apparently considers the subject-object relationship to be rooted in the very nature of "labor" (or in the sphere of material reproduction), unmediated symbolically. This is in sharp contrast to the position I present here, which roots instrumentality in the nature of a particular form of social mediation rather than in the relations of human with nature.

Habermas's decision to grasp modern economic and political processes in systems-theoretic terms complements his attempt to conceptualize modern forms of morality, legality, culture, and socialization in terms of a rationalized lifeworld constituted by communicative action. Apparently, he conceives of the cultural and social constitution of worldviews and forms of life only in terms of overt ("traditional" and "religious") sociocultural forms. Hence—aside from whether relating the modern worldview logically to formal properties of linguistically mediated communication necessarily indicates that it actually is so structured—Habermas's conception of the rationalized lifeworld is extremely underspecified as an approach to modern life. It assumes that because social interaction in capitalism is not mediated by overt traditional forms, it must then be mediated by linguistic communication per se (however distorted by capitalism). By taking the abstract form of commodity-mediated communication at face value, such an approach does not allow for a theory of secular ideologies or for

106. Ibid., p. 318.

an analysis of the great changes in consciousness, norms, and values which have occurred within modern society itself in the course of the past centuries— changes that cannot be grasped simply in terms of oppositions such as "traditional" and "modern," or "religious" and "secular." Moreover, inasmuch as Habermas grounds the systemic and lifeworld dimensions of modern society in two very different ontological principles, it is difficult to see how his theory can explain interrelated historical developments in economy, politics, culture, science, and the structure of everyday social life.[107] In other words, because his theory combines two one-sided approaches, it has difficulty relating the two dimensions purportedly grasped by these approaches.

These problems are rooted, ultimately, in Habermas's appropriation of a systems-theoretic approach, his quasi-ontological distinction between system and lifeworld, his insistence on distinguishing between developmental logic and historical dynamic, and, relatedly, his evolutionary theory. I cannot directly address these complex issues here, in particular, the problems involved in conceptualizing human phylogenetic development in a manner analogous to Piaget's ontogenetic developmental scheme. I would, however, like to draw attention to a fundamental assumption underlying Habermas's approach: he distinguishes between historical logic and empirical dynamic in order to ground his social critique of postliberal society. This implies an assumption that such a critique cannot be grounded in the nature and dynamic of modern capitalism itself. In his discussion of Critical Theory, Habermas points out the limitations of the subject-object paradigm upon which it was based. What he apparently has retained from that tradition, however, is the thesis that capitalism is "one-dimensional," a unitary, negative whole that does not give rise immanently to the possibility of a social critique. This may seem paradoxical inasmuch, as we have seen, one of his theoretical intentions has been to move beyond the fundamental pessimism of Critical Theory. Nevertheless, it has become clear that he has sought to do so by subsuming capitalism within a larger conception of modern society, rather than by rethinking Marx's critique of capitalism as a critique of modernity. In such an approach, the pessimism of Critical Theory is to be overcome theoretically by positing a social realm (in this case, one constituted by communicative action) that both exists alongside, but purportedly is not intrinsically part of, capitalism, and also grounds theoretically the possibility of a social critique. Communicative action in such an approach is analogous to labor in traditional Marxism; as a result, the critique apprehends capitalism only as pathological and, therefore, must ground itself in a quasi-ontological manner, outside of the social and historical specificity of this form of social life.

Both Habermas's implicit understanding of capitalism as one-dimensional and

107. For a similar critique, see Nancy Fraser, "What's Critical About Critical Theory?: The Case of Habermas and Gender," *New German Critique* 35 (Spring–Summer 1985), pp. 97–131.

his appropriation of Parsons's notion of steering media are related to his understanding of Marx. I have shown that Critical Theory's analysis of postliberal capitalism as a society without an intrinsic structural contradiction was based on a traditional conception of labor in capitalism as "labor." What I shall now show is that Habermas's critique of Marx in *The Theory of Communication Action* and, hence, his turn to systems theory—in order to define modern society as one in which important dimensions of social life are integrated quasi-objectively and therefore lie beyond the pale of action theory—also rests upon a traditional reading of Marx.

Habermas interprets the Marxian theory through the lens of the thesis of one-dimensionality. He presents Marx's analysis of capital, of the dialectic of "living labor" (the proletariat) and "dead labor" (capital), as a dialectic of the rationalization of the lifeworld and systemic rationalization. Marx's critique of capitalism, according to his interpretation, was a critique of its disintegrative influence on the lifeworld of the laboring classes. Socialism, then, "lies on a vanishing line of a rationalization of the lifeworld that was *misguided* by the capitalist dissolution of traditional forms of life."[108]

It is important to note that Marx's analysis, understood thus, does not grasp capitalism as double-sided, constituting new forms that point beyond itself; rather, it regards capitalism only as a negative force that destroys and deforms what had emerged as a result of the rationalization of the lifeworld. The possibility of socialism, then, results from the revolt of the lifeworld against its destruction by the system. This, however, implies that socialism represents not a society *beyond* capitalism—a new historical form—but an alternative, less distorted version of the same historical form.

Although, as we shall see, Habermas is critical of what he regards as Marx's specific analysis, his own approach adopts the general topos of the sort of social critique he attributes to Marx. Thus, in discussing the Protestant ethic analyzed by Weber, Habermas describes it as a *partial* expression of ethically rationalized worldviews, as an adaptation to the modern form of economic-administrative rationality—hence, as a *regression* behind the level that already had been attained in the communicatively developed ethic of brotherliness.[109] In other words, Habermas treats capitalism as a particularistic distortion of a universalist potential that was already present at its inception. This view is, of course, parallel to that implied by the traditional Marxist notion of socialism as the realization of the universalistic ideals of the bourgeois revolutions whose fulfillment had been hindered by the particularistic interests of the capitalists.

This traditional motif is also expressed in Habermas's brief account of the "new social movements" of the past several decades. He discusses these movements either as essentially defensive, protecting the lifeworld against systemic

---

108. Habermas, *The Theory of Communicative Action,* vol. 1, p. 343.
109. Ibid., pp. 223–28.

encroachments, or as civil rights movements that attempt to generalize socially the universalistic principles of the bourgeois revolutions.[110] He does not, however, treat these movements as expressing new needs and new possibilities— that is, in terms of a possible social transformation that points beyond capitalism in terms of the potential generated by the capitalist form of life itself.

Habermas's approach, then, can be understood on one level as maintaining some key features of traditional Marxism. At the same time, however, it criticizes as quasi-romantic Marx's specific analysis of capitalism. As I have noted, Habermas's appropriation of elements of Parsons's systems-theoretic approach is related to his evaluation of Marx's theory of value as an inadequate approach to modern society, unable to deal with the two analytic levels of "system" and "lifeworld." Habermas claims that, despite the apparent "two-level" character of the Marxian theory, Marx did not present an adequate analysis of the systemic level of capitalism, inasmuch as he treated this level essentially as an illusion, as the ghostly form of class relations that have become anonymous and fetishized.[111] For this reason, Marx could not recognize the positive aspects of the development of the systemic interconnections of the capitalist economy and the modern state; instead, he envisioned a future society as one based on the victory of living labor over dead labor, of the lifeworld over the system—a society in which the objective semblance of capital has been dissolved. However, Habermas claims, this vision does not grasp the integrity and importance of the systemic level. Moreover, it is unrealistic: Weber was correct to argue that the abolition of private capitalism would not mean the destruction of modern industrial labor.[112]

Habermas's critique presupposes that Marx analyzed capitalism essentially in terms of class relations, and that doing so undermined his attempt to grasp both levels of modern society. In other words, although Habermas's specific criticisms of Marx differ from those in his earlier works, his interpretation of the Marxian analysis of capitalism as quasi-romantic is based upon the assumption that Marx wrote a critique from the standpoint of "labor." Such a critique of capitalism, in Habermas's view, points toward a process of the "dedifferentiation" of spheres of life that had become differentiated in modern society—a process that he considers regressive and undesirable. For this reason, Habermas turns to systems theory in order to conceptualize the quasi-objective dimension of modern society, and attempts to embed this theory in a critical approach.

As I have demonstrated, though, Marx's analysis of labor in capitalism is not at all what Habermas attributes to him. The categorical social forms of commodity and capital do not simply *veil* the real social relations of capitalism,

110. Ibid., vol. 2, p. 343ff.
111. Ibid., pp. 338–39.
112. Ibid., pp. 339–40.

according to Marx; rather, they *are* the fundamental social relations of capitalism, forms of mediation that are constituted by labor in this society. The full
significance of this difference will only become fully apparent in Part III, when
I analyze Marx's concept of capital. As we have seen, however, far from regarding what Habermas terms the "systemic dimension" as an illusion, a projection of "labor," Marx treats it as a quasi-objective structure constituted by
alienated labor. Marx's critique is of the form of this structure and the abstract
form of domination it exerts. The standpoint of his critique is not outside of the
structure; he neither calls for its complete abolition nor accepts its present form
and simply demands that it be limited to its "proper" sphere. Rather, his critique's standpoint is an immanent possibility generated by that structure itself.

That standpoint, as we shall see, is grounded by Marx in the double character
of labor in capitalism. Because Habermas assumes that Marx's critique is made
from the standpoint of "labor"—that is, the standpoint of the "vanishing
lifeworld"—he mistakenly claims that Marx has no criteria by which to distinguish the destruction of traditional forms of life from the structural differentiation of the lifeworld.[113] Marx's critique, however, is not based on what *was*
but on what *could be*. As I shall show, his analysis of the temporal dimension
of capitalism's social forms provides the basis for a theory of the intrinsic social
shaping of the material form of production, the form of growth, and the form
of administration in capitalism. Such an approach allows one to distinguish
between these forms as they exist under capitalism, and the potential they embody for other, more emancipatory forms.

Marx's vision of emancipation, which follows from his analysis, is precisely
the opposite of what Habermas attributes to him. Jumping ahead for a moment,
I shall show that, far from conceiving of socialism as the victory of living labor
over dead labor, Marx understands dead labor—the structure constituted by
alienated labor—to be not only the locus of domination in capitalism but also
the locus of possible emancipation. This makes sense only when Marx's critical
analysis of capitalism is understood as one that points toward the possible *abolition* of proletarian labor ("living labor"), not toward its *affirmation*. In other
words, contrary to Habermas's claim Marx agrees with Weber that the abolition
of *private* capitalism would not suffice at all for the destruction of modern
industrial labor. Nevertheless—and this is a crucial difference—Marx's analysis
does not accept the existing form of such labor as necessary.

In Part III I will demonstrate that Marx's analysis allows for a fundamental
critique of capitalism which entails neither a romantic vision of "dedifferentiation" nor an acceptance of the "iron cage of modern industrial labor"
as the necessary form of technologically advanced production. Instead, it can
provide a critique of the form of growth, of advanced technological production,
and of the systemic compulsions exerted on political decisions in capitalism—

113. Ibid., pp. 340–41.

and does so in a way that points beyond these forms. Such a critique would not simply evaluate negatively the encroachments of the system but would uncover and analyze the social forms underlying its determinate character and its "imperialist" expansion. From the standpoint of such a critique, one could argue that Habermas has no way of distinguishing between the forms of production and growth which developed in capitalism and other possible "differentiated" forms. Habermas's approach, with its static categories of "money" and "power," must accept the forms developed in capitalism as historically final, as the results of "differentiation" per se.[114]

As I continue to unfold Marx's analysis, then, I shall show how it allows for a nontraditional understanding of capitalism as contradictory rather than as one-dimensional. It thereby obviates the need to ground the critique of capitalism and the possibility of its transformation outside of capitalism itself, for example, in a transhistorical, evolutionary logic of history—whether that history is interpreted as a process of the self-realization of "labor" or of linguistically mediated communication.

The issue here is not simply whether Habermas has adequately interpreted Marx. Rather, it is whether the Marxian theory, as I have been reconstructing it, provides the possibility for a theoretical approach that could not only move beyond the weaknesses of traditional Marxism, and the pessimism of Critical Theory, but also avoid the problematic aspects of Habermas's attempt to ground a critical theory adequate to contemporary society. Turning to a theory of the historical specificity of the form of mediation that constitutes capitalism can, as noted, provide the basis for a reinterpretation of capitalism's contradictory character and for a critique of the form of production, of the economy, and, in

---

114. Habermas's final critique of Marx is that he dealt with the real abstraction of capitalist society only in terms of labor, and, hence, too narrowly, rather than thematizing the "systematically induced reification of social relations in general" (ibid., p. 342), which would have allowed for a more general theory, able to deal with bureaucratization as well as with the economy. However, there is a tension between Habermas's understanding of Marx's theory of labor as one of the process of real abstraction characteristic of capitalist society, on the one hand, and his interpretation of Marx's analysis of capitalism essentially in terms of class relations, on the other. Moreover, even here, Habermas's critique is, once again, based on an understanding of labor in capitalism as "labor" rather than as a form of social mediation. Understood in the latter way, the real abstraction of labor in capitalism can indeed be understood as a mechanism that underlies the reification of social relations in general. Finally, Habermas's conception of "power" and "money" as steering media simply signal that a process of abstraction characterizes modern society, and that a contemporary critical theory must take both the economy and the state into consideration. Unlike Marx's theory of labor as a social mediation, however, they do not allow for a distinction among forms of abstraction; nor do they grasp the process of temporal directionality characteristic of capitalism. I shall elaborate these themes in Part III of this work, arguing that Marx's theory is not necessarily one of the primacy of the economic sphere ("money") over the political ("power") but, rather, one of a dialectical historical development that embeds, shapes, and transforms both economy and polity and their interrelations.

general, of the form of interdependence in capitalism—in a way that a systems-theoretic approach cannot. Such a critical theory treats the analysis of capitalism as one of the underlying structures of modernity itself, and allows one to recover the idea of the possible transformation of production and the economy and, hence, of socialism as a historically different form of life.

The notion of the historical specificity of the Marxian critical theory, as well as of the forms of social life it grasps, also refers to history itself, in the sense of an immanent logic of historical development. In Part III, I shall outline how Marx grounds the historical dynamic of capitalism in the double character of its basic social forms. Such a historically specific social explanation of the existence of a historical logic rejects any notion of an immanent logic of human history as yet another projection onto history in general of capitalist society's conditions. The historical specificity of the critique of political economy delineates Marx's final break with his earlier transhistorical understanding of historical materialism and, hence, with notions of the philosophy of history (*Geschichtsphilosophie*). Ironically, Habermas's attempt to reformulate historical materialism in terms of an evolutionary logic of history, which he can posit but cannot really ground, remains closer than Marx's mature theory to Hegel's philosophy of history— precisely the "ballast" from which Habermas seeks to liberate historical materialism.[115]

The theory of historical development implied by Marx's analysis of the social forms of capitalism can also avoid some problems associated with a transhistorical, evolutionary theory of development. The idea that an immanent historical logic characterizes capitalism but not all of human history opposes any conception of a unitary mode of historical development. Yet such a notion does not imply an abstract form of relativism. Although the rise of capitalism in Western Europe may have been a contingent development, the consolidation of the commodity form is a global process, mediated by a world market that becomes increasingly integrated in the course of capitalist development. This process entails the constitution of world history. Thus, according to such an approach, a universal process with an immanent logic of development that provides the standpoint of a general critique does exist; it is historically determinate, however, and not transhistorical.

As a historically specific theory of social mediation, the approach I have been outlining also allows for a theory of determinate forms of consciousness and subjectivity. It could serve as a better basis for a theory of ideology as well as for efforts to address interconnected historical developments in various spheres of social life. Because such an approach can address the constitution of values and worldviews in terms of specific, contradictory social forms, rather than in

115. See Habermas, "Toward a Reconstruction of Historical Materialism," in Steven Seidman, ed., *Jürgen Habermas on Society and Politics* (Boston, 1989), pp. 114–41; *The Theory of Communicative Action*, vol. 2, p. 383.

terms of the cognitive and moral progress of the human species, it could serve as the starting point for attempts to grasp the two-sided character of capitalist development in cultural and ideological terms as well. One could, for example, analyze historical developments such as the spread of witchcraft trials or absolute slavery in the early modern period, or the rise of exterminatory anti-Semitism in the late nineteenth and twentieth centuries, with reference to the two-sidedness of capitalist development, rather than in terms of a presumed historical or cultural "regression" that cannot be justified historically.[116]

The historical specificity of the categories of Marx's mature critique has more general implications for the question of a self-reflexive social epistemology. I have argued that because both the interaction of humanity with nature and essential social relations are mediated by labor in capitalism, the epistemology of this mode of social life can be formulated in terms of categories of alienated social labor. The forms of interaction with nature and of human interaction, however, vary considerably among social formations. Different formations, in other words, are constituted by different modes of social constitution. This, in turn, suggests that forms of consciousness *and* the very mode of their constitution vary historically and socially. Each social formation, then, requires its own epistemology. Put more generally: Even if social theory proceeds on the basis of certain very general and indeterminate principles (for example, social labor as a prerequisite of social reproduction), its categories must be adequate to the specificity of its object. There is no transhistorically valid, determinate social theory.

This historically determinate Marxian approach provides a framework within which the underspecified character of Habermas's notions of system and lifeworld can also be analyzed. As I have shown, Marx argues that capitalism's social relations are unique in that they do not appear to be social at all. The structure of relations constituted by commodity-determined labor undermines earlier systems of overt social ties without, however, replacing them with a similar system. Instead, what emerges is a social universe that Marx describes as one of personal independence in a context of objective dependence. Both the abstract, quasi-objective structure of necessity and, on an immediate level, the much greater latitude of interaction in capitalist society than in a traditional society, are moments of the form of mediation that characterizes capitalism. In a sense, the opposition of system and lifeworld—like the earlier one of labor and interaction—expresses a hypostatization of these two moments in a way that dissolves capitalist social relations into "material" and "symbolic" spheres. The characteristics of the value dimension of the alienated social relations are attributed to the systemic dimension. This conceptual objectification

---

116. I have addressed modern anti-Semitism in these terms as a new form and not as an atavistic mode: See M. Postone, "Anti-Semitism and National Socialism," in A. Rabinbach and J. Zipes, eds., *Germans and Jews Since the Holocaust* (New York, 1986).

leaves an apparently indeterminate sphere of communication which no longer
is seen as structured by a form of social mediation (inasmuch as that form is
not overtly social); rather, it is seen as self-structuring and "naturally social."
Within the framework of this approach, then, the underspecification of lifeworld
as well as system expresses a theoretical point of departure that has retained the
notion of "labor."

The reading of Marx's theory I present here changes the terms of the theoretical problem to which Habermas has responded by reconceptualizing as historically determinate the notion of constitution by labor. This reinterpretation of
the Marxian notion of contradiction moves away from the concept of "labor"
and reconsiders the thesis of capitalism's "one-dimensionality." Interpreting
labor in capitalism as socially mediating allows one to move beyond the fundamental pessimism of Critical Theory in a way that is different from Habermas's: it entails a theory of the social constitution and specificity of production
and of forms of subjectivity in capitalism, and treats critical and oppositional
consciousness as socially determinate possibilities constituted by the dialectical
social forms themselves. In grounding itself socially and historically in this
manner, such a critical social theory could dispense with the last vestiges of
Hegel's philosophy of history. In such an approach, the possibility of emancipation is grounded neither in the progress of "labor" nor in any evolutionary
development of linguistically mediated communication; rather, it is grounded in
the contradictory character of the structuring social forms of capitalist society
in their historical development. At this point, then, I shall turn to a consideration
of Marx's concept of capital and examine the initial determinations of its intrinsic dialectic.

PART III

Toward a reconstruction of the Marxian critique: capital

7. Toward a theory of capital

At this point I can proceed with my reconstruction of Marx's critical theory of capitalist society. Thus far, I have investigated the differences between a traditional Marxist critique from the standpoint of "labor" and the Marxian critique of labor in capitalism, focusing on the categories Marx developed in the initial chapters of *Capital,* in particular on his conception of the twofold character of labor in capitalism, his distinction between value and material wealth, and his emphasis on the temporal dimension of value.

On the basis of this analysis of the commodity form, I shall now outline an approach to Marx's category of capital. Capital, according to Marx, is a self-moving social mediation that renders modern society intrinsically dynamic and shapes the form of the process of production. He develops this category in *Capital* by unfolding it dialectically from the commodity, thereby arguing that its basic determinations are implied by the latter social form. By indicating the intrinsic relation of the commodity and capital forms, Marx seeks both to elucidate the basic nature of capital and to render plausible his point of departure—his analysis of the commodity's dual character as the core structure of capitalism. What characterizes capitalism, according to Marx, is that—because of the peculiar nature of its structuring relations—it possesses a fundamental core that embodies its basic features. In his critique of political economy, he tries to establish the existence of this core and demonstrate that it underlies the intrinsic historical dynamic of capitalism. This core, then, would have to be overcome for this society to be negated historically.

In this chapter I shall present the course of Marx's exposition of the category of capital and the sphere of production. To investigate this exposition in detail would exceed the limits of this work, so in subsequent chapters I shall try instead to clarify some crucial aspects of the social forms Marx unfolds in his treatment of capital by considering them in relation to certain implications of his critical theory's initial categories. Proceeding this way will show how my analysis of these categories implies a reconceptualization of the Marxian dialectic of the forces and relations of production, and thereby sheds new light on Marx's complex category of capital and his understanding of capitalism's overcoming. (This discussion will touch upon aspects of modern capitalism, but only in a very preliminary manner.)

In general, the interpretation of Marx's category of capital I present here will demonstrate further that the Marxian critique does not analyze capitalist society merely in terms of liberal capitalism's overt hallmarks, that is, the bourgeois relations of distribution. Rather, it grasps as intrinsic to capitalism the proletarian-based industrial process of production as well as, more generally, the subsumption of individuals under large-scale social units, and entails a critique of capitalism's productivist historical logic. It thereby implicitly presents socialism as the historical negation of such "postliberal" characteristics of capitalism, as well as of the bourgeois relations of distribution.

Money

In Volume 1 of *Capital* Marx develops an analysis of money and then capital on the basis of his initial determinations of the commodity. He begins by examining the process of exchange, arguing that the circulation of commodities differs formally and essentially from the direct exchange of products. The circulation of commodities overcomes the temporal, spatial, and personal barriers imposed by the direct exchange of products. In the process, a quasi-natural network of social connections develops; although constituted by human agents, it lies beyond their control.[1] The commodity form of social mediation historically gives rise to the independent private producer, on the one hand, and it constitutes the social process of production and the relations among producers as an alienated system independent of the producers themselves, a system of all-round objective dependence, on the other.[2] More generally, it gives rise to a world of subjects and a world of objects. This sociocultural development proceeds with the development of the money form.[3]

Marx structures his investigation of money as a dialectical unfolding, in the course of which he logically derives both the social form of money, leading to his analysis of capital, as well as the forms of appearance that veil that social form. Proceeding from his analysis of the commodity as the duality of value and use value, Marx initially determines money as the externalized manifest expression of the value dimension of the commodity.[4] He argues that in a society where the commodity is the universal form of the product, money does not render commodities commensurable; rather, it is an expression, a necessary form of appearance, of their commensurability, of the fact that labor functions as a socially mediating activity. This does not *appear* to be the case, though, as Marx

1. Marx, *Capital*, vol. 1, trans. Ben Fowkes (London, 1976), pp. 207–9.
2. Ibid., p. 202. As I have suggested, this opposition, as it develops with the development of capitalism, could serve as a point of departure for a sociohistorical analysis of the common opposition between objectivistic social theories and theories of society that focus one-sidedly on human agency.
3. Ibid., p. 183.
4. Ibid., pp. 162, 188.

then indicates in the course of elaborating the various functions of money (as the measure of values, the means of circulation, and as money). He shows that a necessary quantitative discrepancy exists between value and prices, and that something can have a price without having a value. For these reasons, the nature of money in capitalism may be veiled—money may not appear to be an externalized expression of the form of social mediation that constitutes capitalist society (abstract labor objectified as value).[5] Moreover, because the circulation of commodities is effected by the externalization of their double character—in the form of money and commodities—they seem to be mere "thingly" objects, goods circulated by money rather than self-mediating objects, objectified social mediations.[6] Thus, the peculiar nature of social mediation in capitalism gives rise to an antinomy—so characteristic of modern Western worldviews—between a "secularized," "thingly" concrete dimension and a purely abstract dimension, whereby the socially constituted character of both dimensions, as well as their intrinsic relation, is veiled.

According to Marx, the nature of social mediation in capitalism is further obscured by the fact that money has developed historically in such a manner that coins and paper money have come to serve as signs of value. There is no direct correlation, however, between the value of these signs and the value they signify. Because even relatively valueless objects can serve as means of circulation, money does not appear to be a bearer of value. Consequently, the very existence of value as a social mediation, whether located in the commodity or in its expression as money, is veiled by this contingent surface relationship between signifier and signified.[7] This real process of obfuscation is reinforced by the function of money as a means of payment for commodities that had been acquired previously through contracts, and as credit money. In such cases, money no longer seems to mediate the process of exchange; rather, the movement of the means of payment seems merely to reflect and validate a social connection that already was present independently.[8] In other words, social relations in capitalism can seem as though they have nothing to do with the commodity form of social mediation. Rather, these relations can appear either to be pregiven or to be constituted ultimately by convention, by contracts among self-determining individuals.

In this section of his exposition, then, Marx investigates how the money form both expresses and increasingly veils the form of social mediation grasped by the category of the commodity, and he does so in a way that implicitly criticizes other theories of money and society. Marx also unfolds a dialectical reversal in his treatment of money: it is a social means that becomes an end. This discussion serves as a bridge between his analysis of the commodity and that of capital.

5. Ibid., pp. 196–97.
6. Ibid., pp. 210–11.
7. Ibid., pp. 222–24.
8. Ibid., pp. 233–35.

I have shown that Marx analyzes the commodity as an objectified form of social mediation: the commodity, as generalized, is a self-mediating form of the product. Proceeding from this determination, Marx describes commodity circulation as a mode wherein the social production and distribution of goods—which he calls the process of "social metabolism" or "transformation of matter" (*Stoffwechsel*)—is mediated by the "transformation of form" (*Formwechsel*) or "metamorphosis" of the commodities from use values to values and back to use values.[9] In other words, presupposing that the commodity is the general form of the product—hence, that it is intrinsically both a value and a use value—Marx analyzes the sale of commodity *A* for money, which is then used to buy commodity *B,* as a process of "metamorphosis." In the first step, commodity *A* is transformed from the manifest form of its particular, use value dimension into the manifest form of its general, value dimension (money); the latter can be transformed, in a second step, into another particular manifest form, commodity *B*. (The argumentative thrust of this interpretation of commodity exchange becomes clearer later in Marx's text, when capital is treated as self-expanding value that alternately takes on the form of commodities and of money.) This process, for Marx, is one in which production and distribution (the transformation of matter) are effected in a historically specific way by the transformation of form. It expresses the dual character of labor in capitalism, the circumstance that people's relations among each other and with nature are mediated by labor. On another level, Marx initially describes the process of commodity exchange—Commodity *A*–Money–Commodity *B*—as one of selling in order to buy.[10]

In the course of his investigation, however, Marx notes that the nature of commodity circulation is such that the transformation of form, which initially had been determined logically as a social means, a way of mediating the transformation of matter, becomes an end in itself.[11] He grounds this dialectical reversal in a social necessity to accumulate money which springs from the relations of the process of circulation itself, from the fact that when commodity circulation becomes widespread, not every purchase can be effected by a simultaneous sale. Rather, one must possess a hoard of money in order to acquire the means of consumption and to pay debts. Although, in terms of the system's underlying logic, one sells in order to buy, selling and buying become separated, and the externalized value dimension of the commodity—money—becomes a self-sufficient purpose of the sale.[12] With the extension of circulation, everything becomes convertible into money,[13] which thereby becomes a radical social lev-

---

9. Ibid., pp. 198–200.
10. Ibid., p. 200.
11. Ibid., p. 228.
12. Ibid., pp. 228, 234, 240.
13. "Circulation becomes the great social retort into which everything is thrown, to come out again as the money crystal. Nothing is immune from this alchemy" (ibid., p. 229).

eler. It embodies a new, objectified, form of social power that is independent of traditional social status and can become the private power of private individuals.[14]

At this point Marx begins his transition to the category of capital. In discussing the subjective dimension of the emergence of money as an end—the desire to hoard and the "Protestant" virtues of industriousness, abstinence, and asceticism—Marx argues that hoarding money is not a mode of accumulation that is logically adequate to value, to an abstract general form which is independent of all qualitative specificity. Marx elaborates a logical contradiction between the boundlessness of money, when considered qualitatively as the universal representation of wealth that is directly convertible into any other commodity, and the quantitative limitation of every actual sum of money.[15] Marx thus sets the stage for the category of capital, a form that more adequately embodies both the drive for boundless accumulation implicit in the value form, as well as the dialectical reversal described above. With capital, the transformation of (the commodity) form becomes an end and, as we shall see, the transformation of matter becomes the means to this end. Production, as a social process of the transformation of matter which mediates humans and nature, becomes subsumed under the social form constituted by labor's socially mediating function in capitalism.

Capital

Marx first introduces capital, the category with which he grasps modern society, in terms of a general formula informed by his analysis of value and the commodity. Marx had characterized the circulation of commodities as Commodity–Money–Commodity, or C-M-C, as a qualitative transformation of one use value for another, but he presents the circuit of capital as Money–Commodity–Money or, more accurately, M-C-M', where the difference between M and M' is necessarily only quantitative.[16] It should be noted that, like his analysis of C-M-C, Marx's analysis of M-C-M, as necessarily M-C-M', presupposes the commodity as the general form of the product. In other words, with the formula M-C-M', Marx neither tries to prove that investment for gain exists in capitalism, nor tries to ground the historical genesis of capitalist society in the logical unfolding of his categories. Rather, he presupposes the existence of capitalist society and of investment for gain; his intention is to clarify critically, by means of his categories, the underlying nature and developmental course of that form of social life.

14. Ibid., pp. 229–30. This form of social power, which is the initial specification of the power of the capitalist class, is a concrete expression of the abstract form of social domination I have been articulating. They are related but not identical.
15. Ibid., pp. 229–31.
16. Ibid., pp. 248–51.

The formula M-C-M' does not refer to a process whereby *wealth* in general is increased but to a process whereby *value* is increased. Marx calls the quantitative difference between M and M' *surplus value*.[17] Value becomes capital, according to Marx, as a result of a process of the valorization of value, whereby its magnitude is increased.[18] His analysis of capital seeks to grasp modern society in terms of a dynamic process inherent in those social relations which are objectified in the value form of wealth and, hence, in the value form of the surplus. What characterizes modern society, according to this analysis, is that the social surplus exists in the form of surplus value, and that this form implies a dynamic.

These determinations must be further examined. The formula M-C-M' is intended to represent an ongoing process: M' is not simply withdrawn at the end of the process as money, but remains part of the circuit of capital. This circuit, in other words, is actually M-C-M'-C-M"-C.... Unlike the movement entailed by the circulation of commodities and the turnover of money, this circuit implies ongoing growth and directionality; this directional movement, though, is quantitative and without an external telos. Whereas the circulation of commodities can be said to have a final purpose that lies outside of the process—namely, consumption, the satisfaction of needs—the motivating force of the circuit M-C-M', its determining purpose, according to Marx, is value itself, an abstract general form of wealth in terms of which all forms of material wealth can be quantified.[19] This abstract quantitative character of value as a form of wealth is related to the circumstance that it also is a social means, an objectified social relation. With the introduction of the category of capital, another moment of the determination of value as a means is introduced: value, as a form of wealth abstracted from the qualitative specificity of all products (hence their particular uses), and whose magnitude is a function of abstract time alone, receives its most adequate logical expression by serving as the means for more value, for the further expansion of value. With the introduction of the category of capital,

17. Ibid., p. 251.
18. Ibid., p. 252.
19. Ibid. Although M-C-M' describes the movement of the social totality, the circuit C-M-C remains of primary importance for the majority of people in capitalist society, who depend upon the sale of labor power in order to buy means of consumption. To criticize workers for becoming "bourgeois" when they become interested in various "material possessions" is to overlook the ways in which wage labor is an integral aspect of capitalist society, and to blur the distinction between C-M-C and M-C-M'. It is the latter that defines the bourgeois class.

  On the other hand, one purpose of Marx's mode of presentation is to indicate that these two circuits are systemically interconnected. In a society where the commodity is universal and people reproduce themselves by means of the circuit C-M-C, value is the form of wealth and of the surplus; hence, the process of production necessarily will be shaped and driven by the process of M-C-M'. A society based upon the C-M-C circuit alone cannot exist; such a society did not exist as a precursor to capitalism, according to Marx, but is a projection of a moment of capitalist society onto the past. See Marx, *A Contribution to the Critique of Political Economy,* trans. S. W. Ryazanskaya (Moscow, 1970), p. 59.

then, value is revealed as a means to a goal that is itself a means, rather than an end.[20]

Capital, then, is a category of movement, of expansion; it is a dynamic category, "value in motion." This social form is alienated, quasi-independent, exerts a mode of abstract compulsion and constraint on people, and is in motion. Consequently, Marx accords it the attribute of agency. His initial determination of capital, then, is as self-valorizing value, as the self-moving substance that is subject.[21] He describes this self-moving subjective-objective social form in terms of a continuous, ceaseless process of value's self-expansion. This process, like Nietzsche's demiurge, generates large-scale cycles of production and consumption, creation and destruction. Capital has no fixed, final form, but appears at different stages of its spiraling path in the form of money and commodities.[22] Value, then, is unfolded by Marx as the core of a form of social mediation that constitutes social objectivity and subjectivity, and is intrinsically dynamic: it is a form of social mediation that necessarily exists in objectified, materialized form, but is neither identical with, nor an inherent property of, its materialized form, whether in the shape of money or goods. The way in which Marx unfolds the category of capital retrospectively illuminates his initial determination of value as an objectified social relation, constituted by labor, that is carried by, but exists "behind," the commodities as objects. This clarifies the thrust of his analysis of the commodity's twofold character and its externalization as money and commodities.

The movement of capital is without limit, without end.[23] As self-valorizing value, it appears as pure process. In dealing with the category of capital, then, one is dealing with a central category of a society that becomes characterized by a constant directional movement with no determinate external telos, a society driven by production for the sake of production, by a process that exists for the sake of process.[24] *This expansion, this ceaseless motion is, within the framework of Marx's analysis, intrinsically related to the temporal dimension of value.* As

---

20. As I have argued, the development and spread of what Horkheimer described as instrumental reason (and action) should be understood socially—in terms of the development of the peculiar form of social means I have begun to outline—rather than technically, in terms of "labor" and production as such.

21. *Capital,* vol. 1, pp. 255–56.

22. Ibid., pp. 255–57.

23. Ibid., pp. 252–53.

24. Ibid., p. 742. On a very abstract level, these initial determinations of capital provide a socio-historical basis for the linearity of life in modern society, which Max Weber, referring to Leo Tolstoy's works, described pessimistically as follows: "The individual life of civilized man, placed into an infinite 'progress,' according to its own immanent meaning should never come to an end; ... Abraham, or some peasant of the past, died 'old and satiated with life' because he stood in the organic cycle of life. ... Whereas civilized man ... may become 'tired of life' but not 'satiated with life' " ("Science as a Vocation," in H. H. Gerth and C. W. Mills, eds., *From Max Weber: Essays in Sociology* [New York, 1958], pp. 139–40).

we shall see, Marx's concept of self-valorizing value attempts to grasp an alienated form of social relations that possesses an intrinsic temporal dynamic; this alienated form constitutes an immanent logic of history, gives rise to a particular structure of labor, and continually transforms social life while reconstituting its underlying capitalist character. His critical investigation of production in capitalism analyzes how individual labors increasingly become cellular components of a large, complex, and dynamic alienated system that encompasses people and machines and is directed by the goal of production for the sake of production. In short, the capital form of social relations, in Marx's analysis, is blind, processual, and quasi-organic.[25]

How is this directionally dynamic and totalistic form of social relations constituted? Marx approaches this problem by inquiring into the source of surplus value, the source of the quantitative difference between M and M'. Because the object of investigation is a society in which M-C-M' represents an ongoing process, the source of surplus value must be a regular ongoing source. Marx argues against theories that try to locate that source in the sphere of circulation and maintains, on the basis of the determinations of the categories he has developed thus far, that the ongoing increase in the magnitude of value must originate in a commodity whose use value possesses the peculiar property of being a source of value. He then specifies that commodity as *labor power,* the capacity for labor sold as a commodity.[26] (Remember that Marx is speaking of the source of value, not of material wealth.) The generation of surplus value is related intrinsically to a mode of production based on labor power as a commodity. The precondition for such a mode is that labor is free in a double sense: workers must be the free proprietors of their own labor capacity and, hence, of their persons; yet they must be "free" of all the objects needed to realize their labor power.[27] In other words, the precondition is a society in which means of consumption are obtained via commodity exchange, and in which workers—as opposed to independent artisans or farmers—do not own any means of production and are therefore compelled to sell their labor power as the only commodity they own. This is the precondition of capitalism.

At this point in his exposition, Marx states explicitly the historical specificity of his critical social theory's categories. Although the circulation of commodities and money certainly antedate capitalism, according to Marx, it is only in capitalism that labor power becomes a commodity, that labor takes on the form of wage labor.[28] Only then does the commodity form of the product of labor be-

---

25. A more complete investigation of the category of capital than I am undertaking here should explore the possible relations between the capital form, so determined, and the development in the West of organicist and biologistic modes of thought in the nineteenth and twentieth centuries. See M. Postone, "Anti-Semitism and National Socialism," in A. Rabinbach and J. Zipes, eds., *Jews and Germans Since the Holocaust* (New York, 1986), p. 309ff.

26. *Capital,* vol. 1, pp. 261–70.

27. Ibid., pp. 271–73.

28. Ibid., pp. 273–74.

come universal,[29] and money become a real universal equivalent. This historical development, for Marx, signifies an epochal historical transformation: it "embraces a world history."[30] Capitalism marks a qualitative break with all other historical forms of social life.

This section of *Capital* confirms my earlier argument that the logical unfolding of the categories from the commodity through money to capital should not be understood as a necessary historical progression. The commodity of the beginning of *Capital* presupposes wage labor. Marx intends his mode of presentation not as a historical unfolding but as a logical unfolding that proceeds from the essential core of the system. This is further supported by his statement that although merchants' capital and interest-bearing capital historically antedate the modern "fundamental form" of capital, they are logically derivative of this fundamental form in capitalism (and hence are dealt with later in the exposition, in Volume 3 of *Capital*).[31] I shall return below to this theme of the relation of history and logic in Marx's analysis.

This reading contravenes the interpretation, criticized above, that Marx's analysis of value in Volume 1 of *Capital* postulates a model of a precapitalist society, and that his discussion of price and profit in Volume 3 pertains to capitalist society. This implies that value precedes price historically. On the contrary, though: my interpretation suggests that, just as commodity circulation, money, merchants' capital, and interest-bearing capital historically precede the modern form of capital, *prices*—even if not the "prices of production" to which Marx refers in Volume 3—*antedate value*.[32] Value as a totalizing category is constituted *only* in capitalist society.

In this regard, it is significant that it is only when Marx begins to develop the category of capital that he argues against theories that analyze the value of a commodity in terms of its relations to needs. He counters that such theories confuse use value with value and do not consider adequately the nature of production.[33] That such arguments appear at this point in Marx's presentation

29. Ibid., p. 274n4.
30. Ibid., p. 274 (translation amended).
31. Ibid., pp. 266–67.
32. It is the case that, in the manuscript published as Volume 3 of *Capital*, Marx states that it is appropriate to view the values of commodities as historically and theoretically prior to the prices of production (trans. David Fernbach [Harmondsworth, England, 1981], p. 277). [The 'prices of production' are the prices of commodities that are exchanged as the products of capitals; they are specific to capitalist society (ibid., p. 275).] Nevertheless, this statement is contravened both by the logic of Marx's presentation as well as by innumerable statements in which he criticizes political economists such as Smith and Torrens for transposing value, as a category of capitalist society, to precapitalist conditions. I would suggest that "values" in the above statement should be understood loosely, as the exchange values or prices of commodities in precapitalist society. These prices, in my reading, antedate both value, as Marx develops this category in his critique of political economy, and prices of production.
33. *Capital*, vol. 1, pp. 261–62.

implies that the deductive derivation of value he undertakes in the opening chapter of *Capital* is *not* the real basis for his argument concerning value—that value is not a subjective category but is an objectified social mediation which is constituted by labor and measured by labor time expenditure. Rather, the real basis for this position is provided by his unfolding of the category of capital and his analysis of production. Value, in Marx's understanding, far from explaining market equilibrium in capitalism or even grounding a model of pre-capitalist society, comes into its own only as a structuring social category with the constitution of capital as a totalizing form. It is, as we shall see, a category of efficiency, rationalization, and ongoing transformation. *Value is a category of a directionally dynamic totality.*

Finally, one should note that, within the structure of Marx's argument, just as the concept of capital as self-valorizing value retrospectively illuminates his earlier determinations of the twofold character of the commodity, the concept of labor power as a commodity retrospectively illuminates the idea that the commodity as a value is constituted by abstract labor—that is, by labor as a socially mediating activity. This function of labor emerges very clearly with the category of labor power. Nevertheless, Marx's concepts of abstract labor and wage labor should not be conflated. By beginning with the category of the commodity as a social form, rather than with the sociological category of wage labor, Marx seeks to grasp the historical specificity of social wealth and the fabric of social relations in capitalism, the dynamic character of this society, as well as the structure of labor and of production. He does so by means of categories that also grasp socially and historically specific forms of subjectivity. The category of wage labor, however, could not serve as the point of departure from which these various dimensions of capitalist society could be unfolded.

The critique of bourgeois civil society

When Marx introduces the concepts of surplus value and labor power, he begins to shift the focus of his investigation from the sphere of circulation, which he characterizes as being on the "surface" of society, open to public view, to "the hidden abode of production."[34] Before making this shift, he summarizes the subjective dimension of the categories he has developed in his exposition thus far. In other words, he draws attention to the ideas and values that he had implicitly unfolded as immanent moments of the categorial social forms that structure C-M-C, the sphere of circulation. This summary provides important insights into the nature of Marx's critical analysis of bourgeois civil society, to which I have alluded, and the significance of his focus on production.

The sphere of circulation, or commodity exchange, according to Marx,

---

34. Ibid., p. 279.

is . . . a very Eden of the innate rights of man. It is ruled exclusively by Freedom, Equality, Property and Bentham. Freedom, because both buyer and seller of a commodity, let us say of labour-power, are determined only by their own free will. They contract as free persons, who are equal before the law.. . . Equality, because they only relate to each other as commodity-owners and exchange equivalent for equivalent. Property, because each disposes only of what is his own. And Bentham, because each looks only to his own advantage. The only force bringing them together and putting them into relation with each other, . . . is the private interest of each. And precisely for that reason, either in accordance with the pre-established harmony of things, or under the auspices of an omniscient providence, they all work together . . . in the common interest.[35]

What is the nature of this critique? On one level, it locates as socially and historically constituted those structured modes of social action and values which are taken to be "eternal" and "natural." Marx clearly is relating the determinations of civil society—as expressed in Enlightenment thought, theories of political economy and Natural Law, and Utilitarianism—to the commodity form of social relations. He argues that the differentiation of social life in Western Europe into a formal political sphere and a sphere of civil society (whereby the latter functions independently of political control and also is free of many traditional social constraints) is very much bound to the spread and deepening of this form of social relations—as are the modern values of freedom and equality, as well as the notion that society is constructed by the actions of autonomous individuals acting in their own self-interests. By socially and historically grounding the modern individual—which is an unexamined point of departure of Enlightenment thought—and the values and the modes of action associated with civil society, Marx seeks to dispel the notion that they are "natural," that they emerge when people, freed from the trammels of irrational superstitions, customs, and authority, are able to pursue their own interests rationally and in a way consistent with human nature (whereby what is "rational," of course, is seen as independent of social and historical specificity). Moreover, Marx also tries to ground socially the notion of a "natural" form of social life itself: Capitalism differs fundamentally from other societies in that its characterizing social relations are not overt but are "objectively" constituted and, hence, do not appear to be socially specific at all. This difference in the very fabric of social relations is such that the differences between noncapitalist and capitalist societies can seem to be between social institutions that are extrinsic to human nature, hence, "artificial," and those that are socially "natural."[36] By specifying the determining social relations of capitalism, showing that they appear not to be social at all, and indicating that the apparently decontextualized individuals who act in terms of what seems to be their self-interest, are themselves socially and historically constituted (as is the very category of interest), Marx's critical

35. Ibid., p. 280.
36. Ibid., p. 175n35.

theory of capitalist society grounds socially, and thereby undermines, the modern notion of the "naturally social."[37]

However, Marx's critique of the structured modes of action and values rooted in the sphere of circulation does not merely show that they are socially constituted and historically specific. I have noted that he locates circulation on the "surface" of society, unlike the sphere of production, which purportedly represents a "deeper" level of social reality (and in which, as we shall see, the values associated with the sphere of circulation are negated). Although Marx is critical of any theory of capitalism that focuses on the relations of distribution to the exclusion of those of production, he is not only interested in showing that one can find "behind" the sphere of circulation, with its formal equality, freedom, and lack of external force a sphere of production marked by direct domination, inequality, and exploitation; his critique does not simply dismiss the institutions, structures, and values of the sphere of circulation as mere shams. Rather, he is arguing that commodity circulation is only a moment of a more complex totality—and he thereby decries any attempt to consider this moment as if it were the whole.

In taking this sphere as a moment of the totality, however, Marx also accords it real social and historical importance, and not merely as a social basis for capitalism's ideologies of legitimation. The great bourgeois revolutions are a case in point, as is the question of the nature and development of workers' consciousness. For example, it is significant that the relationship of workers and capitalists exists in the sphere of circulation as well as in that of production, according to Marx. That is to say, a defining moment of the nature and development of this relationship is that, in the sphere of circulation it is a relationship of formal equality between owners of commodities.[38] Thus, when Marx discusses the value of labor power as a commodity in terms of the value of the workers' means of subsistence, he emphasizes that the number and extent of workers' necessary requirements, as well as the way in which they are satisfied, are not fixed; rather, they vary historically and culturally, and depend on the habits and expectations of the class of free workers. As Marx puts it, "the value of labour-power contains a historical and moral element."[39] I shall not elaborate on the rich implications of these passages except to note that one constituting moment of the historical and moral element to which he refers is that the workers also are commodity owners—that is, "subjects." This conditions not only the nature of their values (their ideas of fairness and justice, for example) but also their ability and willingness to organize on this basis.

37. This argument could serve as the point of departure for a critique of Habermas's notion, developed in *The Theory of Communicative Action,* that undermining traditional social forms by capitalism allows for the historical emergence of a lifeworld constituted by communicative action as such, that is, social action whose characteristics are not socially determinate.
38. *Capital,* vol. 1, pp. 271–73.
39. Ibid., p. 275.

One could argue, for example, that it is generally only through collective action around issues such as working conditions, hours, and wages that workers actually gain some control over the conditions of sale of their commodity. Hence, despite the widespread assumption that workers' collective action and bourgeois social forms are opposed, commodity ownership can only be fully realized for the workers in collective form; workers, then, can only be "bourgeois subjects" *collectively*. In other words, the nature of labor power as a commodity is such that collective action does *not* stand opposed to commodity ownership, but is necessary to its realization. The historical process of labor power's realization as a commodity paradoxically entails the development of collective forms within the framework of capitalism that do *not* point beyond that society—rather, they constitute an important moment in the transition from liberal to postliberal capitalism.[40]

Marx's analysis of the wage laborer–capitalist relationship and of the constitution of workers' values and forms of consciousness is not, of course, limited to a consideration of the sphere of circulation. Although wage laborers are commodity owners and, hence, "subjects" within the sphere of circulation, according to Marx, they also are "objects," use values, elements of the process of production, within the capitalist sphere of production. This simultaneous determination by both spheres defines wage labor. I have noted Marx's implicit dual determination of the individual constituted in capitalist society—as subject and as the object of a system of objective compulsions. That the worker is at once subject (a commodity owner) and object (of the capitalist process of production) represents the concrete extension, the "materialization," of this dual determination. An adequate treatment of Marx's understanding of the development of workers' consciousness would have to proceed from an analysis of both moments, their interactions, and their historical transformations.[41] I shall not un-

---

40. The analysis of such collective forms in terms of the commodity is related to the interpretation of capital as the adequate expression of the category of value; this could serve as a point of departure for rethinking the relationship between capital and the large-scale bureaucratic social organizations and institutions characteristic of postliberal capitalism. On another level, the relation between effective commodity ownership and the category of the bourgeois subject could also serve as a point of departure for rethinking the process of the extension of the franchise in Western Europe and North America in the nineteenth and twentieth centuries.

41. In this regard, my interpretation of Marx's approach is very different from that of Georg Lukács. In his discussion of the class consciousness of the proletariat, Lukács proceeds from the notion that workers can only become conscious of their existence in society when they first become aware of themselves as commodities (see "Reification and the Consciousness of the Proletariat," in *History and Class Consciousness,* trans. Rodney Livingstone [London, 1971], p. 168ff.). Unlike Marx, who treats the workers as both objects and subjects by analyzing them as both commodities and commodity owners (*Capital,* vol. 1, p. 271), Lukács grounds the possibility of self-awareness and oppositional subjectivity ontologically—that is, outside of the social forms. Marx's categorial analysis seeks to grasp the historical specificity and development of workers' consciousness in terms of the interaction and development of several social dimensions of capitalist society. He analyzes forms of consciousness which remain within the framework

dertake such an investigation in this work; I wish merely to note at this point that, although the values Marx relates to the sphere of circulation, when falsely totalized, serve as the basis for an ideology of legitimation in capitalist society, they also have had important historical consequences for the nature and constitution of modes of social and political critique, as well as of oppositional social movements. They do have an emancipatory moment for Marx, even if it remains within the framework of capitalist society.

This brief discussion of aspects of Marx's critique of bourgeois civil society reinforces and specifies further my earlier argument, that his analysis of the emancipatory values of bourgeois society neither dismisses those values, nor upholds them as ideals that go unrealized in capitalism but will be realized in socialism.[42] Neither of those interpretations does justice to Marx's theory as one

of capitalist society while modifying and transforming it, and suggests determinations of those forms of consciousness which point beyond this society. Lukács, however, essentially abandons the categorial analysis of determinate forms of subjectivity when he deals with the consciousness of the proletariat. Beginning with his notion of the "self-consciousness of the commodity," he tries to unfold an abstract dialectic of subject and object, deriving the possibility of the workers' self-consciousness as historical subjects out of a self-awareness of their social existence as objects (see "Reification and the Consciousness of the Proletariat," p. 168ff.). The difference between these two approaches is related to the distinction, mentioned above, between Marx's analysis of the Hegelian concept of the identical subject-object in terms of a structure of social relations (capital), on the one hand, and Lukács's identification of this concept with the proletariat. Whereas Marx's theory socially grounds the opposition of subject and object, Lukács's sophisticated version of the social critique from the standpoint of "labor" remains within the framework of the subject-object problematic. Lukács considers capitalism as a form of social "objectivity" that disguises the "real" human relations at its core, and conceives of the abolition of capitalism in terms of the realization of the historical Subject. Hence he states that, by knowing themselves as commodities, workers can recognize the "fetish character of every commodity," by which he means that they can recognize the "real" relations among people that lie underneath the commodity form (ibid., p. 169). Marx, as I have emphasized, also maintains that the core of the social formation is veiled. This structuring core, however, is the commodity itself as a form of relations, not a set of relations "behind" the commodity.

I shall examine how Marx's analysis also implies that the sort of consciousness that points beyond capitalism is related to the object character of direct human labor within the process of production. Yet the nature and possible consequences of such consciousness are different than in Lukács's approach. For Lukács, the proletariat realizes itself as the Subject of history by recognizing and abolishing its social determination as an object in capitalism; for Marx, the proletariat is an object and appendage of capital, one that is and remains the necessary presupposition of capital even as it becomes increasingly anachronistic. The possibility Marx seeks is the self-abolition of the proletariat; this class is not, and does not become, the Subject of history.

42. The widespread notion that the ideals of the bourgeois revolutions serve as the standpoint of a fundamental, epochal critique of capitalism, and will be realized in socialist society, can be critically analyzed partly with reference to the idea that organized workers constitute themselves as a collective commodity owner. If collective action and structures per se are misunderstood as being opposed to capitalism, the social actions and ideals of this collective commodity owner can be misunderstood as pointing toward the negation of capitalism itself, rather than its laissez-faire phase.

of the social constitution of cultural ideals and forms of consciousness. Although Marx does, throughout *Capital,* show how the sphere of circulation disguises the nature and existence of value, the opposition he draws between circulation and production, between surface and deep structure, is not identical to that between "illusion" and "truth." The latter opposition is related to the topos of a critique from the standpoint of "labor," wherein the sphere of production represents an ontologically more essential and transhistorical moment, that is distorted in capitalism by circulation but would emerge openly in socialism. In Marx's analysis, however, the spheres of circulation and production are both historically determinate and are constituted by labor in its twofold character. Neither sphere represents the standpoint of the social critique: both surface and deep structure would be abolished with the abolition of capitalism. Their opposition, then, is neither one between illusory appearance and "truth," nor, conversely, between the ideals of capitalist society and their partial or distorted realization. Rather, it is an opposition between two different yet interrelated spheres of that society which are associated with very different sorts of ideals.[43]

As I noted in discussing the opposition between abstract universalism and particularistic specificity, for Marx, overcoming capitalism involves neither the simple abolition of its cultural values nor the realization of those values of bourgeois society he deems emancipatory. Instead, his approach implies that the overcoming of capitalism must occur on the basis of historically constituted values that represent the transcendence of the sorts of internally related, antinomic oppositions—for example, that between abstract equality and concrete inequality—that characterize the capitalist social formation.

The sphere of production

At this point, I can make some preliminary observations about Marx's treatment of the sphere of production in capitalism. Based on my elaboration of the differences between a critique from the standpoint of "labor" and a critique of the character of labor in capitalism, one can say that Marx's assertion regarding production—that it constitutes a more fundamental, "hidden" social sphere behind the "surface" sphere of circulation—is not a statement about the social primacy of the production of the physical means of life. Rather, it refers to the constitution of the social relations, mediated by labor, that characterize capitalism. Within the framework of his analysis, capital—like the commodity—is a form of social relations. The category refers to neither wealth nor wealth-producing capacity in general; nor, understood as a social form, can it be reduced

43. The relationship between these spheres changes historically and varies among capitalist countries. An analysis of their relationship could provide one dimension of an approach to variations and transformations of ideals and values in capitalism, one that focuses on the various ways in which the spheres of production and circulation are mediated—for example, by market coordination or state direction.

to class relations. I have initially determined the capital form of social relations as an alienated, abstract, self-moving Other, characterized by a constant directional movement with no external goal. Marx's analysis of the sphere of production seeks to ground this dynamic by specifying the capital form and investigating the constitution and development of the peculiar, intrinsically contradictory and dynamic form of alienated social relations. Because of the dual character of labor in capitalism, his investigation is necessarily also an investigation of the creation of the surplus product.[44] As we shall see, Marx analyzes the dynamic of capital as a non-linear process that simultaneously is one of reproduction and transformation. In reproducing itself, capital constantly transforms much of social life.

Marx, in locating this dynamic process in the sphere of production, argues that it is rooted in neither the sphere of circulation nor that of the state. His analysis, in other words, suggests that the classical bipartite division of modern society into state and civil society is incomplete: it cannot grasp the dynamic character of the social formation. Marx does not simply identify "civil society" with "capitalism," nor does he posit the primacy of either sphere of the classical bipartite scheme. Instead, he argues that as capitalism develops fully, the spheres of the state and civil society are first constituted as separate but increasingly become embedded in a superordinate dynamic structure, which he tries to grasp with his analysis of the sphere of production. According to this approach, the ongoing changes of the social formation—including the changing relationship of state to civil society, as well as the character and development of the institutions in each sphere (for example, the rise of large-scale hierarchical bureaucracies in both "public" and "private" sectors)—can be understood only in terms of the intrinsic dynamic of capitalist society rooted in the "third," superordinate sphere, the sphere of production.

I shall now follow the category of value, from the sphere of circulation across the "threshold" of the "hidden abode of production," as it were, and will show how, in Marx's analysis, value is not merely a regulator of circulation, nor a category of class exploitation alone; rather, as self-valorizing value, it shapes the form of the production process and grounds the intrinsic dynamic of capitalist society. The possible validity and analytic usefulness of the category of value are not necessarily restricted to liberal capitalism.

Marx approaches his investigation of the capitalist process of production on the basis of his determinations of the commodity. This production process, according to Marx, is twofold in character: just as the commodity is a unity of use value and value, the process of producing commodities is the unity of a "labor process" (the process of production of material wealth) and a process

---

44. It should be noted that, in Marx's analysis, surplus value is not equivalent to profit but refers to the total social surplus (of value), which is distributed in the form of profit, interest, rent, and wages.

of creating value. From this, Marx unfolds the process of production of capital as the unity of a labor process and a ''valorization process'' (the process of creating surplus value).[45] In both cases, the use value dimension is the necessary material form of appearance of the value dimension; as such, it also veils the latter's historically specific social character.

Before examining the specific nature and development of the capitalist process of production, Marx considers the most abstract determinations of the labor process, independent of any specific social form.[46] The fundamental elements of the labor process, according to Marx, are labor (understood as concrete labor, as purposeful activity aimed at the production of use values), and the means of production (the objects on which labor is performed and the means, or instruments, of this labor).[47] In its basic and abstract determinations, the labor process is the universal condition for the transformation of matter, the metabolic interaction (*Stoffwechsel*) of humans and nature and, hence, is a universal condition of human existence.[48]

This section of *Capital* is frequently taken out of its context in Marx's presentation and understood as presenting a transhistorically valid definition of the labor process. This is particularly true of Marx's well-known statement that ''what distinguishes the worst architect from the best of bees is that the architect builds the cell in his mind before he constructs it in wax.... Man not only effects a change of form in the materials of nature; he also realizes his own purpose in those materials.''[49] What is frequently overlooked, however, is that Marx's presentation subsequently entails a reversal: he goes on to show how the labor process in capitalism is structured in such a way that precisely those aspects that initially were presupposed as uniquely ''human''—for example, purposiveness—become attributes of capital.

Recall that, in his analysis of money, Marx examines how the transformation of form (*Formwechsel*), initially determined as a means of effecting the transformation of matter (*Stoffwechsel*), becomes an end in itself. Now, proceeding from his initial, very abstract determination of the labor process, Marx develops this reversal of means and ends further: he shows how the process of the transformation of matter in production is shaped by the goal of the transformation of form, as expressed by the category of capital. In considering the capitalist process of production, he first briefly takes note of the property relations involved—that the capitalist purchases the necessary factors of the labor process (the means of production and labor), and that, consequently, the worker labors under the control of the capitalist to whom his labor, as well as the product,

---

45. *Capital*, vol. 1, pp. 293, 304.
46. Ibid., p. 283.
47. Ibid., pp. 283–84, 287, 290.
48. Ibid., p. 290.
49. Ibid., p. 284.

belongs.[50] Nevertheless, Marx does not treat capitalist production only in terms of ownership, nor does he focus immediately on the production and appropriation of the surplus; rather, he begins to examine the specificity of the capitalist process of production with regard to the form of wealth it produces. In other words, although Marx describes capitalist production as the unity of a labor process and a process of creating surplus value, he initially seeks to grasp it by examining its basic determinations on a prior logical level, as the unity of a labor process and a process of creating value.[51] He places the value form of wealth at the center of his considerations.

Marx proceeds by first analyzing the logical implications of the process of producing value. He then unfolds the capitalist process of production, showing, in the process, how these logical implications become materialized. Marx begins by noting that the elements of the labor process acquire a different significance when considered in terms of the process of creating value. In the first place, the goal of the process of production no longer is the product simply as a use value; rather, use values are produced only because and insofar as they are the bearers of value. The goal of production is not only use value, but value—more precisely, surplus value.[52] This, however, changes the significance of labor in the process of production. Unfolding his earlier categorial determinations further, Marx argues that labor's transhistorical significance as a qualitatively specific purposeful activity aimed at creating specific products is modified in capitalist production. Considered in terms of the process of creating value, labor is significant only quantitatively, as a source of value, without regard to its qualitative specificity.[53] This, in turn, necessarily implies that the qualitative specificity of the raw materials and products are also of no significance in terms of this process. Indeed, Marx maintains that, despite appearances, the real function of raw materials in the creation of value is merely to absorb a definite quantity of labor, and that of the product is only to serve as a measure of the labor absorbed. "Definite quantities of product . . . now represent nothing but definite quantities of labour. . . . They are now simply the material shape taken by a given number of hours or days of social labour."[54] That is, extending the analysis he had begun to develop with regard to commodity circulation, Marx argues that what characterizes capitalist production is that the transformation of matter by labor is simply a means toward the creation of the social form constituted by labor (value). To say that the goal of production is (surplus-)value is to say that that goal is the social mediation itself.

Marx's analysis of the process of production seen as a process of creating value provides an initial logical determination of the indifference, structurally

50. Ibid., pp. 291–92.
51. Ibid., p. 293.
52. Ibid.
53. Ibid., pp. 295–96.
54. Ibid., pp. 296–97.

implicit in capitalism, toward the production of specific products. More important for our purposes, he begins to specify the sphere of production by showing how the process of creating value transforms the elements of the very labor process in which it is expressed. This is particularly significant in the case of labor: Marx's determinations of value and the process of its creation imply that labor, which in the labor process is defined as purposeful action that regulates and directs human interaction with nature, is separated from its purpose in the process of creating value. The goal of the expenditure of labor power no longer is bound intrinsically to the specific nature of that labor; rather, this goal, despite appearances, is independent of the qualitative character of the labor expended— it is the objectification of labor time itself. That is to say, the expenditure of labor power is not a means to another end, but, as a means, has itself become an "end." This goal is given by the alienated structures constituted by (abstract) labor itself. As a goal, it is very singular; it is not only extrinsic to the specificity of (concrete) labor but also is posited independently of the social actors' wills.

Labor, however, is not merely separated from its purpose in the process of creating value; it is also transformed into the object of production. Direct human labor in production, according to Marx, becomes the actual, if covert, "raw material" of the process of creating value. Yet because this process is, at the same time, a labor process, labor may continue to seem to be purposive action that transforms matter in order to satisfy human needs. Its real significance in terms of the process of creating value, however, is its role as the source of value. As we shall see, with the development of capitalist production this significance is increasingly expressed in the material form of the labor process.

Labor, then, as a result of its dual character in capitalism, becomes "objective" in a double sense: its purpose, because constituted by labor itself, becomes "objective," separate both from the qualitative specificity of particular labors as well as from the actors' wills; relatedly, labor in the process of production, because separated from its purpose, is reduced to the object of that process.

Having analyzed thus the logical implications of the process of creating value, Marx proceeds to initially specify the valorization process, the process of creating surplus value. Surplus value is created when the workers labor for more time than is required to create the value of their labor power, that is, when the value of labor power is less than the value this labor power valorizes in the production process.[55] At this stage of Marx's presentation, in other words, the difference between the process of creating value and that of creating surplus value is only quantitative: "If we now compare the process of creating value with the process of valorization, we see that the latter is nothing but the continuation of the former beyond a definite point."[56]

It is significant that Marx analyzes the valorization process essentially in terms

55. Ibid., pp. 300–302.
56. Ibid., p. 302.

of the creation of value: his initial discussion of the capitalist process of production is as concerned with the form of wealth—hence, the form of the surplus—as it is with the surplus itself. This supports my contention that Marx's
analysis of production in capitalism is not based upon a labor theory of *wealth,*
and that his critique should not be understood as one of exploitation alone. In
other words, his investigation of the source of the surplus is not of the creation
by "labor" of a surplus of material wealth, whereby he criticizes the appropriation of that surplus by the capitalist class. Relatedly, Marx does not consider
the process of production in capitalism to be a labor process controlled extrinsically by the capitalist class for its own benefit, which, in socialism, would be
used for the benefit of all. Such interpretations overlook the implications of both
the value form of wealth and Marx's analysis of the twofold nature of the
production process in capitalism—that is, of its intrinsically capitalist (capital-
determined) character. Capitalist production, according to Marx, is characterized
not only by class exploitation but also by a peculiar dynamic, rooted in the
constant expansion of value; it is also characterized by the various determinations of the valorization process outlined above. As we shall see, these determinations are materialized in the concrete form of the industrial labor process.
Marx grounds these distinctive features of capitalist production in the value form
of wealth and, hence, of the surplus. One cannot grasp them adequately only in
terms of the fact that the means of production and the products belong to the
capitalists and not to the workers. In other words, Marx's conception of the
social relations constituted in the sphere of production cannot be understood
solely in terms of class relations of exploitation.

Earlier I examined Marx's conception of the constitution by labor of an "objective" form of social mediation that acquires a quasi-independent existence. I
now have followed the logical unfolding of this mediation to a new level and
found that the nature of value is such that the process of its creation transforms
labor into the object of production while confronting it with a goal outside of
its purpose. What I am beginning to unfold, in other words, are further determinations of the system of social domination which Marx describes as the domination of people by their labor. Unlike more traditional interpretations, labor
as presented here is not only the object of domination but the constituent source
of domination in capitalism.

Marx traces the development of this system of domination by elaborating the
capitalist process of production from the initial determinations I have examined
thus far. He analyzes it in terms of the relationship between its two moments,
that is, between its development as a valorization process and as a labor process.
In pursuing the former process, Marx distinguishes between "necessary labor
time," the amount of time in which the workers create the amount of value
needed for their reproduction, and "surplus labor time," in which the workers
create additional value, above and beyond that "necessary" amount—in other

words, surplus value.[57] Surplus value, created by the working class and appropriated by the capitalist class, is the form of the surplus product in capitalism. Its essential quality is temporal: The sum of ''necessary'' and ''surplus'' labor time makes up the working day.[58] On this basis, Marx proceeds to differentiate between two forms of surplus value—''absolute surplus value'' and ''relative surplus value.'' For the former, the amount of surplus labor time, hence surplus value, is augmented by lengthening the workday; the latter refers to the increase in surplus labor time that is achieved—once the workday has been limited—by the reduction of necessary labor time.[59] This reduction is accomplished by increasing the general productivity of labor (or at least of labor in those branches of industry that produce means of subsistence or their means of production), which reduces the labor time needed to reproduce labor power.[60] With the development of relative surplus value, then, the directional motion that characterizes capital as self-valorizing value becomes tied to ongoing changes in productivity. An immanent dynamic of capitalism emerges, a ceaseless expansion grounded in a determinate relationship between the growth of productivity and the growth of the value form of the surplus.

This historical dynamic of capitalist society, in Marx's analysis, entails a dynamic of both dimensions of the capitalist process of production—of the labor process as well as of the valorization process. The ongoing changes in productivity associated with the production of relative surplus value are accompanied by a radical transformation of the technical and social conditions of the labor process:[61] ''The production of relative surplus-value completely revolutionizes the technical processes of labour and the groupings into which society is divided.''[62] The labor process, then, is transformed as the basis of the valorization process moves from absolute surplus value toward relative surplus value. Marx describes this transformation of the labor process as one from a stage of the ''formal subsumption of labour under capital,''[63] in which ''the general character of the labour process is . . . not changed by the fact that the worker works for the capitalist . . . instead of himself,''[64] to one of labor's ''real subsumption under capital,''[65] where a ''transformation of the mode of production itself . . . results from the subordination of labour to capital.''[66] In the latter stage, the determinations of the valorization process are materialized in the labor process: direct human labor materially becomes the object of production. In other words,

57. Ibid., p. 325.
58. Ibid., p. 339.
59. Ibid., pp. 431–32.
60. Ibid.
61. Ibid.
62. Ibid., p. 645.
63. Ibid.
64. Ibid., p. 291.
65. Ibid., p. 645.
66. Ibid., p. 291.

concrete proletarian labor acquires materially the attributes that Marx accorded it logically at the beginning of his analysis of the valorization process. As the adequate materialization of the valorization process, this form of production, industrial production, is characterized by Marx as the "specifically capitalist mode of production."[67]

Marx's analysis of the "real subsumption" of labor under capital is an attempt to analyze the process of production in developed capitalism as molded by capitalist relations of production (that is, by value and capital); he treats this production process as intrinsically capitalist. This demonstrates that, in his view, the fundamental contradiction of capitalist society—the contradiction between its forces and relations of production—refers not to one between industrial production and "capitalism" (that is, bourgeois relations of distribution) but to one within the capitalist mode of production itself. This, obviously, undermines the traditional conception of the role accorded the working class in the transition from capitalism to socialism.

Marx, then, analyzes both the concrete form of industrial production and the dynamic logic of industrial society in terms of the twofold social forms that constitute capitalist society. This is yet another sign that the full implications of his initial categories emerge only in the course of his analysis of the capitalist sphere of production. I have shown that Marx associates the category of relative surplus value with the real subsumption of labor under capital and with an ongoing historical dynamic; relative surplus value is the form of surplus value adequate to capital, as understood by Marx. Only when this category is unfolded in his presentation does the commodity form of social mediation emerge fully developed. It becomes totalizing, a moment of a social totality that it constitutes; as we shall see, this mediation now becomes a moment of a totality. With the introduction of the category of relative surplus value—even more than in the case of labor power understood as a commodity—the categories with which Marx begins his analysis "come into their own" and retrospectively illuminate his logical point of departure. This is particularly true of the temporal dimension of the categories: only at this point in Marx's argument does the logical unfolding of the categories express a historical dynamic of capitalist society and, in this sense, become "real" as a historical logic. In other words, in Marx's analysis, the development of relative surplus value accords capitalism a dynamic that, although constituted by social practice, has the form of a historical logic. It is directional, unfolds in a regular fashion, is beyond the control of its constituting agents, and exerts an abstract form of compulsion on them. The character of this dynamic can be explained, according to Marx, in terms of the dualistic forms of the commodity and capital. This implies, conversely, that,

67. Ibid., p. 645.

inasmuch as these forms grasp such a logic of development, they are fully valid socially only in developed capitalism.

Marx's mode of presentation, then, involves a complex argument regarding the relation of logic and history. *Capital* begins as a logical unfolding whose point of departure, the commodity, presupposes the category of capital: Marx illuminates capital's essential character by unfolding it dialectically from the commodity. This essential character is such that, with the emergence of the category of relative surplus value, the logical unfolding of the presentation becomes historical as well. Marx's presentation implies that this fusion of the logical and the historical—that is, the existence of a dialectical logic of history—is specific to developed capitalist society. Nevertheless, we have also seen that Marx presents the logical unfolding of the categories *prior* to the emergence of relative surplus value—from the commodity through money to capital—in such a way that it also can be read as a historical unfolding. In so doing, Marx implicitly suggests that the historically determinate logic of history which characterizes capitalism can be read back onto all of history. His presentation shows, however, that what then seems to be a historical unfolding is actually a projection backward, based on a logical reconstruction of the dynamic character of the social form of capital, a dynamic character that it acquires only when it is fully developed.

That the logical and the historical should not be confused, although they become fused once capitalism is developed, is demonstrated very clearly in the last section of Volume 1 of *Capital*. In that section, "Primitive [or "Original"] Accumulation," Marx outlines his analysis of the actual historical developments leading to capitalism.[68] Although these developments can be understood retrospectively as coherent, in no way are they presented in terms of the sort of intrinsic dialectical logic Marx presents in the first sections of Volume 1, when he unfolds the category of capital from the commodity form. Marx's presentation, then, implies that this sort of dialectical logic does not express the actual course of the prehistory of capitalist society—indeed, that such a historical logic does not exist prior to the full development of the capital form. However, it also suggests that such a logic does exist once the capital form is fully developed, and that it can be read back as the prehistory of capitalism. In this way, Marx's mode of presentation implicitly provides a critique of a Hegelian philosophy of history, of human history understood as a dialectical unfolding, by uncovering its "rational core" in a historically specific logic of history. Within the framework of this critique, a general human history does come into being historically (in an alienated form) but does not exist transhistorically. Hence, human history as a whole cannot be characterized in a unitary way—in terms either of an intrinsic logic or its absence.

68. Ibid., pp. 873–940.

8. The dialectic of labor and time

Marx in unfolding the category of capital, then, relates the historical dynamic of capitalist society as well as the industrial form of production to the structure of abstract domination constituted by labor when it is both a productive activity and a socially mediating activity. I shall now specify this relation by examining more closely how, according to Marx's critique, the fundamental social forms of capitalism shape the character of both this historical dynamic and this form of production. Rather than proceeding by directly investigating Marx's analysis of the sphere of production, however, I shall discuss the most salient structural features of that sphere by first taking a "step backward," as it were, and considering further the implications of the initial categories of Marx's analysis. This will clarify certain important characteristics of the capital form which might not be apparent were I to examine the sphere of production more directly. In particular, this will allow me to elaborate the central importance of the temporal dimension of value to Marx's analysis. Such an approach will elucidate the specificity of the dynamic of capital and lay the groundwork for articulating Marx's understanding of the social constitution of the process of production. Once I have analyzed the determinate character of the dynamic of capitalism on this fundamental level, I shall return, in Chapter Nine, to examining central aspects of Marx's treatment of the sphere of production in light of this analysis.

By first considering the implications of Marx's initial categories for an analysis of the dynamic of capital and of the process of production, the interpretation presented in this chapter will be able to clearly locate the basic contradiction of capitalist society—and, hence, the possibility of social critique and practical opposition—in the double-sided social forms grasped by the Marxian categories, rather than between these social forms and "labor."

This approach will make clear how my reinterpretation of Marx's basic categories grounds a reconceptualization of the nature of capitalism, in particular, of its contradictory dynamic, in a way that does not privilege considerations of the market and private ownership of the means of production. It provides the basis for analyzing the intrinsic relationship between capital and industrial production, and for investigating the possible relation between the development of capital and the nature and development of other large-scale bureaucratic institutions and organizations of postliberal capitalist society. (An investigation based on this interpretation would ground socially and specify historically these institutions and organizations, and, in doing so, provide the basis for distinguishing between economic and administrative mechanisms that are bound or related to the capital form, and those that would remain necessary even if capital were abolished.)

The immanent dynamic

I have focused thus far on the centrality to Marx's critical theory of his conception of the dual character of the fundamental social forms of capitalist society, and have tried to clarify the nature of, and distinction between, the value dimension of the forms (abstract labor, value, abstract time) and their use value dimension (concrete labor, material wealth, concrete time). At this point, I can examine their interrelations. The nonidentity of these two dimensions is not simply a static opposition; rather, the two moments of labor in capitalism, as productive activity and as a socially mediating activity, are mutually determining in a way that gives rise to an immanent dialectical dynamic. It should be noted that the following investigation of the dynamic relation of productivity and value presupposes fully developed capitalism; this relation is the core of a pattern that only fully comes into its own with the emergence of relative surplus value as a dominant form.

In examining the significance of the distinction between concrete labor and abstract labor in terms of the difference between material wealth and value, I showed that although increased productivity (which Marx considers an attribute of labor's use value dimension) does increase the number of products and, hence, the amount of material wealth, it does not change the magnitude of total value yielded within a given unit of time. The magnitude of value, then, appears to be a function of abstract labor time expenditure alone, completely independent of labor's use value dimension. Behind this opposition, however, there is a dynamic interaction between the two dimensions of commodity-determined labor, as becomes evident when the following example is examined closely:

The introduction of power looms into England, for example, probably reduced by one half the labour required to transform a given quantity of yarn into woven fabric. The English hand-loom weaver in fact needed the same amount of labour-time as before to effect this transformation; but the product of his individual hour of labour now only represented half a social labour-hour, and consequently fell to one half its former value.[1]

Marx introduces this example in the first chapter of Volume 1 of *Capital* to illustrate his notion of socially necessary labor time as the measure of value. His example indicates that when the commodity is the general form of the product, the actions of individuals constitute an alienated totality that constrains

1. Marx, *Capital*, vol. 1, trans. Ben Fowkes (London, 1976), p. 129.

and subsumes them. Like his exposition of value in Volume 1 more generally, this example operates on the level of the social totality.

It is significant for our purposes that this initial determination of the magnitude of value also implies a dynamic. Let us assume that, before the power loom was introduced, the average hand-loom weaver produced 20 yards of cloth in one hour, yielding a value of x. When the power loom, which doubled productivity, was first introduced, most weaving still was done by hand. Consequently, the standard of value—socially necessary labor time—continued to be determined by hand-loom weaving; the norm remained 20 yards of cloth per hour. Hence, the 40 yards of cloth produced in one hour with the power loom had a value of $2x$. However, once the new mode of weaving became generalized, it gave rise to a new norm of socially necessary labor time: the normative labor time for the production of 40 yards of cloth was reduced to an hour. Because the magnitude of value yielded is a function of (socially average) time expended, rather than the mass of goods produced, the value of the 40 yards of cloth produced in one hour with the power loom fell from $2x$ to x. Those weavers who continued to use the older method, now anachronistic, still produced 20 yards of cloth per hour but received only $\frac{1}{2}x$—the value of a socially normative half hour—for their individual hour of labor.

Although an increase in productivity results in more *material wealth,* the new level of productivity, once generalized, yields the same amount of *value* per unit time as was the case prior to its increase. In discussing the differences between value and material wealth, I noted that the total value yielded in a social labor hour remains constant, according to Marx: "The same labour, therefore, performed for the same length of time, always yields the same amount of value, independently of any changes in productivity."[2] This example clearly indicates, however, that something does change with changes in productivity: not only does increased productivity yield a greater amount of material wealth, but it effects a reduction of socially necessary labor time. Given the abstract temporal measure of value, this redetermination of socially necessary labor time changes the magnitude of value of the individual commodities produced rather than the total value produced per unit time. That total value remains constant and simply is distributed among a greater mass of products when productivity increases. This, however, implies that, in the context of a system characterized by an abstract temporal form of wealth, the reduction of socially necessary labor time redetermines the normative social labor hour. The social labor hour in this example had been determined by hand-loom weaving in terms of the production of 20 yards of cloth; it then was redetermined by power-loom weaving in terms of the production of 40 yards of cloth. Although, then, a change in socially general productivity does not change the total amount of value produced per abstract time unit, it does change the determination of this time unit. Only the

2. Ibid., p. 137.

hour of labor time in which the general standard of socially necessary labor time is met counts as a social labor hour. In other words, *the social labor hour is constituted by the level of productivity.* (Note that this determination cannot be expressed in terms of abstract time. What has changed is not the *amount* of time which yields a value of x but, rather, the *standard* of what constitutes that amount of time.)

Productivity—the use value dimension of labor—does not, then, change the total value yielded per abstract time unit; it does, however, determine the time unit itself. We are thus faced with the following apparent paradox: the magnitude of value is a function only of labor expenditure as measured by an independent variable (abstract time), yet the constant time unit itself apparently is a dependent variable, one that is redetermined with changes in productivity. Abstract time, then, is not only socially constituted as a qualitatively determinate form of time, but it is quantitatively constituted as well: what constitutes a social labor hour is determined by the general level of productivity, the use value dimension. Yet although the social labor hour is redetermined, it remains constant as a unit of abstract time.

I shall investigate the temporal dimension of this paradox below, but at this point it should be noted that Marx's example implies that the two dimensions of the commodity form interact. On the one hand, increased productivity redetermines socially necessary labor time and thereby changes the determinations of the social labor hour. That is, the abstract temporal constant which determines value is itself determined by the use value dimension, the level of productivity. On the other hand, although the social labor hour is determined by the general productivity of concrete labor, the total value yielded in that hour remains constant, regardless of the level of the productivity. This implies that each new level of productivity, once it has become socially general, not only redetermines the social labor hour but, in turn, is redetermined by that hour as the "base level" of productivity. The amount of value yielded per unit of abstract time by the new level of productivity is equal to that yielded by the older general level of productivity. In this sense, the level of productivity, the use value dimension, is also determined by the value dimension (as the new base level).

This process of the reciprocal determination of the two dimensions of social labor in capitalism occurs on the level of society as a whole. It is at the heart of a dialectical dynamic intrinsic to the social totality constituted by commodity-determined labor. The peculiarity of the dynamic—and this is crucial—is its *treadmill effect.* Increased productivity increases the amount of value produced per unit of time—until this productivity becomes generalized; at that point the magnitude of value yielded in that time period, because of its abstract and general temporal determination, falls back to its previous level. This results in a new determination of the social labor hour and a new base level of productivity. What emerges, than, is a dialectic of transformation and reconstitution: the socially general levels of productivity and the quantitative determinations of socially necessary labor time change, yet these changes reconstitute the point of departure, that is, the social labor hour and the base level of productivity.

This treadmill effect implies, even on the abstract logical level of the problem of the magnitude of value—in other words, before the category of surplus value and the wage labor–capital relation have been introduced—a society that is directionally dynamic, as expressed by the drive for ever-increasing levels of productivity. As we have seen, increased productivity results in short-term increases in the amount of value yielded per unit time, which induces the general adoption of the newer methods of producing;[3] however, once these methods become generalized, the value yielded per unit time returns to its older level. In effect, those producers who had not yet adopted these new methods are now *compelled* to do so. The introduction of still newer methods of increasing productivity bring about further short-term increases in value. One consequence of the labor time measure of wealth, then, is that as the temporal constant is redetermined by increased productivity, it induces, in turn, still greater productivity. The result is a directional dynamic in which the two dimensions, concrete labor and abstract labor, productivity and the abstract temporal measure of wealth, constantly redetermine one another. Because, at this stage of the analysis, we cannot explain the necessity that capital accumulate constantly, the dynamic outlined here, does not represent the fully developed immanent historical logic of capitalism. It does, however, represent the initial specification of this logic and delineates the form growth *must* take in the context of labor-mediated social relations.

The reciprocal redetermination of increased productivity and the social labor hour has an objective, lawlike quality that is by no means a mere illusion or mystification. Although social, it is independent of human will. To the extent that one can speak of a Marxian "law of value," this treadmill dynamic is its initial determination; as we shall see, it describes a pattern of ongoing social transformation and reconstitution as characteristic of capitalist society. The law of value, then, is dynamic and cannot be understood adequately in terms of an equilibrium theory of the market. Once one considers the temporal dimension of value—understood as a specific form of wealth that differs from material wealth—it becomes evident that the form of value implies the above dynamic from the outset.

Note that the market-mediated mode of circulation is *not* an essential moment of this dynamic. What is essential to the dynamic of capitalism once it has been

---

3. As I have discussed, people in capitalism do not act directly in this regard on the basis of considerations of value, according to Marx; rather, their actions are shaped by considerations of price. A complete analysis of the underlying structural dynamic of capitalism, as grasped by the critique of political economy, would therefore have to show how individuals constitute this dynamic on the basis of its forms of appearance. Because my intention here, however, is only to clarify—on a very abstract logical level—the nature of this structural dynamic, I shall not address such considerations of the relation of structure and action.

constituted fully is the treadmill effect, which is rooted in the temporal dimension of the value form of wealth alone. If the market mode of circulation does play a role in this dynamic, it is as a subordinate moment of a complex development—for example, as the mode by which the level of productivity is generalized.[4] That such generalization results in a return of the amount of value to its original level, however, is *not* a function of the market; it is a function of the nature of value as a form of wealth and is essentially independent of the mode by which each new redetermination of the abstract temporal frame is generalized. As we shall see, this pattern is a central moment of the form of growth Marx associates with the category of surplus value. To focus exclusively on the mode of circulation is to deflect attention away from important implications of the commodity form for the trajectory of capitalist development in Marx's critical theory.

This investigation of the abstract determinations of capitalism's dynamic suggests that although the market mode of circulation may have been necessary for the historical genesis of the commodity as the totalizing social form, it need not remain essential to that form. It is conceivable that another mode of coordination and generalization—an administrative one, for example—could serve a similar function for this contradictory social form. In other words, once established, the law of value could also be mediated politically. One implication of this abstract logical analysis, then, is that abolishing the market mode of coordination and overcoming value are not identical.

Earlier, we described the category of capital as a dynamic social form. We now have begun to examine more closely the nature of its dynamic character and indicate how it ultimately is rooted in the interaction of value and material wealth, abstract and concrete labor—that is, the interaction of the two dimensions of the commodity form. This dynamic represents the first outlines of the immanent historical logic of capitalism, which results from the alienated character and temporal determination of labor-mediated social relations. It abstractly foreshadows a central characteristic of capital, namely, that it must accumulate constantly in order to exist. Becoming is the condition of its being.

Abstract time and historical time

I have begun to examine how the dialectical interaction between the use value dimension of social labor in capitalism and its value dimension generates a historical dynamic. The interaction between the two dimensions of the commodity form can also be analyzed in temporal terms, with reference to an opposition between abstract time and a form of concrete time peculiar to

4. On another level, market competition also serves to generalize and equalize the rate of profit, according to Marx: see *Capital,* vol. 3, trans. David Fernbach (Harmondsworth, England, 1981), pp. 273–302.

capitalism. In order to clarify the significance of this opposition I shall also extrapolate its implications on a more socially concrete level.

As we have seen, the interaction of the two dimensions of the commodity form involves a substantive redetermination of an abstract temporal constant. This abstract temporal measure of value remains constant, yet it has a changing, if hidden, social content: not every hour is an hour—in other words, not every hour of labor time counts as the social labor hour that determines the magnitude of total value. The abstract temporal constant, then, is both constant and non-constant. In abstract temporal terms, the social labor hour remains constant as a measure of the total value produced; in concrete terms, it changes as productivity does. Yet because the measure of value remains the abstract temporal unit, its concrete redetermination is not expressed in this unit as such. Increased productivity is, to be sure, expressed in the proportional decrease in the value of each individual commodity produced—but not in the total value produced per hour. Nevertheless, the historical level of productivity does bear on the total value produced, if only indirectly: it determines the socially necessary labor time required to produce a commodity; this temporal norm, in turn, determines what constitutes a social labor hour. It has become clear that, with increased productivity, the time unit becomes "denser" in terms of the production of goods. Yet this "density" is not manifest in the sphere of abstract temporality, the value sphere: the abstract temporal unit—the hour—and the total value produced remain constant.

That the abstract time frame remains constant despite being redetermined substantively is an apparent paradox that I have noted. This paradox cannot be resolved within the framework of abstract Newtonian time. Rather, it implies another sort of time as a superordinate frame of reference. As we have seen, the process whereby the constant hour becomes "denser"—that is, the substantive change effected by the use value dimension—remains nonmanifest in terms of the abstract temporal frame of value. It can, however, be expressed in other temporal terms, with reference to a form of concrete temporality.

In order to elaborate the character of this other sort of time, I must examine further the interaction of the use value and value dimensions of labor in capitalism. In a sense, changes in productivity move the determination of socially necessary labor time along an axis of abstract time: socially necessary labor time decreases with increased productivity. But, although the social labor hour is thereby redetermined, it is not moved along that axis—because it is the coordinate axis itself, the frame against which change is measured. The hour is a constant unit of abstract time; it must remain fixed in abstract temporal terms. Hence, each new level of productivity is redetermined "back" as the base level, yielding the same rate of value. Nevertheless, a new level of productivity has indeed been achieved, even if it is redetermined as the same base level. And while this substantive development cannot change the abstract temporal unit in terms of abstract time itself, it does change the "position" of that unit. The entire abstract temporal axis, or frame of reference, is moved with each socially general increase in productivity; both the social labor hour and the base level of productivity are moved "forward in time."

This movement resulting from the substantive redetermination of abstract time cannot be expressed in abstract temporal terms; it requires another frame of reference. That frame can be conceived as a mode of concrete time. Earlier, I defined concrete time as any sort of time that is a dependent variable—a function of events or actions. We have seen that the interaction of the two dimensions of commodity-determined labor is such that socially general increases in productivity move the abstract temporal unit "forward in time." Productivity, according to Marx, is grounded in the social character of the use value dimension of labor.[5] Hence, this movement of time is a function of the use value dimension of labor as it interacts with the value frame, and can be understood as a sort of concrete time. In investigating the interaction of concrete and abstract labor, which lies at the heart of Marx's analysis of capital, we have uncovered that *a feature of capitalism is a mode of (concrete) time that expresses the motion of (abstract) time.*

The dialectic of the two dimensions of labor in capitalism, then, can also be understood temporally, as a dialectic of two forms of time. As we have seen, the dialectic of concrete and abstract labor results in an intrinsic dynamic characterized by a peculiar treadmill pattern. Because each new level of productivity is redetermined as a new base level, this dynamic tends to become ongoing and is marked by ever-increasing levels of productivity. Considered temporally, this intrinsic dynamic of capital, with its treadmill pattern, entails an ongoing directional movement of time, a "flow of history." In other words, the mode of concrete time we are examining can be considered *historical time,* as constituted in capitalist society.

The historical time to which I refer clearly differs from abstract time, although both are constituted socially with the development of the commodity as a totalizing form. I have argued that abstract time, defined as an abstract independent framework within which events and actions occur, emerges from the transformation of the results of individual activity, by means of a total social mediation, into an abstract temporal norm for that activity. Although the measure of value is time, the totalizing mediation expressed by "socially necessary labor time" is not a movement *of time* but a metamorphosis of substantial time into abstract time *in space,* as it were, from the particular to the general and back.[6] This mediation in space constitutes an abstract, homogenous temporal frame that is unchanging and serves as the measure of motion. Individual activity then takes place in, and is measured with reference to, abstract time but cannot change that

---

5. *Capital,* vol. 1, p. 137.
6. See Lukács, "Reification and the Consciousness of the Proletariat," in *History and Class Consciousness,* trans. Rodney Livingstone (London, 1971), p. 90.

time. Although changes in productivity move the abstract time unit historically, that historical movement is not reflected in abstract time. Abstract time does not express the motion of time, but constitutes an apparently absolute frame for motion; its equable constant "flow" is actually static. Consequently, the amount of value yielded per unit time, being a function of that time, remains constant regardless of changes in productivity. The entire frame is reconstituted but does not itself express this reconstitution: the movement of the frame is not reflected directly in value terms.

Historical time, in this interpretation, is not an abstract continuum within which events take place and whose flow is apparently independent of human activity; rather, it is the movement *of time,* as opposed to the movement *in time.* The social totality's dynamic expressed by historical time is a constituted and constituting process of social development and transformation that is directional and whose flow, ultimately rooted in the duality of the social relations mediated by labor, is a function of social practice.

This historical process has many aspects. I shall consider only a few fundamental determinations of this process, but all imply, and provide the ground for, the more concrete aspects of the dynamic analyzed by Marx. In the first place, as noted, the dynamic of the totality entails the ongoing development of productivity, a development that distinguishes capitalism from other societies, according to Marx.[7] It involves ongoing changes in the nature of work, production, technology, and the accumulation of related forms of knowledge. More generally, the historical movement of the social totality entails ongoing, massive transformations in the mode of social life of the majority of the population—in social patterns of work and living, in the structure and distribution of classes, the nature of the state and politics, the form of the family, the nature of learning and education, the modes of transportation and communication, and so on.[8] Moreover, the dialectical process at the heart of capitalism's immanent dynamic entails the constitution, spread, and ongoing transformation of historically determinate forms of subjectivity, interactions, and social values. (This is implied by Marx's understanding of his categories as determinations of forms of social existence, grasping both social objectivity and subjectivity in their intrinsic relatedness.) Historical time in capitalism, then, can be considered as a form of concrete time that is socially constituted and expresses an ongoing qualitative transformation of work and production, of social life more generally, and of forms of consciousness, values, and needs. Unlike the "flow" of abstract time, this movement of time is not equable, but changes and can even accelerate.[9]

A characteristic of capitalism, then, is the social constitution of two forms of

7. *Capital,* vol. 1, pp. 486–89.
8. Ibid., pp. 411–16, 517–44, 575–638.
9. The development of the capital form could, then, serve as the starting point for a sociohistorical examination of changing conceptions of time in the West since the seventeenth century.

time—abstract time and historical time—that are related intrinsically. The society based upon value, upon abstract time, is, when fully developed, characterized by an ongoing historical dynamic (and relatedly, the spread of historical consciousness). In other words, the Marxian analysis elucidates and grounds socially the historically dynamic character of capitalist society in terms of a dialectic of the two dimensions of the commodity form that can be grasped as a dialectic of abstract and historical time. He analyzes this society in terms of determinate social forms that constitute a historical process of ongoing social transformation. The basic social forms of capitalism, according to Marx, are such that people in this social formation create their own history—in the sense of an ongoing, directional process of social transformation. Because of the alienated character of these forms, however, the history they constitute is beyond their control.

Historical time, then, is not just the flow of time within which events take place but is constituted as a form of concrete time. It is not expressed by the value-determined form of time as an abstract constant, as "mathematical" time. We have seen that the social labor hour is moved within a dimension of historical time that is concrete and does not flow equably; yet the abstract temporal unit does not manifest its historical redetermination—it retains its constant form as *present time.* Hence, the historical flow exists behind, but does not appear within, the frame of abstract time. The historical "content" of the abstract temporal unit remains as hidden as does the social "content" of the commodity.

Like this social "content," however, the historical dimension of the abstract temporal unit does not represent a noncapitalist moment; it does not, in and of itself, constitute the standpoint of a critique that points beyond that social formation. As opposed to Lukács—who equates capitalism with static bourgeois relations and posits the dynamic totality, the historical dialectic, as the standpoint of the critique of capitalism[10]—the position developed here shows that the very existence of an ongoing, "automatic" historical flow is related intrinsically to the social domination of abstract time. *Both* forms of time are expressions of alienated relations. I have argued that the structure of social relations characteristic of capitalism takes the form of a quasi-natural opposition between an abstract universal dimension and one of "thingly" nature. The temporal moment of that structure also has the form of an apparently nonsocial and nonhistorical opposition between an abstract formal dimension and one of concrete process. These oppositions, however, are not between capitalist and noncapitalist moments, but, like the related opposition between positive-rational and romantic forms of thought, they remain entirely within the framework of capitalist relations.

Before examining further the interaction of the two forms of time in capitalism, I shall first continue to investigate their differences—in particular, those

10. Lukács, "Reification and the Consciousness of the Proletariat," pp. 143–49.

differences between historical time and the frame of abstract time which are implied by the differences between material wealth and value. As we have seen, the frame of abstract time, intrinsically related to the value dimension, remains constant with increased productivity. The social labor hour in which the production of 20 yards of cloth yields a total value of x is the abstract temporal equivalent of the social labor hour in which the production of 40 yards of cloth yields a total value of x: they are equal units of abstract time and, as normative, determine a constant magnitude of value. Assuredly, there is a concrete difference between the two, which results from the historical development of productivity; such a historical development, however, redetermines the criteria of what constitutes a social labor hour, and is not reflected in the hour itself. In this sense, then, *value is an expression of time as the present.* It is a measure of, and compelling norm for, the expenditure of immediate labor time regardless of the historical level of productivity.

Historical time in capitalism, on the other hand, entails a unique process of ongoing social transformation and is related to ongoing changes in the historical level of productivity: it is a function of the development of the use value dimension of labor in the context of the commodity-determined social totality. It is significant that Marx analyzes productivity in terms of the use value dimension of labor (that is, the social character of concrete labor) as follows:

The productivity of labour . . . is determined amongst other things by the workers' average degree of skill, the level of development of science and its technological application, the social organization of the process of production, the extent and effectiveness of the means of production, and the conditions found in the natural environment.[11]

This means that the productivity of labor is not bound necessarily to the direct labor of the workers; it also is a function of scientific, technical, and organizational knowledge and experience, which Marx regards as products of human development that are socially general.[12] We shall see that in his account, capital unfolds historically in such a way that the level of productivity becomes less and less dependent on the direct labor of the workers. This process entails the development in alienated form of socially general forms of knowledge and experience which are not a function of, and cannot be reduced to, the skills and knowledge of the immediate producers.[13] The dialectical movement of time we have been considering represents the initial determinations of Marx's analysis of capital's historical unfolding.

When the use value dimension of labor is measured, it is—unlike the value dimension—measured in terms of its products, the amount of material wealth it

11. *Capital,* vol. 1, p. 130.
12. Marx, *Results of the Immediate Process of Production,* trans. Rodney Livingstone, in *Capital,* vol. 1, pp. 1024, 1054.
13. See, for example, *Capital,* vol. 1, pp. 443–58, 482, 509, 549.

produces. Not being bound to immediate labor, it is not measured in terms of the expenditure of abstract labor time. The measure of material wealth also can have a temporal aspect, but in the absence of the form of temporal necessity associated with the value dimension, this temporality is a substantive function of production—the amount of time actually required to produce a particular product. This time is a function *of* objectification and not a norm *for* expenditure. The changes in this concrete time of production which occur with the developments of productivity are changes reflecting the historical movement of time. This movement is generated by a process of social constitution related to an ongoing accumulation, in alienated form, of technical, organizational, and scientific knowledge and experience.[14] It follows from the discussion thus far that, within the framework of Marx's analysis, certain *consequences* of this accumulation—that is, consequences of the social, intellectual, and cultural developments that ground the movement of time—can indeed be measured, either in terms of changes in the quantity of goods produced per unit time, for example, or in terms of changes in the amount of time required to produce a particular product. The historical developments *themselves,* however, cannot be measured: they cannot be quantified as dependent variables of abstract temporality (that is, in value terms), even though the requirements of the social form of value mold the concrete form of production in which the accumulation of knowledge, experience, and labor is objectified. The movement of history, then, can be expressed indirectly by time as a dependent variable; as a movement of time, though, it cannot be grasped by static, abstract time.

One important aspect of Marx's conception of the trajectory of capitalist society's historical dynamic has become apparent at this initial stage of the investigation. His fundamental categories imply that, with the unfolding of the dynamic driven ultimately by the commodity form of relations, a growing disparity arises between developments in the productive power of labor (which are not necessarily bound to the direct labor of the workers), on the one hand, and the value frame within which such developments are expressed (which *is* bound to such labor), on the other. The disparity between the accumulation of historical time and the objectification of immediate labor time becomes more pronounced as scientific knowledge is increasingly materialized in production. Consistent with Marx's distinction between value and material wealth, the great increases in productivity effected by science and advanced technology are not, and cannot be, accounted for adequately in terms of abstract labor time expenditure, whether manual or mental—including the time required for research and development, and the training of engineers and skilled workers.

This development can be understood with reference to the category of historical time. As we shall see in considering the trajectory of production, with the development of scientifically and technologically advanced production, in-

14. Ibid., pp. 482, 510.

creases in productivity also express the accumulation of socially general past experience and labor, as well as the frequently discontinuous increases in general knowledge that occur on the basis of this preserved past.[15] The dynamic of capitalism, as grasped by Marx's categories, is such that with this accumulation of historical time, a growing disparity separates the conditions for the production of material wealth from those for the generation of value. Considered in terms of the use value dimension of labor (that is, in terms of the creation of material wealth), production becomes ever less a process of materially objectifying the skills and knowledge of the individual producers or even the class immediately involved; instead, it becomes ever more an objectification of the accumulated collective knowledge of the species, of humanity—which, as a general category, is itself constituted with the accumulation of historical time. In terms of the use value dimension, then, as capitalism develops fully, production increasingly becomes a process of the objectification of historical time rather than of immediate labor time. According to Marx, though, value, necessarily remains an expression of the latter objectification.

The dialectic of transformation and reconstitution

The historical dynamic characteristic of capitalist society, as analyzed by Marx, is not linear but contradictory. It points beyond itself but is not self-overcoming. I have examined, on an abstract and preliminary level, certain differences between production based on the objectification of immediate labor and that based upon historical time. Were it not for the dual character of capitalism's social forms, the development of production could be understood simply as a technical development entailing the linear supersession of one mode of production by another according to the following historical pattern: In the course of capitalist development a form of production based upon the knowledge, skills, and labor of the immediate producers gives rise to another form, based upon the accumulated knowledge and experience of humanity. With the accumulation of historical time, the social necessity for the expenditure of direct human labor in production gradually is diminished. Production based upon the present, upon the expenditure of abstract labor time, thus generates its own negation—the objectification of historical time.

A number of theories of modernity—for example, those of "postindustrial society"—are based on such an understanding of the development of production. This evolutionary understanding is not fully adequate to the nonlinear character of capitalist production's historical development. It presupposes that the form of wealth produced remains constant, and that only the method of its production, understood solely in technical terms, changes. Within the framework of Marx's analysis, such an evolutionary development would be possible only

15. Ibid., p. 508ff.

if value and material wealth were not very different forms of wealth. Because of the double character of capitalism's structuring forms, however, this development represents only one tendency within a much more complex, dialectical historical dynamic. Marx's analysis of value as a structuring social category neither treats the development of production simply as a technical development—whereby a mode of production based primarily on human labor is superseded by one based on science and technology—nor, however, does it ignore the great changes effected by science and technology. Rather, on the basis of the distinctions between value and material wealth, abstract and concrete labor (and, implicitly, abstract and concrete time), Marx analyzes production in capitalism as a contradictory social process that is constituted by a dialectic of the two dimensions of the commodity form.

The interaction of these two dimensions is such that value is not simply superseded by the accumulation of historical time, but continually is reconstituted as an essential determinant of the social formation. This process, which entails the retention of value and the forms of abstract domination associated with it, despite the development of the use value dimension, is intrinsic structurally to the basic social forms of capitalism grasped by Marx's fundamental categories. In examining the most abstract determinations of capitalist society's dynamic in terms of the interaction of these two dimensions, we saw how each new level of productivity both redetermines the social labor hour and, in turn, is redetermined by the abstract time frame as a base level of productivity. Changes in concrete time effected by increased productivity are mediated by the social totality in a way that transforms them into new norms of abstract time (socially necessary labor time) that, in turn, redetermine the constant social labor hour. Note that inasmuch as the development of productivity redetermines the social labor hour, this development reconstitutes, rather than supersedes, the form of necessity associated with that abstract temporal unit. Each new level of productivity is structurally transformed into the concrete presupposition of the social labor hour—and the amount of value produced per unit time remains constant. In this sense, the movement of time is continually converted into present time. In Marx's analysis, the basic structure of capitalism's social forms is such, then, that the accumulation of historical time does not, in and of itself, undermine the necessity represented by value, that is, the necessity of the present; rather, it changes the concrete presupposition of that present, thereby constituting its necessity anew. Present necessity is not "automatically" negated but paradoxically reinforced; it is impelled forward in time as a perpetual present, an apparently eternal necessity.

For Marx, then, the historical dynamic of capitalism is anything but linear and evolutionary. The development—which I have grounded, on a very abstract logical level, in the double character of labor in capitalism—is at once dynamic and static. It entails ever rising levels of productivity, yet the value frame is perpetually reconstituted anew. One consequence of this peculiar dialectic is that sociohistorical reality is increasingly constituted on two very different levels. On the one hand, as I have pointed out, capitalism involves an ongoing transformation of social life—of the nature, structure and interrelations of social classes and other groupings, as well as the nature of production, transportation, circulation, patterns of living, the form of the family, and so on. On the other hand, the unfolding of capital involves the ongoing reconstitution of its own fundamental condition as an unchanging feature of social life—namely, that social mediation ultimately is effected by labor. In Marx's analysis, these two moments—the ongoing transformation of the world and the reconstitution of the value-determined framework—are mutually conditioning and intrinsically related: both are rooted in the alienated social relations constitutive of capitalism, and together they define that society.

The Marxian concept of capital, examined on this very fundamental level, is an attempt to grasp the nature and development of modern capitalist society in terms of *both* temporal moments, to analyze capitalism as a dynamic society that is in constant flux and, yet, retains its underlying identity. An apparent paradox of capitalism, within this framework, is that, unlike other social formations, it possesses an immanent historical dynamic; this dynamic, however, is characterized by the constant translation of historical time into the framework of the present, thereby reinforcing that present.

To analyze modern capitalist society in terms of the domination of value (and, hence, the domination of capital) is thus to analyze it in terms of two apparently opposed forms of abstract social domination: the domination of abstract time as the present, and a necessary process of ongoing transformation. Both forms of abstract domination as well as their intrinsic interrelation are grasped by the Marxian "law of value." I have noted that this "law" is dynamic and cannot be grasped adequately as a law of the market; at this point I can add that it categorially grasps the drive toward ever-increasing levels of productivity, the ongoing transformation of social life in capitalist society, as well as the ongoing reconstitution of its basic social forms. It reveals capitalism to be a society marked by a temporal duality—an ongoing, accelerating flow of history, on the one hand, and an ongoing conversion of this movement of time into a constant present, on the other. Although socially constituted, both temporal dimensions lie beyond the control of, and exert domination over, the constituting actors. Far from being a law of static equilibrium, then, Marx's law of value grasps as a determinate "law" of history, the dialectical dynamic of transformation and reconstitution characteristic of capitalist society.

The analysis of capitalism in terms of these two moments of social reality suggests, however, that it can be very difficult to grasp both simultaneously. Because so many aspects of social life are transformed more and more rapidly as capitalism develops, the unchanging underlying structures of that society—for example, the fact that labor is an indirect means of life for individuals—can be taken to be eternal, socially "natural" aspects of the human condition. As a result, the possibility of a future qualitatively different from modern society can be veiled.

This brief investigation of the dialectic of the two dimensions of the basic forms of capitalist society has shown how, according to Marx's analysis, production based on the expenditure of abstract present time and that based on the appropriation of historical time are not clearly distinguished modes of producing in capitalism (whereby the latter gradually supersedes the former). Rather, they are moments of the developed capitalist process of production which interact in a way that constitutes this process. Consequently, production in capitalism does not develop in a linear fashion. The dialectical dynamic does, however, give rise to the historical possibility that production based on historical time can be constituted separately from production based on abstract present time—and that the alienated interaction of past and present, characteristic of capitalism, can be overcome. It is this possible future separation that allows one to distinguish between the two moments of the sphere of production in the present, that is, in capitalist society.

At this point, I can return to the category of socially necessary labor time. We have seen that this category represents the transformation of concrete time into abstract time in capitalism, and, as such, expresses a temporally normative compulsion. My preliminary examination of capitalism's immanent dynamic has shown how this objective, impersonal compulsion exerted on individuals is not static but is itself continually reconstituted historically. The producers not only are compelled to produce in accordance with an abstract temporal norm, but must do so in a historically adequate fashion: they are compelled to "keep up with the times." People in capitalist society are confronted with a historically determinate form of abstract social necessity whose determinations change historically—that is, they are confronted with a socially constituted form of historical necessity. The notion of historical necessity has another meaning, of course—that history necessarily moves in a determinate fashion. This discussion of Marx's initial categories has shown that, according to his analysis, these two aspects of historical necessity—the changing compulsion confronting individuals, and the intrinsic logic impelling the totality—are related expressions of the same form of social life.[16]

This investigation implies further that the category of socially necessary labor time also has another dimension. Given that value is the form of social wealth

16. It should be clear that the sort of historical necessity grounded socially by the Marxian categories pertains to the development of the social formation as a whole. It does not refer directly to political developments within countries and among countries, for example. These could, conceivably, be investigated in terms of the historical "metalogic" analyzed by Marx; to do so without considering necessary mediations and contingent factors, however, would be reductionist. By the same token, to criticize Marx's analysis from the standpoint of a more contingent plane of historical development is to confuse levels of analysis and social reality which should be distinguished.

in capitalism, socially necessary labor time should be understood as socially necessary in an additional sense: it implicitly refers to labor time that is necessary for capital and, hence, for society so long as it is capitalist, that is, so long as it is structured by value as the form of wealth and surplus value as the goal of production. This labor time, accordingly, is the expression of a superordinate form of necessity for capitalist society as a whole, as well as for individuals, and should not be confused with the form of necessity Marx refers to in his distinction between "necessary" and "surplus" labor time. As we have seen, this is a distinction between the portion of the workday in which the workers labor for their own reproduction ("necessary" labor time) and the portion that is appropriated by the representatives of capital ("surplus" labor time).[17] In this sense, both "necessary" and "surplus" labor time are subsumed under "socially necessary labor time" in all of its ramifications.

The category of value, in its opposition to that of material wealth, then, signifies that labor time is the stuff of which wealth and social relations are made in capitalism. It refers to a form of social life in which humans are dominated by their own labor and are compelled to maintain this domination. The imperatives grounded in this social form, as I shall discuss further, impel rapid increases in technological development and a necessary pattern of ongoing "growth"; yet, they also perpetuate the necessity of direct human labor in the process of production, regardless of the degree of technological development and of the accumulation of material wealth. It is as the ultimate ground of these historically specific imperatives that labor, in its dual character as productive activity and as a historically specific social "substance," constitutes the identity of capitalism, according to Marx.

It should be clear by now that the complex dynamic I have been investigating is the essential core of the Marxian dialectic of the forces and relations of production in capitalism. My reading indicates, first, that this dialectic is rooted in the double character of the social forms that constitute capitalist society—in the value and use value dimensions of labor and of socially constituted time; and, second, that it perpetuates the abstract compulsion of temporal necessity in both its static and its dynamic dimensions. By grounding this dialectic's fundamental features on such an abstract logical level, I have shown that, in Marx's analysis, it is rooted neither in a purportedly fundamental contradiction between production and distribution, nor in private ownership of the means of production—that is, in class conflict; rather, it stems from the peculiar social forms constituted by labor in capitalism which structure such conflict. This understanding of the developmental pattern and possible negation of capitalist society differs greatly from that associated with approaches proceeding from the notion of "labor" that define the contradictory dialectic of capitalism in traditional terms.

We have seen, if only on a preliminary logical level, how the two dimensions

17. *Capital*, vol. 1, pp. 324–25.

of social labor dynamically redetermine and reinforce one another. Nevertheless, in my discussion of the differences between production based on the appropriation of historical time and that based on the expenditure of abstract present time, I have also shown that these two dimensions are fundamentally different. In Marx's analysis, the ground for capitalism's contradictory character is precisely the circumstance that, while these two dimensions are very different, they, nevertheless, are bound together as two moments of a single (historically specific) social form. The result is a dynamic interaction in which these two moments redetermine one another and in such a way that their difference becomes a growing opposition. This mounting opposition within a common framework does not, as I have shown on a very abstract level, result in any sort of linear evolutionary development wherein the underlying basis of the present is quasi-hautomatically overcome and superseded. Even at this level one can see that it would result in a growing intrinsic structural tension.

In the traditional interpretation, capitalist relations of production remain extrinsic to the process of production, which is constituted by "labor." The contradiction between the forces and relations of production is, therefore, seen as one between production and distribution, that is, *between* existing social "institutions" and spheres. Within the framework developed in this work, however, that contradiction is *within* these "institutions," spheres, and processes. This suggests that the capitalist process of production, for example, must be understood in social as well as in technical terms. As I shall elaborate, even the material form of this process can be analyzed socially, in terms of the growing internal structural tension, the "shearing pressure," that results from the two structural imperatives of the dialectic of transformation and reconstitution— achieving ever-higher levels of productivity and producing a surplus of value.

It is the nonidentity of the two dimensions of the basic structuring forms of capitalism, then, which imparts an intrinsic dialectical dynamic to the social formation and unfolds as its basic contradiction. This contradiction both shapes social processes and institutions in capitalist society and grounds the immanent possibility of its historical negation.

My analysis of the dialectic of labor and time has shown clearly that Marx, far from adopting labor and production as the standpoint of a historical critique of capitalism, focuses his critical analysis precisely on the socially constitutive role played by labor in that society. Hence, Marx's idea that capitalism's contradictory character gives rise to a growing tension between what is and what could be does not posit industrial production and the proletariat as the elements of a postcapitalist future. In Marx's understanding the basic contradiction of capitalism is not one between one existent social structure or grouping and another; rather, it is grounded in the capitalist sphere of production itself, in the dual character of the sphere of production in a society whose essential relations are constituted by labor.

The fundamental contradiction of capitalism, then, lies between the two dimensions of labor and time. On the basis of the investigation thus far, I can describe this contradiction as one between the socially general knowledge and skills whose accumulation is induced by the labor-mediated form of social relations, on the one hand, and this form of mediation itself, on the other. Although the value basis of the present and, hence, the abstract necessity expressed by socially necessary labor time, is never automatically overcome, it comes into growing tension with the possibilities intrinsic to the development it has induced.

I shall elaborate this contradiction below, but at this point I wish to return to the question of the historical dialectic. The interpretation I have presented here extends the scope of this dialectic beyond the laissez-faire epoch of capitalism but also limits it to the capitalist social formation. My analysis of Marx's initial categories has shown, if only abstractly, that his conception of the dual character of capitalism's structuring social forms implies a historical dialectic. By socially grounding the directional dialectical dynamic in a way that specifies it historically as a feature of capitalist society, this investigation reinforces my contention regarding the historical determinateness of Marx's categories and his conception of an immanent logic in history.

It also helps to distinguish three modes of dialectical interactions that are intertwined in Marx's analysis. The first, which is best known and most commonly referred to, can be characterized as a dialectic of reflexive constitution through objectification. It is expressed, for example, by Marx's statement at the beginning of his discussion of the labor process in *Capital* that people, by acting on external nature and changing it, change their own nature.[18] In other words, for Marx, the process of self-constitution involves a process of externalization, both for humanity and for individuals. Skills and abilities are constituted practically, through their expression. Marx's conception of history frequently has been understood in terms of such a process.[19] However, my discussion of the twofold character of capitalism's social forms has demonstrated that this process of self-constitution through labor, even when labor is understood broadly as any externalizing activity, does not necessarily entail a historical development. For example, the material interactions of humanity with nature are not necessarily directionally dynamic; there is neither a theoretical ground nor historical evidence for maintaining that the reflexive effects of concrete labor's objectifications must be directional. The sorts of immanent necessity and directional logic that are central to the dialectical development I have been examining are not intrinsic to the interactions of a knowing subject with its objectifications—whether these interactions are understood individually or in terms of the interactions of humanity with nature. In other words, a directional logic is not intrinsic to those activities which can be termed forms of concrete labor.

18. Ibid., p. 283.
19. Lukács can be interpreted in this way: see "Reification and the Consciousness of the Proletariat," pp. 145–49, 170–71, 175–81, 185–90.

A second dialectical interaction in Marx's mature theory is one of the reciprocal constitution of determinate forms of social practice and social structure. In *Capital,* as I have noted, Marx begins to develop a complex dialectic of deep structure and practice, mediated by the forms of appearance of the former as well as by the subjective dimensions of the various social forms. Such an analysis allows one theoretically to overcome objectivistic and subjectivistic interpretations of social life so as to reveal the valid moments and distorted aspects of each.[20] Nevertheless, this sort of dialectic is also not necessarily directional; it can entail the reproduction of a form of social life that has no intrinsic historical dynamic.[21]

Both of these dialectical interactions can exist in some form in various societies. What distinguishes capitalism, according to Marx, is that both become directionally dynamic because they are embedded in, and intertwined with, an intrinsically dynamic framework of objectified social relations, which is constituted by a third sort of dialectical interaction—one rooted in the double character of the underlying social forms. As a result, the social structures of capitalism that constitute and are constituted by social practice are dynamic. Because, moreover, the intrinsically dynamic relations that mark capitalism are mediated by labor, humanity's interaction with nature does indeed acquire a directional dynamic in capitalism. What ultimately gives rise to this historical dynamic, however, is the twofold character of labor in capitalism, not "labor." This directionally dynamic structure also totalizes and renders dynamic the antagonism between producing and expropriating social groupings; in other words, it constitutes such antagonism as class conflict.

My investigation of the implications of the temporal dimension of value, then, has shown that Marx's analysis uncovers the basis of a dialectical developmental logic in historically specific social forms. His analysis thereby shows that there is indeed a form of logic in history, of historical necessity, but that it is immanent only to the capitalist social formation, and not to human history as a whole. This implies that Marx's mature critical social theory does not hypostatize history as a sort of force moving all human societies; it does not presuppose that a directional dynamic of history in general exists. Rather, it seeks to explain the existence of the sort of ongoing directional dynamic that defines modern society, and to do so in terms of historically determinate social forms

20. For example, Marx's analysis of value and price indicates the "rational core" of approaches based on the premise of methodological individualism or of the notion that social phenomena are the aggregate results of individual behavior. At the same time, the Marxian analysis embeds such approaches historically by showing the historically specific social constitution of that which they take to be socially ontological (for example, the maximizing rational actor).

21. Pierre Bourdieu's examination of Kabyle society is a good example of an analysis of the reproduction of such a form of social life in terms of a mutually constituting dialectic of structure and practice (as one of structure, habitus, and practice): see *Outline of a Theory of Practice,* trans. Richard Nice (Cambridge, 1977).

constituted by labor in a process of alienation.[22] This analysis implies that any theory that posits an immanent logic to history as such—whether dialectical or evolutionary—without grounding this logic in a determinate process of social constitution (which is an unlikely proposition), projects as the history of humanity the qualities specific to capitalism. This projection necessarily obscures the actual social basis of a directional dynamic of history. The historical process is thereby transformed from the object of social analysis into its quasi-metaphysical presupposition.

22. The notion that the commodity form is the ultimate ground for capitalism's complex historical dynamic calls into question any transhistorical opposition between a conception of history either as a single, homogeneous process or as the result of the intersections of a variety of social processes with their own temporalities. My effort to ground socially—on a very abstract logical level—the historically dynamic character of capitalism suggests that although capitalism is not necessarily marked by a unitary, synchronous, homogeneous historical process, it is, as a whole historically dynamic in a way that distinguishes it from other forms of social life. The relations among various social levels and processes are organized differently than they would be in a noncapitalist society; they become embedded in a general, socially constituted, temporally directional, dialectical framework.

9. The trajectory of production

I have approached Marx's conception of the nature of capitalist society by examining the implications of his analysis of the commodity as capitalism's fundamental social form. My examination has uncovered the initial determinations of the intrinsic historical dynamic implied by his analysis of commodity-determined labor's double character and value's temporal dimension. In this way it has begun to illuminate Marx's category of capital as referring to a contradictory and dynamic structure of alienated social relations constituted by labor. This approach has supported and further clarified my argument that Marx's theory of the centrality of labor to capitalist society is a critical theory of a determinate mode of social mediation; labor in capitalism has a social significance, within the framework of that theory, that cannot be grasped adequately when labor is understood only as a productive activity mediating humanity and nature.

I shall now reconsider Marx's analysis of the sphere of production in light of this investigation of his critical theory's initial categories, focusing in particular on the issues of economic growth, class conflict, and the social constitution of industrial production. In this way I shall elaborate further the understanding of capital—and, hence, the reconceptualization of capitalism and the nature of its possible overcoming—developed thus far.

Surplus value and "economic growth"

My preliminary discussion of Marx's conception of the dialectic of the forces and relations of production sheds light on an aspect of the dynamic implied by his category of surplus value of particular interest in view of the current intensification of ecological problems on a global scale. The category itself, as we have seen, refers to the value yielded by surplus labor time, that is, the labor time expended by workers above and beyond the time required to create the amount of value necessary for their own reproduction (necessary labor time). The category of surplus value usually has been understood as indicating that the social surplus in capitalism results not from a number of "factors of production" but from labor alone. Such an interpretation maintains that labor's unique productive role is veiled by the contractual character of the relations between non-propertied producers and nonproductive proprietors in capitalism. These relations take the form of an exchange in which workers are remunerated for the value of their labor power—which is less than the value they produce. Nevertheless, this difference in value is not evident. In other words, because exploitation in capitalism is effected by means of such an exchange, it is not manifest—unlike, for example, the expropriation of the surplus in feudal society. The category of surplus value, then, is taken to reveal the nonmanifest exploitation characteristic of capitalism.[1]

While this interpretation does grasp an important dimension of the category, it is one-sided; it concentrates exclusively on the expropriation of *surplus* value, as it were, without considering sufficiently the implications of surplus *value*. I have shown, however, that Marx analyzes the valorization process—the process of creating surplus value—in terms of the process of creating value; his analysis is concerned not only with the source of the surplus but also with the form of the surplus wealth produced. Value, as noted, is a category of a dynamic totality. This dynamic involves a dialectic of transformation and reconstitution that results from the dual nature of the commodity form and from the two structural imperatives of the value form of wealth—the drive toward increasing levels of productivity and the necessary retention of direct human labor in production. We now can extend that analysis further. As we have seen, capital is "self-valorizing value," according to Marx;[2] it is characterized by the need to expand constantly. When value is the form of wealth, the goal of production necessarily is surplus value. That is, the goal of capitalist production is not simply value but the constant expansion of surplus value.[3]

The salient features of this expansion are rooted in the value form of wealth itself. They include, but are not limited to, the unstable and crisis-prone nature of the accumulation of capital, as analyzed by Marx. Precisely these aspects of capital accumulation have been the focus of much attention in the Marxist tradition. In *The Limits to Capital,* for example, David Harvey discusses at length how, within the framework of Marx's analysis, balanced growth is impossible in capitalism.[4] Due to the necessary imbalance between production and consumption, as well as the underlying contradiction between production and circulation, crises are intrinsic to capitalism.[5] Moreover, according to Harvey, because capitalists must attempt to equalize the rate of profit, they allocate social labor and organize production processes in ways that do not necessarily maximize the aggregate output of surplus value in society. This, he claims, is the material basis for the systematic misallocation of social labor and for

1. See, for example, Paul M. Sweezy, *The Theory of Capitalist Development* (New York, 1969), pp. 56–61; and Maurice Dobb, *Political Economy and Capitalism* (London, 1940), pp. 56, 58, 75.
2. Marx, *Capital,* vol. 1, trans. Ben Fowkes (London, 1976), p. 255.
3. Ibid., pp. 714–18, 725ff.
4. David Harvey, *The Limits to Capital* (Chicago, 1982), p. 171.
5. Ibid., pp. 81–82, 157.

the bias in the organization of labor processes that leads capitalism into periodic crises.[6] Harvey also emphasizes that capital itself creates barriers against the tendency toward perpetually accelerating technological and organizational changes.[7] In general, he maintains that capitalists, acting in their own self-interests under the social relations of capitalist production and exchange, generate a technological mix that threatens further accumulation, destroys the potentiality for balanced growth and jeopardizes the reproduction of the capitalist class as a whole.[8]

Although the unstable and crisis-ridden features of capital accumulation certainly are crucial aspects of Marx's theory, in attempting to unfold the fundamental characteristics of capital, I shall focus on another aspect of his analysis of the process of the expansion of surplus value. It is clear that his critique of capitalism's peculiar process of accumulation for the sake of accumulation[9] is not one of distribution alone, that is, a critique of the fact that social wealth is not used for the benefit of all. It is also not a productivist critique—its thrust is not to indicate that the problem with capitalism is that the aggregate output of surplus value is not maximized in a balanced way. Marx's critique is not undertaken from a standpoint that affirms such maximization. Rather, his critique is of the very nature of the growth immanent to capital, of the trajectory of the dynamic itself.

The specificity of the growth entailed by the expansion of surplus value is grounded in the characteristics of value as a temporally determined form of wealth and social mediation. We have seen that because total value created is a function only of abstract labor time expenditure, increased productivity yields a greater amount of material wealth but results only in short-term increases in value yielded per unit time. Leaving aside considerations of the intensity of labor at this point, "a working day of a given length always creates the same amount of value, no matter how the productivity of labour and, with it, the mass of the product and the price of each single commodity produced may vary."[10] Given this temporal determination of value, the expansion of surplus value—the systemic goal of production in capitalism—can be achieved only if the proportion of surplus labor time to necessary labor time is changed. This, as noted, can be accomplished by extending the duration of the work day (the production of "absolute surplus value").[11] Once, however, the length of the work day has been limited (as a result of labor struggles or legislation, for example), surplus labor time can be increased only if necessary labor time is reduced (the production of "relative surplus value"). This reduction, according

6. Ibid., p. 68.
7. Ibid., pp. 121–22.
8. Ibid., pp. 188–89.
9. *Capital*, vol. 1, p. 742.
10. Ibid., p. 656.
11. Ibid., p. 340ff.

to Marx, is effected by increased productivity. Although a socially general increase in productivity does not increase the total value yielded within a given time period, it does decrease the value of the commodities required for the workers' reproduction. In other words, it decreases necessary labor time and, thereby, increases surplus labor time.[12] As a result of both this relation of productivity to the expansion of relative surplus value as well as the short-term increases in value yielded per unit time when productivity is increased, capital, according to Marx, "has an immanent drive and a constant tendency towards increasing the productivity of labour."[13]

This tendency toward ongoing increases in productivity is intrinsic to the expansion of relative surplus value, the form of the surplus adequate to capital. It is generated by the peculiar relationship between the value form of the surplus and productivity. Within the framework of Marx's presentation, this relationship illuminates retrospectively his argumentative intent in determining the magnitude of value in terms of abstract human labor time expenditure. It now clearly appears as an initial determination of capitalism's peculiar dynamic, as the point of departure for Marx's attempt to grasp and elucidate this dynamic. Although increased productivity results in a directly proportional increase in material wealth, it increases surplus value only indirectly, once the working day is limited, by decreasing necessary labor time; it does not result in immediately corresponding increases in socially appropriable wealth or decreases in labor time (as could be the case if material wealth were the dominant social form of wealth). Moreover, because the total value yielded per unit time does not increase with socially general increases in productivity, it represents a limit to the expansion of surplus value: the amount of surplus value yielded per unit time can never exceed this amount, regardless of the degree to which productivity is increased. Indeed, it cannot even reach this limit since, on a general social level, capital can never dispense completely with necessary labor time.

According to Marx, it is precisely this limit—which is intrinsic to the form of wealth whose magnitude is a function of abstract human labor time expenditure—that generates a tendency toward ever-higher rates of increase in productivity. On the basis of his analysis of the abstract temporal measure of value and the consequent indirect relationship between increases in productivity and increases in surplus value, Marx argues that, given a constant rate of increase in productivity, the rate of increase of the mass of surplus value per determinate portion of capital falls as the level of surplus labor time rises.[14] He argues, in other words, that the more closely the amount of surplus value yielded approaches the limit of the total value produced per unit time, the more difficult it becomes to further decrease necessary labor time by means of increased pro-

12. Ibid., pp. 431–33.
13. Ibid., pp. 436–37.
14. Ibid., pp. 657–58; Marx, *Grundrisse: Foundations of the Critique of Political Economy,* trans. Martin Nicolaus (London, 1973), p. 340.

ductivity and, thereby, to increase surplus value. This, however, means that the higher the general level of surplus labor time and, relatedly, of productivity, the more productivity must be further increased in order to achieve a determinate increase in the mass of surplus value per determinate portion of capital.

The significance of this relationship between productivity and surplus value is not limited to the question of Marx's approach to the issue of the tendency of the rate of profit to fall[15] or, more generally, to the problem of whether the expansion of capital can continue indefinitely. It also indicates that the value form of the surplus not only induces ongoing increases in productivity, but that the expansion of surplus value required by capital implies a tendency toward accelerating rates of increase in productivity. Capital tends to generate a constant acceleration in the growth of productivity. Note that, according to this analysis, enormous increases in productivity are effected precisely because higher levels of productivity increase surplus value only indirectly. By the same token, although such increases in productivity result in corresponding increases in material wealth, they do not yield corresponding increases in surplus value. The difference between the two forms of wealth in their relation to productivity means that, on the one hand, the ever-increasing levels of productivity generated by capital accumulation entail directly corresponding increases in the masses of products produced and of raw materials consumed in production. On the other hand, though, because the social form of the surplus in capitalism is value rather than material wealth, the result—in spite of appearances—is not a commensurate increase in the surplus product. The ever-increasing amounts of material wealth produced under capitalism do not represent correspondingly high levels of social wealth in the form of value.

This pattern of growth is double-sided for Marx: it involves the constant expansion of human productive abilities, yet tied as it is to an alienated dynamic social structure, this expansion has an accelerating, boundless, runaway form over which people have no control. Leaving aside considerations of possible limits or barriers to capital accumulation, one consequence implied by this particular dynamic—which yields increases in material wealth greater than those in surplus value—is the accelerating destruction of the natural environment. According to Marx, as a result of the relationship among productivity, material wealth, and surplus value, the ongoing expansion of the latter increasingly has deleterious consequences for nature as well as for humans:

---

15. Although much has been written about the tendency of the rate of profit to fall, what frequently has been overlooked is that Marx treats it in Volume 3 of *Capital* as a "surface" phenomenon that reflects and refracts a more fundamental historical tendency in capitalism—namely, that machines gradually displace living labor in the process of production. As with most of the categories he analyzes in Volume 3, Marx argues that this surface phenomenon was not recognized as such by classical political economy and, instead, was accorded the significance of a more fundamental historical tendency: see *Capital,* vol. 3, trans. David Fernbach (Harmondsworth, England, 1981), pp. 317–75.

In modern agriculture, as in urban industry, the increase in the productivity and the mobility of labour is purchased at the cost of . . . debilitating labour-power itself. Moreover, all progress in capitalist agriculture is a progress in the art . . . of robbing the soil; all progress in increasing the fertility of the soil for a given time is a progress towards ruining the more long-lasting sources of that fertility.[16]

Rooted in his analysis of value in contradistinction to material wealth, Marx's critique of capitalist industry and agriculture is clearly not a productivist critique. Yet that Marx's critique is based on an analysis of the specific form of labor in capitalism rather than "labor," implies that the growing destruction of nature should not simply be seen, conversely, as a consequence of increasing human control and domination of nature.[17] Neither the productivist critique of capitalism nor the latter sort of critique of the domination of nature distinguishes between value and material wealth; both are based on the transhistorical conception of "labor." Hence, each focuses exclusively on one dimension of what Marx sought to grasp as a more complex, two-sided development. Together, then, these positions constitute another theoretical antinomy of capitalist society.

In Marx's analysis, the growing destruction of nature under capitalism is not simply a function of nature having become an object for humanity; rather, it is primarily a result of the *sort* of object that nature has become. Raw materials and products, according to Marx, are bearers of value in capitalism, in addition to being constituent elements of material wealth. Capital produces material wealth as a means of creating value. Hence, it consumes material nature not only as the stuff of material wealth but also as a means of fueling its own self-expansion—that is, as a means of effecting the extraction and absorption of as much surplus labor time from the working population as possible. Ever-increasing amounts of raw materials must be consumed even though the result is not a corresponding increase in the social form of surplus wealth (surplus value). The relation of humans and nature mediated by labor becomes a one-way process of consumption, rather than a cyclical interaction. It acquires the form of an accelerating transformation of qualitatively particular raw materials into "matter," into qualitatively homogeneous bearers of objectified time.

The problem with capital accumulation, then, is not only that it is unbalanced and crisis-ridden, but also that its underlying form of growth is marked by runaway productivity that neither is controlled by the producers nor functions directly to their benefit. This particular sort of growth is intrinsic to a society based on value; it cannot be explained in terms of misdirected views and false priorities alone. Although productivist critiques of capitalism have focused only on the possible barriers to economic growth inherent in capital accumulation, it is clear that Marx criticized both the accelerating boundlessness of "growth"

16. *Capital*, vol. 1, p. 658.
17. See Max Horkheimer and Theodor W. Adorno, *Dialectic of Enlightenment*, trans. John Cumming (New York, 1972), pp. 3–42, 89ff.

under capitalism as well as its crisis-ridden character. Indeed, he demonstrates that these two characteristics should be analyzed as intrinsically related.

The pattern I have outlined suggests that, in the society in which the commodity is totalized, there is an underlying tension between ecological considerations and the imperatives of value as the form of wealth and social mediation. It implies further that any attempt to respond fundamentally, within the framework of capitalist society, to growing environmental destruction by restraining this society's mode of expansion would probably be ineffective on a long-term basis—not only because of the interests of the capitalists or state managers, but because failure to expand surplus value would indeed result in severe economic difficulties with great social costs. In Marx's analysis, the necessary accumulation of capital and the creation of capitalist society's wealth are intrinsically related. Moreover—and I can only touch upon this theme here—because labor is determined as a necessary means of individual reproduction in capitalist society, wage laborers remain dependent on capital's "growth," even when the consequences of their labor, ecological and otherwise, are detrimental to themselves and to others. The tension between the exigencies of the commodity form and ecological requirements becomes more severe as productivity increases and, particularly during economic crises and periods of high unemployment, poses a severe dilemma. This dilemma and the tension in which it is rooted are immanent to capitalism; their ultimate resolution will be hindered so long as value remains the determining form of social wealth.

What I have briefly outlined here cannot, then, be understood simply as "economic growth." It is another indication that Marx does not analyze the process of production and the patterns of technological development and economic expansion of capitalist society in "technical," that is, essentially nonsocial terms; he does not grasp the social dimension as extrinsic (for example, in terms of ownership and control alone). Rather, he analyzes this process and these patterns as intrinsically social, structured by the social forms of mediation expressed by the categories of the commodity and capital.

It should be noted in this regard that, although competition among capitals can be used to explain the *existence* of growth,[18] it is value's temporal determination that, in Marx's analysis, underlies the *form* of that growth. The particular relation between increases in productivity and the expansion of surplus value shapes the underlying trajectory of growth in capitalism. This trajectory cannot be explained adequately in terms of the market and private property, which suggests that, even in their absence, economic growth would *necessarily* assume the form marked by increases in productivity much greater than the increases in social wealth they effect—as long as social wealth ultimately remains a function of direct labor time expenditure. Planning in such a situation, however successful or unsuccessful, would signify a conscious response to the

18. See Ernest Mandel, *Late Capitalism*, trans. Joris De Bres (London, 1975), p. 31.

compulsions exerted by the alienated forms of social relations expressed by value and capital; it would not, however, overcome them.

According to Marx's critical theory, the abolition of the accelerating blind process of economic "growth" and socioeconomic transformation in capitalism, as well as its crisis-ridden character, would require the abolition of value. Overcoming these alienated forms would necessarily involve establishing a society based on material wealth, in which increased productivity would result in a corresponding increase in social wealth. Such a society could be characterized by a form of growth very different from capitalist growth. Marx's distinction between material wealth and value allows for an approach that relativizes the opposition between runaway growth as a condition of social wealth, on the one hand, and austerity as a condition for the ecologically sound organization of production and distribution, on the other, by locating this opposition in a historically specific form of social life. If his analysis of value as the determining form of wealth and of social mediation in capitalist society is valid, then it points to the possibility that this opposition can be overcome.

Classes and the dynamic of capitalism

The theoretical framework developed in this work also transforms the problem of class and class conflict as treated in Marx's mature theory. My discussion clearly has shown that his conception of capitalism's intrinsically dynamic social relations, as expressed by the categories of value and surplus value, refer to objectified forms of social mediation and cannot be understood solely in terms of class relations of exploitation. Nevertheless, class relations do play a very important role in the historical unfolding of that society, according to Marx. Although this work shall not fully address that role, much less deal adequately with the various dimensions and complexities of Marx's understanding of class relations, the investigation thus far suggests the following approach to the problematic of class: The category of class delineates a modern social relation that is mediated quasi-objectively by labor; class conflict in capitalism, according to the critique of political economy, is structured by, and embedded within, the social forms of the commodity and capital.

Marx first introduces class relations in Volume 1 of *Capital* in the course of developing and analyzing the category of surplus value, by presenting the relationship between the capitalist class and the working class. As presented, though, the theoretical status of this relationship is by no means self-evident. It frequently has been taken as a description of the structure of social groupings in capitalist society or, alternatively, as a description of a historical tendency for the population to become polarized into two social groupings, a small capitalist class and a large proletariat. Both of these readings have met with considerable criticism. The first has been criticized as an unwarranted simplification of the structure of social groupings in capitalism; indeed, as is well known, Marx himself presents what appears to be a richer, more variegated picture of social groupings and their politics in his historical and political writings. The second interpretation—that his treatment of class in Volume 1 of *Capital* is a description of a historical tendency—has also increasingly been called into question in light of recent social and economic developments, in particular the decline in the relative size of the industrial working class in advanced capitalist societies and the growth of the new salaried middle classes.

A variety of theoretical responses to these social and economic developments have sought to defend the Marxian analysis of class or to reaffirm the central significance of class in analyzing capitalism. One approach has been to argue that the opposition of the capitalist class and the proletariat presented in Volume 1 of *Capital* is only the first stage of a more complete description. James Becker, for example, argues that the polarized relation of the first volume should be understood as a first approximation, and that Marx's investigations in Volumes 2 and 3 imply a much more complex picture of the structure of social groupings in capitalism and their development.[19] Becker begins his argument by drawing attention to the following criticism of Ricardo by Marx: "What he [Ricardo] forgets to emphasize is the constantly growing number of the middle classes, those who stand between the workman on the one hand and the capitalist and landlord on the other."[20] Having thus shown that Marx does not maintain the position on empirical class polarization that frequently has been attributed to him, Becker proceeds, on the basis of Marx's analysis, to outline a form of "circulatory-administrative accumulation" that has followed historically in the wake of industrial accumulation. It is circulatory-administrative accumulation, according to Becker, that has generated socially the new middle classes and remains the main source of their employment and income.[21] In investigating the relation between qualitative changes in the basic forms of capital (both in circulation and in production) and the development of social classes and their interrelations, Becker tries to indicate that the Marxian analysis is not contravened by the growth of the new middle classes, but that, on the contrary, his analysis is quite capable of accounting for that development.[22]

Thus, Marx's critique of political economy, in its unfolding, does provide the basis for a more differentiated analysis of the historical development and transformation of classes and other social groupings in capitalism than frequently has been assumed. However, I would argue that although the relation of the working class and the capitalist class presented in Volume 1 of *Capital* can be understood as a first approximation, this in no way implies that the full significance of this

---

19. James F. Becker, *Marxian Political Economy: An Outline* (Cambridge, 1977), pp. 203–205.

20. Marx, *Theories of Surplus Value,* part 2, trans. Renate Simpson (Moscow, 1968), p. 573.

21. Becker, *Marxian Political Economy,* pp. 209, 231–35.

22. Martin Nicolaus has also argued, if somewhat differently, that the growth of the new middle strata is implied by Marx's analysis: see "Proletariat and Middle Class in Marx," *Studies on the Left* 7 (1967).

relation should be understood in those terms. Marx did, of course, concern himself with the transformation of the social structure of European society with the development of capitalism—the dissolution or transformation of older social strata and groupings such as the nobility, the peasantry, and the traditional artisanate, and the emergence of newer ones such as the working class, the bourgeois class, and the new salaried middle classes. Nevertheless, his basic intention in *Capital* was not to provide a complete picture of the sociological structure of capitalist society, whether considered statically or developmentally; rather, the significance of the class relation Marx presents in Volume 1 of *Capital* must also be seen in terms of the essential thrust of his argument.

The relationship of the capitalist and working classes generally has been understood to be central to Marx's analysis, as the relation of exploitation that determines capitalist society and that, in the form of class conflict, is the driving force of historical change.[23] In other words, it has been understood as the most fundamental social relation of capitalism. In this work, however, I have argued that Marx conceptualizes capitalism's fundamental relations on a logically deeper level of analysis; his concern is with the constituting social mediation of that society. This raises the question of the relationship in his analysis between class and the specific character of social mediation in capitalism.

In discussing the category of surplus value, I have argued that the strategic thrust of Marx's critical theory is not only to reveal the existence of exploitation by showing that the surplus in capitalism, despite appearances to the contrary, is created by labor and appropriated by nonlaboring classes. Rather, in grasping the surplus as one of value, his theory also delineates a complex dynamic that ultimately is rooted in alienated social forms. This implies that the polarized class opposition between capitalists and workers is significant in Marx's analysis not only because exploitation as such is central to his theory, but also because class relations of exploitation are an important element of the dynamic development of the social formation as a whole. However, those relations do not, in and of themselves, give rise to that dynamic development; they do so inasmuch as they are constituted by, and embedded in, the forms of social mediation I have been analyzing.

This can be clarified by examining the way in which Marx introduces the notion of class conflict in *Capital*. That notion can refer to a very broad range of collective social action; for example, it can refer to revolutionary action or, at the very least, highly politicized social action aimed at achieving political, social, and economic goals through mass mobilizations, strikes, political campaigns, and so on. There also is an "everyday" level of class conflict, however. It is this level that Marx, in his analysis of the forms of surplus value, first introduces as an intrinsic moment of capitalism.

In discussing the length of the workday in capitalism, Marx notes that it is

23. See, for example, Erik O. Wright, *Classes* (London, 1985), pp. 6–9, 31–35, 55–58.

indeterminate; it fluctuates greatly within boundaries that are both physical and social.[24] This is directly related to the character of the relations between the producers and the appropriators of the social surplus in capitalist society—that they are also constituted and mediated by the commodity form. The workday results, at least in principle, from a contract between two formally equal parties regarding the sale and purchase of labor power as a commodity. It is precisely because the relations between the workers and the capitalists are constituted, in part, by such an exchange, according to Marx, that conflict is intrinsic to these relations:

> The nature of commodity exchange itself imposes no limit to the working day, . . . to surplus labour. The capitalist maintains his rights as a purchaser when he tries to make the working day as long as possible . . . and the worker maintains his right as a seller when he wishes to reduce the working day to a particular normal length. *There is here therefore an antinomy, of right against right, both equally bearing the seal of the law of exchange. Between equal rights, force decides.* Hence, in the history of capitalist production, the establishment of a norm for the working day presents itself as a struggle over the limits of that day, a struggle between collective capitalists, i.e. the class of capitalists, and collective labourers, i.e. the working class.[25]

Class conflict and a system structured by commodity exchange, in other words, are not based on opposed principles; such conflict does not represent a disturbance in an otherwise harmonious system. On the contrary, it is inherent to a society constituted by the commodity as a totalizing and totalized form.

Class conflict is rooted in this quasi-objective form of social mediation in several ways. The relationship between workers and capitalists is marked by an inherent indeterminacy regarding, for example, the length of the workday, the value of labor power, and the ratio of necessary to surplus labor time. That such determinations of the relationship are not "given" and, hence, can be the object of negotiation and struggle at any time, indicates that the relationship between producers of the social surplus and its appropriators in capitalism is not based fundamentally on direct force or on fixed traditional patterns. Rather, it ultimately is constituted very differently—by the commodity form of social mediation, according to Marx. It is precisely the indeterminate aspects of this relationship, moreover, that allow for the expression of historically variable needs and requirements. Finally, that this class relationship entails ongoing conflict is also due to the form of the social antagonism involved—one of right against right—which itself is a determination of social subjectivity as well as of social objectivity. As the form of an "objective" social antinomy, it is also a determination of the self-conceptions of the parties involved. They conceive of themselves as possessing rights, a self-conception which is constitutive of the nature of the struggles involved. Class conflict between capitalists and wage laborers is also rooted in the specific ways in which needs and requirements are un-

24. *Capital*, vol. 1, p. 341.
25. Ibid., p. 344 (translation amended, emphasis added).

derstood and articulated in a social context structured by the commodity—that is, in the sorts of social self-understanding and conceptions of rights associated with a relationship that is so structured. These self-conceptions do not occur automatically, but are constituted historically; moreover, their contents are not merely contingent but are implied by the commodity-determined mode of social mediation.

As noted, in the case of labor power as a commodity, the relationship constituted by the commodity form cannot be realized fully as one between individuals. Workers can acquire some effective control over their commodity—that is, effective commodity ownership—only by means of collective action. In this regard, it is significant that Marx, having begun the chapter on the working day in *Capital* by grounding class conflict logically in the circumstance that the relations of workers and capitalists are mediated by commodity exchange, concludes the chapter by discussing the effective introduction of a legal limitation to the working day, which he regards as indicating that the workers as a class have gained some control over the sale of their commodity.[26] The chapter moves from a formal determination of workers as commodity owners to the realization of that determination, that is, to a consideration of the working class as a real, collective, commodity owner. In Marx's analysis, then, the category of the commodity, as it is unfolded in the form of capital, refers not only to the quasi-objective interconnections of atomized individuals, but also to large-scale collective social structures and institutions. Conversely, the development of collective forms is not, in and of itself, opposed to, or in tension with, the structuring social relations of capitalist society. In other words, Marx's theory of capital is not restricted to liberal capitalism. Indeed, in showing that the realization of labor power as a commodity entails the development of collective forms, his analysis implies the beginning of a transition to postliberal capitalist forms.

When workers are able to act collectively as commodity owners the stage is set historically for the form of production that is adequate to capital, according to Marx. The limitation of the workday is an important factor in effecting the transition to the production of relative surplus value and, hence, to the ongoing dynamic involving the determinate interrelations among productivity, surplus value, material wealth, and the form of production we examined earlier. It is within this dynamic framework that the antagonism implicit in the class relationship emerges in the form of ongoing conflicts that, in turn, become moments of the development of the totality. These conflicts are not limited to questions of hours and wages, but occur around a broad range of issues such as the nature and intensity of the labor process, the application of machinery, labor conditions, social benefits, and workers' rights. They become intrinsic aspects of everyday life in capitalist society.

Such conflicts directly affect the ratio of necessary to surplus labor time and, hence, play an important role in the dialectic of labor and time we have ex-

26. Ibid., pp. 342–44, 415–16.

amined. Moreover, because such conflicts are mediated by a totalizing form, their significance is not only local: the production and circulation of capital is such that conflicts in one sector or geographical area affect other sectors or areas. With the spread of the wage labor–capital relationship, the organization of the working class, improvements in transportation and communication, and the growing ease and speed with which capital circulates, such conflicts have ever-more general consequences; the totalizing character of the mediation increasingly becomes realized. On the one hand, this process of totalization means that local conditions of worker-capitalist relations can never be isolated and fixed completely. Consequently, the conditions of this class relation—both locally and more generally—change constantly; conflict becomes an ongoing feature of that relation. Conversely, class conflict becomes an important factor in the spatial and temporal development of capital, that is, in the distribution and flow of capital, which becomes increasingly global, and in the dialectical dynamic of the capital form. Class conflict becomes a driving element of the historical development of capitalist society.

Although class conflict does play an important role in the extension and dynamic of capitalism, however, it neither creates the totality nor gives rise to its trajectory. We have seen that, according to Marx's analysis, it is only because of its specific, quasi-objective, and temporally dynamic form of social mediation that capitalist society exists as a totality and possesses an intrinsic directional dynamic (whose initial determinations we examined as the dialectic of transformation and reconstitution). These characteristics of capitalist society cannot be grounded in the struggles of producers and appropriators per se; rather, these struggles only play the role they do because of this society's specific forms of mediation. That is to say, class conflict is a driving force of historical development in capitalism only because it is structured by, and embedded in, the social forms of the commodity and capital.[27]

27. G. A. Cohen also argues that, as important as class struggles (and related phenomena of exploitation, alliances, and revolution) are to processes of historical change, these struggles themselves do not constitute the trajectory of historical development. Rather, they must be understood with reference to that trajectory. See G. A. Cohen, "Forces and Relations of Production," in J. Roemer, ed., *Analytical Marxism* (Cambridge, 1986), pp. 19–22; and "Marxism and Functional Explanation," in ibid., pp. 233–34. Cohen's conception of the intrinsic dynamic of history, however, is transhistorical. He therefore is unable to ground it in historically specific and, hence, social terms, that is, in terms of historically specific structured forms of social practice. Instead, he separates both the process of production and technological development (which he understands as "technical" phenomena) from social relations, and conceptualizes the history of humanity in terms of the evolutionary development of the former. He then seeks to grasp social development by means of a functional explanation: see "Forces and Relations of Production," pp. 12–16, and "Marxism and Functional Explanation," p. 221ff.

Because of his transhistorical presuppositions, Cohen must posit as necessarily separate precisely those spheres of social life whose "real conflation," as I have argued, characterizes capitalism and accords it an immanent dynamic. Based as it is on the notion of the primacy of the technical, Cohen's understanding of "historical materialism" as a teleological and linear

This approach, then, grounds the idea that class struggle is the impelling force of history in terms of historically determinate forms of mediation. It also seeks to specify the notion of class itself. It is clear that class, in Marx's theory, is a relational category—classes are determined in relation to other classes. The antagonism between producing and appropriating social groupings, structured by their determinate relations to the means of production, is central to his analysis of class. One can, however, further specify the notion of class with reference to the forms of social mediation I have been analyzing. According to Marx, the antagonism of workers and capitalists is structured such that ongoing conflict is an intrinsic feature of their relationship. Nevertheless, the struggle between producing and appropriating social groups does not, in and of itself, constitute them as classes. In Marx's analysis, the dialectical structure of capitalist social relations is centrally significant; it totalizes and renders dynamic the antagonistic relationship between workers and capitalists, thereby constituting it as class conflict between labor and capital. This conflict, in turn, is a constituting moment of the dynamic trajectory of the social whole. Classes, properly speaking, are relational categories of modern society. They are structured by determinate forms of social mediation as antagonistic moments of a dynamic totality and, hence, in their conflict, become dynamic and totalized.[28]

process of productive growth is very dubious historically; moreover, it resembles those forms of materialism that Marx had already criticized in the *Theses on Feuerbach* for not being able to grasp the subjective dimension of life and understand practice as socially constituting. Cohen's transhistorical approach, in other words, is bound to a hypostatized conception of history which does not allow him to ground socially his insight that directional historical dynamic cannot be explained in terms of class struggle and other immediate forms of social action alone.

On the other hand, some criticisms of Cohen—Jon Elster's, for example—try to recover social action but do so at the cost of any notion of a dynamic social structure, and, hence, of a directional historical development. Such approaches conceive of social actors prior to, and independent of, their social constitution. Social relations, within the framework of such methodological individualist approaches, are treated as extrinsic to those actors. (See Jon Elster, "Further Thoughts on Marxism, Functionalism and Game Theory," in Roemer, ed., *Analytical Marxism*, pp. 202–20.) Such one-sided responses to Cohen's position cannot adequately meet his challenge to explain the directional dynamic and trajectory of (capitalist) history.

The opposition of the two positions represented by Cohen and Elster recapitulates the classical antinomy of structure and action, of external objective necessity and individual freedom. In this sense, together they express—rather than grasp—the characteristics of modern, capitalist society. Both approaches lack a notion of historically specific structures of social relations as structured forms of practice that are alienated (hence quasi-independent), are intrinsically bound to determinate worldviews, and constitute and are constituted by social action. In other words, neither position illuminates the historical specificity of capitalist social relations, of capitalism as a form of life.

For other criticisms of both Cohen's and Elster's positions, see Johannes Berger and Claus Offe, "Functionalism vs. Rational Choice?" and Anthony Giddens, "Commentary on the Debate," in *Theory and Society* 11 (1982).

28. The relation of class and totalization was raised by Marx in a different way when he characterized French small peasants as follows: "The great mass of the French nation is formed by

Class conflict between the workers and capitalists as it is developed in Volume 1 of *Capital,* then, is a moment of the ongoing, totalizing dynamic of capitalist society. It is structured by, and constitutes, the social totality. The classes involved are not entities but structurings of social practice and consciousness which, in relation to the production of surplus value, are organized antagonistically; they are constituted by the dialectical structures of capitalist society and impel its development, the unfolding of its basic contradiction.

It is in these terms that the importance of class and class conflict in Marx's analysis must be understood. His argument does not imply that other social strata or groupings—for example, those organized around religious, ethnic, national, or gender issues (and which only sometimes can be understood in class terms)—play no important roles historically and politically. Nevertheless, different levels of historical reality and, therefore, of historical analysis must be distinguished. The level at which class conflict plays a central role in Marx's analysis is that of the historical trajectory of the capitalist social formation as a whole.

I have, of course, been very schematic in outlining this approach to Marx's conception of class and class conflict. I have sought only, in a preliminary fashion, to clarify the theoretical status of the way he presents the relationship of the working class and the capitalist class in Volume 1 of *Capital,* and to indicate that this presentation must be understood with reference to his analysis of social mediation in capitalism.

I shall not be able to consider other important dimensions of this problematic in this work, such as the processes by which a class is constituted socially, politically, and culturally on a more concrete level or, relatedly, the question of collective social and political action. Nevertheless, the approach I have been developing has some implications for these issues, which I can touch upon.

The determinations of class—which I admittedly have only begun to elucidate (for example, the proletariat as owners of the commodity labor power

---

simple addition of homologous magnitudes, much as potatoes in a sack form a sack of potatoes. Insofar as millions of families live under economic conditions of existence that divide their mode of life, their interests and their culture from those of the other classes, and put them in hostile opposition to the latter, they form a class. Insofar as there is merely a local interconnection among these small-holding peasants, and the identity of their interests begets no community, no national bond and no political organization among them, they do not form a class" (*The Eighteenth Brumaire of Louis Bonaparte,* in Karl Marx and Frederick Engels, *Collected Works,* vol. 2: *Marx and Engels: 1851–53* [New York, 1979], p. 187).

In light of my discussion, Marx's description of the peasants as being only partially a class (unlike the workers, for example) should not be understood only in physical and/or spatial terms—that peasants work separately on their small plots, for example, whereas workers are massed in factories, a situation that encourages an awareness of commonalities, the exchange of ideas, the formation of political consciousness, the undertaking of collective action, and so on. Although Marx's conception of class does include this level, another, more abstract logical level is crucial: classes, properly speaking, are structured by the totalizing social mediation and, in turn, act upon it. This process of totalization cannot be grasped adequately in terms of physical proximity: classes are elements of the totalizing dynamic of capitalist society.

and as objects of the process of valorization)—are not simply "positional" determinations, but are determinations of both social objectivity and subjectivity. This implies a critique of approaches that first define class "objectively"—in terms of a position in a social structure—and then address the question of how the class constitutes itself "subjectively"; typically, this involves relating objectivity and subjectivity extrinsically, by means of the notion of "interest."

If the initial determination of class in Marx's approach is not one of objective position but of objectivity *and* subjectivity, the question of the subjective dimension of a particular class determination must be distinguished from the question of the conditions under which many people act as members of a class. I cannot address the latter question here, but as regards the former, the subjective dimension of class cannot—even on the level of its initial determination—be understood only in terms of the consciousness of collective interests if the particular conceptions of these interests, as well as the notion of interest itself, are not grasped socially and historically. I have sought to show how, according to the Marxian categorial approach, consciousness is not merely a reflex of objective conditions; rather, the categories, which express the basic social mediations characteristic of capitalism, delineate forms of consciousness as intrinsic moments of forms of social being. Hence, class determinations, for Marx, entail socially and historically determinate forms of subjectivity—for example, views of society and of self, systems of values, understandings of action, conceptions of the sources of social ills and possible ways of ameliorating them—that are rooted in the forms of social mediation as they differentially constitute the particular class. In this sense, the category of class is a moment of an approach that seeks to grasp the historical and social determinateness of various social conceptions and demands as well as of forms of action.

Social class, then, structured by the social forms and a driving moment of the capitalist social totality, is also a structuring category of meaning and of social consciousness. This is not to say that all individuals who can be "located" similarly have the same beliefs, nor that social and political action "automatically" follow class lines. It does mean, however, that the social and historical specificity of forms of subjectivity and social action can be elucidated in terms of the notion of class. The nature of social and political demands, or the determinate forms of the struggles associated with these demands, for example, can be understood and clarified socially and historically in terms of class, provided that class is understood with reference to the categorial forms.

This approach to subjectivity in terms of class structurings of more overarching determinations of forms of social relations is an attempt, then, to grasp forms of subjectivity in social and historical terms. Moreover—and this is crucial—because it analyzes forms of subjectivity in capitalism and the dynamic structure of capitalist society with the same categories, it also can consider forms of thought critically, in terms of the adequacy of their self-understanding and their understanding of society.[29] The standpoint of such a critique remains immanent to its object (although, as we have seen, the sort of immanent critique involved cannot be grasped adequately as one that opposes the ideals of a society to its actuality). It is against the background of this sort of analysis of the categorial

29. Marx's description, in *The Eighteenth Brumaire,* of the conceptions of the democratic parliamentary opposition in France in 1849 as petty bourgeois is a case in point. It is clear—and Marx is very explicit in this regard—that he is not directly correlating sociological class background and political ideas. Rather, his description is an attempt to illuminate the nature of the ideas themselves. According to Marx, the social and political criticisms and the positive visions of democracy articulated by that parliamentary party avoided dealing with the structural existence of capital and wage labor, and expressed a notion of emancipation that implicitly entailed a world of free and equal commodity producers and owners (even if organized in cooperative form)—that is, a world in which all are petty bourgeois. (See *The Eighteenth Brumaire,* p. 130ff.) In this sense, their ideas can be characterized in terms of that class.

Similarly, Marx's description of the workers involved in the February revolution and the June Days of 1848 as the proletariat (although most of the workers involved were artisans), is not simply an empirical description of the social background of the actors concerned; in other words, it is not part of an attempt to demonstrate a direct correlation between class position and political action. Rather, the use of class terms is an effort to characterize historically and socially the forms of action undertaken and the sorts of demands raised—for example, the "social republic," which Marx characterizes as "the general content of the modern revolution" (ibid., p. 109). By using the term "proletariat," Marx suggests that these demands and forms of action historically represented something new, that they no longer expressed a traditional artisanate, but instead were more adequate, as demands, to the new form that society was taking. At the same time, Marx also characterizes these demands as being in tension with the actual conditions of the workers. Conversely, Marx implicitly treats as artisanal the historical nature of the demands and forms of action of the *same* workers after the revolutionary movement was crushed, which he characterizes as attempts to achieve salvation within the existing conditions of the workers—as opposed to revolutionalizing the old world on the basis of its potential resources (ibid., p. 110). In other words, Marx does not use class merely as a sociological description; he uses it as a social category that also is a category of historically and socially determinate forms of subjectivity, a category that attempts to make sense of changing forms of consciousness and action.

For some recent discussions on Marx's treatment of class in his historical works, see Craig Calhoun, "The Radicalism of Tradition," *The American Journal of Sociology* 88, no. 5 (March 1983), and "Industrialization and Social Radicalism," *Theory and Society* 12 (1983); and Mark Traugott, *Armies of the Poor* (Princeton, 1985).

The approach I outline here points toward an understanding of collective social and political action which proceeds neither from a notion of a collective subject nor from that of socially, historically, and culturally decontextualized individuals acting on the basis of interests. It differs from the sort of class-centered interpretations that seek to correlate directly sociological class background and political action. Such interpretations attribute to a social grouping the sort of quasi-objective character that Marx sees as characteristic of the alienated forms of social mediation in capitalism. This approach also differs, however, from approaches that criticize such forms of class hypostatization even as they basically accept the same framing of the problem insofar as they seek to explain behavior. (This is the case regardless of whether they accord more weight to political or organizational factors, for example, than to social background in establishing a correlation to "political orientation.") This is quite different from an attempt to grasp the historical and social nature of political and social conceptions and forms of action.

determinations of class—as social and historical determinations of social being and consciousness—that questions regarding the more concrete social, political, and cultural constitution of a class, questions of collective action and self-awareness, should be posed. I can do little more than refer to these complex themes, however, and shall not develop them further in this work.

The interpretation I present here strongly modifies the central significance traditionally accorded to class relations of exploitation and conflict. I have shown how, in Marx's mature analysis, class conflict is a driving element of capitalism's historical development only because of the intrinsically dynamic character of the social relations that constitute this society. The antagonism between immediate producers and owners of the means of production does not, in and of itself, generate such an ongoing dynamic. Moreover, as I shall show, the logical thrust of Marx's presentation does not support the idea that the struggle between capitalists and workers is one between the dominant class of capitalist society and the class that embodies socialism—and that such struggle therefore points beyond capitalism. The class struggle, viewed from the workers' perspective, involves constituting, maintaining, and improving their position and situation as members of a working class. Their struggles have been a powerful force in the democratization and humanization of capitalism, and have also played an important role in the transition to organized capitalism. However, as we shall see, Marx's analysis of the trajectory of the capitalist process of production does not point toward the possible future affirmation of the proletariat and the labor it performs. On the contrary, it points toward the possible abolition of that labor. Marx's presentation, in other words, implicitly contravenes the notion that the relation between the capitalist class and the working class is parallel to that between capitalism and socialism, that the possible transition to socialism is effected by the victory of the proletariat in class struggle (in the sense of its self-affirmation as a working class), and that socialism involves the realization of the proletariat.[30] So, although the antagonism between the capitalist class and the working class plays an important role in the dynamic of capitalist development, it is not identical with the fundamental structural contradiction of the social formation as I have begun to articulate it.

Production and valorization

The reconsideration undertaken in this work of the Marxian critique's most fundamental categories and the consequent reinterpretation of the dynamic interactions of the commodity form's two dimensions also casts new light on Marx's analysis of the capitalist process of production. On the basis of what has

30. In terms of my discussion, orthodox variants of traditional Marxism can be understood as forms of thought whose vision of a future society is one in which all would be members of the working class—a vision that necessarily implies the institutionalized universalization of capital (for example, in the form of the state).

been developed thus far, I shall now consider Marx's treatment of the labor process in capitalism with two purposes in mind: first, to clarify important dimensions of his concept of capital which have not yet been considered; and second, to support my claim that his presentation's argumentative thrust implies quite clearly that overcoming capitalism would *not* entail the self-realization of the proletariat. The logic of Marx's presentation docs not support the notion that the proletariat is the revolutionary Subject.

I have established that Marx treats the sphere of production in capitalism not only in terms of material production but also in terms of the underlying forms of social mediation characteristic of this society. He does so by analyzing the process of production as both a labor process (a process of producing material wealth) and a valorization process (a process of creating surplus value). As noted, when Marx first introduces these two dimensions of the process of production, he shows how the significance of the labor process's various elements are transformed when one considers them from the standpoint of the valorization process. Considered in terms of the labor process, labor seems to be a purposeful activity that transforms raw materials by means of instruments of labor in order to achieve determinate ends. However, in terms of the valorization process, labor is significant as a source of value, regardless of its purpose, its qualitative specificity, the specificity of the raw materials it uses, and the products it creates. Labor is separated from its concrete purpose and becomes a means toward a goal given by the alienated structures constituted by (abstract) labor itself. Considered in these terms, labor is actually the object of production.

After Marx provides the initial determinations of the two dimensions of the capitalist process of production, he proceeds to unfold them. As we have seen, he first presents the valorization process, treating it in terms of the production of absolute and then relative surplus value (the latter being the form of surplus value more adequate to the category of capital). He then goes on to examine the capitalist labor process by investigating it in general terms, as cooperation, and then by analyzing more specifically its two major historical forms—manufacture, which is based on the detail division of labor, and large-scale industry, based on industrial machine production.[31] In his discussion of cooperation, manufacture, and large-scale industry, Marx traces how the transformation of the significance of the labor process's elements—which occurs on a formal level when those elements are considered in terms of the valorization process—becomes "realized" or materialized in the concrete form of the labor process itself. He shows that initially the labor process is capitalist only because it is used for the end of valorization; the valorization process remains extrinsic to the labor process itself. As capitalism develops, however, the labor process comes to be intrinsically determined by the process of valorization.[32] Industrial machine-

---

31. *Capital,* vol. 1, pp. 439–639.
32. Ibid., pp. 439, 482, 548.

based production is the form of the labor process adequate to the production of relative surplus value.[33]

This materialization of the valorization process—like the peculiar historical dynamic grasped by the category of surplus value—ultimately is rooted structurally in the dialectic of the two dimensions of the commodity form. In elaborating this thesis, I shall show that, just as the significance of the category of surplus value cannot be understood fully in terms of exploitation, of the appropriation of the surplus product by a class of private owners, the capitalist labor process, as presented by Marx, cannot be understood as a technical process that is used in the interests of a class of private appropriators.

In analyzing the role of labor in Marx's critique, I have devoted a great deal of attention to the implications of labor's historically specific character as a socially mediating activity in capitalism. In outlining the process of production, I shall now consider labor's other social dimension, namely, its social character as productive activity. As I noted in discussing abstract and historical time, the development, in alienated form, of modes of knowledge and experience that are socially general but are not a function of the immediate producers' skills and knowledge is an important aspect of the historical unfolding of capital in Marx's account. This development is a central focus of my examination of his treatment of the labor process: it serves as the point of departure for my interpretation of the category of capital in terms of the intersection of the two social dimensions of labor in capitalism, and it provides the basis for my argument that Marx's conception of socialism does not involve the realization of the proletariat.

Cooperation

Capitalist production, according to Marx, has been marked from its inception by relatively large-scale production. Historically and conceptually, it only really begins when comparatively large numbers of workers are employed at the same time by each individual capital unit (a firm, for example)—that is, when the labor process is undertaken on an extensive scale and yields relatively large quantities of products. Marx maintains that, in its early stages, capitalist production did not entail a qualitative change in the mode of producing, but only a quantitative increase in the size of producing units, in the number of workers simultaneously employed by the same capital.[34] He therefore begins his analysis of the labor process's development in capitalism by discussing, without further determinations, cooperation in general—in other words, production in which large numbers of workers work together in the same process or in connected processes.[35] Marx indicates clearly that he plans to show that capital modifies

33. Ibid., p. 645.
34. Ibid., p. 439.
35. Ibid., pp. 439, 443.

the labor process, eventually rendering it intrinsically capitalist; by the same token, the categories of his critical analysis acquire their full validity and significance only as categories of the developed sphere of production in capitalism. Thus, for example, he states that "the law of valorization . . . comes fully into its own for the individual producer only when he produces as a capitalist and employs a number of workers simultaneously, i.e. when from the outset he sets in motion labour of a socially average character."[36] This passage reinforces my earlier claim that Marx's determinations of value do not refer to market exchange alone but are intended as determinations of capitalist production. We shall see that, for Marx, as capital becomes fully developed, the abstract temporal dimension of value structures production internally: value becomes a determination of a particular form of organizing and disciplining labor within large-scale organizations. By the same token, it is only then that the law of valorization becomes valid.

Marx focuses his discussion of cooperation on the greater degree of productivity it permits. He asserts that cooperation both effects an increase in the productive power of the individuals and entails the creation of a new productive power that is intrinsically collective. As noted, Marx analyzes productivity in terms of the social character of concrete labor which, for him, includes scientific, technical, and organizational knowledge and experience. At this point, he develops this analysis further by considering the increased productivity that results from cooperation in terms of the use value dimension of labor, that is, in terms of labor's social character as productive activity:

The specific productive power [or "force of production," *Produktivkraft*] of the combined working day is, under all circumstances, the social productive power of labour, or the productive power of social labour. This power arises from co-operation itself. When the worker co-operates in a planned way with others, he strips off his individual limits and develops his species capacities.[37]

In Marx's analysis, in other words, the productive power (or "force of production") that arises as a result of cooperation is a function of concrete labor's social dimension. This power is social, however, not only in the sense that it is collective but also in the sense that it is greater than the sum of the productive powers of the individuals immediately involved; it cannot be reduced to the power of its constituting individuals.[38] It is this aspect of concrete labor's social dimension which is crucial to Marx's analysis.

Cooperation benefits the capitalist in several ways, according to Marx. It is a powerful means for increasing productivity and, hence, for reducing the socially

36. Ibid., p. 441.
37. Ibid., p. 447 (translation amended).
38. Ibid., p. 443.

necessary labor time required for the production of commodities.[39] Moreover, the capitalist pays the workers as individual commodity owners, that is, for their independent labor powers, not for their combined labor power; hence, their collective productive power is developed as a "free gift" to capital.[40] It is important to note that this "free gift" is the productive power of labor's use value dimension, which, as noted, is measured in terms of the output of material wealth rather than the expenditure of abstract labor time. That is, Marx is not referring directly to surplus value here; rather, at this point he is drawing attention to the process in which the power of the social dimension of labor as a productive activity—a productive power greater than that of its constituting individuals—becomes the productive power of capital, one for which the capitalist does not have to pay.[41]

> The social and general productive powers of labour are productive powers of capital; but these productive powers relate only to the labour process. . . . They do not directly affect *exchange-value*. Whether a hundred work together, or each one of the hundred works by himself, the value of their product is equal to a hundred days' labour, whether represented in a large or small quantity of products; . . . the productivity of labour does not affect the value.[42]

The process by which labor's productive powers become capital's is one of alienation and is central to Marx's analysis of capital. I previously analyzed alienation in terms of the abstract dimension of labor as a socially mediating activity; I am now referring to the alienation of the social dimension of concrete labor as productive activity. *Both* processes are constitutive of capital. As these processes of alienation develop, the workers are subsumed under, and incorporated into, capital: they become a particular mode of its existence.[43]

This process of alienation of social labor's productive powers has a historical significance that goes far beyond the issue of the private appropriation of the surplus social product by capitalist class: It entails, as we shall see, a process of the historical constitution in alienated form of socially general modes of knowledge and experience that are not limited to the immediate producers' skills and knowledge. This development has very negative effects on the character of much immediate labor, and yet it eventually gives rise to the possible emancipation of people from the sway of their own labor and their reappropriation of the socially general knowledge and power first constituted historically in alienated form.

At this point in Marx's exposition, however, the nature of this process of

39. Ibid., p. 447.
40. Ibid., p. 451.
41. Ibid.
42. Marx, *Theories of Surplus Value,* part 1, trans. Jack Cohen and S. W. Ryazanskaya (Moscow, 1971), p. 393.
43. *Capital,* vol. 1, p. 451.

alienation is not yet clear. The alienated productive power of labor is greater than the sum of its parts, but it still is constituted essentially by the workers immediately involved; hence, when Marx speaks of the "species capacities" that are developed in cooperation, these capacities appear to be those of the collectivity of workers. A mode of socially general knowledge and experience has not yet been constituted within the sphere of production in a form intrinsically independent of the immediate producers. Consequently, it seems that the transformation of the productive powers of labor into those of capital is only a function of private ownership. It is possible at this stage of the categorial unfolding, then, to conceive hypothetically of the abolition of capitalism—of overcoming capital's appropriation of the productive powers of social labor—in terms of the abolition of private property in the means of production alone; the workers could then jointly "own" the collective social power they constitute and cooperatively direct the same labor process that had existed under conditions of private ownership. In other words, the capitalist character of production at this point still appears to be extrinsic to the labor process.

The further course of Marx's exposition reveals, however, that the nature of capital has not yet emerged clearly in his investigation of simple cooperation. His analysis of the labor process does not retain as final the determination of its capitalist nature in terms of private property; he does not merely go on to indicate the emergence of the historical conditions that would allow for the real possibility of private property's overcoming. Rather, Marx proceeds to develop further and transform his determinations of what constitutes capitalism and, hence, what would constitute its negation. Specifically, he presents the development of the labor process in a way that changes the initial, extrinsic, determination of the capitalist character of production. Marx summarizes this development in terms of the alienation of the use value dimension of labor as follows:

It is a result of the division of labour in manufacture that the worker is brought face to face with the intellectual potentialities of the material process of production as the property of another and as a power which rules over him. This process of separation starts in simple co-operation, where the capitalist represents to the individual workers the unity and the will of the whole body of social labour. It is developed in manufacture, which mutilates the worker, turning him into a fragment of himself. It is completed in large-scale industry, which makes science a potentiality for production which is distinct from labour and presses it into the service of capital.[44]

This summary outline implies that capital, as a social form, is intrinsically related to the division of labor and that, as this categorial form is unfolded, its productive power no longer can be understood solely in terms of the individuals who immediately constitute it. Rather, the power of capital comes to embody the alienated power of society in a more general sense. Emancipation, then, the

---

44. Ibid., p. 482.

reappropriation of what had been alienated, no longer adequately can be grasped in terms of the abolition of private ownership alone.

Manufacture

This developmental trajectory of the production process should be examined more closely. Following his discussion of simple cooperation, Marx analyzes manufacture as the specific form of cooperation that characterized the capitalist process of production in Europe from the mid-sixteenth to the late eighteenth century.[45] Whereas simple cooperation leaves the mode of each individual's labor largely unchanged, manufacture revolutionizes the labor process itself.[46] It is marked by a new form of the division of labor, a detail division of labor within the workshop which Marx distinguishes from the division of labor within society.[47] What characterizes manufacture is the fact that the labor process is based on the division of handicraft operations into specialized partial, or detail, operations, which are carried out by specialized workers using specialized instruments of labor.[48] This form of the division of labor ties workers to single, repetitive, simplified tasks, which then are closely articulated and coordinated with one another;[49] it thereby increases greatly the productivity of labor by increasing the specialization of each worker and lessening considerably the amount of time necessary to produce commodities.[50] In this way the manufacturing mode of producing increases surplus value; and it further augments the self-valorization of capital in another way, inasmuch as the simplification of tasks and their consequent one-sided development diminish the value of labor power directly.[51]

Marx does not treat the relationship between manufacture and capital as an extrinsic one; nor does he investigate the former as a mode of producing that, in and of itself, is independent of capital but is used by capitalists for their benefit. Rather, in the course of criticizing Adam Smith for not distinguishing adequately between the division of labor within society and the division of labor within the workshop,[52] Marx asserts that the latter is specific to capitalist society.[53] He then goes on to describe manufacture as "a specifically capitalist form of the process of production [which] is . . . a particular method of creating relative surplus-value, or of augmenting the self-valorization of capital."[54] In other

45. Ibid., p. 455.
46. Ibid., p. 481.
47. Ibid., p. 474ff.
48. Ibid., pp. 457, 486.
49. Ibid., p. 464.
50. Ibid., p. 458ff.
51. Ibid., p. 470.
52. Ibid., pp. 470–75.
53. Ibid., p. 480.
54. Ibid., p. 486.

words, Marx treats it as a labor process that is related intrinsically to capital, in the sense that it is shaped materially by the valorization process.

The material form of the process of production in manufacture, according to Marx, is a consequence of the ongoing drive for increased productivity which marks capitalism. He grounds this drive in the commodity form—in the "objective" imperatives as well as the cultural values and worldviews associated with this form which give rise to attempts to make the labor process as efficient as possible. Marx contrasts historically the emphasis on quality and use value expressed by writers of classical antiquity with the emphasis on quantity and exchange value, expressed in modern theories of political economy and embodied in the material form of manufacture.[55] The latter emphasis does not simply develop historically out of the former as a result of some sort of quasi-natural development of the division of labor; rather, it marks a historical break. It is the expression of a very different, historically determinate, form of social mediation.

The principle of lessening the labor time needed to produce commodities was, as Marx points out, formulated consciously early in the period of manufacture.[56] As an ongoing principle of production, the reduction of necessary labor time— that is, increased productivity—was first effected historically primarily by breaking down the labor process into its constituent parts rather than by introducing machinery. Each resultant partial operation of manufacture, according to Marx, retains the character of a handicraft and, hence, remains bound to the strength, skill, quickness, and sureness of the workers.[57] On the one hand, then, the process of production remains bound to individual human labor; on the other, it becomes more efficient as this individual labor becomes more partial. The result, according to Marx, is the creation of a peculiar "machine" that is specifically characteristic of the manufacturing period—namely, the collective worker, formed out of the combination of a number of individual specialized workers.[58] The individual workers become organs of this whole.[59]

As was the case in simple cooperation, the whole—which, in manufacture, is the collective working organism—is a form of existence of capital. The productive power of the use value dimension of labor, which here results from the combination of various kinds of labor—in other words, the great increase in productivity which is effected by the detail division of labor—is the productive power of capital.[60] In manufacture, the opposition between workers and capital, as an opposition between individual fragmented parts and a whole that is directly social, comes to be embodied in the material form of production itself. Marx leaves no doubt that he regards the subsumption of the individuals under the

55. Ibid., pp. 486–87.
56. Ibid., p. 467.
57. Ibid., pp. 457–58.
58. Ibid., p. 468.
59. Ibid., p. 469.
60. Ibid., p. 481.

collective in manufacture to be extremely negative. Far from being part of, or effecting, a linear and general form of progress, the increasing productive power of the whole is constituted at the expense of the productive power of the individual. It is based upon a process that "converts the worker into a crippled monstrosity by furthering his particular skill . . . through the suppression of a whole world of productive drives and inclinations."[61] With manufacture, the "individual himself is divided up, and transformed into the automatic motor of a detail operation."[62] Moreover, this division of labor expresses a more general development, rooted in the commodity form, that transforms all spheres of life and lays the foundation for the sort of specialization that develops one faculty in people at the expense of all others.[63] Marx's critique, as should be clear by now, is not only that manufacture "increases the socially productive power of labour for the benefit of the capitalist instead of the worker"—a critique of property that could remain extrinsic to the labor process itself—but that "it also does this by crippling the individual worker."[64]

Manufacture, then, has the form of a productive mechanism whose component parts are human beings.[65] It represents a directly social form of production in the sense that the worker can work only as part of the whole. If the need for the workers to sell their labor power had initially been grounded in their propertylessness, in the fact that they did not possess the means of producing commodities, it now becomes grounded in the technical nature of the labor process itself. This "technical" nature is intrinsically capitalist, according to Marx.[66]

The concrete form of this labor process, as noted, is grounded by Marx in the economy of time.[67] In analyzing manufacture, he continues to treat value as a structuring category of the organization of production (which he began to do while discussing cooperation), indicating once again that he does not regard it only as a category of the market. The rule that the labor time expended on a commodity should not exceed the socially necessary labor time is not simply enforced extrinsically by the action of competition, according to Marx; in manufacture, it has become "a technical law of the process of production itself."[68] At this point in his presentation, then, Marx shows retrospectively that the determination of the magnitude of value with which he began his categorial investigation of capitalism is a critical determination of the mode of production as well as of the mode of distribution. The resulting organization of the mode of production—one based on the most efficient possible use of human labor

61. Ibid., pp. 481, 483.
62. Ibid., p. 481.
63. Ibid., p. 474.
64. Ibid., p. 486.
65. Ibid., p. 457.
66. Ibid., p. 482.
67. Ibid., p. 464.
68. Ibid., p. 465.

engaged in increasingly specialized and fragmented tasks—is despotic and hierarchical.[69]

Value, then, is a structuring principle of *both* forms of the division of labor in capitalist society. It structures not only the social division of labor in this society, according to Marx, but the division of labor in the workshop as well: "The planned and regulated *a priori* system on which the division of labour is implemented within the workshop becomes, in the division of labour within society, an *a posteriori* necessity imposed by nature, . . . perceptible in the fluctuations of . . . market prices."[70] Note that Marx does not consider the planned structure of the workshop as a "positive" or "noncapitalist" aspect of modern society opposed to the nonplanned anarchy of the market. He regards precisely this structure of the labor process to be despotic—the despotism of the collectivity, structured by considerations of productivity and efficiency, effected at the cost of the individual. Rather than criticize the sphere of distribution in capitalism from the standpoint of production, Marx analyzes them as interrelated: "In the society where the capitalist mode of production prevails, anarchy in the social division of labour and despotism in the manufacturing division of labour mutually condition each other."[71]

It is clear that Marx is criticizing the "planned" structure of production *and* the market-mediated mode of distribution in capitalism. He roots both in the commodity form as it has been unfolded in the form of capital, and he thereby characterizes capitalism in terms of both poles of an opposition between the apparently decontextualized, atomized individual and the collective whole in which individuals function as mere cogs. (On another level, this opposition is that between private and directly social labor, which I discussed at the beginning of Chapter Two.) His notion of overcoming capitalism, therefore, cannot be understood in terms of overcoming the market alone or in terms of extending to all of society the planned order that prevails in the workshop; Marx describes this order in terms of the complete subjugation of the worker to capital (understood not in terms of private property but as an organization of labor that increases its productive power).[72] Instead, his analysis implies that overcoming capitalism would require overcoming *both* the "planned," organized, bureaucratic despotism generated in the sphere of production and the anarchy of the sphere of distribution, whereby the former is accorded critical primacy.[73]

69. Ibid., pp. 476, 481.
70. Ibid., p. 476.
71. Ibid., p. 477.
72. Ibid.
73. Marx's analysis of the structuring of production and the trajectory of capitalist development by the commodity form allows for the possibility that such structuring could occur in the absence of the market. Thus, within such a theoretical framework, the encroachment in the twentieth century of an organized, bureaucratic mode of regulation upon areas formerly regulated by the market should not be understood as a development within capitalism that points beyond it; rather, it can be grasped as an extension of the large-scale institutions associated with capital

At this stage in Marx's exposition, however, the conditions of this possibility are not yet evident. Manufacture is a sort of "intermediate stage" in Marx's presentation of the capitalist process of production. Understanding its "intermediate" character illuminates the strategic thrust of his presentation and the implications of his initial categories for his understanding of capital and the possibility of its overcoming. On the one hand, as we have seen, in manufacture the capitalist character of production is no longer extrinsic to the labor process—hence one no longer can conceive of the abolition of capital in terms of the abolition of private property alone, as was possible in the case of simple co-operation. Marx's critical comments on the detail division of labor clearly imply that his conception of emancipation includes the historical overcoming of the labor process that has become molded by capital. On the other hand, however, the possibility that this labor process can be overcome has not yet emerged at this stage of his presentation. In spite of the differences between manufacture and simple cooperation, they share a common characteristic: the alienated whole (capital) is greater than the sum of its parts, yet it is still constituted by the immediate producers.

In order to clarify this point, let me pose the following hypothetical scenario, which underlines the historical character of capitalism's possible negation and is relevant for reconsidering "actually existing socialism": An attempt is made to create a socialist society on the basis of the form of production that characterizes manufacture. Not only is capitalist private property abolished but value is replaced by material wealth as the form of social wealth. The purpose of increased productivity is no longer to increase surplus labor time expenditure but, rather, to yield a greater degree of material wealth in order to satisfy needs. Nevertheless, such a change in the goal of production does not involve a fundamental transformation in the labor process. We have seen that value, according to Marx, is based on direct human labor time expenditure. Yet, at this stage in the development of capitalism, productivity and, hence, the production of material wealth are also essentially based on direct human labor, made more efficient by the detail division of labor. In other words, the primary productive force is the organization of human labor itself. In such a situation, production necessarily remains based on direct human labor, regardless of whether the goal of increased productivity is an increase in surplus value or an increase in material wealth.

So long as human labor remains the essential productive force of material wealth, then, production for the purpose of creating material wealth at a high level of productivity necessarily entails the *same* form of the labor process as when the goal of production is an increase in surplus value. The distinction between these two forms of wealth has little significance here; in both cases,

at the cost of the bourgeois sphere of distribution, as a change in the form in which the law of value prevails historically.

the labor process is based on the detail division of labor as developed in capitalist manufacture. The one-sided, repetitive, fragmented nature of labor can be abolished in such a situation only by lowering considerably the level of productivity and, hence, of general social wealth. Although Marx's analysis does not affirm the labor process in capitalism, it certainly does not entail a romanticizing critique of this labor process which refers back to a purported precapitalist "wholeness"—one that, if effected, would be socially and economically disastrous. Nevertheless, at this stage in Marx's presentation, the conditions are not yet present for a possible historical overcoming of the labor process in which the detail division of labor could be abolished while a high level of productivity was maintained.

It has become clear that a central aim of Marx's categorial analysis is to determine the emergent possibility for precisely such an overcoming of the capitalist labor process. This possibility is implied by the categories of Marx's analysis but, as I have argued, they should be understood as categories of fully developed capitalism. Only from that standpoint can the "intermediate" character of manufacture in Marx's presentation be understood. Although manufacture's labor process is shaped by capital, the hypothetical scenario above demonstrates that the difference between value and material wealth, so central to Marx's categorial analysis of developed capitalism, is not yet practically relevant to the form of production. In other words, although the labor process of manufacture is molded by the valorization process, it is not—when viewed from the standpoint of fully developed capitalist production—the fully adequate materialization of the valorization process and, hence, does not fully express the specificity and contradictory nature of capital's drive toward increased productivity.

I have noted that, considered in terms of the initial determinations of the labor process, labor functions as an active productive force that transforms matter in order to produce material wealth; however, it serves as the "actual" raw material, the object, of the valorization process. This inversion is real, rather than metaphoric in Marx's analysis, and it holds for all forms of capitalist production. Nevertheless, it is not fully materialized in manufacture. Although labor has become fragmented in manufacture and can exist only as part of the whole (that is, workers have become parts of the productive apparatus), the workers still make use of the tools rather than vice versa. Manufacture is essentially a complex form of handicraft, wherein the labor of each worker is no longer that of a craftsman but, rather, a specialized aspect of that labor. The labor of the collective worker has the character of that of a "supercraftsman." The form of the labor process is such that direct human labor—even if only in collective form—still seems to be the active, creative principle of the labor process, rather than its object.

In Marx's categorial analysis, in other words, when the primary productive force used to increase productivity is the organization of human labor itself, the labor process does not yet express the specific function of direct human labor in capitalism as a source of objectified labor time. Similarly, the productive power of the use value dimension of labor—of socially general knowledge and experience—is not yet expressed in a form that potentially could become independent of direct human labor. Consequently, the dual nature of capital, at this stage of the exposition, is not yet clear, and the contradiction *within* capitalist production has not yet been unfolded. At this stage of Marx's exposition, then, the capitalist process of production does not yet embody the possibility of its own negation.

His exposition has, however, begun to indicate what this possibility would entail. The labor process would embody the central contradiction of capital, according to Marx's categorial analysis, when the alienated social totality that is greater than its parts could no longer be understood solely in terms of the individuals immediately involved in its constitution, and when overcoming capital could no longer be understood in terms of the reappropriation by workers of that which they constituted. At that point, the distinction Marx draws between value and material wealth would become relevant. Manufacture set the stage historically for such a form of the labor process—for large-scale machine-based production.[74]

Large-scale industry

It is with the development of large-scale industrial production that capital comes into its own, according to Marx. He analyzes this mode of producing as the adequate materialization of the valorization process, as the embodiment of the twofold character of the underlying social forms of capitalism, and thus as the adequate expression of the specific, contradictory nature of capital's drive toward ever-increasing levels of productivity. This implies, conversely, that the full significance of Marx's conception of the dual character of production in capitalism emerges only with his analysis of industrial production.

In order to clarify this aspect of Marx's investigation, I shall briefly consider further its argumentative intent. We have seen that Marx, in his treatment of manufacture, is highly critical of the labor process that emerges with the development of capitalist society; he describes it as intrinsically capitalist and seeks to grasp its determinate features as intrinsically shaped by capital. However, at this point in his presentation, this characterization has not yet been grounded convincingly. The value form of the social surplus may indeed generate an ongoing drive for increased productivity, but a labor process for which material wealth is the goal cannot yet be distinguished from one for which value is the goal. Hence, one cannot yet fully discern that production is *not* a technical process that is used by a class of private appropriators in their interests and

74. *Capital*, vol. 1, pp. 458, 461, 489–91.

could be used by workers in their own interests. If this were the case, the negative character of work in capitalism described by Marx would simply be a necessary concomitant of a high level of productivity—an unfortunate, but unavoidable, price that must be paid for a high level of general social wealth, however such wealth is distributed. Yet, as we shall soon see, Marx intends, in investigating large-scale industry, to call into question the purportedly necessary relation between high levels of productivity and fragmented, empty work. He tries to demonstrate that the form of the industrial labor process cannot be grasped adequately in technical terms, in terms of the requirements of high levels of productivity alone, but that it *can* be elucidated socially, with reference to the duality of the essential social forms of capitalism.

Marx begins his investigation of large-scale industry by first examining it in terms of the production of material wealth, that is, in terms of the use value dimension of labor in capitalism. By extending his analysis of the historical development in capitalism of concrete labor's social character (which he had begun in his investigation of cooperation and manufacture), he shows that the production of material wealth is only one aspect of the developed capitalist labor process. What characterizes the use value dimension of labor in industrial production, according to Marx, is that it is constituted in a form that becomes increasingly independent of the labor of the immediate producers. He briefly traces the course of this historical development in terms of the development of machine production, beginning with the starting point of the eighteenth-century industrial revolution—the supersession of the worker, who handles a single tool, by a working machine.[75] (The latter is a mechanism operating with several similar tools; the number of tools it brings into play simultaneously is independent of the organic limitations that confine the tool use of the handicraftman.)[76] Marx then describes the development of motive mechanisms (for example, the steam engine) that, like the working machine, exist in an independent form, emancipated from the limits of human strength, and, unlike water- or animal-power, are entirely under human control.[77] The development of such motive mechanisms allows, in turn, for the development of a machine system—a sort of "division of labor" among machines modeled on the division of labor in manufacture.[78] According to Marx, the latter must be adapted to the worker and is, in this sense, "subjective," but the former, is "objective": the production process is analyzed into its constituent elements with the aid of the natural sciences and without regard to earlier, "worker-centered," principles of the division of labor.[79] A further stage in this historical process of overcoming direct human labor's centrality to the labor process is the production of machines by

75. Ibid., p. 494.
76. Ibid., pp. 494–97.
77. Ibid., pp. 498–99.
78. Ibid., p. 501.
79. Ibid., pp. 501, 508.

machines, which provides the "adequate technical foundation" of large-scale industry.[80] These developments result in a system of machinery, which is described by Marx as a vast automaton driven by a self-acting prime mover.[81] (I shall have occasion below to discuss the parallels between this description and Marx's earlier description of capital.) He summarizes the development of machine-based production as follows:

As machinery, the instrument of labour assumes a material mode of existence which entails the replacement of human strength by natural forces, and the replacement of routine based upon experience by the conscious application of the natural sciences. In manufacture, the organization of the social labour process is purely subjective: it is a combination of one-sided, specialized workers. Large-scale industry, on the other hand, possesses in the machine system an entirely objective organization of production, which confronts the worker as a pre-existing material condition of production.[82]

When Marx describes the development of large-scale industry in terms of the replacement of human strength by natural forces, he is referring not only to the harnessing of natural forces such as steam and water but also to the development of socially general productive forces. Thus, he characterizes as "natural forces of social labor" the productive forces resulting from cooperation and the division of labor, noting that—like natural forces such as steam and water—they cost nothing.[83] In this regard, he observes that science also is like a natural force; once a scientific principle is discovered, it costs nothing.[84] Finally, in discussing the objectified means of production, Marx asserts that aside from the costs of depreciation and of the auxiliary substances consumed (oil, coal, and so on), machines and tools do their work for nothing; the greater the productive effectiveness of the machine compared with that of the tool, the greater the extent of its gratuitous service.[85] He relates this productive effectiveness to the accumulation of past labor and productive knowledge, describing large-scale industry as a form of production in which "man [has] succeeded in making the product of his *past labour* . . . perform gratuitous service on a large scale, like a force of nature."[86]

Note that what Marx refers to here as the "natural forces" that replace human strength and traditional skills in machine-based production are precisely those socially general powers in terms of which he earlier had formulated the social character of concrete labor—namely, "the level of development of science and

80. Ibid., p. 506.
81. Ibid., p. 502.
82. Ibid., p. 508 (translation amended).
83. Ibid.
84. Ibid. The first part of this sentence ("Wie mit den Naturkräften verhält es sich mit der Wissenschaft.") does not appear in the English translation. It can be found in *Das Kapital,* vol. 1, *Marx-Engels Werke,* vol. 23 (Berlin, 1962), p. 407.
85. *Capital,* vol. 1, p. 510.
86. Ibid. (emphasis added).

its technological application, the social organization of the process of production, [and] the extent and effectiveness of the means of production.''[87] One aspect of the development of large-scale industry, then, entails the historical constitution of socially general productive capacities and modes of scientific, technical, and organizational knowledge that are not a function of, and cannot be reduced to, workers' strength, knowledge, and experience; it involves as well the ongoing accumulation of socially general past labor and experience. This historically constituted aspect of the use value dimension of labor in capitalism is like a ''natural force'' inasmuch as it is independent of direct labor, costs nothing, and increasingly replaces human toil as the central social factor in the transformation of matter, the social ''metabolism'' of humanity with nature that is a necessary condition of social life. With the development of large-scale industry, then, the incorporation into production of these ''immense forces of nature''[88]—that is, the acquired ability to tap the powers of nature and objectify and make use of the past—increasingly supersedes direct human labor as the primary social source of material wealth. The production of material wealth increasingly becomes a function of the objectification of historical time.

This historical development of concrete labor's social character fundamentally distinguishes large-scale industry from manufacture. Not only does it raise the productivity of labor enormously, but to the extent that it renders the production of material wealth essentially independent of direct human labor time expenditure, it also undermines the technical need for manufacture's characteristic division of labor, both within the workshop and throughout society.[89] In other words, this historical development implicitly points to the possibility of a different social organization of labor.

This possibility, however, is not realized in large-scale industry. Indeed, the actual structure of industrial production is very different from the possibility implied by an abstract consideration of the development of labor's use value dimension alone. Although society's productive forces are highly developed with capitalist large-scale industry, the form in which those forces are constituted historically does not liberate the workers from partial, repetitive labor, according to Marx. On the contrary, it subsumes them under production and turns them into cogs of a productive apparatus, parts of specialized machines.[90] He describes the resulting mode of producing as a form entailing even more fragmented and specialized labor than had been the case in manufacture.[91] Factory work, he notes, ''does away with the many-sided play of the muscles, and confiscates every atom of freedom, both in bodily and intellectual activity.''[92] In general, the actual form of machine

87. Ibid., p. 130.
88. Ibid., p. 509.
89. Ibid., pp. 545–47, 614–16.
90. Ibid., p. 547.
91. Ibid., p. 614.
92. Ibid., p. 548.

production has extremely negative consequences: work is fragmented further, women and children are employed in repetitive, low-paying jobs, the intellectual level of work is lowered, and either the work day is lengthened or the intensity of labor is increased.[93] These negative effects, moreover, are not restricted to the locus of immediate production: this mode of production undermines the security of workers and involves the creation of a disposable working population that is held in reserve for the requirements of capitalist exploitation.[94] It adversely affects the health, the general level of intellectual capacities and moral sensibilities, and the family life of the working population.[95] Marx summarizes the negative effects of large-scale industry on the workers, on the nature of labor, and on the social division of labor by contrasting the potential embodied in machine production with its actual consequences:

Machinery in itself shortens the hours of labour, but when employed by capital it lengthens them . . . ∞ itself it lightens labour, but when employed by capital it heightens its intensity . . . ∞ itself it is a victory of man over the forces of nature, but in the hands of capital it makes man the slave of those forces . . . ∞ itself it increases the wealth of the producers, but in the hands of capital it makes them paupers.[96]

In capitalist industrial production, then, the productive forces of society are developed in a form that dominates people and is inimical to their development—a form very different from that conceivable when the development of labor's use value dimension is considered alone. Instead of leading to the abolition of the fragmentary division of labor characteristic of manufacture, the actual development of the social character of concrete labor is such that "the capitalist form of large-scale industry reproduces the same division of labour in a still more monstrous shape . . . in the factory proper . . . and everywhere outside the factory."[97]

93. Ibid., pp. 517–23, 533.
94. Ibid., pp. 557–68, 580–88, 618.
95. Ibid., pp. 517–26, 619–21. Although Marx describes at length the "terrible and disgusting" effects of the "dissolution of the old family ties within the capitalist system" on the working population in the first half of the nineteenth century (p. 620), he does not regard those ties as a model of intimate human relations that should be reestablished. Neither, of course, does he regard the entrance of large numbers of women and children into processes of production structured by alienated labor to be, in and of itself, a positive, progressive, or beneficial development. Rather, consistent with his analysis of the two-sided character of capitalism, he regards it as a development that both is negative and yet gives rise to conditions that could allow for a possible future "higher form of the family and of the relations between the sexes" (p. 621).

   The approach developed in this work could, in my view, serve as a fruitful point of departure for investigating the historically changing nature in capitalist society of the structuring of the family, of work, and of their interrelation (as well as their implications for the structuring of gender). Such an approach could consider these themes in terms of the development of the quasi-objective form of mediation constituted by labor.
96. Ibid., pp. 568–69.
97. Ibid., p. 614.

This "monstrous" division of labor is a central focus of Marx's analysis. On the one hand, his investigation of the development of labor's use value dimension and the contrast he draws between its potential and its actual form indicate clearly that the division of labor in large-scale industry, unlike that in manufacture, is not a necessary technical concomitant of increased productivity. For this reason, he sharply criticizes as "economic apologists" those who—understanding industrial production in purely technical terms and so failing to distinguish between "the capitalist application of machinery" and "machinery itself"— can conceive of no other utilization of machinery than the capitalist one, and who therefore decry all critics of the capitalist system of industrial production as enemies of technical progress.[98] On the other hand, despite his use of terms such as the capitalist "utilization" and "application" of machinery, Marx does not regard the relationship of capitalism and industrial production to be extrinsic. What renders large-scale industry capitalist is not private ownership alone; rather, as I shall elaborate, industrial production is intrinsically capitalist inasmuch as it is a valorization process as well as a labor process.[99] Its ultimate goal is not material wealth but surplus value. Although this duality is characteristic of earlier forms of capitalist production as well, according to Marx, only with large-scale industry do the differences between value and material wealth, abstract labor and concrete labor, become significant and come to constitute the form of the labor process itself. The thrust of Marx's analysis of industrial production, then, is to show how the division of labor characteristic of large-scale industrial production is neither grounded in technical necessity nor contingent, but is an expression of its intrinsically capitalist character. That is to say, one important aim of his categorial critical theory is to grasp the capitalist mode of industrial production in social terms—in terms of his analysis of the forms of social mediation that structure capitalism—and thereby to articulate the disparity between the possibilities implied by the development of labor's use value dimension in capitalism and the actual historical development of the forces of production.

Before proceeding, it should be noted that from the standpoint of such a social analysis of production, approaches that grasp capitalist industrial production solely in technical terms are like those that understand labor in capitalism only in terms of the interactions of people with nature. In both cases, the concrete dimension is not understood as the materialized form of the social mediation; instead, the fetishized form of appearance of the social mediation is taken at face value. This is the case of those criticisms of capitalist production that focus exclusively on private property and the market, as well as of theories that treat industrial development as a process of "modernization" without acknowledging the social category of capital.

98. Ibid., pp. 568–69.
99. Marx, *Results of the Immediate Process of Production,* trans. Rodney Livingstone, in *Capital,* vol. 1, pp. 983, 1024; *Capital,* vol. 1, p. 645.

I shall now turn to the relationship between Marx's conception of the basic social forms that characterize capitalism and his analysis of large-scale industry. In tracing the unfolding of Marx's categories, we saw that his temporal determination of the magnitude of value becomes fully significant only when the category of relative surplus value is introduced; similarly, it is only when he analyzes large-scale industry that the full significance of his determination of value as the objectification of (abstract) human labor becomes clear. As noted, because the goal of capitalist production is surplus value, it gives rise to an incessant drive for increased productivity, which leads eventually to the supersession of direct human labor by the productive powers of socially general knowledge as the primary social source of material wealth. At the same time—and this is crucial—capitalist production is and remains based on human labor time expenditure precisely because its goal is surplus value.

Marx grasps capitalist industrial production in terms of this duality: as a process of creating material wealth, it ceases to depend necessarily on direct human labor; yet, as a process of valorization, it necessarily remains based on such labor. Large-scale industry is defined by the rise of productive powers that no longer are a function of direct human labor—yet this in the context of such labor's continued importance. With the development of this mode of production, living labor gradually ceases to be the active, regulating force of production. We have seen that, from the standpoint of Marx's analysis of the valorization process, direct human labor is significant as a source of value, regardless of its qualitative specificity and the level of productivity; the goal of the expenditure of labor is the objectification of labor time itself. It is precisely when the production of material wealth stops depending on direct human labor, even as such labor remains integral to the process of production, that this function of human labor as the mere source of objectified labor time comes to be expressed in the form of the labor process itself:

> Every kind of capitalist production, in so far as it is not only a labour process but also capital's process of valorization, has this in common, that it is not the worker who employs the conditions of his labour, but rather the reverse, the conditions of labour employ the worker. However it is only with the coming of machinery that this inversion first acquires a technical and palpable reality.... [T]he means of labour confront the worker during the labour process as capital, dead labour, which dominates and soaks up living labour power.[100]

Marx sees industrial production, then, as the adequate materialization of the valorization process—a process in which material wealth is produced as a means of generating surplus value rather than as the ultimate goal of production; hence, a process in which living labor serves as the object of production and the source of value. In this sense, the ultimate function of the forces of production is to

100. *Capital*, vol. 1, p. 548 (translation amended).

"soak up" as much living labor power as possible. This process is expressed materially in large-scale industry by the fragmented nature of work and also—because the productive forces no longer are a function primarily of direct human labor—by the growing difference between the relation of the objectified forces of production to the formation of value and their relation to the formation of material wealth.[101] The machine enters as a whole into the labor process, giving rise to great quantities of material wealth, but it enters into the valorization process only in that it either transmits gradually to products the value that went into its creation or changes the proportion of surplus labor time to necessary labor time by reducing the labor time necessary to reproduce the workers.[102] As noted, this analysis implies that, with industrial production, the growth in material wealth resulting from ever-higher levels of productivity far outstrips the growth in surplus value—particularly once machines are themselves produced by machines, which greatly increases the gap between their wealth-creating capabilities and the amount of labor time expended in their construction.[103]

The growing disparities effected by the development of the forces of production, between the increases in material wealth and in surplus value, is an expression of the growing differences between the productive powers of the use value dimension of labor and living labor. Earlier, I touched upon Marx's notion of the relationship between the forms of social relations that characterize capitalism and the development of immensely powerful productive capacities, along with the worldviews and conceptions of reality that are related to this development. What is important to our investigation at this point is the determinate form of this development. In the context of a mode of production in which living labor remains essential to production, and machinery is used as a means of increasing surplus value, the productive powers of labor's concrete dimension are constituted in opposition to living labor as productive powers of capital:[104]

The separation of the intellectual powers of the production process from manual labour, and the transformation of those powers into powers exercised by capital over labour, is ... finally completed by large-scale industry erected on the foundation of machinery. The narrow skill of the individual machine operator, whose labour has been emptied of all content, vanishes as an infinitesimal quantity in the face of the science, the gigantic natural forces, and the social mass labour embodied in the machine system, all of which constitute the power of the "master."[105]

The capitalist process of production induces the historical development of powerful, socially general productive powers, according to Marx; however, this process of historical constitution—which I described as the accumulation of

101. Ibid., p. 509.
102. Ibid., pp. 492, 502.
103. Ibid., pp. 509–17.
104. Ibid., pp. 508–9, 544ff.
105. Ibid., pp. 548–49 (translation amended).

historical time—is effected as a process of alienation. These powers come into being historically in alienated form, as powers of capital, of the "master."

I discussed this process of the alienation of labor's use value dimension while examining Marx's treatment of cooperation and manufacture, and shall further investigate its structural grounds below. What is important at this point is that in large-scale industry the social productive powers of concrete labor—which Marx refers to as "species capacities" constituted in alienated form as a "free gift" to capital—are not only greater than the sum of the productive powers of the immediate producers but are no longer constituted primarily by them. Unlike manufacture, the powers of the social whole no longer express in alienated form the knowledge, skills, and labor of the collective worker but, rather, the accumulated collective knowledge and power of humanity, of the species. Hence, as the passage cited above clearly indicates, with the development of large-scale industry, the powers of capital cannot be considered those of the collective worker in alienated form, but have become greater than the latter.

Another aspect of this development is a decline in the skills and powers of the individual workers as well as—and this is crucial—of the collective worker. As the production of material wealth increasingly becomes a function of socially general technical, organizational, and scientific knowledge, rather than of the skills, knowledge, and labor of the immediate producers, the combined labor of the workers stops being like the labor of a "supercraftsman," as was the case in manufacture. Production no longer is a form of handicraft, based ultimately on the labor of the workers. Nevertheless, because the socially general productive powers are developed as those of capital—hence, within the framework of a system that presupposes the expenditure of immediate labor time—the objectified forces of production in large-scale industry do not, *on a total social level,* tend to replace direct human labor in production. Rather, they are used to extract higher levels of surplus value from labor that has ceased to be essential to the production of material wealth and, hence, progressively loses its character as skilled handicraft labor or as a specialized aspect of such labor.

Thus, there is a structural antagonism between the alienated forces of production and living labor, wherein the former become more developed while the latter becomes increasingly empty and fragmented: "Even the lightening of labour becomes an instrument of torture, since the machine does not free the worker from labour, but rather empties his labour of all content."[106] The logic of large-scale industrial production, then, implies a long-term decline in the skills of the workers.[107] I have already noted that, according to Marx, the func-

---

106. Ibid., p. 548.
107. Ibid., pp. 559–64. The long-term tendency for the skills of workers in industrial capitalism to decline has been investigated at length by Harry Braverman in his classic study, *Labour and Monopoly Capitalism: The Degradation of Work in the Twentieth Century* (New York and London, 1979). Braverman has been criticized for underemphasizing workers consciousness and struggles in modifying and guiding the development of the labor process itself. However,

tion of human labor as the source of value in the valorization process becomes expressed materially in the industrial labor process. At this point I can add that, as it does so, labor becomes increasingly empty, little more than the simple expenditure of energy.

This socially constituted, antagonistic relationship between the objectified forces of production and living labor shapes the form of the industrial process of production. In the case of manufacture, the differences between value and material wealth are not yet significant for the form of the labor process. This form, therefore, can be explained in terms of the drive for increased productivity alone. The form of the industrial labor process, however, cannot be accounted for only in those terms. Its antagonistic and contradictory character, according to Marx, emerges from the mounting tension between the two tendencies generated by the double character of the underlying social mediation—the ongoing drive for increased productivity and the necessary expenditure of direct labor time. This tension results in the development of a productive system that confronts the workers as an objective system into which they are incorporated as component parts:[108]

In ... manufacture, the worker makes use of a tool; in the factory, the machine makes use of him. There the movements of the instruments of labour proceed from him, here it is the movements of the machine that he must follow. In manufacture the workers are part of a living mechanism. In the factory we have a lifeless mechanism which is independent of the workers, who are incorporated into it as its living appendages.[109]

With the development of large-scale production, the workers have become the objects of a process that itself has become the "subject," according to Marx. He refers to the factory as a mechanical automaton that is a subject, composed of various conscious organs (the workers) and unconscious organs (the means of production), all of which are subordinated to its central moving force.[110] In other words, Marx describes the industrial factory in the same terms that he earlier used to describe capital, thereby implying that the former should be

as David Harvey has pointed out, Braverman's analysis, like Marx's, is concerned with the broad sweep of the history of capital accumulation and whether one can speak of long-term unidirectional changes in the labor process (*The Limits to Capital* [Chicago, 1982], pp. 106–19). That is, the issue is not only one of whether workers are subjects or objects of history, or even whether class struggle modifies the development of the labor process; rather, it is, on a higher level of abstraction, whether capitalism has a historical trajectory. As I have argued, such a trajectory, which Marx attempts to grasp with his conception of the social forms constitutive of capitalism, cannot be explained with reference to class struggles alone. Related issues are whether such a trajectory of development points toward the possible overcoming of capitalism and, further, whether this possibility entails the self-realization of the proletariat or, rather, the abolition of proletarian labor.

108. *Capital,* vol. 1, pp. 508, 517.
109. Ibid., p. 548.
110. Ibid., pp. 544–45.

regarded as a physical expression of the latter. By analyzing large-scale industry thus, Marx seeks to understand in social terms a system characterized by enormous productive forces, on the one hand, and fragmented, empty, direct human labor, on the other. The nature of work and of the division of labor in industrial capitalism are not necessary, if unfortunate, by-products of any technologically advanced method of producing wealth, according to Marx; rather, they are expressions of a labor process molded by the process of valorization.

Although I have shown that Marx relates the antagonistic character of industrial production to the dual imperatives of valorization, a full explanation of how these dual imperatives are effected—that is, how the drive for increased productivity in capitalism is such that, on a total social level, direct human labor is retained as an integral element of production—would exceed the bounds of this work. That would require explaining how value operates as a socially constituted form of abstract domination, although the actors are unaware of its existence. Such an explanation would, in turn, require an elucidation of Marx's analysis of the dialectic of structure and action, hence, a deeper investigation of the relationship between his level of analysis in Volume 1 and that in Volume 3 of *Capital*.[111]

Nevertheless, in my earlier discussion of the dialectic of transformation and reconstitution I did uncover, albeit on a logically abstract level, one dimension of such an explanation—namely, the fundamental *structural* grounds in Marx's analysis for the ongoing reconstitution of valorization's dual imperatives and, hence, for the antagonistic form that capitalist production takes. At this point, I shall return briefly to a consideration of this dialectic which, as noted, ultimately is rooted in the temporal determination of the magnitude of value. In examining the interaction of the two dimensions of the commodity form, we saw that increased productivity does not increase the amount of value produced in a social labor hour but, rather, redetermines that hour historically; the forms of necessity associated with value thereby are reconstituted rather than superseded. In other words, the dialectic of the two dimensions of labor and of time in capitalism is such that value is reconstituted as a perpetual present, although it is moved historically in time. This reconstitution, as I suggested, is the most fundamental determination of the structural reproduction of the relations of production, that is, of the basic social forms that remain constitutive of capitalism, despite the tremendous transformations characteristic of this social formation.

With regard to the process of production itself, one aspect of the form of necessity intrinsic to value is the expenditure of abstract human labor time in production. The reconstitution of the abstract time frame by the development of social labor's productivity thus involves structurally reconstituting the necessity that such labor time be expended. In other words, the dialectic of transformation and reconstitution, which is rooted in the basic structuring forms of capitalism,

111. Ibid., p. 531n71.

is such that the expenditure of human labor in the immediate process of production remains necessary regardless of the degree to which productivity is developed. Consequently, although the development of large-scale industry entails the historical development of concrete labor's social character in a form that is independent of the immediate producers, production based on objectified historical time does not simply supersede production based on the present, that is, the expenditure of direct labor time. Instead, the latter is continually reconstituted as an essential, necessary element of capitalist production. This is the fundamental structural ground for the "incessant reproduction, [the] perpetuation of the worker, [which] is the absolutely necessary condition for capitalist production."[112]

The reconstitution of value and the redetermination of social productivity entailed by the dialectic I have outlined are the most basic determinations of a process of reproducing the relation of wage labor and capital which is both static and dynamic; this relation is reproduced in a way that transforms each of its terms. This process of reproduction, as analyzed by Marx, ultimately is a function of the value form and would not be the case were material wealth the defining form of wealth. It is, as we have seen, an aspect of a necessary treadmill dynamic, in which increased productivity results neither in a corresponding increase in social wealth nor in a corresponding decrease in labor time, but in the constitution of a new base level of productivity—which leads to still further increases in productivity. Even at this very abstract logical level, one can derive some features of the industrial labor process and proletarian labor from the implications of this dialectic. The dynamic reconstitution of the necessity of value-producing labor (wage labor) is such that it implies, at the same time, the transformation of the concrete nature of that labor. Considered abstractly and on a total social level, the effect of increased productivity on direct human labor, within a framework characterized by the structural retention of such labor in production, is to render that labor more uniform and simple and to intensify its expenditure. It imparts to human labor a concrete form that begins to resemble the initial determinations of its fetishized social form (abstract labor)—the expenditure of muscle, nerves, and so on. In other words, the increasing fragmentation of proletarian labor, according to Marx, is related intrinsically to the dialectical pattern wherein such labor remains necessary as the source of value even as it becomes ever less significant as the source of the social productive forces that are alienated as capital. The development of tremendous social powers in a form that is alien to the workers and controls them, and the related long-term tendency for proletarian labor to become one-sided and empty, are the fundamental grounds for Marx's statement that "in proportion as capital accumulates, the situation of the worker, *be his payment high or low,* must grow worse."[113]

112. Ibid., p. 716.
113. Ibid., p. 799 (emphasis added).

These developments clearly do not derive from private ownership of the means of production alone, in Marx's analysis, but are rooted in the deep structure of the social relations I have been investigating. One can now see more clearly that, in developing the category of capital out of that of the commodity, Marx lays the foundation for analyzing the concrete form of the developed capitalist process of production—what he terms the "production of relative surplus value" or the "real subsumption of labor under capital"—as a materialization (on the level of society as a whole) of the twofold movement grounded in the underlying social forms. This process of production is both a process of the production of material wealth, increasingly based on socially general knowledge, and a process of the production of value, based on immediate labor time expenditure. Hence, to analyze its concrete form is to examine a mode of production that, on a deep level, embodies the contradictory structural imperatives of achieving ever-higher levels of productivity and producing a surplus of value. Historical changes in the concrete form of fully developed capitalist production can, according to such an approach, be grasped in terms of a growing "shearing pressure" generated by these two increasingly opposed imperatives. This results in a mode of production characterized by the material opposition of the general to the particular, by the increasing fragmentation and emptying of human labor with increased productivity, and the reduction of workers to cogs of a productive apparatus. In short, large-scale industry is not a technical process that is used for purposes of class domination and increasingly comes into contradiction with that form of domination, according to Marx; rather, as constituted historically, it is the materialized expression of an abstract form of social domination—the objectified form of the domination of people by their own labor. Large-scale industrial production is intrinsically capitalist—"the specifically capitalist mode of production (in which machinery, etc. becomes the real master of living labour)."[114]

In the course of this investigation, I have shown that the strategic intent of Marx's law of value is not merely to explain the conditions of market equilibrium but, rather, to grasp capitalist society in terms of a "law" of history, a dialectic of transformation and reconstitution. This dialectic entails both a particular logic of "growth" as well as a determinate material form of production. In this regard, Marx's categorial analysis in *Capital* can be understood as an attempt to ground socially and historically the double-sided nature of capitalist progress, which he earlier had described as follows:

In our day, everything seems pregnant with its contrary. Machinery gifted with the wonderful power of shortening and fructifying human labour, we behold starving and overworking it. The new-fangled sources of wealth, by some weird spell, are turned into

114. Marx, *Results of the Immediate Process of Production,* p. 983.

sources of want.... All our invention and progress seem to result in endowing material forces with intellectual life, and in stultifying human life into a material force.[115]

Substantive totality

Capital

In examining Marx's analysis of industrial production as the materialization of the twofold character of the form of social relations characterizing capitalist society, I have also been elucidating his concept of capital. We have seen that Marx's category of capital cannot be understood in "material" terms alone, that is, in terms of the "factors of production" controlled by the capitalists; nor can it be grasped fully in terms of the social relation between the capitalist and working classes, structured by private ownership of the means of production and mediated by the market. Rather, the category of capital refers to a peculiar sort of social relation, to a dynamic, totalistic, and contradictory social form that is constituted by labor in its duality as an activity mediating people's relations with each other and with nature.

Marx first conceptually determines this totalistic form in terms of the value dimension, as self-valorizing value, and then unfolds it as a directionally dynamic structure, the social basis of a determinate pattern of historical development. Yet his concept of capital cannot be grasped fully in terms of the value dimension alone, for, as we have seen, the use value dimension of labor in capitalist society is constituted historically as an attribute of capital. In the cases of cooperation and manufacture, this appropriation of concrete labor's productive powers by capital can seem to be a matter of ownership and control, that is, a function of private property, because these powers are still constituted by direct human labor in production and, hence, can seem only extrinsically related to capital. Marx's analysis suggests, however, that although private property may have been central to this process of alienation in the historical emergence of capitalism, it does not remain structurally central once large-scale industry has developed. In the latter situation, the social productive powers of concrete labor appropriated by capital no longer are those of the immediate producers; they do not exist first as powers of the workers which are then taken from them. Rather, they are socially general productive powers and their alienated character is intrinsic to the very process of their constitution—indeed, the condition for their coming into being historically is precisely that they are constituted in a form that is separate from, and opposed to, the immediate producers. This form, as should be clear, is what Marx seeks to grasp with his category of capital. Capital is not the mystified form of powers that "actually" are those of the workers; rather it is the real form of existence of "species capacities," no longer those

115. Marx, Speech at the Anniversary of the *People's Paper,* April 14, 1856, in Robert C. Tucker, ed., *The Marx-Engels Reader* (2d ed., New York, 1978), pp. 577–78.

of the workers alone, that are constituted historically in alienated form as socially general powers.

If the social dimension of concrete labor that is constituted as a "free gift" to capital cannot be apprehended adequately in terms of the powers of the immediate producers, and the process of its alienation cannot be apprehended adequately in terms of private property, this process of alienated constitution must be located on a deeper structural level. The initial determinations of such a structurally grounded process of alienation were already implied by the dialectic of labor and of time outlined above. As we have seen, this dialectic promotes the development of socially general productive powers; these productive powers, however, are only apparently means at the disposal of the producers, to be used for their own benefit. As we noted in analyzing the treadmill dialectic, these powers neither give rise to an increase in the dominant form of social wealth produced per unit time nor transform positively the structure of labor. Instead, because increased productivity structurally reconstitutes the determinations of value, these productive powers serve to reinforce the abstract compulsions exerted on the producers; they heighten the degree and intensity of exertion required, as well as the fragmentation of labor. In this sense, they function as attributes of labor's abstract dimension, and have become means that dominate the producers. This process is structurally grounded in the double character of the commodity form itself as I have unfolded it. The dialectic wherein each new level of productivity is redetermined as the base level of the abstract temporal frame of reference, which functions as a socially general compelling norm, can be conceptualized as a process in which the social character of labor as a productive activity structurally becomes an attribute of the totality—which although constituted by social practice, is opposed to, and dominates, the individuals. In this way the concrete dimension of labor is "appropriated," as it were, by its abstract dimension.

This structural appropriation of labor's use value dimension by its abstract dimension is the fundamental expropriation of the capitalist social formation. It logically precedes, and does not fundamentally result from, the sort of concrete social expropriation associated with private ownership of the means of production. Implicit in Marx's mode of presentation—that is, in his unfolding the category of capital from that of the commodity—is the argument that the form of mediation effected by labor induces an enormous increase in the productive powers of the use value dimension of labor, while constituting these productive powers in alienated form. (This process of alienated constitution obviously cannot be adequately grasped in terms of the market and private property. Once again, then, we see that Marx's categories of value and capital engage a deeper structural level of modern life than do traditional Marxist interpretations of capitalist society's basic features.)

In finding, first, that Marx's category of capital refers to the alienated totality constituted by the mediating function of labor in capitalism and, second, that as "self-valorizing value" the abstract totality "appropriates" as its attribute the social character of productive activity, I have shown that capital, according to Marx, like the commodity, has a double character—an abstract dimension (self-valorizing value) as well as a concrete or substantive social dimension (labor's social character as productive activity). *Capital is the alienated form of both dimensions of social labor in capitalism,* confronting the individuals as an alien, totalistic Other:

> Capital is not a thing, it is a definite social relation of production pertaining to a particular historical social formation, which simply takes the form of a thing and gives this thing a social character. . . . Capital is the means of production as transformed into capital, they being no more capital in themselves than gold or silver are money. It is the means of production monopolized by a particular section of society, the products and conditions of activity of labour-power, which are rendered autonomous vis-à-vis this living labour-power and are personified in capital through this antithesis. *It is not only the workers' products which are transformed into independent powers,* the products as masters and buyers of their producers, *but the social powers and interconnecting form of this labour also confront them as properties of their product.*[116]

As the alienated form of both the abstract social bond constituted by labor, and the historically constituted productive powers of humanity, capital as a totality is both abstract and concrete; moreover, each of its dimensions is general. In examining value earlier, I analyzed it as an abstract, general, homogenous social mediation; it is now clear that this mediation induces the development of productive powers and determinate modes of knowledge that are socially general (whereby, as we have seen, the abstract and concrete forms of generality differ). On another level, capital can also be grasped as the objectified duality of abstract time and historical time, as a totality in which historical time is accumulated in an alienated form that oppresses the living. Capital is the structure of the history of modern society, a constituting social form which is constituted in such a way that "the tradition of all the dead generations weighs like a nightmare on the brain of the living."[117]

I can now expand on my earlier discussion of the Marxian notion of the dialectic of the forces and relations of production. If value is the fundamental category of capitalist social relations of production, and if labor's use value dimension encompasses the forces of production, then capital can be understood as an alienated structure of labor-mediated relations of production which promotes the development of socially general forces of production while incorporating them as its attributes. *The dialectic of the forces and relations of production*—the fundamental determinations of which I analyzed as the dialectic of transformation and reconstitution—*is, then, a dialectic of two dimensions of capital* rather than of capital and forces extrinsic to it. This dialectic is at the

116. *Capital,* vol. 3, pp. 953–54 (emphasis added).
117. *The Eighteenth Brumaire,* p. 103.

heart of capital as a dynamic, contradictory social totality. Far from denoting only the means of production owned by a class of private expropriators, Marx's category of capital refers to an alienated, dualistic structure of labor-mediated relations in terms of which the peculiar fabric of modern society, its abstract form of domination, its historical dynamic, and its characteristic forms of production and of work can be understood systematically. For Marx, capital, as the unfolded commodity form, is the central, totalizing category of modern life.

Earlier, I described industrial production in Marx's analysis as intrinsically capitalist. I now can extend that description: *Industrial production is the materialization of capital* and, as such, is the materialization of *both* the forces and the relations of production in their dynamic interaction. Clearly, this analysis has moved very far away from the traditional Marxist understandings of the forces and relations of production in capitalism and their contradiction.

As a moment of the dialectic of capital, the use value dimension—that of the accumulation of historical time, of socially general knowledge and powers—is neither identical with, nor completely independent of, the abstract value dimension; rather, the use value dimension is shaped by the abstract value dimension in their interaction. This implies, on the one hand, that although the totality is necessarily alienated, it is not one-dimensional but has a dual character; the totalized whole is not a noncontradictory unity. On the other hand, it indicates that the form in which the use value dimension has been constituted historically is not independent of capital, and should not be seen as the locus of emancipation.

We have already seen that the species-general knowledge and power to which the dynamic of capital gives rise develop in alienated form and in opposition to the individuals. Hence, one cannot justifiably attribute to Marx, as Habermas has done, the notion that the rapid development in industrial capitalism of science and technology automatically effects social progress and human emancipation.[118] Contrary to the assumptions of productivist Marxism, against which Habermas was reacting, the development of science and technology does not, in Marx's approach, represent a sort of linear progress that simply would be continued under socialism. Even leaving aside the question of the relation between social form and form of scientific thought, we have seen that Marx does not treat the development of science and technology as a purely technical development or as a social development that is independent of, and opposed to, capitalist relations of production. On the contrary, the forms of socially general knowledge and power developed under capitalism, according to his analysis, are socially formed and are incorporated into the process of production as attributes of capital. They reinforce the domination of abstract time, thereby functioning as moments of a dialectical process that retains direct human labor in production

118. Jürgen Habermas, *Knowledge and Human Interests,* trans. Jeremy Shapiro (Boston, 1971), pp. 50–51.

while emptying it concretely and intensifying it temporally. Industrial capitalism's "liberation" of general human productive capacities from the limits of individual strength and experience, in other words, is effected at the expense of the individuals.

In generating this antagonistic relation between socially general human productive capacities and living labor, capital shapes each. That the use value dimension of social labor is constituted in alienated form means that it operates structurally to the detriment of the immediate producers, and further that, like workers' concrete labor, it is shaped intrinsically by the dialectical processes outlined above. Hence, although it is not identical with the value dimension, it could not serve as the basis for human emancipation in the form in which it has been constituted historically.

The notion that elements of the historically constituted substantive social dimension—determinate modes of socially general scientific, technical, and organizational knowledge and practice—are shaped by that of value is of central significance for a critical theory that seeks to analyze postliberal modern society as capitalist. It lends depth to my discussion in Chapter Four of the social basis for what Horkheimer described as the increasingly instrumental character of social life in the modern world, that is, the transformation of the world into a world of rationalized means, rather than of ends.

I argued earlier that the process of increasing instrumentalization described by Horkheimer ultimately is rooted in the character of labor in capitalism as a socially mediating activity and, hence, in the nature of value as a form of wealth that is also a form of social mediation. When the goal of production is surplus value, production is no longer a means to a substantive end, but a means to an end that itself is a means and, therefore, is purely quantitative. Consequently, production in capitalism is for the sake of production; the process of production of any given product is only a moment in a never-ending process of the expansion of surplus value.

This goal informs the nature of production itself. As we have seen, according to Marx's analysis of capitalist production, the abstract temporal compulsion associated with value also determines the concrete form of the labor process. Beginning with manufacture, value becomes a structuring principle of the organization of large-scale production; production is organized according to the most efficient possible use of human labor engaged in increasingly specialized and fragmented tasks for the end of greater productivity. In other words, the use value dimension of labor becomes structured by value.

Although I cannot fully analyze this process, I can suggest, on the basis of what I have developed thus far, that it is also grounded structurally in the dialectic of labor and of time. The socially general modes of scientific, technical, and organizational knowledge and practice that emerge in the course of capitalist development are constituted historically in a social context that is determined by an abstract, homogeneous, quantitative social dimension and, hence, is geared toward ongoing increases in productivity and efficiency. Not only are the various aspects of labor's use value dimension developed and utilized in order to serve the ends given by the value-determined framework, but they also function structurally to reinforce and reconstitute this framework—that is, they function as attributes of capital. This function, however, is not extrinsic to their character: They not only serve to redetermine the value dimension but, in turn, are determined by it. This suggests, then, that the dialectical interaction of the two dimensions of labor in capitalism is such that the substantive dimension comes to be structured intrinsically by the characteristics of the value dimension.

What I have called the "appropriation" of the use value dimension by that of value thus can be seen as a process in which the use value dimension is structured by means of the sort of formal rationality whose source is the value dimension. The result is the tendency in modern life which Weber described in terms of the growing (formal) rationalization of all spheres of life, and which Horkheimer sought to articulate in terms of the growing instrumentalization of the world. Because this process increasingly entails the substantive dimension of labor and social life—that is, the administrative rationalization of both production and the institutions of social and political life in postliberal capitalism—Horkheimer located its source in labor per se. However, the ultimate ground of this substantive development is not the concrete dimension of labor but, rather, its value dimension. Although the latter does shape the former in its image, my analysis has demonstrated that the two are not identical. This nonidentity of the two dimensions of capital is the basis of the fundamental contradiction that underlies its dialectical dynamic: it gives rise to the possibility of the future separation of these two dimensions and, hence, to the historical possibility that the modes of socially general knowledge and powers developed under capitalism might be transformed. In the process, these modes of knowledge and power could become means at the disposal of people rather than socially constituted means of abstract domination.

This approach, then, is an effort to ground the historical process of instrumentalization, which Horkheimer took to be an indication of the growing *noncontradictory*, one-dimensional character of postliberal capitalism, in the *contradictory* character of the structuring forms of capitalism. It suggests that the loss of meaning (or "meaningfulness") that has been associated with this process of rationalization or instrumentalization is a function neither of technologically advanced production per se nor of secularization as such; rather, it is rooted in modes of social life and production that are structured by forms of social relations that mold both production and people's lives into segments of an ongoing process with no substantive end. Such an approach theoretically allows for the possibility that a secular form of life based on technologically advanced production could exist without being shaped by instrumental reason—one, that is, which could have more substantive meaning for people than the form of life structured by capital.

The proletariat

I can now return to the questions of the historical role of the working class and capitalism's fundamental contradiction, as they are implicitly treated by Marx's mature critical theory. In focusing on his analysis of the structuring forms of social mediation constitutive of capitalism, I have shown that class conflict does not, in and of itself, generate the historical dynamic of capitalism; rather, it is a driving element of this development only because it is structured by social forms that are intrinsically dynamic. As noted, Marx's analysis contravenes the notion that the struggle between the capitalist class and the proletariat is one between the dominant class of capitalist society and the class that embodies socialism, and that socialism, therefore, entails the self-realization of the proletariat. This idea is bound inextricably to the traditional understanding of capitalism's fundamental contradiction as one between industrial production and the market and private property. Each of the two major classes of capitalism is identified with a term of this supposed contradiction; the antagonism between workers and capitalists is then seen as the social expression of the structural contradiction between the forces and relations of production. This entire conception rests on a notion of "labor" as the transhistorical source of social wealth and constituting element of social life.

I have criticized the underlying assumptions of this conception at length by elucidating the distinctions Marx makes between abstract and concrete labor, value and material wealth, and by demonstrating their centrality to his critical theory. On the basis of these distinctions, I have developed the dialectic of labor and of time which is at the core of Marx's analysis of the pattern of growth and of the trajectory of production characteristic of capitalism. Far from being the materialization of forces of production alone that structurally are in contradiction with capital, proletarian-based industrial production is shaped intrinsically by capital, according to Marx; it is the materialized form of both the forces *and* relations of production. Hence, it cannot be grasped as a mode of producing that, unchanged, could serve as the basis for socialism. The historical negation of capitalism in Marx's mature critique cannot be understood in terms of a transformation of the mode of distribution in a way that would be adequate to the industrial mode of producing developed under capitalism.

By the same token, it has become clear that the proletariat is not, in Marx's analysis, the social representative of a possible noncapitalist future. The logical thrust of Marx's unfolding of the category of capital, his analysis of industrial production, completely contravenes traditional assumptions regarding the proletariat as the revolutionary Subject. For Marx, capitalist production is characterized by an enormous expansion in social productive powers and knowledge that are constituted within a framework determined by value and, hence, exist in alienated form as capital. As industrial production becomes fully developed, these productive powers of the social whole become greater than the combined-skills, labor, and experience of the collective worker. They are socially general, the accumulated knowledge and power of humanity constituting itself as such in alienated form; they cannot adequately be apprehended as the objectified powers of the proletariat. "Dead labor," to use Marx's term, is no longer the objectification of "living labor" alone; it has become the objectification of historical time.

According to Marx, with the development of capitalist industrial production, the creation of material wealth becomes ever-less dependent on the expenditure of direct human labor in production. Nevertheless, such labor does continue to play a necessary role inasmuch as the production of (surplus-)value necessarily depends on it; the structurally grounded reconstitution of value which we examined above is, at the same time, the reconstitution of the necessity of proletarian labor. The result is that as capitalist industrial production continues to develop, proletarian labor becomes increasingly superfluous from the standpoint of the production of material wealth, hence, ultimately anachronistic; yet it remains necessary as the source of value. As this duality plays itself out, the more developed capital becomes, the more it renders the very labor it requires for its constitution empty and fragmented.

The historical "irony" of this situation, as analyzed by Marx, is that it is constituted by proletarian labor itself. In this regard, it is significant that Marx, in considering the political economic category of "productive labor," does not treat it as a social activity that constitutes society and wealth in general—in other words, he does not treat it as "labor." Rather, he defines productive labor in capitalism as labor that produces surplus value, which is to say, contributes to the self-valorization of capital.[119] He thereby transforms what had been a transhistorical and affirmative category of political economy into one that is historically specific and critical, grasping what is central to capitalism. Instead of glorifying productive labor, Marx argues: "The concept of a productive worker . . . implies not merely a relation between the activity of work and its useful effect . . . but also a specific social relation of production . . . which stamps the workers as capital's direct means of valorization. . . . To be a productive worker is . . . not a piece of luck, but a misfortune."[120] In other words, productive labor is the structural source of its own domination.

119. *Capital,* vol. 1, p. 644.
120. Ibid. This confirms, once again, that the centrality of proletarian labor to Marx's analysis of capitalism should not be taken as an affirmative evaluation on his part of its ontological primacy to social life, or as part of an argument that workers are the most oppressed group in society. Rather, it is central to his analysis as the fundamental constitutive element of the abstract and dynamic form of social domination characteristic of capitalism—that is, as the focus of his critique. Marx's analysis of commodity-determined labor and its relation to the notion of the subject also suggests a historical-structural approach to issues such as which activities became recognized socially as labor, and which people in society were considered subjects. This interpretation could contribute to the discussion of the sociohistorical constitution of gender, and would change the terms of many recent discussions regarding the relation

In the Marxian analysis, the proletariat thus remains structurally important to capitalism as the source of value, but not of material wealth. This is diametrically opposed to traditional understandings regarding the proletariat: far from constituting the socialized productive forces that come into contradiction with capitalist social relations and thereby point to the possibility of a postcapitalist future, the working class, for Marx, is the essential constituting element of those relations themselves. *Both* the proletariat and the capitalist class are bound to capital, but the former is more so: capital conceivably could exist without capitalists, but it could not exist without value-creating labor. According to the logic of Marx's analysis, the working class, rather than embodying a possible future society, is the necessary basis of the present under which it suffers; it is tied to the existing order in a way that makes it the object of history.

In short, Marx's analysis of the trajectory of capital does not in any way point toward the possible self-realization in a socialist society of the proletariat as the true Subject of history.[121] On the contrary, it points to the possible abolition of the proletariat and the labor it performs as a condition of emancipation. This interpretation necessarily involves a fundamental rethinking of the relation of working-class struggles in capitalist society to the possible overcoming of capitalism—an issue to which we can only allude in this work. It indicates that the possible historical negation of capitalism implied by Marx's critique cannot be understood in terms of the proletariat's reappropriation of what it has constituted and, hence, in terms of the abolition of private property alone. Rather, the logical thrust of Marx's presentation clearly implies that this historical negation should be conceived as people's reappropriation of socially general capacities that are not ultimately grounded in the working class and had been constituted historically in alienated form as capital.[122] Such reappropriation would be possible only if the structural basis of this process of alienation—value, hence, proletarian labor—were abolished. The historical emergence of this possibility depends, in turn, upon the underlying contradiction of capitalist society.

> of the Marxian critique to issues of the social and historical position of women, racial, and ethnic minorities, and other sorts of groups. Such discussions have tended to proceed from, or react to, traditional Marxist positions. (This tendency has been expressed, for example, in the framing of questions such as whether housework is as important to society as factory work, or whether class—as opposed to gender, race, or other social categories—necessarily is the most relevant category of social oppression.)
>
> 121. Jean Cohen also argues against the postulate of the proletariat as revolutionary Subject. However, she identifies this traditional Marxist position with Marx's analysis of the capitalist process of production: see Jean Cohen, *Class and Civil Society: The Limits of Marxian Critical Theory* (Amherst, Mass., 1982), pp. 163–228.
>
> 122. This analysis contravenes interpretations of Marx that attribute to him the quasi-romantic notion that overcoming capitalism entails the victory of "living labor" over "dead labor." See Jürgen Habermas, *The Theory of Communicative Action,* vol. 2: *Lifeworld and System: A Critique of Functionalist Reason,* trans. Thomas McCarthy (Boston, 1987), p. 340. As I shall elaborate in the following section, Marx's analysis implies, on the contrary, that the possibility of a qualitatively different future society is rooted in the potential of "dead labor."

Contradiction and determinate negation

We now can turn to this contradiction. My examination of Marx's treatment of industrial production in *Capital* has clearly contravened the traditional interpretation of his conceptions of capitalism's basic contradiction and the relation of the proletariat to capitalism and to socialism; it has shown that, in Marx's analysis, industrial production is the materialized form of capital, and that the proletariat does not embody a possible future beyond the domination of capital but, rather, is the necessary presupposition of that domination. The investigation has thereby confirmed retrospectively the significance of the differences between a critique based upon the notion of "labor" and one whose critical focus is the historically specific character of labor in capitalism. Yet the intrinsic shaping of production by capital and the subsumption of the proletariat does not mean that capitalism is one-dimensional in Marx's view. Rather, I have shown that he does grasp this society as being fundamentally contradictory, although he does not locate its contradiction between the modes of producing and distribution. This suggests that the abolition of liberal capitalism's relations of distribution is not a sufficient condition for the abolition of capital, and allows for an approach to postliberal forms of capitalism based on an analysis of the essentially contradictory character of this social formation.

Capitalism's fundamental contradiction, as suggested by the logic of Marx's presentation, is rooted in its basic structuring social forms. I shall not try to work out the historical unfolding of this contradiction in its objective and subjective dimensions at this point; rather, I shall only try to clarify, on an abstract logical level, Marx's conceptions of the general character of this contradiction and some essential aspects of the determinate historical negation of capitalism, as they have been implied by my investigation thus far.

Marx's conception of the structural contradiction of capitalist society, which necessarily is one between what is historically specific to this society and what points beyond it, cannot be understood as one between capital and dimensions of social life presumed to be independent of it. My investigation of the dialectic of the two dimensions of both labor and time in capitalism has shown that the concrete dimension of social labor is constituted as an attribute of the value dimension. Both the concrete and abstract social dimensions of labor in capitalist society are dimensions of capital, according to Marx; neither of them, in their existent form, represents the future.

Although no existing social form represents the determinate negation of capitalism, Marx's presentation nevertheless does point toward the possibility of such a negation. The trajectory of development he presents implies a growing tension between the two dimensions of the basic social forms of capitalism, that is, between the socially general knowledge and capacities whose accumulation in alienated form is induced by the form of social mediation constituted by labor, on the one hand, and that form of mediation itself, on the other. We have seen that value, a historically specific form of social mediation that is also a form of wealth, is the ultimate basis of capital, of the totality. In its dialectical interaction with the use value dimension of the commodity form, it continually is reconstituted; yet the development of the sphere of production also points toward the possible historical overcoming of value. Inasmuch as value necessarily is bound to the expenditure of direct human labor time, it becomes an ever-narrower basis for the tremendous increases in productivity it induces.

To the extent that one chooses to speak of "fetters" on the forces of production, this notion does not refer primarily to the market or private property hindering the full development of industrial production. Indeed, the very notion of the full development of the forces of production certainly does not refer mainly to the possible production of a still greater mass of products (for, as noted, it is precisely runaway productivity that characterizes one moment of capital expansion). Rather, the underlying fetter, in Marx's conception, is that the general powers of humanity *must,* in a system structured by value, be used to squeeze as much surplus labor time from the workers as possible—although, increasingly, they *could* be used to increase social wealth directly and transform the detail division of labor. This systemic compulsion results in determinate modes of "growth" and of production. Hence, the fetters imposed by the capitalist relations of production should be seen as intrinsic to these modes themselves, and not as external factors that hinder their development.

These fetters become more constraining with the accumulation of historical time. Marx's presentation indicates that, in the course of capitalist industrial development, a growing gap emerges between the socially general productive capacities that are constituted as capital and the value basis of the totality. Yet this gap does not signify the linear supersession of the existent form by a newer one. The dialectic of the mutual transformation and reconstitution of the two dimensions of capitalism's structuring social forms is such that this society does not, and cannot, evolve in a quasi-automatic fashion into a fundamentally different form of society; similarly, the latter cannot emerge automatically out of any sort of collapse of the present system. Rather, the growing gap I have outlined has two opposed moments. On the one hand, as structured by value, it becomes expressed as an increasingly antagonistic opposition between the objectified totality and individuals: the former becomes increasingly rich and powerful, while much individual labor and activity becomes emptier and powerless. In Marx's account, people are not liberated by, but are subsumed under, the growth in productive capacities that come into being as capital. On the other hand, though, the same development—which signifies a growing disparity between the conditions for the production of material wealth and those for the production of value—makes proletarian labor more superfluous as a source of material wealth. In rendering proletarian labor potentially anachronistic from the standpoint of the production of material wealth, it renders value itself potentially anachronistic.

Clearly, then, Marx's presentation of the development of capitalist production implies the possible abolition of value and proletarian labor. (The latter becomes increasingly superfluous in terms of the potential of the use value dimension, although it remains constitutive of value.) My analysis has shown that although both dimensions of social labor in capitalism are dimensions of capital, according to Marx, it is value that constitutes the foundation of capitalism and is necessarily bound to it. The use value dimension is, to be sure, constituted in a form that is shaped by capital; unlike value, however, it is not bound necessarily to capital. The logic of Marx's presentation suggests that the abolition of value would allow what had been constituted as social labor's alienated use value dimension to exist in another form: in other words, the logical thrust of Marx's presentation indicates that the accumulation of historical time occurs in an alienated form that reconstitutes the necessity of the present; at the same time, it suggests that this accumulation also undermines the necessary moment of the present which it helps to reconstitute and thereby gives rise to the historical possibility of a fundamental transformation of the organization of social life.

This implies a distinction in Marx's analysis between the manifest form of the use value dimension, which is structured by value and is an integral aspect of the growing instrumental character of social life, and the latent potential of that which has been so constituted. It suggests that Marx's notion of capitalism's fundamental contradiction is ultimately one of a contradiction between the *potential* of the species-general capabilities that have been accumulated, and their *existent, alienated form* as constituted by the dialectic of the two dimensions of labor and of time. The relation between the existent and its determinate potential is central to Marx's conception of the possible overcoming of capitalism. Because the growing opposition between the two dimensions of social labor in capital is one between two moments of the same social form, it results in a growing tension or an economic and social shearing pressure between the existent and its determinate form. This tension both reinforces capital and gives rise to the possibility that the two constitutive dimensions of the structuring relations of capitalism be separated. It points toward the possible separation of society from its capitalist form. It is this structurally generated gap between what is and what could be, according to Marx's analysis, that allows for the possible historical transformation of capitalism and, relatedly, provides the immanent grounds for the possibility of the critique itself. Social necessity comes to be divided historically into what is and remains necessary for capitalism and what would be necessary for society were it not for capitalism.

Marx's critique, then, is not "positive." Its ultimate standpoint is not an existent social structure or grouping that is held to be independent of capitalism; indeed, it is not the existing form of either term of capitalism's basic contradiction, however one interprets this contradiction. We have seen that Marx's presentation indicates that general historical emancipation is grounded not in the possible full realization of the already extant form of production but, rather, in the possibility of its overcoming. This critique is rooted not in what is but in what has become possible—but cannot be realized within the existing structure of social life. Within the framework of such a critical social theory, the possible realization of freedom is not "guaranteed" by any existing structure or social grouping whose full development is checked by the relations of production. Neither, however, is it a historically indeterminate possibility. Instead, it entails the determinate negation of the existing order—the creation of new structures that have emerged as historical possibilities but require the abolition of the basic foundation of the capitalist order as a condition of their real and effective social existence. As we have seen, precisely that which grounds the possibility of a new organization of society, according to Marx—namely, objectified historical time—reinforces, in its existent form, capitalism's system of abstract domination. An essential aim of his critical theory is to elucidate this paradoxical structural development and thereby contribute to its possible transformation. The standpoint of Marx's "negative" critique, then, is a determinate possibility that emerges historically from the contradictory character of the existent order and should not be identified with the existing form of either of this order's dimensions. In this sense, the standpoint of the critique is temporal, rather than spatial.

This interpretation of capitalism's basic contradiction implies, of course, an understanding of capitalism's determinate negation very different from that implied by the traditional interpretation. In the traditional interpretation, overcoming capitalism's basic contradiction involves the open realization of labor's centrality to social life. I have argued quite to the contrary that, according to Marx, labor's constitutive centrality to social life characterizes capitalism and forms the ultimate ground of its abstract mode of domination. This approach interprets Marx's notion of capitalism's basic contradiction in terms of a growing tension between a form of social life mediated essentially by labor and the historically emergent possibility of a form of life in which labor does not play a socially mediating role. I have shown that the logic of the historical development he outlines points toward the possible historical overcoming of value and, hence, of the objective, quantifiable mode of social mediation constituted by labor. This would entail overcoming the form of social domination that lies at the heart of capitalism, the sorts of abstract, objective compulsions that characterize capitalism's necessary patterns of growth and mode of production. The trajectory of capitalist development, according to Marx's analysis, implies a possible determinate historical negation that would allow for the constitution of another, non-"objective," form of social mediation, a different form of growth, and a mode of technologically advanced production no longer shaped by value's imperatives. People, rather then being dominated by, and subsumed under, their own socially general productive capacities, could then make use of them for their own benefit.

One aspect of this determinate negation of capitalism, then, is that social life would no longer be mediated quasi-objectively by the structures we have examined but, rather, could be mediated in an overtly social and political fashion. In such a society, a political public sphere could play a more central role than in capitalism, for it could not only be free from the distorting effects of the enormous disparities of wealth and power that characterize class societies, but also free from a number of fundamental constraints that Marx analyzed as features of capitalism (rather than of the "economy").

For example, the logical thrust of Marx's presentation implies that if the value basis of production were abolished, material wealth would no longer be produced as the bearer of value but would itself be the dominant social form of wealth in a situation of technologically advanced productive capabilities. Given Marx's analysis of capital, this would mean that the nature and consequences of economic growth could be quite different than under capitalism. Increased productivity would not increase social wealth indirectly by decreasing necessary labor time, thereby generating a tendency toward runaway growth as a condition of economic "health"—as is the case when value is the dominant form of wealth; rather, it would result directly in increased social wealth. In such a situation, there would be no gap between the amount of material wealth produced and the amount of social wealth. On a systemic level, this would not only overcome the most fundamental ground for the existence of poverty (in terms of the "wealth" of society) in the midst of apparent plenty (the mass of goods produced); it would also allow for a form of economic growth not necessarily diametrically opposed to the long-term ecological interests of humanity.

The logical trajectory of Marx's categorial analysis also points toward the possible transformation of the structure of production, considered on a general social level. We have seen that, for Marx, the nature of industrial production—or, better, the gap between the potential of the growing productive knowledge and experience of humanity and the antagonistic form of capitalist production with its extreme detail division of labor—is rooted in the dialectic of the two dimensions of capital and, hence, ultimately in the value form. The strategic thrust of Marx's critique in this regard is to show that the relation between high levels of productivity and fragmented, empty work is a historically determinate relation that, as capitalism develops, becomes grounded less in technical necessity and more in a specific form of social necessity. Capital both maintains this relation as necessary and renders it potentially dispensable; it reconstitutes proletarian labor while making it increasingly insignificant as the social source of material wealth. The abolition of value, in such an analysis, would involve the abolition of the two imperatives of valorization—the necessity for ever increasing productivity and the structural necessity that immediate labor time be expended in production. This would allow both for a great *quantitative* change in the social organization of labor—that is, a socially general large-scale reduction in labor time—as well as for a fundamental *qualitative* transformation of the structure of social production and the nature of individual labor as well. The potential of the use value dimension, no longer constrained and shaped by the value dimension, could be used reflexively to transform the material form of production. As a result, a great deal of work that, as the source of value had become increasingly empty and fragmented, could be abolished; any remaining one-sided tasks could be rotated socially. In other words, Marx's analysis implies that the abolition of value would allow for a socially general transformation of production that would entail the abolition of proletarian labor—through both the transformation of the nature of much work in industrial capitalism, and the abolition of a system in which people are tied for much of their adult lives to such work—while maintaining a high level of productivity. It would allow for a form of production based directly on the appropriation of historical time.

Marx's critical analysis of industrial production, then, points to the possible abolition of much one-sided labor as well as to the possibility that labor could be redefined and restructured so as to be more interesting and intrinsically rewarding. It suggests that so long as direct human labor is the immediate social basis of ongoing surplus production, there will necessarily be an opposition between social wealth (whether in the form of material wealth or of value) and the labor that produces it, in as much as the former is created at the expense of the latter. This opposition becomes most pronounced in the value-based system of production. Nevertheless, the contradictions of that system, according to Marx, point to a possible transformation of production that could overcome the older opposition between social wealth and labor. His analysis points in the direction of the possible creation of modes of individual labor that, freed from the constraints of the detail division of labor, could be fuller and richer for the individuals. Moreover, they could be varied; people would not necessarily be tied to one sort of labor for most of their adult lives.

Overcoming the antagonistic opposition of individuals and society does not, then, entail the subsumption of the former under the latter. On the contrary, Marx's analysis demonstrates that precisely such subsumption already exists— as a feature of capital. Overcoming this antagonistic opposition requires overcoming a concrete structure of labor in which the "poverty" of individual labor is the presupposition of social wealth; it requires a new structure of labor in which the wealth of society and the "wealth-creating" possibility of labor for the individual are parallel, not opposed. Such a structure becomes a possibility, in Marx's critical analysis, when the growing contradiction of capitalism gives rise to the historical possibility that the productive capacities that had been constituted in alienated form could be reappropriated and reflexively utilized on the sphere of production itself.

The possibility that social labor, in a postcapitalist society, could be more interesting and rewarding does not, however, express a utopia of labor. It is not tied to the notion of labor's constituting centrality to social life; rather, it is predicated upon the historical *negation* of that socially constituting role played by labor in capitalism. Moreover, Marx's analysis of labor's mediating role in structuring work and production in capitalism can be extended to the structuring of play, leisure, and their relation to work, as well as to the relation of public life and work, on the one hand, and private life, on the other. This suggests that overcoming this historically specific form of mediation would not only allow for a new structuring of work, but for a fundamental restructuring and resignification of social life in general—not only for the favored (or marginal) few, but for most.

This possible transformation of production and labor rests, as we have seen, on the distinction implied by Marx's analysis between the existent form of the use value dimension, which is molded by value, and its latent potential. Because the possible reappropriation by people of the use value dimension of labor that was constituted in alienated form depends on the abolition of value, this reappropriation implicitly presupposes a separation of the two dimensions of the basic social forms of capitalism; this, in turn, implies a possible transformation of the elements of the use value dimension. In other words, the approach I have outlined can treat the existent forms of those elements as instrumental in character—because they are shaped by value—and, yet, allow theoretically for the possibility that, if value were abolished, what was constituted historically as the concrete dimension of capital (including scientific and technical forms of knowledge, for example, in addition to the mode of producing) could exist in another form. Thus, Marx's analysis suggests that the abolition of value would allow for a different mode of technologically advanced production, one not structured intrinsically in the antagonistic way that marks the sphere of production in capitalism; this analysis also suggests the possibility of a more general reshaping and restructuring of the scientific and technical knowledge that has been developed within the context of capitalism's alienated social forms. More generally, Marx's critique of capitalism allows for a position that neither affirms scientific and technical knowledge in their existent forms as emancipatory nor implicitly calls for their abstract negation. Rather, by analyzing socially the emancipatory potential of what had been constituted historically in alienated form, the Marxian critique seeks to grasp critically what exists in a way that points beyond it historically.

One strand of Marx's analysis, then, can be summarized as follows: The dynamic of capital generates the development of productivity in a concrete form that remains an instrument of domination. Yet its growing potential forms the basis for an eventual transformation of society, of the mode of social mediation, and of the social organization of production, in such a way that the structure as well as the goal of production would change fundamentally. The possibility of this reflexive transformation of the sphere of production provides the basis for a social critique that can move beyond the antinomy of two kinds of social criticisms. The first is a critique of alienated labor and the alienation of people from nature that rejects industrial technology per se in the historically impossible hope of a return to a preindustrial society; the second is a critique of the inequitable and unjust distribution of social power and of the great mass of goods and services produced in capitalism, which accepts as necessary the linear continuation of capital-determined production.

In considering the meaning of the abolition of wage labor implied by the logic of Marx's presentation, I have focused on the concrete dimension of this abolition—that is, on the possible abolition of proletarian labor and, relatedly, on the possible transformation of the labor process itself—in order to make clear how fundamentally my interpretation differs from that of traditional Marxism. At this point, however, I should note that Marx's categorial analysis of capitalist production's development also points to the possible abolition of the other aspect of wage labor, that is, of the system of distribution based on the exchange of labor power for wages with which means of consumption are acquired. We have seen that proletarian labor becomes increasingly insignificant as the social source of material wealth, even as it is systemically reconstituted as the source of value. Leaving aside the question of exploitation, this means a gap emerges between the significances of wages considered in value terms and considered in terms of material wealth. Once the socially general productive capacity of concrete labor become greater than that of the sum of individual labors, a growing discrepancy arises between labor time inputs and material outputs. The system of wages, considered from the standpoint of material wealth, becomes a form of socially general distribution and only appears to be remuneration for labor time expenditure. It no longer has a basis in the production of material wealth; its systemic retention is a function of the value dimension alone. Because there is no longer a necessary relation between labor time inputs and the production of material wealth, the abolition of value under these conditions would also allow for the development of another mode of social distribution—one in which the acquisition of means of consumption would not be an "objective" function of the expenditure of labor time.[123]

Thus, a central aspect of the realization of the potential of the accumulated use value dimension of labor, once freed from the constraints of value, is that the social surplus no longer would have to be the product of the direct labor of a class of people subsumed under the process of production, people's labor no longer would be a quasi-objective means of acquiring means of consumption. This is an important feature of Marx's conception of socialist society as overcoming human prehistory. It follows, then, that the most basic condition for

123. André Gorz's discussion, in *Paths to Paradise*, of the possibility of a guaranteed income is based on an approach that is similar to the interpretation of the abolition of value presented here. He argues that when increased output is achieved with falling labor costs, that increase can only be socially distributed if it gives rise to the creation and distribution of means of payment corresponding to its own volume (which would be the case if material wealth were the socially dominant form of wealth), and not to the value of labor expended. He maintains further that the essential function of a guaranteed income for life would be to distribute to everyone the wealth created by society's productive forces as a whole and not by the sum of individual labors. See *Paths to Paradise: On the Liberation from Work,* trans. Malcolm Imrie (Boston, 1985), p. 42.

overcoming class society is not the abolition of a set of property relations—hence, of a class of private expropriators—but a fundamental transformation of the mode of social mediation and its related mode of production. Such a transformation would involve the abolition of the class whose direct labor in production is the source of the surplus. In the absence of such a transformation, class society would continue to exist, regardless of whether or not the expropriators of the surplus could be considered a class in the traditional Marxist sense.

Modes of universality

This approach to the possible transformation of existent social forms, implied by Marx's critical analysis of the twofold character of the structuring relations of capitalism, also has implications for the relation of determinate forms of universality to capitalism and its possible historical negation. As noted, modern modes of social and political generality and of universalistic ideas are not the historical results of transhistorical evolutionary or teleological processes, for Marx. Rather, they emerge historically and are shaped within a context constituted by the underlying structuring social forms of capitalism. Their relation to those forms is intrinsic; that is, they are grounded socially and historically in determinate forms of social life.

We have seen that Marx's analysis of the commodity as the fundamental structuring principle of social practice and thought in modern capitalist society provides a point of departure for a critical sociohistorical approach to the character of modern universality and equality. With the historical emergence of capital—of the commodity as a totalizing social form—a mode of social mediation comes into being that is abstract, homogeneous, and general: each instance of that mediation (that is, each commodity considered as a value) is not qualitatively determinate but a moment of a totality. At the same time, each commodity, considered as a use value, is qualitatively particular. As a form of practice, the commodity form of social mediation generates a social form of equality that potentially is universal, establishing commonality among objects, among labors, among commodity owners, and potentially among all people. The form of this universality, however, is abstracted from the qualitative specificity of particular individuals and groups; the commodity form generates an opposition between an abstract, homogeneous form of universality and a form of concrete particularity that excludes universality.[124]

Such an analysis avoids treating the form of universality that becomes dom-

---

124. An example of this opposition is the classical distinction in liberal capitalist society between the person as a citizen, equivalent to, and indistinguishable from, all other citizens, and the person as a concrete person, embedded in specific social relationships. One could also argue that a more mediated expression of this opposition is the way in which gender differences are constituted and conceived in capitalist society.

inant in capitalist society quasi-metaphysically as the Universal per se, in favor of treating it as a socially constituted, historically specific form of universality that *appears* in transhistorical form as the Universal. This approach does not simply oppose the reality of capitalist society to its ideals but provides a historical analysis of these ideals themselves. An analysis relating the modern, abstract form of universality to the value dimension of the commodity form does not necessarily imply a dismissal of this form of universality, but does allow for a social analysis of its ambivalent character—that, as noted, this form of universality has had positive political and social consequences and, yet, in its opposition to all particularity, it has also been an aspect of abstract domination.

In analyzing universal forms in social and historical terms, Marx's analysis does not consider all modes of universality constituted in capitalism to be tied necessarily to value. On the basis of the distinction between value and use value, his theory also suggests the historical constitution of a parallel form of universality, one that is not abstract and homogeneous and does not necessarily exist in opposition to particularity. In considering the category of concrete labor, I noted how the abstract general social mediation that structures capitalist society also gives rise to this other form of generality; activities and products that may not be deemed similar in other societies become socially organized and classified as similar in capitalism—for example as varieties of (concrete) labor or as specific use values. This generality, however, is not a totality but a whole, made up of particulars. This sort of generality is also evident in Marx's conception of the development of species-general modes of knowledge and capacities that are constituted historically in the course of capital's development. Because this socially substantive general dimension comes into being within a framework determined by value, it is structured accordingly: it becomes part of the abstract, rationalized, technical-administrative world constituted by capital. On the other hand, according to Marx's analysis, this substantive general dimension is not identical with value and, hence, with abstract homogeneous universality—although, as the concrete dimension of capital, it is shaped by value. Consequently, the growing tension between the potential of the use value dimension of labor in capitalism and the actuality of the world constituted by value can also, on one level, be seen as allowing for a potential separation of the two forms of generality. On this extremely preliminary level, then, the Marxian critical theory implicitly addresses the historical constitution of two sorts of generality. One is an abstract, homogeneous sort of generality, rooted in the value dimension and related intrinsically to a conception of humanity that is general, abstract, homogeneous, and therefore necessarily in opposition to concrete particularity as its antithesis; the second is another sort of generality that is not homogeneous. Although the latter is constituted in alienated form, according to Marx, his analysis suggests that, in a postcapitalist society, it could exist in a form freed from the structuring of value and, hence, not necessarily opposed to particularity—a form that could be related to the development of a new conception of humanity as general and, yet, variegated.

This analysis of value-determined universality is like Marx's treatment of capital-determined production. For Marx, overcoming of capitalism entails neither the abolition of all forms of technologically advanced production nor the realization of the form of industrial production developed under capitalism. Similarly, it neither entails the eradication of universality nor can it be adequately understood in terms of the effective extension to all people of the abstract, homogeneous form of universality that develops as a moment of the mode of social life structured by the commodity. Rather, his analysis points toward the possibility that another dominant form of universality might be constituted.

This preliminary discussion of the two forms of socially constituted universality implied by Marx's categorial analysis lends depth to my discussion of the role accorded the working class in the critique of political economy, and has more general implications for a consideration of various social movements in terms of the forms of universality we have outlined. In the Marxist tradition, the proletariat frequently has been seen as a universal class and, on this basis, has been contrasted to the capitalist class, whose interests are deemed particularistic in that they do not coincide with (or are opposed to) those of society as a whole. It is because of its universal character that the proletariat has been thought of as the representative of a possible future society. My discussion of the social grounding of modes of universality implied by Marx's analysis indicates, however, that the relation of capitalism to its possible historical negation should not be understood in terms of this sort of opposition between particularity and universality, for this opposition itself is characteristic of capitalism's social forms. Rather, capitalism's relation to its possible negation should be seen in terms of different dominant forms of universality. The relation of the universality represented by the proletariat to the possible overcoming of capitalism should not, then, be approached only quantitatively, in terms of the extent to which universality is realized. It should, instead, be considered qualitatively, in terms of the sort of universality the class represents.

We have just seen that, with his analysis of capital's double character, Marx implicitly grounds socially the historical constitution of two very different modes of generality—one in the objective form of social mediation grasped by the category of value, and the other as an aspect of the use value dimension. The latter, according to Marx, is generated historically by the abstract form of mediation but is separable from it. It seems clear that, within this framework, the universality represented by the proletariat ultimately is that of value, however inclusive or collective its form. Far from representing the negation of value, the proletariat essentially constitutes this abstract, homogeneous form of wealth, the social mediation whose generality is opposed to qualitative specificity. Moreover, in discussing Marx's treatment of the workers as subjects and as objects of production, I showed that his determination of them as subjects was as (collective) commodity owners. These preliminary determinations imply that the extension of the universalistic principles of bourgeois society to larger segments of the population—that is to say, the realization of these principles—which has, in part, been effected by working class movements, as well as by those elements of women's movements and minority movements that have struggled for equal rights, should not be understood as a development that points beyond capitalist society. Although such movements have greatly democratized capitalist society, the form of universality they have helped constitute is one that, for Marx, remains tied to the value form of mediation and, ultimately, stands in opposition to individual and group specificity.

If capitalism's basic contradiction is not one represented by the social opposition of the working class and the capitalist class, and if overcoming capitalism does not entail the realization of the abstract form of universality associated with this society, then the question of the nature and the sources of historically constituted forms of subjectivity that point beyond the existent order must be rethought. In outlining some dimensions of capitalism's basic contradiction—and, hence, the nature of its determinate historical negation—as they are implied by Marx's analysis of the capitalist sphere of production, I have touched upon a series of tensions that I described in terms of a growing gap between the possibilities generated by the development of capital and its actual form. This gap gives rise to a sort of shearing pressure that structures the institutions of capitalist society and shapes its course of development. My discussion of this shearing pressure has focused primarily on the structure of production and nature of work in capitalist society and, to a lesser extent, on the social constitution of modes of universality. Nevertheless, the tensions Marx grounds in the dual character of capitalism's underlying social forms should be understood not only in "objective"—for example, economic and social—terms, but also in "subjective" terms as well, with reference to changing forms of thought and sensibilities. A fuller examination of capitalist society along these lines would, of course, require a more concrete level of analysis; on no level, though, should its emphasis on contradiction, however redetermined, be understood as assuming an automatic breakdown of capitalist society or the necessary emergence of oppositional or critical forms of consciousness pointing beyond the existing social formation. The interpretation I presented here does, however, suggest that the Marxian analysis implies an approach to *qualitative historical changes* in forms of subjectivity and in structures of needs—one that could account for such changes, not merely in terms of the social backgrounds of the actors involved, but also as possibilities constituted by the development of the social forms at the core of capitalism. In other words, the Marxian analysis implies a social theory of subjectivity that is historical.

Although I cannot elaborate such a sociohistorical approach here, I will point out that Marx's analysis of capitalism implies that an important element of such an approach should be the growing contradiction between the necessity and nonnecessity of value-creating labor, the notion that precisely what constitutes the social formation and is necessary to it—labor acting as a socially mediating activity—becomes increasingly unnecessary in terms of the potential of what it constitutes. This, in turn, suggests the existence of a growing gap between the sort of labor people continue to perform in a society mediated by labor and the sort of labor they could perform, were it not for this "necessity" of capitalism.

One could, for example, investigate changing attitudes toward labor and what constitutes meaningful activity in terms of this contradictory development. This would involve an analysis of the historical emergence of new needs and forms of subjectivity in terms of a growing structural tension between the increasingly anachronistic character of the structure of work (and of other institutions of social reproduction), and their continued centrality in modern society. Such an analysis could, for example, begin to investigate the emergence in the 1960s of "postmaterialist" values on a mass scale with reference to such a tension, and examine the subsequent ebb of such values in terms of a series of crises and structural transformations in advanced industrial capitalist countries which dramatically reestablished the "necessary" connection between labor, as presently defined, and material reproduction. This approach could also help to illuminate changes in the definitions of and relations among public, private, and intimate spheres of modern social life, as well as a recent phenomenon noted by theorists as diverse as Daniel Bell and André Gorz—namely, the increasing importance of consumption to self-identity. This latter issue should not be understood only in terms of the growing dependence of capitalism on mass consumption (a position that frequently regards such consumption merely as generated and manipulated by advertising, for example); nor should such a study reify consumption in a culturalist manner as the site of identity and resistance, analogous to the traditional Marxist reification of production. Rather, it should also analyze the increasing subjective importance of consumption in terms of the decline of work as a source of identity, and relate this decline to the ever-more anachronistic character of labor's structure and to the negative effects of production for the sake of production on the character of much work. The idea that labor's necessary role as a socially mediating activity and, with it, a determinate structure of production become anachronistic even as they are continually reconstituted could also serve as the basis for an analysis of deeper historical changes in conceptions of morality and of self.

This general approach could be a useful point of departure in reconceptualizing the relation of the working class to the possible overcoming of capitalism. We have seen that, according to Marx's analysis, the proletariat is an essential element of value-determined relations of production and, as such, is also rendered anachronistic as capitalism develops. Overcoming capitalism, then, must also be understood in terms of the abolition of proletarian labor and, hence, the proletariat. This, however, renders very problematic the question of the relation of working-class social and political actions to the possible abolition of capitalism; it implies that such actions, and what is usually referred to as working-class consciousness, remain within the bounds of the capitalist social formation—and not necessarily because workers have been materially and spirtually corrupted, but because proletarian labor does not fundamentally contradict capital. The political and social actions of working-class organizations have been historically important in the processes by which workers have constituted and defended themselves as a class within capitalism, in the unfolding of the wage labor–capital dynamic, and, especially in Western Europe, in the democratization and social humanization of the capitalist order. However militant the actions and the forms of subjectivity associated with the proletariat asserting itself have been, though, they did not and do not point to the overcoming of capitalism. They represent capital-constituting, rather than capital-transcending, forms of action and consciousness. This would be the case even if the structure of wage labor were to become truly global—which it is becoming as a result of capital's current form of globalization—and if the workers were to organize accordingly. The issue is not simply the degree to which the capital–wage labor relation has become globalized (although, at a more concrete level of analysis, the spatial extension of capital does have important consequences). It is also not simply an issue of "reformism"; the fundamental problem is not that politics based on the existence of labor power as a commodity leads to trade-union consciousness. It is, rather, that capital rests ultimately on proletarian labor—hence, overcoming capital cannot be based on the self-assertion of the working class. Even the "radical" notion that the workers produce the surplus and, therefore, are its "rightful" owners, for example, points to the abolition of the capitalist class—but not to the overcoming of capital. That would require overcoming the value form of the surplus and the capital-determined form of the labor process.

These considerations can serve as a point of departure for an examination of the objective and subjective conditions for the abolition of proletarian labor and, hence, for the abolition of capitalism. It could illuminate historically, for example, different sorts of workers' dissatisfaction or lack of identification with their work. However, this interpretation also highlights a dilemma when one considers the possible relation of working-class organizations to the overcoming of capitalism. It suggests that there is no linear relation or direct continuity between actions and polities associated with the working class asserting itself (however radically or militantly), on the one hand, and actions and policies that would point beyond capitalism, on the other. Indeed, this approach implies that there is a deep tension between actions and policies that represent workers exclusively as workers (and therefore are completely focused on jobs as defined within the existing socioeconomic framework as the necessary means of individual reproduction) and those that would go beyond such an exclusive definition. It suggests that if a movement, concerned with workers, were to point beyond capitalism, it would both have to defend workers' interests and have to participate in their transformation—for example, by calling into question the given structure of labor, not identifying people any longer only in terms of that structure, and participating in rethinking those interests. However, I can do no more than mention these themes and problems here.

Inasmuch as the idea of a growing tension between the necessity and non-necessity of value-constituting labor refers to the form of social mediation, its implications are not limited to an investigation of the structure of work itself. A final example I have already touched upon of what one could investigate in terms of this understanding of capitalism's contradiction is that of changing conceptions of, and attitudes toward, universality. The notion of the different forms of socially constituted universality implied by Marx's analysis of the development of the structuring forms of the social formation could serve as the basis for a sociohistorical investigation of some strains of new social movements—for example, of the feminist movement—that are attempting to formulate a new form of universalism, beyond the opposition of homogeneous universality and particularity. This approach, then, could also serve as the point of departure for rethinking the relation of the new social movements and identity-based politics of recent decades to capitalism and its possible overcoming. These various examples, however, are intended only as suggestions. At the preliminary logical level of the present study, I cannot adequately undertake an investigation of such possible implications of my interpretation.

To sum up my discussion of the determinate negation of capitalism as it is implied by Marx's critique: This negation cannot, in any way, be grasped in terms of a transformation of the bourgeois mode of distribution alone. Socialism, according to Marx, also involves another mode of production, one not organized as a metamachine based essentially upon direct human labor. It, therefore, would allow for new modes of individual labor and activity that are richer and more satisfying, and for a different relation of work to other realms of life. The possibility of this transformation ultimately is rooted in the possibility of a determinate historical negation—in the abolition of an objective mode of social mediation and the abstract compulsions associated with it, a mode of social mediation that ultimately is constituted by labor, and that constitutes the quasi-automatic directional dynamic of the capitalist social formation and its form of production. Hence, the determinate historical negation of value envisioned by Marx as a historical possibility could free humans from the alienated sway of their own labor, while allowing labor, freed from its historically specific social role, to be transformed so as to enrich rather than impoverish individuals. Freeing the forces of production from the compulsions imposed by the form of wealth based upon direct labor time entails freeing human life from production. In light of the traditional interpretation, it is ironic that Marx's analysis implies that most individuals' labor could become more satisfying and self-constituting only when labor is no longer socially constitutive.

Marx's understanding of the abolition of the capitalist form of labor and of production, then, refers not to production in any narrow sense but to the very structuring principle of our form of social life. Relatedly, his critique of capitalism is not one of social mediation per se but of the specific form of mediation constituted by labor. Value is a self-mediating form of wealth, but material wealth is not; the abolition of the former necessarily entails the constitution of new forms of social mediation, many of which presumably would be political in nature (which by no means necessarily implies a hierarchical, state-centered mode of administration).

Central to Marx's conception of the overcoming of capitalism is his notion of people's reappropriation of the socially general knowledge and capacities that had been constituted historically as capital. We have seen that, according to Marx, such knowledge and capacities, as capital, dominate people; such reappropriation, then, entails overcoming the mode of domination characteristic of capitalist society, which ultimately is grounded in labor's historically specific role as a socially mediating activity. Thus, at the core of his vision of a postcapitalist society is the historically generated possibility that people might begin to control what they create rather than being controlled by it.

The development of the social division of time

At the beginning of this work, I asserted that the notion of the historical specificity of value, which Marx develops in the *Grundrisse,* provides a key to interpreting his mature critique of political economy. I have shown that this idea is indeed the essential core of Marx's analysis in *Capital* of the nature of modern capitalist society and its possible determinate negation. At this point I shall briefly recapitulate what I have developed in this chapter and reconfirm the essential continuity of Marx's analysis in the two texts, by summarizing his conception of the trajectory of capitalist production in *Capital* in terms of temporal categories introduced in the *Grundrisse*—that is, in terms of the development of what I shall call the "social division of time." In the process, I shall emphasize the central significance of the notion of historical nonnecessity. As we have seen, the growing historical nonnecessity of value-constituting labor— that is, the necessary presupposition of capitalism and the constituent of its characteristic form of abstract social necessity—is essential to Marx's understanding of capitalism's fundamental contradiction as one between what is and its own potential (rather than between what is and what also is).

In a passage from the *Grundrisse* quoted at the beginning of this work, Marx states:

Capital itself is the moving contradiction, [in] that it presses to reduce labour time to a minimum, while it posits labour time, on the other side, as sole measure and source of wealth. Hence it diminishes labour time in the necessary form so as to increase it in the superfluous form; hence posits the superfluous in growing measure as a condition—question of life or death—for the necessary.[125]

My investigation of *Capital* permits us now to grasp these temporal categories. Marx's opposition of "necessary" and "superfluous" labor time is not identical to that of "necessary" and "surplus" labor time. The former opposition refers to society as a whole, whereas the latter refers to the class of immediate producers. In Marx's theory, the existence of surplus production—more than is necessary to satisfy producers' immediate needs—is a condition of all "historical" forms of social life. One can distinguish in every historical form between the amount of production required to reproduce the laboring population and an additional amount, expropriated by nonlaboring classes, "necessary" for society as a whole. According to Marx, in capitalism the surplus is value, rather than material wealth and is not expropriated by means of direct domination. Instead, expropriation is mediated by the form of wealth itself, and exists in the form of a nonmanifest division between that portion of the workday in which the workers labor for their own reproduction ("necessary" labor time) and that portion which is appropriated by capital ("surplus" labor time). Given the distinction between value and material wealth, so long as the production of material wealth depends largely on the expenditure of direct labor time, both "necessary" and "surplus" labor time can be considered socially necessary.

This, however, ceases to be the case as the production of material wealth comes to be based on socially general knowledge and productive capacities rather than on direct human labor. In such a situation, the production of material wealth may bear so little relation to the expenditure of direct labor time that the total amount of socially necessary labor, in *both* its determinations (for individual reproduction and for society generally), could be greatly reduced. The result, as Marx put it, would be a situation characterized not by the "reduction of necessary labour time so as to posit surplus labour" but rather by "the reduction of the necessary labour of society in general to a minimum."[126]

My examination of the dialectic of the two dimensions of capitalism's underlying social forms has shown, however, that a general reduction of socially necessary labor that would be fully commensurate with the productive capacities developed under capitalism cannot occur, according to Marx's analysis, so long as value is the source of wealth. The difference between the total labor time determined as socially necessary by capital, on the one hand, and the amount of labor that would be necessary, given the development of socially general productive capacities, were material wealth the social form of wealth, on the other, is what Marx calls in the *Grundrisse* "superfluous" labor time. The category can be understood both quantitatively and qualitatively, as referring both to the duration of labor as well as to the structure of production and the very

125. *Grundrisse,* p. 706.
126. Ibid., (translation amended).

existence of much labor in capitalist society. As applied to social production in general, it is a new historical category, one generated by the trajectory of capitalist production.

Until this historical stage of capitalism, according to Marx's analysis, socially necessary labor time in its two determinations defined and filled the time of the laboring masses, allowing nonlabor time for the few. With advanced industrial capitalist production, the productive potential developed becomes so enormous that a new historical category of "extra" time for the many emerges, allowing for a drastic reduction in both aspects of socially necessary labor time, and a transformation of the structure of labor and the relation of work to other aspects of social life. But this extra time emerges only as potential: as structured by the dialectic of transformation and reconstitution, it exists in the form of "superfluous" labor time. The term reflects the contradiction: as determined by the old relations of production it remains labor time; as judged in terms of the potential of the new forces of production it is, in its old determination, superfluous.

It should be clear that "superfluous" is not an unhistorical category of judgment developed from a position purportedly outside of society. It is, rather, an immanent critical category that is rooted in the growing contradiction between the potential of the developed forces of production and their existent social form. From this point of view, one can distinguish labor time necessary for capitalism from that which would be necessary for society were it not for capitalism. As my discussion of Marx's analysis has indicated, this distinction refers not only to the quantity of socially necessary labor but also to the nature of social necessity itself. That is, it points not only toward a possible large reduction in total labor time but also toward the possible overcoming of the abstract forms of social compulsion constituted by the value form of social mediation. Understood in these terms, "superfluous" is the historically generated, immediate opposite of "necessary," a category of contradiction that expresses the growing historical possibility of distinguishing society from its capitalist form, and, hence, of separating out their previous necessary connection. The basic contradiction of capitalism, in its unfolding, allows for the judgment of the older form and the imagination of a newer one.

My analysis of the dialectic of transformation and reconstitution has shown that, according to Marx, historical necessity cannot, in and of itself, give rise to freedom. The nature of capitalist development, however, is such that it can and does give rise to its immediate opposite—historical nonnecessity—which, in turn, allows for the determinate historical negation of capitalism. This possibility can only be realized, according to Marx, if people appropriate what had been constituted historically as capital.

The understanding of the determinate negation of capitalism implied by the unfolding of Marx's categories in *Capital* parallels what he presents in the *Grundrisse*. In the latter, he characterizes a possible postcapitalist society in terms of the category of "disposable" time: "on the one side, necessary labour time will be measured by the needs of the social individual, and, on the other, the development of the power of social production will grow so rapidly that, even though production is now calculated for the wealth of all, *disposable time will grow for all.*"[127] Marx defines "disposable" time as "room for the development of the individual's full productive forces, hence those of society also."[128] This is the positive form taken on by that extra time, freed by the forces of production, which under advanced capitalism remains bound as "superfluous." The category of superfluous time expresses only negativity—the historical nonnecessity of a previous historical necessity—and therefore still refers to the Subject: society in general in its alienated form. The category of disposable time reverses this negativity and gives it a new referent: the social individual.[129] It presupposes the abolition of the value form of social mediation: only then, according to Marx, can (nonalienated) labor time and disposable time complement one another positively as constitutive of the social individual. Overcoming capitalism, then, would entail the transformation not only of the structure and character of social labor but also of nonworking time, and of their relation. In the absence of the abolition of value, however, any extra time generated as a result of the reduction of the workday is determined negatively by Marx, as the antithesis of (alienated) labor time, as what we would call "leisure time": *"Labour time as the measure of wealth* posits wealth itself as founded on poverty, and disposable time as existing *in and because of the antithesis to surplus labour time.*"[130]

The trajectory of capitalist production as presented by Marx can be viewed, then, in terms of the development of the social division of time—from socially necessary (individually necessary and surplus), through socially necessary and superfluous, to the possibility of socially necessary and disposable (which would entail overcoming the older form of necessity). This trajectory expresses the dialectical development of capitalism, of an alienated form of society constituted as a richly developed totality at the expense of the individuals, which gives rise to the possibility of its own negation, a new form of society in which people, singly and collectively, can appropriate the species-general capacities that had been constituted in alienated form as attributes of the Subject.

The development of the social division of time is in Marx's analysis a function of the complex dialectic of the two dimensions of capitalism's underlying structuring forms. As I have argued, by grounding capitalism's directional dynamic in the twofold character of the fundamental structures of this society, Marx breaks with any notion of a single transhistorical human history with an immanent principle of development; further, he demonstrates

---

127. Ibid., p. 708.
128. Ibid.
129. For a discussion of disposable time which focuses on a possible system of rotational employment, see Becker, *Marxian Political Economy,* p. 263ff.
130. *Grundrisse,* p. 708.

that this directional dynamic cannot be taken for granted but must itself be grounded by a theory of social constitution. Within the framework of this interpretation, the emergence of capitalism can be seen as an ever-less random development with the rise and full unfolding of the commodity form—but not as the unfolding of an immanent principle of necessity. The history of the capitalist social formation, however, does have an immanent, as opposed to a retrospective, logic, according to Marx; as a result of its form of social mediation, capitalism is marked by a form of historical necessity. Yet the dialectic of its underlying social forms is such that capitalism points beyond itself to the possibility of a future society based on a different form of social mediation, one that would be neither quasi-objectively constituted nor traditionally given. Marx's analysis implies that a society so constituted would allow people a greater degree of freedom over their lives, individually as well as collectively, and could be considered a situation of historical freedom. To the degree that one can speak of a notion of human history in Marx's mature works, then, it is not in terms of a single transhistorical principle; rather, it refers to a movement, initially contingent, from various histories to History— to a necessary, increasingly global, directional dynamic constituted by alienated social forms which is structured in a way that it points toward the possibility of historical freedom, toward the possibility of a future society free from any quasi-objective directional logic of development.

The specificity of capitalism's dialectical dynamic, as analyzed by Marx, entails a relationship of past, present, and future very different from that implied by any linear notion of historical development. The dialectic of objectified present time and objectified historical time can be summarized as follows: In capitalism, objectified historical time is accumulated in alienated form, reinforcing the present, and, as such, it dominates the living. Yet, it also allows for people's liberation from the present by undermining its necessary moment, thereby making possible the future—the appropriation of history such that the older relations are reversed and transcended. Instead of a social form structured by the present, by abstract labor time, there can be a social form based upon the full utilization of a history alienated no longer, both for society in general and for the individual.[131]

For Marx, then, the historical movement of capitalism, driven forward by social conflicts structured by the dialectic of labor and of time, can be expressed in terms of the development of the social division of time, and results in the possibility that the social meaning of time be transformed: "The measure of

---

131. One could draw a parallel between this understanding of the capitalist social formation's history and Freud's notion of individual history, where the past does not appear as such, but, rather, in a veiled, internalized form that dominates the present. The task of psychoanalysis is to unveil the past in such a way that its appropriation becomes possible. The necessary moment of a compulsively repetitive present can thereby be overcome, which allows the individual to move into the future.

wealth is then not any longer, in any way, labour time, but rather disposable time.''[132]

Realms of necessity

I have shown that Marx's mature critical theory is based on an analysis of the historically specific role of labor in capitalism as constituting the peculiar, quasi-objective mode of social mediation that structures this society. Yet several commonly cited passages in Volume 3 of *Capital* seem to call into question some central propositions of the interpretation presented here—in particular, that over-coming capitalism would involve overcoming value, a self-mediating form of wealth, and, relatedly, alienated labor. I shall therefore close this chapter and, with it, this stage of the investigation, by considering these passages in light of what I have developed thus far, in order to show that they actually are consistent with my interpretation.

Central to my reading has been the argument that value is a determinate form of wealth, historically specific to capitalism, and that it is temporally determined. One aspect of the abstract form of social domination constituted by labor as a socially mediating activity was shown to be the sort of objective necessity exerted by the form of abstract time. In Volume 3 of *Capital,* however, it seems as if Marx maintains that, even after the overcoming of capitalism, such a temporal determination of wealth would be retained:

After the abolition of the capitalist mode of production, but still retaining social production, the determination of value continues to prevail in the sense that the regulation of labour time and the distribution of social labour among the various production groups, ultimately the bookkeeping encompassing all this, become more essential than ever.[133]

Despite Marx's use of the term "value" at this point in his posthumously published manuscript, his statement that the regulation of labor time would remain important in a (technologically developed, globally interdependent) postcapitalist society should be distinguished from the notion that value would remain the form of wealth. I can begin to clarify this distinction by turning to a passage in the *Grundrisse* where he addresses the same question of the role of the regulation of labor time expenditure in a postcapitalist society:

Thus, economy of time, along with the planned distribution of labour time among the various branches of production, remains the first economic law on the basis of communal production. It becomes law, there, to an even higher degree. However, this is essentially different from a measurement of exchange-values (labour or products) by labour time. The labour of individuals in the same *branch of work,* and the various kinds of work, are different from one another not only quantitatively but also qualitatively. What does

132. *Grundrisse,* p. 708.
133. *Capital,* vol. 3, p. 851.

a solely *quantitative* difference between things presuppose? The identity of their qualities. Hence, the quantitative measure of labours presupposes the equivalence, the identity of their quality.[134]

It is significant that Marx explicitly distinguishes the "planned distribution of labour time" from the "measurement of exchange-value by labour time," which he then discusses in terms of the qualitative equation of various kinds of labors. The difference between the two is that the form of wealth based on labor time expenditure is related intrinsically to a quasi-objective form of social mediation, according to Marx. In such a situation, time is not a descriptive measure, but has become a quasi-independent objective norm. *This* grounds the dialectic of labor and time and, hence, the logic of development and form of material production that characterize capitalism in Marx's analysis. This dialectic, and the forms of abstract social necessity related to it, are functions not of an economy of time as such but of the temporal form of wealth. By the same token, not every economy of time implies a self-mediating form of wealth. Marx clearly distinguishes the two.

Marx's statement that considerations of labor time would remain important in a postcapitalist society does not, therefore, mean that the form of wealth itself would be temporal rather than material. On the contrary, it is another example of his thesis that what was constituted historically in an alienated form that dominates people—in this case, the economy of time—could be transformed and controlled by people for their benefit, were the labor-constituted mode of mediation abolished. These passages, then, do not contravene my assertion that the distinction between value and material wealth, and the notion that overcoming capitalism entails the abolition of the former form of wealth and its supersession by the latter, are central to Marx's critical analysis. As he notes in Volume 3 of *Capital*, several pages prior to the passage cited above,

it depends upon the productivity of labour how much use-value is produced in a definite time, hence also in a definite surplus labour-time. The real wealth of society, and the possibility of constantly expanding its reproduction process, therefore, do not depend upon the duration of surplus-labour, but upon its productivity and the more or less copious conditions of production under which it is performed.[135]

This passage shows clearly that Marx thought the form of wealth in a postcapitalist society would be material wealth. Although an economy of time would remain important, this time presumably would be descriptive. Within the framework of Marx's analysis, as I have presented it, the differences between such a socioeconomic order and one dominated by the temporal form of wealth would be considerable. In the postcapitalist society constituted as a determinate possibility by the trajectory of capital, increases in social wealth could be di-

134. *Grundrisse,* p. 173.
135. *Capital,* vol. 3, p. 820 (translation amended).

rectly proportional to increases in productivity—hence, the relation between considerations of time expenditure and wealth production could be essentially different than in a situation where value is the social form of wealth. Moreover, because the process of production no longer would possess a double character as a labor process and a valorization process, it would not necessarily be based on the extraction of labor time from the workers; nor would its form be molded structurally by the necessary role of direct human labor in production as the essential source of wealth (in the form of value). Hence, the process of production could be fundamentally transformed. As I have shown, the dialectic of capital, in Marx's analysis, points to the possibility that the previously necessary presupposition of social wealth could be overcome—that humanity, as it were, could free itself from Adam's curse.[136]

Marx's notion of a possible postcapitalist economy of time, therefore, and his analysis of capitalism in terms of a temporal form of wealth are not identical and should be distinguished. The trajectory of capitalist development, as he analyzes it, implies both that a possible postcapitalist society would be based on material wealth, and that it would also be characterized by an economy of time. In short, as Paul Mattick noted, when Marx refers to value in the passage from Volume 3 cited at the beginning of this section, "the term value in this connection is a mere manner of speech."[137]

Just as one must distinguish between an economy of time and the domination of time, in Marx's mature theory, one must also, in considering the relation between labor and social necessity, distinguish between transhistorical social necessity and historically determinate social necessity. An example of the former sort of necessity, for Marx, is that some form of concrete labor, however determined, is necessary to mediate the material interactions of humans and nature and, hence, to maintain human social life. Some such activity, according to Marx, is a necessary condition of human existence in all forms of society.[138] Marx's implicit notion of the latter sort of necessity, according to my interpretation, refers to the sorts of abstract, impersonal compulsions exerted by capitalism's objectified, alienated forms of social relations that ultimately are constituted by labor as a socially mediating activity. His analyses of the trajectory of capitalist production and the historical constitution of tremendous productive capacities as capital can also be described in terms of the development

---

136. The emphasis on the overcoming of alienated labor as a condition of human emancipation is central to the thought of Herbert Marcuse, who was one of the first to recognize the significance of both the *Economic and Philosophic Manuscripts of 1844* and the *Grundrisse*. Because the historical dimension of Marcuse's analyses has sometimes been overlooked, his positions have been attributed a higher degree of romanticism than is the case. See Herbert Marcuse, "The Foundation of Historical Materialism," in *From Luther to Popper,* trans. Joris De Bres (London, 1972), pp. 3–48; and *One-Dimensional Man* (Boston, 1964).

137. Mattick, *Marx and Keynes: The Limits of the Mixed Economy* (Boston, 1969), p. 31.

138. *Capital,* vol. 1, p. 133.

of this second form of social necessity. The historical development of capitalism, then, of a society based upon an abstract, quasi-natural form of social domination, entailed not only the supersession of direct, personal forms of social domination but also the partial overcoming of the domination of humans by nature. In other words, to the degree that, with the development of capitalism, humanity freed itself from its overwhelming dependence on the vagaries of its natural environment, it did so by the non-conscious and unintentional creation of a quasi-natural structure of domination constituted by labor, a sort of "second nature"; it overcame the domination of the first, of the natural environment, at the price of constituting the domination of this second nature.

As a result of its dual character, then, commodity-determined labor, in Marx's analysis, is bound to two different forms of necessity, one transhistorical, and one specific to capitalism. This should be borne in mind when one considers the following frequently cited passage from Volume 3 of *Capital:*

> The realm of freedom actually begins only where labour, which is determined by necessity and external goals, ceases; thus in the very nature of things it lies beyond the sphere of actual material production. . . . Freedom in this field can only consist in socialized humans, the associated producers, rationally regulating their material interchange with Nature, bringing it under their common control, instead of being ruled by it as by a blind force; and achieving this with the least expenditure of energy and under conditions most favorable to, and worthy of, their human nature. But it nonetheless remains a realm of necessity. Beyond it begins that development of human power, which is an end in itself, the true realm of freedom, which, however, can blossom forth only with this realm of necessity as its basis.[139]

This passage refers to two different sorts of freedom—that from transhistorical social necessity and that from historically determinate social necessity. The "true realm of freedom" refers to the first form of freedom. Freedom from *any* form of necessity must necessarily begin outside of the sphere of production. There can, however, be a form of freedom within this sphere as well, according to Marx: the associated producers can control their labor rather than being controlled by it. In terms of what I have developed thus far, it is clear that he is not referring here to control over production in any narrow sense but to the transformation of the structure of social production and the abolition of the abstract form of domination rooted in commodity-determined labor—that is, to the abolition of historically determinate social necessity. We have seen that, for Marx, overcoming the value form of social relations would mean overcoming alienated social necessity. Humanity could thereby free itself from the sorts of quasi-natural social compulsions discussed above, for example, the form of runaway productivity associated with capital accumulation and the increasing fragmentation of labor—in short, the various aspects of social and historical automatism. In Marx's view, then, the abolition of alienated labor would entail

---

139. *Capital,* vol. 3, p. 820 (translation amended).

overcoming historical necessity, the historically specific social necessity consti- tuted in the capitalist sphere of production; it would allow for historical freedom. ''Historical freedom'' can be used to characterize Marx's conception of a society in which people are free of alien social domination, whether its form is personal or abstract, and in which it would be possible for the associated individuals to make their own history.

In Marx's conception, historical freedom involves the liberation from histor- ically determinate social necessity and allows for an expansion of the ''true realm of freedom.'' However, it does not and cannot entail freedom on a total social level from any sort of necessity: society, for Marx, cannot be based on absolute freedom. One remaining constraint is nature. Although the labor of individuals need not be a necessary means for acquiring means of consumption, *some* form of social production is a necessary precondition of human social existence. The form and extent of this transhistorical, ''natural,'' social necessity can be historically modified; this necessity itself, however, cannot be abolished. Even when direct human labor in production no longer would be the primary source of social wealth, and society no longer would be structured by a quasi- objective form of social mediation constituted by labor, social labor would have to be performed, according to Marx. For this reason, as I noted early in this work, he maintains that, however playful individual labor may become, labor on a socially general level can never acquire the character of pure play.

The abolition of alienated labor, implied by Marx's analysis of capitalism, does not, then, signify the abolition of the necessity of all forms of social labor, although the character of such labor, the amount of labor time (and life time) required, and the various possible modes by which the social distribution of labor could be effected could be considerably different than in a society domi- nated by historical necessity. Within the framework of Marx's analysis, then, the continued existence of the necessity of labor as a condition of human social life should not be identified with alienation, with the abstract forms of labor- constituted social domination I have analyzed. The former necessity is rooted in human life itself—in the circumstance that humans are part of nature, but are so mediately, inasmuch as they also regulate their ''metabolism'' with their natural environment by means of labor.

There is an additional aspect of the last passage quoted that deserves mention. That the labor-mediated interaction between humanity and nature is a necessary precondition of human social life highlights one dimension of Marx's critique of capitalism which usually is overlooked. We have seen that, according to Marx, material wealth is constituted by (concrete) labor and nature, but value is a function of (abstract) labor alone. As self-valorizing value, capital consumes material nature to produce material wealth—not as an end, however, but as a means of expanding surplus-value, of extracting and absorbing as much surplus labor time from the working population as possible. This transformation of mat- ter into units of objectified time is a one-way, rather than a cyclical, process of productive consumption. In this respect, capital-determined production is like slash-and-burn agriculture on a "higher" level; it consumes the sources of material wealth and then moves on. Capitalist production, in Marx's words, "only develops the techniques and the degree of combination of the social process of production by simultaneously undermining the basic sources of all wealth—the earth and the worker."[140] The enormous increases in productivity induced and required by capital are due precisely to the fact that the creation of more material wealth is not an end but a means of lowering necessary labor time. One consequence of the value form, then, is that capital is characterized by a movement toward boundless expansion; as we have seen capitalist production is for the sake of production. This accelerating drive of capital is a function of a form of wealth based on the expenditure of direct labor time. We have seen that this basis becomes less significant and ever-narrower as a source of material wealth, while remaining necessary as a source of value, according to Marx. The boundless strivings of capital and its narrow basis are tied to each other, yet this is not manifest. The dream implied by the capital form is one of utter boundlessness, a fantasy of freedom as the complete liberation from matter, from nature. This "dream of capital" is becoming the nightmare of that from which it strives to free itself—the planet and its inhabitants.

Humanity can fully awaken from this somnambulistic state only by abolishing value. This abolition would entail abolishing the necessity for productivity to be constantly increased in the form discussed above, and would allow for a different structure of labor, a higher degree of control by people over their lives, and a more consciously controlled relationship with the natural environment. Marx's assertion that some form of labor is a transhistorical social necessity is a critique of conceptions of absolute freedom, a critique based on a recognition of the boundedness of humanity as a mediate part of nature. It suggests that a situation of historical freedom would also allow for a consciously regulated process of interaction with nature, a relationship with nature that should not be understood in terms of the romanticized "harmony" that expresses the subjection of humanity to the blind forces of nature, or the "freedom" that entails the blind subjugation of nature.

Marx's critical theory frequently has been criticized as "Promethean," as a theory based on the dangerously utopian proposition that people can shape their world as they choose. The analysis of modern society in terms of labor-mediated social relations presented in this work calls into question one assumption such criticisms make—namely, that whether people shape their world around them is a matter of choice. Marx's analysis can be understood as a very powerful and sophisticated attempt to show that, with the development of the commodity as a total social form, people already "make" the world around them. This indicates retrospectively that people earlier also constituted their world; the form in

---

140. *Capital,* vol. 1, p. 638 (translation amended).

which people make the world under capitalism, however, is very different from earlier forms of social constitution. The modern, capitalist world, according to Marx, is constituted by labor, and this process of social constitution is such that people are controlled by what they make. Marx analyzes capital as the alienated form of historically constituted, species-general knowledge and skills and, hence, grasps its increasingly destructive movement toward boundlessness as a movement of objectified human capacities that have become independent of human control. In terms of what I have developed in this work, Marx's conception of the overcoming of capitalism can be understood in terms of people gaining control over such quasi-objective developments, over processes of ongoing and accelerating social transformation, which they themselves have constituted. Within such a framework, then, the issue is not so much whether people should try to shape their world—they already are doing so. Rather, the issue is the way in which they shape their world and, hence, the nature of this world and its trajectory.

10. Concluding considerations

The purpose of this work has been to reinterpret Marx's mature critical theory by closely examining its most basic categories and, on this basis, to begin reconceptualizing the nature of capitalist society. An important concern of this reinterpretation has been to show the extent to which significant differences exist between Marx's theory and traditional Marxist interpretations. Indeed, I have shown that Marx's theory can provide a powerful critique of such interpretations, one that embeds them socially by analyzing them with the same categories with which it critically analyzes capitalism. This reinterpretation of Marx's analysis, in other words, allows for a critique of traditional Marxism that, at the same time, expresses another critical theory of capitalism. It also transforms the terms of discourse between Marxian theory and other sorts of social theory.

The key to the reinterpretation of Marx's theory developed here has been the distinction between a critique of capitalism from the standpoint of "labor," traditionally understood, and one based on a critical analysis of the historically determinate character of labor in capitalism. My investigation has shown that the former conception lies at the heart of traditional Marxism, and that the Marxian analysis should not be understood in these terms. We have seen that Marx's analysis of the historically unique character of labor as a socially mediating activity in capitalism is central to his investigation of the social relations and forms of subjectivity that characterize this society. According to Marx, the dual function of labor in capitalism as abstract labor and as concrete labor, as an activity that mediates people's relations with one another and with nature, constitutes the fundamental structuring form of social life in capitalism—the commodity. He treats the commodity as a socially constituted and constituting form—"subjective" as well as "objective"—of social practice. Marx's theory of the centrality of labor to social life in capitalism, then, is a theory of the specific nature of the form of social mediation in this society—one that is constituted by labor and has a quasi-objective character—rather than a theory of the necessary social primacy of the labor-mediated interactions of humans with nature. This focus on social mediation, rather than on "labor" (or class), means that Marx's social theory of knowledge, relating labor and consciousness, should be understood as one that grasps forms of social mediation (constituted by structured forms of practice) and forms of subjectivity as intrinsically related. Such

385

a theory has nothing in common with a reflection theory of knowledge or with the notion that thought is "superstructural." It also contravenes the common identification of a "materialist" theory of subjectivity with a theory of interests alone.

My investigation has shown that, on the basis of his conception of the twofold character of the commodity form of social mediation, Marx reconstructs the fundamental features of capitalist society. His categorial analysis characterizes modern social life in terms of several salient features, which it tries to interrelate and ground socially. These features include the quasi-objective, "necessary" character of social domination—that is, the impersonal, abstract, and pervasive nature of a form of power with no real personal or concrete institutional locus— the ongoing directional dynamic of modern society, and its labor-mediated form of interdependence and of individual material reproduction. At the same time, Marx's categorial analysis seeks to explain some of the apparent anomalies of modern social life as intrinsic aspects of its structuring social forms: the continued production of poverty in the midst of plenty, the apparently paradoxical effects of labor-saving and time-saving technology on the organization of social labor and social time, and the degree to which social life is controlled by abstract and impersonal forces despite the growing potential ability of people to control their social and natural environment.

Thus, Marx's analysis of the commodity as the contradictory unity of both abstract and concrete labor, value and material wealth, is central to his conception of capitalism and of what its abolition would entail. It provides the conceptual basis for the dialectic of transformation and reconstitution outlined above, and thereby allows for a critical social and historical analysis of the form of economic growth, the nature and trajectory of production, distribution and administration, and the nature of work in capitalist society. Marx's basic categories not only ground a social analysis of these fundamental features of capitalist society, but do so in a way that relates them intrinsically to a growing gap that separates the powerlessness and fragmentation of individual labor and existence from the power and richness of the social totality. My investigation of Marx's analysis of the sphere of production has demonstrated that his critique of this opposition between the social totality and individuals is not simply a critique of historical processes of social "differentiation" per se, undertaken from the standpoint of a romanticized conception of the immediate unity of individual and society. Rather, his critique is based on an analysis of the specificity of this opposition in capitalism. He analyzes it as a function of the alienated form in which socially general human capacities and knowledge are historically constituted in capitalism, and explains this alienated form in terms of the nature of labor-mediated social relations. On the basis of his analysis of capital, then, Marx provides a powerful critique of the specific character of the opposition constituted in capitalist society between an objectified general social dimension and individuals. He thereby contravenes the notion that this opposition, as it is materialized in the form of capitalist industrial production, for example, is a necessary concomitant of any technologically advanced mode of production based on a highly developed social division of labor. In this way, his analysis suggests the possibility of a fundamentally different mode of "differentiation."

The historical development of capitalist society, according to this approach, is socially constituted, nonlinear and nonevolutionary. It is neither contingent and random, as historical change might be in other forms of societies, nor a transhistorical evolutionary or dialectical development; rather, it is a historically specific dialectical development that originates as a result of particular and contingent historical circumstances but then becomes abstractly universal and necessary. This historical dialectic entails ongoing and accelerating processes of the transformation of all aspects of social life, on the one hand, and the ongoing reconstitution of the most fundamental structural features of capitalism, on the other. It is important for our purposes to recall that the dialectic of transformation and reconstitution, in Marx's analysis, is grounded ultimately in the difference between value and material wealth, that is, in the double character of the constituting social mediation of capitalism. Although the market may serve as the means by which that dialectic is generalized in bourgeois capitalism, the dialectic itself cannot be explained completely in terms of bourgeois relations of distribution.

In Marx's analysis, then, the twofold character of labor, rather than the market and private ownership of the means of production, constitutes the essential core of capitalism. His presentation of the trajectory of production, for example, indicates that bourgeois relations of distribution had been of central significance in the early development of capitalism; once that society is fully developed, however, these relations become less structurally central. Indeed, my investigation has shown that an exclusive focus on those bourgeois aspects of capitalism can veil the crucial significance in Marx's analysis of the distinctions between abstract and concrete labor, value and material wealth.

A "labor theory of wealth," for example, may be able theoretically to ground class exploitation; a theory that emphasizes that production in capitalism is for the sake of profit, rather than use, may be able to show how this goal engenders the introduction of technical innovations in production; and a traditional Marxist approach may be able to provide an account of the crisis-ridden character of the capitalist process of social reproduction. However, all of these theoretical goals can be achieved while ignoring the fundamental distinctions that Marx introduces at the beginning of his exposition. As I have shown, though, Marx's theory also entails a critique of the character of economic growth in capitalism and of the nature and trajectory of the capitalist process of production, its intrinsic opposition between objectified socially general knowledge and living labor. This critique, which is also one of the quasi-objective and directionally dynamic character of social compulsion in capitalism and the structuring of the social universe in terms of an opposition of abstract and concrete dimensions, is based ultimately on Marx's critical analysis of the double character of labor in capitalism. It is very different than a critique of capitalism from the standpoint of "labor," transhistorically understood.

Moreover, Marx's analysis of capital treats the concept of totality in a way that is at odds with traditional Marxism as well as with many current criticisms of Marxism. We have seen that the Marxian theory analyzes capital as a social totality, as an alienated form that ultimately is constituted by the labor-mediated form of social relations. Hence, it entails a critique of the social totality. It does not affirm totality in the manner of traditional Marxism, as that which is to be realized in socialism once the particularism of bourgeois society is overcome. Unlike many current positions that also critically associate totality with domination, however, the Marxian theory does not deny its social existence; rather, this theory analyzes totality as a function of the dominant form of social mediation, and seeks to indicate the possibility of its overcoming. Within the framework of such an approach, both the affirmation of totality and the denial of its existence serve to maintain the domination of capital.

The differences between the Marxian critique and traditional Marxism are, then, considerable. Indeed, the two are in many respects opposed; much of what is affirmed by the latter is grasped critically by the former. Thus, we have seen that Marx's theory does not consider class relations, structured by private ownership and the market, to be the social relations most fundamental to capitalism. Similarly, the critical thrust of his categories of value and surplus value is not simply to ground a theory of exploitation. Marx's theory neither affirms the capitalist process of production in order to criticize the patterns of capitalist distribution, nor implies that the proletariat is the revolutionary Subject that will realize itself in a future socialist society. For Marx, the intrinsic contradiction of capitalist society is neither, structurally, between capitalist relations and industrial production, nor, socially, between the capitalist class and the working class—with the second term in each case taken to be intrinsically independent of capitalism, pointing toward a possible socialist future. On a more general level, Marx's theory does not assert that labor is the transhistorical structuring principle of social life; it does not grasp the constitution of social life in terms of a subject-object dialectic that is mediated by (concrete) labor. Indeed, it provides *no* transhistorical theory of labor, class, history, or the nature of social life itself.

My investigation of the categories of Marx's self-reflexive critique has revealed a conception of the nature of capitalism and its overcoming very different from that of traditional Marxist interpretations. We have seen that labor in capitalism, far from being the *standpoint* of Marx's critique, is its *object*. In his mature theory, the critique of exploitation and the market is embedded within the framework of a far more fundamental critique, in which the constituting centrality of labor in capitalism is analyzed as the ultimate ground for the abstract structures of domination, the increasing fragmentation of individual labor and individual existence, and the blind runaway developmental logic of capitalist society and large-scale organizations that increasingly subsume people. This critique analyzes the working class as an integral element of capitalism rather than as the embodiment of its negation. By pointing to the possible overcoming of value, the Marxian critique points to the possible overcoming of the structures of abstract compulsion characteristic of capitalism, the possible abolition of proletarian labor, and the possibility of a different organization of production, while suggesting that they are related intrinsically.

At the beginning of this work, I suggested that the historical developments of the past half-century—such as the development and more recent crisis of state-interventionist postliberal capitalism, the rise and subsequent collapse of "actually existing socialist" societies, the emergence of new social, economic, and environmental problems on a global scale, and the appearance of new social movements—have made clear the inadequacies of traditional Marxism as a critical social theory with emancipatory intent. They demonstrate the need for a fundamental reconceptualization of capitalist society. The Marxian theory, as I have reinterpreted it, could provide a fruitful starting point for such a fundamental rethinking of the nature of capitalism and its possible historical transformation.

Because the approach I have outlined shifts the focus of the critique of capitalism away from an exclusive concern with the market and private property, it could serve as the basis for a critical theory of modern, capitalist society which would be more adequate to postliberal capitalism and could provide a basis for an analysis of "actually existing socialist" societies. I have shown, for example, that the contradiction between the forces and relations of production developed in *Capital* is not essentially one between industrial production and liberal capitalist institutions, and that it does not point toward the realization of the former. Far from providing a critique of the market and private property from the standpoint of industrial production and the proletariat, Marx's theory furnishes the basis for an analysis of the industrial process of production as intrinsically capitalist. The Marxian categories of commodity and capital seek to express the internal organizing principle of large-scale industrial production as well as the quasi-automatic dynamic of capitalism. Moreover, they also provide a point of departure for analyzing postliberal forms outside of the sphere of immediate production, such as collective forms of social organization. Indeed, we saw that the full development of the commodity form actually implies the development of such collective social forms. Recall that the commodity only becomes totalized once labor power becomes commodified; however, the logical determination of labor power as a commodity is realized historically only when workers exercise effective control over that commodity. They can do so, within the framework of Marx's analysis, only as collective commodity owners; the totalization of value requires collective forms of organization.

The Marxian analysis of capitalism, then, is not bound necessarily to liberal capitalism; rather, it implies that the full development of the categorially grasped social forms of capitalism points beyond its liberal phase. Moreover, although this book has focused on the structuring of the process of production, the implications of Marx's categorial analysis extend far beyond the sphere of immediate production. I have shown that his analysis of the structuring of social life by the commodity is not restricted to this sphere: he analyzes the commodity as the most fundamental and general social mediation of capitalist society. I have also shown that Marx conceives of value as a social form that is not manifest but is determining of a deep structural level of modern social existence, and operates behind the backs of the social actors. Value, according to Marx, is constitutive of consciousness and action and, in turn, is constituted by people, although they are unaware of its existence. Its workings, therefore, need not be limited to the sphere of immediate production, where it purportedly is generated. This implies that the analysis I have outlined of the large-scale hierarchical form of organization generated by the commodity and capital, in which people are subsumed as cogs of a rationalized mega-apparatus, is not restricted to the sphere of immediate production.

These considerations suggest that Marx's theory allows for a general critical social analysis of the development of the massive, rationalized, bureaucratic organizations of production and administration characteristic of advanced capitalism on the basis of a systematic analysis of the structuring of social life by the commodity form.[1] In other words, it allows for an analysis that could ground

1. David Harvey also argues that the important transformations in twentieth-century capitalism do not necessarily obviate the Marxian analysis, but can be understood in terms of that analysis: see *The Limits to Capital* (Chicago, 1982), pp. 136–55. Proceeding from the insight that Marx's notion of the equalization of the rate of profit, developed in Volume 3 of *Capital,* depends on the ease with which capital can be moved, Harvey argues that the dramatic changes in the organizational forms of firms in the past century are related to the concentration and centralization of capital. This concentration and centralization was rooted in the law of value, and, conversely, improved the operation of the law of value (pp. 137–41). The rise of large-scale bureaucratically organized capitalist firms proceeded apace with great improvements in transport, communication, and banking techniques—all of which lowered the barriers to competition and facilitated the movement of capital (p. 145). Harvey maintains that managerial coordination does not contradict the law of value. Referring to Alfred Chandler's account of the "managerial revolution" (*The Visible Hand: The Managerial Revolution in American Business* [Cambridge, Mass., 1977]), Harvey claims that, by the turn of the century, the volume of economic activities had reached a level that made administrative coordination more efficient and profitable than market coordination (p. 146). He points out that large firms are able to switch capital and manpower from one line to another very quickly and efficiently. Moreover, since the 1920s, large firms (led by General Motors in the United States) have decentralized internally, according each subdivision financial accountability. Harvey concludes that modern managerial structure has generated a form that has the effect of equalizing the profit rate administratively (pp. 148–49).

The extent to which administrative modes of distributing value (by equalizing the profit rate) presuppose the existence of competition at some level—whether national or international—is a question I cannot address here. Harvey's approach is to argue that although market coordination

socially, and grasp as intrinsically contradictory, what Weber analyzed as the rationalization of all spheres of social life in the modern world.[2]

Such an analysis would not share the fundamental presuppositions underlying the Frankfurt School's analysis of postliberal capitalism as a one-dimensional, completely administered, social universe. My investigation of Marx's analysis of the process of production has shown that his understanding of the contradictory nature of capitalist society is very different than the traditional understanding that informed Friedrich Pollock's attempt to grasp the qualitative changes in twentieth-century capitalism. An analysis based on Marx's theory would grasp as capital-determined and internally contradictory precisely those important qualitative developments that, according to Pollock, indicate that the fundamental contradiction of capitalism has been overcome even though an emancipatory transformation of society has not been achieved.

The interpretation outlined in this work of Marx's conception of the contradictory character of the structuring forms of capitalism, and the dialectic of transformation and reconstitution it implies, also allows—on a very abstract logical level—for an analysis of recent developments that appear to mark a new phase of capitalist development. By recovering the notion of a dialectical historical development on a more essential level than that of the mode of distribution, such an approach is less linear than Pollock's treatment of the supersession of liberal capitalism by state capitalism. It could, therefore, serve as a point of departure for understanding what may be a new transition in the development of capitalism, characterized by a weakening of state-centered forms in the West, and a collapse of state-controlled forms in the East—that is, by the partial reversal of the trend toward growing state control that marked the transition from liberal to organized capitalism. From this perspective, Pollock's analysis of this transition treated as linear what now appears to have been a moment of a more dialectical development. The approach I have presented could be more adequate to that development and could begin to establish the basis for conceptualizing the similar historical trajectories of state-interventionist capitalism and

---

no longer is essential to capitalism, competition does remain central. What changes is the locus of competition—it shifts, for example, to capital markets, where competition is for money capital. This competition is a means by which the discipline of capital can be imposed upon firms as well as states (pp. 150–55). Harvey's approach to the viability of the law of value in the twentieth century is sophisticated and illuminating. Unlike my approach, however, Harvey does not focus on the specificity of value as a temporally determined form of wealth. In considering the process of accumulation for the sake of accumulation in capitalism, he concerns himself primarily with competition and private property, rather than with the distinctions between abstract and concrete labor, value and material wealth. Hence, Harvey does not ground the dynamic of production and its material form in the contradiction I have outlined; similarly, his emphasis on competition leaves unclear how he would analyze "actually existing socialist" societies.

2. Lukács, as we have seen, undertakes such a task in *History and Class Consciousness,* trans. Rodney Livingstone (London, 1971). However, his approach is undermined by his traditional assumptions regarding labor, totality, and the proletariat.

"actually existing socialism" as two quite different variations of a common phase of the global development of capital.

Rethinking the nature of capitalism means reconceptualizing its overcoming. The Marxian theory, as interpreted here, suggests an approach that neither affirms the existent forms of social production and administration as necessary concomitants of "modernity" nor calls for their abolition; instead, it points beyond the opposition of these two positions. We have seen, for example, that Marx does not treat the process of production in technical terms but analyzes it socially, in terms of two social dimensions that, although intertwined in capitalism, conceivably could be separated. As a critical theory of modern society, the Marxian theory analyzes social domination as intrinsic to the process of production and other "institutions" of this society. It does so in a way that does not look yearningly to the past but does distinguish conceptually what is indistinguishable on an immediate, practical level in capitalism—namely, what *is* necessary because of capital for a society with technologically advanced production and a highly developed social division of labor from what *would be* necessary for such a society were capital abolished. Marx's critique of political economy is a critical theory of modernity whose standpoint is not the precapitalist past but the possibilities developed by capitalism which point beyond it. Inasmuch as Marx's critique seeks to ground socially and is critical of the abstract, quasi-objective social relations of capitalism, and the nature of production, work, and the imperatives of growth in that society, it could provide the basis for an analysis of contemporary developments which could address more adequately than has traditional Marxism the sources of many current concerns, dissatisfactions, and aspirations.

This approach, with its understanding of the contradictory character of capitalism, allows one to distinguish among three major forms of socially constituted critique and opposition in capitalism. The first is rooted in what people consider traditional forms, and is directed against the destruction of these forms by capitalism. The second bases itself on the gap between the ideals of modern capitalist society and its reality; this form characterizes a broad range of different movements, ranging from liberal, civil rights movements to working-class movements (once the working class has been constituted). The interpretation I present delineates a third major form of critique and possible opposition—one based on the growing gap between the possibilities generated by capitalism and its actuality. This approach could serve as a fruitful basis for an analysis of the new social movements of recent decades.[3]

---

3. Even on a logically abstract, preliminary level, however, the historical development of values, needs, and concerns that seem to point beyond capitalism should not be interpreted as linear. The transition to a new phase of postliberal capitalism, for example, seems to have reestablished the apparently necessary connection between existing forms of work and individual reproduction, and has helped shift what seems to have been a growing concern with the nature of working activity in the direction of the notion of fulfillment through consumption. See T. J. Jackson Lears,

The Marxian critique, as interpreted here, also implies an approach to the question of the conditions for democracy in a postcapitalist society, which I can only touch upon at this point. First, it provides the basis for an analysis of the social limits to democracy in capitalist society which goes beyond the traditional critique of the gap between formal political equality and concrete social inequality. The traditional position argues that the minimization of the enormous disparities of wealth and power that are rooted in the capitalist relations of distribution is a necessary social condition for the meaningful realization of a democratic political system. In light of what I have presented here, such considerations can be seen to apprehend only one aspect of the social limits to democracy in capitalist society. What also must be grasped are the constraints to democratic self-determination that are imposed by the abstract form of domination rooted in the quasi-objective, totalizing, historically dynamic form of social mediation that constitutes capitalism.

We have seen that, for Marx, this form of social domination shapes the nature of growth, the form of social production and reproduction, and the relations of humans with nature in capitalist society. These processes, however, do not appear to be social at all, so discussion of their transformation can appear to be wildly utopian. Marx's analysis, however, insists that these constraints are social: they neither are technical in nature nor necessary aspects of modernity. Moreover, the forms of compulsion rooted in the commodity and capital are not static but, rather, dynamic. The abolition of this aspect of the capitalist relations of production is not only desirable, according to my reconstruction of the Marxian analysis, but is necessary if humanity is to free itself from a dynamic form of social domination, the effects of which are becoming increasingly destructive.

Unlike many traditional interpretations, moreover, this conception of the social conditions for democratic self-determination need not have statist implications. We have seen that, for Marx, the basic relations of production of capitalism are not equivalent to the market and private property; hence, the supersession of the market and private property by the state would not signify the overcoming of value and capital. Indeed, the term "state capitalism," which Pollock used but could not ground, can be justified to describe a society in which capitalist relations of production continue to exist while bourgeois relations of distribution have been replaced by a state-bureaucratic mode of administration that remains subject to the compulsions and constraints rooted in capital.

The differences between the Marxian and the traditional Marxist approaches in this regard parallel their differences with regard to the issue of social mediation. I have shown that the Marxian critique is of a determinate form of social mediation, constituted by labor; it is not a critique of social mediation per se.

"From Salvation to Self-Realization," in Richard W. Fox and T. J. Jackson Lears, eds., *The Culture of Consumption* (New York, 1983).

Whereas the latter sort of critique tends to equate mediation with the market and points to its replacement by administration, the Marxian critique allows quite readily for the possibility of political modes of mediation in a postcapitalist society—that is, for a conception of a political public sphere in socialism that lies outside of the formal state apparatus.

My intention, however, has not been to elaborate a full theory of the nature, development, and possible overcoming of advanced capitalist society, or to elaborate an approach to "actually existing socialist" societies. This work is preliminary, a work of theoretical clarification and reorientation on a fundamental logical level. My intention here has primarily been to provide as coherent and powerful a reinterpretation of the categorial foundations of the Marxian theory as possible, distinguishing it from traditional Marxism, and suggesting that it may be able to provide the foundation for an adequate critical analysis of the contemporary world. I have elucidated the underpinnings of such an analysis— the basic categories and orientations in terms of which it would seek to grasp capitalism and understand its historical trajectory.

Although this reinterpretation of the basic categories of Marx's mature critical theory renders plausible the notion that his theory could serve as the basis for a powerful critical social theory of the contemporary world, I do not claim to have demonstrated the adequacy of this theory as an analysis of capitalist, or modern, society. My reinterpretation does, however, transform fundamentally the terms with which the question of the adequacy of Marx's categorial analysis must be posed. In general, this question has been discussed within the framework of the traditional interpretation, that is, as if his categories were transhistorical categories of a social critique from the standpoint of "labor," categories of a critical political economy rather than a critique of political economy. Thus, for example, most debates regarding the validity of Marx's "labor theory of value" have considered it as a theory of prices or of exploitation, based on a transhistorical conception of "labor." In the process, they have conflated what I have shown to be distinctions fundamental to Marx's theory, such as those between value and material wealth, abstract labor and concrete labor.[4] The question of the validity of a transhistorical "labor theory of social wealth" is, however, very different than that of the adequacy of a historically specific "labor theory of value." The question of the validity of historically specific, dynamic, and temporally bound categories is quite different than that of categories purported to be valid transhistorically. Moreover, my investigation has revealed that precisely the fundamental distinctions that are conflated in traditional Marxism constitute the basis for Marx's attempt to grasp what he saw as the essential features of capitalist society. In other words, the object of Marx's theory, its

4. For a recent brief overview of such discussions, see Michael W. Macy, "Value Theory and the 'Golden Eggs': Appropriating the Magic of Accumulation," *Sociological Theory* 6, no. 2 (Fall 1988). Macy tries to reformulate Marx's critique of political economy in terms of the concept of alienation, but accepts the transhistorical interpretation of the categories of that critique.

critical focus, is different than that of theories that do not distinguish between value and material wealth. For both reasons, the adequacy of Marx's critical theory cannot properly be evaluated, whether positively or negatively, on the basis of arguments that basically translate its categories into the terms of political economy.

The question of the adequacy of Marx's theory must, then, be formulated in terms of the purported historical specificity of its categories and the nature of its object. We have seen that, with his categorial analysis, Marx attempts to grasp capitalist society in terms of an underlying form of social mediation, constituted by labor, that has a twofold character, and generates a complex directional dialectic. On this basis he seeks to analyze and ground socially what he clearly regards as fundamental characteristics of this form of social life, in a way that shows them to be intrinsically related. These characteristics include the quasi-objective and dynamic nature of social necessity in capitalism, the nature and trajectory of industrial production and of work, the specific pattern of economic growth, and the particular form of exploitation (as well as the changing forms of subjectivity) characteristic of capitalism.

It is with reference to these characteristics of capitalist society that the question ultimately must be posed of the explanatory power of Marx's historically specific categorial analysis. I have examined his analysis of value as a form of wealth and of social mediation; and I have tried to elucidate Marx's argument that, despite appearances, value—which is a function of immediate labor time expenditure—rather than material wealth, is the dominant social form of wealth in capitalism. I have shown how his theory implies that value is reconstituted structurally as the core of capitalism, even as it gives rise to conditions that render it anachronistic—and, therefore, that capitalist society is shaped by the dialectic of the value and use value dimensions of capital and by the shearing pressure between them. In this way, this work is an attempt to clarify the nature and basic contours of Marx's theory of value and its relation to what he saw as capitalism's fundamental characteristics. It has done so, however, only on a preliminary logical level. Such a theory would have to be developed further before one could adequately address the question of its viability.

One important theoretical issue that would have to be examined is the relationship of structure and action. In elucidating the dialectic of transformation and reconstitution at the heart of Marx's analysis of capital, I noted that, as presented, the dialectic grasps only the underlying structural logic of the dynamic. A more complete account would involve investigating further how value is constituted by people and can be operative, although they are unaware of its existence. Marx's analysis implies that, although social actors are unaware of the essential structuring forms of capitalist society, there is a systematic relationship between these forms and social action. What mediates the two is that the underlying social forms (for example, surplus value) appear necessarily in manifest forms (for example, profit) that both express and veil them and serve as the basis for action. As noted, a more complete discussion of this problem would entail reexamining the relationship of Marx's analysis in Volume 1 of *Capital* to that in Volume 3, and would also require investigating whether one can then show that people, acting on the basis of the immediacy of the manifest forms, reconstitute what Marx claims are the underlying social forms of capitalism.

Other aspects of the Marxian analysis would have to be further developed before its explanatory power could be more adequately assessed. For example, in order to explore further the issue of whether the underlying pattern of growth in capitalism can be grasped adequately by the dialectic of what Marx analyzes as the two dimensions of the constituting social mediation of that society, it would be necessary to investigate his analysis of circulation in Volume 2 of *Capital* and his analysis of the interpenetration of circulation and production in Volume 3. One would need to do so, moreover, on the basis of the fundamental distinction, which I have emphasized, between value and material wealth. This would, at the same time, entail rethinking Marx's analysis of the structural basis of crises in capitalism.

Such an analysis would be necessary in order to explore the viability of Marx's categories in grasping the temporal and spatial dimensions of the expansion of capital—that is, the interrelated processes of the qualitative transformation of capitalist society and the changing nature of capitalist globalization. An important starting point for such an undertaking would be the analysis, which I have begun, of Marx's category of value as a structuring category of the organization of large-scale production under conditions of the real subsumption of labor under capital. This analysis, if developed further, could serve as the basis for a more intensive investigation of a problem I have noted several times—the possible relation between the structuring of industrial production by a dialectic of the value and use value dimension of capital, as analyzed by Marx, and the large-scale rationalized and bureaucratized organization of social production and administration in industrial capitalism. Such an investigation would be an important step toward two ends: first, determining whether the Marxian theory could indeed provide the basis for an approach capable of grasping qualitative changes in the nature and development of capitalist society; and second, whether it could serve as basis for an analysis of qualitative historical changes in subjectivity, in forms of thought and sensibilities. In so doing, such an investigation could also serve as the point of departure for analyzing the latest transition of capitalism alluded to above, and could further our understanding of the new social movements of the past decades. The theory of social mediation I have outlined here might also be able to provide the basis for a fruitful reconceptualization of the social constitution and historical transformation of gender and race in capitalist society.

Finally, further elaboration of my reinterpretation would need to address the implications, for any understanding of the possible overcoming of capitalism, of the argument that (according to the logic of Marx's analysis) the proletariat is not the revolutionary Subject.

Such extensions and elaborations of this reinterpretation would be necessary in order to examine further the adequacy of Marx's categorial analysis as the basis for a social theory of contemporary society—to investigate further the explanatory power of Marx's conception of value as a form of wealth and social mediation constituted by abstract labor time expenditure, to examine his notion that value becomes increasingly anachronistic and yet remains structurally central to capitalism, and to evaluate his analysis of the directional dynamic and institutions of capitalism in terms of this intrinsic tension.

I have argued that, although Marx's theory of value—the contention that, despite scientific developments and their technological applications, social wealth in capitalism remains a function of labor time expenditure—seems highly implausible at first glance, it can be judged only in terms of what it attempts to explain. I have sought to indicate that the Marxian theory of value is not one of the constitution and appropriation of a transhistorical form of wealth but, rather, is an attempt to explain in social terms such features of capitalist society as the nature of its historical dynamic and of its mode of production. This reinterpretation, of course, is not a "proof" of Marx's theory of value; it does, however, indicate that the question of its adequacy is not quite as simple as, at first glance, it may have appeared.

In general, then, the plausibility of the Marxian theory, as I have presented it, depends on whether it adequately characterizes the essential features of modern society, and whether its categorial analysis of capitalism's basic social relations adequately explains these features. What is at issue is the question of the nature of capitalism. This question can be conceived, on one level, in terms of the plausibility of the proposition that capitalism and socialism are distinguished not only by the way in which social wealth is appropriated and distributed, but also by the nature of this wealth itself and its mode of production. My investigation has shown the far-reaching ramifications of this latter proposition. I have shown that, within the framework of Marx's analysis, value is a form of wealth that is not extrinsic to production or to other social "institutions" in capitalism but, rather, is intrinsic to them and shapes them; as a form of mediation, it generates a process of ongoing transformation and reconstitution. Socialism, then, cannot be understood as a society with a different mode of appropriating and distributing the same form of social wealth, based on the same form of production; instead, it is determined conceptually as a society in which social wealth has the form of material wealth. Hence, it is conceived of as a very different sort of society, one free from the sorts of socially constituted abstract compulsions (in the form of both abstract time and historical time) that are characteristic of capitalism. This, in turn, implies the possibility of a mode of technologically advanced production and of a highly developed social division of labor that are structured differently than in capitalism. This reformulation of the distinguishing determinations of capitalism and socialism is rich, theoretically powerful, and germane to contemporary conditions—enough so to warrant further serious development of the theoretical approach I have presented here.

In conclusion, it should be noted that the interpretation I have presented here not only calls into question traditional Marxist approaches but also raises issues of significance for social theory in general. I have presented Marx's theory as a self-reflexive, historically determinate theory, as an approach that is conscious of the historical specificity of its categories as well as of its own theoretical form. In addition to being historically determinate, the Marxian critique is a theory of social constitution—the constitution, by a determinate form of social practice, of a historically specific form of social mediation that lies at the core of capitalist society and that is constitutive of forms of social objectivity and subjectivity. On the one hand, it is a theory of the social constitution of a determinate directional dynamic; it explains this dynamic in terms of a process by which historically determinate social practices and historically specific social structures are mutually constituting. By analyzing capitalist society's historically dynamic structures and institutions in terms of a form of mediation constituted by labor, the Marxian theory both accords quasi-independent social reality to such structures and analyzes them as socially constituted (by forms of social practice that, in turn, are molded by those structures). It thereby calls into question, as one-sided, positions that proceed from the social reality of such structures without grasping them as socially constituted, as well as those that emphasize the process of social constitution in a way that dissolves structures of mediation into congeries of present practices.

On the other hand, the Marxian theory is also a social theory of consciousness and subjectivity, one that analyzes social objectivity and subjectivity as intrinsically related; it grasps both in terms of determinate forms of mediation, objectified forms of practice. Even as a social theory of consciousness, however, it is historically specific: Because of its analysis of the specificity of the form of social mediation, the Marxian theory suggests that the contents of consciousness, as well as the form of the social constitution of meaning, are historically specific in capitalism. It implies that meaning is not necessarily constituted in the same way in all societies, and thereby calls into question transhistorical and transcultural theories of the constitution of meaning and, hence, of "culture."

What gives Marx's theory of social constitution its power is precisely that it is historically determinate. Marx does not present it as a general, indeterminate theory with purported universal applicability but, rather, in a form that is inseparable from the basic social forms constitutive of capitalist society. This mode of presentation itself provides a powerful, if implicit, critique of any theoretical approach that universalizes what was unfolded by Marx in a theoretically rigorous manner as a determinate aspect of capitalist society—including the theory of this society.

Marx's analysis of modern society as capitalist, then, is a theoretically sophisticated attempt to grasp this society from the viewpoint of its possible transformation by means of a socially self-reflexive, historically determinate theory of social constitution. We have seen, for example, that Marx's category of capital can ground socially the directional dynamic of capitalist society, the character of economic "growth," and the nature and trajectory of the production process in capitalism. His analysis implicitly demands of other theoretical positions that they provide a social account of these features of capitalist society. It does so, moreover, in a way that questions any approach that treats industrial production solely in technical terms, as well as those that either simply presuppose the existence of history or hypostatize as a transhistorical development what the Marxian theory analyzes as a socially constituted, historically specific form of history. More generally, Marx's approach implicitly is critical of all transhistorical theories, as well as of theories that address either social structures or social practices without grasping their interrelations.

The question of the adequacy of Marx's theory, then, is not only a question of the viability of his categorial analysis of capitalism. It also raises more general questions regarding the nature of social theory. Marx's critical theory, which grasps capitalist society by means of a theory of the constitution by labor of a directionally dynamic, totalizing mediation that is historically specific, is a brilliant analysis of this society; and it is, at the same time, a powerful argument regarding the nature of an adequate social theory.

Selected bibliography

Works by Marx (in German)

Sources used which appear in *Marx-Engels Werke* (*MEW*), Berlin, 1956–1968
Marx, Karl. *Briefwechsel*, vols. 27–39.
  Das Elend der Philosophie, vol. 4.
  Das Kapital 1–3, vols. 23–25.
  Der achtzehnte Brumaire des Louis Bonaparte, vol. 8.
  Kritik des Gothaer Programms, vol. 19.
  Lohn, Preis, Profit, vol. 16.
  Lohnarbeit und Kapital, vol. 6.
  Ökonomisch-Philosophische Manuskripte, supplementary vol. 1.
  Randglossen zu Adolf Wagners "Lehrbuch der politischen Ökonomie", vol. 19.
  Theorien über den Mehrwert, 1–3, vols. 26.1–26.3.
  Thesen über Feuerbach, vol. 3.
  Zur Judenfrage, vol. 1.
  Zur Kritik der Hegelschen Rechtsphilosophie, vol. 1.
  Zur Kritik der Hegelschen Rechtsphilosophie: Einleitung, vol. 1.
  Zur Kritik der politischen Ökonomie, vol. 13.
Marx, Karl, and Friedrich Engels. *Die Deutsche Ideologie*, vol. 3.
  Die Heilige Familie, vol. 2.
  Manifest der Kommunistischen Partei, vol. 4.

Other sources used
"Fragment des Urtextes von *Zur Kritik der politischen Ökonomie*." In *Grundrisse der Kritik der politischen Ökonomie*. Berlin, 1953.
Grundrisse der Kritik der politischen Ökonomie. Berlin, 1953.
Resultate des unmittelbaren Produktionsprozesses. Frankfurt, 1969.
"Ware und Geld." *Das Kapital*, vol. 1, 1st ed. In *Marx-Engels Studienausgabe*, vol. 2, edited by Iring Fetscher. Frankfurt, 1966.

Works by Marx (in English)

Marx, Karl. *Capital*, vol. 1. Translated by Ben Fowkes. London, 1976.
  Capital, vol. 2. Translated by David Fernbach. London, 1978.
  Capital, vol. 3. Translated by David Fernbach. Harmondsworth, England, 1981.
  "Contribution to the Critique of Hegel's Philosophy of Law." In Karl Marx and Frederick Engels, *Collected Works*, vol. 3: *Marx and Engels: 1843–1844*. New York, 1975.
  "Contribution to the Critique of Hegel's Philosophy of Law: Introduction." In Karl Marx and Frederick Engels, *Collected Works*, vol. 3: *Marx and Engels: 1843–1844*. New York, 1975.
  A Contribution to the Critique of Political Economy. Translated by S. W. Ryazanskaya. Moscow, 1970.

"Critique of the Gotha Program." In Karl Marx and Frederick Engels, *Collected Works,* vol. 24: *Marx and Engels: 1874–1883.* New York, 1975.

Economic and Philosophic Manuscripts of 1844. In Karl Marx and Frederick Engels, *Collected Works,* vol. 3: *Marx and Engels: 1843–1844.* New York, 1975.

The Eighteenth Brumaire of Louis Bonaparte. In Karl Marx and Frederick Engels, *Collected Works,* vol. 11: *Marx and Engels: 1851–1853.* New York, 1979.

Grundrisse: Foundations of the Critique of Political Economy. Translated by Martin Nicolaus. London, 1973.

"Marginal Notes on Adolf Wagner's *Lehrbuch der politischen Ökonomie.*" In Karl Marx and Frederick Engels, *Collected Works,* vol. 24: *Marx and Engels: 1874–1883.* New York, 1975.

"On the Jewish Question." In Karl Marx and Frederick Engels, *Collected Works,* vol. 3: *Marx and Engels, 1843–1844.* New York, 1976.

The Poverty of Philosophy. In Karl Marx and Frederick Engels, *Collected Works,* vol. 6: *Marx and Engels: 1845–1848.* New York, 1976.

Results of the Immediate Process of Production. Translated by Rodney Livingstone. In *Capital,* vol. 1 (Fowkes).

Speech at the Anniversary of the *People's Paper,* April 14, 1856. In *The Marx-Engels Reader,* edited by Robert C. Tucker. 2d ed., New York, 1978.

Theories of Surplus Value, part 1. Translated by Emile Burns. Moscow, 1963.

Theories of Surplus Value, part 2. Translated by Renate Simpson. Moscow, 1968.

Theories of Surplus Value, part 3. Translated by Jack Cohen and S. W. Ryazanskaya. Moscow, 1971.

"Theses on Feuerbach." In Karl Marx and Frederick Engels, *Collected Works,* vol. 5: *Marx and Engels: 1845–1847.* New York, 1976.

Value, Price, and Profit. In Karl Marx and Frederick Engels, *Collected Works,* vol. 20: *Marx and Engels: 1864–1868.* New York, 1985.

Wage Labor and Capital. In Karl Marx and Frederick Engels, *Collected Works,* vol. 9: *Marx and Engels: 1849.* New York, 1977.

Marx, Karl, and Frederick Engels. *The German Ideology.* In Karl Marx and Frederick Engels, *Collected Works,* vol. 5: *Marx and Engels: 1845–1847.* New York, 1976.

The Holy Family. In *Writings of the Young Marx on Philosophy and Society,* edited by Lloyd D. Easton and Kurt H. Guddat. Garden City, N.Y., 1967.

Manifesto of the Communist Party. In Karl Marx and Frederick Engels, *Collected Works,* vol. 6: *Marx and Engels: 1845–1848.* New York, 1976.

Other Works

Adorno, Theodor W. *Drei Studien zu Hegel.* Frankfurt, 1970.

"Introduction." In *The Positivist Dispute in German Sociology,* translated by Glyn Adey and David Frisby. London, 1976.

Negative Dialectics. Translated by E. B. Ashton. New York, 1973.

"On the Logic of the Social Sciences." In *The Positivist Dispute in German Sociology,* translated by Glyn Adey and David Frisby. London, 1976.

Spätkapitalismus oder Industriegesellschaft. In *Gesammelte Schriften,* vol. 8. Frankfurt, 1972.

Althusser, Louis. *For Marx.* Translated by Ben Brewster. New York, 1970.

"Lenin Before Hegel." In *Lenin and Philosophy,* translated by Ben Brewster. New York and London, 1971.

Althusser, Louis, and Etienne Balibar. *Reading Capital.* Translated by Ben Brewster. London, 1970.

Anderson, Perry. *Considerations on Western Marxism.* London, 1976.

In the Tracks of Historical Materialism. Chicago and London, 1983.

Arato, Andrew. "Introduction." In *The Essential Frankfurt School Reader,* edited by Andrew Arato and Eike Gebhardt. New York, 1978.

Arato, Andrew, and Paul Breines. *The Young Lukács and the Origins of Western Marxism.* New York, 1979.

Ariès, Philippe. *Centuries of Childhood.* New York, 1962.

Arnason, Jóhann Páll. *Zwischen Natur und Gesellschaft: Studien zu einer Theorie des Subjects.* Frankfurt, 1976.

Aron, Raymond. *Main Currents in Social Thought,* vol. 1. Translated by Richard Howard and Helen Weaver. London, 1965.

Aronowitz, Stanley. *The Crisis in Historical Materialism: Class, Culture, and Politics in Marxist Theory.* New York, 1981.

Avineri, Shlomo. *The Social and Political Thought of Karl Marx.* London, 1968.

Backhaus, H. G. "Materialien zur Rekonstruktion der Marxschen Werttheorie" (Parts 1, 2, 3). In *Gesellschaft: Beiträge zur Marxschen Theorie,* nos. 1, 3, 11. Frankfurt, 1974, 1975, 1978.

"Zur Dialektik der Wertform." In *Beiträge zur Marxistischen Erkenntnistheorie,* edited by A. Schmidt. Frankfurt, 1969.

Bahr, Hans Dieter. *Kritik der politischen Technologie.* Frankfurt, 1970.

Becker, James F. *Marxian Political Economy: An Outline.* Cambridge, 1977.

Beer, Max. *Allgemeine Geschichte des Sozialismus und der sozialen Kämpfe.* Erlangen, 1973.

Bell, Daniel. "The Cultural Contradictions of Capitalism." In *The Cultural Contradictions of Capitalism.* New York, 1978.

Benhabib, Seyla. *Critique, Norm, and Utopia: On the Foundations of Critical Social Theory.* New York, 1986.

Berger, Johannes, and Claus Offe. "Functionalism vs. Rational Choice?" *Theory and Society* 11, no. 4 (1982), pp. 521–26.

Berlin, Isaiah. *Karl Marx: His Life and Environment.* 2d ed. London, 1952.

Bilfinger, Gustav. *Der bürgerliche Tag.* Stuttgart, 1888.

Die babylonische Doppelstunde: Eine chronologische Untersuchung. Stuttgart, 1888.

Die mittelalterlichen Horen und die modernen Stunden. Stuttgart, 1892.

Böhm-Bawerk, Eugen von. "Karl Marx and the Close of His System." In *"Karl Marx and the Close of His System" by Eugen Böhm-Bawerk and "Böhm-Bawerk's Criticism of Marx" by Rudolf Hilferding,* edited by Paul M. Sweezy. New York, 1949.

Bologh, Roslyn Wallach. *Dialectical Phenomenology: Marx's Method.* Boston, London, and Henley, 1979.

Borkenau, Franz. "Zur Soziologie des mechanistischen Weltbildes." *Zeitschrift für Sozialforschung* 1 (1932): 311–35.

Bottomore, Tom. "Introduction." In *Karl Marx.* Oxford, 1973.

"Sociology." In *Marx: The First Hundred Years,* edited by David McLellan. New York, 1983.

Bourdieu, Pierre. *Outline of a Theory of Practice.* Translated by Richard Nice. Cambridge, 1977.

Brandes, Wilhelm. *Alte Japanische Uhren.* Munich, 1984.

Brandt, Gerhard. "Ansichten kritischer Sozialforschung, 1930–1980. Gesellschaftliche Arbeit und Rationalisierung." In *Leviathan,* Sonderheft 4. Opladen, 1981.

"Max Horkheimer und das Projekt einer materialistischen Gesellschaftstheorie." In *Max Horkheimer heute: Werke und Wirkung,* edited by Alfred Schmidt and Norbert Altwicker. Frankfurt, 1986.

Braudel, Fernand. *Capitalism and Material Life, 1400–1800.* New York, 1975.

Braverman, Harry. *Labour and Monopoly Capital: The Degradation of Work in the Twentieth Century.* New York and London, 1974.

Burawoy, Michael. *The Politics of Production.* London, 1989.

Calhoun, Craig. "Industrialization and Social Radicalism." *Theory and Society* 12, no. 4 (1983), pp. 485–504.

"The Radicalism of Tradition." *The American Journal of Sociology* 88, no. 5 (March 1983), pp. 886–914.

Carus-Wilson, Eleanora. "The Woolen Industry." In *The Cambridge Economic History of Europe,* edited by M. Postan and E. E. Rich. Cambridge, 1952.

Castoriadis, Cornelius. *Crossroads in the Labyrinth.* Translated by Kate Soper and Martin H. Ryle. Cambridge, Mass., 1984.

"From Marx to Aristotle, from Aristotle to Marx." *Social Research* 45, no. 4 (Winter 1978), pp. 667–738.

Chandler, Alfred. *The Visible Hand: The Managerial Revolution in American Business.* Cambridge, Mass., 1977.

Cipolla, Carlo M. *Clocks and Culture, 1300–1700.* London, 1967.

Cohen, G. A. "Forces and Relations of Production." In *Analytical Marxism,* edited by J. Roemer. Cambridge, 1986.

Karl Marx's Theory of History: A Defence. Oxford, 1978.

"Marxism and Functional Explanation." In *Analytical Marxism,* edited by J. Roemer. Cambridge, 1986.

Cohen, Jean. *Class and Civil Society: The Limits of Marxian Critical Theory.* Amherst, Mass., 1982.

Colletti, Lucio. "Bernstein and the Marxism of the Second International." In *From Rousseau to Lenin,* translated by John Merrington and Judith White. London, 1972.

Marxism and Hegel. London, 1973.

Cornu, August. *Karl Marx und Friedrich Engels: Leben und Werk.* 3 vols. Berlin, 1954.

Crombie, A. C. "Quantification in Medieval Physics." In *Change in Medieval Society,* edited by Sylvia Thrupp. New York, 1964.

Debord, Guy. *Society of the Spectacle.* Detroit, 1983.

Dobb, Maurice. *Political Economy and Capitalism.* London, 1940.

Dubiel, Helmut. "Einleitung." In *Friedrich Pollock: Stadien des Kapitalismus,* edited by Helmut Dubiel. Munich, 1975.

Theory and Politics: Studies in the Development of Critical Theory. Translated by Benjamin Gregg. Cambridge, Mass., and London, 1985.

Durkheim, Emile. *The Division of Labor in Society.* Translated by George Simpson. New York and London, 1964.

The Elementary Forms of Religious Life. Translated by Joseph Ward Swain. New York, 1965.

Edgley, Roy. "Philosophy." In *Marx: The First Hundred Years,* edited by David McLellan. New York, 1983.

Eisenstadt, S. N. "The Structuring of Social Protest in Modern Societies: The Limits and Direction of Convergence." In *Yearbook of the World Society Foundation,* vol. 2. London, 1992.

Elias, Norbert. *The Civilizing Process.* Translated by Edmund Jephcott. 2 vols. New York, 1978, 1982.

Elson, Diane. "The Value Theory of Labour." In *Value: The Representation of Labour in Capitalism,* edited by D. Elson. London, 1979.

Elster, Jon. "Further Thoughts on Marxism, Functionalism and Game Theory." In *Analytical Marxism,* edited by J. Roemer. Cambridge, 1986.

Making Sense of Marx. Cambridge, 1985.

Euchner, Walter, and Alfred Schmidt, eds. *Kritik der politischen Ökonomie heute: 100 Jahre "Kapital."* Frankfurt, 1968.

Eyerman, Ron, and David Shipway. "Habermas on Work and Culture." *Theory and Society* 10, no. 4 (July 1981), pp. 547–66.

Fetscher, Iring. "The Changing Goals of Socialism in the Twentieth Century." *Social Research* 47 (Spring 1980), pp. 36–62.

"Das Verhältnis des Marxismus zu Hegel." In *Marxismusstudien,* vol. 3. Tübingen, 1960.

Marx and Marxism. Translated by John Hargreaves. New York, 1971.

Überlebensbedingungen der Menschheit. Munich, 1980.

"Vier Thesen zur Geschichtsauffassung bei Hegel und Marx." In *Stuttgarter Hegel-Tage 1970*, edited by H. G. Gadamer. Bonn, 1974.

"Von der Philosophie zur proletarischen Weltanschauung." In *Marxismusstudien*, vol. 2. Tübingen, 1959.

Von Marx zur Sowjetideologie. Frankfurt, Berlin, Bonn, 1957.

ed. *Marx-Engels Studienausgabe*, vol. 2. Frankfurt, 1966.

Foucault, Michel. *Discipline and Punish: The Birth of the Prison*. Translated by Alan Sheridan. New York, 1977.

The Order of Things. New York, 1973.

Fraser, Nancy. "What's Critical about Critical Theory? The Case of Habermas and Gender." *New German Critique* 35 (Spring–Summer 1985), pp. 97–131.

Gaines, Jeremy G. *Critical Aesthetic Theory*. Ph.D. diss., University of Warwick, 1985.

Giddens, Anthony. *Central Problems in Social Theory: Action, Structure, and Contradiction in Social Analysis*. Berkeley and Los Angeles, 1979.

"Commentary on the Debate." *Theory and Society* 11, no. 4 (1982), pp. 527–39.

A Contemporary Critique of Historical Materialism. London and Basingstoke, 1981.

"Labour and Interaction." In *Habermas: Critical Debates*, edited by John B. Thompson and David Held. Cambridge, Mass., 1982.

Godelier, Maurice. *System, Struktur und Widerspruch im "Kapital."* Berlin, 1970.

Gorz, André. *Critique of Economic Reason*. Translated by Gillian Handyside and Chris Turner. London and New York, 1989.

Paths to Paradise: On the Liberation from Work. Translated by Malcolm Imrie. Boston, 1985.

Strategy for Labor: A Radical Proposal. Translated by Martin A. Nicolaus and Victoria Ortiz. Boston, 1967.

Gould, Carol C. *Marx's Social Ontology*. Cambridge, Mass., and London, 1978.

Gouldner, Alvin. *The Two Marxisms: Contradictions and Anomalies in the Development of Theory*. New York, 1980.

Gramsci, Antonio. *Selections from the Prison Notebooks*. Edited and translated by Quentin Hoare and Geoffrey Nowell Smith. New York and London, 1971.

Gross, David. "Time, Space, and Modern Culture." *Telos* 50 (Winter 1981–82), pp. 59–78.

Grossmann, Henryk. *Das Akkumulations- und Zusammenbruchsgesetz des kapitalistischen Systems*. Frankfurt, 1970.

"Die gesellschaftlichen Grundlagen der mechanistischen Philosophie und die Manufaktur." *Zeitschrift für Sozialforschung* 4 (1935), pp. 161–229.

Marx, die klassische Nationalökonomie und das Problem der Dynamik. Frankfurt, 1969.

Gurevich, Aaron J. "Time as a Problem of Cultural History." In *Cultures and Time*, edited by L. Gardet et al. Paris, 1976.

Gurjewitsch, Aaron J. *Das Weltbild des mittelalterlichen Menschen*. Translated by Gabriele Lossack. Munich, 1980.

Habermas, Jürgen. "Between Philosophy and Science: Marxism as Critique." In *Theory and Practice*, translated by John Viertel. Boston, 1973.

Communication and the Evolution of Society. Translated by Thomas McCarthy. Boston, 1979.

Knowledge and Human Interests. Translated by Jeremy Shapiro. Boston, 1971.

"Labor and Interaction: Remarks on Hegel's Jena *Phenomenology of Mind*." In *Theory and Practice*, translated by John Viertel. Boston, 1973.

Legitimation Crisis. Translated by Thomas McCarthy. Boston, 1975.

"A Reply to My Critics." In *Habermas: Critical Debates*, edited by John B. Thompson and David Held. Cambridge, Mass., 1982.

"Technology and Science as 'Ideology.' " In *Towards a Rational Society*, translated by Jeremy J. Shapiro. Boston, 1970.

The Theory of Communicative Action. Volume 1: *Reason and the Rationalization of Society.* Translated by Thomas McCarthy. Boston, 1984.

The Theory of Communicative Action. Volume 2: *Lifeworld and System: A Critique of Functionalist Reason.* Translated by Thomas McCarthy. Boston, 1987.

"Toward a Reconstruction of Historical Materialism." In *Jürgen Habermas on Society and Politics,* edited by Steven Seidman. Boston, 1989.

Harvey, David. *The Condition of Postmodernity: An Enquiry into the Origins of Cultural Change.* Oxford and Cambridge, Mass., 1989.

The Limits to Capital. Chicago, 1982.

Heath, L. R. *The Concept of Time.* Chicago, 1936.

Hegel, G. W. F. *Phänomenologie des Geistes.* Frankfurt, 1970.

"Preface" to the *Phenomenology.* In *Hegel: Texts and Commentary,* edited by Walter Kaufmann. Garden City, N.Y., 1966.

Wissenschaft der Logik. 2 vols. Frankfurt, 1970.

Heilbroner, Robert L. *The Nature and Logic of Capitalism.* New York, 1985.

The Worldly Philosophers: The Lives, Times, and Ideas of the Great Economic Thinkers. 5th ed. New York, 1980.

Held, David. *Introduction to Critical Theory.* London, Melbourne, Sydney, Auckland, Johannesburg, 1980.

Heller, Agnes. *The Theory of Need in Marx.* London, 1976.

Hilferding, Rudolf. "Böhm-Bawerk's Criticism of Marx." In *"Karl Marx and the Close of His System" by Eugen Böhm-Bawerk and "Böhm-Bawerk's Criticism of Marx" by Rudolf Hilferding,* edited by Paul M. Sweezy. New York, 1949.

Finance Capital: A Study of the Latest Phase of Capitalist Development. Edited with an introduction by Tom Bottomore. From translations by Morris Watnick and Sam Gordon. London and Boston, 1981.

Review of *Der soziale Gehalt der Marxschen Werttheorie* by F. Petry. In *Archiv für die Geschichte des Sozialismus und der Arbeiterbewegung,* no. 8, edited by C. Gruenberg. Leipzig, 1919.

"Zur Problemstellung der theoretischen Ökonomie bei Karl Marx." *Die Neue Zeit* 23, no. 1 (1904–1905).

Hirsch, Joachim. *Staatsapparat und Reproduktion des Kapitals.* Frankfurt, 1974.

Hirsch, Joachim, and Roland Roth. *Das neue Gesicht des Kapitalismus.* Hamburg, 1986.

Horkheimer, Max. "The Authoritarian State." In *The Essential Frankfurt School Reader,* edited by Andrew Arato and Eike Gebhardt. New York, 1978.

Dawn and Decline: Notes 1926–1931 and 1950–1969. Translated by Michael Shaw. New York, 1978.

"Die Juden in Europa." *Zeitschrift für Sozialforschung* 8 (1939), pp. 115–36.

The Eclipse of Reason. New York, 1974.

"Traditional and Critical Theory." In *Critical Theory,* translated by Matthew J. O'Connell et al. New York, 1972.

Horkheimer, Max, and Theodor W. Adorno. *Dialectic of Enlightenment.* Translated by John Cumming. New York, 1972.

Howard, Dick. *The Marxian Legacy.* New York, 1977.

Hyppolite, Jean. *Studies on Marx and Hegel.* Translated by John O'Neill. New York, 1969.

Jay, Martin. *The Dialectical Imagination: A History of the Frankfurt School and the Institute for Social Research, 1923–1950.* Boston and Toronto, 1973.

Marxism and Totality: The Adventures of a Concept from Lukács to Habermas. Berkeley and Los Angeles, 1984.

Kant, Immanuel. *Critique of Pure Reason.* Translated by Norman Kemp Smith. New York and Toronto, 1965.

Kaufmann, Walter, ed. *Hegel: Texts and Commentary*. Garden City, N.Y., 1966.

Kautsky, Karl. *Karl Marxs oekonomische Lehren*. Stuttgart, 1906.

Keane, John. "On Tools and Language: Habermas on Work and Interaction." *New German Critique* 6 (Fall 1975), pp. 82–100.

Kellner, Douglas. *Critical Theory, Marxism, and Modernity*. Baltimore, Md., 1989.

Kolakowski, Leszek. *Main Currents of Marxism: Its Rise, Growth, and Dissolution*. 3 vols. Translated by P.S. Falla. Oxford, 1978.

Toward a Marxist Humanism. Translated by Jane Zielonko Peel. New York, 1968.

Korsch, Karl. *Die materialistische Geschichtsauffassung*. Frankfurt, 1971.

Marxism and Philosophy. Translated by Fred Halliday. New York and London, 1970.

Kosik, Karel. *Die Dialektik des Konkreten*. Frankfurt, 1967.

Krahl, Hans Jürgen. *Konstitution und Klassenkampf*. Frankfurt, 1971.

Kulischer, J. *Allgemeine Wirtschaftsgeschichte des Mittelalters und der Neuzeit*. 2 vols. Munich, 1965.

Landes, David S. *Revolution in Time: Clocks and the Making of the Modern World*. Cambridge, Mass., and London, 1983.

Lange, Oskar. "Marxian Economics and Modern Economic Theory." In *Marx and Modern Economics*, edited by David Horowitz. London, 1968.

Lash, Scott, and John Urry. *The End of Organized Capitalism*. Madison, Wisc., 1987.

Lears, T. J. Jackson. "From Salvation to Self-Realization." In *The Culture of Consumption: Critical Essays in American History, 1880–1980,* edited by Richard W. Fox and T. J. Jackson Lears. New York, 1983.

Lefebvre, Henri. *The Sociology of Marx*. Translated by Norbert Guterman. New York, 1969.

Le Goff, Jacques. "Labor Time in the 'Crisis' of the Fourteenth Century." In *Time, Work, and Culture in the Middle Ages,* translated by Arthur Goldhammer. Chicago and London, 1980.

"Merchant's Time and Church's Time in the Middle Ages." In *Time, Work, and Culture in the Middle Ages,* translated by Arthur Goldhammer. Chicago and London, 1980.

Leiss, William. *The Limits to Satisfaction: An Essay on the Problem of Needs and Commodities*. Toronto and Buffalo, 1976.

Lichtheim, Georg. *From Marx to Hegel*. London, 1971.

Marxism: An Historical and Critical Study. New York, 1965.

Lowe, Adolf. "M. Dobb and Marx's Theory of Value." *Modern Quarterly* 1, no. 3 (1938).

Löwith, Karl. *From Hegel to Nietzsche: The Revolution in Nineteenth-Century Thought*. Translated by David E. Green. Garden City, N.Y., 1967.

Lukács, Georg. *History and Class Consciousness*. Translated by Rodney Livingstone. London, 1971.

The Ontology of Social Being. Translated by David Fernbach. London, 1978.

Luxemburg, Rosa. *The Accumulation of Capital*. Translated by Agnes Schwarzschild. London, 1963.

McCarthy, Thomas. *The Critical Theory of Jürgen Habermas*. Cambridge, Mass. and London, 1978.

McLellan, David. "Politics." In *Marx: The First Hundred Years,* edited by David McLellan. New York, 1983.

The Thought of Karl Marx: An Introduction. London and Basingstoke, 1980.

Macy, Michael W. "Value Theory and the 'Golden Eggs': Appropriating the Magic of Accumulation." *Sociological Theory* 6, no. 2 (Fall 1988), pp. 131–52.

Mandel, Ernest. "Economics." In *Marx: The First Hundred Years,* edited by David McLellan. New York, 1983.

The Formation of the Economic Thought of Karl Marx. New York and London, 1971.

Late Capitalism. Translated by Joris De Bres. London, 1975.

Marxist Economic Theory. London, 1968.

Marcuse, Herbert. *Counterrevolution and Revolt*. Boston, 1972.

Eros and Civilization: A Philosophical Inquiry into Freud. New York, 1962.

"The Foundation of Historical Materialism." In *From Luther to Popper*, edited and translated by Joris De Bres. London, 1972.

One-dimensional Man: Studies in the Ideology of Advanced Industrial Society. Boston, 1964.

"Philosophy and Critical Theory." Translated by Jeremy J. Shapiro. In *Critical Theory and Society*, edited by Stephen Bronner and Douglas Kellner. New York and London, 1989.

Reason and Revolution: Hegel and the Rise of Social Theory. Boston, 1964.

"Some Social Implications of Modern Technology." *Studies in Philosophy and Social Sciences* 9 (1941), pp. 414–39.

"Über die philosophischen Grundlagen des wirtschaftswissenschaftlichen Arbeitsbegriffs." In *Kultur und Gesellschaft*, vol. 2. Frankfurt, 1965.

Márkus, György. "Die Welt menschlicher Objekte. Zum Problem der Konstitution im Marxismus." In *Arbeit, Handlung, Normativität*, edited by Axel Honneth and Urs Jaeggi. Frankfurt, 1980.

Marramao, Giacomo. "Political Economy and Critical Theory." *Telos* no. 24 (Summer 1975): 56–80.

Mattick, Paul. *Kritik der Neomarxisten*. Frankfurt, 1974.

Marx and Keynes: The Limits of the Mixed Economy. Boston, 1969.

"Nachwort." In *Marx, die klassische Nationalökonomie und das Problem der Dynamik*, by H. Grossmann. Frankfurt, 1969.

Mauke, Michael. *Die Klassentheorie von Marx und Engels*. Frankfurt, 1970.

Meek, Ronald. *Studies in the Labour Theory of Value*. 2d ed. New York and London, 1956.

Mehring, Franz. *Karl Marx: The Story of His Life*. Translated by Edward Fitzgerald. Ann Arbor, Mich., 1962.

Mészáros, István. *Marx's Theory of Alienation*. London, 1970.

Mill, J.S. *Principles of Political Economy*, vol. 1. 2d ed. London, 1849.

Moore, Stanley. *Marx on the Choice between Socialism and Communism*. Cambridge, Mass. 1980.

Müller, Rudolf Wolfgang. *Geld und Geist: Zur Enstehungsgeschichte von Identitätsbewusstsein und Rationalität seit der Antike*. Frankfurt, 1977.

Müller, Wolfgang. "Habermas und die 'Anwendbarkeit' der 'Arbeitswerttheorie.' " *Sozialistische Politik* no. 1 (April 1969), pp. 39–54.

Mumford, Lewis. *The Myth of the Machine*. New York, 1966.

Technics and Civilization. New York, 1934.

Murray, John Patrick. "Enlightenment Roots of Habermas' Critique of Marx." *The Modern Schoolman* 57, no. 1 (November 1979), pp. 1–24.

Marx's Theory of Scientific Knowledge. Atlantic Highlands, N.J., 1988.

Needham, Joseph. *Science in Traditional China: A Comparative Perspective*. Cambridge, Mass., and Hong Kong, 1981.

Needham, Joseph, Wang Ling, and Derek de Solla Price. *Heavenly Clockwork: The Great Astronomical Clocks of Medieval China*. 2d ed. Cambridge, 1986.

Negri, Antonio. *Marx beyond Marx: Lessons on the "Grundrisse."* Edited by Jim Fleming. Translated by Harry Cleaver, Michael Ryan, and Maurizio Viano. South Hadley, Mass., 1984.

Negt, Oskar, and Alexander Kluge. *Geschichte und Eigensinn*. Frankfurt, 1981.

Nell, E. "Value and Capital in Marxian Economics." In *The Crisis in Economic Theory*, edited by D. Bell and I. Kristol. New York, 1981.

Nicolaus, Martin. "Introduction." In *Karl Marx, Grundrisse*, translated by Martin Nicolaus. London, 1973.

"Proletariat and Middle Class in Marx." *Studies on the Left* 7, no. 1 (Jan.–Feb. 1967): 22–49.

"The Unknown Marx." *New Left Review*, no. 48 (March–April 1968), pp. 41–61.

Offe, Claus. *Disorganized Capitalism: Contemporary Transformations of Work and Politics*. Edited by John Keane. Cambridge, Mass., 1985.

Strukturprobleme des kapitalistischen Staates: Aufsätze zur politischen Soziologie. Frankfurt, 1972.

Ollman, Bertell. *Alienation: Marx's Conception of Man in Capitalist Society.* 2d ed. Cambridge, 1976.

Petry, Franz. *Der soziale Gehalt der Marxschen Werttheorie.* Jena, 1916.

Piccone, Paul. "General Introduction." In *The Essential Frankfurt School Reader,* edited by Andrew Arato and Eike Gebhardt. New York, 1978.

Piesowicz, Kazimierz. "Lebensrhythmus und Zeitrechnung in der vorindustriellen und in der industriellen Gesellschaft." *Geschichte in Wissenschaft und Unterricht* 31, no. 8 (1980): 465–85.

Piore, Michael J., and Charles F. Sabel. *The Second Industrial Divide: Possibilities for Prosperity.* New York, 1984.

Pirenne, Henri. *Belgian Democracy.* Translated by J. V. Saunders. Manchester, 1915.

Polanyi, Karl. *The Great Transformation.* New York and Toronto, 1944.

Pollock, Friedrich. "Bemerkungen zur Wirtschaftskrise." *Zeitschrift für Sozialforschung* 2 (1933), pp. 321–53.

"Die gegenwärtige Lage des Kapitalismus und die Aussichten einer planwirtschaftlichen Neuordnung." *Zeitschrift für Sozialforschung* 1 (1932): 8–27.

"Is National Socialism a New Order?" *Studies in Philosophy and Social Science* 9 (1941): 440–55.

"State Capitalism." *Studies in Philosophy and Social Studies* 9 (1941): 200–25.

Postone, Moishe. "Anti-Semitism and National Socialism." In *Germans and Jews Since the Holocaust,* edited by Anson Rabinbach and Jack Zipes. New York, 1986.

"History and Critical Social Theory." *Contemporary Sociology* 19, no. 2 (March 1990): 170–76.

"Necessity, Labor and Time." *Social Research* 45 (Winter 1978), pp. 739–88.

Postone, Moishe, and Barbara Brick. "Critical Pessimism and the Limits of Traditional Marxism." *Theory and Society* 11 (1982), pp. 617–58.

Postone, Moishe, and Helmut Reinicke. "On Nicolaus's 'Introduction' to the *Grundrisse.*" *Telos* 22 (Winter 1974–75): 130–48.

Reichelt, Helmut. *Zur logischen Struktur des Kapitalbegriffs bei Karl Marx.* Frankfurt, 1970.

Reinicke, Helmut. *Ware und Dialektik.* Darmstadt and Neuwied, 1974.

Ricardo, David. *The Principles of Political Economy and Taxation.* Cambridge, 1951.

Ritsert, Jürgen. *Probleme politisch-ökonomischer Theoriebildung.* Frankfurt, 1973.

Robinson, Joan. *An Essay on Marxian Economics.* 2d ed. London, Melbourne, Toronto, 1967.

Roderick, Rick. *Habermas and the Foundations of Critical Theory.* New York, 1986.

Rosdolsky, Roman. *The Making of Marx's "Capital."* Translated by Pete Burgess. London, 1977.

Rubin, Isaak Illich. *Essays on Marx's Theory of Value.* Translated by Milos Samardzija and Fredy Perlman. Detroit, Mich., 1972.

Rubin, Isaak Illich, et al. *Dialektik der Kategorien: Debatte in der UdSSR (1927–1929).* Translated by Eva Mayer and Peter Gerlinghoff. Berlin, 1975.

Sahlins, Marshall. *Culture and Practical Reason.* Chicago, 1976.

Sapir, Edward. *Language: An Introduction to the Study of Speech.* New York, 1921.

Sartre, Jean-Paul. *Critique of Dialectical Reason.* Translated by Alan Sheridan-Smith. Edited by Jonathan Rée. London, 1976.

Sayer, Derek. *Marx's Method: Ideology, Science, and Critique in "Capital."* Atlantic Highlands, N.J., 1979.

The Violence of Abstraction: The Analytic Foundations of Historical Materialism. Oxford and New York, 1987.

Schlesinger, Rudolf. *Marx, His Times and Ours.* London, 1950.

Schmidt, Alfred. *The Concept of Nature in Marx.* Translated by Ben Fowkes. London, 1971.

History and Structure: An Essay on Hegelian-Marxist and Structuralist Theories of History. Translated by Jeffrey Herf. Cambridge, Mass., 1981.

"Zum Erkenntnisbegriff der Kritik der politischen Ökonomie." In *Kritik der politischen Ökonomie heute: 100 Jahre Kapital,* edited by Walter Euchner and Alfred Schmidt. Frankfurt am Main, 1968.

Schmidt, Alfred, and Norbert Altwicker, eds. *Max Horkheimer heute: Werke und Wirkung.* Frankfurt am Main, 1986.

Schumpeter, Joseph. *Capitalism, Socialism and Democracy.* New York and London, 1947.

History of Economic Analysis. New York, 1954.

Shaikh, Anwar. "The Poverty of Algebra." In *The Value Controversy* by I. Steedman, P. Sweezy, et al. London, 1981.

Sherover-Marcuse, Erica. *Emancipation and Consciousness: Dogmatic and Dialectical Perspectives in the Early Marx.* Cambridge, Mass., 1986.

Simmel, Georg. *The Philosophy of Money.* Translated by Tom Bottomore and David Frisby. Boston, London, Melbourne, and Henley, 1978.

Smith, Adam. *An Inquiry into the Nature and Causes of the Wealth of Nations.* New York, 1937.

Sohn-Rethel, Alfred. *Geistige und körperliche Arbeit.* Frankfurt, 1972.

Intellectual and Manual Labor: A Critique of Epistemology. Translated by Martin Sohn-Rethel. Atlantic Highlands, N.J., 1978.

Warenform und Denkform. Frankfurt, 1971.

Sweezy, Paul M. *The Theory of Capitalist Development.* New York, 1969.

Thomas, Paul. "The Language of Real Life: Jürgen Habermas and the Distortion of Karl Marx." *Discourse: Berkeley Journal of Theoretical Studies in Media and Culture* 1 (Fall 1979): 59–85.

Thompson, E. P. "Time, Work-Discipline, and Industrial Capitalism." *Past and Present* 38 (Dec. 1967): 56–97.

Thomson, George. *The First Philosophers.* London, 1955.

Thrupp, Sylvia. "Medieval Industry, 1000–1500." In *The Fontana Economic History of Europe,* vol. 1, edited by Carlo M. Cipolla. Glasgow, 1972.

Tönnies, Ferdinand. *Karl Marx: His Life and Teachings.* Translated by Charles P. Loomis and Ingeborg Paulus. East Lansing, Mich., 1974

Traugott, Mark. *Armies of the Poor: Determinants of Working-Class Participation in the Parisian Insurrection of June 1848.* Princeton, N.J., 1985.

Tuchscheerer, Walter. *Bevor "Das Kapital" entstand: Die Herausbildung und Entwicklung der ökonomischen Theorie von Karl Marx in der Zeit von 1843–1858.* Berlin, 1968.

Tucker, Robert C. *The Marxian Revolutionary Idea.* New York, 1969.

Uchida, Hiroshi. *Marx's "Grundrisse" and Hegel's Logic.* Edited by Terrell Carver. London and Boston, 1988.

Vranicki, Predrag. *Geschichte des Marxismus.* 2 vols. Frankfurt, 1972.

Vygodski, Vitali Solomonovich. *The Story of A Great Discovery.* Berlin, 1973.

Walton, Paul, and Andrew Gamble. *From Alienation to Surplus Value.* London, 1972.

Weber, Max. *Economy and Society: An Outline of Interpretive Sociology.* Edited by Guenther Roth and Claus Wittlich. Translated by Ephraim Fischoff, Hans Gerth, A. M. Henderson, Ferdinand Kolegar, Guenther Roth, Edward Shils, and Claus Wittich. Berkeley, Los Angeles, and London, 1978.

The Protestant Ethic and the Spirit of Capitalism. Translated by Talcott Parsons. New York, 1958.

"Science as a Vocation." In *From Max Weber: Essays in Sociology,* edited by H. H. Gerth and C. W. Mills. New York, 1958.

"The Social Psychology of the World Religions." In *From Max Weber: Essays in Sociology,* edited by H. H. Gerth and C. W. Mills. New York, 1958.

Wellmer, Albrecht. "Communication and Emancipation: Reflections on the Linguistic Turn in Critical Theory." In *On Critical Theory,* edited by John O'Neill. New York, 1976.

Critical Theory of Society. Translated by John Cumming. New York, 1971.

Wendorff, Rudolf. *Zeit und Kultur: Geschichte des Zeitbewusstseins in Europa.* Opladen, 1980.

Whitrow, G. J. *The Nature of Time.* Harmondsworth, Eng. 1975.

Whorf, Benjamin L. *Language, Thought and Reality.* Cambridge, Mass., 1956.

Wiggershaus, Rolf. *Die Frankfurter Schule: Geschichte, theoretische Entwicklung, politische Bedeutung.* Munich and Vienna, 1986.

Williams, Raymond. "Culture." In *Marx: The First Hundred Years,* edited by David McLellan. New York, 1983.

Winfield, Richard. "The Dilemmas of Labor." *Telos* 24 (Summer 1975), pp. 113–28.

Wittgenstein, Ludwig. *Philosophical Investigations.* Translated by G. E. M. Anscombe. New York, 1958.

Wolff, Robert Paul. *Understanding Marx: A Reconstruction and Critique of "Capital."* Princeton, 1984.

Wright, Erik O. *Classes.* London, 1985.

Zeleny, Jindrich. *Die Wissenschaftslogik bei Marx und "Das Kapital."* Frankfurt, 1970.

Index